The boys are generally well. No
body in the Reg't much sick
We have no deaths now. hav'nt
had over 3 in over 4 months
We are Veteran Soldiers now
Col Jones is in fine health and loves
to play Cards as much as ever
Tell them who may enquire that
we are all well.   There is a great
deal of dissatisfaction in the Army
here growing out of the Cotton trade
I am afraid it will ruin our Army
and demoralize the Citizens
I am seriously alarmed about it—
this is entre nous. (between us).
Love Kisses &c to the Children
          Yours truly
          E P Petty

Journey
to
Pleasant Hill

JOURNEY

The Civil War Letters of

TO

Captain Elijah P. Petty

PLEASANT

Walker's Texas Division CSA

HILL

Edited by NORMAN D. BROWN

With an introduction by O. SCOTT PETTY

Pictures by JOHN GROTH

The University of Texas
INSTITUTE of TEXAN CULTURES
San Antonio

Editor's Note

TO PRESERVE THE FLAVOR of Petty's style and that of the era itself, the manuscript has been edited in accordance with the following guidelines. If a sentence ends at the right margin of the letter, Petty almost never uses punctuation; if within a line, he uses a half-inch space or a dash (or no break at all). The dashes—with spaces on either side in the old-fashioned way—have been preserved, periods added where appropriate and first words in sentences capitalized. Only series commas have been added for clarity; the few other commas are Petty's own.

His *c*'s and *s*'s vary so much in caps and lower-case that the caps have been, to a great extent, eliminated, whereas his other less numerous capitalization quirks have been left intact along with frequent twists of spelling. His inconsistent use of superior letters (Gen^1, 8th) has been duplicated. Letters or words in brackets have been added where the meaning of a word or sentence might be unclear. Petty's initial misspellings of proper names have been corrected in brackets (Alexandr[i]a), but not thereafter. In general, the original form has been kept as far as is possible and still maintain readability.

O. Scott Petty's dedication to family and history made the preservation and publication of these letters possible.

Copyright © 1982 by THE UNIVERSITY OF TEXAS INSTITUTE OF TEXAN CULTURES

Library of Congress Catalogue Card Number 82-82398
ISBN 0-933164-94-7
ISBN 0-933164-95-5 (*special*)

Design and Production by WHITEHEAD & WHITEHEAD, *Austin, Texas*
Calligraphy by KATE BERGQUIST
Manufactured in the United States of America
FIRST EDITION

This book has been printed on acid free paper which will not yellow with age.

CONTENTS

MAPS

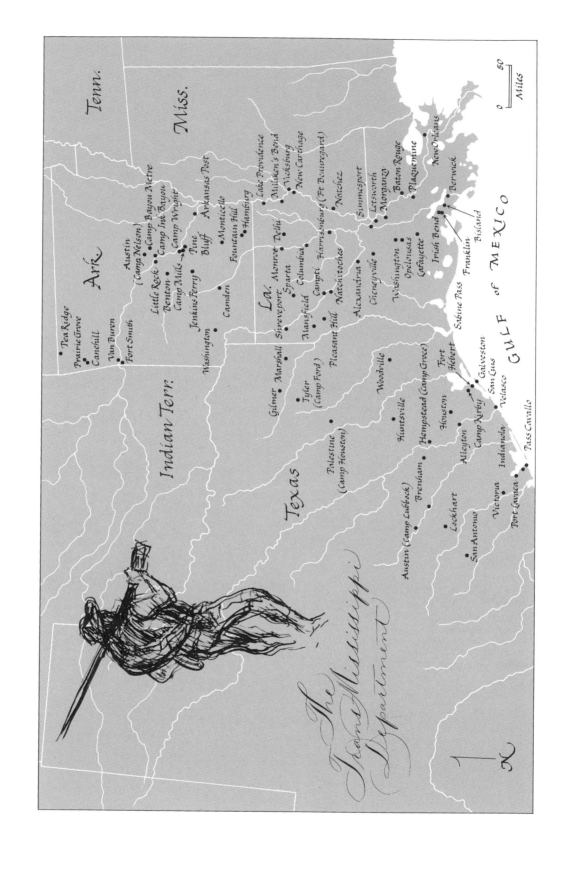

The Trans-Mississippi Department

Tenn.

Miss.

Ark.

Tea Ridge
Prairie Grove
Cane Hill
Van Buren
Fort Smith

Austin (Camp Nelson)
Little Rock
Benton
Camp Mills
Jenkins Ferry
Washington
Camden

Camp Bayou Metre
Camp Ink Bayou
Camp Wright
Pine Bluff
Arkansas Post
Monticello
Fountain Hill
Hamburg

Lake Providence
Milliken's Bend
Vicksburg
New Carthage

Harrisonburg (Ft Beauregard)
Natchez
Simmesport
Letsworth
Morganza
Baton Rouge
Plaquemine
New Orleans
Berwick

La.

Monroe
Delhi
Sparta
Columbia
Campti
Natchitoches
Alexandria
Cheneyville
Washington
Opelousas
Lafayette
Irish Bend
Franklin
Bisland

Shreveport
Mansfield
Pleasant Hill

Gilmer
Marshall
Tyler (Camp Ford)

Indian Terr.

Texas

Palestine (Camp Houston)
Huntsville
Woodville
Brenham
Hempstead (Camp Groce)
Houston
Fort Hébert
Galveston
San Luis
Velasco

Austin (Camp Lubbock)
Lockhart
San Antonio
Victoria
Port Lavaca
Indianola
Pass Cavallo
Camp Kirby

Sabine Pass

GULF OF MEXICO

0   50
Miles

N

PREFACE

In his book, *The South to Posterity: An Introduction to the Writing of Confederate History* (1939), Douglas Southall Freeman noted: "The first historians of the Confederacy were, of course, those who wrote home of the events they had witnessed, those who supplied the press with its reports, and those who determined they would preserve letters or paste newspaper articles in scrapbooks."[1] One of the first things a Johnny Reb did after getting settled in camp was to write his homefolk about his new life in the army. And, thereafter, until discharge, death or war's end, he continued to write frequent and informative letters about his experiences in camp, on the march, in battle and in prison. At the same time he received cherished letters from his family and friends telling of life at home. According to Professor Bell Irvin Wiley, the historian of the common soldier of the Confederacy and the Union, "Never in the history of the South has there been such a tide of letter writing as that which was raised by the Confederate War, for on no other occasion has so large a proportion of the people been away from home for so long a time. Letters written by soldiers were more apt to be preserved than those received in camp, and these faded missives, now reposing by the thousands in private possession and in public repositories, constitute a valuable and largely neglected source for the South's social history."[2]

Since Wiley's *The Life of Johnny Reb: The Common Soldier of the Confederacy* was published in 1943, the neglect he spoke of has largely been remedied by scholars who have cited Confederate letters in their articles and books. In addition, many collections of these letters have been edited for publication. Other equally valuable collections, however, remain unpublished; and Confederate correspondence in private possession continues to come to light. One such trove, the letters of Captain Elijah P. Petty of Bastrop, Texas, to his wife Margaret; daughter Ella; and sons Frank, Don and Van, is in the possession of one of Petty's grandchildren, O. Scott Petty of San Antonio, Texas. Through the generosity of the Petty family, The Institute of Texan Cultures is privileged to make these letters available to the general public.

Elijah Parsons Petty was born in Dover, Stewart County, Tennessee, on January 1, 1828, one of nine children born to John Hewing and Theora Bruton Petty. His father, who was of Scottish descent and had relatives in Glasgow, was born on December 10, 1795, and his mother on February 25, 1805. They were married in 1821 at Dover and kept an inn there from 1840 to 1850. They then migrated to Texas, settled at Indianola and, a few years later, moved to Seguin, where they spent the remainder of their lives. [3]

Two days after turning 21, Elijah married Margaret Elizabeth Pinner, the daughter of Dr. Joseph and Sallie R. (Acree) Pinner of Dyersburg, Tennessee. "One day young Elijah rode up on horseback to her home and Margaret climbed upon the back of his horse and they rode off and were married in Stewart County, Tennessee, January 3, 1849," wrote Mary Estelle Petty Tucker, Elijah and Margaret's great-granddaughter. "This episode has been told to me by my mother, Estelle E. Petty, who knew 'Didy' (Margaret Pinner Petty) well and by my cousin, Alf McDonald, in whose home Margaret Petty often stayed." [4]

Margaret Petty's mother came from a wealthy family and lived in a two-story house built with wooden pegs, with plastered walls and brass doorknobs. Called "Edelweiss," the house was built in the early 1800's on a beautiful site in District Eight on the Cumberland River. Margaret was born in Stewart County on August 19, 1832, into a large family. [5]

Petty had been studying law, and on February 20, 1849, he appeared before two circuit court judges, Will Fitzgerald and W. A. Martin, with a "Certificate of Recommendation" signed by William Cook, clerk of the Stewart County Court, stating that "the Court was fully satisfied that said E P Petty is a man of good moral character and that he had attained the age of Twenty one years." After examining Petty, "touching his qualifications to practice law," Fitzgerald and Martin issued him a license to practice in any of the courts of law and equity in Tennessee. On April 10, 1849, Petty and W. Lowe of Springfield signed an agreement to practice law together in the circuit courts of Stewart County as equal partners under the name and style of Lowe & Petty, "dividing equally between us any amounts of fees we may thus realize." The partnership was to continue until January 1, 1850, "and no longer unless by special agreement endorsed by us on the back of this instrument. . . ." On March 13, 1850, the two men mutually agreed to continue their partnership on the same terms for 12 months, retroactive to January 1.

On September 13, 1850, Petty was "regularly Initiated Passed and Raised to the Sublime degree of Master Mason in Dover Lodge No. 39"; on February 26, 1851, he joined the Dover Division of the Sons of Temperance. [6]

The Pettys' first child, Ella Pene, was born on December 2, 1849. In the late summer of 1851 the family left Tennessee by covered wagon for Texas. The trip took six weeks. After a short stay in Seguin they moved on to Bastrop, the county seat of Bastrop County, arriving there on December 27, 1851. One of the oldest settlements in Texas, Bastrop was located on the left bank of the Colorado River at the crossing of the Old San Antonio Road between Bexar and Nacogdoches. Four more children were born to the couple in Texas: Cyr Frank, born August 30, 1853; Sallie Belle, born October 5, 1855 (who lived only three years, dying on November 13, 1858, of "congestion of the lungs"); Don Green, born October 4, 1857; and Van Alvin, born August 19, 1860. [7]

On October 29, 1851, Petty received a license to practice law in "the several District and inferior Courts" of Texas from District Court Judge William E. Jones at Lockhart in Caldwell County. His law office in Bastrop was over L. C. Cunningham & Company's store. A card in the Bastrop *Advertiser*, dated January 7, 1854, stated: "E. P. PETTY, Attorney and Counsellor at Law, Bastrop, Texas, Respectfully solicits the patronage of the public. The most satisfactory references can be given if required." In 1855 Petty formed a partnership with George Washington Jones, a lawyer of great ability and a forceful speaker. Jones had previously been in partnership with H. Armington. The two men promised to "Give their joint attention to all business pertaining to their profession that may be entrusted to them." In January 1856 Governor Elisha Pease, with the advice and consent of the Texas Senate, appointed Petty to the office of Notary Public for Bastrop County. On November 25, 1857, Petty was enrolled as an "Attorney and Counsellor" of the Texas Supreme Court and was "permitted and authorized to appear plead and practice" in all Texas courts. [8]

In a February 16, 1864, letter to his wife's brother, Dr. Thomas Jefferson Pinner, Petty recalled his political stance during the tumultuous months of 1860–1861 which saw Abraham Lincoln's election to the presidency; the secession of seven Lower South states, including Texas; and the formation of the Confederate States of America:

I was a Breckenridge & Lane Sub Elector for the 2nd Judicial District of Texas. Then upon the election of Lincoln I took the stump for Secession — spoke, electioneered, legged wire, worked and voted for Secession. Attended the Texas Convention [as a spectator] and lobbied for it and when Texas over the opposition of Gov Houston and his satel[l]ites went out of the Union on the 2 March 1861 (just two days before Lincoln was inaugurated) I rejoiced and shouted. [9]

In the flood tide of patriotism which swept over Texas during the first months after the Civil War began at Fort Sumter in the harbor of Charleston, South Carolina, there was an irresistible rush to arms. Volunteer military companies organized everywhere. By May 3, 1861, the Bastrop Volunteers Infantry had been formed with George Washington Jones as captain, and Stephen C. Ferrell, James Priest and Blackstone H. Davis as lieutenants. Among those carried on the muster roll were William A. Highsmith, Chas. William Miller, Joseph D. Sayers and Elijah P. Petty, all destined within a short time to command their own companies. Sayers would serve as governor of Texas from 1899 to 1903. On June 1 the company numbered 95 men of all ranks. It was assigned to the Twenty-sixth Brigade, Texas State Troops.[10] On September 28, 1861, the "Bastrop Lubbock Guards" was organized in Beat No. 2 with John Finney as captain and Petty as first lieutenant, and was likewise assigned to the Twenty-sixth Brigade.[11] Ordered to the defense of Galveston in late October, the unit became Company B in Major Jared E. Kirby's Third Texas Infantry Battalion, a six-month command that served on the Texas coast. Petty became the battalion's adjutant. Mustered out on April 24, 1862, he enlisted at Bastrop on May 13, 1862, for the war and joined the Seventeenth Texas Infantry Regiment as captain of Company F.[12] Colonel R. T. P. Allen, the superintendent of the Bastrop Military Institute, commanded the regiment; and George Washington Jones was the lieutenant colonel. After marching to Little Rock, Arkansas, in the summer and fall of 1862 the regiment became part of the Third Brigade in a Texas infantry division commanded by Brigadier General Henry E. McCulloch. About three months after its organization Major General John G. Walker assumed command of the division, and it was known thereafter as Walker's Texas Division. The division, the largest unit of Texans in the war, made a reputation for long marches over the frequently muddy roads of Arkansas and Louisiana, and earned the sobriquet of "Walker's Greyhounds."

The vast Confederate Trans-Mississippi Department theoretically covered almost 600,000 square miles, embracing Missouri, Arkansas, the western four-fifths of Louisiana, Texas, the Indian Territory (Oklahoma) and the short-lived Confederate Territory of Arizona (roughly the southern two-fifths of the modern states of Arizona and New Mexico). It was never more than a peripheral theater of military operations, and its fate depended upon the shifting fortunes of the armies defending the Confederacy's heartland east of the Mississippi River. Historians, whose major interests lay in the "Eastern" theater (Virginia, Maryland and Pennsylvania) or the "Western" theater (embracing all the other

Southern states east of the Mississippi), have had relatively little to say about the war west of the river, especially after the fall of Vicksburg, Mississippi, on July 4, 1863. Yet, as Professor Robert L. Kerby has pointed out, "the Trans-Mississippi was the most extensive military department in the Confederacy; it was, at least potentially, a recruiting ground and a source of supply for the East; its very existence was a factor which the Union high command had to weigh when planning campaign strategy; it did enjoy some unique advantages and encounter some unique problems; and its history does serve to complement and refine the history of the Confederate States."[13]

Petty's letters to his family begin with one to his wife on November 5, 1861, after he arrives at Camp Kirby near Galveston and, except for three periods, two lasting about seven weeks and the other about ten weeks, when he was either at or near home or his wife was visiting him in camp, continue on a regular basis until April 2, 1864. The letters allude to army life in camp and on the march; to wartime conditions on the home front; to social relationships with citizens near camp; to the faltering morale of the rank and file in the face of Confederate defeats; to the increasing number of desertions; and to judgments concerning generals, military strategy and tactics. Petty's literate prose style and the moral values governing interfamily and other social relationships which he forcibly expresses provide valuable insights into the cultural and social history of the Old South's educated middle class.

The fighting was often as fierce in the Trans-Mississippi Department as in the other two theaters, and Walker's Texas Division played a conspicuous part in four hard-fought battles: Milliken's Bend, Mansfield (Sabine Cross Roads) and Pleasant Hill, Louisiana, and Jenkins' Ferry, Arkansas. However, the reader who hopes to find graphic descriptions of these engagements in Petty's letters will be disappointed. He was severely wounded in the right shoulder at Milliken's Bend on June 7, 1863, and went home on sick leave, thus removing any necessity to describe the fighting in a letter. Tragically, Petty was killed at the battle of Pleasant Hill, April 9, 1864. The battle of Mansfield was fought on April 8. I have bridged the gap in his letters from June 4 to August 17, 1863, with an in-text account of Milliken's Bend and the efforts of Walker's Division to relieve Vicksburg, besieged by Major General Ulysses S. Grant's Federal forces, from west of the Mississippi. I have also described the division's movements from April 3 to April 9, 1864. In addition, an epilogue traces the subsequent history of the division to its disbandment at Camp Groce near Hempstead, Texas, on May 20, 1865.

According to local tradition, as Petty lay dying in the Childers mansion in the village of Pleasant Hill, he requested that he be buried in the yard. It was not until 25 years later, in 1889, that his family learned exactly where he was buried. His grave was then marked with a tombstone, the only monument on the battlefield.

Frank

Margaret and Don

Van

Ella

Captain Elijah P. Petty

NOTES

[1] Douglas Southall Freeman, *The South to Posterity: An Introduction to the Writing of Confederate History* (New York: Charles Scribner's Sons, 1939), p. 1.

[2] Bell Irvin Wiley, *The Life of Johnny Reb: The Common Soldier of the Confederacy*, 2nd ed. (Baton Rouge: Louisiana State University Press, 1943, 1978), p. 192 (hereafter cited as Wiley, *Life of Johnny Reb*).

[3] Van Alvin Petty, "Memo of the family of Elijah P. and Margaret E. Petty," and "Memorandum of Petty family. Fathers Ancestors," San Antonio, July 7, 1927, enclosed in Van Alvin Petty to Kitty Ford, July 8, 1927; Wilfred Richardson to O. Scott Petty, May 23, 1981, both in possession of O. Scott Petty, San Antonio, Texas. The other children of John and Theora Petty were: George Bolivar Petty,

born Dover, Tennessee, in 1826, who married Mary Eliza Buckner and died in Seguin in 1859; Dewitt C. Petty, who married Mary Elizabeth Holland, April 25, 1867, and died in Seguin in 1906; Calvina (Callie) Adaline Petty, who married John L. Cochran, October 5, 1852; Donie (Fredonia) Lydia Petty, born Stewart County, Tennessee, who married Andrew Dove of Indianola, Texas, and died on February 15, 1874, at Seguin; Theora Jane Petty, who married Charles Cabaniss Howerton on October 5, 1858; and Johnnie Petty, who was married twice, first to Lowellen Robinson and then to Rufus F. Evans, and died on July 23, 1907. John H. Petty died in Seguin on August 23, 1863, and Theora Petty died there on April 17, 1878.

[4] Mary Estelle Petty Tucker (Mrs. Reagan Tucker), "Elijah Parsons Petty," typescript dated March 21, 1965, in possession of O. Scott Petty. Van Alvin Petty was Mrs. Tucker's grandfather. This biographical sketch was published in Susan Merle Dotson, comp., *Who's Who of the Confederacy: A Symposium by the Members of the Albert Sidney Johnston Chapter No. 2060, United Daughters of the Confederacy* (San Antonio: Naylor Company, 1966), pp. 241–46 (hereafter cited as Dotson, comp., *Who's Who of the Confederacy*).

[5] *Ibid*; Petty, "Memo of the family of Elijah P. and Margaret E. Petty." The other children of Joseph and Sallie R. Pinner were John R., Wm. W., Mary E., Elbert, Thomas Jefferson, Sallie O. and Joseph C. The date of Joseph Pinner's death is not known. Sallie died at Dyersburg, Dyer County, Tennessee, in 1888 and was buried in Stewart County. Van Alvin Petty, "Memorandum of Pinner family. Mothers Ancestors," San Antonio, July 7, 1927, enclosed in Van Alvin Petty to Kitty Ford, July 8, 1927, in possession of O. Scott Petty; "The Last Will and Testament of Mrs. Sallie R. Pinner, dec'd., Probated July, Term, 1888, Will L. Wilkerson, Clerk," typescript in possession of O. Scott Petty.

[6] Documents in possession of O. Scott Petty.

[7] Petty, "Memo of the family of Elijah P. and Margaret E. Petty."

[8] E. P. Petty's Law License, Issued October 30 [29]th A D 1851; Appointment, Notary Public, issued January 1, 1856; License, Texas Supreme Court, issued November 25, 1857, in possession of O. Scott Petty; Bastrop *Advertiser*, May 27, 1854; March 14, 1857.

[9] Elijah P. Petty to Dr. Thomas Jefferson Pinner, February 16, 1864, in possession of O. Scott Petty.

[10] Muster Rolls Bastrop Volunteers Infantry, Capt. G. W. Jones, May 3, June 1, 1861, Confederate Muster Rolls, No. 781, Texas State Archives, Austin, Texas.

[11] A List of Officers Elected, upon the Organization of the Militia in Precinct No. 2 of Bastrop County, Confederate Muster Rolls, No. 921, Texas State Archives, Austin, Texas; Commission of E. P. Petty as first lieutenant of Militia Company in Beat No. 2 Bastrop County a part of the 26th Brigade Texas Militia, September 28, 1861, signed by Governor Edward Clark at Austin, October 17, 1861, in possession of O. Scott Petty.

[12] Compiled Service Record of E. P. Petty, National Archives, Washington, D. C.

[13] Robert L. Kerby, *Kirby Smith's Confederacy: The Trans-Mississippi South, 1863–1865* (New York: Columbia University Press, 1972), pp. 1–2, 431 (hereafter cited as Kerby, *Kirby Smith's Confederacy*).

ACKNOWLEDGMENTS

I wish to thank O. Scott Petty of San Antonio for giving me the opportunity to edit his grandfather's letters. He and his wife Edwina and son Scott Jr. wanted a book that would meet scholarly standards and have the best design, illustrations and production possible. They selected the distinguished artist, John Groth of New York City, to illustrate the book and approved the selection of Fred and Barbara Whitehead of Austin to design it.

Jack R. Maguire, Executive Director of The University of Texas Institute of Texan Cultures—San Antonio, recommended me to the Petty family as editor, worked out the financial arrangements for publishing the book and kept in close touch with the project as it proceeded. I consulted with John L. Davis and Thomas W. Cutrer of The Institute; and Dr. Cutrer kindly supplemented my annotations with 13 footnotes including those on Confederate finance, mail service, refugees, food shortages, Hardee's *Tactics*, court-martial procedures and the battle of Chattanooga. Sandra Hodsdon Carr of The Institute staff copy edited the manuscript.

Terry G. Waxham of Shreveport, Louisiana, guided me over the Mansfield and Pleasant Hill battlefields in June 1981 and generously provided newspaper clippings, photographs of Captain Petty's grave and battlefield scenes, and copies of letters from Confederate and Federal soldiers who participated in the Red River Campaign. Terry's father, H. G. Waxham, drew detailed maps of the Mansfield and Pleasant Hill battlefields, based upon personal exploration and earlier maps. Regrettably, these could not be reproduced for this book as drawn; however, Fred Whitehead used them as basic sources in drawing the maps which do appear. Fred also prepared the maps of the Trans-Mississippi Department, Galveston, Milliken's Bend and the Red River Campaign.

Goode D. Edge, Historic Site Manager, Mansfield State Commemorative Area, met with me at the recently renovated park museum to discuss the project and provided copies of documents in the museum.

Mrs. Lenna Jenkins and her sister, Mrs. Daisy Hunter, two of Captain Petty's grandchildren, gave a coffee in Mrs. Jenkins's lovely old home, Beau Sejour, during my visit to Mansfield.

Robert W. Boldrick of San Antonio, my research assistant at an early stage of the project, provided useful information for the footnotes, especially on family genealogy, medical terms and literary works. The staffs of the Barker Texas History Center Library, The University of Texas at Austin and the Texas State Archives were helpful in locating information on Captain Petty and Walker's Texas Division.

Norman Brown

THE QUESTIONS I am most frequently asked are how I came to publish these letters 118 years after they were written—where were they all of those years, how and when did they come into my possession, and why am I publishing them now?

Elijah Parsons Petty was a lawyer living in Bastrop, Texas, with his wife Margaret and his children, Ella Pene (age 11 years), Cyr Frank (age 7 years), Don Green (age 3 years) and Van Alvin (age 8 months; and later to become my father), when the Civil War broke out. He immediately volunteered, telling his wife that he would write to her at every opportunity to keep her informed of everything of interest that happened until he returned or was killed. He faithfully kept that promise.

After Captain Petty was killed on April 9, 1864, Margaret continued to live in their home in Bastrop and worked to support the family and educate her children. Later, when her children had grown, married and had homes of their own, she would visit each in turn. On September 15, 1905, she moved into our home in San Antonio and lived with us until her death on August 15, 1911.

On May 18, 1929, my father Van Alvin passed away. The metal box of Captain Petty's letters was stored in his home until 1947 when they came into my possession. The first thing I did when I got the box was to open it and inspect the letters. I found that bugs had been nibbling at them, but, fortunately, no great damage had been done. I cleaned them, sealed the box with adhesive tape and inspected them occasionally to be sure all was well. I knew the letters were valuable historically and wanted to share them with other members of the family, but I also felt they should all be kept together.

I had the letters for about 20 years before finding time to work with them. Preparing them for copying was a slow and tedious process since most were in their original envelopes and quite fragile. They had to be steamed very carefully before being unfolded, and then placed between the pages of large books with a sheet of soft white paper on each side and kept under pressure until they were dry. For steaming, I used a thermally insulated picnic chest which I kept in my study. At night I would set a pan of boiling water in the bottom and lay a few of the letters on a rack above the water and let them steam overnight, then get up extra early the next morning and put them to press before going to the office.

My wife Edwina deserves an extra star in her crown for putting up with me for the several years it took to do this job. She tolerated without complaint my untidy study with steaming apparatus on the floor and stacks of books used as presses all over the place. For her help, advice, encouragement and patience I am most grateful.

In 1973 I made 47 xerox copies of the letters, had them bound in six volumes and presented a set to each of Captain Petty's grandchildren and great-grandchildren (or to an heir of those deceased), and to a few libraries and other people. No sooner had the letters been delivered than I began to hear from people who wanted to buy copies, and I had to reply, "There ain't no more." Publication of these letters in 1973 served two purposes: it shared them with Captain Petty's descendants, and it ensured their preservation.

Captain Petty had a brilliant mind, was well educated and of high moral character, and was quite a philosopher. His letters were more than a history of the war—they were often filled with advice to his wife on how she should raise their children and to his children on how they should behave. He told her how to live in his absence, and how to conserve and invest her money. He would often philosophize on various subjects, and for this reason I felt that his letters should be shared with the general public.

In November 1978 I employed Mrs. Ronald (Bonnie) Flake, a journalist, to transcribe the letters. Captain Petty's handwriting was beautiful, and most of the letters were written with pen. Paper, however, was scarce and often of poor quality. Wallpaper was sometimes resorted to for stationery, and by the end of the war a pencil often replaced the pen. More than a century of fading and insect damage made the reading no easier. Bonnie finished the job in about nine months—Thanks, Bonnie.

On November 14, 1979, I took copies of the letters to Jack Maguire, executive director of The Institute of Texan Cultures, and asked his advice on how best to have them published. Mr. Maguire gave them to his chief historian, Dr. John L. Davis, and asked him to study them. Dr. Davis was most enthusiastic about the letters and recommended that The Institute publish them under their logotype, provided that I would employ an editor who was familiar with Civil War history to write a narrative and annotate the letters and that I would pay for the publishing of a book of which The Institute would be proud. To these conditions I heartily agreed.

The search for an editor began, and on April 7, 1980, Dr. Norman D. Brown, associate professor of history at The University of Texas, accepted the job. Mrs. Harry (Hazel) Ransom put us in touch with John Groth who, on September 23, 1981, agreed to illustrate the letters and so began a course of research in Confederate uniforms, arms and accoutrements. The next step was to find a book designer, and we are indebted to William Wittliff for putting us in touch with Fred and Barbara Whitehead, who accepted the assignment on November 1, 1981. That completed our organization.

THANKS

BESIDES THOSE already acknowledged, I wish especially to thank Lewis A. Davis for the inestimable help he has given me ever since the beginning of this project. I also thank Louise and Scott Petty Jr., Mary Estelle Petty Tucker (Mrs. Reagan Tucker), Van A. Petty III, Lenna Petty Jenkins (Mrs. Ned Jenkins), Daisy Petty Hunter (Mrs. Frank Hunter), Harvey McDonald, Mrs. T. A. Richardson, Frank Merritt, Mrs. Lewis Edge and Mrs. J. W. Hines. At my request they spent untold hours searching for whatever might be helpful. Lenna Petty and Daisy Hunter, Captain Petty's only other living grandchildren, entertained Dr. Brown, John Groth and me at coffee in Lenna's beautiful old Southern mansion, Beau Sejour, where we met many younger members of the Petty family.

I am indebted to Jack and Pat Maguire, Dr. John Davis and Dr. Tom Cutrer especially and other members of The Institute of Texan Cultures for the magnificent job they have done in producing this book.

The following people helped greatly, for which I thank them: Iris Haese, Dennis Hoerster, Rynda Naegelin, Patton White, Robert Boldrick, Charla Hatter, Alan Eaks, William Taylor, Bruce Lawrence, Susan Payne, Keith Watkins, Joe O. Parr Jr., H. Willard Lende Jr., Goode Edge and Terry Waxham.

So many people have contributed in some way that I may have overlooked someone. If so, the oversight was unintentional. Thank you all. I hope everyone enjoys reading this book as much as I have enjoyed putting it together.

O. Scott Petty
June 23, 1982

Journey to Pleasant Hill

I reckon you think I dont intend for you to need for money—this is so. All I make is for my family and I want them to get the benifit of it. I can take care of myself. I dont want my family stinted for any thing nor shall they be if I can help it — I hardly realized the love I have for you all until this cruel war forced a separation. I did'nt know that you all composed so great a portion of my happiness and that you are so necessary to me. But it is so and I must do my part to take care of and preserve you.

Elijah P. Petty to Margaret Petty, February 12, 1863

I will state that I was a Secessionest per se. Spoke, electioneered and voted for it. Helped to carry Texas triumphantly out of the accursed old Union. Have been in the army over two years. Have fought and bled in our glorious Cause and am now ready to fight and bleed again. Am a soldier for this war determined to be a free man or a dead man. Never expect to sheath my sword or cease fighting until our independence is acknowledged and our glorious Chivalrous Confederacy takes her stand as proud nation among the nations of the earth.

Elijah P. Petty to Sarah Olivia Pinner, January 4, 1864

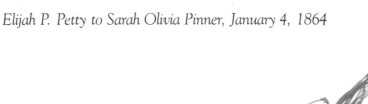

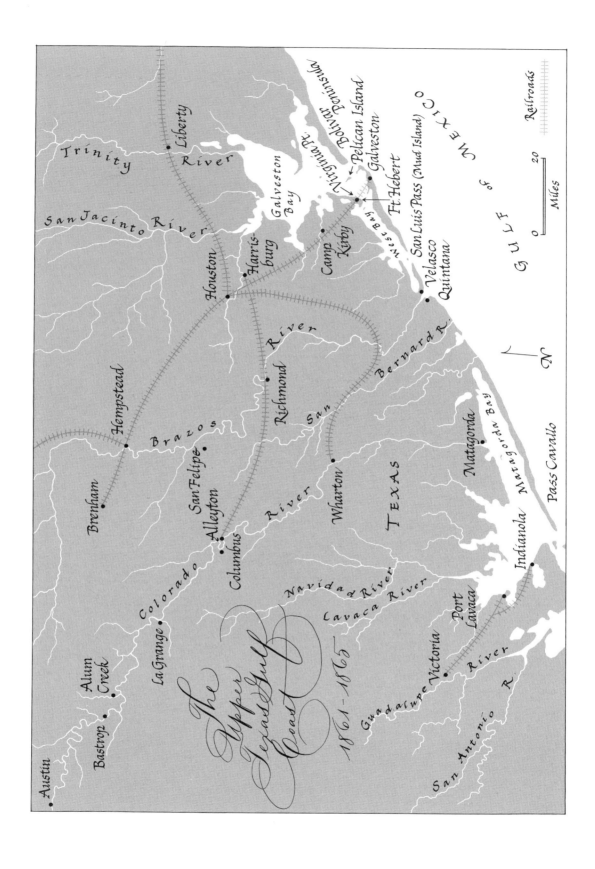

The
Upper
Texas Gulf
Coast
1861-1865

Austin

Bastrop

Alum Creek

La Grange

Colorado

Trinity River

Liberty

San Jacinto River

Brenham

Hempstead

Houston

Harris-burg

Galveston Bay

Virginia Pt.

Bolivar Peninsula

Pelican Island

Galveston

Ft. Hebert

Camp Kirby

West Bay

San Luis Pass (Mud Island)

Velasco

Quintana

Brazos

San Felipe

Alleyton

Columbus

Richmond

San

River

Bernard R.

GULF of MEXICO

N

Railroads

Miles

0   20

Colorado River

Wharton

TEXAS

Navidad River

Lavaca River

Matagorda

Matagorda Bay

Pass Cavallo

Indianola

Port Lavaca

Victoria

Guadalupe River

San Antonio R.

CHAPTER ONE

The Defense of Galveston

ON APRIL 19, 1861, PRESIDENT ABRAHAM Lincoln established a naval blockade of the Confederacy. Texas ports were not guarded by such brick forts as protected Savannah, Charleston, New Orleans and Mobile; few heavy guns were to be found in the state, none mounted for coastal defense. Helpless before a sea assault, Texans could only breathe an uneasy sigh of relief because the Federal government initially had only 42 ships for the entire blockade. When Colonel John S. Ford captured Brazos Santiago and Fort Brown on the Río Grande in February 1861, 12 of the captured guns were immediately sent to Galveston, where Sidney Sherman, a San Jacinto veteran, had been placed in command of the city's fortifications. In April he was replaced by Captain John C. Moore, a West Point graduate and college professor from Tennessee, who later rose to brigadier general. Moore soon received additional cannon taken during March at Fort Clark in west Texas. On July 2 a Federal warship, the U.S.S. *South Carolina* under Commander James Alden, arrived off Galveston to enforce the blockade. Moore deputized an officer to visit Alden under a flag of truce "for the purpose of requesting you to inform me of the object of your visit." In reply Alden sent Moore a copy of a declaration of blockade "with the single remark that I was sent here to enforce it, which I should do to the best of my ability." Alden armed the schooners *Dart*, *Shark* and *Sam Houston* from among his first ten captures along the Texas coast and was thus able to extend the blockade to Sabine Pass with only his own ship's crew and guns.[1]

With the Federal blockade a reality, enlistments in coastal artillery

units increased, each company being rushed to the Gulf Coast immediately upon mustering into service. In Galveston the Third Battalion
Texas Artillery, composed of seven companies, was organized under
Major Joseph J. Cook, a graduate of the United States Naval Academy.
A citizen's committee from Galveston, consisting of William Pitt
Ballinger, John S. Sydnor and M. M. Potter, left on July 25 for Richmond, carrying a request from General Earl Van Dorn, then commanding in Texas, for heavy ordnance. They arrived in Richmond on August
4. The previous day *South Carolina* shelled Galveston after a tender
returning from a cruise to the southward was fired upon by two of
the Confederate batteries. There was no great damage, although one
civilian was killed. When eight foreign consuls and vice-consuls in the
city protested Commander Alden did not resume his bombardment, and
the blockade continued as before. Meanwhile, Major Josiah Gorgas, the
chief of the Confederate Ordnance Bureau, offered the Galveston committee four 10-inch Columbiads, two 8-inch rifled pieces and two soon-
to-be-completed 8-inch rifled pieces, adding that gun carriages and some
32-pounders could be secured in New Orleans. These guns did not reach
Galveston until January 1862.[2]

On August 14, 1861, Paul O. Hébert of Louisiana was appointed a
brigadier general in the Confederate army and was assigned to command
the Department of Texas, replacing Van Dorn. That same day Commander W. W. Hunter of the Confederate navy was ordered to proceed
to Galveston for duty "as superintendent in charge of the works for the
defense of the coast of Texas." Hunter was authorized to appoint two
acting master's mates and one acting gunner to serve under his command. After his arrival in Texas Hunter made an elaborate survey of the
waters of Galveston Bay, which was of great service in the Confederacy's
subsequent military operations. According to Governor Francis R. Lubbock of Texas, "Hunter was a gallant officer, whose scientific knowledge
and zeal contributed much to our success in that quarter."[3]

General Hébert assumed command on September 16, 1861, with his
headquarters at Galveston. One of his first actions was to authorize
Commander Hunter to employ "such light-draft vessels, propelled by
steam or otherwise, as was deemed necessary for the defense of Galveston Harbor and the adjacent coast." The naval officer was also authorized to employ such commanders, mates, engineers, seamen and deck
hands, as the service required.[4]

As a West Point-trained engineer Hébert was appalled by the state's
Gulf Coast defenses. On September 27 he complained to Secretary of
War Leroy Pope Walker: "I regret to say that I find this coast in almost a
defenseless state, and in the almost total want of proper works and arma-

ments; the task of defending successfully any point against an attack of any magnitude amounts to a military impossibility." The port of Galveston was partially defended by a few open sand works, mounted with guns of calibers ranging from 18-pounders to 32-pounders, which were totally inadequate to resist a bombardment by heavy guns. The few large guns now on the way, "should they not arrive too late," would in some measure increase the efficiency of the harbor defenses. "On a coast like this, however, where in calm weather a landing can be effected at any point, and the bays in the rear and flank of Galveston island reached in that manner or by the pass at the west end, the problem of defense, considering the means available to that effect, is certainly one of very difficult, if not impossible solution."[5]

Hébert assigned Colonel John C. Moore, First Regiment of Texas Volunteers, to command the Military District of Galveston which comprised Galveston Island, Virginia Point, the adjacent bay coast and the peninsula of Bolivar. Before leaving Texas Van Dorn had requested Governor Edward Clark to furnish three regiments of infantry, one each for Galveston, Victoria and Fort Brown; seven companies of artillery (one light) for Fort Brown, Saluria, San Luis, Galveston and Sabine Pass; and five companies of cavalry, one for Sabine Pass and the coast to Bolivar Point, three for Galveston and one for the coast west of the city. General Henry E. McCulloch, who commanded the department until Hébert's arrival, directed the troops intended for Galveston and Sabine Pass to report to Colonel Moore for muster and orders. Hébert felt still more men were needed for coastal defense, and so, on October 7, he issued the following grandiloquent proclamation "To the Men of Texas":

TEXANS: It is more than probable that your State will soon be invaded by the sea-coast. The enemy's resources for such an attack would seem to be formidable. Yours to meet and defeat it lie almost entirely in your own strong arms, brave hearts, and trusty rifles.

Our infant Government has achieved wonders; but yet it must largely rely upon the States that created it and which have so gallantly sustained it to strain every nerve for their own individual protection. Look not to Richmond, then, for all your military inspiration and guidance. Remember the days of yore, when your own red right hands achieved your independence; and while some of your hardy sons are prepared to share the glory to be won in Virginia, Kentucky, and Missouri, and others to guard the highway to the Pacific which they have won against superior arms and numbers, be it your portion of the duty which you owe to them and yourselves to keep your soil free from the enemy's touch and to pre-

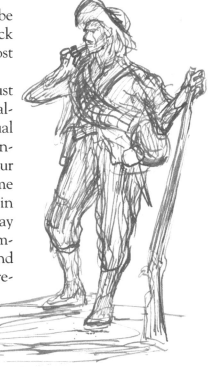

serve unsullied the fame of the Texas ranger. Let every man, then, clean his old musket, shot-gun, or rifle, run his bullets, fill his powder-horn, sharpen his knife, and see that his revolver is ready to his hand, as in the trying but glorious days when Mexico was your foe.

Organize at once into companies, if possible into battalions, and report to me promptly at Galveston and San Antonio your locality, your number, your arms, ammunition, and equipments, and your distance by day's travel, by railroad or otherwise, from the principal points on the coast.

Be ready to march at a moment's notice, and wait for orders. Rely upon it that I shall not fail to call you when needed; and when I call, I know that you will come. I am too near to San Jacinto's field to doubt for a moment that even against overwhelming numbers you will gladly rally to the defense of your homes, your families, and your liberties.

Our enemy may succeed, from his superior armaments, in ravaging your sea coast; but, God willing and you aiding, he will never hold a foot of your soil — never![6]

Privately Hébert remained gloomy and apprehensive. "As an engineer, I can but too well appreciate the defenseless state of the sea coast, see plainly what is needed generally, but of course can only deplore my inability to remedy the evil," he wrote his friend, Attorney General Judah P. Benjamin. "I much fear that I have brought my little military reputation to an early grave." These forebodings were soon realized.[7]

Among the companies responding to Hébert's appeal was the "Bastrop Lubbock Guards," organized in Precinct No. 2 of Bastrop County on September 28, 1861. The men chose the following officers: John M. Finney, captain; E. P. Petty, first lieutenant; J. Person, second lieutenant; J. H. Allen, third lieutenant; T. C. Biddle, first sergeant; R. T. Anderson, second sergeant; W. A. Perkins, third sergeant; and S. Black, fourth sergeant. The Bastrop County Court gave $185.00 from the school fund to furnish blankets to the company. The Bastrop Lubbock Guards were ordered to Galveston in late October 1861 and became Company B in Major Jared E. Kirby's Third Texas Infantry Battalion, a six-month command that served on the Texas coast and was mustered out on April 24, 1862. Nearly all of the battalion's members reenlisted in Waul's Legion.[8]

Petty's letters home begin with one to his law partner, George Washington Jones.

Camp Kirby Bayou Dickerson[9]
November 3rd AD 1861 CS1

Dear Wash[10]

Here is a copy of the correspondence between Col Nichols[11] &
Genl Hebert[12] in reference to the construction of the term emergency.

Galveston Oct 16th 1861

To Genl P. O. Hebert
Com Mil Dept of Texas
General

I am applied to for your construction of the oath the members of
my regiment are required to take. Will you favour me with your
construction of the condition "and longer if in the Opinion of the
Genl Commanding an emergency exists for further service and then
until discharged by proper Authority."

Very Respectfully
Your Obt Servt
E. B. Nichols
Col 5 Regt T V

This "emergency" is one under which no brave man would disband and go home without disgrace.

P. O. Hebert
Brig Genl

I send you this so that you may be in possession of all the information accessible to me upon this point. We have all been sworn in — Have taken an oath, a copy of the Nichols oath as interpreted or construed by Kirby[13] & Hebert and are satisfied with it. We reached the Station[14] 2½ miles from here on Friday night last and our luggage was thrown out into the mud (by the Scoundrel of a conductor) without ceremony or care where we had to sleep that night. Yesterday (Saturday) we reached this place and find comfortable quarters etc. with plenty to eat. There is but one other company here yet. Capt McDade's from Hempstead.[15] We are looking for three other companies in a day or two. So far we are well pleased with Maj Kirby & the men here seem to be gentlemen.

We are having quite a pleasant time so far (Save & except friday night) but are in a hubbub fixing up & hence must write a short letter for the present.

Your obt Servant etc
E. P. Petty

P.S. Address me at Galveston care of Maj Kirby Bayou Dickerson.

E.P.P.

Camp Kirby Dickerson Bayou
November 5th AD 1861 C.S.1

Dear Wife

At the risk of tiring you with my too numerous letters I again write proposing to give you a brief sketch of every thing since leaving home. On the day we started [Monday, Oct. 28] we only travelled 10 miles camping on Alum Creek at John Armstrongs. The teams were not able to carry the waggons any further. We bought corn at 57 cents per bushel from Wm Dickson — Howard Allen and myself had been detailed to go forward and make preparation for camping — We went to Jim Walkers and bargained for corn if we could reach it — We also went to old man Farmer's and did likewise and also procured another waggon to haul our tricks after which we returned to camp making 26 miles travel that day or 16 more than the company. Tuesday morning we started by day — Road good, we travelled finely — At Farmers received 9 additional men, got to Evergreen [Washington Co.] at noon, received two more recruits. Corn given to us today by old man Burns — Afternoon travelled 10 miles. Corn given to us to night — Wednesday morning 2 of our waggon mules gone — Put two men afoot and their mules in the waggon and started — Corn given us today by James Shepherd 11 miles from Brenham. Reached Brenham about 4½ O'clock — Unfurled our banner[16] and marched majest'ckly through the town. Had to buy corn to night at 40 cents per bushel. Thursday morning started at 9 O'clock on Extra Train for Hempstead — which place we reached about 11 O'clock a.m. with our banner fluttering gloriously in the breeze. Just as the cars stopped we discovered wheeling into the plaza Capt Highsmiths Company[17] with their banner floating out beautifully — We all formed on the platform & when Capt H. halted I gave the Command three Cheers for the Bastrop Cavalry. When the boys made the Welkin ring Capt H's company returned 3 cheers for the Bastrop Lubbock Guards after which they dismounted and there was a general mingling & shaking hands of friends. We staid in Hempstead 2 hours during which time it blew and rained most furiously and about half the boys of both Companies besides several that did'nt belong to either Company got good & mellow. About 8 or 10 of Capt H's men had quit him on the Change from State to Confederate service and his men set to seduce our boys and get them in to fill up his Command and before I found it out had about a dozen disaffected and several had expressed their determination to quit us and join him — I however with persuasion, remonstrance and some curses prevailed upon the men and they all remained. It is due to Capt H to say that he had nothing to do with it, that he discourged it with his men and was the first to give me notice of what was going on — We left Hempstead at one Oclock p.m. 2 miles below H. is Col [William H.] Parson's Camp [Camp Groce] — When we passed it it was raining furiously but the men was on the road side in numbers and Cheer after Cheer went up on Car & in Camp — I formed Col Parsons acquaintance at Hempstead. He is a verry pleasant affable gentleman and did some tremendous bragging on the Bastrop boys[18]— He examined our flag and compared with Capt H's and pronounced our's much the neatest and prettiest — We reached Houston at 8 O'clock. It was dark, cold, muddy & wet — We quartered in a large Cotton Shed and spent a pleasant night under all the circumstances. Friday we spent in Houston & several of the boys got considerable drunk but acted the gentlemen — At 3 O'clock we left our Cotton Shed for the Depot of the Galveston R R about 1 mile

— We marched in regular order with our banner in the breeze through Houston — At the Cars Major Kirby met us, made a stirring speech and we were sworn in by Lieut [J.] Sparks of the Confederate Army. I forgot to state that we had hardly got into our cotton shed on the night before when recruiting officers for other Companies and regiments were amongst us trying to disaffect our men and enroll them — This they kept up until Capt Finney and myself invited the gentlemen to leave our Camp and not return any more.

They had our men considerably disaffected and at one time I thought we were going under entirely but thanks to our zeal and the good sense of the Company all were sworn in — We left H at 5 Oclock and reached Dickerson Bayou at about 8 Oclock at night.

Capt Finney and Lieut Camp[19] staid over at Houston & I had charge of the Company — We crossed the Bayou from the Station when the infernal conductor stopped the cars (contrary to his promise) in the muddiest and worst place he could have found and tumbled every thing we had into the mud — breaking and otherwise damaging our things to a great extent. In tumbling out the things they piled up against the cars and he was about to start them the result of which would have been to tumble every thing into a creek of running water. I told him if he did a d---d Scoundrel I would put a rail on the track and throw his d---d concern in the creek and called upon the boys to get a rail — This sort of brought him to his senses & he waited 10 or 15 minutes on us. The boys wanted to crucify him on the spot — One drew his knife, another his pistol etc but they were stopped I thinking it better to submit to the outrage rather than get into a difficulty and ruin the good reputation of our County but I have given some of the soldiers a Carte blanch to whip the Scoundrel whenever the oppertunity offers — There we were in the mud and dark, cold and without fire, and Bob Rice, Bunt Dabney and W. R. Shearn sick — About this time a soldier from Maj Kirby's Command appeared amongst us and said he would show us a house near by where there was a good pile of wood but he did not think the man would sell it. I called for 10 men to go with me after the wood — Also took the sick with me. We found the house, the wood and the owner but he refused to sell his wood. I told the boys to take it any how, to keep an account of it and I would pay for it. You bet they rolled with big loads of wood then — I then told the man that I had three sick men and that I wanted them to stay in his house — This he also refused. I told him that it was no use of talking it had to be so. Finally he consented to every thing, took the sick, made coffee — Gave them good beds & treated them well etc. We soon had good fires, cooked and eat our

Suppers, stretched our tents and our limbs & slept as soundly and as snugly as we ever did in our lives — Next morning Saturday we paid the old fellow, struck our tents — Put all our baggage in a boat which Maj Kirby had sent us and marched to this place about 2 miles where we were received with military eclat by the Company which was here ahead of us. We reached here about noon Saturday. This place is on the South side of Dickerson Bayou about 21 miles by R R from Galveston. This is a low, flat, wet, muddy, sticky prarie Country with verry little timber. It is a cold, clamy, crawfishy soil & produces verry little but sweet potatoes and pumpkins which grow finely. On the Bayou however it is a sightly country and there are some fine residences. It is principally occupied by rich citizens from Galveston as a summer resort. They seem now to be occupying them permantly. The place we are at is a large beef packery. They are not now at work at that beef packing business but are preparing to begin it in a short time. So I expect we will have to leave it. There is house room enough for the Battalion here with 3 verry large Cisterns. The Bayou water is not regarded as healthy (though at this season it is fresh) and is only used for washing. There is one family living here and I have engaged the lady to do my washing — I could'nt think of doing it myself — This part of my letter is strictly private — _____ has not kept his promise to me at all and has been drinking considerably since leaving home — So has Lieut _____ & Seargent _____ — F & C were tight when they got in from Houston. Sunday they all got pretty tight and had a general playing of cards & betting. Sunday night _____ lost about 15 dollars. Monday morning I was appointed officer of the day and of course had full control of the Company. The first order I issued was prohibiting gaming under penalty of double duty, standing guard etc. I was appealed to, remonstrated with and told that I was about take all the privileges the poor soldier had away etc. I was inexorable and drove gaming from the public gaze — The boys had to sneak out in out houses and play if they played at all. Monday evening Capt F, Lieut C and Seargent B went to Galveston as they say on business as I think on a frolick and so I am still in Command of the Company and have I think broken up gambling. I have no trouble now with the men — They all respect me and if their actions speak any thing love me. I am mild and kind and free with them and we are getting along like a band of brothers. I drill them moderately though sufficiently and they are learning fast. I think that soon we will have an efficent Company.[20] Capt F. will return in the morning when my authority ceases. Capt F as well as all the officers are liked, respected and loved by all the men — We are all a band of brothers and the other soldiers quartered here had to ask which were the officers and further remarked that they never saw such a Company before that they could'nt tell the officers from the men — Their officers are stiff, starchy and reserved. We are doing fine — All the sick are now well — We have plenty to eat and good appetites to eat it with. There are two Companies here and two other parts of Companies. We only number 56 and had to borrow & splice on a part of the other Companies to make ours full so that we could report and draw rations. Some of us may come up recruiting soon if so I will endeavour to get to come. Jim Cunningham is here with a part Company & if he fails to get his full will unite with us — We are 3 miles by land from the bay and 7 miles from by the Bayou. We are stationed here to defend the R. R. bridge 2 miles above here — War steamers can come in 17 miles of this place and their gun boats can come up to the bridge without even going any way near Galveston and it is thought that if they attempt to attack Galveston that a simultanious attempt will be made to seize the bridge at this point, cut off communication & reinforcements from Galveston and not only starve out or capture that place but have the R R to Houston & the up Country — So you see that this is an important post and is likely to be a hot one too — Well if they come they will find out that we are here, that's all —

I must stop. My hand is tired and I am sleepy besides it late so adios — my dear.

E. P. Petty

P.S.
My little ones God bless them how are they etc.

E.PP

Camp Kirby Dickerson Bayou
November 7th 1861

Dear Daughter

I have concluded to send you a few lines both for pleasure and for pastime. There is nothing transpiring here that is of particular interest. We are just here drilling some and loafing more. We drill about 3 hours per day and the boys spend the ballance of the time some in running to the Depot — some in singing and dancing — some in sailing on the Bayou & others boat riding and some in gaming & such other pastime as their fancy may select. When I have command of the Company I prohibit gaming but when Capt. Finney is in command it runs rife — Last night some of the boys were engaged in singing some good old Camp Meeting songs. The noise disturbed Capt. F. and he ordered it stopped — I told him that he had better stop a game of cards that was going on in his presence — and let the men sing — that one was pleasant recreation whilst the other was contaminating and ruinous in its effects — He concluded to stop neither and so the men continued their songs and their game. Capt. F. says however that he intends to stop gaming — I hope he will — Lieutenant McLester[21] and 4 of our men have gone down to Galveston and will be back to day — When it comes to my turn to run about I will come up home I think — You dont know how much I miss you all. Your bright faces, innocent smiles and amusing & pleasant prattle — But my Country needs my services and I would be worse than no man and unworthy of my wife and children if I refused or failed to respond to her call[22] — I must close as the man starts to the office. Kiss the little & big ones & write to me.

Truly
E P Petty

Alliton[23] 28th Novr 1861

Dear Mag

We arrived here this evening safe and sound — Had quite a pleasant trip down — Have only 3 recruits.

I send by the waggon one half barrel Sugar house molasses for which I paid 50 cents per gallon or $12.00 for the whole. Its freight up will be nothing I suppose as the waggon goes back empty.
I thought it best to lay in while I had the money & could save freight.
We go down in the morning   no news up to night by the cars —

Truly yours etc
E. P. Petty

P.S
35 vessels off the mouth of the Mississippi River, also fighting at Pensacola.[24]

E.P.P.

Camp Kirby
Dickerson Bayou
Decr. 5th 1861

Dear Wife

As Capt Finney will return to Bastrop on tomorrow I take the oppertunity of sending you a short letter. I was quite sick yesterday notwithstanding which I drilled part of the day and at 4 O'clock PM.

acted as Adjutant to the Major in dress parade and he says acquitted myself with honor though it was my first effort in the new position. The Major's wife & two other ladies were present and hence I was on my p's & q's and put forward my best foot. I am quite well to day and will act as Adjutant again this evening and the Major has requested to assist him in organizing the Battalion which perhaps I will do. The health of our Camp is now good with but little exception. The weather is fine but our Water has run short. The Cisterns at Tallow Town[25] are empty and the Bayou has become salt for want of rain and we are using tank water which is good at present. When this fails we will have to dig a well. If it should rain soon it will save us this necessity. We are making cartridges — moulding bullets, rubbing up guns & pistols & sharpening knives for the purpose of welcoming the Lincolnites "with bloody hands to hospitable graves"[26] when they see fit to make a foray on Galveston. There is no appearance of a fleet off Galveston yet. A council of war was held there a few days ago & it was determined that the place was indefensible and hence all the guns were moved to the Main land at Virginia Point[27] and every body run when the guns went except a few Yankees and Dutch who remain to welcome the Lincolnites when they come.[28] The soldiers however have not all gone but a regiment or so is still in possession of the place. Genl Hebert's family is on this Bayou and he comes up every evening on a special train to see his wife. He is up to day & out hunting so it does'nt seem that he is verry apprehensive of an attack soon.[29] Dec^r-6th All well in camps this morning so far as I know. Had dress parade yesterday evening — I acted as adjutant — It went off verry well — after parade Maj K called upon me to drill the Battalion which I did for one hour. It went off quite well for the first time. Our Company did first rate. There is some prospect of rain today — hope it will. We are out of Coffee & cant get for love or money. If you can buy & send me some by Capt F do so. Sherman Reynolds had some when I was up — also send some rye[30] or Barley to mix in. My love & kisses to my little ones & compliments to Mrs Turner & family. Thine truly

E. P. Petty

Camp Kirby
Decr 8th 1861

My Dear Ella

I know of no better way of spending a Sabbath hour than in writing to my little duck of a daughter. I am just in from Tallow Town where we had dress parade, I acting as adjutant to the Battalion which by the way is a very prominent position as much if not more than Major though the rank is not so high — I am only acting temporarily as an accomodation to Major Kirby. There were several ladies out to see us and they have promised to visit our Camp this evening. I hope they will do so as it is a great relief to the Soldiers to be cheered by the presence of the ladies. We dont get as much news here as you do at home except from Galveston. It quite exciting down there now — as on friday last 3 more vessels loaded with troops appeared before that place. They haven't attempted to land yet but have been figuring around as though they were going to and keep the people all in alarm. Nearby every body has left the place and the Gen[l] has had all the big guns moved over to Virginia Point so that the Lincolnites can't Capture them.[31] Col Morre's [Moore's] Regiment has also been removed to Houston so that it can go either east or west if necessary.[32] There isn't over 1500 or 2000 troops now on the island. Genl Hebert has just issued orders to have the Rail Road & Telegraph from Virginia Point to Houston guarded night and day to prevent injury to them and to prevent the enemy in case of an attack on Galveston from cutting off comunication & reinforcements. Things look like a fight down this way and you need not be surprised to hear of one at any day. We have been spending two days in making cartridges, pouches etc so as to be ready at a moment to go to Galveston or fight here. We are pretty poorly provided with every thing except baggage and that will be in our way if we have a fight. I think I shall go down to Galveston in a few days to take observations if we are not ordered down soon. If we

fight my dear Ella your father will be found in the front rank, let it cost what it may if he keeps his senses & can get there. I have no news to write particularly. You have heard that Caravajal has attacked Matamoros and is likely [to] carry the place if he has not already done so.[33] Poor Mrs Graves ran away from Texas to get out of war & trouble and jumped right into it. They dont hurt women and children in war however unless it is accidentally done.

Give my love to all my little ones & wife and respects to Mrs. Turner & family & others. Write soon & often.

Yours truly
E. P. Petty

Camp Kirby
Dec[r] 10th 1861

Dear Margaret

Your's of the 5th inst has just been received — I sent a letter yesterday to Ella and one a few days ago to you in which I gave all I could find out about the prospects ahead. I now give you the news from Galveston up to yesterday morning (the 9th). There was no vessel in sight except a tender belonging to the blockading vessel, even the blockader the Santee had withdrawn[34] So that for the present all is quiet and the prospect of a fight removed. It is my opinion that the appearance of the vessels here was a feint and that the point of attack on Texas will be the Rio Grande so as to cut off & capture a large train of guns & munitions comeing to us across Mexico, also to cut off our Mexican trade and reach San Antonio by that route and this opinion seems to be gaining amongst military men in these parts — all we can do is to be ready — wait & see. There has been no order for the removal of Parson's Regiment here. There is a rumor and it is but a rumor that Parson's Regiment will be sent to San Antonio to be in readiness to meet this anticipated Western invasion. People are getting thick on Dickerson Bayou now being refugees from Galveston. Some of the officers in this Battalion have had their wifes down here for a few days and the ladies seemed to have passed the time agreeably — We have had no rain or cold weather here since we have been down. The trees are yet green. This is quite a pleasant country now but when it rains I had rather be delivered. I am in fine health since my days sickness last week and am hard at work drilling our Company in the morning and the Battalion in the evening. I am doing more work than any five men in the Battalion. Lieut Camp had the sick Head ache this week & suffered much but is now well. Oscar Nash had a chill & fever yesterday to day is better — There is no sickness of any consequence here. I send you a news paper with latest news. You will find in it the Matamoras fight. Poor Mrs Graves. How my heart bleeds for her. See the destruction of her brother Anton's property. I wish she was back in Bastrop.[35] Remember me kindly to my friends & kiss my little ones for me — I only wrote this to post you in matters this way and rely upon it that I give you the news correctly as I have it.

Yours Truly
E. P. Petty

Camp Kirby Dickerson Bayou
December 11th AD 1861 CS1

Dear Ella

I have nothing of any consequence to write and only do so to pass time pleasantly. Camp life would be monotonous to me if I were not kept so busy in drilling haveing to drill both Company and Battalion and when I am not engaged at this I feel like writing to you or your ma — Camp life is rough — one hears many things which will not bear repeating and will hardly bear listening to. I promised you all when I left home that I did not intend to loose my character and standing as a citizen but intended when I returned to assume my place and be the citizen again. I intend to fulfil this promise to the letter. I thought last week that before now there would have been a battle fought at Galveston and I so wrote to you and your ma — but at present the prospect is not quite so good, the ships except the blockade all having left for the West so that I now have no idea any thing about it. Hope that they will have too much sense to attack us — It is cold to night — the north wind blows cold to night and the rain is now pattering on my tent. It is the first winter we have had. It now rains hard and we will have a chance to try our tents. A poor fellow in Capt Whitehead's Company[36] died last night with quinsy[37] after a very short illness and we buried him this evening with military honors. I superintended the burial honors (the first I ever saw) and did it up like a book. It was a sad scene to bury a poor soldier far from friends & home with no dear ones to follow him to his last resting place. Capt Whitehead has several sick in his company. There is one or two sick with chills & fever in our Company. Oscar Nash and Cummings Burleson have chills, a few others are grunty a little but of no consequence. It rains furiously — good as it will fill our cisterns & give us some good water again. I send you a song "Dixie" — the boys sing it beautiful down here.[38] There is nothing of interest here to write. My love & kisses to all.

Yours truly
E.P. Petty

Dixie, the War Song

1. Away down at Dickerson Station
   There we had an organization
     Away away away in Dixie
   Major Kirby was our guide
   The Bastrop boys stood by his side
     Away away away in Dixie
       In Dixie land I'll take my stand
       And live and die for Dixie

2. Orders came from Genl Hebert
   For Kirby's boys to move to the car
     Away away away in Dixie
   And away down to Galveston
   There to have a little fun
     Away away away in Dixie etc

3. They wanted us to shovel sand
   In our own sweet & happy land
     Away away away in Dixie
   But Maj Kirby gave Command
   My boys shall not shovel sand
     Away away away in Dixie etc

4. They learned us there to double quick
   And swore it was the verry lick
     Away away away in Dixie
   And in the abscence of Major Kirby
   They drilled away both late and early
     Away away away in Dixie

5. Major Kirby is the Man
   To lead us on in Dixie land
     Away away away in Dixie
   He has brought us all safe thus far
   And bids defiance to Genl Hebert
     Away away away in Dixie etc

6. Company A has Captain McDade
   Of the Yankee boys is not afraid
     Away away away in Dixie
   He left his home and family
   To fight for honor and liberty
     Away away away in Dixie etc

7. There's Captain Finney bold & true
   In drill he sometimes puts us through

Away away away in Dixie
To all his boys kind and free
Here's to our Capt three times three
    Away away away in Dixie
8. Captain Whitehead of Company C
    The most gallant man of all the three
        Away away away in Dixie
    When honor and liberty are at stake
    On Yankee scamps his mark will make
        Away away away in Dixie
9. There's adjutant Petty among the rest
    We believe that he is the best
        Away away away in Dixie
    And when upon the battle field
    He'll prove himself as true as steel
        Away away away in Dixie etc

Camp Kirby. Dickerson Bayou
December 15th 1861

Dear Margaret

I have received but one letter from home since leaving and I am sure that I have written some 5 or 6. Dont understand me as grumbling but if you knew how much good it did me to get a letter from you and Ella you would write more of them even if it was but a line or two. Since I wrote last things have been quiet in these parts until yesterday and today — Yesterday morning a large Steamer joined the blockader and up to this morning was still there. I have heard this evening from a gentleman who left Virginia Point since 12 O'clock and he says that on last night the alarm gun was fired and the troops were up arms in hand all night, but it was extremely foggy and nothing was attempted — that some time this morning the Ship which was heavily laden with troops sai[lle]d down towards the West end of the island and there is some alarm about an effort to land to night — of course this creates some little stir in military quarters and we have to hold ourselves ready to go down at a moments notice. There is no knowing what a day may bring forth in this quarter. I intend to keep you fully posted as far as I can find out. Madam rumor is rife in reports, some few true and many eronious — I give them all to you as I get them and you must judge for yourself — I would not be astonished either way fight or no fight and I want you to be prepared for either issue — Another item of news (and it is important) is that the New York Herald has in a recent publication a full report of the number of Troops in Texas from Galveston to Hempstead — their locality, efficiency and names of officers. They are as well posted as Gen¹ Hebert himself So you see that we have spies in our midst. It would do me much good to catch one or more so as to have a hanging spell some morning before breakfast. There is verry little sickness in our Camp — a few chills and fever cases. Capt Whitehead has some considerable sickness yet amongst his men and in Capt McDade's Company sickness is on the increase owing to the increase of number and the offensiveness of the Beef Packery. We had Battalion inspection the other day. Major Stith inspector for the State was here to inspect our arms etc.[39] Major Kirby called upon Lieut [W.O.G.] Wilson of Capt McDade's Company to act as adjutant. After inspection Major Stith called upon them to manoeuvre the Battalion. This they (Maj K. & Lieut W) would'nt near undertake and so Lieut Petty was called upon and for about an hour put them through the Battalion drill under the observation of Maj S. who is an old & experienced officer — After

it was over Maj. S. voluntarily called upon me and stated in the
presence of Maj K & others that I was about the best drill officer he
had seen and that in his report to Genl Hebert he would give me a
commendatory notice and to day I was up at the Depot when the cars
passed and Major S was on them on his way from Galveston and he
called me to the window and in the presence of several gentlemen told
me that he had done so. I tell you these things not to be told to others
out of the family but that you may have some idea of how I am
deporting myself down here. It makes me proud to know it myself and
happy to communicate it to my family. I have bought me a fine
Uniform Coat. Gave twenty five dollars for it. You never saw the like
of brass buttons and when I get it on I feel quite <u>malicious</u>. I enjoy
splendid health & cheerful spirits. My love to my little ones & respects
to friends.

Yours truly
E. P. Petty

Decr 16th 1861

P.S. Private — I am terribly mortified this morning from this cause —
Whilst in attendance upon divine service on yesterday (Sunday) Oscar
F Nash shot a pig belonging to the proprietor of the land upon which
we are located and I have just issued a warrant for his arrest. It is
mortifying in the extreme and I am surely troubled much about it.
It is the first thing that has happened since we left home that I can
seriously complain about.

E. P. Petty

Camp Kirby Decr 18th 1861

Dear Wife

I received night before last [from] Mr Sid Person your letter & also
Ella's of the 14th & 13th also one pair of wollen sock — Also I received
yesterday your letter of 10th inst. These make three letters from home
received by me since my return here. I have verry little to write in
addition to what I have already stated in my numerous letters (I think
I have written at least six). There is no present imminent prospect of a
fight in these parts, all the vessels save the Santee (the blockader)
having left Galveston for parts unknown to me. So it goes one day

vessels & excitement and the next vessels all gone and quiet restored. I sometimes think that after a while we will have a fight and sometimes I dont but most of the time I think we will — I cant tell however much more if any than you can up there. In fact I believe rumor is more rife in Camps than elsewhere. In the last week we have received nine recruits making our number now — officers & men — seventy five. We sent one man — Cummings Burleson — home sick. He was quite sick. I dont know what ailed him — I heard from him at Brenham. He was better. We have another man — George Smith — quite sick — He has a pretty severe attack of pneumonia. He is some better today but quite sick and is anxious to go home and if he should be able to stand the trip I think I will send him up next Saturday. I am so sorry for his father — just lost one son in Kentucky — Ferrills Company[40] — and now another quite sick. Oscar Nash is unwell — has a furlough & will stay up a few days to recruit his health etc. Talking of Oscar — I wrote you that I had him under arrest for shooting a hog. I want you to keep these little misgivings of our soldiers to yourself. I dont want to tell tales out of school — Oscar made full atonement for his offense. Paid for the hog etc — The owner Mr Harris & his wife interceded for him & I released him — Spilby Garrett is having Chills. Mr [W.] Morgan is also with a chill to day —

these with the exception of some little cramp colic & the like constitute our sick list — The ballance are quite well. I enjoy splendid health — I think that sickness is diminishing in all the camps here. We have plenty to eat — I have to my own astonishment got so I can use tea and dont miss coffee at all. Keep your own coffee at home — you will need it worse than I will. You ask about the ½ barrel of Molasses — I sent it in Tom Hill's waggon — the same that carried the letter to you about it. I told the negro — that the first time his master's waggon went to town to carry it up to you, that if you got it by Christmas it would do — It will be forthcomeing in due time I suppose. You asked about buying things at Galveston or Houston & sending up etc. I can buy from our Sutler any thing I want on my Confederacy pay but the prices are exorbitant in the extreme, at least 100 per Cent higher than they were in Bastrop when I left and hence I dont think I will buy any thing down here more than I am compelled to. Dont spend any more money than is absolutely necessary — When the little money you have is gone you loose one of your best friends. On the 31st of this month we are to be paid off our wages in full to that date. My pay will be two months' wages which at $90 per mo. makes $180. From this I shall have to deduct my expenses, say $20 per mo., $25 for my military coat and $10 which I shall spend in having a photograph taken showing me from head to feet with full rigged regimental on. This will be taken in picture frame for wall hanging & will be beautiful. I will send it up just as soon as I can have it taken and get a chance — The artist is now here but is quite busy for the present. My Coat is exactly like Capt Finney's so you can form some idea of it. Tom Biddle is just now starting our musical band over to Tallow Town to have it ambrotyped. As to hiring a negro — I want you to do so if you can. Of course Mrs Turner can help you & you could get along without one until I come home but when she leaves you know we must have one and it will be cheaper and a better chance to get one now than at that season. I have written to Harvey Wilbarger, Old man John Price, Newton G. Alsup and H K McDonald to call upon you and pay you all the money they could and that you would receipt them for it. Wily Tom was to bring the pork in when it was seasonable to do so. I dont want it at such a time as that it would spoil. I think Jim Weaver will bring in the promised beef yet. Jim has never disappointed me when he promised positively. It may be so warm is the reason. Do the best you can to provide — I will send up all my money that I can spare when I get it. I have heard of Mrs Highsmith's being up at Parson's Regiment. If Capt Finney was at home I would go up & see her and may be so I will do so when he does come. God bless the little Children, how it makes my heart yearn for them to hear of their affection for their "poor old daddy." I think of them much more than they do of me. I read Ella's letters to the boys in Camps and the general opinion is that she is spunkier than her father. This is all I know and can write for the present.

Your's truly
E. P. Petty

P.S. Send me by Oscar Nash the best vest I have.

E.P.P.

Camp Kirby Decr 20th 1861

My Dear Ella

Capt Finney & M^r Jo Sims reached camp last night and brought me your Ma's & your letter with a sack of coffee & rye. I am much obliged to you & her for them. I sent your Ma a letter by Charley Caldwell who I expected reached Bastrop to day. I also sent you a present — "Gentle Annie Songster" which James Cunningham gave me to send to you. You must learn the songs and sing to me when I get home[41]— You want know when I am comeing home. This I cant answer — I reckon not until my time is out in the spring. I would love to see you all every day but the affairs of Camp are such as to require my constant attention. The men expect it of me and I must not throw them off. I wish it was otherwise, so that I could enjoy the society of my wife and children more. Capt Finney & Lieut Camp have gone down to Galveston to night so that you see I am necessary here — Capt Whitehead has just got up to night from Galveston and says that two more ships appeared before Galveston this evening. What they are and what they are after I will not even guess, but suppose that they are not after much good. We sent a few days ago all the sick men we had in camps home where they could be better taken care of. I send you some verses "The Child's Wish" which please carefully read and cherish. It goes home to most any child and you and your brothers can realize it fully if your minds can comprehend its import. Your's can I am sure.[42] I want you to take a little more pains in your writing and spelling, as I exhibit your letters verry frequently. I want you to study your books assiduously and attentively also your music. Be obedient to your teachers, polite to those who are your elders, pleasant & agreeable to your equals and kind & attentive to those younger and above all be obedient to your Mother and kind to your brothers. They are all in all to you. You must love, honor & cherish them above all others. This advice will do for Frank as well as you & I want you to instruct him in it. When Don gets older he will understand it. In the mean [time] give the bent of their minds that direction. You know that I love you all & will advise you what I think best. I will write to you & keep you posted.

Bob Rice had a chill to day & has fever to night. I hope he will be better in the morning. I have just learned to night that Gen¹ Hebert will be up to review our Battalion tomorrow.

Yours truly
E. P. Petty

The Child's Wish!

1 Oh I long to lie dear Mother
   on the cool & fragrant grass
   With the calm blue sky above my head
   And the shadowy clouds that pass
2 And I want the bright bright sunshine
   To play around my head
   I'll close my eyes and God will think
   Your little child is dead
3 Then Christ will send an angel
   To bear me up to him
   He'll bear me slow and steady
   Far through the ether dim
4 And then he'll gently lay me
   Close by the Savior's side
   And when I think that I am in heaven
   My eyes I'le open wide
5 And I'le look around the angels
   Who stand around the throne
   Till I find my own dear sister
   For I know she must be one
6 Then I'le put my arms around her
   And look into her eyes
   And remember all I say to her
   And all her sweet replies
7 And when I find her, Mother!
   We'll go away alone

I'le tell her how we mourned for her
All the while that she's been gone
8 And then I'le ask the Angel
To bear me back to you
He'll bear me slow and steady
Down through the ether blue
9 And you'll only think dear Mother
That I've been out to play
And have gone to sleep beneath the tree
This sultry summer day

Galveston Texas
Decr 25th 1861

My Dear Wife

You will see by the above heading that I am spending my Christmas here. I have been laboring hard since I came from home and I concluded to relax by visiting this place and taking a view of our mortal enemy. Through a spy glass from an observatory on one of the highest buildings in this City I have seen for the first time our enemy the blockader together with another small vessel near her. I have also seen again the "Stars and Stripes" — glorious old flag but now the emblem of hate & tyranny. I could see the vessel plain though she was about seven miles off — I could see the port holes for her guns etc. I have visited all the notable places around here and also been out to one Christmas party and one tea party etc and when I get back to Camps & quiet I will try and give you some of the particulars of my trip. "I could'nt afford to give you all." I am quite well and left all well in Camps. I came down day before yesterday & will go up to morrow. I saw preparations in camps for some frollicking about head quarters and concluded to dodge it for myself — Lieut McLester & Jim Cunningham are with me. M^{c}L is comeing up home in a few days on business when I will try & write again. I merely write this much to keep up the times and also keep you posted. I enclose you the latest news.[43] You will see that it is verry important and if true the rotten U.S. Government will go under for 90 days. If England demands the restoration of our Ministers and an apology for the insult to her flag the U.S. will be in a dilema — If she refuses war is the consequence & of course England & the Confederate States can soon settle the question for her. If she complies — she disgraces herself in the eyes of the world — demoralizes her own people and will not be worth barking at by the dogs. This is glorious news & I could enjoy it with a zest but it comes blended with bad — the death of Col Terry.[44] That was a terrible lick to us — The name of Terry had become a terror to the Yankees and his death will discourage us and give them renewed confidence etc. & hence it becomes a blow that will be felt. I want you to hold yourself in readiness to come down if I send for you. I don't know that I will but I may. I want to show you the prettiest city in the Confederate States, Galveston — I will write you further after awhile — Kiss my loved ones and believe me truly

Yours Etc
E. P. Petty

Camp Kirby
Dec[r] 27th 1861

My Dear Ella

I received your letter of the 23rd last night and on the night before or rather on yesterday morning one from your Ma dated the 20th & 21st. I have concluded to answer both letters in one and hope your Ma will be satisfied with it particularly as I wrote one to her from Galveston 2 days ago. I am in good health. Yesterday we started another man home sick — Walter Clark from the Yegua [a district of Bastrop County]. There are one or two more complaining in camps — and perhaps one will have to be sent home. The ballance are generally well. The health of the other camps is much improved. I spent my Christmas in Galveston and you cant imagine how bad I wanted my family with [me]. I would have given almost any sum of money to have had you there. I saw on Monday last premonitory signs of a big spree in camps, beginning at head quarters & running all through the whole system and so Lt McLester & myself concluded to make our escape in time — We took the cars Monday evening & reached Galveston about 8 O'clock at night & stopped at the Washington Hotel. Tuesday morning we found some friends & with them visited Genl. Hebert's Head Quarters and registered our names, official position, date of arrival, Hotel where to be found etc all of which is required by official orders. I then visited the Quarter Master Department and put in a requisition for a tent to which I am entitled. After this I struck out for sight seeing & pleasure generaly. Visited the Soldiers quarters, the wharves and shipping etc — Found Professor Hancock[45] & with him went up on top of his son in law's store (four stories high) & on to the

observatory & with a large glass looked at our Mortal Enemy, Lincoln's blockader. She was about seven miles off — and I could see her pretty plain — her spars & ropes — The stars & stripes and the piercings or port holes for her guns. She was sitting like a duck on the water not caring a fig what became of any thing. There was another small three masted vessel near her equally as quiet as the blockader. In the evening we went out to see Col E.B. Nichols Regiment drill which I witnessed until about four o'clock. They did'nt manuever as well as I expected. They went through 2 or 3 common place manuevers after which they passed in review before Genl Hebert & closed the scenes — I also saw a couple of squads of men going through the drill of the piece with 2 six pound Cannon which was quite new & interesting to me — I saw the twin sisters, the 2 cannon used by the Texans at the battle of San Jacinto — They were iron 6 pounders. At the Annexation of Texas to the Union they were ceded to the U.S. Government and went into the Arsenal at Baton Rouge Louisiana and at the Secession of that state her citizens seized the arsenals and these guns among the rest. The Legislature of Louisiana had the Twin Sisters refitted & reequipped and made them a present to Texas and they are now in Galveston in good order & ready for service in defence of our liberty again.[46] Lt McLester & myself were invited to tea by Mrs Fanny Armstrong (Hancock) which we accepted and spent a verry pleasant

evening in the family — at 8 O'clock we had another engagement at
the house of Mr. Hughes, large Commission Merchant of the firm of
Mathew Hughes & Landers. We met some nice young ladies & several
married ones & several gentlemen, had egg nog & cake in abundance
& enjoyed ourselves elegantly until about 11 O'clock — On Christmas
Morning the Soldiers were allowed holiday and a good many of them
got drunk — a good many were arrested and carried to the guard
house. There was verry little shooting of Christmas guns for the want
of powder. This morning I visited the Catholic Cathedral which was
opened for the public. It was quite a curiosity to me [47]— I cant
describe it to you on paper — my descriptive powers are not sufficient
but it was magnificent with its tall gothic windows painted with
variegated colors, its crucifixes & crosses, its forms of Jesus & Mary, its
long white tapers, its fine pictures of the diferent scenes connected
with the crucifixion, its font of Holy Water and its large fine Organ. It
would be of vast advantage to you to visit it. In the evening I went
back to services and staid & witnessed the ceremonies awhile — It was
strange to me to see men, women & little children comeing in &
going to the font of Holy Water — dipping in the tips of their fingers
& crossing themselves. I went out to the batteries on the Gulf and saw
the big 32 pound guns, looking out grimly on the gulf and frowning at
the blockade — with large piles of balls lying near etc. A sentinel at

each gun to keep off intruders would meet us & keep us at a respectable distance. I stood upon the sea side and witnessed the angry surf roll in at my feet for half hour with profound pleasure. It was a grand sight to witness old Ocean foaming with wrath and bellowing at your feet. It was day when I returned (Thursday morning) and I saw the fortifications made at Eagle Grove (the Island side of the bridge) and at Virginia Point. They look pretty & strong and I think will command & secure the bridge in case of attack — The long rows of white tents and clouds of smoke arising at Virginia Point showed beautiful and told of many a soldier deprived of the comforts of home besides myself. In Galveston and within a few hours reach I think there must be some 5 or 6 000 soldiers so that Lincoln must come pretty strong to defeat us — I got back to camps 9½ O'clock yesterday (Thursday) morning & found an invitation by Maj Kirby for the whole battalion to take Dinner with him [at] Tallow Town. We marched the company over through the rain and to the table in the rain. It rained all the time they were at dinner. They said it was a first rate dinner notwithstanding. I with the officers were invited to dine in the house with Col. Kirby's Mother, Wife, daughter & some 2 or 3 other ladies who were visitors. I hav'nt set down to a wedding supper or dinner in Texas that is equal to that dinner. Every thing that woman's delicate taste could suggest or man's whimsical appetite could desire was there — meats from roast turkey to pickled hog's brains — pies & cakes in superabundance — were on that table — all it lacked of being a wedding was the bride, the bridgegroom & the parson. I think I shall go up to Harrisburg[48] in the morning to see Mrs Highsmith & Capt Highsmith — I shall stay up 2 days if I go. It was impossible for me to come up Christmas — It is with a squeeze that I can get away from camps for a few days — I have become a necessity here and cant be spared. I want you to write to me often without being so particular about my answering every one. You need'nt become so jealous of your Ma and be scared about my writing to her so often. I knew your Ma a good while before I did you and loved her first and longest and you must continue to let this be the case — I love you and the other children as well as any body could love their children — Aye I even sometimes think that I am foolish about you but your Mother I love because she is the mother of my darling little children — I love her for her sake — for your sake and for my own — so dont fret if I write most to her — You can read them all & that will do you as much good — Kiss all the children & your Ma for me & believe me truly

Yours etc.
E.P. Petty

Dear Wife

    I merely have time to drop you a line as I did not know until last night that Mr. McLester was going home & we have no candles here to write by. I went up to Houston Saturday to the Terry procession. It was a grand affair & when I have more time will give you the particulars. I came back to Camp Parsons⁴⁹ & spent Saturday night & the Sabbath. Saw Mrs Highsmith etc. She is quite well. I shall not have any time or opportunity to leave Camps any more soon. I am going to work again. I am in the enjoyment of fine health except I have a <u>set fast</u> on the end of my tongue & that boil which set me crazy whilst at home has not got well yet. I would (if I can get a boarding place here for you) like very much for you & the children to come down a while. What do you think of it — Consult your feelings etc & write to me what time it would suit you to come down. I will study & write you more about. They are now calling me to breakfast.

Yours truly & hastily
E.P. Petty

Dear Margaret

    Just as soon as I can have my photograph executed I will send it up to you. Major Kirby says he must have one and promises to give me one of his. I think you had better wean Van — it will be better for your health. Your health is all important to you — Dont fret about people not helping you — Help yourself — Live economical & with what money you have you can weather the storm — Keep your gold close — Husband your resources & it will all be well. I cant send up much money for the present as every thing is high — I bought me a sword at Galveston — It cost me $18- in cash — so I now am nearly out of money — and if I dont get my pay soon will have to draw on you. Hire a negro by all means if you can get one — Your health wont permit you to do otherwise — keep the children at home until spring & exercise them in domestic matters. You can do as you please about music lessons — I had rather you had Kept your coffee at home but I had might as well have it as loafers — If loafers crowd you feed <u>scant</u> & they will fall off — <u>Starve them out</u>. I was afraid that you could'nt get along with Mary. I know I could'nt. She is too ill & impudent. I am glad you got the molasses — Is it a good article — Have you tried it. Do the best you can for yourself and children and when you want any advice write to me for it — Write often — give my love to the little ones & don't let them forget that they have a poor old daddy in the service of the Country defending their home, their lives & liberty.

Truly yours
E.P. Petty

Camp Kirby Jany 1st 1862

Dear wife

I received your letter of the 26th ult last night. If you could imagine how much pleasure it afforded me to get a letter from you or Ella and with how much avidity I devoured its contents you would not be so fraid to write or be in the least alarmed about boring me with letters. This is my birthday as you will see by the heading above and as a fit new year and birthday from me to you (it ought to come from you to me) I send you my photograph by Mr Biddle. The artist was hurried and it is not as well done as it might yet it is pretty fair and will answer — In my last I told you of my trip to Houston to the Terry procession. It was a grand procession.[50] There was about 2500 soldiers in it besides the Masonic Order and Citizens — The program was 1st Masonic order. 2 Corpse borne on Caison — 3 Terry's Saddle horse led by his negro who was with him in Kentucky with his Saddle, Sword etc. 4 His brothers and Son who was with him when he was Killed. 5 Col Moore's Regiment. 6 Capt Mechling's Artilery Company looking beautiful with Cannon & Caisons.[51] 7 Two or 3 Companies from Galveston & Virginia Point. 8 Citizens. 9 Col Parsons Regiment — Judge Campbell pronounced a touching and appropriate eulogy upon the deceased[52]— The procession then reformed & escorted his remains to the R Road to be carried to his residence — His wife did not come in to Houston at all. In the evening I went down to Col Parson's Regiment where I spent the night and all day Sunday. I saw Mrs Highsmith & Fanny. They are well and Mrs H is nearly crazy to see you she said. She begged me to send you. I would like to do so but I am fearful that the weather will set in bad and this would be a miserable country for you to be in for it would be so muddy that you could not get about to enjoy yourself — I may do so yet but at present am undetermined about it. I came home Sunday night and Tuesday morning early I with Maj Kirby took Genl Heberts special train for Galveston to witness the reviews of the troops at Galveston & Virginia Point — We left here at 6 O'clock, reached Galveston at ¼ past 7

O'clock. The review then came off at 10, at Virginia Point at 12 — I took dinner at V. P. with Col Nelson[53] and I think we sat at the table 2 hours and had at least four changes of plates — every thing that was good to eat and drink from Oysters to Cakes & from water to Champaign wine was there and we lunched and munched, feasted, drank and cracked jokes and toasted until about 3½ O clock P M. Then we came home at four and reviewed, inspected & mustered our entire Battalion before night. So you see that although I am denied the pleasure of the society of my wife & children yet I endeavor to keep myself busy and draw pleasure out of surrounding circumstances. To day I have spent (although it is my birthday) in making out the muster and pay rolls for this Battalion and in drilling the Battalion. I am not near through with my work but quit it to write to you — I am now acting & temporarily and will perhaps act permanently as Adjutant for this Battalion — Whilst at Galveston there arrived two of the larger guns. It is so for I saw and handled them myself — One is a ten inch Columbiad — carries about a 64 pound ball. The other is a rifle cannon — carries about 64 pound conical ball & about a 32 pound round ball — The Columbiad weighs 9027 pounds, the rifle Cannon 8500 pounds. I saw also 3 beautiful breach loading cannons — the prettiest guns that I ever saw — I also heard full particulars of the Royal Yacht affair. Capt Chubb[54]— 40 men on 2 launches attacked the R Y on 2 sides and succeeded in capturing her after a severe Conflict — Two of our men were slightly wounded — Two of the enemy were killed, one a Lieutenant, and eight wounded — Capt Chubb & crew have been sent to New York[55] — A ship loaded with tobacco run through the blockade into Galveston a day or two ago.

Another one also loaded with tobacco attempted to do so but was captured[56] — A day or two ago a steamer run the blockade into Sabine — She came in under Brittish Colors.[57] She brought 45 tons of Cannon powder — a large lot of rifle powder — 7 000 000 Caps (percussion), 5 000 Cannon primers — a large lot of coffee, dry goods, bagging rope etc — This is important for Texas — Hurrah for us — There is but one Vessel off Galveston now and things are quiet. Col Henry E. McCulloch[58] is calling for Six Months Men for the Lower Rio Grande. The Seige of Matamoras is still going on — Caravajal will finally succeed in subduing the place I hope — He is a friend of Texas & the South — At Matamoras they made a breast work of about a thousand sacks of coffee and got it shot to pieces — So another supply of coffee has been cut off — If Tom does'nt bring your pork soon get Wash Jones to see him about it. Also about the beef — give my respects to Wash & family & my friends. I send you a paper with latest news — Kiss all the babies for me.

Yours truly
E.P. Petty

Camp Kirby
Jany 5th 1862

My Dear Ella

I received your's and your Ma's letters of the 29th and 31st ult last night. I am glad to hear that you are in good health and that you are getting along so well in this world. Notwithstanding your good health and good circumstances I expect you miss your poor old daddy verry much. I know that he misses you all and wishes that the state of the Country would allow him to return to the bosom of his family and remain there but alas I am fearful that it will be a long time before our troubles are over. I am in the enjoyment of splendid health. I have never seen such pretty weather in my life. We have had no cold or wet weather down here yet. I hav'nt seen a particle of ice this winter. The trees are yet more than half covered with foliage there not having been frost enough to kill the leaves. It looks like the Lord was on our side so far as cold weather is concerned though we need rain badly. Our Company is getting along finely. There is not a case of sickness now in it. There is but one in Capt McDade's and but four in Capt Whitehead's. This does not include those whom we have sent home sick but only those who are present. [*Page missing*] and so we were on tip toe of expectation and are so yet as our men are still required to stay there. It must be some news that the schooner brought in that caused the orders. This is all the news from Galveston except that 5 more of those larger & long expected Cannons have arrived making seven in all now safe in Galveston.[59]

Your Ma wanted to know if I had heard from Seguin — She has asked the question several times and inadvertently I over looked it not thinking much about it. When I returned from Bastrop I found a letter here from Pa and a few days afterwards I received one from [Andrew] Dove.[60] These are the only letters I have received from them. They were all well. That is about all the news in the letters. I enclosed you Dove's letter. Pa's I have lost or would sent it. I will not close this letter until morning and if any thing turns up before then I will write it to you —

Sunday night after roll call —

No news from Galveston or elsewhere to day. Tell Ma to send or go to Mr Bean, get my watch — Pay the bill and send it to me by Mr McLester or Biddle also to send me a vest as I need one. Mr. Levi Moore who has been here a few days will carry this letter up together with some news papers which I send.

Yours truly
E.P. Petty

Camp Kirby
Jany 8th 1862

Dear Margaret
Your's and Ella's of the 3rd inst was received last night — As to the best mode of saving the pork when you get it you must be the judge taking into consideration the time it is received and the state of the weather. I somehow think that Weaver will yet bring in that beef. If he does not I shall be disappointed verry much. We are all quite well in Camps there not being a case of sickness in our camps and those who were sick in the others are convalescing. We had some rain here at last but not enough to do any good. Make Wash Jones get you a negro. I do not want you to do your own work as long as I am able to do otherwise! When I cant do any better I must submit to it & so must you. You ask me about the people down here, their houses etc etc. When you come down you can see for yourself and be the better judge.

There is a great deal of aristocracy here amongst the citizens. They are the elite from Galveston. They have got their furniture etc., good houses and live high, run to Galveston every few days etc and live like Lords. Jo Sims & I tried to day to make arrangements to board you & Abby with some of them but failed in [this] oweing to the crowd boarding with them from Galveston. We succeeded however in getting rooms at Mr Harris who lives about a quarter of a mile below here on the Bayou. They have some few negroes — only a tolerable house but comfortable and make no pretensions to aristocracy but are good social, friendly, respectable citizens and I think you will be quite comfortable there. Jo Sims & I will meet you at Brenham on next Monday night week (the 20th). Jo has written to Abby to get Mr Grimes' Hack & if she cant get that to take her carriage — He has a good carriage horse & double harness. You can furnish Sam and all of you can come to Brenham — Get James Townsend to come with you & drive the team back. Come by the way of Evergreen. There is a good place to stay at 10 miles this side of Evergreen, Mr Burns — this will be 35 miles — then the next day 30 miles to Brenham. Start on Sunday & be out two days. We will be there Monday night unless the cars fail to make the connection. If they do we will be there on Tuesday. Hire you a little negro or Dutch girl to nurse for you. Dont fail in this respect if possible — Write to me immediately & let me know all about it — Dont bring too much baggage but bring your best. Unless something turns up I will write no more.

Yours Truly
E. P. Petty

Camp Kirby Jany 13th 1862

Dear Wife

It is cold this monday morning and as I have no fire place to my tent will have to write a short letter. The health of our camp this morning is fine not a case of sickness on hand. There is some few cases of sickness in Capt Whitehead's company and several cases in Capt McDade's. The sickness in Capt W's grows out of the negligence of the men to clean up their ground or camps and also their own uncleanliness. That of Capt McD's from their situation at Tallow Town where they have to breath the Malaria arising there from which is enough to kill an elephant.[61] Maj Kirby got up a petition to Genl Hebert signed by nearly all the officers to remove the Command from this place. I was in Command Co B at the time & refused to sign it but the men clamored so for a change that I finally signed it under protest. It went up to Genl H. who sent Dr Riddell here to examine the locality, amount of sickness etc which he did last Saturday. His report will determine our case. I have not heard the result yet — suppose we will find out to day or tomorrow. My opinion is that Tallow Town will be condemned and Capt McD's Co. moved over this side the Bayou close to our camps and that the Command will not be removed from this locality.[62] Maj Kirby's plan is to move the Command to the neighborhood of Hempstead, where he thinks it will be more healthy and cheaper to the Government and where Maj K will be at home and also Capt McD's men will be near home. I have been and am now opposed to any change — We are well fixed here and have a pretty place in a good nice neighborhood and to leave here and go up the Country looks like running and to go below here is very objectionable to me. It makes no difference where we go so far as your trip down here is concerned. You & Mrs Sims must meet us at Brenham at the specified time (Monday the 20th) and we will conduct you to our Camps. I learn that Measels have broken out amongst the troops at both Virginia Point and Houston and I am fearful that if removed from here Genl H. will send us to one of those points. On Saturday night last at Houston Bunt Dabney of our Company shot and I expect killed Bob White of Capt Highsmith's Company. There were three of our boys present and they say that Bob White was charging upon Bunt with a large knife and that Bunt shot in self defense. He shot him with an army six shooter slug ball. The ball entered his abdomen a little on the right below his ribs and came out near his back bone. Bob was not dead when the boys left but the D^r said could not live the night out. It occurred at a house of prostitution — White was drinking and I expect Bunt was also making another example of the calamitous evils of women & wine. Bunt is now here or hereabouts. Major Allen is now here.[63] He came down to go into the service provided he could get a position. When he came here it was his intention to apply for the Adjutancy of this Battalion but finding that I was acting and expecting the position he says he will not interfere with me. In a few days the question of the Adjutancy will be submitted to the Battalion when I hope that I may be the choice. The appointment belongs to Major Kirby but for some considerations he has determined to leave it to a vote of the Battalion. The rank is that of 1st Lieut with one hundred dollars per month salary. It is the prettiest and most prominent position in the Battalion and I have taken a good deal of pains to qualify myself for the position and dont intend to give it up without a struggle. Capt McDade's son is my opponent for the place — I think that I have the advantage of him because I have drilled the battalion & filled the place so that they see I am qualified for it. This he has not done. I may be mistaken. We shall see.[64] On the meat question it is best & I expect the only way to save it to take the bone out. Mrs Turner can save it that way I think. You asked me how far Mrs Highsmith was from Camp Parson's etc. She is at Harrisburg 2 miles by Rail Road & 3 miles by Dirt Road from the Regiment. She was well pleased & is anxious that you stop one day with her as you come down. I dont expect you can do so however — I will see as I come up — I send you a paper. Read the article from "Kirby's Battalion" signed "Bastrop." I don't know who is the author of the article but he indulges in too much laudation of the officers etc. I send it to you so you can see at least what our private thinks of us. You will learn it all when you come down. At present adios.

E. P. Petty

P.S.   Jany 14th 1862
I have just received yours & Ella's per Lt McLester — I sent you a letter per Mr Jim Moore, also one by mail since I sent my photograph

— Bob White died the next night after he was shot — On last night two ships loaded with cotton was to run the blockade from Galveston — It was a fine night for the business as it was cloudy & hazy & a norther was blowing.

E. P. P.

[There is a gap of ten weeks in Petty's letters, from January 14 to March 24, 1862. During at least part of that time his wife was staying near the camp. The return of Kirby's Battalion for the month of February 1862 lists Petty as "Absent with Leave."]

In January 1862 Galveston's batteries were increased from eight to thirteen heavy guns, with the additions being the pieces acquired by the citizens' committee in Richmond. Hébert continued to garrison both Fort Point and Pelican Spit, covering the harbor mouth. Federal warships off the Texas coast in early 1862 numbered only five. On January 18 *Midnight* and *Rachel Seaman* shelled the shore batteries at Velasco and Pass Cavallo, testing their strength and range. Lieutenant James Trathen, commanding *Midnight*, reported that "One object has been gained in this instance, making the enemy expend his ammunition." Colonel Joseph Bates, commanding at Velasco, wrote: "While the enemy remains on their vessels, with their long-range guns, &., they can annoy and harass us, but when they come on land we will whip them certain." On January 25 the U.S.S. *Arthur*, Acting Lieutenant John W. Kittredge, captured off Pass Cavallo the schooner *J. J. McNeil*, bound from Veracruz, Mexico, to Indianola, Texas, with a cargo of coffee and tobacco. Lieutenant George W. Ingram of the Twelfth Texas Cavalry wrote his wife on February 11: "One of Old Abe's largest War Steamers with some others of less Magnitude are lying off the Island & are watching Galveston about as close as a wolf would a sheep fold and I suppose feel about like a wolf looks and attack is expected." However, no attack materialized.[65]

Late in February what Governor Lubbock termed "a vexatious little affair" occurred near Camp Aransas on the coast. Unexpectedly one afternoon the Federals appeared in the vicinity with two launches and captured a sloop bound for Corpus Christi, taking from her medicine and other articles intended for the Confederacy. Captain B. F. Neal, in charge of the camp, ordered out his company and, pursuing, exchanged several shots with the launches, driving them back to the ships. Somewhat chagrined at their escape, Neal reported: "The enemy is becoming quite bold and daring, and will destroy the commerce of these bays unless checked in his buccaneering . . . . They have the advantage of us, possessing better boats and being more accustomed to them than we are." Neal had two six-pounders but no powder. "This was an illustration of our disadvantages in the war," Lubbock noted in his memoirs.[66]

On February 28, 1862, Kirby's Third Texas Infantry Battalion had 8 officers and 186 men "present for duty," 221 "aggregate present" and 250 "aggregate present and absent." It formed part of the First Brigade of Texas Volunteers at Galveston, commanded by Colonel Ebenezar B. Nichols. The other units in the command were Nichols's own six-month regiment, the Ninth Texas Infantry; Allison Nelson's Tenth Texas Infantry; Theodore Oswald's Fourth Texas Infantry Battalion; Joseph W. Speight's First Texas Infantry Battalion; Xavier B. Debray's Texas Cavalry Battalion; Cook's Artillery; and William Edgar's Light Battery. The command had a total of 2,831 officers and men "present for duty," 3,850 "aggregate present" and 4,037 "aggregate present and absent."[67]

Galveston Mar 24th 1862

My Dear Ella

I have verry little news that is good to write. I send herein an extra which contains terrible news for us.[68] It seems now that we cant whip any thing and if every Department of our Government is as weakly governed and has as little energy as this I do not wonder at our mishaps and defeats for I do tell you that there is not energy enough here to pull a setting goose off of her nest nor honesty enough to save even a pound of pickled beef. This place is to be evacuated as I gather from all that I can see transpiring around. They are moving the guns away from Pelican Spit[69] also the men. They are moving the men and guns from the Island.

We have just received orders to move to Virginia Point to which place we will go in a day or two. It worries me nearly for I have not sold my horse and there is no fit place there to keep him. Just about like my luck. A great many of our boys are sick. One of Capt McDade's men died yesterday and there is another that will die soon I think. Direct your letters to me at that place Virginia Point.

Yours truly
E.P. Petty

P.S. I send you the original song of Dixey.

Dear Margaret

I have been to Va Pt to day looking after quarters for our men etc. I found all ready and we will go up about Saturday — Our quarters are verry good for Spring and Summer. We will be in houses. I hardly think now that we will be discharged until the expiration of our time — of this however I cannot be certain. Col Nelson's reg[t] will leave the last of this or the first of next week.[70] We & Speights' reg[t][71] have to take their place and guard the bridge & batteries. We had a north wind about five days last week which blew nearly all the water out of the bay. The tide was lower than it had been for years — right opposite to Judge Jones residence near Va Pt[72] they found the remains of a wrecked vessel which had on board several Cannon — a large iron box supposed to contain Ammunition etc — They succeeded in getting a howitzer and a long six pound iron cannon off before the tide returned. The howitzer is worthless but the 6 pounder is in a perfect state of preservation and is a verry fine gun. I saw it myself & examined it. They saw another howitzer and another large gun supposed to be a 32-pounder but could not get them off. Neither could they get the iron box. Harry Litle of our Company says it was the Tobin a Texas war vessel which foundered in the Sep[t] gale of 1837. (25 years ago.)[73] It was the gale that swept the water over this Island.

Capt Whiteheads men at Va Pt wade out in the bay and when they find the red fish on the bars sunning them selves kill them with knives, oyester shells etc — The other day one of them came across a porpoise on the shoals and mounted him and tried to hold him. The fish struck

out for deep water — the fellow holding on and yelling for help —
When the fish got where it was deep enough to use himself he gave his
tail a flirt and threw the man about 20 feet — The man lost his hat
and shoes. I was out on the beach the other day. The gulf was perfectly
smooth — no surf rolling in. I could see the porpoises rolling up &
down, a thing you so much desired whilst here but could not. I wished
verry much that you were with me. I have made an arrangement here
so that I can draw about $250- at Bastrop on my salary for you in a
few days. I will write & send you the papers. I got your letter. This will
make the third one I have written home. I have'nt sold Charly [his
horse] yet. I am afraid he is going blind. Just my luck you know — I am
in fine health. I hate to leave here. A good many of the boys are sick.
I send this by Tom Biddle.

> Yours truly
> E.P. Petty

Galveston Mar 27 1862

Dear Margaret

Enclosed I send you Jack Nash's note for prin & inst $262.67 first
April. Also his letter requesting me to pay it and send it up that he
had the money for me.

I have settled the note so please send for the money immediately
and when you get it keep it until I come up — Get Wash Jones or
some body else to go immediately for the money as something may
happen to prevent my getting it.

I sent you a letter of yesterdays date by Sg^t Biddle. I did'nt have the
note then. We are so so and go to Va Pt next Tuesday. I now believe
that we will be discharged in about 2 weeks.

> Nous Verrons
> E.P. Petty

Bastrop County
March Th 20th 62
E P Petty Esqr

Dear Sir

I wish to pay E B Nichols I think a bout $250 hundred dollars or he
has a note on me if you will take it up. I will pay you the money So

soon as you Send it up here or come up. I have it for him and would like to pay him your friend. No gold or silver here.

John D. Nash

Galveston Texas
March 28th 1862

Dear Margaret

    The evening I left home I met Hanke and he wanted to buy my ranch out by Nash's or Eastland's and I told him that I would think the matter over and write to him about it etc. I want you to see him immediately and make the trade for me if you can. Hanke wanted to put in for part payment his place. You know Snelling has an interest in the Land. I am willing to sell him the land for seven hundred and fifty dollars and take his place at two hundred & fifty or three hundred dollars at most provided Snelling is willing to take Hanke's place for his interest in the land — So you will have to see Snelling and Hanke both before a trade can be struck. Hanke's place and Snelling's use of the land whilst living on it will pay him for his outlays etc I think verry well. The ballance that would be comeing on the land say $450 or $500 — Hanke would have to pay in cash or its equivalent — or I would take half cash & the ballance secured by Mortgage on the land giving him twelve months if he would pay me 10 per cent interest from date. You had better (perhaps) let Wash Jones read this letter and make the trade for you or assist you in making it. If Wash isn't there dont show it to any body else but see the parties yourself and make the trade if it is makeable. If you can get any gold or silver save and save it good & hold on to it like death to a sick negro.[74] See Snelling and just ask him if he will (in case the trade can be made) take Hankes place for his interest in the land — It will give him a homestead — save him rent & will be better for him generally. Be wary and shrewd in your trade. Do your best. I want to try your skill at trade etc. Write to me if you received a note which I sent you on Jack Nash for near $260 and did you get the money on it. Write me in full what Hanke & Snelling say about the trade etc. We are moderately well. I am quite so. I dont know when we will go to Va Pt now — I am just from there and barracks are not ready for us. I rode Charly over the bridge. He didn't like it much. His eye is no better and I am thinking that I can't sell him. Not on account of his eye so much as the want of money. There is none here.

Yours truly
E. P. Petty

Dear Margaret

I have just received yours of the 29th ult enclosing Pa's letter. Dont fret my dear over small matters. You have plenty to go on, plenty of money, plenty of friends and shall never suffer as long as my head is hot. So be of good cheer, lay aside jealousy and dont fret at the good luck of others. I expect Dewit, Dove & Cochran felt the sting of my letter. I hope they did. I have just written to Charley Howerton to send you some money by mail, that you were in need of it.[75] I have also written to Harvey Wilbarger and John McDavid to the same effect & hope some of them will pay you some money. I sent you a note the other day on Jack Nash. Did you get it & have you got the money. If you [have,] pay Gillespie, Johnson, Orgain and Olrich their debts or a part of them. I also wrote to you to see Hanke & sell him my Sandy tract of land. What have you done about it. Are Ella & Frank at School. If not have them there and give them all the education possible. It looks gloomy as though hard times were ahead of us. Things are now in such a fix that we will have to do a good deal of hard fighting to straighten them out. Keep every thing together as much as possible — get some hogs, chickens etc and go to earning a living. You must look ahead for yourself now — I am in for the war in some shape or other and so there is no particular dependence to be placed on me in that line. Galveston is beginning to look pretty now — The trees & every thing is getting green and flowers are blooming all over it and so it both looks & smells pretty. I rode out on the beach to day to enjoy its grandeur. I rode Charly in and let the breakers burst over him. He stood it fine and seemed to say, glorious. Charly is as blind as a bat in one eye and it makes him quite scary. Capt Chubb has been at home about a week and day before yesterday he made us a speech before Tremont house giving a narration of his fight, capture and captivity. He said that they killed seven, that they got and wounded eight men. They were verry cruelly treated for a good while after that verry kind. He says that they are moving Heaven & Earth for our subjugation, that they are sanguine of success and that we have an awful job ahead of us & must be up & doing.[76] I am boarding at the Palmetto. I don't like the table as well as Mrs Stephens but have a kind & most admirable land lady. I am much pleased with her. I visit the girls verry frequently & enjoy the change from the dull monotony of the soldiers life verry much. There are many items which would interest you but which I cant write — We have four pretty sick cases in the hospital [H. M.] Farmer, [A.] Gillen, Piper & Payne. There is a great deal of

Coughs & Colds amongst the boys. Friday we move to Virginia Point
— A good many of the boys are glad of the change. I cant say that I
am entirely pleased but it is all right — Col Speights Battalion leaves
in the morning en route for Arkansas so you see that there is very
few of us left here. Nichols Reg^t & our Command are determined
regardless of consequences to go home when our time is out. Love to
all.

Truly thine
E. P. Petty

April 3 1862

Enclosed I hand you an order from J. C. Sims on his wife for twenty
five dollars drawn in your favour. Please call upon her and get the
money immediately & keep it.

Yours Truly
E. P. Petty

Fort Hebert Va Pt[77]
1 O'clock Apl 6 1862

Dear Margaret

Your's of the 1st and Ella's of 30 ult has just been handed to me. The
particulars of our Comeing here & you will see in Ella's letter enclosed
herewith. I am truly glad you got the money from Mr Nash. I wrote
you the other day to pay some debts with. (If you did not get that
letter I now say to you to pay Gillespie, Morgan etc, Mr Orgain, Mr
Oelreich, Mr Dimon and John Johnson their accounts or a part of
them saving for yourself enough money to get along upon without
encroaching upon your reserved rights you know what. I also enclosed
you a draft by Jo Sims on his wife in your favour for twenty five dollars.
This was money I loaned Jo — I hope you were as lucky with this as
with the other and hope that you got gold or silver. Take care of your
money for God's Sake. It may be your best friend and only friend. I
also wrote to you to sell Hanke my land. What did you do about it —
Biddle will have a happy time recruiting I hope. He is a good
recruiting officer in a horn. The boys are not disposed to reenlist until
discharge [and] return home and I am not disposed to press them.
Finney has now gone above to get a Com^n from Col Waller to raise a
Cavalry Co.[78] I hope him success. Write me all the local items.

Truly yours
E. P. Petty

Fort Hebert
Virginia Point
Sunday April 6th 1862

My Dear Daughter

I have very little of interest to write to you. Last friday our
Command bid adieu to the City and City life and like a swarm of bees
settled down on this point. I am not at all pleased with our change.
Our duties here will be much heavier than in town and I am fearful
that we will have more sickness — We find a good deal of sickness in
the Hospital here such as flux & typhoid fever. I never saw the like of
fish, crabs, oysters etc that the soldiers are getting here and to this I
attribute the sickness and I have warned our boys against it. The
novilty in the change from the City here compensates at present for
the inconveniences of the place & the boys seem to be as well or
better contented than in town. I am boarding my horse at Judge
Jones'. He has a beautiful place one of the most lovely places I have
seen down here — fine residence, beautiful shrubbery, elegant shell
walks and good fruit trees besides magnificent sea views and a nice &

beautiful farm. I wanted to board myself with him but for the present he declined to board me on account of the sickness of his wife. In a few days he says perhaps he will board me. We (McLester, Cunningham, Williamson & myself) are now boarding at an Irishman's and by the way we are faring quite well — equally so far as food is concerned as when in town. I heard that a Steamer came into the blockader on yesterday morning the first vessel of any sort that has come in for some time — I suppose that she is a supply ship. The cotton vessels still continue to run out here. On yesterday Mr Fleigs cotton schooner passed here for the West end for the purpose of running out there. This morning I heard some pretty heavy guns down that way and am afraid that she attempted to go out and was fired upon but the wind & tide both being unfavourable I am in hope that she did not and that the firing was only to scale or clean out the guns.

Since I began this letter your letter of the 30th ult and your Ma's of the 1st inst has been handed to me. I was much gratified in their perusal. Hurrah for Frank tell him to push up. I want to see how much he can learn by the time I come home and Dont forget yourself whilst the learning is going on — remember that your education cost me much trouble & money and when you loose time I loose money. I am sorry that you have such bad luck with chickens. I am also sorry to hear of the sickness in the family. You must write as often as you can and give me all the news about crops & folks & soldiers etc. I dont know when I shall be at home. I wish they would discharge us now. I am tired of this service & hope the next I may chance to engage in will be a little more active and congenial with my feelings.

Truly yours
E. P. Petty

Fort Hebert April 7th 1862

Dear Mag

Upon reflection I countermand the orders given for the payment of certain debts & if you have not paid any of them do not do so.

Yours Etc
E. P. Petty

[Probably about April 7, 1862]
Ft Hebert Va Pt

Dear Mag

I drop you a line this morning I hope the last one I shall ever send you from Va Pt. Our Q M Cunningham goes to Houston to day for the money to pay us off & will return tomorrow. The Mustering officer will come down on tomorrow to muster us out of the service. It will take us two or three days to fix up our Muster & pay rolls, discharges etc. So I think about Wednesday or thursday next we will bid farewell to these mundane parts and go to our homes rejoicing.

This is about all of interest I have to write. I am quite well. It is as Cold as Chloe. [79]

Yours Most truly
E. P. Petty

Fort Hebert Va Pt
April 8th 1862

Dear Margaret

I write a line this morning simply to inform you. to inform you. well it makes no difference what but you will see I am quite well and hope to continue so whilst I remain in this God forsaken place. I am doing first rate at my new boarding house and I am inclined to believe that the Irish are pretty clever folks. Dont tell Mrs Turner — There are five or six persons trying to raise Companies out of the Kirby Battalion. I have concluded to wait until they all get satisfied and then take the remnants and from what I can see the remnants will be better than the bolt — Capt Finney made his Co a speech yesterday but I dont think it went down to his entire satisfaction. He is promising all who will enroll with him furlough but those who will not he refuses. The biggest part will not go home. I do not know what the result of all this may be. Time will determine. I sent you a letter yesterday by Pitch Barrett — and I write you to save your money and not pay any debts. Dont pay any thing until I come up. Write verry often.

Yours Etc
E. P. Petty

Fort Hebert Va Pt
April 10th 1862

Dear Margaret

Your's of the 5th inst has just been received. In reference to the land trade I leave it to you and Snelling. I know ole man Smith well and he is a good old man and I suppose is very good for any contract which he will make. At least the land can be made good for itself. If the land is sold I want some money in the trade — The price I fixed in the trade proposed for Hanke was & is the minimum price. I will take no less. So you can take that as a basis and operate on it always going above never below — I dont care much if I dont trade just at this time. I have plenty so far to live upon without selling it. I have no particulars to write. I have written you two letters this week one by L. P. Barrett and one by Capt Finney both of which you will recieve before this. I am still well and doing well. We had a verry cool Norther tuesday & verry little rain. I learn that you had fine rain. Charley jumped out yesterday and run away. He went about 15 miles up the Bay. A negro caught & brought him in last night. No indications of an emergency down in these parts yet. We are all bent on comeing home 1st May unless there is a Yankee fleet in sight. Everything in <u>Statu Quo</u> here.

Truly yours
E. P. Petty

P.S. I have just learn that on last night a grocery Keeper at Galveston shot & killed one of Capt. Dupree's soldiers and that on this morning the soldiers hung him for it. Col Kirby is raising a regiment for Carter's Brigade & has I learn 5 Companies.[80] Evening of the 10th

E. P. Petty

Houston April 14th 1862

Dear Margaret

I am just on my way back to Camps from a visit to Col Kirby's. I have not accomplished fully the object of my mission — Col K offered me a Com[n] to raise a Co for his regiment and insists that I shall do so. I refused for the time to do so and so left but I have been tolerably incredibly informed the Lt Moore will beat Col Allen[81] for Col and if so I shall go with Kirby.[82] Col K. also told me that if I failed to raise a Co. I should be his adjutant but rather I would raise a Co — I send you glorious news — It has changed the faces of every body down here. Now if they will press the foe back out of Tenn & Ky all will be well.[83] I can write no more now. I have had a pleasant trip & am quite well.

Truly your's
E. P. Petty

Ft Hebert April 22/62

Dear Ella

Just a line. I have the orders to muster us out of the service, which will take place just as soon as the Mustering Officer L[t] Steele[84] fixes the time which I think will take place this week. There is no news here of interest. I will be at home soon but cant stay long as you will see by my bills sent up some days ago.

The Conscript law[85] which you will see in the extra here enclosed would not let me stay if I so desired by my Country needs my services and she shall have them. I will see you soon.

Yours ever truly
E. P. Petty

Notes

[1] Alwyn Barr, "Texas Coastal Defense, 1861–1865," *Southwestern Historical Quarterly*, XLV (July 1961), pp. 1–4 (hereafter cited as Barr, "Texas Coastal Defense"); Navy Department Naval History Division, *Civil War Naval Chronology, 1861–1865* (Washington: Government Printing Office, 1971), pt. 1, p. 19 (hereafter cited as *Civil War Naval Chronology*); R. Rush et al., eds., *Official Records of the Union and Confederate Navies in the War of the Rebellion*, 31 vols. (Washington: Government Printing Office, 1894–1922), series I, XVI, pp. 575–78 (hereafter cited as *Official Records Navies*).

[2] Barr, "Texas Coastal Defense," pp. 5–7; O. M. Roberts, "Texas," in *Confederate Military History*, 12 vols., ed. General Clement A. Evans (Atlanta: Confederate Publishing Company, 1899), XI, p. 71 (hereafter cited as Roberts, "Texas"); *Civil War Naval Chronology*, pt. 1, p. 21; *Official Records Navies*, series I, XVI, pp. 605–10.

[3] R. N. Scott et al., eds., *War of the Rebellion: A Compilation of the Official Records of the Union and Confederate Armies*, 128 vols. (Washington: Government Printing Office, 1880–1901), series I, IV, pp. 97–98 (hereafter cited as *Official Records Armies*); *Official Records Navies*, series I, XVI, pp. 835–36; Francis R. Lubbock, *Six Decades in Texas: The Memoirs of Francis R. Lubbock, Confederate Governor of Texas*, ed. C. W. Raines (Austin: Ben C. Jones & Co., 1900; Pemberton Press, 1968), p. 344 (hereafter cited as Lubbock, *Six Decades in Texas*).

[4] *Official Records Navies*, series I, XVI, p. 840. On November 4 Hébert assigned Hunter to "the immediate command of the naval defenses of the port of Galveston, and of all vessels in the employ of the Government." *Ibid.*, pp. 848–49.

[5] Paul O. Hébert to Leroy Pope Walker, September 27, 1861, *Official Records Armies*, series I, IV, pp. 112–13.

[6] *Ibid.*, pp. 107–8, 113, 115–16. "Unless Galveston is defended, the war may be brought to our own doors and firesides," warned the Bellville *Countryman*. "We should as soon have the Comanches among us as the invading army of Lincolnites. Let us meet them at the threshold of Texian soil. Let them never obtain a foothold on Texian ground, and the re-enactment of the scenes of Maryland, Kentucky and Missouri will be avoided." While it was desirable that every man should take such arms as he could get, "by all means have a Bowie knife," the paper advised. "The latter may be used in the hands of a Texian as offset and reconvention to the Yankee bayonet." Bellville *Countryman*, October 2, 1861.

[7] Paul O. Hébert to Judah P. Benjamin, October 31, 1861, *Official Records Armies*, series I, IV, pp. 130–31.

[8] A List of the Officers Elected, upon the Organization of the Militia in Precinct

No. 2 of Bastrop County, Confederate Muster Rolls, No. 921, Texas State Archives, Austin, Texas; D. L. Vest, *Watterson Folk of Bastrop County* (Waco: Texian Press, 1963), p. 85 (hereafter cited as Vest, *Watterson Folk of Bastrop County*); Marcus Wright, comp., *Texas in the War, 1861–1865*, ed., notes by Harold B. Simpson (Hillsboro: Hill Junior College Press, 1965), pp. 22, 109n (hereafter cited as Wright, comp., *Texas in the War*).

[9] Dickinson Bayou, its correct name, rises in western Galveston County and flows into Galveston Bay. It is named for John Dickinson, landowner in the area during the Republic of Texas and founder of the town of Dickinson. Camp Kirby, named for Major Jared E. Kirby, was located approximately four miles from its mouth. The soldiers encamped at this point patrolled down the Bayou to Galveston Bay. Bill Windsor, *Texas in the Confederacy: Military Installations, Economy and People* (Hillsboro: Hill Junior College Press, 1978), p. 23 (hereafter cited as Windsor, *Texas in the Confederacy*).

[10] George Washington Jones was born in Marion County, Alabama, September 5, 1828. His boyhood was passed on a farm in Tipton County, Tennessee. In 1848 he came with his parents to Texas and located on the Colorado River ten miles below Bastrop, where he taught school and farmed for two years. He then went to Bastrop and studied law under Phil Claiborne, a prominent lawyer in the Austin area in the 1840's, 1850's and 1860's. In 1853 Jones was defeated by a small majority for the Texas House of Representatives, but three years later he was elected District Attorney. At the end of his first term he declined to be a candidate for reelection. The following year he was an unsuccessful candidate for the state senate.

"George Washington Jones was the most outstanding figure, not only in Bastrop County, but in the State," wrote Mrs. Mary McDowall of Bastrop. "He was a lawyer of great ability, and a forceful speaker. When Wash Jones was trying a case in court, school would not keep. Every boy went to the courthouse. I remember on one occasion the Girls' School did not keep. It was the trial of the murderer of Charles Kirk. Colonel Jones was an old friend of our family, and I have sat and listened to many of his and uncle's [Henry Crocheron] conversations. Unfortunately, he was addicted to drink — the spree kind." According to Mrs. McDowall, in the 1850's there were two young lawyers in Bastrop named Rose, usually called "the Roses." "The wife of one taught school. A great lawyer, Wash Jones, shot and killed one of the Roses on the street. Mrs. Rose went away."

During the presidential campaign of 1860 Jones espoused the cause of Stephen A. Douglas, the candidate of the northern Democracy, and fought vigorously against secession the following year; but, when the voters declared in its favor, he cast his lot with them, remarking, "It is a foolish undertaking, but I will fight it out with my people." By May 3, 1861, the Bastrop Volunteer Infantry had been formed with Jones as captain. On March 30, 1862, he was mustered into the Confederate army at Camp Terry as a private in Captain J. Z. Miller's company, was elected lieutenant colonel of the Seventeenth Texas Infantry on June 9, 1862, and after the battle of Milliken's Bend, June 7, 1863, took Colonel R. M. T. Allen's place and was promoted to colonel in September 1864. According to Frank Brown, "he was an abble [able], brave, and vigorous commander, and was greatly admired for his courage in action." After the war Jones was a member of the constitutional convention, and in 1866 he was elected lieutenant governor on the James Throckmorton ticket but was removed by General Philip Sheridan "as an impediment to reconstruction." In 1876 he was the Greenback candidate for Congress in the fifth district but was defeated. However, he was elected in 1878 and reelected in 1880. In 1882 he was the Greenback candidate for governor but was defeated by John Ireland and was again defeated by Ireland in 1884. Thereafter, he declined to be a candidate for any office. Jones died at Bastrop on July 11, 1903. *History of Texas Together with a Biographical History of Milam, Williamson, Bastrop, Travis, Lee and Burleson Counties* (Chicago: Lewis Publishing Company, 1893), pp. 671–72; *Biographical Encyclopedia of Texas* (New York: Southern Publishing Company, 1880), p. 215; Rev. Homer S. Thrall, *The People's Illustrated Almanac, Texas Hand-Book and Immigrants' Guide for 1880* (St. Louis: N. D. Thompson & Co., Publishers, 1880), p. 128; Frank Brown, "Annals of Travis County and of the City of Austin (From the Earliest Times to the Close of 1875)," Chapter XI, p. 54, typescript in Texas State Archives; Mary McDowall, "Little Journey through Memory's Halls," pp. 31, 94, typescript in McDowall Family Papers, The University of Texas Archives, Austin, Texas (hereafter cited as McDowall, "Little Journey through Memory's Halls"); Compiled Service Record of George Washington Jones, National Archives, Washington, D.C.

[11]Ebenezar B. Nichols came from New York to Texas in 1838. After a period of military service he settled in Houston and, in partnership with William Marsh Rice, became a prominent merchant and citizen. He moved to Galveston in 1850. A member of the Secession Convention, Nichols was there made a state commissioner to raise and disburse funds for the public safety. Nichols accompanied Colonel John S. Ford in his expedition to the lower Río Grande Valley. Hébert appointed him colonel of a six-month infantry regiment at Galveston and on December 7, 1861, assigned him to the command of the Military District of Galveston. He also served on General John B. Magruder's staff at the battle of Galveston, January 1, 1863, and Nichols's home was Magruder's headquarters. Nichols died at his home in Galveston on November 30, 1872. Julia Beazley, "Ebenezar B. Nichols," in *The Handbook of Texas*, 3 vols., ed. Walter Prescott Webb, H. Bailey Carroll and Eldon Stephan Branda (Austin: Texas State Historical Association, 1952, 1976), II, pp. 278–79 (hereafter cited as Webb, Carroll and Branda, eds., *Handbook of Texas*); Roberts, "Texas," pp. 16, 38–41; *Official Records Armies*, series I, IV, p. 155.

[12]Born in Louisiana on December 12, 1818, Paul Octave Hébert attended West Point and graduated at the top of his class in 1840. He served with distinction in the Mexican War and became governor of Louisiana in 1852. He was commissioned colonel of the First Louisiana Artillery early in 1861. Appointed brigadier general August 14, 1861, he commanded successively the Department of Texas, the Galveston defenses and the Subdistrict of North Louisiana.

Aristocratic and imperious in manner, he does not seem to have been very popular among the Texas troops. They seem mostly to have pronounced his name "E-bar" or "A-bar," the closest their speech could come to his Creole name. Governor Lubbock is quite critical of Hébert in his memoirs: "Really, General Hebert appeared somewhat bewildered at the magnitude of the task assigned him, and not to have matured, at least at the beginning of my administration, any definite line of policy." In 1862 John B. Magruder replaced Hébert as commander of the Department of Texas. "General Hebert is a good-looking creole," Lieutenant Colonel James Arthur Lyon Fremantle of the British army noted in his journal on May 11, 1863: "He was a West-Pointer, and served in the old army, but afterwards became a wealthy sugar planter. He used to hold Magruder's position as commander in chief in Texas, but he has now been shelved at Monroe [Louisiana], where he expects to be taken prisoner any day. From the present gloomy aspects of affairs about here, it seems extremely probable that he will not be disappointed in his expectations." Ezra J. Warner, *Generals in Gray: Lives of the Confederate Commanders* (Baton Rouge: Louisiana State University Press, 1959), pp. 131–32 (hereafter cited as Warner, *Generals in Gray*); Lubbock, *Six Decades in Texas*, p. 346; Walter Lord, ed., *The Fremantle Diary: Being the Journal of Lieutenant Colonel James Arthur Lyon*

Fremantle, Coldstream Guards, on His Three Months in the Southern States (Boston: Little, Brown and Company, 1954), p. 70 (hereafter cited as Lord, ed., *Fremantle Diary*).

[13] One of Austin County's leading citizens, Jared E. Kirby owned Alta Vista plantation east of Hempstead in present-day Waller County. Prairie View University is located on the plantation. Kirby raised an infantry company for the defense of Galveston. "The speech of Col. (now Capt.) Kirby on Monday last at the Courthouse, was well received," reported the Bellville *Countryman* on October 9, 1861. "The Col. demonstrated most clearly, as we think, the importance of making a vigorous defense at Galveston, thereby defending our own thresholds and our own friends. In defending Galveston, we are only fighting the enemy at the 'outer gate.' Unless we can stay his approach at the coast, we may soon expect him at our own homes. Col. Kirby expects to start this week for Galveston with his company." After arriving in Galveston Kirby was promoted to major and commanded the Third Texas Infantry Battalion, a six-month outfit raised by authority of Special Order No. 52, Department of Texas, dated October 22, 1861. It served on the Texas coast and was mustered out on April 24, 1862. Corrie Pattison Haskew, comp., *Historical Records of Austin and Waller Counties* (Houston: Premier Printing & Letter Service, Inc., 1969), pp. 61, 102; Wright, comp., *Texas in the War*, pp. 22, 109n; Bellville *Countryman*, October 9, 1861.

[14] The Dickinson station of the Galveston, Houston and Henderson Railroad, a line completed in January 1860.

[15] Captain James W. McDade commanded Company A (formerly Kirby's company) in the Third Texas Infantry Battalion. The company was mustered into Confederate service on October 20, 1861. McDade and Dr. R. R. Peebles had founded Hempstead in 1858, 2,000 acres of land being conveyed to the townsite company by Peebles and his wife Mary Ann, who acquired the tract through her first husband, Jared E. Groce Jr. The chartering for the Houston & Texas Central Railroad was the immediate inspiration for the establishment of the town.

"The men in Kirby's company were in good health and spirits last Friday when the editor left," reported J. T. Kimbrough, the editor *pro tem* of the Bellville *Countryman*, on October 23, 1861. "There had been a few cases of chills and fever, but they yielded readily to quinine, of which there was plenty on hand. They have excellent quarters and room for two or three hundred more, with good cistern water to drink and a good chance to fish, etc." J. P. Ousterhout, the proprietor of the *Countryman*, who was serving in McDade's company, reported from Camp Kirby on December 21 that "Capt. McDade has been authorized by Gen. Hebert to increase his company to one hundred and fifty men. We have now one hundred and twenty and recruits are coming in daily." Muster Roll of Capt. J. W. McDade's Company from Austin County, in Bellville *Countryman*, March 8, 1862; *ibid.*, January 1, 8, 1862; Frank Mac D. Spindler, "The History of Hempstead and the Formation of Waller County, Texas," *Southwestern Historical Quarterly*, LXIII (January 1960), pp. 405–10.

[16] This was the flag presented by the ladies of Bastrop to the Bastrop Volunteers on June 15, 1861. Mary (Nicholson) McDowall, writing in 1926, remembered the occasion:

> On a never-to-be-forgotten day the Bastrop volunteers, under the command of Colonel [Captain] Wash Jones, were drawn up on the campus of the Military Institute. In the rear of the volunteers, Captain Gillespie's cavalry was stationed. On the gallery of the Institute (the old Academy . . .) was a large

group of citizens — men, women and children, with fire and enthusiasm on every face. I (Mary Ann Nicholson), stepped to the front, bearing a beautiful silken flag, and making *my* speech, of which I now recall only the words, 'Liberty or death,' presented the flag to Colonel Jones in the name of the ladies of Bastrop . . . . Colonel Jones received the flag in the name of the volunteers. His speech was such as only Wash Jones could make. Mrs. Jones told me afterwards that the Colonel shed tears when I presented the flag; *he* knew what war meant; I did not.

"Captain Petty of Bastrop, took a Company down into Louisiana," Mrs. McDowall continued. "This Company carried the flag which I had presented to the first volunteers. When the war closed, it was returned to me — faded, battle torn, a rag, and with it a poem. Captain Petty was killed in Louisiana. In some way the flag and the poem were lost." McDowall, "Little Journey through Memory's Halls," pp. 50–51, 54.

The restored flag is displayed in the Confederate Museum on the grounds of the Texas Capitol in Austin. It bears the motto "Fearless Faithful."

[17] Captain Malcijah Benjamin Highsmith (Kige) was the son of Capt. Samuel Highsmith of the Texas Rangers. The Bastrop Volunteer Cavalry organized under Highsmith in July 1861 and served as part of William H. Parsons's Twelfth Texas Cavalry Regiment. Muster Roll Capt. M. B. Highsmith's Co. Bastrop Cavalry. Mustered into the Service of the State by W. H. Parsons aide de Camp and Mustering officer of the 4th Texas Regiment Camp Tarrant Aug. 30th 1861, Confederate Muster Rolls, No. 1313–1, Texas State Archives, Austin, Texas; Vest, *Watterson Folk of Bastrop County*, pp. 83–85.

[18] Colonel William H. Parsons was born in Alabama. In 1845 he withdrew from Emory College in Oxford, Georgia, and served in the Second United States Dragoons under the command of Zachary Taylor during the Mexican War. According to a letter written by M. B. White in 1861, Parsons was a prominent lawyer in Waco before the Civil War and an "able writer" with whom White had "a corresponding acquaintance" that "grew out of both writing for the Galveston News." In 1860–

1861 Parsons published a newspaper, *The Southwest*, at Waco. On July 25, 1861, Governor Clark authorized Parsons to organize a regiment of mounted troops for state service in the Ninth Military District, composed of the counties of Ellis, Hill, Navarro, McLennan, Limestone, Freestone, Bell, Falls, Johnston and Williamson. On September 1 the regiment, designated the Fourth Cavalry, was organized and the field officers chosen.

Parsons established a tent camp near Rockett in Ellis County and put his officers to drilling the men, continuing the drill until the following April 1862 in various parts of Texas. On September 30 General Hébert accepted Parsons's regiment into the Confederate army. On October 28 Parsons, following instructions, asked his men to enlist for 12 months of Confederate service. The soldiers had originally enlisted for 12 months of state service and were to serve only in Texas. All accepted but 40. Among them were 14 men from Highsmith's company. Highsmith wrote to Governor Edward Clark, asking that the 14 men from his company be honorably discharged or given state service, adding that they were all good soldiers and fine citizens but were not prepared for Confederate service. Considerately, he also arranged for his men to draw their pay.

Organized as the Twelfth Texas Cavalry, the regiment spent the fall and winter of 1861–1862 near Houston at Hempstead and on Sim's Bayou. From there it proceeded by easy stages to Pine Bluff, Arkansas; Memphis, Tennessee; and Little Rock, Arkansas. The Federals were encountered for the first time on May 17, 1862, at Searcy Lane, between Little Rock and Batesville on White River. A brigade was next organized, composed of the Twelfth, Nineteenth and Twenty-first Cavalry regiments and Pratt's Battery, and with the addition of Colonel Charles Morgan's battalion, constituted what was known as Parsons's Texas Cavalry Brigade, a title it maintained until the end of the war. The unit served in Arkansas and Louisiana. Parsons practiced law after the war and spent much of his later life in Washington, D. C. Margaret R. Edwards, "William H. Parsons," in Webb, Carroll and Branda, eds., *Handbook of Texas*, II, p. 342; *Official Records Armies*, series I, IV, pp. 95–96, 113–14; Vest, *Watterson Folk of Bastrop County*, pp. 88–89; Wright, comp., *Texas in the War*, p. 115n; John Q. Anderson, ed., *Campaigning with Parsons' Texas Cavalry Brigade, CSA: The War Journals and Letters of the Four Orr Brothers, 12th Texas Cavalry Regiment* (Hillsboro: Hill Junior College Press, 1967), p. 2n (hereafter cited as Anderson, ed., *Campaigning with Parsons' Texas Cavalry Brigade*); George H. Hogan, "Parsons' Brigade of Texas Cavalry," *Confederate Veteran*, XXXIII (January 1925), pp. 17–20; Johnnette Highsmith Ray, ed., "Civil War Letters from Parsons' Texas Cavalry Brigade," *Southwestern Historical Quarterly*, LXIX (October 1965), pp. 210–23 (hereafter cited as Ray, ed., "Civil War Letters from Parsons' Texas Cavalry Brigade").

[19] J. T. Camp was a second lieutenant in Company B, Third Texas Infantry Battalion. Muster Roll of the Bastrop Lubbock Guards, Company B, Kirby Battalion, in Bellville *Countryman*, January 25, 1862.

[20] Jno. Duff Brown was elected first lieutenant of Captain Ben Shropshire's company in Nichols's six-month regiment. "I studied military tactics and drilled pretty hard most of the term," he wrote. "Captain Shropshire was an able lawyer, and passed the larger part of the time, or at least much of it, in Houston on courts martial, leaving me in command of the company. Unused to the ways of military discipline, so entirely different from the freedom of home, the men were impatient, at times a little irritable, and always extremely curious about everything. They made life a burden with innumerable questions, often puerile beyond belief." John Duff Brown, "Reminiscences of Jno. Duff Brown," *Texas Historical Association Quarterly*, XII (April 1909), p. 308.

[21] H. McLester Jr. was second lieutenant in Company B, Third Texas Infantry Battalion. Like Lieutenant Camp, he had joined the company since it was organized on September 28, 1861. Muster Roll of the Bastrop Lubbock Guards, Company B, Kirby Battalion, in Bellville *Countryman*, January 25, 1862.

[22] One of McDade's company, in a letter from Galveston dated November 9, 1861, complained about the failure of some Austin County men to come to the city's defense. "For the information of some of the readers of the Countryman, I will say that Galveston is a very much threatened and very important point on the coast of Texas," "Travis" wrote. "And I know the above information has been given over and again by the Countryman with a plentiful sprinkling of thunder, but the afore-said readers *must have skipped it else they would have been down here.*" "Travis" also complained that "there are those even in this city — young men who apparently have nothing to do — who promenade the streets dressed up in 'store clothes,' with nice kid gloves on their hands and pomade on their hair, who refuse to enter the ranks in defense of their Island City home." Bellville *Countryman*, November 20, 1861.

[23] Located on the Brazos River near the town of Columbus, Colorado County, Alleyton was the western terminus of the Buffalo Bayou, Brazos and Colorado Railroad and was a principal shipping depot for Confederate troops and materials. Windsor, *Texas in the Confederacy*, p. 8.

[24] The *Civil War Naval Chronology* reports: "November 22, 1861: Two days of combined gunfire commenced from U.S.S. *Niagara*, Flag Officer McKean, U.S.S. *Richmond*, Captain Francis B. Ellison, and Fort Pickens against Confederate defenses at Fort McRee, the Pensacola NavyYard, and the town of Warrington, terminating the following day with damage to Confederate positions and to U.S.S. *Richmond*." *Civil War Naval Chronology*, pt. 1, p. 37.

[25] Old Tallow Town was the site of a beef packery. Workers of the Writers' Program of the Works Projects Administration in the State of Texas, *Houston: A History and Guide* (Houston: Anson Jones Press, 1942), p. 153.

[26] An allusion to a much-admired speech by Congressman Thomas Corwin of Ohio in 1848 during the Mexican War: "If I were a Mexican I would tell you, 'Have you not room in your own country to bury your dead men? If you come into mine we will greet you with bloody hands, and welcome you to hospitable graves.'"

[27] Virginia Point was located near the railroad bridge on the mainland opposite Galveston Island. "The strategic location of this post made an excellent site for a Confederate headquarters for several commanding officers throughout the war. The garrison, also called Fort Hebert, had a large General CSA Hospital and barracks." Windsor, *Texas in the Confederacy*, p. 36.

[28] The German immigrant population of Texas was generally Unionist and abolitionist in sentiment. They were thus regarded with suspicion and hostility by Confederate sympathizers and sometimes persecuted.

[29] On the contrary, Hébert's despondency was growing. On November 15 he had written the Secretary of War as follows: "There is no doubt but that the defense of Galveston, or any other point on this coast, in the event of a formidable attack, is a very difficult if not an impossible matter; yet an effort must be made in that direction and this place held as long as possible. It is a cotton port, and if in the possession of the enemy would be a nucleus for the disaffected, of which there are, I am sorry to say, many in the State. As a matter of necessity connected with the defense and possession of the island, I have directed the planking of the railroad bridge,

connecting with the mainland, so as to admit of the passage of troops. The heavy guns, so long on the way, have not yet reached this place."

Rumors of the proposed evacuation of Galveston began to reach Lubbock at the capital, and, with his low opinion of Hébert, it was easy for him to believe they had some foundation. To encourage the general, Lubbock wrote him a letter dated December 7, offering to share the responsibility of burning Galveston, if he thought best, on its evacuation. "If . . . it is found impossible to prevent the enemy from taking possession of the island, then I would suggest, as a dernier resort, that the city of Galveston be entirely destroyed, — buildings and everything else which can afford them comfort, convenience, or shelter. Every cistern (wooden or brick) should be entirely destroyed, the water turned out, and the cisterns made wholly unfit for use again. The stock, including horses, cattle, and sheep, to be driven from the island, and every spear of grass burned." Hébert, in his answer, thanked Lubbock for his proffered cooperation but said nothing of his suggestion as to Galveston. Lubbock, *Six Decades in Texas*, pp. 346–49.

[30] Referring to the cereal grain, which was added to improve flavor and "stretch" the very expensive coffee beans.

[31] "Galveston will be almost uninhabited in a few days longer both by citizens and soldiers," Lieutenant George W. Ingram of the Twelfth Texas Cavalry wrote his wife from Camp Parsons on December 13. "Evry train & evry Steamboat that leaves that place for Houston is loaded with the citizens & goods & household affairs of evry description. This has been going on for about two weeks. One Regiment of Infantry have been moved to Houston and a large amount of ammunition. Nearly all of the cannons have been moved from the Island to Virginia Point & in the event that there is an attack made by the enemy on Galveston the Soldiers will fall back on Virginia Point after having fired & reduced the city to ashes. This I <u>know</u> is the plan of Gen. Hebert. Those big guns that you have heard so much about have never reached Galveston and it is too late now to save the city. No successful defense could be made against a large fleet & resistance on the Island would be useless sacrifice of life on our part. An attack has been expected for about two weeks. I feel sure that an attack will be made sometime during the winter. It may not be made at Galveston before they try some other point, but prospect of an early attack is strong. Another fleet has left the northern ports. It will attack some ports on the Gulf Coast & the probability is that they will try Galveston next." Henry L. Ingram, comp., *Civil War Letters of George W. and Martha F. Ingram* (College Station: Texas A&M University, 1973), pp. 14–15 (hereafter cited as Ingram, comp., *Civil War Letters*).

[32] George Fleming Moore organized the Seventeenth Texas Cavalry Regiment. This regiment was dismounted in July 1862 and was captured at Arkansas Post, January 11, 1863. After being exchanged in April 1863 the Seventeenth Texas Cavalry (dismounted) was assigned to what became known as Granbury's Texas Brigade, Cleburne's Division, Army of Tennessee. Moore resigned his commission in 1862 to accept an appointment as an associate justice of the Texas Supreme Court. Wright, comp., *Texas in the War*, pp. 26, 117n.

[33] Matamoros, a city of Tamaulipas, Mexico, was across the Río Grande from Fort Brown. With its Gulf port of Bagdad, it was an important source of supply for Texas and the Confederacy during the Federal blockade of Southern ports.

Tamaulipas and the other northern states of Mexico were subject throughout the 19th century to the rule of semi-independent governors. Conflict among these *caudillos* and the national government resulted in nearly constant political unrest. In 1861 Tamaulipas was divided between the *rojos*, supporters of Jesús de la Serna, and the *amarillos* (*crinolinos*) of Cipriano Guerrero. In November 1861 General José María Jesús Carbajal, a native Texan from San Antonio, led the *rojos* against the *crinolinos* at Matamoros. Carbajal and de la Serna were Southern sympathizers.

[34] On September 17 the U.S.S. *South Carolina* was relieved by the sailing frigate *Santee*, commanded by Captain Henry Eagle. Commander Allen of *South Carolina* left the two prize schooners, *Sam Houston* and *Anna Taylor*, in Eagle's charge, and transferred 23,000 pounds of bread, 75 barrels of salt provisions and 25 barrels of whiskey. "I consider the blockade of this port to be effectual, as we are so near the bar as to prevent any ingress or egress without our knowledge," Eagle informed Flag-Officer Wm. W. McKean, the commander of the West Gulf Blockading Squadron. Henry Eagle to Wm. W. McKean, October 19, 1861, *Official Records Navies*, series I, XVI, pp. 733–34.

Santee's battery consisted of "2 64-pounders 106 cwt; 10 8-inch 63 cwt; 20 32-pounders 57 cwt; 16 32-pounders 33 cwt; 2 heavy 12-pounders; 1 30-pounder Parrott rifle; 1 11-inch Dahlgren smoothbore; 1 100-pounder Parrott rifle." Windsor, *Texas in the Confederacy*, p. 72.

[35] Mrs. Graves, a Bastrop lady of German ancestry, followed the example of many Texas Germans in leaving for Mexico when Texas seceded. Her brother Anton, or Antonio, Erhard was a member of the large German-American merchant community at Matamoros.

[36] Captain J. W. Whitehead's company was Company C, Third Texas Infantry Battalion. There is a company muster roll in the Bellville *Countryman*, February 1, 1862.

[37] Quinsy was a general term for diseases characterized by extreme pain in the throat: diphtheria, tonsillitis and others, frequently fatal in the 19th century.

[38] Daniel D. Emmett, a native of Ohio and one of the foremost minstrels of the antebellum era, composed "Dixie" as a "walk 'round" song. He explained that he had used "Dixie's Land" as Northern showmen used it to refer to the South. After the song's first performance by Bryant's Minstrel Troupe in New York City on April 4, 1859, it became so popular that several versions were printed and several writers claimed authorship. Emmett had difficulty acquiring a copyright. "Dixie" was the South's most popular patriotic song, and variations and parodies were numerous. David C. Roller and Robert W. Twyman, eds., *The Encyclopedia of Southern History* (Baton Rouge: Louisiana State University Press, 1979), pp. 364–65 (hereafter cited as Roller and Twyman, eds., *Encyclopedia of Southern History*).

[39] The Confederate Index in the Texas State Archives lists a Captain Maclin S. Stith, Home Guard, Reserve Company, Beat 3, Wharton City, Twenty-second Brigade, Texas Militia, August 1861.

[40] Company D, Eighth Texas Cavalry, was commanded by Captain Stephen C. Ferrell. It was recruited largely from Bastrop County, with contingents from Hays, Travis and Burleson counties. Thomas S. Lubbock and Benjamin Franklin Terry organized the Eighth Texas (better known as Terry's Texas Rangers) at Houston on September 9, 1861. The advance units left for Virginia on September 11 but were rerouted at Nashville, Tennessee, to Kentucky and fought the entire war in the West with the Army of Tennessee. Wright, comp., *Texas in the War*, p. 114n; Leonidas B. Giles, *Terry's Texas Rangers*, rpt. ed. (Austin: Pemberton Press, 1967), pp. 13–15. Giles was a member of Company D.

[41] To supplement sheet music Southern presses issued pocket songbooks, or "songsters," containing the words of sentimental and patriotic tunes. "Letters,

diaries and reminiscences of soldiers indicate that the great flood of new songs published during the war made little dent on Rebel ranks," stated Bell I. Wiley. "The list of camp favorites was fairly small and it was made up to a large extent of melodies familiar before the war." Wiley, *Life of Johnny Reb*, p. 152.

[42] The Pettys' third child, Sallie Belle, died in Bastrop in 1858 at the age of three. This is the special significance which Petty wants Ella to realize. Ella was eight when her sister died.

[43] The Houston *Telegraph* of December 25 contains a notice of the so-called "Trent Affair." On November 8, 1861, the U.S.S. *San Jacinto* forced the British mail steamer *Trent* to surrender two passengers, Confederate diplomats James Mason and John Slidell, who were on their way to England. The two men were held in Boston until January 1, 1862. *San Jacinto's* captain, Charles Wilkes, became a national hero. The incident provoked great indignation in England, but war was averted when Secretary of State William H. Seward ordered Mason and Slidell released on the grounds that they were "personal contraband" and that, therefore, Wilkes had made a mistake in not bringing in the *Trent* also. Mark Mayo Boatner III, *The Civil War Dictionary* (New York: David McKay Company, Inc., 1959), p. 847 (hereafter cited as Boatner, *Civil War Dictionary*).

[44] Benjamin Franklin Terry, the organizer with Thomas S. Lubbock of Terry's Texas Rangers, was killed in the regiment's first fight at Woodsonville, Kentucky, December 17, 1861, and the command passed to Lubbock, who was ill at the time and died before he could assume his duties. Colonel John A. Wharton then became its commander. The Rangers had a fine record, fighting at Shiloh, Bardstown, Perryville, Murfreesboro, Chickamauga and Knoxville.

[45] William J. Hancock was the first superintendent of the Bastrop Academy. In the 1850's he moved his family to Houston.

[46] The "Twin Sisters," two iron field pieces, were gifts from the people of Cincinnati, Ohio, to aid the Texans in their struggle with Mexico. Major A. G. Dickinson, commanding at San Antonio, on November 30, 1863, wrote Major S. T. Fontaine, chief of artillery and ordnance for Arizona, New Mexico and Texas: "The

'Twin Sisters,' I am informed are at or in a camp in the vicinity of Austin. They are in a deplorable condition, and I am fearful could not be used," and, continuing, referred him to Colonel John S. Ford for further information. This is the last official mention of the guns; they disappeared after November 1863 and are reported to have been buried near Harrisburg in August 1865 by five of General John B. Magruder's discharged soldiers. "'Twin Sisters,'" in Webb, Carroll and Branda, eds., *Handbook of Texas*, II, pp. 812–13; Ernest W. Winkler, "The 'Twin Sisters' Cannon 1836–1865," *Southwestern Historical Quarterly*, XXI (July 1917), pp. 61–68; Lubbock, *Six Decades in Texas*, pp. 372–73.

[47] In 1839 the land for the first Catholic church in Galveston was purchased, but it was not until 1841 that construction was begun on a frame building, some 50 by 22 feet in size, which was the predecessor of the present cathedral. Hardly was this church finished before a hurricane practically demolished it, indicating the need for a more substantial building. The Rt. Rev. John Mary Odin, D. D., Bishop of Claudiopolis and Vicar Apostolic to Texas, went to Europe in 1845 and brought back French, German and Irish priests to help carry on his work. "My trip into Belgium has secured for me five hundred thousand bricks which will be transported free to Galveston," he wrote. "I hope to construct soon a beautiful church at Galveston, the principal city of the diocese." The cornerstone was laid for St. Mary's Cathedral on March 14, 1847, the work was rushed to completion, and St. Mary's was consecrated on November 28, 1848. In 1847 the whole of Texas was made a diocese, and Odin was named the first Bishop of Galveston. He was made Archbishop of New Orleans on February 15, 1861. Joseph Schmitz, "John Mary Odin," in Webb, Carroll and Branda, eds., *Handbook of Texas*, II, p. 302; Priests of the Seminary, comps., *Diamond Jubilee, 1847–1922 of the Diocese of Galveston and St. Mary's Cathedral* (Galveston: Knapp Brothers, Printers, 1922?), pp. 102–3; Douglas R. Zwiener and Elisabeth Darst, *A Guide to Historic Galveston* (1966), pp. 16–17.

[48] The original settlement on Buffalo Bayou, Harrisburg was still an independent town in 1861. It has since been completely absorbed by the growth of Houston.

[49] Camp Parsons, named for Colonel William H. Parsons of the Twelfth Texas Cavalry, was located at Sim's Bayou about eight miles below Houston and 30 miles from Galveston, and on the left side of the railroad between the two cities. Anderson, ed., *Campaigning with Parsons' Texas Cavalry Brigade*, p. 13.

[50] "The Obsequ[i]es of Col. Terry," Houston *Tri-Weekly Telegraph*, December 30, 1861.

[51] William T. Mechling was born in Pennsylvania and was graduated from West Point in 1848. He served on frontier duty in Texas and New Mexico as a member of the Third and later the Eighth United States Infantry. For unknown reasons he was dismissed from the army in 1855 and took up farming in Bexar County, Texas, where his battery of light artillery was raised during the early fall of 1861. Captain Mechling was succeeded in command by Horace Haldeman in the spring of 1862 and was assigned to staff duty. The battery was assigned to the First Brigade, Walker's Texas Division, and fought in the battles of Mansfield (April 8, 1864) and Pleasant Hill (April 9, 1864). Later that year it was assigned to the Fourth Artillery Battalion, Trans-Mississippi. Lester Fitzhugh refers to it as "Mechling's-Haldeman's Texas Battery." Wright, comp., *Texas in the War*, pp. 42, 133n, 135–36n; Alwyn Barr, ed., "William T. Mechling's Journal of the Red River Campaign, April 7–May 10, 1864," *Texana*, I (Fall 1963), pp. 363–64.

[52] "Eulogy of Judge R. C. Campbell Over the Remains of Col. B. F. Terry," ten-page typescript in The University of Texas Archives, Austin, Texas. Also, Houston *Tri-Weekly Telegraph*, January 1, 1862.

[53] Allison Nelson was born in Fulton County, Georgia, March 11, 1822. Trained as a lawyer, he was a member of the Georgia legislature in 1848–1849 and was also mayor of Atlanta in 1855, but his primary interest was in military affairs. He was captain of a company of volunteers in the Mexican War, espoused the cause of Cuban independence and was appointed a brigadier general by Narciso Lopez. He was in Kansas during the border troubles, and after moving to Texas in 1856 he made a reputation as an Indian fighter. He was elected to the Texas legislature in 1859 and to the secession convention in 1861. Elected colonel of the Tenth Texas Infantry, he was promoted brigadier general to rank from September 12, 1862. Nelson was assigned to command the Second Division of General T. H. Holmes's infantry in Arkansas, consisting of his own and Colonel Flournoy's brigades on September 28, 1862, but died of fever in his camp near Austin, Arkansas, on October 7, 1862. Warner, *Generals in Gray*, pp. 223–24.

[54] On October 9, 1861, Commander Hunter made an agreement with owner Thomas Chubb and the crew of the schooner *Royal Yacht* to serve in the defense of Galveston "for the compensation of $1,350 per month from the day of the acceptance of this agreement by the Confederate States of America." On November 8 a boat expedition under Lieutenant James E. Jouett from the U.S.S. *Santee* surprised and captured the crew of *Royal Yacht* and burned the vessel off Galveston. "We took a few stand of arms, 13 prisoners, and her colors," Jouett reported. "As our pilot was shot down and the schooner had received a shell between wind and water, I did not deem it advisable to attempt to bring her out; we therefore burned her, after spiking her gun, a light 32-pounder. After this we returned to the ship. I regret to state that 1 man was killed, 2 officers and 6 men wounded, one mortally, who has since died." *Royal Yacht*, however, was not destroyed in the attack. A Confederate boarding party extinguished the fires after the Federal sailors had departed. The schooner did suffer considerable damage to her deck, beams, masts and sails.

Eighteen years after the event Jouett, who was wounded early in the engagement, revealed to the Secretary of the Navy that he had been deserted by the second launch taking part in the attack and had been faced with a mutinous crew. *Official Records Navies*, series I, XVI, pp. 757–58, 844; Mitchell S. Goldberg, "A Federal Naval Raid into Galveston Harbor, November 7–8, 1861: What Really Happened?" *Southwestern Historical Quarterly*, LXXXVI (July 1972), pp. 58–70.

[55] Captain Thomas Chubb was a Galveston shipmaster accused of acquiring free Negroes and selling them as slaves. On one occasion he was charged with hiring a crew at Boston and selling it into slavery at Galveston. Following his capture on board *Royal Yacht*, he was condemned to be hanged as a pirate for his slave trading. He escaped death by being exchanged before the penalty could be carried out.

Chubb returned to Texas, resumed command of *Royal Yacht*, painted and overhauled her, and made her as good as new. On May 17, 1862, Captain Eagle of *Santee* sent a midshipman under a flag of truce to demand Galveston's surrender. Chubb was dispatched to meet the Federal ship's boat. As the boat came near *Royal Yacht* the Yankee sailors, looking up, recognized Chubb, and exclaimed: "Why, there's Captain Chubb!" "Yes," replied the captain, "this is Captain Chubb that was hung for a pirate, and this (pointing to the boat) is the *Royal Yacht* that was burned and sunk, all as good as new." Chubb then reached down and helped the midshipman on board, "who appeared anything but pleased with his reception." C. Richard King, "Andrew Neill's Galveston Letters," *Texana*, III (Fall 1965), p. 205; Houston *Tri-Weekly Telegraph*, May 23, 1862.

[56] On December 30, 1861, the U.S.S. *Santee* captured off Galveston the schooner *Garonne*, 14 tons, bound from New Orleans to Brownsville, Texas, with 165 small

bales of tobacco. *Civil War Naval Chronology,* pt. 1, p. 40; *Official Records Navies,* series I, XVII, pp. 42–43.

[57] Sabine Pass, Texas, was at the mouth of the Sabine River between Texas and Louisiana. There was a Confederate military installation there.

[58] Henry E. McCulloch was born in Rutherford County, Tennessee, December 6, 1816. He accompanied his older brother Ben to Texas in the fall of 1835 but was sent back to help his father for another two years. In 1838 he returned to Texas, joining his brother at Gonzales, where he aided in surveying and locating lands. He was one of Captain Mathew Caldwell's scouts, and was in the battle of Plum Creek against the Comanches. He served as first lieutenant in John Coffee (Jack) Hays's Texas Rangers and took part in the battles of the Salado and the Hondo, and in the Somerville expedition against Mexico in 1842–1843. In 1843 McCulloch was elected sheriff of Gonzales County. During the Mexican War he commanded a company of Texas Rangers, serving with Captains Samuel Highsmith and Shapley P. Ross against the Indians. He was again mustered into service as captain of a company of Rangers on November 5, 1850, to protect the settlers west of San Antonio against Indian raids and was mustered out by Captain James Longstreet at Fort Martin Scott in November 1851. McCulloch served as a representative from Guadalupe County in the Fifth Texas Legislature in 1853 and was elected to the state senate in 1855. In 1859 President James Buchanan appointed him United States marshal for the eastern district of Texas, and he was holding this position when the war came. He aided Ben McCulloch in forcing the surrender of the Federal troops in Texas and was commissioned colonel of the First Texas Mounted Riflemen on April 15, 1861. In September 1861 he succeeded Van Dorn in command of the Department of Texas until the arrival of Hébert, who assigned him to command in the vicinity of San Antonio, including coast points. He was promoted brigadier general to rank from March 14, 1862. A week previously his brother Ben had been killed at the battle of Elkhorn Tavern or Pea Ridge, Arkansas. On June 12, 1862, he took command of all the troops within Texas east of the Brazos River and north of the old San Antonio road, with headquarters at Tyler. In the fall of 1862 he was assigned to the duty of organizing an infantry division of four Texas brigades (one was soon detached for other service) at Camp Nelson, Arkansas. Major General John G. Walker relieved McCulloch from command about three months after the organization, and the Texan was given the Third Brigade in what became known as Walker's Texas Division. After taking part in the battle of Milliken's Bend in June 1863 McCulloch returned to the command of the Northern District of Texas. Warner, *Generals in Gray,* p. 201; Roberts, "Texas," p. 244–45; Sid S. Johnson, *Texans Who Wore the Gray* (Tyler?, c. 1907), p. 54 (hereafter cited as Johnson, *Texans Who Wore the Gray*); Jack W. Gunn, "Henry E. McCulloch," in Webb, Carroll and Branda, eds., *Handbook of Texas,* II, pp. 106–7.

[59] These were the heavy guns, drawn by oxen, so long on the way from Alexandria, Louisiana. Lubbock, *Six Decades in Texas,* p. 346.

[60] Andrew Dove was Petty's brother-in-law in Seguin, Texas.

[61] On January 15, 1862, J. T. Kimbrough, the editor *pro tem* of the Bellville *Countryman,* told his readers: "We made a flying trip to Dickinson's Bayou on last week, and enjoyed two day's camp life in Capt. McDade and Capt. Finney's Companies, and found the health, joviality, and contentedness of the Camps to be almost universal, indeed we may say the latter was all life and gayety, but some few cases of fever prevailed, but to no dangerous extent and most of the subjects appeared to be on the mend. The Battalion appears on drill every evening at two

o'clock, and drill for about two hours. All appeared to understand the commands and perform them like veteran soldiers. After roll call morning and evening, the men are at leisure and some amuse themselves fishing in the Bayou, which proves to be anything but unprofitable sport, for they frequently add to their rashions a bounteous supply of fine fish. Others employ their time in reading, singing, and *other camp amusements*." Bellville *Countryman*, January 15, 1862.

[62] Petty was mistaken in his opinion that the command would not move. "Capt. J. W. McDade's and Capt. J. M. Finney's companies have been removed to comfortable quarters on Galveston Island," the Bellville *Countryman* reported in early February. "Persons writing to their friends in those companies will address them accordingly." Bellville *Countryman*, February 8, 1862.

[63] Major Robert (Bob) Allen was the son of Colonel Robert T. P. Allen, a West Point graduate, who had founded the Kentucky Military Institute. In 1857 Colonel Allen founded the Bastrop Military Institute with himself as superintendent. Bob Allen served as commandant of cadets. In her reminiscences Mary McDowall noted that "Major Robert Allen was very unpopular. He had a way of finding out all the mischiefs or pranks, and this the boys disliked. One night while going his rounds of the barracks (slipping around, the boys said), upon opening a door a basis [basin] of water fell on him. Of course, no one knew who was guilty." Mrs. McDowall also recalled that Allen was "a marvelous mathematic teacher." McDowall, "Little Journey through Memory's Halls," pp. 41–42. Mrs. McDowall's recollection that Bob Allen was unpopular with the cadets is confirmed in a letter from Cadet Isaac Dunbar Affleck to his father, dated January 28, 1861: "I am getting along better now than when I wrote you, but they have not as good a school now as they had last year. Maj. Allen has charge of the school now, while Col. is at Austin, but none of the boys like him, he does not treat the boys with any respect at all, and some are going to leave pretty soon." Robert W. Williams Jr. and Ralph A. Wooster, eds., "A Cadet at Bastrop Military Institute: The Letters of Isaac Dunbar Affleck," *Texas Military History*, 6 (Spring 1967), p. 92.

[64] Petty received the appointment as adjutant of Kirby's Battalion. On February 10, 1862, Kirby wrote Major Samuel Boyer Davis, A. G.: "Finding it indispensable for the good of the service that I should have an Adjutant to assist me in the administration of my military duties, I with pleasure and great confidence recommend E. Petty 1st. Lieut. of Com. B. Kirbys Battalion to the position of Adjutant of said Battalion. Hoping it may meet the approbation of the Commanding General and that the appointment may be made I remain your obt. svt." On February 14 Petty wrote Major Davis: "I herewith enclose you my appointment as adjutant of the Kirby Battalion which appointment requires me to report my acceptance thereof to Head Quarters. I hereby express my acceptance of the position and if a commission is necessary please send it to me and if not return me the written evidence of my appointment. Your obt servt." Compiled Service Record of E. P. Petty, National Archives, Washington, D.C.

[65] Barr, "Texas Coastal Defense," pp. 8–10; *Civil War Naval Chronology*, pt. II, p. 8; Ingram, ed., *Civil War Letters*, p. 17.

[66] Lubbock, *Six Decades in Texas*, p. 383. On April 5 a launch from the U.S.S. *Montgomery*, Lieutenant Charles Hunter, captured and destroyed near San Luis Pass the schooner *Columbia* loaded with cotton. The captured crew and passengers were put ashore, after which the warship stood out to sea. On April 22 two boats from the U.S.S. *Arthur* captured a schooner and two sloops at Aransas Pass but were forced to abandon the prizes and their own boats when attacked by two Confederate sloops and troops. *Ibid.*, pp. 383–84; *Civil War Naval Chronology*, pt. II,

pp. 45, 51; *Official Records Navies*, series I, XVIII, pp. 18, 104–8, 448–50.

[67] These figures are taken from a morning report of the First Brigade of Texas Volunteers, February 28, 1862, *Official Records Armies*, series I, IX, p. 701.

[68] The outlook was distinctly bleak for the Confederacy at this time. The defeats of the late winter, Forts Henry and Donelson, Tennessee; the collapse of the South's first line of defense in Kentucky; the loss of Roanoke Island and a sizable portion of eastern North Carolina; and the Confederate defeat at Pea Ridge or Elkhorn Tavern, Arkansas, which probably meant the permanent loss of Missouri—all were leaving their mark on Southern morale.

[69] Fort Pelican Island was located in Galveston harbor and was commanded by Captain John H. Manly. Windsor, *Texas in the Confederacy*, p. 27.

[70] The Tenth Texas Infantry had been ordered to Arkansas.

[71] Joseph W. Speight, a prominent educator, Mason and public official, was one of the early settlers of Waco, Texas. In the summer of 1861 he raised the First Texas Infantry Battalion, which was composed primarily of McLennan County men. This battalion was augmented and reorganized in 1862 as the Fifteenth Texas Infantry Regiment. The regiment formed part of Polignac's Texas Brigade, Mouton's Division, in the Red River Campaign of 1864. Wright, comp., *Texas in the War*, pp. 21, 81, 107n; Lester N. Fitzhugh, "Texas Forces in the Red River Campaign, March–May, 1864," *Texas Military History*, 3 (Spring 1963), p. 18 (hereafter cited as Fitzhugh, "Texas Forces in the Red River Campaign").

[72] William Jefferson Jones, a native of Virginia, arrived at Galveston, Texas, on November 9, 1837. During 1838 and 1839 he held a commission under President Mirabeau B. Lamar to raise a battalion of three companies for frontier defense; and in June 1839 he was ordered to join Colonel Edward Burleson with two of his companies engaged in the Cherokee War. After the Indian campaign he was appointed judge of the Second Judicial District, which position he held for several years. Jones married Elizabeth Gibson and moved to Columbus on the Colorado, where he practiced law, farmed and raised stock. After the annexation of Texas he formed a law partnership with Robert Jones Rivers and in 1852 moved to Virginia Point. He died at his residence on May 10, 1897, and was buried at Virginia Point. Amelia W. Williams, "William Jefferson Jones," in Webb, Carroll and Branda, eds., *Handbook of Texas*, I, p. 927.

[73] The *Handbook of Texas* contains no mention of any Texas Navy ship called *Tobin* but does record that the 125-ton schooner *Brutus* was lost in a storm at Galveston in October (not September) 1837. Webb, Carroll and Branda, eds., *Handbook of Texas*, I, p. 232. It is possible that *Tobin* may have been the *Brutus's* former name.

[74] Lieutenant Colonel Arthur J. L. Fremantle, on leave from Her Majesty's Coldstream Guards, toured the Confederacy in the spring and summer of 1863 and noted the precipitous depreciation of the value of Confederate currency. Given "four times the value of my gold in Confederate notes" at Brownsville, Texas, in April, he was offered six to one for gold only two months later in Charleston and eight to one in Richmond. Rebel war clerk, John B. Jones, recorded an even more startling decrease in the value of Confederate money following the twin disasters of Vicksburg and Gettysburg in July and the lifting of the siege of Chattanooga in November of 1863. "While in the beginning of the year only three Confederate dollars were needed to buy one in gold, by the end of 1863 it took twenty." By December cornmeal cost $20 per bushel and whiskey $15 per quart. One half a cord

of wood sold for $20 and a load of coal for $31.50. A man's suit cost $700 in Confederate currency, and a pair of boots sold for $200.

The depreciation of Confederate money was at first very gradual but became more rapid as the probability of Southern independence became more remote and as gross mismanagement in the Confederate Treasury Department became more evident. With the failure of the government to secure appreciable foreign loans or to market cotton successfully on a scale large enough to support the Southern war effort, "money was manufactured by machinery to meet the wants of the Government," observed Richmond *Examiner* editor Edward A. Pollard, "and paid out as rapidly as it was needed." This money had no metallic backing and was not legal tender. It was, rather, a promissory note: the pledge of the government to pay the bearer in dollars "two years after the ratification of a treaty of peace between the Confederate States and the United States of America."

At first patriotism provided a partial demand for these notes, but soon almost everyone began to attempt to convert their Confederate paper into goods. This lack of faith in Southern currency drove precious metals, already scarce in the South at the war's beginning, out of circulation almost entirely, following the law of finance which makes base currency drive out of circulation one less base. Commodities, too, were affected by this lack of faith, as many Southerners attempted to invest their notes in goods. Those with unbounded faith in the success of the Confederate cause purchased Negroes, and others bought land or livestock, but the amount of property available for purchase became increasingly small in proportion to the vast amounts of paper in circulation.

Distrust of notes of circulation also sent prices into a wild inflationary spiral. Paper dollars that by the beginning of 1864 were worth but six cents in coin were by the end of that year valued more nearly by weight than by denomination. At the close of the war all Confederate currency turned to dead leaves. Lord, ed., *Fremantle Diary*, p. 22; John B. Jones, *A Rebel War Clerk's Diary*, ed. Earl S. Miers (New York: Sagamore Press, Inc., 1958), pp. 520–22; Edward A. Pollard, *The Lost Cause: A New History of the War of the Confederates* (New York: E.B. Treat and Company, 1867), pp. 420–28 (hereafter referred to as Pollard, *The Lost Cause*).

[75] Dewitt Clinton Petty was Elijah Petty's younger brother in Seguin, Texas. The others are brothers-in-law: Andrew Dove married Fredonia Lydia Petty, John L. Cochran married Calvina Adaline Petty, and Charles Cabaniss Howerton married Theora Jane Petty.

[76] See note 55.

[77] "Located on Virginia Point near the railroad tressel [trestle] which linked Galveston with the mainland. This fortress, also called Fort Virginia Point, was first fortified in November, 1861. Armament at that time consisted of 3 24-pounder smoothbores and one 8-inch howitzer, all mounted on siege carriages with the platforms designed to give an angle of fire of 90 degrees. During the early stages of the war the garrison was considered only a battery consisting of a wall of earth, 12 feet at the crown and 20 feet at the base, extending 70 yards on both sides of the railroad tressel. After the evacuation of Galveston, Fort Hebert was heavily fortified and strengthened." Windsor, *Texas in the Confederacy*, pp. 20–21.

[78] Colonel Edwin Waller Jr. operated a plantation in Austin County near Hempstead in present-day Waller County. When Colonel John S. Ford raised the Second Regiment of Texas Cavalry in May 1861, Waller was selected as major. In June 1861 he left Camp Leon near San Antonio with a detachment of the Second Regiment for El Paso, on an expedition that was supposed to take him through New Mexico and Arizona to California. Before Waller and his men reached El Paso the com-

mand of the expedition shifted to Lieutenant Colonel John R. Baylor. The Confederate cavalry, under Baylor and Waller, gained a success against Federal troops at Fort Fillmore near Mesilla, New Mexico. In January 1862 Waller left west Texas with an escort of ten men to return to San Antonio. He then went to Richmond and received authority to raise a regiment of mounted men for three years or the war, with orders to report to Van Dorn in Arkansas. He began to recruit volunteers, offering a bounty of $50. Each volunteer must furnish his own horse, equipment for the horse and such small arms as he could get. Waller wanted to arm one company, at least, with double-barrelled shotguns. He promised to pay each volunteer for the arms he furnished, $12 a day for use of the horse and the horse's value if killed in action. Rifles and revolvers would be furnished in Arkansas to those men who had none. "Texians your homes and hearthstones are now threatened from the North," Waller said in his advertisement in the March 26, 1862, issue of the Houston *Tri-Weekly Telegraph*. "You are called to the rescue. The services of this Regiment are particularly wanted by the gallant Van Dorn to beat back the invader. Come now, come at once, come to the rescue and let us win our liberties by our valor. Here is a service that Texians delight in. This regiment like the brave Rangers of Terry's will be assigned duty in the teeth of danger. Come with me, and I will lead you right where your habits and disposition will enable you to make the best fight in your power." The command was organized as Waller's Thirteenth Texas Cavalry Battalion and left Hempstead on July 1, 1862, for Louisiana, crossing the Sabine River on July 20 and arriving at Berwicks Bay on August 31. Charles Spurlin, ed., *West of the Mississippi with Waller's 13th Texas Cavalry Battalion, CSA*. Hill Junior College Monographs in Texas and Confederate History No. 6 (Waco: Texian Press, 1971), pp. iii, 1–2; "CAVALRY! FOR ARKANSAS!!," one-page recruitment broadside signed by Wm. H. Russell, Broadside 346, Texas State Archives, Austin, Texas.

[79] Chloe in pastoral and other literature is a name for a maiden, especially one beloved.

[80] The Reverend George Washington Carter, the president of Soule University, a Methodist school in Chappell Hill, Washington County, resigned his office in May 1861 and later got permission from the War Department to raise a regiment of Texas Lancers. Carter authorized recruiting officers to raise enough companies to increase his command to brigade strength. Recruits were enlisted for three years or the war

and were told to meet at Hempstead in early April 1862, where they would organize. Thirty companies assembled. Meanwhile, Carter returned from Richmond with orders to reorganize his regiment into a cavalry brigade containing three regiments, to be styled the Twenty-first (First Texas Lancers), Twenty-fourth (Second Texas Lancers) and Twenty-fifth (Third Texas Lancers), and to be commanded respectively by himself and two other Methodist ministers, F. C. Wilkes and Clayton C. Gillespie. Carter, as senior colonel, would also command the brigade. The reorganization took place at Camp Hébert, three or four miles southeast of Hempstead, on April 24, 1862. Norman D. Brown, ed., *One of Cleburne's Command: The Civil War Reminiscences and Diary of Capt. Samuel T. Foster, Granbury's Texas Brigade, CSA* (Austin: University of Texas Press, 1980), pp. xxxviii-xl.

[81] Robert Thomas Pritchard Allen was born in Maryland in 1813. He attended West Point, graduating in 1834. Allen ranked fifth in a class of 36. (His class produced no Civil War generals of note.) Allen served on topographical duty, July 17, 1834, to January 22, 1836, and in Florida against the Seminole Indians, being present at the skirmish of Okihumphy Swamp, March 30, 1836. He resigned from the army on July 31, 1836, and was employed by the government as a civil engineer supervising harbor improvements on Lake Erie, 1836–1838. In 1838 he became a Methodist minister. He was Professor of Mathematics and Civil Engineering in Allegheny College, Pennsylvania, 1838–1841, and in Transylvania University, Kentucky, 1841–1845. He was superintendent with the rank of colonel of the Kentucky Military Institute, 1847–1849, 1851–1854. Allen served as a special agent of the United States Post Office Department for California and Oregon, 1849–1850, and was the owner and publisher of the San Francisco *Pacific News* in 1850. In 1857 he and his son, Robert D., came to Bastrop, Texas, and established the Bastrop Military Institute. "Colonel R. T. P. Allen was a West Pointer; rather small, very quick and alert," wrote Mary McDowall. "The cadets loved and honored him, but were in the habit of calling him 'Raring Tearing Pitching Allen' behind his back. He was a Methodist minister, very devout. His wife was related to Jay Cook[e]. She called her husband 'old man.' One morning she found the Colonel in the parlor on his knees at his morning devotions. He was wanted by some one. She said, 'Get up, old man, I haven't time to pray, and you shan't.'"

In the summer of 1861 Allen was placed in command of a camp of instruction at Camp Clark, Texas. Later that year he went to Virginia and for a few days commanded the Fourth Texas Infantry Regiment of the Texas Brigade. But his fame as a martinet had preceded him to Virginia, and the Texans there refused to accept him as their commander. "The first attempt at giving a Colonel to the 4th Regiment, was the appointment of R. T. P. Allen, a citizen of Bartrop [Bastrop], Texas, and the President of the Military Institute at that place," wrote the regiment's chaplain, Reverend Nicholas A. Davis. "This gentleman, although a man of thorough military education, was not acceptable to either men or officers. He had been in command of the Camp of Instruction, at Camp Clark, Texas, and the men had there with remarkable unanimity, come to the conclusion that he did not suit their views as a commander. A protest against this appointment was made by the officers of the Regiment, and Colonel Allen returned to Texas." According to Mark Sanders Womack, a member of Company G, the men resented Allen requiring them to do menial tasks. In protest several of them forced him to mount his horse without a bridle, and then using switches whipped the horse "out of the regimental grounds amid the hoots and jeers of the boys." Womack added: "That Colonel was never seen again." John Bell Hood was appointed in Allen's place. The Secretary of War offered Allen a captaincy of artillery, which he declined. Returning to Texas, Allen resumed his position as superintendent of the Bastrop Military Institute.

On February 3, 1862, the War Department requisitioned 15 infantry regiments from Texas to fill the state's quota. In compliance with this order Governor Lubbock issued a call on February 26 for the 15 regiments, stating in his proclamation that unless the call was complied with and Texas's quota furnished, he would resort to a draft. Allen decided to raise one of these regiments.

This biographical sketch of Allen is compiled from the following sources: Bvt. Major-Gen. George W. Cullum, *Biographical Register of the Officers and Graduates of the U.S. Military Academy at West Point, N. Y. From Its Establishment, in 1802, to 1890 with the Early History of the United States Military Academy*, 3 vols., 3rd ed. rev. and ext. (Boston: Houghton Mifflin and Company, 1891), I, p. 569 (hereafter cited as Cullum, *Biographical Register of the Officers and Graduates of the U.S. Military Academy*); Wright, comp., *Texas in the War*, pp. 21-101n; McDowall, "Little Journey through Memory's Halls," pp. 40–41; Rev. Nicholas A. Davis, *The Campaign from Texas to Maryland* (Richmond: Office of the Presbyterian Committee of Publication of the Confederate States, 1863), p. 17; Harold B. Simpson, *Hood's Texas Brigade: Lee's Grenadier Guard* (Waco: Texian Press, 1970), pp. 61–62; Bellville *Countryman*, November 27, 1861; Lubbock, *Six Decades in Texas*, pp. 378–79.

[82] Kirby failed to raise enough companies to form his own regiment.

[83] Petty is referring to the battle of Shiloh, Tennessee, April 6–7, 1862. Confederate General Albert Sidney Johnston launched an attack on General Ulysses S. Grant's exposed encampment between the Tennessee River and Shiloh Meeting House two miles to the southwest and by nightfall had driven the Federals to the very banks of the river at Pittsburg Landing. The Confederate triumph, however, was short-lived. Johnston's death on the field was a severe blow to Southern morale, and the timely arrival of Federal reinforcements under General Don Carlos Buell gave Grant a decided advantage. In the next day's fighting General P. G. T. Beauregard, who succeeded Johnston in command, was forced to order a retreat to Corinth, Mississippi. Initial stories in the Confederate press, based on the first day's fight, reported a glorious victory for the South. Petty probably sent his wife a copy of the Houston *Telegraph's* extra of April 12, 1862, which carried the following headline:

A GLORIOUS VICTORY
5000 Prisoners Taken!
One Hundred Cannon Taken.
Twenty Thousand Arms Taken.
Gen. A. S. Johnston Killed

[84] The Confederate Index, Texas State Archives, lists a Third Lieutenant A. L. Steele, Labadie Rifles Volunteer Company, Washington City Infantry, Captain J. S. Lauderdale, Texas Militia, June 1861.

[85] On April 16, 1862, President Jefferson Davis approved an act of the Confederate Congress calling for conscription of every white male between 18 and 35 years of age for three years' service. Later acts raised the age limit to 50. There were no specific exemptions; however, by an act of April 21 the Congress exempted government officials, ferrymen, pilots, employees in iron mines and foundries, telegraph operators, ministers, printers, educators, hospital employees and druggists, among others. There were a number of later revisions in exemptions.

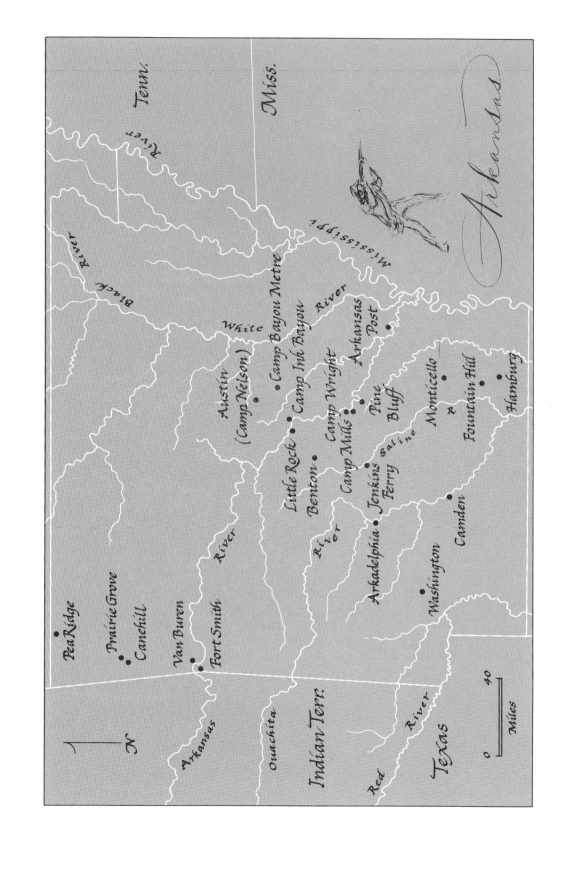

CHAPTER TWO

This Is an Awful Arkansas

IN RESPONSE TO GOVERNOR LUBBOCK'S call for 15 infantry regiments to fill the state's quota, the superintendent of the Bastrop Military Institute, Colonel R. T. P. Allen, placed the following notice in the March 26, 1862, issue of the Houston *Tri-Weekly Telegraph:*

Mr. Editor: Having received many letters from various parts of Western Texas, asking me to raise a regiment under the Governor's call for 15 regiments of infantry for the war, I desire to say through your paper (for everybody reads the Telegraph) that I desire to raise such a regiment.

Companies preparing to serve under my command will please communicate with me personally or by letter, at Camp Lubbock, near Austin. Recruits will also be received singly or in squads, and assigned to companies. We will be ready to receive and provide for all that report themselves.

Twenty years constant experience in the drill enables me to promise that my regiment shall not fall behind the foremost in proficiency of drill and efficiency of preparations for the field. There will probably be two regiments or more at this camp, and it is hardly necessary for me to add that they, as at other camps, will have the right by law to elect their field officers.

R. T. P. Allen

P. S. — The camp near Austin is one of the five appointed by the Governor for the rendezvous of the 15 regiments; I have charge of the camp, will supervise the instruction there, and be in constant attendance for the purpose of mustering into the Confederate service those presenting themselves.

R. T. P. A.

"See card of Col. R. T. P. Allen," the *Telegraph* directed its readers. "We commend this accomplished officer to the new regiments now forming, and shall consider any regiment fortunate that secures his leadership. He is a thorough soldier as well as a christian gentleman."[1]

One of the Texans who responded to Allen's appeal, so lacking in the usual rhetorical bombast, was Elijah P. Petty, who joined Allen's regiment, designated the Seventeenth Texas Infantry, as captain of Company F. He enlisted on May 13, 1862, at Bastrop for the war and was mustered in the same day.[2] The regiment was organized at Camp Terry near Austin on June 9, 1862. Allen was elected colonel; George Washington Jones, lieutenant colonel; and John W. Tabor, major. Allen received 66 votes in Petty's company, and M. W. Sims, no votes; Jones, who was unopposed, likewise received 66 votes; Tabor received 58 votes; T. O. Kidd, four votes; Cyrus Coffee, three votes; and H. M. Bouldin, no votes.[3]

In Petty's company the other officers were: J. L. Cunningham, first lieutenant; H. N. Litle, second lieutenant; H. McLester, third lieutenant; W. M. Miller, first sergeant; O. G. Coulson, second sergeant; S. K. Jones, third sergeant; J. T. McDonald, fourth sergeant; Augus Gillis, fifth sergeant; J. P. Person, first corporal; T. F. Mayo, second corporal; George Smith, third corporal; and J. E. Gage, fourth corporal. There were 63 privates as of June 7, 1862.[4]

On February 24, 1862, following the loss of Forts Henry and Donelson in Tennessee, Secretary of War Judah P. Benjamin ordered Hébert to push forward "with all possible rapidity" to Van Dorn at Little Rock all the troops defending the Gulf Coast, except those necessary to man the batteries. This order did not apply to the troops on the Río Grande or "western frontier." "No invasion of Texas is deemed probable," Hébert was told, "but if any occurs its effects must be hazarded, and our entire forces must be thrown toward the Mississippi, for the defense of that river and of the Memphis and Charleston Railroad." Hébert received Benjamin's order on March 14 and proceeded to forward such troops as could be equipped and armed to Arkansas "as rapidly as the necessary transportation could be obtained." "You have already been instructed as to the disposition of the armed troops organized in Texas and not wanted in that state," General Robert E. Lee wrote Hébert on May 26, 1862. "I presume those ready for the field are en route for Arkansas." On August 8, 1862, Hébert wrote General Henry H. Sibley at San Antonio that Nelson's infantry regiment and Parsons's cavalry regiment were in Arkansas; that Randal's, Carter's, Wilkes's, Gillespie's, Burnett's and Burford's cavalry regiments, Garland's infantry regiment, Waul's Legion (a mixed command) and Haldeman's Battery were en route to Little Rock; and that Flournoy's, Young's, Speight's, Roberts's, Hubbard's, Clark's, Waterhouse's, Ochiltree's and Allen's infantry regiments were ordered there.[5]

Meanwhile, in April 1862 General Van Dorn took his entire army across the Mississippi River, assuring the 20,000 men they would be brought back to Arkansas as soon as the impending battle on the Tennessee had been fought. They all consented to go, and the mounted men were persuaded to leave their horses behind. Many of the soldiers never got back home, and Arkansas was left undefended; moreover, Van Dorn was too late for the battle of Shiloh, fought on April 6 and 7. The main Federal force in Arkansas under General Samuel Curtis was already at Batesville, and scouting parties were within 35 miles of Little Rock. The people of Arkansas, feeling that the Richmond government had abandoned them, were fast becoming despondent. In May 1862 one of the state's senators, Robert W. Johnson, arrived in General Beauregard's camp at Corinth, Mississippi, to ask for help. General Thomas C. Hindman, a resident of Helena, Arkansas, who had commanded a brigade at Shiloh, was assigned to command in Arkansas on May 26 under orders issued by Beauregard. Impressing supplies, raiding the Memphis banks for a million dollars and commandeering steamboats, Hindman arrived in Little Rock on May 31 and went to work with great energy to raise and equip an army for the defense of the state. He had all the cotton in the state collected and ordered it burned if the enemy approached, started new manufactures, enforced martial law (including the use of a passport system) and fixed prices. A host of provost marshals sprang into existence. When discontent arose in his conscript army, Hindman had nine men shot without trials. In all of this he claimed he was supported by everyone except "Tories, speculators, extortioners, and deserters, and a few smaller politicians." As a result, Curtis was forced to retire to Helena, looting as he went, and the Confederacy reasserted itself on the Western border.[6]

Petty's letters home resume on July 12, 1862, just as the Seventeenth Texas Infantry at Camp Texas received orders to move to Tyler in Smith County, Texas, and prepare for active field service.

Camp Texas⁷ July 12 1862

Dear Margaret

We have just received orders to move with as little delay as possible to Tyler Smith County Texas and prepare for active Service in the field. It is impossible for me to say or even conjecture at what time we will leave here as nearly every thing has yet to be prepared but it will be done I suppose speedily. Please put my clothes all in a good state of readiness for marching. Go and see the Cabinet maker Fehr and get him to make me immediately a Camp Chest after the Style of the one made for Capt Allen.⁸ I want it made good & substantial and quick. I will be at home the last of the incoming week when I will inform you more fully of matters. I reported this morning 35 on the sick list present & absent. Mostly measels some quite sick.⁹ Good news from Virginia and Arkansas.¹⁰

Yours truly
E. P. Petty

My Co is 131 strong.

In camp under a post oak
10 miles from Wheelock Robertson County Augt 29th 1862

Dear Margaret

You see from the caption the place from which I write — We are getting along elegantly — Some few of the boys have sore feet — Some complain of sore muscles etc. Verry few are sick. We travelled quite slow at first to harden ourselves & the mules — Saturday we reached the spring head Main Street 1½ miles, Sunday we camped at Becks 7½ miles, Monday at Judge Garretts Mill 10 miles, Tuesday Lexington 14 miles, Wednesday 4 miles from Caldwell 17 miles, Thursday Mordys [?] ferry on Brazos 15 miles & Friday (today) this place 14 miles, total 79 miles. I bought two mules to complete my teams and we have had no trouble with them. The most of the men are footing it and go through like old Soldiers — There are thirty (30) of my Company absent most of them sick. It has rained on us nearly every day since we left and yet it has been so light that the roads are not heavy. We have had no trouble about water or provisions except yesterday evening we did not get a beef and have had no meat for dinner today though we have had bread, milk & butter in abundance. The meat is now here and cooking say 2 O'clock. It threatens to rain

hard today. I suppose it will. We are about 2 days behind Capt Allens
Company. I have rode some every day but one. My feet are a little sore
not enough to prevent my full performance. I will write again as
chance may determine. I will mail this at Wheelock. Kiss my babes.

Truly Yours Etc
E. P. Petty

Aug 29 1862

P.S. Wheelock 30th Augt We are here 10 O'clock a.m. All quite well.
It rained like thunder yesterday & last night. We are now soldiering.

E. P. P.

Centreville Leon Co Sept 3rd 1862

Dear Ella

  I wrote to your Ma from Wheelock — On this side of Wheelock
about 5 miles on Sunday morning early one of my waggon wheels
broke all to pieces so that we had to return to Cedar Creek 1½ miles
on this side of Wheelock where we remained until Monday when we
left Cedar Creek at 9 o'clock and travelled Monday 17 miles and
tuesday 18 to 3 miles of Centreville and to day to this place where
intend to stay until tomorrow morning to rest our teams as we drove
yesterday and the day before rather hard. We are now in about 95
miles of Tyler. We have had good roads up to this time as a general
thing but learn that there is about 20 or more miles of sand ahead of us
— We have rain on us every day since we left home and I have been
soaking wet several times. The boys all stay well and enjoy themselves
admirably. Active moving service suits us all much the best. Tell Ma
that on Cedar Creek I saw Linn, Holly, Sassafras, Birch & Persimmon
trees and on Boggy [Creek] in this County Iron wood, Red oak,
Spannish oak, Sweet gum, black gum & the other trees above
mentioned. Around Centreville the Clay hills and Persimmon sprouts
& black berry briars reminded me of old Stewart County very much.
About Wheelock I found a great abundance of fine peaches and have
had as many as I could eat and also fine peach cobblers — we are
getting along finely and tomorrow morning will start for Tyler via
Magnolia, Palestine etc. May be so I will write home from Palestine.
My love to all.

Yours affectionately
E. P. Petty

Fort Houston Sept 6th 1862

My Dear Wife

We are now safe & sound in Eastern Texas 3 miles from Palestine in Anderson County at a place called Fort Houston a little fort by that name having once been located here in the days of the Republic. This is a sandy bushey Country so close that I can hardly get my breath it seems. There are a great many rich men in these parts but so far as my experience is conserned I find them cold, distant, unaccomodating & I believe rascally. If I want favours I hunt the poor — and I am sure to get but from the rich of this section deliver me.

Tomorrow we will go into Palestine. I am told by my advance guard of Scouts who have been that far ahead that it is a beautiful place — quite sizeable, the largest place we have yet past the other towns all being little dried up places — We are now in 53 miles of Tyler about 4 or 5 more days journey.

We have no cases of sickness in the Companies, so much for being in active life. If we had been at Camp Terry there would have been some dozen or more cases. I will write again from Tyler. We can get no news up here not so much as at home. There are no goods over this way. There are more goods in one store in Bastrop than in all the stores on the route this far and at Robertson. Let me hear from you at Tyler.

Yours Truly
E.P. Petty

P.S. Sept 7th Since writing the above I have taken a jaunt into the city of Palestine — It is a beautiful place situated in the rolling red land of Eastern Texas. It is as large or larger than Bastrop. This red rolling country & timber reminds me of Tennessee — I can look around & see — White oak, Black oak, red oak, Spannish oak, Sweet gum, black gum, persimmon, Sassafras, ash — ironwood, Birch, Sumach, Summer grapes, May pops, Mullen Stalks etc. etc. What do you think — I climbed up into a black gum tree and gathered some summer grapes. They were delicious. They are nearly as large as Mustang's.

E.P.P.

P.S. 8 O'clock A.M. Palestine Sept 7th 1862 I am now at the waggon shop here having a waggon mended. Broke again — last Sunday I had the same waggon mended at Wheelock — this Sunday here in

Palestine — The Co have gone 1½ miles beyond town & will wait until I come up. Capt Allen is about 2 miles from here with his Co. and Capt McDowell is near behind.[11] I am afraid that we will all get together. There is'nt a single case of sickness in Capt Miller's[12] or my Co's (and I believe none in either Capt A or McD's.) and we have been wet every day since we left home and slept in wet clothes & blankets at night — Yesterday was the dryest day we have had & it sprinkled some on us. Excuse bad writing as I wrote on my knees.

Truly yours
E.P. Petty

In Camp 5½ miles North of Tyler
September 11th AD 1862

Dear Wife

About 9 O'clock A.M. today we marched through the Streets of Tyler and about 11 O'clock reached this place which is in the woods ½ mile from the road leading on to Little Rock. We have the thicket to clear up and the ground to grub for our encampment having selected a place new and as remote as possible from where others had been. There are now four Companies here. Capt Allen's, Capt Bouldins,[13] Capt Millers and Capt Petty's. Three others will be in tomorrow, Capt Arnetts,[14] Capt Ryans,[15] & Capt McDowells. There are not many soldiers here or hereabouts & those only fragments of regiments left here sick all the rest having gone to Arkansas. We have orders to go on just as soon as possible so that as soon as 10 ox waggons & oxen can be purchased for us to transport provisions etc we will be off. The Q Master says he can have them ready by next Monday week. I am much pleased with the Country since I crossed the Trinity river. The country is rich & fertile and the general character of land & timber reminds me of Tennessee. In addition to the trees etc about which I have written to you I have seen Maple, Chinkapin, White blossom dog wood (how beautiful) & have seen some small apple orchards though I dont think apples do well here. I am delighted with Anderson County and its shire town Palestine — I think however that it is not so healthy as our section. It is a much better Country over here than I expected to see. We have had a pleasant & agreeable trip over with verry little to mar or annoy us. The health of the entire command is good — I dont like the prospects here however and if we have to lay here long I am fearful there will be sickness. The news of another glorious victory for us at Mannassus [Manassas] has just reached here in which Lee & Stonewall Jackson whipped Pope & McClelland,[16] also that Genl Bragg had met & captured Genl Buell with his entire Command at Sommerville Alabama. If true glorious indeed and I am ready wicked as I am to return thanks to God.[17] Excuse bad writing. I am sitting in the front of a waggon and the mules which are tied to it eating and jerking it about so that I can hardly write at all. I received today your's of the 3rd inst & Ella's of the 31st ult. Was glad to hear from you — Sorry to hear that you had sickness & trouble — hope you will have no more — Cheer up, dont despair or be discouraged. Keep all things right and when I give the infernal Yankees their just deserts I will return home to cheer up your spirits and make home happy once more but whilst absent remember that I am in the service of my Country fighting for liberty & human rights — serving God in an acceptable form and that when I do meet the Yanks I will make them drink the bitter waters of dark damnation for forcing me away from the Comforts of home and the loved ones there. Take good care of my children — train them up in strict honesty and uprightness to respect their parents and those older than themselves— to do due honor to age — to love and cherish one another — to give every person their proper rights. Educate them <u>well</u>. Keep them at school — Encourage them by every means to learn and last though not least impress them with and encourage them in a bitter and unrelenting hatred to the Yankee race — They are our implacable enemies. They have invaded our country and devastated it and are continuing to do so. They have murdered our best citizens & continue to do so and all because we insist upon the unalienable right of self government and as

I am in eternal hostility to them I think it but right that my children who suffer as I suffer and as my country suffers should be indoctrinated with an implacable hatred to so vile and cursed race.

I will write as often as convenient — Dont fail to write every week — Mr [Samuel] Fleming is quite well, in fact all are well.

Kiss my babes & believe me truly

Yours Etc
E. P. Petty
Sept 11th 1862

Camp Near Tyler Sept 18th 1862

My Dear Daughter

I intended to have written to you some days ago but on last Monday (the 15th) I went back near Palestine to try and buy some shoes for my Company & returned to Camps yesterday evening — To day & for 2 or more days I will be exceedingly busy making out muster rolls etc as the QM intends paying us all up to 1st July in the early part of next week — You may depend I dont have much leisure time here and I am glad of it. In the first place it is more healthy to keep stirring and second it occupies my mind so that I am not grieving over home affairs etc. Up to this date I have received but one letter from home — I am sure you have written & I suppose it is the irregularity of the mail. It comes to Tyler but once a week from Austin and 3 times a week from Houston — I am very anxious to hear from you — Wish I could get a letter every day. I have been to Tyler 5 or six times — I dont fancy the place much nor the people — It is not larger than Bastrop nor so pretty. There is'nt any thing in it to sell. There is more goods in Bastrop than all Eastern Texas. They have fine water over here — Springs in nearly every hollow and cold water at that but it is all Calyente. You can taste the iron in every dipper full — I think it is quite sickly over here — You can see many a pale face and hear many an ague & ake. The soldiers have suffered awfully here — Hundreds of them have died and many are sick here now. There are seven Companies of our Regiment here now. When they reached here there were none were sick — Yesterday morning 57 men reported on the sick list — I dont know what to day but suppose more. In my Co to day there is about 10 on the sick list, 1 with fever, 1 or 2 with chills, 1 mumps, several with diarrhea etc but none much sick. If we stay here ten days longer I am fearful there will be an increase. From my information we will leave next week (May be t[o]ward the last) for Little Rock. I understand that our troops are leaving Little Rock perhaps for St. Louis or some other point in Missouri — I regret very much that we are not with them for I long to settle my accounts with the Yankees. Have you heard the news? It comes in here thick & fast and glorious — I dont know how much reliance can be placed in it — I am satisfied if ⅓ is true.[18] The news is first that [we] defeated and utterly routed the combined Yankee Armies of Pope, McCelland [McClellan], Banks, Seigel etc on the memorable plains of Mannassas, that we have taken Washington city and that glorious old Stonewall is Marching 40000 men on Baltimore,[19] 2nd that Genl Kirby Smith has taken Cincinnatti Ohio and hence Whiskey will now be plenty[20] and 3rd that the citizens of St. Louis Mo have risen, captured the city and seized all the federal arms, munitions etc[21] and 4th that Buell is making a hasty retreat from Tennessee.[22] If ⅓ is true it is glory enough for me and all that is necessary to finish the job is for the Allen Regiment to reach the scene.

If I had time I would write you a longer letter but you must excuse me now. I send you herein Miss Mollie E. Moore's address to Speight's Regiment & Capt Herrings reply. I received this from the hands of Miss Mollie herself. Miss Mollie is a poetess — You have seen her poetry in the Houston Telegraph — She is a tall slender girl about 17 years old — blue eyes, light or flaxen hair — rather red complexion —

prominent forehead — quite gay and fascinating — She promised me to pay me a visit at camps — Hope she will do so[23] — Has a cousin in my Company, W.H. Black (Lem Black's son). After receiving this letter write to me at Little Rock Ark.

Yours truly
E. P. Petty

My Dear Wife

In a few days Cicero Nash[24] will leave for home and when he returns will bring clothing etc for the companies from Bastrop County. I find that I shall greatly need some shirts — Please get something good & substantial and make about four and send me by him — Also send me one or two pairs of good winter gloves or gauntlets. I am in splendid health — weigh 130 lbs or did when I reached this place. We have an abundance to eat & all good — Get no flour however. Will not until we start to move. Good crops made over here. No troops here besides ours except a few conscripts & some sick. If you have any earlier or better chance to send shirts and gloves do so. Kiss my little ones all. God bless them for me — I will send you some papers as I can pick them up. Write often.

Truly yours
E. P. Petty

P.S. Bob Fore wants his mother to send by Nash such things as she knows he may need — tell her so.

E. P. Petty

Camp "Bush Whack" Near Tyler
September 23rd 1862

Dear Wife

I am sick today & was also yesterday. I tore up my little finger nail about 10 days ago and it is very sore and painful and I have caught a severe cold and have some fever with it and I have I fear strong symptoms of the piles — and — well I'll quit at that. I am better to day than yesterday. I took about 4 fingers of brandy yesterday and went into a cold spring & bathed which I think helped me. I am not laid up nor have I ceased from the full discharge of my duty and more. We will leave here during the latter part of the present week. I think some of the waggons (the ox) will start on tomorrow. Orders have reached

here to hasten on to Little Rock. I think a movement on St. Louis is intended. There are a good many of the boys unwell but none serious. We have two cases of mumps in my Company — I dont think that we will have to leave any sick here — There is a great difference in the temperature here and at Bastrop. We have heavy dews and the nights are cold & chill. One night I was cold under 5 blankets. This is why I have caught cold. The more I see of this regiment the more I think it is one of the finest in the service. If we just had a Colonel to suit us we would do fine service. The Col question is between us. I dont want it made public but Col Allen grows more detestable to the regiment every day. He has'nt 50 friends in the regiment. The other night the boys concluded to give Col Jones a serenade by way of showing Col Allen unmistakably what they thought of him. By mistake they went to Col Allens tents & yelled for Jones. Jones not being there did not appear — they made the Welkin ring for Jones — Finally a few weak voices cried for Allen but in an instant it was overwhelmingly drowned with Jones Jones etc. — Some of the boys who had found Jones tent now raised a yell and the crowd poured down there. Jones made a speech. They then called for Maj Tabor. He appeared & made a short talk then they cried for Petty. I of course appeared and spoke after which they dispersed. — There were at least 800 men in the turn out showing to Col Allen & all others who was their favorite. Col Allen has been in the best humor ever since that I ever saw him. He sees his course wont do. Lt Litle will leave in the morning for Bastrop to collect up clothing for our Company and forward it on, also to carry back to our families the money which each may have to send. I wrote to you some time since to send me four good shirts and two pairs of gloves one woollen & one pair buck skin gauntletts — Send them and in addition send me four pairs of good stout drawers. I send you by Lt Litle One hundred & twenty-five dollars. I think it better for you to invest your Confederate money in some sort of property. Buy a negro if you can or something else that wont deteriorate its value — If the war should end Confederate money will go down immensely. It makes no difference what the issue may be — Keep enough to meet your current expenses and invest the ballance. The news comes in glorious.[25] Stonewall Jackson has had a fight with Genl. Wool at the Relay House in 12 miles of Baltimore which resulted in the total defeat of Genl. Wool's army. The Marylanders are flocking to Genl Jacksons standard. Ella can now sing "Maryland my Maryland." The tide has absolutely turned in our favour and our victorious colums are pressing onward. Wash Jones will remain at Tyler for some time as Commander of the Post. He has sent for his wife and will carry her on with him.

We have been paid off to day up to 30th June last which made $177.66 for my part. Glass is a most consumate liar and scoundrel. He leid all the way out here and tried to swindle the Companies and no doubt but did do it considerably. Keep it to yourself as I dont want to circulate reports against him. Dont trust him a fingers lenght or he will swindle you.

Write to me at Little Rock until further directed. I have received but 2 letters from home.

Give my love to all friends & kiss my babes.

Flemming and Lum Owens are well.

Your's truly
E. P. Petty

Gilmer Upshur County
Sept 29th 1862

My Dear Wife

I am now at a private house in this good city — I wrote to you by Lt Litle that I had been taken sick and I believe the length of time. If not I was taken with fever & piles both on last Monday (this day one week). Lt Litle left on Wednesday. I went to Tyler with him and returned to Camps by noon quite sick & feeble & in pain. I had determined if possible not to take medicine and so ground my teeth and grunted — The same evening beginning at one Oclock I sat on Court Martial about 2 hours which fatigued me much. That night I got much better. My fever[26] abated but piles did not — Next morning felt much better — Received orders with joy to start for Little Rock by ten o'clock. Started at one after eating hearty & feeling verry well — Had marched hardly a mile when the fever came on like an avalanch and it was all I could do even with the help of a horse to make Camps 8 miles. I subsided, sent for the Doctor & called for medicine which was administered in profusion. Next day took quinine and eat watermelons and had high fever at sun down. Heard that Capt Highsmith & wife were near and after night rode four miles to see them and back to camps that night making it near 12 o'clock. Next morning rose early with fever and went on to where Highsmith & wife were, taking quinine & suffering more than I told them with both piles & fever — Of that interview they have no doubt given you the particulars so I wont attempt to say any thing about it. After I left them I rode about 4 or 5 miles where I was compelled to fall by the way side one of the sickest of the sick where I lay for six hours — Late in the evening I was much better. The fever was subsiding and the piles were relieved entirely — With great difficulty I rode to camps 6 miles further. The fever though not so high continued all night. On Sunday we lay up and I did not abandon my bed but took quinine until I knocked the fever into fits. To day I came here early & have staid here all day & intend to stay here a day or two to recuperate — I have taken lots of quinine to day & have no fever — Am now 8 oclock at night sweating copiously & feeling well. I am mighty feeble and look terrible bad — I dont want you to see me now. You would say I was from Arkansas. With prudence all will be well — I have no prudence but a good Doctor at my elbow who curses me every fifteen minutes. This is enough on my own self when my Company are so much worse off than I. They began to fall as with an epidemic at the camp near Tyler and when we started, had to leave five or six in Hospital that were not able to travel — Others who were sick concluded to try it a while & in a short time we had all the horses occupied & waggons as many as they could carry. This morning at roll call I had 30 men reported for duty besides 8 waggoners out [of] 100 which I have along. We have established a Hospital here and I will have to leave not less than 10 may be more. The others though not fit for duty will try & worry along rather than be left. I have more sickness than any other Company by odds but there is an annoying amount in every one — The Col has been sick — Maj Tabor is quite sick & is here with me — I left at Tyler Fred Hermes, H. Josting,

Lewis Harris, Daniel[?] Morris, Julius Byers & to wait on them Riley Gwinn — I shall leave at this place as far as I now know — Steve Snelling, Henry Boese, Sam Wilson, Ben Decherd, Wate Farmer, George Farmer, Ras Barrett, Tom Irvine & to wait on them John Person & F. A. King — Dave Morris is as sick as any of them but will try to go on. The diseases are billious intermittent fever and chill & fever & Diarrhea I think mostly brought on by eating green fruit which they have found in the shape of apples, grapes & water melons in great abundance over here.

You must excuse my bad writing — I have good paper, ink, pen, table, room, candle etc but my little finger on my right hand is painfully sore and I have to hold it off the table and further I am under the influence of quinine and am nervous. This is a mighty poor Country here. God has long since forgot that he made [it] even if he had a hand in it at first. I am disgusted with it all and would'nt give my Western Prarie House for all the ballance of the world that I have seen or expect to see this trip. I have just heard of another of Stonewall Jackson's victories. He captured Harpers Ferry with the Command etc. 11 000 fed prisoners, 2 000 negroes, 15 thousand stand small arms, 46 cannons and $2 000 000 worth of property.[27] Huzzah for Stonewall. He's the man for the times.[28] When you write give me all the news items in & about Bastrop etc etc. Give my love to the Children. I dont know when you will next hear from me but as the most practicable place.

Your's truly
E. P. Petty

Gilmer Tuesday Sept 30th 1862
10 o'clock AM

Dear Wife

As I hav'nt mailed my letter yet I concluded to add a few more lines this morning. I feel pretty well this morning — Have taken quinine and am in fine perspiration. Maj Tabor is also better. May be I dont worry him some. He devilled me when I was quite sick and I am now paying him with interest. I have just visited our Hospital here. There has been about 40 cases left out of the Regiment. A Lt & other officers with waggon & provisions were left with them also Dr Lewis so that when they recover they have transportation etc. In addition to those I wrote you which I had left I find in hospital Wm. H. Black, Levin Jones & Rev Wm. Rivers from my Co and Elisha Jones to wait on them. This makes from my Company in hospital here 11 sick & 3 waiters total 14 men & 1 Capt Clouby. <u>Aint this the devil.</u> This is more of a town than I at first thought. It is some place it is and there seems to be some clever folks here and I believe they will pay some attention to our sick. I have sold my watch for $30 cash. I am satisfied. It cost me $25. I am living in clover at this place if the blamed Doctor would let me eat it but every once & a while he turns loose to cursing me & wont let me eat. The train left here this morning on its wearisome way to Little Rock. I will follow in a day or two and the sick when they can.

Most truly thine
E. P. Petty

P.S Write to Pa. I hav'nt time. I wrote to him from Tyler.

Petty

Camp 10 miles from Arkansas Line
Bowie County Texas Oct 5th 1862

Dear Margaret

I have an oppertunity per Adolph Erhard[29] to write you a line. I am now sound and well except my little finger which is yet quite sore. I laid over at Gilmer 3 days. I left then on last thursday morning and overtook the Regiment friday evening. The health of the whole command is improving. Active service and travelling is the greatest medicine at last. I have about 25 of my Company behind sick — some at Tyler — some at Gilmer and some on the road. In a day or two we will start back a waggon and an ambulance after them. My piles left me as suddenly as they came and with blue mass[30] and quinine I knocked the fever into fits. Our negro cook Jo is sick and we have our cooking to do. This is the last night I expect soon to spend in Texas as we will cross the line tomorrow. We are now about 30 miles from Fulton [Ark.] and 45 from Washington [Ark.]. The troops at Little Rock are leaving supposed for Missouri.[31] Curtis has left or is leaving Helena.[32] We will have a hard time in Missouri this winter but wherever the Yankees are I am for following. I received your's of the 15th ult. You will find plenty of paper in the old Ledgers and day books in my office. A Large book with Geo P. Shaws name on the out side has a great deal of paper in it. You can use it all but a few pages next to the accounts which I want to figure upon. Go to the office and use any leaves of any of the old Ledgers etc except the books belonging to

Morris' estate.[33] Write to me at Little Rock until further orders. If you can invest your Confederate money in some good property. Write as often as possible and oftener too.

Yours truly
E. P. Petty

Dear Ella

You are going to school with Frank. I want you both to do your best. Study assiduously and let me see when I come home how smart my children have been. Dont think that I am not comeing home for I will come perhaps when you least expect me. You do not know or perhaps do not realize how much trouble and expense I am at to give you learning & what anxiety I feel upon that subject. I want you to obey your ma in all things — She will not require any thing not right of you. Keep good company — Abstain from association with the low bred and vicious — Love and cherish your brothers above every body else your ma excepted. I want you to take music lessons of Miss Mary Nicholson[34] if she teaches. If she does not and Mr Olreich will give you lessons at some private house take them from him. I dont want you to take them at his house. Kiss all the little rats for me and tell them to think of Pa who thinks of them much. Write to me & believe me truly

Yours truly
E. P. Petty

Camp 3½ Miles East of Washington
Arkansas October 10th 1862

Dear Wife

We reached this place yesterday and will lay over here to day for the purpose of drawing rations etc. Although there is an abundance of flour and bacon at the Quarter Master's in Washington they will not give us either and will issue corn meal & beef. Washington & vicinity are quite pretty. The people seem tidy, intelligent and thrifty and there are some beautiful and tasty residences. It is decidedly the prettiest place I have seen and the country around is rich & fertile but with all this it shows that it is sickly. Tallow faces and cadaverous countenances show the ravages of chills & fever. Two nights ago we camped on a lake in Lafayette County Ark the other side of Red River and the boys had some exceeding rich sport seigning the lake with a brush seign (I dont know if I spelled seign right). They caught about a waggonload of buffalo fish verry fine, fat & well flavoured. The water became quite muddy. It was'nt over waist deep and the fish could be plainly seen running & popping their heads up. They got after them with sticks & knives & caught many — One monster alligator gar came plunging & puffing along — About 20 men attacked him with clubs. They fought him for about 50 yards when one man mounted him with his knife and he was finally killed — He measured 7 feet 3 inches and weighed 174 pounds. One mile from Washington I found Pas Turner and Rhem Castleman.[35] Rhem is nearly blind with sore eyes. They have been here a week. Rhem cant bear the light & lays in a dark room. He could'nt see well enough to recognize any one. Could only do it by the voice. He could'nt get a Doctor in Washington to attend on him. Last night I sent him a Doctor from camps and medicine. It will be ten days or two weeks before he can safely travel even with good luck. The health of this Command is decidedly improving — I have but one or two sick men along now and they can travel. My cook is well again — I heard that our sick at Gilmer were nearly all well and sent back waggon and ambulance for them. I learn that the Feds are advancing in force from Helena on White river and that our army had moved out to meet them.[36] Warm times are expected down there. In fifteen or twenty days we will be with them perhaps in time for the fun — I understand that they have the arms for us when we get there and that

we will be immediately initiated. The object is to clean out Arkansas & move at once into Missouri and release that state from bondage so that her patriotic sons may enter the service.[37] I am myself once more and am eating full rations & doing full duty though I look thin & pale so the boys say. It has been raining ever since yesterday and is now turning cold with North wind blowing — It sounds somewhat like a norther & feels a little that way. Every thing is wet & muddy and I think this must be Arkansas. We meet many emmigrants going to Texas. Imagine my mortification yesterday when everybody else was receiving letters that I got none. So save me the pain by writing often. Love to all & Kisses to children.

Yours truly
E. P. Petty

In Camp 5 miles from Arkedelphia [Arkadelphia]
Clark Co Ark Oct 14th 1862

Dear Ella

We have just struck camp at this place on the Caddo river 5 miles from Arkedelphia on the road to Little Rock and about 70 miles from the latter place. We marched to the suburbs of Arkedelphia and Col Allen marched us off to this point without giving us a chance to see the place. One man from each Mess went in to do the trading etc for the messes. They report that it [is] quite a pretty place larger than Washington and about twice the size of Bastrop. The private residences in the vicinity are quite pretty. This is a very rich & fertile county and there is a great deal of wealth in it. I believe that it is better than Hempstead County. We have been making some heavy marches in the last five days. On Sunday we marched over 20 miles over a verry bad road, yesterday about 17 miles. What the hurry is I cant see unless it be that Col Allen wants to make himself appear a Stonewall Jackson so that in the glimmering distance he may be a Brigadier General. It stove nearly all the men up myself amongst the rest. My feet are so sore that I walk like a string halted horse. My health is splendid now. The day I wrote Ma from Washington I was weighed upon two pairs of scales. On one I weighed 132, on the other 136 so you see that I am heavier than I ever have been. I think I would weigh more to day.

Since the rain we have had cold clear weather nearly to the frosting point so we have had a splendid time for marching. We will be at Little Rock in 5 days with good luck. I have several cases of mumps in my company and it seems to be on the increase. It will run through the company before it ceases. There are still a good many sick in the regiment. We left about 12 at Washington — none of my men however. Out of 100 men which I had at Tyler I only now have about 75 the ballance are on the road sick and out of the 75 men along there are only about 60 fit for duty — None are seriously sick however but unwell enough to escape duty.

How do you and Frank get along at school — I hope well. You know Ella that you are my only daughter and I set great hopes by you. That my daughter be smart, intelligent, respicable, neat & tidy is the object of my life and you do all in your power to accomplish this object and my boys God bless them I hope to live to see respectable, intelligent, honest, virtuous and useful members of society. They must study not only books but animate and human nature in all its various phases. I need not say any more to you on this point. You are old enough & sensible enough to comprehend it all. I have just heard the news here that our Army under Genls Price and Van Dorn had been defeated near Corinth with the loss of 10000 men.[38] Sad & as ever if true and one that hurts just now and one that will protract the war. I hear no more of the federals in Arkansas. I am disposed to think that they will not do much here this winter.

I will write again from Little Rock. Hope to receive several letters from you & Ma when I get there. I have been from home now 2 months & have received but 3 letters. This dont suit me and if you dont do better I will have to fall off in my correspondence.

Love to all & kisses to Ma & children.

Truly yours
E. P. Petty

Camp 4 miles from Little Rock Ark
October 19th A D 1862

My Dear Wife

I have just received yours of the 24 & 25 ult and 3rd inst. You may depend it afforded me great pleasure. The last letter I had received previous to these was dated 15th Sept — So it had been over a month since I had heard from home. I am glad you got the money I sent. You will all need it worse than I will. I suppose I still have near one hundred dollars on hand which will do me until I make another draw. We are now camped in four miles of Little Rock. We reached here today at about 9 o'clock A M and will remain here until next Tuesday when we will move up in about a mile of the city. I hav'nt seen the city yet. Will try to go in tomorrow when I will mail this letter. Charley Morgan came out to see us to day. He looks pretty well and says that he is getting along well. He informs me that there are no arms for us, that our army will not go to Missouri until the feds are expelled from Arkansas, that they are 15 000 strong at Helena, 17 prisoners were captured last week and brought in to his camp etc. We have no orders and I cant form an idea of what will become of us. I will write as soon as I can form an idea or get information. Judge Terrell is now in camps and I am told looking well. I will see him presently. He is on Genl McCullochs staff.[39] This is a hard old Country here. Since leaving Arkadelphia we have travelled over the poorest and most God forsaken Country I have ever seen and the people oh God deliver me.[40] We have a miserable camp here worse than it was at Tyler. We passed in a few miles of the celebrated Hot Springs. I wanted to see it verry much but could not. Two days ago we passed through the little town of Benton. I never saw the like of women and children. They waved handkerchiefs etc at us from one end of the town to the other and hurrahed for Texas. We sent up cheer after cheer. I saw many women crying & weeping. It made me feel bad. I have witnessed this weeping at other places. It made me curse in my heart the Lincoln dynasty. We had a death in the Regiment to day, Richard Watson of Walnut Creek in Capt Miller's Co, congestive chill — There is a good deal of sickness still in the regiment. The health of my Co is improving. I have several present unfit for duty but no verry sick cases. I have just learned that our sick at Gilmer Texas are all nearly well and I suppose are now on their way to this place. Glass is a liar & scoundrel. The truth is we went the old road through the man's place. The fence was down and there were neither corn or cotton or any thing else to injure. The fellow was an overseer & was crusty and

insulting to the boys and at night some 15 or 20 of them went up and took 3 of his bee gums — He reported to us and we paid him $5 a gum and put the boys on 4 days roots for it. The man treated us well and we (the Capts) treated him well & so Glass has knowingly lied. I stopped this letter to eat some peach cobler & apple pie. I learn that there is plenty of cider in Little Rock & I intend to spend a dollar for cider tomorrow. I shall subscribe for one of the Little Rock papers for you tomorrow. I have seen Judge Terrell — he looks well. If I find any thing worthy to be written I will put in a post script on tomorrow in Little Rock. I forgot to say that I am well and hearty. A. Jack Hamilton is appointed Governor of Texas and is to return with 50 000 men to take possession etc.[41] Kiss the babes. Lt McLesters respects etc.

Truly yours
E. P. Petty

Oct 20th 1862 — 3 o'clock P M

Dear Wife

I have just returned from a visit to the far famed city of Little Rock. I spent the day there — paid one dollar for dinner and one dollar for horse feed. Maj Tabor paid $5 for a small bottle of brandy cherries. Every thing is in the same proportion. Little Rock is quite an extensive place prettily laid off and verry well built. There is scattered over it a good many dilapidated building[s] which gives it a tint of decay. I visited Maj Charley Morgan's camp and saw the federal prisoners. They brought in 8 or 10 more last night. I was introduced to the Yankee Major and shook him by the hand — So I have had hold of the hand of a wild Yankee but he was safe and unarmed or I should have run off — I found him quite cheerful & pleasant. The privates were playing cards with cards that had the Star spangled banner on their backs. They did'nt seem to care a cent which way the chances went. I have good news and bad news at the same time — The good is that after the fight at Corrinth in which Gens Price & Van Dorn were worsted that Genl Price was reinforced by our exchanged prisoners — renewed the fight — defeated the federals and took 11 000 prisoners.[42] The bad is that Galveston Texas has been captured by federals. If this latter is the case I fear for Texas.[43] Jack Hamilton has been appointed Military Governor of Texas and is to be accompanied by Cassius M. Clay with 50 000 troops to take possession of it[44] — This is but the beginning of his forays I fear and if it is with all her troops gone Texas will be easily overrun.[45] In that event you will have to be verry

circumspect — Keep your money and arms and amunition about your
person or beyond their reach. You must act the part of a true Texan
Matron while you do every thing to protect yourself — your children,
your property etc. You must do no act, say no word, give no look
that will encourage or comfort our enemies — Remember that your
husband is sacrificing his personal ease & comforts & if needs be his
life etc to rid the Country of the hated scoundrels and that they are
oppressing your beloved Country. I tried to get a paper in town to day
for you but they would'nt receive any more subscribers so I am denied
that pleasure —

This is all I have to write now.

Your's truly
E. P. Petty

Oct 20th 1862

Since writing my letter Charley Denney has come into camps on his
way home and I have concluded to send it by him — I am still in fine
health. We have cold nights here, much cover is necessary — Since
the rain I mentioned at Washington it has been clear & cold and I
believe there has been some little frost as I see the potatoes nipped.
You speak of the ladies laughing at my speech etc. This is all greek to
me. I never made such a speech that I remember or used such

language. When & where was it. You speak of moving to Long's place. You had better [stay] at home. If you leave the place it will go to rack and will be ruined forever. I think it will be better and cheaper to stay in your own house. I only make this suggestion. You must be the judge for yourself. Be sure to get plenty of forage for your stock and lay in a good supply of meat for yourself & children — get some body to buy it for you.

Yours truly
E. P. Petty

Little Rock Arkansas
Sunday Oct 26th 1862

Dear Ella

I have concluded to spend an hour this Sabbath evening in writing a few lines to my dear sweet little daughter though I have verry little of interest to communicate. We have been ordered forward to Austin 30 miles further on to which point we will begin to turn next tuesday morning (the 27inst). We would go in the morning but would have to ferry the Arkansas river & by waiting until the next day they will have a pontoon bridge (a bridge of boats) made so that we can march men and waggons over without hindrance or delay. Our regiment has been brigaded — we are now a part and parcel of the 2nd [actually 3rd] Texas Brigade Trans Mississippi District. In the Brigade are the regiments of Cols Flournoy, Fitzhugh, Waterhouse and Allen together with one battery of field artilery.[46] Col Flournoy as senior Col commands for the present the Brigade.[47] I can tell you nothing further of our destination etc for the present. When I reach Austin I can perhaps find out. There are at Austin about 16 regiments of Texas Troops. The Arkansas troops have been sent up towards Missouri. I saw Chauncy Johnson to day just from Austin. He looks tolerable slim, has been sick a good deal. He says there is much sickness amongst the troops. He says that about Austin is the healthiest portion of the state that he has seen — Col Parsons has just had another little brush with the feds. He caught about 250 out chicken stealing etc and attacked them, routed them capturing about 32 prisoners. I did not learn how many feds killed but Parsons lost five killed. Dont know who they were. The prisoners were brought here and paroled and have gone home — —[48]

Parsons is a trump. The feds never make a play but he catches them. They hate him as the devil.

The health of this regiment is not improving any. There is a good deal of sickness in it. Capt Miller lost another man since we came into town, James Hare from Walnut Creek, and Capt Mabry[49] has lost two which makes four since we have been in the vicinity of Little Rock. There is a verry large Hospital here and I suppose from what I can see that there must be 800 cases in it. Little Rock is a beautiful place handsomely laid off & elegantly built. It is very near as pretty as Galveston though not quite so large. On Last Wednesday night Col Allen and his officers were invited to a social party by Mrs Brown at the Arsenal. We went & had quite a nice time. Her father Col Falkner is the original Arkansas Traveller and had the whole represented in pictures and hung on his wall so I have seen and shook hands with the Arkansas traveller.[50] Night before last (the day having been quite warm but a little hazy) the north wind came up just like one of our Texas Northers. It blew furiously all night — About sun up yesterday it began to hail and in about half an hour to snow strait out. It kept this up until about 10 O clock. The ground was covered with snow — There had'nt been frost to kill the leaves and it looked odd to see snow and green leaves mixed — To day it is clear but cold. Arkansas has the honer of showing me this sight for the first time in the fall. Since I wrote on the 20th I have been quite sick again. I was unwell that day but thought nothing of it. The fever however seized on to me again and lasted me until yesterday. It was a rail road fever. I took medicine day before yesterday but it did no good and [I] got up and set into talking and gourmandizing — I believe that cured me. I am free of disease now and feel quite well. My love to all.

Truly yours etc
E. P. Petty

Camp Nelson Near Austin
November 4th 1862

My Dear Daughter

I am just in the receipt of yours and your Ma's of the 20 ult. Was rejoiced to hear that you were all well and perhaps enjoying yourselves. I wrote Ma a letter by Mr Stroud dated 31st ult and headed it Camp Hope. — We are at the same place yet but the name has been changed to Camp Nelson[51] after Col Nelson of Texas who died here about 2 or 3 weeks ago. Col N was about the best man ever Texas sent out and was the best and most efficient Officer in Arkansas and his loss will be more greatly felt and is more mourned than any man who could have fallen in this army. In the letter I sent by Mr Stroud I enclosed two one dollar Texas Treasury Warrants which I told Ma to divide equally between my little children.

Six or Seven thousand stand of Arms have at last reached Little Rock and we have sent down after enough for our regiment and hope that we shall succeed in obtaining them — We have some stirring news here. The feds about 18000 strong have seized Fayetteville in the exteme North Western part of this state. Genl Hindman with about 10 or 12000 troops has fallen back before them, has burned Ft Smith on the Arkansas river and is retiring before them and I suppose has called for reinforcements & arms — The feds 9000 strong have also seized Pocahontas in the extreme North Eastern part of the state and our forces are falling back before them. They have also a large force supposed to be about 12 or 15000 strong at Helena on the Mississippi river with Gun boats etc with River facilities to throw in as many troops as they please at that point and from all their movements I believe (so do others) that it is their intention to push three Columns on Little Rock — one from Fayetteville, one from Pocahontas & one from Helena so you see the news is exciting and active. Stirring times are anticipated here this fall & winter. I think that in less than 10 days our command will be on the move either to Ft Smith or towards Pocahontas. You wanted me to be in one big fight you said — I think that before I see you again I shall smell gun powder frequently — I dont think Texas will be invaded this winter. I believe the landing etc at Galveston was intended as a ruse to keep Texas troops at home whilst they invade this Country. There is a great deal of sickness here amongst the troops.[52] They are dying around us fast. At almost all hours of the day you can hear the guns firing the salute over some soldier gone to his long home far away from friends & home. It is sad to sit and listen at these death tones. It is the only thing that alarms me. I am afraid of Camp sickness. The Yankees and their big guns &

ships have no terrors for me compared to these. Since our regiment reached this place two men have died, one of Capt Mabry's and one of Capt Bouldins men — I expect that one of Capt Miller's men will die to day. At least he is very low. His name is Ringer. I have about 20 cases of sickness present in my Company but none dangerous. The cases are mostly mumps & chills. I left one man at Little Rock quite sick but I heard last night he is nearly well again. My sick from Gilmer I heard from last night. They were at Sulphur fork Red river on their way up — will be here next week — Our regiment looks as large as two of these here — but I am afraid that sickness will bring us down to their size. Our regiment is the best drilled regiment in Arkansas and astonished these fellows here very much.

Every thing is exceedingly scarce and high over here and these people (although we have left our own homes and state and walked six hundred miles to defend them and theirs) are heartless enough to charge the verry maximum price. What do you think of spool cotton at 75 per spool, pins at $3.^{00} per paper, meals of victuals at $1.^{00} per meal — board $3.^{00} per day and almost every other thing at those rates. The Goverment (Genl Holmes)[53] has fixed a tariff of prices on such Country produce as the Army needs. Whilst this is right as far as it goes, yet the tariff ought to have been placed upon every other thing or upon nothing. It is unfair to force the farmers to take $1.^{00} per bushel for his Corn and allow the merchant to charge $3.^{00} for a paper of pins or the grocer to charge him $5.^{00} for a bottle of brandy cherries. The rule ought to be made to work both ways. Yet the tariff only reaches the Country produce and the merchant is at liberty to swindle as much as he pleases.

I am glad that you and Frank are doing so well at your studies — Press on, beat all your school mates & when I come home astonish me with your proficiency and learning — You will have to take old folks place after a while — then prepare for it while you have the chance. If your poor old daddy was to die or get killed over here in Arkansas you would not perhaps have no such oppertunities as have been and are now being furnished you to qualify yourselves for the duties of life — so while the light burns and the oppertunity offers take advantage of it & press on assiduously to the prize and when peace spreads her balmy wings over our happy and dis-enthralled South you can say that we were educated and grew up in the stormy times of this second revolution. God bless my little children how I want them to grow up honorable and respectable and how I wish I was with them to protect their footsteps and prevent them from falling into unbidden paths. I have all faith in the teaching and promptings of your Dear Mother and with your present sense & knowledge of right and what she has & will continue to teach I think it will all be well with you and that when I return home I will still be as I ever have been proud of my Dear little Children. Give my love to all my friends — Kiss my little ones and Ma for me. Write to me often. Address until other wise directed at Little Rock Arkansas as that is a distributive office and wherever the regiment may be sent the letters will follow.

Yours truly
E.P. Petty

Camp Nelson Novr 8th 1862

Dear Wife

Enclosed I hand you letter from Wm B. Young of Hempstead which explains itself — If Tom Biddle has not paid you the money delay no time in calling upon him for it and dont fail to urge him beyond reason to pay it. I fear that the money will be lost to you unless you press Tom hard. I have no faith in him and if he can keep from paying it I believe he will do so — I have no verry particular news to write from these parts — I have just heard that the feds are again leaving this state but hardly credit the report — I did think a few days ago and I hav'nt changed yet that in a short time we would have fun in Arkansas if you call fighting fun. I think they will make a combined effort on this State this winter and that we will have all that we can stand up to even if we dont have to Skedaddle over to Texas. We are now armed with plain Muskets (a pretty fair and efficient arm) and are quite busy cleaning up and drilling the Manual. We have only, out of 800 muskets, 500 bayonets which only gives a little over half bayonets. This is to be verry much regretted as the bayonet is a verry efficient weapon. We hold ourselves now in readiness to move at any moment. We feel and look now like soldiers. I fear that we are going to have trouble about our transportation — As soon as we reached Austin the Brigade Quarter Master called for all of our waggons but one to each company — Col Allen refused to give any up and made application to Genl McCulloch who referred the matter to Genl Holmes at Little Rock. We have not yet heard Genl Holmes' decision but to day I learned that Col Flournoy commanding our Brigade had issued an order to Col Allen to give up the waggons — Whether he does it on his own responsibility or by orders from Genl Holmes I dont know. It makes no difference. Col Allen has determined to refuse to do so and the regiment are determined to stand by him in it — Upon Col A's refusal to comply he will be arrested — that places Lt Col Jones in command who will also refuse — He will be arrested and Maj Tabor will be in command. He will also refuse & be arrested and then all the Captains in their turn and the subalterns will likewise refuse and be arrested so that I would not be surprised if in two weeks Allen's regiment was all under arrest unless something turns up to reconcile matters — I had just as live be crucified one way as another. If I give up my clothing I will freeze and I believe I prefer being shot for disobedience to orders. I am in hopes & believe that it all will be settled. Dont say any thing about it for the present. The weather is cold and clear here. We have lots of frost & ice. It is a great deal colder than in Texas. I am getting along finely now — health fine — frosty mornings brace me up — think I shall fatten this winter — got me a good overcoat — good sword. Ready to fight Yankees now. Spoiling for a fight — reckon wont spoil but once[54] — Got fine brass band for our regiment — Cost about $500 — I paid $15 — It is splendid — Can fight with that music. Two deaths in regiment yesterday — heap of sickness — Health of my Co improving — Swapped off _____ — He is always unfit for duty — Lazy trifling fellow — Would give him for a dog & then kill the dog & make money — Will swap of[f] _____ I reckon if Morgan[55] will have him. Our Gilmer boys hav'nt come up yet. Give my love to all — Write to me at Little Rock.

> Yours truly
> E. P. Petty

"Sunny Side" Private residence of
Mr. Cowan 5 miles from Austin
Arkansas November 22nd 1862

My Dear Wife

In the last ten days I received two letters from you, one of which I never opened & hence know nothing of it[s] Contents. The other & last was dated Nov 4th. I am all the time glad to hear from home and your little pettishnesses exhibited occasionly in your letters shan't hinder me. I don't remember how I expressed myself about the arrival of the mail etc and my not receiving a letter at Washington Ark — I did not expect to get a letter there by mail but here is the fact as it occurred and as I ought to have written it. Adjutant Hunt had been left behind the regiment at Tyler — He brought up all the mail for the Regt that accumulated at Tyler. He overtook at Washington with it &

nearly every body but me got letters hence my great disappointment. That explanation will satisfy you, wont it. If not get my picture & kiss it. May be that will cure the snakebite. As for writing every week & sometimes twice a week I have done my duty faithfully and without cause of complaint — until the last two weeks. I have written none in two weeks. This is the first time I have put pen to paper in that time. On Tuesday morning the 11th Novr I went out to drill as well as I have been in 12 months — drilled with life and vigour never enjoyed any thing better. About 10 oclock returned in from drill. Before I reached my tent I felt mighty bad — went to my tent immediately and lay down — A chill came on that lasted me about 4 hours followed by a rail road fever which continued almost unremittedly until the 18th Novr. It was a severe attack of typhoid pnuemonia — that fell disease that was destroying without mercy so many of my fellow Soldiers around me. The disease seemed to be malignant and did not readily yield to medicines — besides there were over 100 cases in the regiment and medical aid was hard to get. There I was in my little uncomfortable tent fiercely attacked with quite an uncomfortable prospect in view and just at that time what hurt me worst was — we had been starving on poor beef for some time and just about 2 hours before I was taken sick I had bought a hog. Gave $12 and I plainly saw that I had no showing at that hog. I could get to see the Doctor once or twice a day. I took 5 doses of medicine before I could get my bowels to move — one large dose of pills, 3 dozes of Calomel, one of Salts & one of oil. I lay in camp about 3 days and was removed to this place where I have been since. Dr Gorman came out & stays with me & some other of my boys who are sick here — About 4 days ago I missed the fever but oh such a weak creature as I. The first day I tried to sit up it was almost a failure. I tried to walk. My feet would go as without guides. To day I walked out into the yard. It was all I could do but it shows I am strengthening. I am just now at that point where a false step or an imprudent action would relapse me and knock my heels sky high. I am Cautious. You will laugh at that but when I tell you that my foretatstes of these matters of sickness have taught me a lesson perhaps I would'nt have learned at home at youl see that I am in sober earnest. I have somewhat come to the conclusion that I am frail as well as other mortals. John W Wilson [Hauptsbend?], John J. Huling and Henry A Biggs of my Co are all here quite sick with same disease — Biggs came out sound & well to wait on me and after two days faithful service he was taken even worse than I — Geo Smith, Saml Wilson, Shields Hogan and Somerville Baker of my Co are also here sick but not confined to their beds — John Smith, Wm McPhaul are our nurses & waiters, Dr Gorman our physician. We have about 20 men out at private houses sick, as yet have not lost a single case though I am fearful that Sam Jones will die from what I can [tell]. Two days ago orders were received to dispose of those not able to travel — to cook two days rations and be ready every one that was able to walk to move in a moment — A thousand camp reports as to cause, destination etc was in circulation — all conjecture. 2 days have elapsed and up to last account yesterday only one brigadge had moved and that in the direction of Little Rock. I hav'nt heard from camp to day. Suppose more have gone. From the best information I can gather the White and Arkansas rivers are both up. The feds have come up both perhaps, at least White river, in gun boats and are landing troops for the purpose of getting around our forts down there.[56] I also understand that Col Parsons has fallen back to Des Arc about 35 miles from here. This grand retreat from here to Little Rock may be a precautionary measure so that if the forts fall & with them the river, then our army will be safe on the other side and next our supplies but this retreat leaves about 1000 or 1500 sick here who if an enemy were near could be made prisoners of war easily. I dont know what it all means — our authorities do I suppose and I am willing to trust them. It is sinful to see the number of soldiers dying here. Great stout fine young men dying and that for the want of the proper attention — Allen's Reg[t] is receiving its full share of sickness & death. I dont know the daily proportion of deaths of the regiment but it must be as many as two — One day the number went up to 5. There are over 100 of typhoid pnuemonia cases and then embracing all others number about 250. This is awful. I believe that mine up to this time has been the only Co but has lost some — God has prospered us through much tribulations. I am very weak — Have done myself injustice perhaps in attempting to write so much. Excuse impirfections. Remember me Kindly to friends. Kiss my babes. I am not in a condition to write them any good advice now.

believe me truly
E. P. Petty

Bayou Metre[57] Dec[r] 3 1862

My Dear Wife

    Your's of the 18th was received yesterday. I am proud to learn that you are so provident that you manage the affairs of a family so well and I hope that by the time I return home you will be such an adept in these matters that I will have no trouble of the sort on my hands that you will do it all. I approve any thing you do — I think your hog trade was magnificent provided you dont loose them all. They will have to be watched and taken good care of or they will all run wild or some body will get them and in either case they will be lost to you. You had better buy you about 25 or 30 bushels of Sweet potatoes. You can bury them and use that old hay in covering them up so as to keep the frost off — You had better buy about 100 lbs of salt for if the feds get Corpus Christi salt will be an object[58] — You can get it ground some where, say on Jonathan Burlesons mill. You had better buy 100 lbs of sugar — the feds may get that sugar country in Texas and sugar will be scarce and high. Look at all these things and see what you think of them. I only suggest — I am not now the head of the family and dont pretend to dictate. Your advice about my health etc is good and I approve it all but for the life of me I cant help eating any and every thing without regard to quantity and quality. I must eat if I am sick for it but my eating has never yet affected me in the least. I experience no inconvenience from it. This is an awful Arkansas. The most forlorn and God forsaken Country under the sun. Nearly every body in it are leaving for Texas. You never saw or heard the like of people, negroes and every thing that is on the road to Texas — I am afraid that our country and people will be ruined by the admixture of such a population. I am in hopes that most of them will stop in Eastern Texas and not pollute our fair west with their presence and persons.[59] It is an awful country and an awful population here in Arkansas, ignorant, selfish, hoggish and almost despicable. They are a curse to any country. They are suited & naturalized to this climate & country & ought to be compelled to stay here. Our clothing nor Lt Litle have reached here yet and I have heard nothing definite from them. A good many of our officers have resigned and are trying to resign and go home — Dr Lewis and Capt Arnett, Cousin John R King have resigned & gone home. Capt Bouldin and Lt Rucker[60] are trying to resign — all on account of health they say. It may be that we are getting to close to the Yankees. I am going to stick it out until some thing worse happens than has yet. Lt Priest[61] of Capt Millers Co is about to die at Des Arc. He sent for his son here who went down last night. I expect that Flemming[62] will be elected Lieutenant in place of Bob Anderson dead. He is a candidate with fair prospects. I will do some sly legging for him. I have told you & Ella all I know and more too.[63] I hear no news from Texas so write it. Your letters come pretty regular in about 12 days — Kiss my babes for me. My kind regards to friends.

Yours truly
E. P. Petty

My Dear Ella

I received your letter with news papers a few days ago and your Ma's letter of the 18th ult yesterday. The Army here is now encamped on Bayou Metre about 6 miles below the rail road leading from Little Rock to Duvals Bluff on White River and Memphis, about 8 miles from Brownsville and about 20 miles from Austin. It moved down here about a week ago. We are camped about a quarter of a mile from the grand prarie of Arkansas in a low, flat, wet, marshy country. There has been but little rain here this fall and none in two weeks and yet the wagons bogged down and had to be pulled out by hand and by doubling teams etc. There are three brigades here.[64] Genl Deshler's brigade[65] of which Darnell's regiment is part having gone to Arkansas Post about 100 [?] miles or more below Little Rock.[66] The health of the army is not much if any on the improve — Our regiment left at Austin, sick & nurses, 262 men. There have died in the regiment about 50 men. At last I have lost two men out of my Company. Sargt. Sam Jones & Drake Tucker — Jones died last week and Tucker Monday last — Capt Miller has lost 8 men. Dick Watson, Jim Harl, Whitehead, Frank Dyer, Sam Meridith, Ringer Lt. Bob Anderson & Stewart. The Dutch company is the only one that has lost no men. I have at Austin & vicinity now about 20 men sick & nurses etc. Some quite sick and the ballance not able for duty. I have about 60 men here and about 45 able for duty — not much the matter with the others. I had a light spell of typhoid pnuemonia myself. I lay in camp at Austin from tuesday until Saturday then I went into the Country to Mr Cowan's where I staid 16 days. On last Monday the 1st day of December I came here and rejoined the company. I am well but weak & thin and am not doing any hard duty yet nor will not for a few days. I have a tremendous appetite and make corn bread & blue beef disappear in great quantities — I eat any and every thing I can get hold of without regard to quantity or quality. I am prudent in every thing but eating — At Austin I got some fine apples for $1.⁰⁰ a dozen. They did me more good than any thing I have found but pork & turnips — Tell Ma that my pulse has never got right yet and I am afraid never will. For four or five or more days after I was taken sick I was in a perfect elyseum. When I shut my eyes the most beautiful pantomimes would pass before me and I would comment upon them as they appeared to the great edification of all present. I was in my full senses and enjoyed it verry much. A part of the time I was out of my right mind and knew nothing. The whole appears now like a blissful dream. Thank God I am well and at my post again — I resolved and swore that I would not die and sure enough I did'nt. I did'nt come to Arkansas to die — I think that God would never resurrect me here. If this was all the country in controversy in this war the winner would be ruined. I have no news here. The feds are idle in this State — I dont have any idea of their movements if they are making any. The small pox I learn is near us in a private family and I expect we will leave here in a few days. Continue as you say you are to be a good, studious, obedient girl and you will make a useful & happy woman.

Your's truly
E. P. Petty

Camp Bayou Metre Arkansas
Sunday December 7th 1862

Dear Wife

A line this Sunday evening will perhaps prove agreeable to you. I am quite well again but have not fully recovered my strenght and vim. I have verry little or no news to write. Camp is full of rumors as to our destination, some vague, some contradictory and some nonsensical, none reliable. One rumor is that Gov Lubbock[67] has petitioned for Darnell's, Flournoy's and Allen's regiments to be sent back to Texas and that probably we will be sent. Another that we will be or are ordered to Vicksburg. Another that we will be sent to Genl Hindman who is now falling back before the federals in the neighborhood of Ft Smith[68] — Another that we will take up winter quarters here — this is the most nonsensical rumor of all. I want to go any where to get out of these Arkansas Swamps. Since I wrote you & Ella of the 3rd it has rained and snowed both — On the 4th about day it clouded up and by ten oclock a drizling rain set in which continued until about moon down — say 3 O clock on the morning of the 5th when it began to snow and from that time until sun up I dont suppose it ever snowed harder [or] faster in larger flakes and more any where or under any circumstances — By sun up notwithstanding the ground was warm and wet the snow was about 3 inches deep every where. About 10 o clock it was as clear as you ever saw, not a cloud to be seen and it has been clear ever since — Oh what a slosh we had. The ground at best is low & mucky and with the snow and rain we had an awful time. The roads are almost impassable. We are safe from the federals for they cant possibly get to us and they are safe from us for we cant get out of this place —The great danger is starvation as we have our provisions and forage to bring in here. Our clothing wagons got in the 5th in the

snow. I received by your providence and kindness 3 prs drawers,
3 shirts, 2 pr socks, 1 pr pants, 1 pr Suspenders, cloth for a suit of
clothes, 1 pr boots — which came in acceptable time. Muncho
gracious (many thanks). By some sort of unaccountable hook or crook I
have lost my Flemming overshirt out of my trunk. It has nearly ruined
me as I have but one left. I will try and buy one from Bob Wilkins
who has four if I cant find mine. The news reached here last night that
the feds had taken Virginia Point Texas and that they were landing
large bodies of troops at Galveston.[69] If this is true it alarms me for the
safety of Texas. I have not thought really that Texas would be invaded
but this looks like it would. If it is so prepare yourself for the worst —
Nerve yourself for the crisis. Your gold if you have any wear next your
skin all the time and dont let a human being know that you have it for
in Tennessee the[y] strip the women for their money when they suspect
that they have it around them — Also keep your pistol and amunition
concealed — Keep your Confederate money out of their way for they
will destroy it. If they come you may expect to be robbed so conceal
yourself as well as you can. Jack Hamilton is an awful scoundrel and
will not be apt to spare the family of his enemy — Trust to the Lord
until the breeching breaks and then look out for yourself — Keep a
steady nerve and open eye, a listening ear and a valliant heart and you
will weather the storm if it comes. But I hope Texas has yet enough
brave hearts & strong arms to prevent an invasion.

Your's truly
E. P. Petty

Camp Bayou Metre
December 9th 1862

Dr Wife

    This Tuesday morning is beautiful in the extreme though the night
was cold and frosty — not a cloud to be seen since the snow storm
about which I have written you. I felt quite unwell all day yesterday
but acted as officer of the day and was quite active. The cause was
eating some half cooked hominy which did not agree with me. To day
I am quite well. We will leave here in a very short time. Yesterday
evening orders were read on dress parade for commanders of regiments
to hold their commands ready to march at a moments notice. The
impression is that Vicksburg is our destination. If so we will smell gun
powder and hear it thunder. I am satisfied to go wherever we can do
the Confederate States the most good. If at Vicksburg we can stab the
enemy to the heart or some other vital point, the hand that is laid
upon Texas will paralize so that where ever the most service can
be done is the place for me. My feelings, inclinations and all my
yearnings are to be in Texas if she is invaded. My all is there — All
that is near and dear to me is there and I want to be there to protect it
but I belong to the Confederacy and where ever the Authorities
think it best for me to go I submit to. I have the largest company now
present in Allen's Regiment. My sick are getting well and comeing in
fast. I have only lost two men by death. I report a larger Co present
and more men for duty than any Captain. Lt Priest of Capt Miller's Co
died of typhoid fever last friday. This makes 2 Lts and 8 privates Capt
Miller has lost — Capt Mabry has lost 10 men & Capt Ryan 11, Capt
Allen 5, Capt Boudlin 9 or 10, Capt Arnett 1 Lt and 7 or 8 men
etc etc. There has been over 50 died out of the regiment. There are
a great many sick at Austin yet. Our regiment left 262 sick when
it moved besides a few that was at Little Rock and I suppose this
Division left at Austin near 2000 men besides a larger number at Little
Rock. I have about 20 up at Austin and 4 at Little Rock none however
dangerously sick. Whilst I am writing this letter your's of the 26th and
Ella's of the 24th November have been handed to me. I am glad to
hear that you all are well and that you are exhibiting so much energy
in the management of home affairs. I wish I was there to look after
matters — Dont depend upon getting any body to do things for you for
nothing. They wont do. There is'nt much patriotism left at home. I
would'nt give a sou for it all and they will rob the soldiers wives of the
small pittances which they may have. I expect to draw some more pay
soon. If so I will try and send you some more. I am now broke —

spent all my money when sick. If I can draw all that is due me I can send you three hundred dollars perhaps more — Be economical with your money yet live and have plenty. Let the morrow provide for tomorrow — Flemming is a little unwell is taking medicine some. I think he had a chill and some fever. Negro Jo Wilkins has a spell of chills occasionly — I am now physicking for a chill he had yesterday. I dont believe that he can stand the service — He is too old and I believe that I will send him home the first chance I get. I can hire a Dutchman for 10 dollars per month to cook. Jo Webber has just heard that his wife has had twins and he is in ecstacies about it. Joe stays well though he is verry fearful that he never will see Texas again — He wants you to go & see his wife occasionly — Do so — Write often. My love to all & respects to friends.

Truly your's
E. P. Petty

Camp Bayou Metre Dec[r] 10th 1862

My Dear Wife

This morning about 3 o'clock we received orders to cook 1 days rations and prepare to move immediately[70] — All was bustle & confusion. By 8 o'clock we received orders to strike tents and load up. By 9 oclock we received orders to unload and every man to carry his bedding and clothes upon his back, the ballance to be left to be sent and deposited at Little Rock — Then there was a set of mad men in Allens Regiment — but as we could'nt do justice to the subject we did'nt cuss much — Some burnt their surplus clothing — After loading the men with clothing & two blankets with guns, cartridge boxes, haversacks and canteens I determined to put all the ballance in the wagon (they only allow one wagon to the Co) which I did and stood ready to move — About 12 o'clock orders came not to move until morning — so we had to unload and pitch tents again — Such vacilating is common I suppose in the army but it is disagreeable to the men — The orders are for Genl McCulloch to move his division with as little delay as possible to Vicksburg Mississippi and report to Genl Pemberton commanding at that place.[71] Vicksburg will be the scene no doubt during this winter and coming spring of one or more of the most terrible conflicts that have or will occur during this war and the soldiers at that place will necessarily be compelled to suffer much. The feds are making every effort to open the Mississippi river and Confeds to prevent it. Our communication of course will not be so frequent and convenient as at present but I want you to continue to write as often as at present so that I can get one from home as often as possible. I will continue to write as I have done and you will receive them frequently. I send by Mrs Jones who goes home now two hundred dollars. I havnt drawn any pay yet but I borrow this & will pay when I draw. When I cross the Mis. river I expect that my oppertunity for sending money will not be verry good as I expect the fed gun boats will swarm on the river ere long. You will need money worse than I and all I can send you I will do so. Take care of your money. Invest it to the best advantage so that it will make most for you and my dear little ones. As long as I can turn a wheel I do it for you & them not for myself alone. It may not be long before you will be thrown upon your own resources and I know something of the difficulties you will have to encounter and so far as possible will attempt to meet and obviate them — Dont be discouraged by this remark for I dont have as much fears in encountering the enemies guns etc at Vicksburg as I do of the malaria and diseases of this God forsaken and accursed country — I may be killed and I may die. My chances are as good as any bodies but I do not bargain for either and think yet that I will return to the bosom of my family to enjoy many years of tranquility and happiness in a glorious and independent Confederacy. Take care of my children — educate them well — raise them (I know you will) up to be virtuous, honest and upright so that they may make good and useful members of the Government. Write to me at Vicksburg Mississippi thus — Capt E. P. Petty — Allen's Reg^t — 3 Brigade McCulloch's Division. God bless you & yours & mine

E. P. Petty

P.S. I am quite well. I send you three hundred dollars upon reflection.

EPP

Camp Ink Bayou Pulaski Co Ark
December 14th 1862

Dear Wife

We are encamped in 5 miles of Little Rock en route according to orders for Vicksburg but whether we will reach that point is difficult for me to say. There is so much publicity given to the order sending us to Vicksburg that I am inclined to think that our destination is elsewhere perhaps to reinforce Genl Hindman near Ft Smith who has recently had a fight with the feds driving them several miles killing 1000 taking

400 prisoners and a train of wagons & otherwise thrashing them generally.[72] We left Camp Bayou Metre the morning of the 12 and marched 4 miles through grand prarie in the rain — The 13th we started and marched 18 miles in the rain and mud[73] — It was the awfullest march I ever saw. The men were compelled to carry their clothing, blankets and guns say about 35 or 40 pounds — The water and mud was about from shoe mouth to half leg deep. The men fagged and broke down from heft of load and distance of march. They could not stand to be loaded like mules and walked like horses. The wagons bogged continually and such another time you can hardly imagine. Amongst those nearly broken down was myself — I had not entirely recovered my strenght and besides I carried my overcoat, six shooter, sword, canteen of water, haversack with dinner and a sick man's gun. I made out to reach camps nearly as soon as any but I [was] road foundered, foot sore, leg weary, hip shot and as near broke down as a man could well be. That night I received an order from head quarters (Capt Allen Comd'g) to report myself next (this morning) at head quarters early in the morning and get a horse to ride (today) — This was welcome news to me and I availed myself with alacrity of the chance to ride. To day we have marched 8 miles — the road awful. Since we have our camps pitched it has set into rain again and is now pouring down — weather quite warm. The men stood it well to day — I stood it finely and am quite well. The march will do me good and I will fatten on it if they dont run me down on forced marches — Tomorrow we will go into Little Rock and then perhaps will learn more of our destination — I think it will be to Hindman — I wrote you a letter [by] Mrs Wash Jones who started home on the 12th inst in

which I directed you to write to me at Vicksburg — You need not do so until further directed but continue to write to me at Little Rock — If we leave there the letters will follow and in time I can inform you where to write to me — I sent by Mrs Jones to you $300. — Dispose of it to the best and most judicious advantage for yourself and family — Act upon your own judgement as though you had no husband to consult — Whatever you do will meet my approbation — I am willing to believe that you have as much sense and judgement as your mother and I know she made things count whenever she touched them. You have frequently advised me in matters of trade etc. which advice I did not follow and many times have rued it — Now follow your own judgement — It was as good now aye it will be better than when you advised me — It will be sharpened and improved by responsibility and by action — I have no fears — but your gold, if you have any, husband. Keep it with a misers grip for the present — We do not know what a day may bring forth — Herein I enclose you a gold dollar which I have accidently got hold of in Arkansas — I send it to you to be taken care of — Keep it close — Keep the children at school — Encourage them to learn by praise, rewards and all sort of other encouragements — Keep them clad as decently as possible and all the time in good genteel society — I write you as usual at every oppertunity so that you may know how and where I am — Co F is still the largest Co in Allen's regiment though when we got orders to go to Vicksburg 15 were sent to the hospital at Little Rock and others were and are now candidates for that place. _____ astonished me more than any body. He was immediately taken sick and wanted to go to the hospital — the Surgeon sent him — He did'nt want to go to Vicksburg. He though[t] he never would see Texas any more — This is private about the boys going to the hospital — I hope I may be mistaken as to the motives that governed them. I hope they were sick and not cowards.[74] I understand that there are a good many deaths at Austin yet — from four to five per day. I have lost no more men — The health of the regiment is improving I believe — I am glad to get out of these swamps — I am willing to go any[where] to get away from here and for a change — I got your letter by Kige [Malcijah Highsmith] — He sent it to me from Little Rock — I have not seen him — I got your letter written 26 about 2 days before the one of the 27 by Kige — Your letters reach me quite regular particularly when we are stationary — Every thing is quiet in the neighborhood of Helena — Our Cavalry Brigade will be left there to watch and check them — At Arkansas post there are about 12 regiments — Hindman has about

20 000. I have no further news — Kiss my little chaps for Pa — Kind regards to friends.

Truly Yours
E. P. Petty

P.S. Flemming was elected 2nd Lt of Millers Co by acclamation — Tell Mrs Lt Flemming of the fact and congratulate her for me — I had a small finger in that pie.

E.P.P.

P.S. Bob Wilkins requests you to inform his folks to continue to write to him at Little Rock.

I sent you three hundred dollars by Mrs Jones about a week ago. There is getting to be such a plethora of Confederate money that it is bound to depreciate So to prevent loosing to much you had better invest you[rs or] a part of it. If you ca[n get] good cheap land buy it [or any] thing that you want & can manage. I also sent you one dollar in gold in a letter since Mrs J went — Also some time ago I sent you $2 Texas money in a letter by R Stroud — Did you get [it] and in this letter I send two — one dollar Confederate bills — They are for the children. Divide equally between them.

Take care of every thing — Guard & protect my children & believe me ever truly

Yours Etc
E. P. Petty

Little Rock Arkansas
Sat'y Decr 20 1862

Dear Wife

We reached this place on last Monday on our route under orders to Vicksburg — Here the order was countermanded and it was thought we would proceed at once to Genl Hindman at Ft Smith but in this we have so far been disappointed. [75] Genl Holmes and his staff 2 or 3 days ago proceeded by Steam Boat to Ft Smith to investigate (I suppose) the true state of matters up there and see if we are needed. I have just seen a Captain of Artilery who was in the fight with Genl Hindman and he reports that we whipped the feds badly and that they were retreating into Missouri and that there was no prospect of any more fighting in that quarter unless we pursued them into Missouri so I think our destination is yet involved in great doubt — We are on the breeze of chance and where and when we will go is involved in the future. We are now encamped on the bank of the Arkansas river 2 miles below Little Rock and on the opposite side of the river. This is the prettiest, dryest and best Camp we have had in this state — On the river the Steam boats are plying every day. On the rail road just behind & in sight goes the hissing locomotive while 2 miles off in beautiful panorama appears in full view the City of Little Rock. The river is a beautiful stream ½ mile wide from bank to bank and since we have been here it has been in fine boating stage covering up all the bars and filling out to the banks. It is now falling and the bars begin to show to the great relief of these folks here for in every rise of the river the[y] see visions of gun boats, Yankees etc etc. The health of the troops is improving — though since I wrote last I have lost one man certain and another reported dead making in all 4 deaths for my Co. J. B. Watson is dead certain and J. E. Hudson is reported dead both from above Austin Texas and both in the hospital at Little Rock. I have 13 men at Austin Ark and about the same number at Little Rock, sick and nurses — I have in camps over sixty men the largest company here. Some of the companies look mighty small — not over 30 men in camps — The Allen Regiment here now does'nt look like the Allen regiment that left Texas some time ago. I have a good many applications by the boys to be transferred back to Texas to some of the regiments in that state all of which I have refused up to this time as a precident of that kind would perhaps take all my men away as they are all verry anxious to get back to Texas by any means. I am living fine now buying pork at 20 cents per pound for my mess — So are all the other messes. Butter is worth one dollar per pound, chickens one dollar — eggs one dollar per dozen etc etc. The poor soldier gets 11 dollars per month for wages and has such prices to pay for all he gets. It['s] hard that we have to leave our own State unprotected and march long and weary marches to defend these people and then for the scoundrels to skin us to death for every thing. I am quite well and have been since I wrote to you though I still have the Arkansaw Tingo. I have been hard at work this week — I am one of the board to examine Candidates for promotion and newly elected officers — We have examined 14 in the last 2 days Flemming amongst them. It is a good thing for him that I was on the board. In fact I would not have accepted it but for his sake. His examination was deficient and he would have been rejected but I obtained a new hearing & got a week

longer to prepare himself. I intend to protect and save him — He shall
be 2nd Lt. We put the boys through a pretty rigid examination —

Little Rock Arkansas
December 23rd 1862

Dear Ella

Your's and your ma's of the 1st and 4th inst has been to hand for 2
days but I have had no time to answer any sooner. In fact I started
your ma a letter the same day I received yours and there was no
necessity of replying any sooner. I have been very busy for a few days
in examining officers and drawing money and paying off my company
— They have just paid us off to the last of August leaving now due us
near 4 months wages. I have nothing particularly interesting to write
now but do to pass time and keep up the chain of correspondence with
"home sweet home." We are still here near Little Rock in a state of
uncertainty waiting for orders and hoping that they will come for us to
go somewhere. We dont care much where so we are on the move
— For a week and every since we came to this place we have had
delightful weather clear and warm. It is now cloudy and threatning
rain though warm. The boys call the clouds & rain orders to move —
This morning before day I awoke and it was sprinkling rain. I heard
one fellow call out "get up boys — cook one days rations — here is
orders to move" — It so happens that our marches have began on
rainey days and this is the reason of the saying — I wrote to ma that I
understood that James E. Hudson of my Company was dead. It is so
he is dead and this makes 4 men I have lost. I learn that E.R. Jones
who is in the hospital is verry low and will in all probability die. I
hope not but it begins to look like Co F's time has come at last. Col
Speight's regiment a part of McCulloch's Division started this morning
for Genl Hindman — It is reported that a part of the Texas troops here
will be sent to Texas — Pres Mauldin of Lockhart Texas arrived here
yesterday with dispatches from Genl McGruder [Magruder] to Genl
Holmes and dame rumor says it is a demand for troops for the defense
of Texas[76] — I hope so and hope that Col Allen's regiment will be
sent. I wrote to you that we had been ordered to Vicksburg and had
got this far on our road and were stopped for the purpose of going to
Genl Hindman. That order was also countermanded and here we have
remained. Genl Hindman had a considerable fight with the feds near
Cane Hill[77] — Our loss in killed, wounded & missing is reported to be
about 1500, that of the federals reported about 4000. Our wounded

were expected last night at Little Rock. I dont know whether they came or not. I am myself again — am hearty and well and weighed a few days ago 131 pounds. I think now I will weigh more. I believe now that I am done with sickness and will get fat. Tell Frank & Don & Van to think of their poor old father away off in the swamps of Arkansas struggling for liberty and to follow his example. Be a good and dutiful child obedient to your mother and kind to your brothers — Remember thy Creator in the days of thy youth — Be studious and assiduous in the way's of wisdom — Cultivate good manners — Seek the society of the good and eschew that of the evil — Consult your mother before doing anything and obey her admonitions and advice for she is older and much more experienced that [than] you and when I return from the war (as I shall do) I can have the comfort & consolation of having a good, intelligent, honest and upright household. Write to me often — Dont wait for me to write. I am too busy to write every day. I write every liesure moment I have and sometimes encroach on my business hours as I am now doing. It is now raining and threatning to be bad weather — Dont you pity us poor soldiers who have to sleep on the damp, cold ground and be exposed in all sorts of weather. My love to all my family & respects to my friends.

Yours truly
E. P. Petty

My Dear Wife

   I enclose in this letter a letter to Pa with $50 which I propose (as you will see by reading his letter) to loan to him. Times are no doubt hard with the old man and I can accommodate him without inconvenience to my family and at the same time make a good investment of that much money. I also enclose you $12 in small notes Confederate money and one dollar in gold for yourself — the gold you can sink and the Confederate money you can invest — which you had better do pretty soon. You ask where Allen's deed is — It is in my large black pocket book in letter A box. The box is in your wardrobe. We gave up the office long ago with the understanding that our books could remain unless they should be in the way — I wish you would get the key from Dr Ploeger and get all the books except the Morris Estate books and carry them home — The large ledger belonging to the estate of Shaw has enough blank paper in it to last you an age and the verry best kind at that — such as I pay here 25 cents per sheet for. You can leave Wash Jones' law books and the Morris estate books in the office. Dont fail to attend to this immediately. I saw Kige [Malcijah] Highsmith at Little Rock since I came here — He stayed in Little Rock about a week before joining his company — He lost his pocket book and as he says $700 — $500 of his own and $200 sent by him — At the same time he lost his pocket book — a man of this command lost his six shooter. They suspicioned a fellow, followed him to Des Arc, got the Six Shooter but did not get the money and got no trace of it. Tomorrow will be Christmas and a lot of us today will send over & get some whisky at $40 per gallon to have a frolick tomorrow. It goes in a mans life any how so here goes — Hurrah for the Confederacy[78] — I have just been informed that we have been [or will?] be immediately ordered to the Arkansas Post about 100 miles by land & 200 by water below here. We have batteries erected there to defend the river and the up country from Gun Boats — We have already 12 regiments down there and eleven more (our division) are to go down. If we go there our occupation will be to fight gun boats and [skedaddle in the] swamps. I am [told Bayou Metre is] a paradise by the side of [it — There] are swamps all around & [every where.] Hurrah for us. We will get somewhere after a while.[79] Genl Walker[80] commands our Division and Genl McCulloch our Brigade — So Col Rearing Tearing Pitching Allen[81] after all his eagerness to leave Texas and his Stone Wall Jackson marches on the route has fallen short of his mark and has been over looked by those in high places — "Oh what a fall was there my Countrymen." Col A does not increase much in popularity with his command. Mrs Allen & Bunt Dickerson have gone home — When they came up their trunks & clothing etc were left behind at Tyler and they were here near 2 months with scanty clothing so little & so common that they did not feel like visiting. This was the main reason of their return home — a few days before they left their trunks reached Little Rock but they did not find it out — After they had been gone about a week Col A found the clothing — Now his wife & Bunt goes home without clothing & Col A has a large lot of female clothing on hand. He is terribly fretted about it and takes on woefully. In addition to the money I send you I enclose thirty dollars ($20 and $10 bills) which you will please deliver to Jo Weber's wife. He sends it to her through me. Of course it could'nt go right unless I sent it. Tell M^rs W that J is nearly if not quite well again and will be ready for duty in a day or two. I will indulge him awhile for fear of setting him back. The health of the troops is improving. I am quite well again and about as heavy as ever. Dont sell my Piney Creek land if you have not done so — Dont sell any thing now unless you can get gold & silver for it. We have enough Confederacy on hand under the present circumstances. I also enclose you one hundred & sixty dollars ($100 and 3 $20 bills) which you will please give to Lieutenant H. N. Litle — It is his pay for the months of July and August — Tell him that I felt authorized and took the responsibility of signing his name and drawing his money. Tell him further that I have been compelled to leave his trunk at Little Rock. It was the orders that all surplus baggage etc should be deposited at Little Rock. If I can send his trunk home to him I will do so. If not it will be left in Little Rock. They have ruled us down to one wagon & the boys have their Knap sacks to pack. Orderly Sargent Supple of Co I will deliver this letter and money to you. He is a clever gentleman (though odd & peculiar). Treat him kindly.[82] Take care of yourself & my little ones — Dont be imprudent with your health nor desponding in spirits — What is to be will be & [neither] you nor I can change it — So give your energies & services to the rearing & education of your children & let me take care of myself. Write —

Yours truly
E. P. Petty

P.S. Write to Pa and send him the money.

EPP

My Dear Wife

 I wrote you a letter a few days ago by Sargent Supple and sent you some money. I also enclosed some money ($160) for Lt Litle. If you have not paid it over to him deduct fifteen dollars to pay the expenses on his trunk which I have just started to him on a wagon. It will cost that amount to get it home and I thought it better to send it than to deposit it here for the benefit of the Arkansians. I sent the trunk on a wagon to Belton where it will be sent to your care on the stage. I have paid the expenses to Belton — you will pay from Belton to Bastrop. Please when you write specify all the money you have received from me so that I may know whether you get it when I send it — We are now in active service. On the 27th we received orders to move — On Sunday 28 struck tents early and marched to the ferry at Little Rock but could not get over until late in fact only a part of the regiment crossed. Our orders were to go to Pine Bluff — The orders were that the baggage and those not able to walk must go down on a Steam Boat. I declined sending any baggage preferring to bog down with mine — We marched out to our old camp back of the city. I had not been on the old ground half an hour before I was taken with the fever — the verry same kind of an attack which I had there before. I had fever all night and all day yesterday and part of last night — Yesterday we laid all day at that camp — This morning orders came soon to move — We started after early breakfast and went 4 miles on the Pine Bluff road — pitched our tents and began to cook dinner. Before we got through dinner orders came to return to Little Rock immediately and cross to the north side of the river — We got to the river about 4 O clock and the regiment crossed over to night. The reason of our hasty return etc is the news that the federals have taken Van Buren and Ft Smith and that Genl Hindman is retreating and I conjecture that our destination is up there. When orders came this morning I was on my heels ready to march — made the trip out and back, felt verry well of it — Concluded that I would stay in the City to night and sleep on a bed at the tune of $4.^{00} per day. Eat quite a hearty supper to night and then went out into the city and drank over a pint of Cider and dont feel any the worse for it all yet. The day I was taken with this infernal fever (28th) I felt better than I had since I left home and weighed 134 pounds more than I ever did in my life before. I think I will go right strait up again now. Unless matters grow much worse than they have been I shall neither resign nor ask for furlough for now is the time for every man to be at his post if he expects the Confederacy to survive for my opinion is that this winter and spring campaign will settle the question. I have only been sick about 40 days since I left home — If I did not have so much energy and such recuperative powers I would have been a Victim to the diseases of this infamous Country but I expect to survive it all and return to my home in the course of human events. I received yours of the 14th inst a day or two ago but as I had just written thought it would need no immediate reply. I was sorry that you were so much distressed on account of my sickness — Just as soon as I was able to sit up I wrote you a letter giving you the particulars etc — You have received it ere this and are satisfied. I dont know when you will hear from me again — Continue to address me at Little Rock as the letters will follow — My health is improving — Allen's regiment were more cheerful to day than they have been for 3 months. They were devilling every body and could raise the yell verry often. It is an evidence that they are improving in health — They feed us well on both beef and pork, no flour but meal.

Give my respects to friends — My love to my little one.

Your's truly Etc
E. P. Petty

Wednesday Decr 31 1862

I am quite well this morning not the least inconvenienced by my supper or my cider and have tried a considerable break fast this morning and before leaving the city will try some more cider. The Rhapahannock [Rappahannock] news is cheering[83] while the news here is discouraging — I expect that we will go up and put the Yanks through. If so we will make a spoon or spoil a horn. Tell Ella to be a good girl and keep her underclothes clean and Frank to be a good boy & keep his nose clean and not wipe it on his coat sleeve.

E P Petty

Little Rock Ark Jany 4th 1862 [1863]

My Dear Ella

Yours of the 20th ult was received on yesterday. I was then in camp 4 miles north of Little Rock on the Van Buren and Ft. Smith road — To day I am in camp 4 miles south of Little Rock on the Pine Bluff road — On last Tuesday we camped upon this ground and while at dinner received the news that the federals had taken Van Buren with 4 of our Steam Boats and had burned the boats and also orders to march to reinforce Genl Hindman in that vicinity — We immediately started, crossed the river at Little Rock and moved 4 miles when our orders were countermanded on the grounds that the federals had retreated from V.B. towards the Missouri line. On last night we got orders to move and to day (Sunday) have come this far. I suppose we are on the way to Pine Bluff (and may be so to Vicksburg). It rained in torrents yesterday and the roads are miserable — It is to day clear and warm. This has been the pleasantest winter so far that I ever saw — We had two Snows it is true but it was warm, they soon melted away and the weather cleared up. I am astonished at its mildness in this latitude. It is well for the poor soldier that the weather is good for there are enough besetments on his path any how. If we go to Pine Bluff I expect we will fare better than in this region as the country has not been so exhausted of every thing eatable as this there having been verry few soldiers quartered in and around that place. I also expect it will be warmer and perhaps healthier than here. What will be done with us when we get to P.B. is a matter of conjecture — We may be kept there as a reserve for the Arkansas Post or to check any movements that may be made up White river or any other move from Helena or we may be on our way to Vicksburg that being on the road to the latter place or it may be that we will go into winter quarters. It does seem that we are to go bobbing around and are to have no chance of meeting the Yankees.⁸⁴ Within the last hour and even since I have begun this letter it has clouded up and promises to rain perhaps before tomorrow morning. I am fearful it will. The health of the regiment is about the same. I have 60 men including officers in camp some 3 or more of them unfit for duty — At Austin I have about 7 and at Little Rock about 6 or 7 more. The ballance of the company are back in Texas on one pretence or another. Some sick and most of them playing the Opossum. Lt McLester's health is not good. He has been puny for several weeks and looks very bad. I have entirely recovered from my recent attack and am quite myself again. It only lasted me about 2 or 3 days. My usual energy and activity carried me through. I am quite sorry you got such reports of my sickness in November as to have distressed you all so. I was verry sick true but the Doctors never gave me up that I ever heard of. If Dr. Gorman of my Co[85] had not been with me and staid all the time with me and nursed me close I would have run a much closer risk than I did but knowing that I was seriously and perhaps dangerously attacked I determined to have medical aid at hand all the while and did so. Dont be distressed about me any more. I think I will now get on and if you hear distressing tales & reports through others dont believe them until they are confirmed. I am sorry to hear of the bad luck of having your corn eat up. That is truly distressing and Ma had better supply its place at once. I am also sorry of the continued and repeated sickness of my family. It is as distressing to me as for you to hear of any sickness. I am writing this letter with the hope of sending it from Little Rock but if I should fail to get a chance to send it there I will do so from Pine Bluff. Writing more from that place. My love to all for the present. Good bye.

Yours ever
E. P. Petty

In Camp — Jefferson County Arkansas
9 miles above Pine Bluff Jany 7th 1862 [1863]

My Dear Wife

Yours of the 22nd and 23rd and Ella's of the 23rd ult all came safe to hand on the 5th inst. We are now on the march to Pine Bluff and have struck camps here for the night where and when I begin this letter to be finished if I find anything to write about at Pine Bluff to which place we will go on tomorrow. We are getting along finely now. Our sick are convalescing and comeing up, the spirits are cheerful and bouyant and things are decidedly more promising than they have been for a long time — We learn that provisions are more abundant and cheaper about Pine Bluff than about Little Rock or Austin. I hope it is so as my living is costing me pretty smartly now having every thing to buy at tall figures. I wrote to you that I had sent Lt Litle's trunk to Belton and that I had paid the charges to Belton from here. I sent the trunk as stated but did not pay the charges. It went by Mr. White who says he will write to Lt L. stating the bill of charges etc, when he can send him the money etc. I put in the trunk two pairs of my drawers and one pair of old socks. They are good and you can save them for me when I return. The news from across the Mississippi River is cheering — one victory succeeds another.[86] I do hope that the Yankees will proffit from experience and give up the fruitless effort of trying to subjugate a great & good people who have determined and sworn never to be conquered but to struggle on for ages or be free and independent. I am again well and hearty. My appetite about which you lecture me lengthily and sensibly is splendid and never fails me — All other friends may desert me and scorn me but it ever true and faithful sticks to me. Then should I throw it off or scorn and detest it or should I not rather nurture and cultivate it like I would a true friend. Your advice is no doubt good and well timed but I am most too far away for it to have much influence over me and you know when at home I was always risky and you may be sure it is the case here. I am fond of eating and will eat & am to find out for the first time that my appetite has been the cause directly or remotely of any of my sickness. I think it is produced by acclimation — I came here from a dry and healthy climate to a wet and unhealthy one and the process of acclimating is the sole cause — I am determined to return home so you need not let dreams and such shock your nerves. The age for superstition is passed and gone I hope forever and it is time that dreams and prognostics should be discarded. Dreams are the off spring of a diseased and fevered imagination or the listless wanderings of the fancy after reason has been dethroned by the God of Sleep. I dont know what all your dreams were but I intend to contradict the whole of them. I intend to come home but I hope not on sick furlough for I hope now my sickness is at an end. You think I ought not to sacrifice myself for my Country or my men — what did I go into the service for but to sacrifice myself if necessary. Now is the time of all others the most in which my Country and my men need my services and if my intentions were to do any good now is the time to accomplish it. The men were sick and low spirited. Their comrads were dieing all around them. Then it was that they needed my presence and influence to cheer them up and look to their comfort and safety. They needed just such an example of energy of mind to bring them back to health and cheerfullness. The mind has a great deal to do with the progress of disease. If a man will determine to live ten chances to one he will do so. If he gives up ten to one he dies and hence the beneficial influence of my example. Again the men could not get sick furloughs and it would be wrong for the Captain to do so when they could not and desert them in such a time. If I alone had been sick I would have taken furlough and come home. Again from now until this campaign is over is the darkest period of this war and the Country now needs and demands the services of every one of her citizens to sustain her in the struggle — My Country! I could not and would not abandon thee under such circumstances. No, my life, my family, my all are staked on the die I have cast and I will not abandon thee and damned be he that does!

Jany 8th 1862 [1863]

We are now encamped about 4 miles west by south of Pine Bluff with the expectation of staying here a few days. In the present posture of affairs there is no telling how long we will stay here nor when we will go. So you can continue to write to me at Little Rock until further directed. Little Rock is a central position and a distributive office and our mail will follow me wherever we may go. The most of the road from L. R. to this place is fine and weather being pleasant we have had an agreeable trip. I have never seen such a winter any where. We have had one or two bad spells of weather. The ballance has been pleasant and agreeable. It has been quite muddy and particularly so in the Swamps but when we strike any thing like high ground it is fine. The country from L. R. here is poor and piney — the settlements being hovels (with some rare exceptions) and squalid poverty meeting you on every hand. I haven't been to P. B. yet but those who have visited it say that it is quite a business [busy?], flourishing and pretty place. I think that I will go in in a day or two. We are away out here in the woods away from every body and every thing. The water is bad and at some distance off. The wood is good and abundant. The ground where the camps are situated is pretty good but swampy around. What they want with us here is more than my imagination can fix up. We will know some time. I am in splendid health again and as buoyant and cheerful as you ever saw and more sanguine of success in this fight. Although I have been sick about 40 days since I left home I can't get bad enough to take sick furlough and hence have no idea when you will see me. Keep the children at school all the time possible. Keep a keen eye to your finances — Accumulate all the property possible if the children do claim it. I can make plenty more and all I make is for my family. I send herein a little letter for Don — read it to him — and I send $2.00 to buy Van a pig. He shall be even with the other children.

Yours Truly
E. P. Petty

My Dear Little Son Don
    You wanted Pa to write to you did you! Well here it is God bless

your little Soul. Pa has'nt forgot you yet nor will he ever do so. You must be a good boy. Mind what Ma says. Do what she tells you. Love Ella & Frank & Van. Dont tease and fret you[r] little brother Van — he is less than you are and you should take care of him. Dont quarrell with your sister and brothers nor get mad & pout but be a good boy and keep your face strait and pretty so that when your Pa comes home he can be proud of his dear little son Don. Dont forget Pa. So good bye for the present.

E. P. Petty

Jany 9th 1862 [1863]

Master Van Alvin Petty
Bastrop Texas
I am verry well to day. I shall go to P.B. with Cousin Wm. G. King in his buggy to day. He is quite well. No News.

E.P. Petty

Pine Bluff Ark Jany 10th 1863
3 O'clock P M

Dear Wife

I sent you a letter yesterday and would not write so soon but for the news and the army movements now transpiring around me. At 12 O'clock to day we got news that on this morning the fight opened at Arkansas Post the enemy having appeared there during last night with some 5 gun boats and 15 transports loaded with troops and on this morning opened the fight as I suppose by both water & land.[87] The news came by telegraph to P. B. to Genl Walker and by Col Jones & Capt Allen brought out here. Orders were issued immediately for us to move at 2 O'clock PM to day but inasmuch as our wagons were out forageing the move was necessarily postponed until day light in the morning. According to orders therefore we leave for the fight at day light on tomorrow. If we go by land it will take two or three days to go down. If by water we will get there tomorrow night — I dont know which way we will go — Some 3 or 4 of my Co will be sent to the hospital being unable to go — About 50 from the regiment will be sent to the hospital some being unable and some I suppose unwilling to face the music. I dont know how I will stand the fire but I have made this promise to and request of my men that if any of them show the white feather I will shoot them with my own hands and if I show it for them to shoot me instantly. So soon as the thing comes to a head and I have a chance I will give you the result of it. In the mean time be of good Cheer. Believe no idle rumors or reports and wait to hear from me. It will all be right with me. I am in good fighting condition. I am good, well, weigh 135 pounds in good & cheerful spirits — sanguine of success, my fighting tools in trim, plenty of amunition and will have in my Company about 55 men may be more. I am in rather bad fix for Officers. Lt Cunningham is now absent at Pine Bluff sick and I hardly think will be able to go with me. Lt McLester is puny and hardly fit for service though at his post — Orderly Sargent [Woods B.] Miller is absent sick near Little Rock. Sargent Tom McDonald is at Pine Bluff sick so you see that my officers are deficient but my men are all officers and I think will fight as well without as with officers and besides I will try and do enough to supply deficiencies.

I saw yesterday a sight which I never saw before and which I hope never to see again. 3 men of Co A Flournoy's Regiment were Caught stealing a hog and they were by orders of Genl McCulloch dishonorably discharged from the service and drummed out of camps. The different regiments of the Brigade were formed on their respective parade grounds in two ranks about 15 steps apart each rank facing inward. Every officer & private able to be up was required to be at his place. The men were then marched through every command in the following order viz 1st An officer on horse back, 2nd The Band playing the rogues march, 3rd The 3 men with their Knap sacks etc, 4th A company of soldiers with bayonets charged towards the rogues, then 5th Genl McCulloch. After they were drummed entirely through the Brigade was formed in close order when Genl McC made a speech — stating that it was done on his order and responsibility, that he intended to preserve the reputation of Texas and the Texans or die and called upon the men to sustain him. He called upon all who were willing to sustain him to hold up their hats. Nearly every hat in Allen's regiment went up like a rocket but I am sorry to say that in some of the other regiments many a hat remained on its wearer's head — At the conclusion of the speech three cheers were given for Genl McC. It was painful to witness this scene — three young men in the flush of youth and manhood disgraced before the world and will have to go back to their homes ruined men — their families mortified and their children if any scandalized. The young men belonged to Capt Saunder's Co from Bell County Texas.[88] Two were brothers named Wiseman, the name of the other I do not now remember. I am

told that the young Wiseman were good moral men at home, irreproachable in character and of good respectable parentage — how my heart bleeds for their parents.[89] — The news from across the Mississippi still comes cheering and if we can respond by a good and glorious defeat in this state I think the dawning of peace will be near at hand. God send us a good chance at the scoundrels and then you will hear from us. The news of a prospect of a fight was received by the regiment with cheers — great animation of spirit prevails on all sides and all are making active preparations to give the Yankees a warm reception on Arkansas soil. We will receive them "with bloody hands to hospitable graves." I have nothing further to write at present — take good care of my little ones. — Be of good cheer — Remember me kindly to friends and believe me truly as ever

Your's etc
E. P. Petty

P.S. I am told that the guns can be heard at Pine Bluff distinctly if you will go out into the river on a boat. The Yanks came up to the Post on the back water from the Mississippi river —

E. P. Petty

Camp Skedaddle Jany 12th 1863

Dear Wife

I wrote you from Pine Bluff on the 10th inst that the Arkansas Post had been attacked by the feds on the 9th inst and that we were going to reinforce the Post. The feds appeared before the post on friday night 9th inst with several gun boats and numerous transports — From the best information we can get about 5 gun boats and 50 transports. They demanded the surrender of the place and gave them until 6 Oclock Saturday morning to consider. Genl Churchhill (cmd'g the Post) declined to Surrender the fight then opened between the gun boats and fort. 2 of the gun boats soon run by the fort and took their station above — 1 ran up opposite to it and the ballance took station below. The fight lasted all day Saturday and all day Sunday. Some time during Sunday the boats silenced the fort by knocking the work to pieces and dismantling our guns. In the meantime the enemy had landed a large force below the fort and they had been firing on our men behind the breastworks — When the fort fell their transports moved up the river above our men and landed a heavy infantry force and attacked our men in the rear and where they were not protected by breastworks. The enemy below made by land from ten to fifteen different charges and were repulsed with heavy loss — Our boys standing behind the works mowed them down like grass but when the enemy attacked them with an overwhelming force in the rear they could not resist successfully any longer and the White flag was hoisted and the whole command surrendered with the exception of about 300 who escaped by flight. The number that surrendered was near 4 000 nearly if not quite all Texans.[90] We are now halted in about 30 miles of the Post[91] — What our action will be I cant say — Our generals have been in Council of War to day but have revealed nothing. We have met numbers of stragglers to day who fled from the fort — some after and some during the action. 5 of Morgan's Co. have for the present attached themselves to my Co. viz Carroll Billingsly (he was not in the fight), James Allen (Old Jerry's Son), Bat Lane (Gill's Son in law, Lane's son), Norwood and Barnhart. Others from other commands have joined other companies. They lost all they had but what was on their backs. The reports of the killed and wounded on our side is variously estimated. Some say about 100. Others put it as high as 1 000. I expect it was heavy. That of the enemy is variously conjectured. None put it under 2 000. Some as high as 4 000 — all say that the ditches were full and the ground covered with their dead bodies. It is no doubt much heavier than ours as they were exposed and we were behind our works. Our forces in the fort was about 5 000. The enemy from all appearances and all conjectures had not less than 30 000. All say the woods was literally full of Yankees, that they attacked the works from 10 to 15 times and every time with fresh troops while our boys fought all the time without much relief. It is said our boys made a most gallant defense that it was one of the hardest fights of the war — that Genl Deshler's brigade continued to fire for near 2 hours after the White flag had been hoisted not wishing to surrender at all. I dont know the fate of but few of Morgan's Co. John Buchanan escaped and went to Pine Bluff to day. Black Davis and Pass Turner were sick and not in the fight but are supposed to be captured. Jim Allen left the works at 12 O'clock Sunday and when he left none had been killed. The infantry charge was made after that time. Bob Fore was in the works — I expect captured may be killed — The feds fired upon and burned the hospital though the Yellow flag[92] was floating over it and burned up in it 4 sick men a barbarity that none but heathens and Scoundrels ever indulge in. I expect they were big mad though as they had just attacked Vicksburg and had been signally repulsed and concluded to turn with an overwhelming force upon Arkansas and eat her up for breakfast. I expect it is well for us that we did not reach the fort for I expect they had force enough to have captured all of us — What we will now do I cant tell — So Soon as the river rises their boats will ascend and we cant offer them any resistance. The Post is the key to all Arkansas and they now have a bill of sale to it. It is to Arkansas what Fort Donaldson [Donelson] was to Tennessee. I expect and hope that while the river is down so that gunboats cant come up that we will move down in close proximity to the enemy and fight

over every inch of ground on this river before they shall have it.[93] I expect we will have action and stirring times from this on for some time to come — From here to Pine Bluff (25 miles) is the best farming country I have ever seen. It is in a high state of Cultivation and hundreds of negroes. The people are generally alarmed and many are skedaddling for other parts. We have issued and are issueing ammunition so as to be ready — I dont feel as much alarmed & concerned in the enemy's [vicinity?] as I did over in Texas nor do I believe any of the men do. They are all eager for a fight and sorry that they could not get to the fort. I understand that a gun boat is some 12 or 15 miles below us to night. It is now 9 O'clock and perhaps before day we will be awakened by the bursting of bombs instead of the drum — We are right on the bank of the river. It is all right. We are ready and willing for the fray. Let it come. Dont suffer yourself alarm on my account. I will come out right side up with care. Take care of my little one's and I will look after the Confederacy. I will write as soon and often as possible.

Believe me truly your's etc
E. P. Petty

Pine Bluff Jany 22nd 1863

Dear Wife

I have just mailed a letter to Ella of this date but finding a chance to send one direct home by Black Davis who starts in the morning have concluded to write a few lines and enclose with it some money which you can invest in something that will profit you & your family. I send you two hundred dollars in Confederate money in one hundred dollar bills. I could send more but think it best to keep some on hand for emergencies. I expect that we will shortly be paid up to 1st Jany. If so I can send some more money. I gave Ella a full description of my trip towards the Arkansas Post and refer you to her letter for it. From this place down is the finest farming country that I ever have seen but it is low and verry muddy and we had a hard time. It is the hardest soldiering I have ever experienced. We took the rain, the snow, the cold and the mud without tents and with thin covering to sleep under of nights but I enjoyed and stayed good well. In sending of my things when I remained with the expectation of fighting I only retained a small blank book to write to you in (this is a leaf from it), a box of matches to kindle fires with, my pistol & amunition to fight with and your picture to cheer me up (and to kiss). When the enemy pressed in the ballance all went and I never expected to see them any more but fortunately I have got the most of them again and am up in the world again. There is no news of interest here to day. I have just seen Maj Morgan who is up from the Post.[94] All the feds have departed. They carried away all of our sick & wounded, burnt every thing at the Post and filled up & levelled the fortifications. Capt M. Nutt[95] who was taken prisoner wrote his wife and his letter was inspected and sent out by the feds that our loss in killed and wounded was 125 and that of the feds 2500. They paid dearly for that little victory. Such victories generally ruin the victor. This town and country looks like it had been sacked every body and every thing having abandoned it except the Army. I expect from all I can see and learn that we will get into a fight before this campaign closes. I didn't start out to write a letter and am protracting this to long [*one line illegible*] send some money. From what I can learn Texas money and even Bastrop County money is better than Confederate money.[96] If it is so you had better get all you can & take care of it. Of all these things however you must be the Judge and act accordingly. Do the best you can and I will be satisfied. Take care of the little ones and kiss them for me. Our friends here are well.

Yours truly
E. P. Petty

Camp Mills Arkansas[97]
January 29th 1863

Dear Wife

The last letter I have received from home was yours of the 23rd Decr 1862 and was received by me on the 6th of January I believe. You may from this judge my anxiety to hear from you — Over 3 weeks and no tidings from home great Goodness — It is no fault of yours I am sure but of the general derangement of mails created in these parts by the fall of the Arkansas Post since which time there has been no Post officer or Mails at Pine Bluff all having stampeded in afright leaving us to depend upon the uncertainties and irregularities of Couriers for our mails and while below here playing bluff with the enemy we did not so much as have Couriers. The Courier is due this evening from Little Rock and I am waiting for him with an anxious heart hoping to be paid up in full for all my 3 weeks of disappointment.[98] I have no particular camp news to write and the other and outside news you get earlier and more fully than I do. Since the fall of the Arkansas Post desertion has been the order of the day with the Feds. They have been pouring into Col. Carter,[99] to Pine Bluff & to Little Rock by ones, twos, in squads and by Companies to be paroled and sent home until I am informed near 1 000 have been paroled. Some reports say (and they have some appearance of being official) that Col Carter has paroled near 1400 and has sent up for more blank parol[e]s as he is informed that half have not come in that are on their way. From my best information at least 500 have come in and surrendered amongst them some officers and one major.[100] They say that they will no longer fight under Lincoln's proclamation[101] and the people at home will sustain them. I think the true secret is their dread of Vicksburg. They tried it and were used up and now to be led against it again is more than they can stand. They know and feel that Vicksburg is a gaping Hell for Yankee souls, that it is the great highway to damnation for all who seek to conquer Southern Liberty and hence the cowards had rather desert than face the music but they needs must tell a specious tale to curry favour with us here. I have no faith in the scoundrels though I am glad to see their army demoralized. Whilst desertion is the order with the Yanks we too are having some of it. Some of our men are leaving too but in verry small numbers so that it does'nt amount to any. I hope the scoundrels will be caught and shot. I dont want our Southern society disfigured with the slime of deserters or traitors.[102]

We have sent and are sending down towards the Post several Companies of Sharpshooters to annoy the gunboats and transports if they attempt to ascend the river and to pick off pilots and others who show themselves. Capt Millers Co will go from our regiment as his co (being the left flank co) is armed with Enfield rifles. I hope the expedition may prove advantageous. The enemy are now attacking Vicksburg & if they are unsuccessfull which I am sure they will be we may look for them up this way again

Jany 30 — AD 1863

There is no news here to day. Our Commissary Department here has been trying to starve us out but I hope they wont succeed. We have for a week been living on poor beef (dog meat) & corn bread and a verry small quantity of meat at that. I cant eat the meat so I have been living on bread & water. Once & awhile we get some Sugar and Molasses. Since we have been in Arkansas the men have spent half their wages in provisioning themselves when it was the duty of the government to do it. It is hard for the private to serve for $11 per month and buy his own clothes and board himself. It is becomeing unbearable and the men will not submit much longer.

Yesterday I received your's & Ella's of the 3rd inst with Houston Telegraph enclosed. I had seen and heard of the Galveston fight and was much gratified thereby.[103] Today I have walked into Pine Bluff (4 miles) and found the roads bad. After getting in town it set in to raining and oh what a time I had comeing out. I tried to find out about the federal desertions and from all the information I could get we have paroled about 2000 deserters since the fall of the Arkansas Post. I am in fine health: weigh about 140 pounds and look about as well or better than you ever saw me. I have some men yet in hospital. Have lost no more — only 5 in all — The regiment has lost over 100. Some Companies have lost 18 or 20 men. I have over 60 men in Camps. Capt R D Allen is now our Major by the resignation of Maj Tabor to the great regret and mortification of the regiment. I sent you two hundred dollars the other day by Black Davis. As old Sam is about to die you had better buy a good buggy horse. I will send you some more money the first chance to pay for one. Take good care of all things — This war will end some of these days and I want to find things in good order at home. Take care of my little ones. God bless them all. Kiss them all for Pa. Write often and long and send me some Texas papers.

Yours truly
E. P. Petty

P.S. I bought you a Cook book which I will send you as soon as I can.

Petty

I send this for you to write me one so write soon.

Camp Mills Febry 3rd 1863

My Dear Daughter
    I wrote to Ma 3 days ago and gave you all the news I had. I have verry little now to write but thought I would keep my hand in and also discharge my duty. I have just learned this morning that Genl Kirby Smith supersedes Genl Holmes in this Department.[104] I am truly glad of that. I look upon Genl H as a dilapidated old Granny and a drunkard besides. He has done no good nor ever will here. The confidence of the soldiery and people have departed from [him]. Genl S has a world wide reputation, has won it deservedly at Mannassas and

other battle fields and will beget a confidence and impart an energy that will result in good to the Confederacy. I have also learned to day that for the present the Yankees have declined to attack Vicksburg and that while waiting for reinforcements they intend to exercise their elbows in Arkansas trying to gobble us up. I am sorry of this. Vicksburg is the great highway from the U.S. to hell for Yankee souls. I therefore wanted them to attack it and begin at once upon their long journey. V. is impregnable and another failure and overwhelming defeat there would go a long way towards peace I think. If they come up here we will try and give them a warm reception. We "will welcome them with bloody hands to hospitable graves." There is no camp news here of much interest. The health is pretty good better than it has been for some time though I am fearful — Our trip toward the Arkansas Post and exposure down will prove deleterious to us yet as I notice amongst the troops much cold and coughs.[105] We are now camped 4 miles from Pine Bluff on the Little Rock road in a flat marshy pine woods. Wood & water are convenient and this is about all that can be said in favour of the location. On the meat and bread question as a general thing we have plenty. Occasionly we are scarce of good meat for a day or two but never of bread. We only have corn meal. We have had no flour for a long time and so worn out am I on corn bread that when I return home I shall feel insulted whenever Ma sets cornbread before me. I shall live on flour bread the ballance of my life.[106] I am now in fine health heavier and better looking than you ever saw me. I stick close to my command and do my duty as a soldier. I'll feel the better by it when I come home. I notice in your letters evidence of great carelessness in your writing and in your grammar. You leave out a great many words and leave me to guess at your meaning and you use a great many ungrammatical sentences — Of all things in the world let your writing be perfect. Read your letters and see the mistakes and correct them. Dont be in such a hurry about it — You know how to write but you hurry over it. Correct these faults if you want to be a pretty writer or smart writer.

Tell Ma that Judge Terrell intends starting home in a few days and I will try and send her some more money. I sent her $200 by Black Davis — She must buy a good buggy horse if she can find one. I will send her the money to pay for it. Press on in your studies. Be kind and gentle to your little brothers & obedient to your mother. Think more of home and home folks and home things than anything else. Cherish your love for your poor old daddy and believe me truly yours

E. P. Petty

My Dear Wife

Your's of the 11th and 13th inst has just come to hand. You were not more astonished at receiving a mule than I was when I received your letter announcing the fact. The mule belongs to Lt Litle. It was worked out here in the clothing wagons and I received instructions from Lt L. that if I could not get two hundred dollars for it to send it back. Mrs Allen had concluded to go home and I thought it a good chance to send it. (I did not then know that Mrs Jones was going). So I arranged it with Col Allen that she was to carry the mule home and deliver it (not to you) to Lt Litle at his house. Since receiving your letter I called upon Col A and read it to him and told him I was unwilling to have you imposed upon not only in taking care of but in the expense of feeding the mule. He instructed me to write to you (and said he would write to his wife immediately) to send the mule to his house to be sent by his negro to Lt Litle and that he would pay all expenses — So make an estimate of how long you have had the mule and the amount of corn and fodder consumed and send it to Mrs A with request that she either supply its place with more or pay you the market price for it. If this is done all right. If not I will try my hand on the Col again. I furnished old Jo with $20 when he started and he had about $20 of his own so I dont see how his expenses could have been so heavy but as Dr Wilkins does'nt intend to charge for him and as you have already footed the bill let it go and say no more about it. We can afford to be fleeced that sum. Dont fail to get some beef if possible. I am afraid that your meat rations will be short. I want you to put me in your requisition and draw rations for me as I expect to be home during the summer. If you could get a whole beef and half dried & half pickled it would be the best idea I think. Encourage the children to raise pigs, chickens etc so that they may feel like they were citizens & owners of property. On the other provision question it is bad to be extorted upon but you have to submit to present prices so you had better [get] any thing you need and it is cheaper and less trouble to buy by the quantity than by retail. For God's sake dont fail to have plenty to eat as long as money last and as long as I can raise a cent it shall come home. I dont want my wife & children stinted and when I come home (and I shall most certainly come) I dont want to see nor hear of corn bread nor have any thing to drink but good old rio coffee & milk. You ask me about the propriety of drawing provisions from the Commissary — I answer buy what you use — Let those who need it draw from there but you have plenty of money and use it. I dont want it said that my wife & children are benificiaries to a charitable concern — so let the charitable or commissary affair go and buy what you want. You need'nt be alarmed about my health. I think I am getting along first rate now though for about three days I have been a little unwell and believe that on the night of the 5th inst I had an Arkansas Chill. You ought to have heard me then preach Arkansas' funeral I should have said cursed it. Before that I weighed 140 pounds and I dont think I will fall under that perhaps go over. I feel quite well now and as long as I can get any thing to do I enjoy this life and to day I have been drawing and paying off my company two months wages and bounty. This is a good way to spend the sabbath dont you say. A soldiers life (unless he is in the presence of the enemy and actively engaged) [is a] dull, monotonous life and dont suit me. I wish it were over with me for I sigh for home and home comforts once more. The rains have come and the floods descended in Arkansas and all the rivers have been over their banks so as to interupt travel and mail transportation. This is the reason that neither you or I have received letters any more regular. On the 5th inst we had another Snow here about 4 or 5 inches deep with pretty cold weather — This makes the 4th snow this winter so you see that we are in a pretty cold climate and are undergoing some of the hardships of a soldiers life. We will have great tales to tell our children when we get home. Wash Jones has been unwell for some time though he is going about and attending to his duties. There is not much sickness in the regiment now but little in my Co. I lost another man on the 6th inst with Pnuemonia John T. Huling of Austin Texas substitute of Dick Wilkins. He was a good fellow and I regret his death. I wrote you a few days ago that I would send you some money by Judge Terrell. The Judge carries this letter to Austin where he will mail it and I have concluded to enclose you only ten dollars Texas Treas'y Warrant. I will send you some money by Wm Higgins and Benj Snodgrass who will start home next week. I dont know how much but all I can spare. I sent you $200 by Black Davis. Since I commenced this letter Col A has sent me the note herein enclosed with request that y[ou] send it up with the mule — Send also a note with the bill of expenses as they must foot the bill. Tell Frank that I am astonished and mortified that he should be lazy with his books, that I did not think he would treat me so — After I have to expose myself so much to get money and then spend so much to buy him clothes, victuals, books and tuition it is too bad for him to neglect his studies so. He must do better or I will be mad way over here in Arkansas. Kiss all of them for Pa. Give my love & respects to all friends etc

Your's truly
E. P. Petty

Dear Wife

Your's of the 19th ult came to hand on the 9th inst. You ask what interest Snelling has in the Piney Land. The title is all in me but Snelling paid (and of course is entitled to that much interest) near $350 on the purchase money the place costing us $750. It had better not be sold now but if it is Snelling will be entitled to his proportion of the price. See him and find out what he will take for his interest and write to me and if I think it about right will fix up the papers and send you. Make him put it to the lowest figure. Dont be alarmed about some one prowling around your house of nights. It is some body trying to steal something perhaps. May be a dog hunting something to eat. At all events be it what it may, man, beast or hobgoblin, all you have to do is to keep a valliant heart and a steady nerve. Trust in God and keep your powder dry and give them h——l whenever you get the oppertunity. Dont imagine to yourself that you are afraid — Fear makes cowards of the most of us and when you talked so much about it in your letter I could'nt help laughing sure enough as you predicted — Why you aint in half the danger that I am in and yet I sleep sound of nights as though all was peace and I was at home on my own downy couch. It wont do. Never let your Children know that there is such a word in the dictionary as fear and particularly dont teach it by example. I sent you a letter by Judge Terrell a few days ago in which I gave you a statement of the mule transaction. Just between you and me I think Mrs Allen knew all about the matter and sought that as a convenient way to get rid of sending the mule home or of feeding it a few days and believing so she must foot the bill of expenses as I stated to you in that letter and if she is a lady she wont hesitate a moment in doing so. I am glad that Tanner had the manliness to report Stroud. Stroud is represented by his old company here as being a most consumate coward and has been trying under various pretexts to slide out of the Service. I want all such forced in. You can pursue whatever course you please in reference to selling or swapping your place off — Do what you think best about it. I am sorry that you and your neighbors get on so badly. It is about as I expected however and I expect the least you have to do with them perhaps the better. I expect Higgins or Dr Wilkins are about the best advisers you could have. I dont think that they will be governed by selfishness in their counsil and I expect they would be the best men to assist you in investing your money. Of this however you must be the Judge. In Judge Terrell's letter I enclosed you ten dollars Texas Treasury Warrant — I also sent by mail some time since two dollars to be invested in a pig for Van. Did you get it. I want the children to feel like they are citizens and property holders — It will give them a better opinion of themselves — William Higgins and Ben Snodgrass are going home and I will send this letter by them. They were appointed drill masters with the rank of Lieutenant by Genl Hebert in Texas and came on here as such. Genl Holmes now refuses to recognize them as such and they go back to Texas to report to Genl McGruder with hopes that he will. Howard Allen is in same fix but his father refuses to send him back hoping I think to stick him in some company here as Lieutenant when a vacancy occurs. This is my guess and of course is private. He cant foist him on the F Company without a rebelion. I dont know that he will try. Think he is too smart for that. I send by the boys (H. and S.) two hundred dollars for you and one hundred & sixty for Lieut Litle total three hundred & sixty dollars. Please find some way to send Lt L's to him or send him some word about it. You can do so through the Eggleston's perhaps. I reckon you think I dont intend for you to need for money — this is so. All I make is for my family and I want them to get the benifit of it. I can take care of myself. I dont want my family stinted for any thing nor shall they be if I can help it — I hardly realized the love I have for you all until this cruel war forced a separation. I did'nt know that you all composed so great a portion of my happiness and that you are so necessary to me. But it is so and I must do my part to take care of and preserve you. John Person has obtained a transfer from my Co. to Lane's Co Debray's regiment at Galveston[107] by reason of his broken leg and will go back to Texas in a few days. The money I send for Lt Litle is his wages for the months of September and October 1862 so state to him. His trunk was sent to Belton by a Mr White — The freight has not been paid. I sent some few things in it a pair or two of drawers and a pair or two of socks. I wish I could get a chance now to send some clothing home. I would send the cloth for a suit as I have no chance to have it made also some of my winter clothing so as to lighten my trunks. Wash Jones is still puny though about. I am in fine health again. My 3 days sickness that I wrote you about in Judge Terrell's letter reduced me 5 pounds so that about 2 days ago I only weighed 135 pounds — Think now I will go to about 138 as I know I am gaining by my feelings. Bob Wilkins has been sick for a few days but is nearly well again. McLester had a long puny spell and fell off near 20 pounds — He is now well and has nearly recovered himself. Jim Cunningham is now in Pine Bluff sick though nearly well. He has been sorter sick for some time. The health of the regiment is now pretty good and if we could get a fight would make the fur fly. I am glad to see you display your qualities as Commissary for the family — You are doing admirably — I want you to include me in the requisition for rations and I want mine in flour and rio coffee & milk & butter. I think I shall have the pleasure of joining you around the festive board this comeing summer. Remember me kindly to friends and kiss the Small Pettys for me. I will kiss the old one myself when I come home.

Your's truly
E. P. Petty

Camp Mills Febry 14th 1863

Dear Wife

By way of post script your's and Ella's of the 25th and 28th ult with paper have just been recd. Since writing mine of the 12th which you will find herein I have another draw of money both for myself and Lt Litle and now instead of the amount as therein stated I send you for yourself four hundred ($400) dollars and for Lieut Litle Three hundred & twenty ($320) dollars making total Seven hundred & twenty ($720) dollars. This pays Lt Litle up to 1st January 1863. I expect he will be dismissed from the Service for continued abscense and disability from Sickness. He ought to have resigned long ago and has done the public service injustice by not doing so. I concluded to weigh yesterday to see how I was getting on and weighed 139½ pounds heavy so you see that I am up in the world again. I am quite well. Wash Jones is better — All getting along well though it rains nearly every day and we are in a swamp. We would shake here mightily in the Spring. I have no news of interest here to write. There are some gun boats in this river below the Post. It is thought that they are there to keep their men from deserting and running their transports up here and giving them up. This is only a guess. I am sorry for M^rs & Mr Denny but from what I can hear here am not surprised that Charley should be involved. They say in his old Co that he will take things that dont belong to him.

Camp Mills Febry 19th 1863

Dear Daughter

I received a few days ago both yours and your Ma's of the 25th & 28th Jany last. I have been waiting for over a week for William Higgins and Benjamin Snodgrass to start home — have had a letter written to send by them together with some money for your Ma. They have been waiting for John Fort who has nt yet had his papers fixed up so that he can start. Now William is sick and it may be some days before they start. I will send by them the letter and money as it is all ready and will mail this to you so as not to keep you in suspense about a letter. We are still at Camp Mills but will perhaps move a short distance tomorrow to try and better our condition for we are now in a perfect swamp. Cant go ten steps from your tent without getting in the mud & water. We have been here nearly a month and it has rained 2 or 3 times a week and some times oftener. To day it is clear and a regular March wind is blowing. It reminds me of spring and does'nt seem right that the people should be in strife butchering each other like savages but that they should be at home farming. I am in fine health. Weighed last Sunday (4 days ago) 141½ pounds, and have no doubt but would weigh more now. 2 weeks ago I had a chill and fever and for 3 days was quite unwell. Fell off to 135 pounds but got good well and went up to my present weight. I think I am now acclimated to Arkansas and can stand it.

I saw this week Bob Hall, Wesly Puryear and Black Carter just from Bastrop — Hall & Puryear came out to buy negroes on speculation I think. Well they have missed it. Negroes are awful high here and the present state of affairs does not lessen the price in the least — Carter will start home tomorrow but will go down the river by Parson's regiment. There is verry little prospect here of a crop as nearly all the negroes have been run off. There is no news from the Yankees. Some gun boats are in this river near the Mouth but are making no efforts to come up. We have the river lined from its Mouth to Pine Bluff with sharp shooters and flying artilery and will annoy them exceedingly if they attempt to come up.

There is some sickness with the troops yet but few deaths. Press on in your studies — Make an accomplished lady of yourself — Be scrupulously honest in every thing. Wrong no body out of a cents value — Teach your brothers the same. I hope I will be at home this summer and I want to see how much my children improve in one year. Kiss all for me and believe me truly

Your affectionate father
E. P. Petty

I have writen to you about the fall of Arkansas Post and the part we took in it. You have it all in this. I have nothing more to write.

Your's truly
E.P. Petty

Pine Bluff Febry 22 1863

Dear Wife

Various things have detained Higgins & Snodgrass so that they have not yet started. I think that they will be off now in a day or two. We moved camps to day (Sunday as it is) and are now on the river about 3 miles above this place. We have now a pleasant camp. It has been cloudy nearly the whole of this month and rained nearly ¼ the time and snowed once. The people here say that the winter has been unseasonably cold and wet. We have all been exposed and suffering a great deal here in Arkansas. I have been detailed as Judge Advocate of a Court Martial[108] which convenes in this place tomorrow and have come in here to night to secure a boarding house and be ready for work in the morning. Judge Advocate is the same as prosecuting Attorney. I dont know how long the Court will last. Maybe for a month or more. I have engaged board at a Mrs Stakes at two ($2) dollars per day. This comes pretty high but is cheaper than some houses charge and is as cheap as I can get it. I shall be as full of business now as I can manage and sorter after the old style maybe so I will be better contented as a mind constantly employed brings true contentment.

One week ago today I weighed 141½ pounds and I have been since and am now in the verry finest sort of health and expect I weigh more now. There is seemingly no prospect of any fighting here. We are doomed to rot in idleness. This is too bad. Kiss the brats for me. Truly

E.P. Petty

Pine Bluff Ark
March 1st 1863

My Dear Wife

On this Sunday evening I have concluded to write you a short letter. I havent received a letter from you in about 3 weeks — the last one bearing date Jany 28th. The reason I have no doubt is the high waters as it has rained in torrents here and all the water courses are up and when once the Arkansas rivers get up there is no knowing when they will be down again. I have seen a good deal of wet weather and verry muddy country but never any thing to compare with this country. It rains every few days and Oh God the mud. If the Yankees were to come now we could'nt get away with our trains. I have been living in Pine Bluff just a week and am living pretty well — about 3 days I board[ed]. Since then we have been keeping batchelors ranch. It cost me $2 a day to board and it costs about $1.00 per day to board my self — and I live much better (except the bed) than when I boarded. We rented a large fine house here for $20 per month have a cook from the regiment and Jo Weber to wait on us. Our mess here is composed of Col Allen, Maj Allen, Howard Allen, Pass Turner, Capt Mabry and myself. We work at our Court Martial every day hard and at night we go to see the ladies. I have been close in my company ever since I came to Arkansas — Did my duty faithfully without trying to visit or make the acquaintance of the ladies. Now whilst I am here on Court Martial I intend to make up for lost time. There are lots of women here of all kinds, Married, Widows, grass widows and single. We tried last [week] four cases and have now on hand enough to keep us I think a month may be longer. I went up to see my company to day. They are well and cheerful looking forward anxiously to a speedy peace. Every body nearly seems to think that the dawn of peace is upon us but I must confess that I am unable to discern the streaks. I hope it may be my obtuseness of vision that prevents me and that really peace is near by but I cant discern the signs with all my ken. There is no local news here that I know of. Arkansas is now nearly free from the Yankees. There may be some gunboats near the mouth of this river but we are watching them. Our sharp shooters are stationed on the river from its mouth to this place a distance of near 80 miles. We have also light artilery and Cavalry down there who occassionly pitch into their transports. Then woe be to the unlucky transports which start for Pine Bluff or Little Rock. I am in splendid health never finer in my life and in the enjoyment of exuberant spirits. Yet I sigh for the pleasures of home and comforts of wife and children. God bless them all. How I want to see and embrace them. Kiss them again and again for me. I send this by a man going to Burleson County — a discharged Soldier.

Ever truly yours
E. P. Petty

Pine Bluff Ark March 4th 1863

My dear Wife

I am still here hard at work in the Court Martial. We are getting along pretty well. Have disposed of 8 cases up to this time. The other Court Martial have sentenced 4 men to be shot. The sentence was published to day and will be carried into execution in a few days. I am hard hearted enough to want to see a military execution and after I do I will try and give you description of it. They are to be shot for desertion. It has become a military necessity to shoot some body for this offense as an example to prevent the disintegration of our Army. We have just received news here that the enemy have again attacked our Gibralter Vicksburg and were repulsed with a loss of 16000 killed and 10000 prisoners. I am disposed to believe that there has been a fight there and that the enemy as a matter of course have been defeated but the above figures may be considerably changed by the facts.[109] For a few days the weather has been beautiful but cool and the roads are getting passable. This is a country of greater extremes than our own changeable Texas. One day the streets here may be a loblolly of mud and water and in three days they will be disagreeably dusty particularly if the wind blows. I had a funny dream the other night. It was that the war was over, that I started home 1st May and reached there about the last of May, that you refused to kiss me because you said I had been hugging and kissing the Arkansas girls. Now was'nt that funny but the funniest thing of all will be that I intend to kiss some of them before I do leave for it shall never be said that I left Arkansas where kissing is so cheap and did'nt take any stock at all but you know this is all a joke and if a man cant joke his own wife who can he joke. I still keep in splendid health and fine spirits. I feel and

know that we have got the Yanks where the wool is short, that we will whip this fight, that our deliverance is as certain as he who sits on the eternal throne and guides the destinies of the wor[l]d. They day may be far off but it will come. It may be near. I hope it is. I think this campaign will end it. Keep every thing to rights and agoing. — Kiss the children. God bless them for their Pa. Remember me kindly to friends. Tell Mrs Turner that Pass is all right. Pass Turner, Capt Mabry & myself run together here.

Truly your's
E. P. Petty

P.S. I hav'nt had a letter in over 3 weeks nearly 4 weeks.

E. P. P.

Pine Bluff Mar 13th 1863

My dear Wife

I have just returned from witnessing one of the horrors of war. The Military execution of two men for desertion. They were shot to day about 3 O'clock PM in the presence of the entire Division of the army here. The Division was drawn up in 3 sides of a hollow square fronting the river the open side on the river in a large field just in the lower edge of Pine Bluff — The procession was formed as follows — Band of music — The executioners 24 men with Lieutenant and Sargts — The Priest with the two prisoners on either arm — A wagon with two Coffins — About two Companies as guard. The procession was formed at the Court House and marched to the music of the "Dead March" to the Square — Marched all round the square on the inner side then to the graves which had been dug in the Centre. The Sentence was then read. The Priest prayed with and exhorted them — after which the Commands to ready, aim & fire was given when 24 muskets rung forth their Melancholly Sounds 12 of which were Charged with blank and 12 with Shot Cartridges. The poor fellows fell over on their faces, gasped a little and were gone. They were examined by physicians, found to be dead and were buried on the fatal spot. This is a melancholly and tragic end for them but it is the just doom of the deserter. I had rather see a hundred killed in battle than these poor devils here.[110] I have no news to write. Every thing is getting along finely here. This army is in good health and fine spirits and will be efficient in service. I am still here on duty in the Court Martial and am enjoying myself as well as possible here. We have good comfortable quarters, plenty to eat and I have some leisure time to spend with the ladies — But to spend an hour or so with the ladies though agreeable and pleasant is verry unsubstantial happiness to me. I sigh for home and home happiness with the society of my wife and children but I am afraid that I will have acquired such a rambling disposition that I will not be contented when I come home. You sent me a sheet of paper to write you a letter. Paper is rather scarce here true but I have made out thus far to get plenty and have enough now I expect to last me until I get some more. You need'nt send me any more. I have just been paid two months more wages. If I can buy a negro I will do so but negroes are harder to get and higher here than in Texas. I will send you the money if I dont buy soon. I write every week some times oftener. It affords me great pleasure to write home.

Yours truly
E. P. Petty

Pine Bluff Ark. Mar 15th 1863

My dear daughter

    On the 13th inst I started a letter to your Ma in which I gave her all the news. As for news now you will find a dearth in this letter as nothing has happened here of verry great moment. I have just learned to day that Genl Hebert is to take command of our Division here in

the place of Genl Walker our present Commander. This will cause almost universal regret in our Division with officers & men. Genl W has made a universally favourable impression here and is very much respected and I may almost say loved while Genl H is almost universally detested and disrespected.[111] We run off from Texas to get from under him and now he has followed here and seeks to command us. If any thing can be done to prevent it it will be done but if not we must as good soldiers submit for the good of the country. I have also learned that Genl Kirby Smith is on his way here to assume command of the Trans Miss Dept. This will indeed be gratifying news as every body soldier and citizen are tired of the Old Granny Genl. as Gen Holmes is universally styled. Nobody expects any thing of him. No body cares any thing for him & nobody has any respect for him and hence for the sake of the country and the efficiency of the Army we hail the advent of such a Genl as Kirby Smith and the retirement of Genl H. Genl Smith come with a military prestige surpassed by but verry few and we look for stirring times when he comes. Genl Hindman has been relieved of his command here and ordered to report for duty at Vicksburg. Genl H though somewhat severe is one of the best officers that we have ever had here and to his efforts more than any other one man do we owe for the safety of Arkansas. He has been the most slandered man in the Confederate Government and is worst sinned against than sinning. He is an able and efficient though unfortunate officer — and I hope he may be properly appreciated. While I say this of his public character I must say that from all I know of him I am no great admirer of his private character.[112] We have a very efficient though small army here. I mean our Division. They are well clad, well fed, well drilled, well disciplined, well officered, well armed, generally healthy, generally contented and will make their mark whenever the opportunity offers.[113]

I gave you all an account of the Court Martials we have in Session here. We have so reduced the business now that the Court is ordered to adjourn which I suppose we will do on tomorrow. Our Court was only auxiliary to the first one appointed and as we have worked hard for 3 weeks we have accomplished the purpose of our appointment and must subside. I go out of it without regret and will return to my Company (family) with pleasure. On last friday the 13th inst two men were shot here for desertion. I gave a description of this lamentable affair in my letter to your Ma of that date. On next friday one man is to be shot for desertion and I am informed that on the next succeeding friday there are to be six men shot I suppose for desertion. It is an

awful thing to think about shooting a man in the prime of life in
the full flow of health but the sight was not as impressioned [?] as the
thought. I saw them shot down as stoically as I would a hog. It may be
because I knew that they had abandoned or forfeited all claim to life or
even respect as the deserter is most denounced by our laws and is most
to be detested. One was hit with four balls in the breast and fell over
on his face and struggled a few moments. The other was hit with four
balls in his breast and one in his eye. He fell over backwards and
expired instantly. The executioners stood about 8 steps from them
twelve with ball and twelve with blank cartridges. The men were
caused to kneel without any bandages over their eyes — poor fellows.
They have gone to heaven I hope as the Catholic Priest was present
and shrived their souls. Pine Bluff is a pretty place about four times as
large as Bastrop. It is very well laid off and handsomely built with a
fine Court house and some neat churches. The people are generally
social and clean though they have learned how to charge the soldiers.
This seems to be perfectly natural elsewhere as well as here. This is the
head of navigation in the low stages of the Arkansas river and hence
its growth and prosperity. It is not the little Pine Bluff that you and
your Ma saw about eleven years ago. Instead of that it is a large
prosperous thriving town not so large however nor near so pretty as
Little Rock. I think the river lands here the best farming lands I have
ever seen but the back lands are uninviting and the occupants more
so. These folks here dont look like our folks in Texas as a general thing
though in Little Rock and Pine Bluff they have some splendid society.
There is a great disposition amongst all classes here to emigrate to
Texas and I am fearful that our beautiful prarie state will be over run by
an inferior class of people as we call them here <u>short horned stock</u> and
stock that have <u>hair on their fetlocks</u>. God save us from the scourge is
my daily prayer when I pray at all.

Well how do you come on with your studies. There are three that I
fear you neglect too much judgeing by your letters. Orthography,
writing and grammar. You dont take enough pains with your letters.
You are in too great a hurry. You dont write and compose as well now
as you did a year ago. You dont pay enough attention to spelling. Get
your dictionary and when you dont know how to spell a word or its
deffinition look it out. Then dont leave out so many little "the's" and
"its" etc and then have singular verbs with singular nouns and plural
verbs with plural nouns etc. Dont neglect these little rules. They are
all important. I dont do this to scold you but to call your attention to
them. Press forward in all your studies. Be a good girl. Keep <u>good</u>

company or none — revere & respect age. Be courteous to equals and respectful to those below you. Kisses to children & love to Mammy.

Ever yours,
EP Petty

Camp Wright Near Pine Bluff Ark.
March 19th 1863

Dear Wife

Your's of the 24th and 28th ult has just been received. They find me in the enjoyment of fine health and exhuberant spirits. The army too is in fine health and cheerful spirits. We are now in a good trim to meet our invaders. The weather is fine and Springlike. The trees are putting forth. The fruit trees are all in bloom. It is quite warm. We are now drilling 4 hours a day beside the recitation of one hour by the officers. We closed our Court Martial on the 17th inst after a session of twenty-three days. As our decisions have not been published I cant tell you what we did but can say that we did not shoot any body. Two men have been shot — one to be shot tomorrow and seven on the succeeding friday making ten in all — All sentenced by Court Martial No 1. My pay on the Court Martial was as follows $2.⁵⁰ per day besides fire wood at the rate of three cords per month and three rooms. For the rooms and wood they paid me $9.00 per room per month and for the wood $4.00 per cord. They pay me the money as I did not have the rooms and wood so that what I will get will be about $90.⁰⁰ and my expenses have been about $35 leaving me on the Court Martial speculation $55 clear money at the same time. My wages as Captain was going on as usual. We may have to go back and reconvene the Court so as to revise some of our decisions. I think we will. I had rather be in Camps drilling etc than in town on Court Martial. This is a verry dark corner of the world over here. We get no news here. Genl E Kirby Smith has assumed command of the Trans Miss Dept and Grany Holmes has retired to parts unknown I hope. I dont want to see nor hear of him any more.[114] Genl Walker still commands our Division. This with your letters have made me happy. I think now we will do something besides shuffle around in uncertainty at least I hope so. Genl Hebert is placed in command of a Brigade in this Division instead as I wrote to Ella over the Division.[115] Benj. Decherd has got a furlough of fifty days and will start home in a day or so I expect. I may send this letter by him. I could send by him some more money but I believe I will not as I may get a chance to buy a negro here. You speak of buying a negro their and ask my advice about it. I say that if you can get one do so — You know how much money you will need. I have sent you by Ben Snodgrass four hundred dollars. This will do for pocket money or pin money. If I can buy a negro here I can get the money to pay for it without drawing upon you perhaps so that you may have two negroes. On the horse question do as you please. Buy or not as it suits you. If I could get a furlough for 100 days I would not mind trying to come home but to start on 50 days, spend about 20 days going and 20 coming back with about 10 or 15 days stay at home with about $300 expenses is more than I am willing just now to undertake — However if we dont get in active service I will try and come home about July or August if I can get furlough. You speak of my patriotism etc. I hope I have enough to stand square up to my duty in any emergency. What would you think of a Captain to whose care you had entrusted your son if in the hour when he most needed him at his post to aid, assist and comfort that son he would abandon him and leave him to the charge of others to whom you did not look to. You would never forgive him if that son died — Sons were entrusted to my care and mine alone for none but I could have raised the Company at that time. Thus I could not and would not abandon them though I suffered sorely myself — and I have my reward in a clear conscience, the love of my Company, the good will of their parents and friends, the confidence of the Country and the approving smile and loving Kiss of my dear wife — hav'nt I? Yes. You smile and I'll kiss your picture. It is all right — God too has rewarded me with fine health. I had a very pleasant time in Pine Bluff — made the acquaintance of many interesting ladies amongst them Lum Owen's connections verry fine and verry nice folks two young ladies with whom I had a nice time. My boys with few exceptions are quite well. Billy Craft, George Dabney and Polk Condry are in the hospital at Pine Bluff but are doing quite well. They had a fire in Pine Bluff yesterday which burned up one Block of buildings say 7 or 8 houses on the north side of the square. The fire originated in a bakery. The damage was not much as the buildings were not much account. The state of affairs in Bastrop are getting truly bad. Men fighting — men insulting women etc. I think there will be no danger of any one insulting you. It is a good deal sometimes the way a woman conducts herself as to whether she will be offered indignities or not. I am in hopes that the Perkin's difficulty will result in running Fousher into the army if it is possible for such a thing to be done. The fellow is a[s] justly bound to be in the army as I am yet he skulks behind some little appointment to stay at home. I am sorry for Mr and Mrs Denny but Charley ought to be severely punished I have no doubt. Love & kisses to brats.

Truly yours Etc
E. P. Petty

Pine Bluff Ark Mar 24th 1863

My Dear Daughter

I have been in town two days in attendance on Court Martial this week. We were ordered back to revise one of our decisions. We are now through and I concluded as I did not intend to go to camp to night that I could not spend the evening more pleasantly than writing to my dear little daughter. I am staying in town to attend a candy party to night to which I have been invited. I hope that I can be able to while away a few hours amongst the Arkansas Ladies. I am boarding at Mr Lytle's who is a relative of Mrs Flemming and by the by there is a beautiful Miss Mat Lytle here with whom I have spent some pleasant moments and hope to spend a few more in the same pleasant way. I received your two letters of the 24th & 28th ult several days ago. I received Ma's of the 3rd inst by Mr Fuller a few days ago. I expect now that I have received all the letters written to me from home. You ask me which I had rather Ma would buy a negro & buggy horse or you a piano? Well just at this juncture of affairs I would say by all means buy the negro and horse. They will be of more service now than it is possible for a piano to be. They will assist in taking care of and supporting my sweet wife and my blessed little brats. The negro will keep my darling little daughter out of the kitchen perhaps and enable her the better to pursue with assiduity her studies and the accomplishment of her mind — I want you to be accomplished as far as possible in all the branches of education music included. This you can do without being the owner of a piano. You know that I never have and never would with hold from you any thing that would be of service or pleasure to you when I could consistently get it for you but you must now recolect that your little brothers must like your self be supported and educated and if I expend all my money on you it would not be fair towards them and you know that as I am now situated life is uncertain and if I were to die or be killed the financial affairs of my family would be at a stand still and perhaps my dear little children and my wife might suffer. So I want while matters are as they are now to expend my money for such things as will be of most use to my family. So the piano question must rest for the present and when the war closes if I am fully able to do so with justice to others I will then buy you one. I hope you fully appreciate my condition and will cheerfully submit to what must be so at present. Because I cannot now buy you a piano you must not relax in your music or other studies. Endeavour to make good use of the oppertunity that I am now enabled to furnish you in the pursuit of the useful and good studies. Avoid works of fiction, novels and light trashy reading until you get your mind well supplied with warp and then if you have the time you can take in the filling. The novels of this latter day are trifling and demoralizing. There are but few works of fiction worth reading and they ought not to be read until one's education is complete. Also learn the useful arts of housekeeping, cooking etc. They will be of inestimable benefit to you in after life. If you should accidentally be rich and have others to wait on you, You will at least know how it ought to be done and have it well done but if you should be poor, then you will repent not having learned these things in your young days when the oppertunity was afforded. Not only this but you can help ma in her house hold duties. This you ought to do with alacrity. She has been so kind to you, has taken care of you when you could not take care of yourself, taken so much pains to learn you and show you and fix you up for society and board & clothe you and all this kind of thing that you ought to do all you can to assist her and lighten her burdens.

I dont know what will be the disposition made of the troops here this spring and summer. I think some grand move is on hand but what and when I cant form an idea. Genl E Kirby Smith has assumed command of the Trans Miss Department. Genl Price[116] is on his way here with a part of his command. Genl Holmes retains Command of the Dept of Arkansas, Genl Walker Command of our Division. The Cavalry who had been stationed down towards the Mouth of this river that is Cols Carter and Burford's commands[117] and Major Morgan's squadron[118] with Pratt's Battery[119] have been ordered forward to Batesville on White river to respond to Genl Marmaduke[120] who is now there with about 5000 Cavalry all I suppose for the purpose of getting ready to move upon Missouri as soon as the weather is favourable and when Genl Price gets here with his troops. I suppose some troops may be kept here and I am afraid it will be ours for I assure you I dont want to spend the summer in inactivity in these swamps here and if there is any chance dont intend to. If it should be so that we are kept here on this river there will be a petition for furlough sent up to Head Quarters signed by me but if we get into active service you need not expect to see me soon. I am now weaned from home and it is better that I stay.

Our Command is in fine health and spirits now, never better in the world and never more anxious to meet the infernal invaders of our land and our rights. All that we are now afraid of is that we will not be allowed to do so but will kept here to rot in idleness in these Arkansas Swamps.

I am pleased with your description of your Concert for the benefit of sick soldiers. I am glad that old Bastrop continues so magnanimous and patriotic but your concert and the Tabeleaux fall far short of the reality. If you could see the hospital scenes that I have seen with the poor soldiers sick and dying away from home, kindred and friends you would think that your scene was tame in fact was no likeness at all. The hospital scenes are the most horrible we have in the Army and most tries the poor soldiers but all the death and sickness and wounds and destruction of property consequent upon war I fear will not compare in injurious consequences with the evils that are to

follow in the general demoralization of society. Parents have sent bright and promising sons to the war with high hopes that they will return covered with glory and live useful citizens of the Common wealth and instead of having their bright hopes realized they will receive back moral wrecks bloated with infamy and vice to darken the pages of the goverment and bring down this gray hairs with sorrow to the grave. To some extent our army & country will be relieved of this as there is no liquor to be had and hence one great source of crime etc is shut off but there are vices enough and snares enough the Lord knows to ruin forever many a promising Youth.[121] I am tremulous for the times and fear the day when my sweet little daughter will be old enough to go into Society lest she should come in contact with characters of this kind. You cannot be too careful of your company. Abstain from the least appearance of vice. Keep none but the society of the good and gentlemanly. I don't mean perfect for none are perfect but I mean persons who are honest, who are gentlemanly, who do not stoop to little things, who are as wise as the times will allow — Who do not dissipate, Who do not gamble. Who are well bred and who know how to behave themselves in the presence of ladies. Listen to your Ma on questions of this sort. Your parents are older, wiser and have more judgment about the selection of your company than you can possible have hence listen to them. They have experience, they know and can find out more than you can. They will be more influenced by judgment and less by passions than you. Hold your head up. Look aloft. Dont grovel or associate with your unequals. Take your poor old father's advice who is now in the army exposed, struggling — facing disease and death in all shapes that he may secure a home, a country, a name and a competency for his dear family. You know that I would'nt say or do any thing but what would benefit or please them. They are what I live for. They are my happiness. Dont then do any thing that would cause me a pang or for which you might blush or that would cast a slur upon you or the family. When in company be modest, retiring, unassuming, mild and pleasant. You dont know how much these will add to your accomplishments. Be polite and respectful to all but familiar and sociable to such only as are worthy. I have said this much because you are getting old enough to understand and appreciate these things. Not only this but as you are getting your education it is as easy to learn these useful and important lessons now as at a future time and now is the best and safest time for you to learn them — I have written to both you and Frank lately. You have received the letters by this time I suppose. I have also written by Pass Turner to Ma, Don & Van. I want you all to write me long letters and give me all the little items of news about Bastrop. They may seem very unimportant to you but will be very interesting to me.

Kiss them all for me over & over again. I will write when I can. You have not reason to complain at my not writing yet and I hope you will have none. Respects to friends.

I am my darling daughter
yours truly & forever
E. P. Petty

Camp Wright, Ark.,
Mar 26th 1863

My dear Son Frank,

I sent you a letter the other day which I suppose you have received before this.

I got through at town yesterday and came to camp here. I hope I wont have to go in there to Court anymore as I got tired of staying there and being away from my company.

They had another fire in Pine Bluff last night and from appearances it must have been quite a large one but I have not heard the particulars and do not know what is [it] amounts to.

We have fine weather here now. The spring is opening beautifully.

There is considerable farming going on here now particularly alon[g] the river, above Pine Bluff.

Our Camp (Wright) is on the river 3 miles above Pine Bluff and is the prettiest and most comfortable and convenient camp we have had in Arkansas.[122]

We have plenty to eat and are healthy and in fine spirits.

We do not know whether we will have to stay here this summer or what will become of us.

The 7 men who were to be shot on tomorrow have been reprieved. I am glad of it — we have shot enough for example. I think that there will now be but little more desertion in this army —

I sent home by Pass Turner some letters and two books for Ma & Ella. I sent by John D. Nash my C.K. Hall Coat.[123] Tell Ma to take care of it for me. If I get a chance I will send some things home —

How do you get along now My Dear Son? Are you studying your books closely? Are you a good honest boy? Do you keep away from bad boys? Do you mind Ma? Do you do every thing that is right and abstain from doing anything that is wrong.

Do you remember every day your Pa who is away over in Arkansas

after the infernal Yankees? Yes, you must do all these things.
Your Pa loves you & thinks of you every day & night.
Kiss the children & Ma for me & write when you can.

> Yours truly
> E.P. Petty —
> Capt. Co.F. Allen's
> Regiment

Camp Wright Mar 28th 1863

My Dear Wife

I received your's of the 7th inst two days ago and intended on tomorrow (Sunday 29th) to answer it but Wesley Puryear having arrived in camp this evening and intending to start home in the morning and John Person intending to go with him I thought I would write a few lines by them. I send by John Person the piece of cloth — the present by McNeill — which you sent me some time since — I have as much and perhaps more clothes than I will need at least than I can carry with me if we get into active service. So I have concluded not to have it made up now. When I need it I can write you word and you can make it up for me — I also sent a few days ago by John D. Nash my heavy coat (C K Hall coat) also by Pass R Turner two books "A Cook & Confectioner" and "Bigland's Natural History."[124] These things will lighten my trunk considerably and give me room in it. I am glad Mrs. Allen sent you the money. I dont care what she thinks. I know that what she did was an imposition upon you and that it was right to pay it and I am inclined to believe that she knew it and did it on purpose. By what arithmetic did you make your Calculation. You say "25 days at $1.^{50} per day comes to $35.^{00}." Not according to my Count. When I was at School it made $37.^{50} So you have lost $2.^{50}. Well let it go now — I am glad to get as much as I did without further trouble. You give me fits about cursing — Well I have so far forgotten myself or have become so wreckless as to swear again. I am sorry for it and wish it was other wise. I confess that I was terribly distressed when the Arkansas Post fell. I did not think that five thousand Texans would have surrendered to any force much less to 40000 Yankees. We were on the way to relieve them and they knew it and hence when we met the news of its surrender I felt indignant and no doubt swore vehemently. I expect it all turned up right at last for I believe with Pope "that what is is right"[125] and with the old hardshell Baptists "that what is to be will be" and I am now reconciled to my lot. I have written Ella and Frank and will start it by mail in the morning. I am exceedingly well and hearty. On the ration question I was thinking about furlough when I wrote. If we get into active service I will not seek one but if we are left here inactive I intend to try for one. I have no news. My Company generally well etc. My love and kisses to the babes and oh how I would like to kiss you for myself.

Yours truly
E. P. Petty

Camp Wright Ark
Mar 30th 1863

My Dear Wife

    Batt Lane who belonged to Capt. H. S. Morgan's Co. and who is now temporarily attached to my Co. has obtained a furlough for fifty days and will start home 1st April next and I have concluded to write you a few lines by him. For the three last days we have had verry bad weather. It rained, it thundered, it lightened, it hailed, it snowed, it blew and was generally bad and stormy and I am afraid the result will be that the fruit here and the crops and fruit of Texas will all be killed or badly injured. This Country still stays wet and muddy. As the spring opened I hoped that the weather would settle and the roads get good but up to this time such is not the case and if the Yanks were to come we would have to fight as we would have no place to run on. I started you a letter yesterday by John Person also the present McNeill gave me the 7 yds cloth. Also I sent by Mail this morning letters to Ella & Frank which you will perhaps receive before you get this. I send the cloth back because it would cost me a great deal to have it made and besides I have no use for it now. I have more clothes now than I can use even after sending off what I have. If hereafter I should not [need] it I can write home for it and you can make it up and send it to me. I bought a nice Alpaca summer coat last week — it cost me ten dollars. I have now here four coats and three pairs of pants. My trunk is now full — and over flowing. I expect I shall send some more clothing home the first good chance I get. If we get to moving around it will be impossible to carry them and I will have to leave them besides experience has taught me that it is not good for a soldier to have too many clothes. In my letter to Ella I gave her much good and wholesome advice that I felt was necessary for her to learn. She is now getting large enough to begin to think of these things and it will be easier for her to learn them now than hereafter and better than for her to repent not having learned them. I want you to impress these lessons upon her. Dont let her keep company or associate with the unworthy. Warn her against it. Set all her ideas against anything mean, grovelling and contemptible — Make her think well of herself and thus she will be slow to do any thing that will lower that estimation. This war will play such havoc with the Morals of the Young men and boys and I fear for the future. You cannot guard these points to vigilantly Also give the other children magnified ideas of all that is good, honest & noble and depreciated notions of vice & wickedness. Make them think (as it should be) that your opinion and mine upon any subject is right and should be to them the law. Give them exalted ideas of themselves and of their parents that they are as good if not better than any body else. This is the right way to fix for them a high Standard and when once fixed they will never lower it. I feel more my responsibility as parent now than ever and it troubles me that I am not at home to bring my children up to the proper appreciation of morals, virtue, honesty, themselves & parents. But in you I have every confidence and can willingly & freely trust because I know that you appreciate the good and eschew the evil and with you I can safely trust them. Yet I cant help saying as much as I have because I feel that I must add my mite to bring them up as they should live. Make them believe that their parents are better than any body else and that they are as good as their parents so that when they come to mingle with the world their notions will be modified to about the right standard that is to believe themselves as good as any body else. Mixing with Mankind always tends to lower the standard of self estimation. Mankind are so corrupt and selfish that one almost looses confidence in himself. In order then that their estimate of themselves may not be brought too low let it be fixed high up — the higher the better. I am quite well and hearty — So are the troops here. All gay, confident and in cheerful spirits. Woe be to the unlucky Yanks that come in contact with Walkers Division. Love and kisses to children. I will kiss your picture for myself.

Truly yours etc
E. P. Petty

Mar 31st 1863

P.S. Since writing the foregoing we have had an election for 3rd Lieutenant in my Co. to which position Thomas J. Beavers was elected almost unanimously. I have also just heard that the prisoners captive at Arkansas Post have been exchanged and assigned to duty on the other side of the Mississippi river. I hope that they have been exchanged.[126]

E.P. Petty

Pine Bluff Ark April 5th 1863

My Dear Wife

I am again in Pine Bluff having been ordered here to relieve Capt Haldeman Judge Advocate of Court Martial No 1[127] and to act in that capacity to that Court. I dont know how long I will have to stay here perhaps not longer than one week may be much more. I hope not long however as I much prefer being with my company which to me now is and feels like my family. I received your letter of the 16th & 17th a few days ago. Sorry to hear of Dr Ploeger's death but it was not at all unexpected to me for I had looked for it years ago. Sorry to hear that you have lost old Sam. Hope you can yet buy a buggy horse. It pained me to hear of your sickness. I hope you will [take] especial care of yourself for my sake if not for your own and the children's sake for I expect to return home some of these days and hope to spend many pleasant and happy hours and days and years with you. You advised me as to my health which was all right and which advice I took in many essential points as little as you think I did and I now on that license assume to advice you so my dear wife be exceedingly careful with yourself. If you absolutely need medicine take it of course but abstain from it as much as possible. It will do thee harm. As long as medicine was abundant in the army the soldiers died by scores. By now it is scarce they are well and hearty. Much medicine wont do. I abstain from it. I had rather have a spell of sickness than to take a dose of pills. I am now stout and hearty. Never have been salivated my constitution sound — my fibers hard and elastic no injuries arising from the too frequent use of medicine. The reason I said lay in some provisions for me was that I expected some time during this summer to get a furlough unless we go into active service and I think the prospect for our command to get in to it is slim. There will be a movement of the troops in Arkansas I think upon Missouri but I am fearful that Walkers Division will be kept in the disagreeable duty of waiting here and hereabouts for the Yankees to come to them. I cant tell yet what will turn up yet. Time will show and I will try and adapt myself to the circumstances. We are all doing fine here now — the people are making considerable preparations for farming here and I think we will continue to do well. I hope this ungodly war will end but I never have hugged to my bosom the delusive idea that it would end soon. We have got it to whip. That will be the shortest way to end it. I have never had any bosom companions (body lice). Some of the troops have but I have managed to keep scrupulously clean & they dont stay on clean persons. They are an awful pest. You must excuse a short letter now as I have just sent five home one for each of you which contain all the news.

Truly yours etc
E. P. Petty

Pine Bluff Ark Apl 8ᵗʰ 1863

My dear Wife

I am just in the receipt of yours of the 21ˢᵗ ult. and though I now get your letters regularly and may safely count on getting one each week yet I look forward with fond anticipation to the mail and when I shall have the to me exquisite [pleasure] of devouring the lines from you. I believe that I become the more anxious each week to get them. At one time not long since I did fondly anticipate a visit home this spring or summer but now I am becoming alarmed about it. They have detailed me to act as Judge Advocate of a Court Martial here which I thought would detain me perhaps a week or two but the cases are fast accumulating. Eight new ones were sent in to day and I have now on hand business enough for one month and the Lord knows how much more will be in by the time we dispose of these. The Office of Judge Advocate is the most important by far connected with Courts Martial requiring some legal capacity and some considerable experience that when once they get a man at work understandingly, considerable risk [?presc]nts in changing. Therefore unless I can m[anufac]ture some good excuse I exp[ect I] am [?in for] it for the ballance of this C[ourt Martial.] [W]ell as I am from military necessity co[mpelle]d to stay here I am determined to make the [most] of it and enjoy myself to the full extent of all the oppertunities which this place affords and I must tell you that they are large and ample. Beautiful young ladies in swarms. Nice children in gangs. Matronly women in throngs. All lovely, charming, lively and intelligent abound here and hereabouts and with such bewitching inducements and enticements who can withhold himself particularly when by pursueing the opposite course all the enjoyment would be the dull ro[u]tine of the Court Martial or the roll of the drum and heavy tramp of the drill all of which I have long since become sick and tired of. And besides you know my motto contained in the Poet Moores beautiful verse —

"'Tis sweet to think that wherever we rove
We are sure to find something blissful and dear
And that when we are far from the lips we love
We have but to make love to the lips that are near."[128]

My name would not be E.P. Petty if I did not haunt the ladies — enjoy
their society — dance when I am danced to and enjoy myself generally
with them. It makes me the more appreciate the charms of my own
sweet wife which are s[eco]nd to none [?] and after a gay and pleasant
tet[e-a-]tete with [them?] I go to my trunk, take out [the p]icture of [my
swe]et wife. Admire her cha[rms and kis]s it over [aga]in and make an
honest confession by taking [back what I] have said to others. Kiss it
again and feel a better and happier thing — I do enjoy myself here and
intend to continue to do so as long as the chances are afforded but my
Dear Wife let me assure you that I shall never be guilty of any thing
that if known would tinge the cheek of her I love best and of my dear
little children. No Never Never. This is enough on the Arkansas girl
question. I am convinced that I have heretofore judged Arkansas
harshly and that it has its redeeming qualities. I have never passed
myself as a young man yet. All ways own up like an honest man and
get along [. . .] The fleas you say are getting bad. I would have some
compassion on them and beg you not to be so cruel and wasteful as to
destroy them all. And particularly to save me some seed had it not
been that I am satisifed that they cut short your letter and robbed me
of some pleasure. Hence now I say without compassion "lay on McDuff
and damned be he who first cries, enough!"[129] Kill Kill Kill until your
vengeance and mine are fully gratified. I did laugh at you about your
scare not that I thought you were a coward. Oh no. I never thought
that but I wanted to stir you up to strengthen your nerves to excite
your valour so that [your nat]ural timidity might not stand [in the] way
[? of your duty and] so that you might shoot any that should offer to
interfere [with your] reserved rights or interfere with you [either to]
alarm or injure you. When I g[et so]me leisure time I will fix up the
papers so that you can buy Snelling's interest in the land and will send
them to you. Negroes are high here and can with difficulty be bought
yet I will try to get one or more. I have on hand here of my own
money about $400 and will be paid some more before long and can get
as much more as I want. Lt. Flemming has paid me the money on his
note. You will therefore please deliver the note to Mrs Flemming and
tell her to destroy it and so inform her husband.

Flemming is here now and has been for several days. He looks better
than I ever saw him. Everybody nearly is looking well. I am in
splendid health.

Give my respects to friends and love to my children and tell them not to forget their <u>poor old daddy</u> away out here in Arkansas.

Truly yours
E.P. Petty

Pine Bluff Arkansas
April 12th 1863

My Dear Ella

I am left alone here at Mr Lytle's this Sunday night every body having gone to Church and I did not know of a more felicitous way of spending the hour than in writing to my dear daughter and revelling in the sweet reminiscenses of home and home witcheries and pleasures. There is hardly a moment of my time unless I am quite busy or fast asleep but what I think of my dear wife and loving children and I frequently catch myself singing (you know I sing well) that good old song.

> "Home sweet home my happy home"
> "Oh how I long for thee"
> "My Sorrows when shall they have an end"
> "Thy joys when I see"[130]

I dive into the giddy mazes of pleasure on every and all occasions and enjoy myself to the full extent of all the circumstances verry frequently manufacturing and inventing circumstances not otherwise afforded, yet when I want true substantial and holy happiness such as is not evanishing I return to the family altar where my hearts dearest treasures are and then with exquisite feelings enjoy such as this fleeting and unsubstantial world does no where else supply. The longer I stay from my home the more I appreciate you all the higher, I raise you in my standard of estimation and the more vivid and glorious you are in my memory. Oh how I long to be at home so that I can take you all in my arms and say

> "I am monarch of all I survey"
> "My right there is none to dispute"[131]

Then my cup of happiness would be full. I know that you are all getting along well and have plenty but there must be a vacancy about the household altar that none can fill but myself. Well how do you get on with your studies. I hope you fully appreciate the time and oppertunities now afforded you and are pressing up the hill of learning and science with rapid steps. Time is precious to you. Oh! do not then waste the moments as they swift[l]y fly but take advantage of them in storing you mind with useful and valuable information such as will make you an ornament as well as a benefit to society. Dont waste your moments in idleness and more dont expend your time in pursuits and studies that will vitiate instead of elevate your taste — gather the wheat and reject the chaff. Your young mind is like a blank sheet of paper. If you take pains and form your letters well, select a good subject, write correctly and tastefully about it, express good ideas, couch it in fine and well selected sentences, attend well to your capital letters and your punctuation and do not have blots & blemishes on it you will have a nice letter and one that you will not be ashamed to show to any person. So with your mind if take pains with it, cultivate it properly — fill it with well selected information, govern your passions and emotions well so as to leave no blots and blemishes upon it you will be a pleasure to your parents, a happiness to yourself, an ornament and blessing to society. Then be careful my daughter be dilligent — be assidious, be vigilant ever watching your words & actions that you may say or do nothing improper. Be vigilant to do good. Never do wrong. If you should accidently do wrong be hasty in repairing it ever remembering that you do not live for yourself but to contribute your small mite either for the weal or woe of those who may be connected with you by ties of Consanguinity or affinity. Then my daughter wont you remember all these things for your dear parents sake, for your own sake, for the sake of others who may chance to be associated with you in this world and for the sake of your future destiny. Be dutiful and obedient to your parents, kind and loving to your brothers. Affable and sociable with your friends and polite to every body reverencing age & respecting youth. Do all this my daughter it will do thee much good and oh! how it will console the heart of your poor old daddy who has suffered and will suffer so much anxiety for you. Read this letter to Frank and tell him to take well the lesson to himself as far as it can be made applicable. Our Army is all here yet no prospect that I see of a move. We are now all pleasantly situated, healthy and of exuberant spirits with itching palms for Yankee scalps praying & hoping for the hour when chance may send us the oppertunity of giving the rascals a nice thrashing.

I am still in Pine Bluff on Court Martial and the Lord only knows when I will be relieved. I have asked and begged to be relieved but I suppose the authorities think that I can do more good in that capacity than in any other and their will be done not mine. I came to the war to do whatever was required of me and I intend to do so. When my masters say do this I do it and when they say abstain from doing that I abstain. I am fearful that I will get so in the habit of obedience to

Masters and superiors that I will have to have a Master or Mistress at home and so will have to obey implicitly all the orders and edicts that Ma may issue. Well you know that aint much hardship to me as I have always done so (over the left) and always expect to do so (in a horn). I dont know what is to be my destiny here this summer. Where and when we will be sent is uncertain. We are forced to the disagreeable necessity of waiting for the Yankees here. I dont see much chance for me to get home. I cant frame an excuse (unless I lie) to come home. You all are getting along well without me, have plenty of money and every thing else and if you hav'nt you know I have and could send it to you and hence what could I say to get a furlough. That I want to see my family and my family wants to see me. If this were good every married man in the service would go home and break up the Army for you know that the married men are the bone and sinew and the stay of the Army. I dont know what I will do. I suppose take my chances and avail myself of any lucky circumstances which may turn up — but be assured that if I can I will come home some time this summer. Give my love with multiplied kisses to all and believe me truly yours

E. P. Petty

Pine Bluff Ark Apl 16th 1863

My dear Wife

Your's of the 27th & 28th ult came to hand in proper time. I went to cyphering about a week ago to try and give you a surprise. Col Allen applied for orders to return to Texas with two others of his officers to collect and bring up the absentees from his regiment — His application was approved and orders issued. He then selected Capt Mabry and myself to accompany him. Genl Walker refused to approve his selection as both of us were on the Court Martial. On this morning both of us went to Genl W in person, set forth our cases & made our strenuous appeal to him but he was inflexible. He said that he could neither spare us from the Court or from our Companies — That he would like verry much to gratify us personally but that we need not think of going home. He then handed me 43 new cases for the Court and told me I could go to work. I intended to surprise you for when you were in expectancy of a letter I would present the letter writer to your infinite astonishment. I intended to surprise Ella by attending her examination and I intended to surprise the Children — God bless them all by presenting them with their same old daddy (slightly improved) who left them some eight months ago in search of

Yanks scalps. But alas for human expectation that is subject to disappointment. I am now condemned without the benefit of clergy to remain in this goodly city and work in the Court Martial until some dispensation of Providence or the kind consideration of some official Gentleman shall have the goodness to relieve me. There is one consolation in this matter however and that is the importance that the authorities attach to me or us. Col Allen wants us to go because we are the only officers (he says) that he can fully rely upon or that can possibly answer his purpose. Whilst Genl Walker says that we are so essentially important to the Confederate Government both with our Companies and in the Court Martial that he cant possibly dispense with our services. My prospect and hope for getting off this Court have gone glimmering. There are now 70 cases in the Court and since I have been here this time tried on an average, but two per week. If we could dispose of one per day and have no more to accumulate it would take 70 days to clean up the docket but they are accumulating rapidly. When I came here two weeks ago there were 12 cases. 3 have been disposed of & 70 now remain. So I am here stuck and the only hope I now have to get off is for the Yankees to come and break up the lay out. I cant surprise you now. When I can do so the Lord knows and as he has quit communicating with me I suppose he will not tell me and therefore you will have to excuse me for not telling you. I am sorry to hear that you have lost your horse and hope that you may yet find him. Buy you another. Get Higgins or Dr Wilkins to buy one for you. On the money question do what you think is best but always keep enough on hand to prevent your suffering, to buy clothing & provisions and to educate the children. I want them attended to as well as if they were mine. So therefore dont neglect their comfort, pleasure or improvement. If I keep well I can make plenty of money so I want no stinting of either yourself or my children. I may send you some money by Col Allen who starts home on tuesday next. I cant find anything here to invest money in. Every thing here is enormously high. I have some surplus money on hand that I saved to come home on. Now I dont need it and will send it to you. Dont press the collection of your debts now — let them stand for the present. If any body offers to pay however dont refuse. We have staked our all on the issue of the Confederacy and lets sink or swim with it. Whilst this is the case I think that others besides us might bear a part in it and not force it upon the Soldiers widow. Let them therefore keep their Confederate money and bear their part of the losses if losses there must be. Since I wrote to you I have met a number of my old Tennessee friends who live here and hereabouts. Anthony Rodgers, Peter

Rodgers, Joseph Rodgers, James L. Riggs, Columbus Lee, The Atkins, Capt John Petty's family who by the way are distant relatives of mine, Mrs Sledge alias Williamson, Old Man Thompson who merchandized at Seguin is also here. Besides these old Lang Syne Acquaintances I have made many new and very pleasant ones here and the Lord being willing and no special obstacles being placed in the way I intend to make many more. I am enjoying myself admirably here. I visit the ladies as much as I can with propriety and in their refined society I wear off the rough manners contracted in camp. It was a God send for me to come to Pine Bluff. I had almost forgotten how to demean myself in the presence of the ladies. I had been so long out of their society and in that of other men like myself that I had nearly forgotten that I was a citizen, that I had a wife and children at home and that I would have to return and associate with them and communicate my manners etc to them but now since my association here with ladies of refinement and good standing (and I have and will not associate with any other sort if I know it) I feel that my sentiments are more elevated, my taste more refined — my moral atmosphere more pure and holy. I realize to the fullest extent that I am still as I ever have been and ever hope to be a gentleman of the first water. My appreciation of my wife and children is more vivid and deep and I know that I can return to you without either mental or moral deterioration. I have no news. Multiplied kisses to my brats & respects to friends. Yours etc

E. P. Petty

Pine Bluff Ark Sunday Night 10 Oclock
April 19th 1863

Dear Wife

Col Allen will start home in the morning so I have concluded to finish my letter to night & send it by him. I have no additional news to write. The health of this command still improves. Mine was never finer in my life. The business of our Court Martial is rapidly increasing so that it looks like it might become permanant. It has already been too permanant for my good. If it had not have been for the Court Martial I believe that I should have started home with Col Allen on tomorrow. While it has been a great pleasure to me in this case it has proved the most detrimental and has robbed me of my greatest happiness that is in visiting my own sweet wife and loveing children. If I can possibly get out of the Court I intend to ask for furlough but this is a very doubtful road to travel. I have just heard of Jim Gatlin. He lives about 30 miles above here. I intend to write to him to come and see me. When we were encamped on Bayou Metre we were in about 3 miles of Jim's farm. He is rich and doing well. I hope to see him soon.

I send in this letter one hundred two dollar bills making two hundred dollars. I have some three hundred dollars left which I will keep for emergencies. They pay me up every two months — I have been paid up to 1st April. I want you to have the money. I dont know what may become of me. A soldiers fate is uncertain. I may like Darnells men take a trip Chicago or elsewhere.[132] Then my money will be of no service to me and you would loose the benefit of it. If I need any more here I can borrow it and draw on you. I wrote to you that Flemming had paid me the amount of his note. So give Mrs F. the note so that she can destroy it and write to Lt F. Remember me kindly to friends — God bless & preserve you all for my future pleasure and happiness and also for yours.

Truly yours
E. P. Petty

[1] Houston *Tri-Weekly Telegraph*, March 26, 1862. Allen's card was dated Bastrop, March 19, 1862.

[2] Compiled Service Record of E. P. Petty, National Archives, Washington, D.C.

[3] Election Returns from Captain E. P. Petty's Company for Field Officers — Regt Organized at Camp Terry Near Austin, June 9, 1862, Confederate Muster Rolls, No. 1557, Texas State Archives, Austin, Texas.

[4] Muster Roll of Capt. E. P. Petty's Company "F," Colonel R. T. P. Allen's Regiment Texas Volunteer Infantry, Camp Terry, June 7, 1862, Confederate Muster Rolls, No. 1557, Texas State Archives, Austin, Texas.

[5] Judah P. Benjamin to Paul O. Hébert, February 24, 1862; Hébert to George W. Randolph, April 19, 1862; Robert E. Lee to Hébert, May 26, 1862; Hébert to Henry H. Sibley, August 8, 1862, *Official Records Armies*, series I, IX, pp. 700, 707, 713, 729–30.

[6] Colonel Thomas L. Snead, "The Conquest of Arkansas," in *Battles and Leaders of the Civil War*, 4 vols., ed. Robert Underwood Johnson and Clarence Clough Buel (New York: Thomas Yoseloff, 1956), III, pp. 441–45 (hereafter cited as Snead, "Conquest of Arkansas"); Michael B. Dougan, *Confederate Arkansas: The People and Policies of a Frontier State in Wartime* (University: University of Alabama Press, 1976), pp. 90–94 (hereafter cited as Dougan, *Confederate Arkansas*).

[7] The precise location of Camp Texas is unknown. Windsor, *Texas in the Confederacy*, p. 35.

[8] Captain Robert D. Allen, Company A, Seventeenth Texas Infantry.

[9] Disease did not wait long to strike the soldiers; and its initial onslaughts were the most devastating. During the early months of the army it was not uncommon for half the men of a regiment to be sick at the same time, and frequently the ratio was higher. "Most of the men who wore the gray were from the country, and this helps explain much of the sickness which plagued the Confederates," wrote Bell I. Wiley. "The country boys were tough, but they had not been immunized to the diseases common to children of towns and cities. Consequently they were besieged with these illnesses when they went to the army, while their city comrades of softer constitutions enjoyed comparatively good health. Pertinent also was the fact that townsmen knew better how to take care of themselves than the rustics did." Wiley, *Life of Johnny Reb*, p. 246.

[10] In the Seven Days Battle (June 25–July 1, 1862) Robert E. Lee's Army of Northern Virginia forced the Federal Army of the Potomac under George B. McClellan to retreat from in front of Richmond to the protection of gunboats on the

James River. In the North McClellan and his army were the subject of agitated controversy. Southerners rejoiced that Richmond had been held, when earlier its fall had appeared imminent. It is not known what "good news" had been received from Arkansas.

[11] Captain S. J. P. McDowell, Company K, Seventeenth Texas Infantry.

[12] Captain J. Z. Miller, Company B, Seventeenth Texas Infantry.

[13] Captain Hillery M. Bouldin, Company I, Seventeenth Texas Infantry.

[14] Captain C. C. Arnett, Company G, Seventeenth Texas Infantry.

[15] Captain Hillary H. Ryan, Company D, Seventeenth Texas Infantry.

[16] On August 3 McClellan, without being actually removed from command, was ordered to embark his army at Harrison's Landing on the James River for Aquia Creek on the Potomac. He was then to join the rash and boastful John Pope, whose Army of Virginia lay along the Rappahannock River with its principal base at Manassas. No greater blunder could have been made. By a single stroke the pressure on Richmond was removed and McClellan's army tied up in an operation that would last a month. Lee turned his attention to Pope, whom he completely outmaneuvered by sending Thomas J. "Stonewall" Jackson to his rear to destroy his supplies at Manassas and then defeated in the second battle of Bull Run or Manassas, August 29–30. The rout of the Federal army was almost as complete as at the first battle of Bull Run or Manassas the year before.

[17] The rumor was false. On June 27, 1862, General Braxton Bragg relieved Beauregard as commander of the Confederate Army of Tennessee. In late August he launched an invasion of Kentucky. Buell, commanding the Federal Army of the Cumberland, was forced to evacuate central Tennessee and retreat in haste in order to save Louisville.

[18] "Very early in the conflict the most fantastic tales began to pervade the Confederacy," Bell I. Wiley stated. "Robert M. Gill wrote to his wife Bettie from Louisville, Kentucky, on April 29, 1861, in all seriousness. 'It is reported by a gentleman here just from Washington City that Abe Lincoln had been drunk for thirty six hours & was still drunk when he left.' And throughout the war rumors of even more extravagant proportions from sources considered wholly reliable were accepted without question by campfire idlers and passed on with enriched detail and growing inaccuracy: General Kirby Smith in possesson of Cincinnati; Lincoln and his whole cabinet captured by Jeb Stuart; General Grant killed; General Beauregard accompanied on the march by 'a train of Concubines & wagon loads of champaigne'; the Confederacy recognized by England and France; peace to be concluded in six weeks." Wiley, *Life of Johnny Reb*, p. 169.

[19] Lee now decided that the time had come to carry the war into the enemy's territory, and early in September he crossed the Potomac River into Maryland. He had no intention of attacking Washington but meant rather to cut some of the important railroad connections between the East and the West, rally Maryland to the Confederate cause and then invade Pennsylvania. McClellan, who after Pope's debacle resumed command of all the troops around Washington, gave chase. By chance, a copy of Lee's plans for the Maryland campaign, "Special Orders No. 191," fell into McClellan's hands. It was revealed that Lee had sent Stonewall Jackson back across the Potomac to capture Harpers Ferry. If McClellan had been capable of prompt action, he might have won a magnificent victory over the divided Confederates. But his habitual caution gave Lee time to concentrate his army behind

Antietam Creek at Sharpsburg, Maryland. Jackson, after capturing Harpers Ferry and about 12,000 Federals, rejoined the army in time for the bloodiest one-day battle of the war (September 17). It could hardly be said that either side "won," but two days later, Lee crossed back into Virginia unpursued.

[20] In early August Confederate General E. Kirby Smith invaded Kentucky from east Tennessee and won a small but impressive victory at Richmond (August 30). On September 15 Smith appeared before Covington, Kentucky, on the Ohio River across from Cincinnati but retired rapidly.

[21] This rumor was false.

[22] See note 17.

[23] Mollie Evelyn Moore [Davis] is regarded as the first Texan ever to make her living by literary efforts. Born in Alabama in 1844, she moved to Tyler, Texas, with her parents when a child. The family's beautiful home was called "Sylvan Dell." By 1861 she had a poem in nearly every issue of the Houston *Telegraph* and counted numerous admirers. Her two older brothers, Tho. O. Moore and Hartwell Moore, enlisted in the Confederate army — the first named in the Seventh Texas Infantry and the second in the First Texas Infantry of Hood's Texas Brigade. "Mollie E. Moore's patriotism was aroused to the highest pitch by the call to arms and by the stirring scenes around her," wrote Sid S. Johnson. "Her Southern heart leaped in the very exuberance of patriotic ardor. Her pen gave forth verses and songs for the departing soldiers, and this writer remembers well the occasion of her presenting in Tyler a flag to Co. K. of the Third Texas Cavalry and the noble poem she read with such beauty of expression."

In 1874 Miss Moore married Major Thomas E. Davis of Virginia; and they shortly moved to New Orleans, Louisiana, where he became the editor-in-chief of the *Picayune*, and she became an influential literary and social figure. She continued to write poems, novels and children's books with Texan and Southern settings and had a national reputation by the time of her death in 1909. C. W. Wilkinson, "Mollie Evelyn Moore Davis," in Webb, Carroll and Branda, eds., *Handbook of Texas*, I, pp. 470–71; Johnson, *Texans Who Wore the Gray*, pp. 176–78.

[24] Cicero Nash was a first lieutenant in Captain J. Z. Miller's Company B, Seventeenth Texas Infantry.

[25] See note 19.

[26] Unsanitary conditions, poor nutrition and lack of medical understanding made "camp fever" a prevalent cause of death and debilitation in every 19th century war. The "medicine" Petty refers to is likely some purgative containing mercury or other toxic substances, unpleasant in application as well as in effect. Quinine, in contrast, actually has some beneficial effect; it controls the symptoms of malaria ("intermittent fever") and can lower body temperature to break fevers of nonmalarial origin. In generous doses it causes nervousness and irritability, as does caffeine. The handwriting on this letter shows its effects.

[27] See note 19.

[28] According to Thomas L. Connelly, there were other Confederate generals who "rivaled and sometimes surpassed" Robert E. Lee in popularity during the war. "His main competitor for hero status among Confederates was General Thomas Stonewall Jackson. Even after his death Jackson's popularity matched Lee's, and only in the Reconstruction era did Lee surpass him. Before Lee assumed command

of the Army of Northern Virginia, Jackson's success in the Shenandoah Valley campaign had made his name a Southern byword." Thomas L. Connelly, *The Marble Man: Robert E. Lee and His Image in American Society* (New York: Alfred A. Knopf, 1977), p. 18.

[29] Adolph Erhard of Bastrop was the brother of Mrs. Graves and Anton Erhard of Matamoros.

[30] Blue mass is mercury metal, absorbed onto paper shreds or flour and rolled into pills. It was used for many ailments. Mercury is poisonous, a powerful emetic and purgative, and the pills have no other medicinal value.

[31] On September 30, 1862, General Theophilus H. Holmes, commanding the Trans-Mississippi Department, issued the following order: "Brigadier-General McCulloch, with his entire infantry force, Haldeman's and Edgar's batteries, and the cavalry of his division, will move immediately to Devall's [Duval's] Bluff, take post near that place, and report by telegraph to Major-General Hindman for further instructions." Colonel Parsons's cavalry brigade was placed under McCulloch's orders. *Official Records Armies*, series I, XIII, p. 978.

[32] General Samuel R. Curtis pushed the Confederates out of Missouri in February 1862 and defeated Van Dorn's numerically superior force at Pea Ridge, Arkansas, on March 7–8, 1862. For a time he threatened Little Rock but finally withdrew to Helena on the Mississippi, where he arrived on July 13. That autumn he was given command of the Department of the Missouri but had a falling out with Governor William Gamble and was removed by Lincoln in May 1863. He then commanded the Department of Kansas and later that of the Northwest until the end of the war. Ezra J. Warner, *Generals in Blue: Lives of the Union Commanders* (Baton Rouge: Louisiana State University Press, 1964), pp. 107–8 (hereafter cited as Warner, *Generals in Blue*).

[33] As with almost all other collections of Confederate letters, the stationery used by Captain Petty shows a marked deterioration in quality as the war drags on. Although Petty never used any but plain paper and envelopes, many Southerners in 1861 were writing letters on sheets of fancy design, inscribed with warlike emblems and mottos and even some fervidly pro-Southern doggerel verse. As these writing materials ran out with the war's first year, paper of any kind began to be valued at a premium. "In fact," declared Bell Wiley, "the declining fortunes of the Confederacy may be strikingly traced in degeneration of the stationery used by ordinary soldiers." Soldiers and their families were driven increasingly to the expedient of using old wrapping paper, fly pages from books and journals, and even wallpaper as the growing scarcity of standard writing materials, combined with the South's spiraling rate of inflation, boosted the price of a single quire of paper to $5 and "a bunch of envelopes" to $3, this when the pay of a Rebel private was $11 per month.

Although Petty does not make mention of their scarcity, other basic writing materials, too, were in short supply. Ink, according to Wiley was "scarce, pale, and expensive," and, like many other items in the blockaded Confederacy, was often manufactured at home from inferior ingredients. Polk berries and oak galls were common ingredients for ersatz Rebel ink.

Pens and pen staffs, too, were increasingly hard to come by as the war progressed, with Southern letter writers making use of quills made of goose or turkey feathers or pieces of cane. One enterprising Texas soldier learned to write home with a corn-stalk pen. "When it wont write on one Side I turn it over on the other. pen points are worth a dollar a peace," he commented, and "Scarce at that." Wiley, *Life of Johnny Reb*, pp. 194–96.

[34] Miss Nicholson, later Mrs. William McDowall, was for a long time a popular teacher and social figure in Bastrop. Her unpublished memoirs, "A Little Journey through Memory's Halls," furnish a good deal of information about other townspeople mentioned in these letters. Margaret Belle Jones, comp., *Bastrop: A Compilation of Material Relating to the History of the Town of Bastrop With Letters Written by Terry Rangers* (Bastrop, 1936), pp. 28–32.

[35] Privates Paschal R. Turner and R. M. (Rhem, Rheum) Castleman, both from Bastrop County, belonged to Captain H. S. Morgan's company of the Eighteenth Texas Cavalry Regiment, commanded by Nicholas H. Darnell.

[36] In early October 1862 about 25,000 Texas and Arkansas troops of all arms, "the bone and sinew of Texas and Arkansas, all dressed in their home-spun suits," assembled at Clarendon Heights on the White River in mud and water knee-deep to oppose a rumored Federal advance; but, according to Private J. P. Blessington of the Sixteenth Texas Infantry, "with the exception of some of Colonel Parson's Cavalry stampeding and giving a false alarm, there was no enemy nearer to us than the garrison at Helena, on the Mississippi River, some fifty miles distant." On the morning of October 9 the concentration broke up, with Henry McCulloch's and Allison Nelson's troops returning to Little Rock and General Thomas J. Churchill's brigade of Arkansans and Colonel Robert Garland's brigade of Texans ordered to Arkansas Post. [J. P. Blessington,] *The Campaigns of Walker's Texas Division. By a Private Soldier* (New York: Lange, Little & Co., Printers, 1875), pp. 40–42 (hereafter cited as Blessington, *Walker's Texas Division*). Ironically, Brigadier General Eugene A. Carr, the Federal commander at Helena, was expecting a Confederate attack: "If we should be attacked by an overwhelming force coming through the hills the gunboats could be of no great assistance to us, and the carnage would be great," he advised Curtis. "All the soldiers that are available are constantly at work on the fort, but there is no prospect of finishing it in a week." Eugene A. Carr to Samuel R. Curtis, October 12, 1862, *Official Records Armies*, series I, XIII, pp. 314–15.

[37] General Theophilus H. Holmes, the new commander of the Trans-Mississippi Department, reached Little Rock on August 12, 1862. He ordered General Thomas C. Hindman to concentrate the greater part of the Confederate troops in Arkansas near Fort Smith on the western border of the state and to organize an expedition into Missouri. Hindman assumed command of the 9,000 to 10,000 troops in northwestern Arkansas on August 24. With this force he moved to the Missouri border and took position along the line between that state and Arkansas. On September 10 Hindman was recalled to Little Rock to help organize the troops in that neighborhood for his expedition. In his absence Federal General John M. Schofield advanced with his "Army of the Frontier," driving the Confederates before him into the mountains of Arkansas. Hindman returned to Fort Smith on October 15 and was about to take a strong position near Fayetteville, where reinforcements were hastening to him, when Schofield again advanced. Hindman hastily retreated to the Arkansas River, where he wrote Holmes that with another division he could "move into Missouri, take Springfield, and winter on the Osage at least." On October 21 President Davis wrote Holmes of tentative plans to have Confederate armies join together to drive the Federals from Tennessee and Arkansas and recapture Helena, Memphis and Nashville. Schofield, having accomplished the object of his expedition, returned to Missouri with two divisions, leaving Kansan James Blunt with another division in the vicinity of Fayetteville to guard the mountain passes. On November 20 he turned over command of the Army of the Frontier to Blunt and went to St. Louis. Snead, "The Conquest of Arkansas," pp. 446–47; E. B.

Long with Barbara Long, *The Civil War Day by Day: An Almanac, 1861–1865* (Garden City: Doubleday & Company, Inc., 1971), p. 280 (hereafter cited as Long, *Civil War Day by Day*).

[38] On October 3 Confederates under Earl Van Dorn and Sterling Price attacked William S. Rosecrans's Federals from northwest of Corinth, Mississippi. After heavy fighting and piecemeal assaults the Federals were driven into strong redoubts closer to the city. At nightfall the issue was still in doubt. The next day the Confederates renewed their heavy attacks against the well-posted Federals. They were eventually repulsed and withdrew in the early afternoon. Federal losses were 2,520 out of about 23,000 effectives; Confederates, 4,233 out of probably 22,000 total troops. The Southerners succeeded in taking some of the pressure off Bragg in Kentucky by preventing reinforcements being sent to Buell, but they failed to capture a strategic rail and road center or to smash Rosecrans and thus force Grant back toward the Ohio. Long, *Civil War Day by Day*, pp. 274–75.

The battle of Perryville, Kentucky, was fought on October 8, 1862. Bragg yielded the field to the Federals, but Buell lost the opportunity for a significant victory by following too slowly. Bragg retreated into east Tennessee, leaving his dead and wounded on the field. Thus two major Confederate thrusts north had been halted and pushed back.

[39] Alexander Watkins Terrell was born in Patrick County, Virginia, on November 23, 1827. He came to Texas from Missouri in 1852 and practiced law at Austin with Andrew Jackson Hamilton before becoming judge of the Second District Court in 1857. Commissioned a major in the First Texas Cavalry Regiment, Arizona Brigade, he later commanded Terrell's Texas Cavalry Regiment. General E. Kirby Smith promoted Terrell to brigadier general on May 16, 1865. After the war Terrell fled to Mexico, where he served with the French forces of Emperor Maximilian as "Chief of Battalion." He then returned to Texas and had a distinguished career as a Texas legislator between 1875 and 1893. He served as American minister to Mexico, 1893–1897. Terrell died on September 8, 1912, at Mineral Springs. Wright, comp., *Texas in the War*, pp. 93–94n.

[40] Texas soldiers generally expressed great contempt for Arkansas and her people. The Bellville *Countryman* published the following anecdote to illustrate this contempt: "Some time since two soldiers belonging to a Texas regiment in that State, were discussing the probabilities of a much longer continuance of the war, one of them remarked that he knew the reason the war did not end. 'Well,' said he, 'Jeff Davis wants Lincoln to take Arkansas, and Lincoln isn't willing to take the State as a gift, he'd rather fight about it first.'" Bellville *Countryman*, January 3, 1863.

[41] Andrew Jackson Hamilton was born in Huntsville, Alabama, on January 28, 1815. He was admitted to the bar in Talladega, Alabama, in 1841. He moved to La Grange, Texas, in 1846. In 1849 Governor Peter Hansborough Bell appointed him attorney general of Texas. Hamilton practiced law in Austin with Alexander Watkins Terrell and was a member of the Texas House of Representatives in 1851 and 1853; in 1856 he was an elector on the Democratic ticket. He served in the Thirty-sixth Congress and sided with Sam Houston in opposition to secession. Upon his return from Washington he was elected to the legislature on a Union ticket but refused to take his seat under the Confederacy. He fled to New Orleans in 1862 and then to Washington. Lincoln appointed him military governor of Texas with orders to reestablish Federal authority in the state. However, the Federals failed to win control of the state, and Hamilton did not exercise any functions of his office. In April 1863 he addressed a war meeting at Faneuil Hall, Boston, and the following year issued from New Orleans an address to the people of Texas urging them to lay down their arms and withdraw from the Confederacy.

President Andrew Johnson appointed Hamilton provisional governor of Texas in July 1865, and although he later broke with Johnson to become a Republican he was regarded as a conservative on racial questions. In 1866 James W. Throckmorton defeated him for governor. Hamilton resumed his law practice, and in 1866 was appointed associate justice of the Texas Supreme Court. That year he was a delegate to the Loyalist Convention in Philadelphia and to the Republican National Convention in 1868. He ran for governor in 1869 on the Conservative ticket but was narrowly defeated by E. J. Davis. Poor health caused his retirement from public life. He died in Austin on April 11, 1875. "Andrew Jackson Hamilton," in Webb, Carroll and Branda, eds., *Handbook of Texas*, I, p. 759; Kenneth B. Shover, "Andrew Jackson Hamilton," in Roller and Twyman, eds., *Encyclopedia of Southern History*, p. 568.

[42] This rumor was false.

[43] On October 4 Federal naval forces under Commander William B. Renshaw in *Westfield*, including the steamers *Harriet Lane*, *Owasco* and *Clifton* and the mortar schooner *Henry James*, bombarded and captured Galveston, meeting only feeble resistance. Renshaw reported: "The guns of a formidable-looking battery on Pelican Island, from which we anticipated a heavy fire proved to be 'quakers' [wooden guns], and the bursting of an XI-inch shell from *Owasco* over their heavy X-inch columbiad, mounted on Fort Point, causing a panic in the fort, will account for the ease with which this important capture has been made." The Confederate defenders were commanded by Colonel Joseph J. Cook; they withdrew under a truce agreement to the mainland in order to protect property and lives in Galveston and because there was no particular advantage in staying on the island as long as the bay was occupied by superior Federal warships. Inasmuch as Renshaw had warned that "[he] would hoist the United States flag over the city of Galveston or over its ashes," the defenders had little choice but to withdraw. However, Renshaw had no force to put ashore to consolidate his gains, and his control of Galveston was tacit rather than actual. Rear Admiral David G. Farragut, commanding the West Gulf Squadron, wrote Secretary of the Navy Gideon Welles on October 15: "I am happy to inform you that Galveston, Corpus Christi, and Sabine City and the adjacent waters are now in our possession. . . . All we want, as I have told the Department in my last dispatches, is a few soldiers to hold the places, and we will soon have the whole coast." William B. Renshaw to David G. Farragut, October 5, 1862, *Official Records Navies*, series I, XIX, pp. 254–55; Farragut to Gideon B. Welles, October 15,

1862, *ibid.*, pp. 253–54; *Civil War Naval Chronology*, pt. II, pp. 100–1; Charles C. Cumberland, "The Confederate Loss and Recapture of Galveston, 1862–1863," *Southwestern Historical Quarterly*, LI (October 1947), pp. 110–15 (hereafter cited as Cumberland, "Confederate Loss and Recapture of Galveston").

⁴⁴Cassius Marcellus Clay was a truculent Kentucky abolitionist and Republican politician. In 1862 he was recalled as minister to Russia and was made a temporary major general of volunteers, but he refused to fight until the government should abolish slavery in the seceded states. "I shall strike only for liberty, and will never draw the sword for the protection of rebels' slaves," he defiantly declared. Clay returned to Kentucky in the fall of 1862 on a mission to the legislature but was temporarily diverted into military service during the Confederate invasion of the state. He did no fighting. Clay left for Russia again in 1863 where he remained until 1869. On Clay, see David L. Smiley, *Lion of White Hall: The Life of Cassius M. Clay* (Madison: University of Wisconsin Press, 1962).

The Bellville *Countryman* carried the following news item in its edition of November 8, 1862: "Jack Hamilton is said to have received the appointment from Lincoln of Military Governor of Texas, with his capitol at Galveston. Cassius M. Clay is to command the military forces. We may therefore anticipate that Texas will be invaded this winter for Jackson has given them full information concerning the condition of our State." However, Smiley doesn't mention any plan to send Clay to Texas.

⁴⁵On October 28, 1862, Secretary of War Edwin Stanton sent a confidential dispatch to the governors of New York and the New England states announcing that General Nathaniel P. Banks "has established his headquarters in New York to organize a Southern expedition." It was the government's intention that he should make a landing on the coast of Texas, but early in November there occurred a sudden shift in administration policy. On the 8th Banks was given command of the Department of the Gulf, superseding Ben Butler, and was told that Lincoln "regards the opening of the Mississippi River as the first and most important of all our military and naval operations and it is hoped that you will not lose a moment in accomplishing it." After this had been done other operations might be considered, such as breaking up the railroads at Jackson and Marion, Mississippi, or an expedition up the Red River to secure the cotton and sugar of that area and to establish a base for an advance on Texas. Ludwell H. Johnson, *Red River Campaign: Politics and Cotton in the Civil War* (Baltimore: Johns Hopkins Press, 1958), pp. 19–22 (hereafter cited as Johnson, *Red River Campaign*).

⁴⁶In October 1862 Brigadier General Henry E. McCulloch was ordered to organize the Texas infantry then assembled at Camp Nelson, near Austin, Arkansas, into a division of four brigades. A battery of light artillery was attached to each brigade. The division was officially known as McCulloch's Division, until Major General John G. Walker took command, when it assumed the name of Walker's Texas Division, and was known by that name until the end of the war. The Fourth Brigade, commanded by Colonel James Deshler, was detached from the division shortly after its organization and sent to Arkansas Post. As of December 12, 1862, McCulloch's Division was the First Division, Second Corps, Army of the Trans-Mississippi Department, and was composed as follows:

First Brigade, Col. Overton Young
12th Texas, Col. Overton Young (Lt. Col. Benjamin A. Phillpot)
18th Texas, Col. William B. Ochiltree
22d Texas, Col. Richard B. Hubbard

13th Texas Cavalry (dismounted), Col. John H. Burnett
Haldeman's Battery, Capt. Horace Haldeman

Second Brigade, Col. Horace Randal
11th Texas, Col. Oran M. Roberts
14th Texas, Col. Edward Clark
15th Texas, Col. Joseph W. Speight
28th Texas Cavalry (dismounted), Col. Horace Randal (Lt. Col. Eli H. Baxter Jr.)
Gould's Sixth Texas Cavalry Battalion (dismounted), Maj. Robert Gould
Daniel's Battery, Capt. James M. Daniel

Third Brigade, Col. George Flournoy
16th Texas, Col. George Flournoy (Lt. Col. James E. Shepard)
17th Texas, Col. Robert T. P. Allen
19th Texas, Col. Richard Waterhouse
16th Texas Cavalry (dismounted), Col. William Fitzhugh
Edgar's Battery, Capt. William Edgar

Official Records Armies, series I, XXII, pt. 1, pp. 903–4; Blessington, *Walker's Texas Division*, pp. 45–59.

[47] George M. Flournoy was born in Louisville, Georgia, on November 30, 1832. He attended the University of Georgia and graduated from law school at Tuskegee, Alabama, in 1853. He moved to Austin, Texas, the following year and opened a law practice. He was attorney general of Texas in 1862 but resigned the following year to join the Confederate army. In 1862 he organized the Sixteenth Texas Infantry Regiment. Wright, comp., *Texas in the War*, p. 107n.

[48] On October 11, 1862, a portion of Parsons's Texas Cavalry Brigade, 100 men under Lieutenant Colonel De Witt Giddings of the Twenty-first Texas, had a skirmish with Federal cavalry near the forks of a road eight or nine miles from Helena, Arkansas. General Eugene A. Carr, commanding at Helena, reported "the loss of several men killed and Major [Benjamin] Rector, with about 30 missing, the killing of several of the enemy, and the capture of a lieutenant colonel [Giddings], and 12 other Texans." Eugene A. Carr to Samuel R. Curtis, October 12, 1862, *Official Records Armies*, series I, XIII, pp. 314–15.

Henry Orr of the Twelfth Texas in Parsons's Brigade gave a Confederate view of the skirmish in a letter to his sister Mary: "The day the command left for the Bluff, Col. Giddings with 100 men started on a scout towards Helena. They attacked about the same number of Feds in the vicinity of Helena, several days ago, and were thrashing them badly when a reinforcement came in to their rear, and they had to get away. They brought with them, however, 15 prisoners (Iowaians), one of which is a major. It is believed that Col. Giddings was taken prisoner with five soldiers, for when last seen the Feds were in hot pursuit of them. The boys say they killed between 20 and 30 of the Feds and lost not one that they know of, and but two or three slightly wounded. I saw the prisoners. They were a good looking lot; set free to talk and seemed not to care much for being in the hands of the Rebels. They say they are tired of the war." Anderson, ed., *Campaigning with Parsons' Texas Cavalry Brigade, CSA*, p. 80.

[49] Captain Seth Mabry, Company E, Seventeenth Texas Infantry.

[50] During the political campaign of 1840 in Arkansas Sandford (Sandy) C. Faulkner was canvassing the state with three other Democrats. They lost their way and came to the ramshackle hut of a squatter, who played on a three-stringed fid-

dle the first part of a familiar tune, the last part of which he did not know. The squatter was unfriendly until Faulkner played on the old battered fiddle the other half of the tune, which brought about a complete change in the old man's attitude. As the story went, Faulkner was immediately given the only dry spot in the kitchen, feed for his horse and a turn at the whiskey jug.

Returning to Little Rock, Faulkner told the story of "The Arkansas Traveler" in public for the first time, at the barroom of the Anthony House. The dialogue, with its violin accompaniment, soon became a popular favorite. The tune was nationally current by 1845 and in print by 1847; the dialogue was nationally current by 1851 and in print by 1860. "It cannot be definitely established that Faulkner originated either the dialogue or the music," wrote Margaret Smith Ross. "At least three other people have been credited with the authorship of 'The Arkansaw Traveler' or almost identical pieces. . . . It is doubtful if Faulkner himself ever made any statement about it. It was probably enough for him that Arkansans, then as now, took it for granted that he was the original traveler."

When the Civil War broke out Faulkner was appointed Military Storekeeper and served at the Little Rock arsenal until the city was occupied by the Federal army in 1863. He then went to Tyler, Texas, where he remained until the war was over. He died in Little Rock in 1874. Margaret Smith Ross, "Sandford C. Faulkner," *Arkansas Historical Quarterly*, XIV (Winter 1955), pp. 301–14.

[51] "Camp Nelson was located about two miles east of Austin, in a belt of woods skirting the valleys running east and west, shut in by high acclivities," J. P. Blessington stated. "The country here is a succession of high, rock hills, and deep, dark, narrow defiles, surrounded on all sides by these frowning hills. The camp was protected from the cold, piercing, wintry winds; yet it also seemed like imprisoning the men to winter them here, far distant from any communication with friends at home." Blessington, *Walker's Texas Division*, p. 44.

[52] The men of McCulloch's Division long remembered Camp Nelson, because of the severe winter which caused much illness and many deaths. "Dysentery and fevers of various kinds made many victims," Blessington recalled. "The hospital was filled with sick. The sickness was owing a great deal to the impure water we had to use. Fully 1,500 men died at Camp Nelson." B. H. Carroll of Company A, Seventeenth Texas Infantry, stated that the division "lost more men from measles and pneumonia in one winter at Little Rock than in all the battles in which it was engaged." Blessington, *Walker's Texas Division*, p. 44; Miss Mamie Yeary, comp., *Reminiscences of the Boys in Gray, 1861–1865* (Dallas: Press of Wilkinson Printing Company, 1912), p. 124 (hereafter cited as Yeary, comp., *Reminiscences of the Boys in Gray*).

First Lieutenant Edward Cade, a surgeon in Randal's Twenty-eighth Texas Cavalry (dismounted), wrote his wife from Camp Nelson on November 8: "It snowed here 25th Oct. Ice every morning. The Army dying up like rotten sheep. Our regiment dont exceed 150 men fit for duty; balance sick and weak from former sickness . . . ." Eight days later, he wrote: "The army still remains here perfectly inactive. They are now very well fed. Fresh pork, Beef, a little Bacon, potatoes, flour, meat, and molasses and Sugar are regularly issued to the troops. Before this diet was issued their health was very bad. As it is there is hardly an hour in the day but what you hear numbers of volleys that are fired over the graves of poor fellows who have died far away from friends and relatives. Sick men in the army are horribly treated. Men become so selfish they will not wait on their nearest relatives or friends." John Q. Anderson, *A Texas Surgeon in the C.S.A.* (Tuscaloosa: Confederate Publishing Company, Inc., 1957), pp. 25–26 (hereafter cited as Anderson, *A Texas Surgeon*).

[53] Theophilus Hunter Holmes was born in Sampson County, North Carolina, November 13, 1804, and was graduated from West Point in 1829. He resigned from the army April 22, 1861, to cast his lot with the Confederacy. He was successively appointed brigadier general on June 5, 1861, major general on October 7, 1861, and lieutenant general to rank from October 10, 1862. He commanded a brigade at First Manassas and a division during the Seven Days. His poor performance at the division level led to him being exiled to the command of the Trans-Mississippi Department, from which he was ultimately relieved by General Edmund Kirby Smith. Warner, *Generals in Gray*, p. 141.

[54] Although Petty was "spoiling for a fight," other Texas soldiers, going into winter quarters again, with the implication of another season of fighting, expressed feelings of war weariness. One wrote his sister from Arkansas in late November 1862 that he had "enough of Yanks." "I would to God," he added, "that I could do my share of fighting and come home though I see no chance for that." But he consoled himself with the observation, "There is one thing Sure the war cant go on always I will either go up the flew or come home before a grait while." Several weeks later, this soldier wrote another member of his family: "Well Leiza I wish I could tell when this custiard [cursed] war will come to an end. I fear the time is so fare off we will be a ruined people." His brother was even more outspoken. "God speed the day when that time [war's end] shall come," he wrote, "for I am tired of camp life, especially in this country. it is no pleasur to be away from my folks and if this war dont stop before next fall I am coming home you can look for me in twenty days after white frost." Wiley, *Life of Johnny Reb*, p. 130.

[55] Captain H. S. Morgan commanded a company in the Eighteenth Texas Cavalry Regiment (dismounted). The regiment was captured at Arkansas Post, January 11, 1863.

[56] Brigadier General Alvin P. Hovey, the Federal commander at Helena, decided to make "a dash upon the Post of Arkansas" and on November 16 embarked 6,000 infantry and 2,000 cavalry on steamboats. Arriving at the mouth of the White River on the 19th, he landed his cavalry under General Cyrus Bussey on the north side and directed him to proceed to the ferry near Wild Goose Bayou and opposite Prairies Landing. Colonel George F. McGinnis was sent with his Eleventh Indiana Volunteers on the steamboat *Rocket* to destroy a ferry boat at Napoleon used by the Confederates. The fleet began an ascent, but the river fell at least five feet within two days, and the boats could not get over a new bar with only 30 inches of water in the channel. Hovey prepared to march overland but received a letter on the 20th from his chief-of-staff, Colonel Norton P. Chipman, "intimating that other movements might require our forces at another point." Realizing that he could not accomplish his objective in less than eight or ten days, he immediately recalled his cavalry which had reached within eight miles of Arkansas Post and returned to Helena on the night of November 21. "I deeply regret that we could not have been permitted to consumate our plans," Hovey stated in his official report, "as I feel confident that we should have captured the Post, with a large number of prisoners and stores." *Official Records Armies*, series I, XIII, pp. 358–60.

[57] Bayou Metre was about six miles below the railroad from Little Rock to Duval's Bluff on White River, about eight miles from Brownsville and about 20 miles from Austin. (See Petty to Ella, December 3, 1862).

[58] Alone, the great saline at Saltville in southwest Virginia was capable of producing the 300 to 450 million pounds of salt required per year by the Confederacy.

Unfortunately for the states of the lower South, importation of that vital commodity from Virginia, England and the West Indies was most often less expensive than the development of its own sources. Early in the Civil War the Union blockade interdicted the foreign supply, and as Union armies cut deeply into the already strained Southern transportation network, shipments from Virginia became increasingly costly and problematical. To aggravate the situation, speculators and profiteers quickly cornered the principal production sources of the Deep South and created an even greater scarcity by artificial means. Within two years the prewar price of one cent per pound had run up to 25 cents per pound in gold, and with the fall of Vicksburg and Port Hudson in July 1863, the Trans-Mississippi was cut off from all eastern salt at any price.

The arid alkali sections of south and west Texas were dotted with dead lakes from which, during the summer months, salt deposits had merely to be scraped as the waters dried. As the Natchez *Daily Courier* pointed out in September 1861, "There should not be such a hue and cry about the want of salt. There are lakes in Texas (not lately discovered . . .) which will yield almost enough of the article for the consumption of the Southern States." Transportation of salt from west to east Texas, however, presented the same degree of difficulty as transportation from Virginia. The hundreds of miles from the Trans-Pecos region or from the Staked Plains to the settled areas of the state not only traversed deserts, escarpments, hills and forests, but were also the hunting grounds of the fierce Comanche who pushed back the Texas frontier by a hundred miles from 1861 to 1865.

Some salt was produced within the civilized portion of Texas in 1861. In the hill country of central Texas the Falls Creek saline in Llano County yielded 20 to 30 bushels a day, and a spring on the Colorado River in Lampasas County supplied a bushel of weak brine every minute for reduction at Swenson's Saline. Steen and Brooks salines in Smith and Grand Saline in Van Zandt County also produced a weak brine which brought some relief to the people of northeast Texas, but ironically, not until after the war did the citizens of that region learn of the huge deposit of solid rock salt which lay beneath the surface of Van Zandt County.

The wartime output remained too meager to provide all of the salt which Texans needed for seasoning food, tanning hides, dyeing cloth and the all-important function of curing meat in the days before canning and refrigeration. Thus the price of this prime necessity continued to rise for the duration of the war. Pollard, *The Lost Cause*, p. 427; Ella Lonn, *Salt as a Factor in the Confederacy* (Tuscaloosa: University of Alabama Press, 1965), pp. 28–31, 238.

[59] Following the Battle of Wilson's Creek, Missouri, in August 1861, Confederate sympathizers in southern Missouri and northern Arkansas began to flee their homes in large numbers and make their way into Louisiana and Texas. The loss of New Orleans one year later made Louisiana only marginally safer than her northern neighbor as a haven from Union harassment. By the summer of 1863, with the fall of Port Hudson and Vicksburg, the entire eastern and southern portions of the state were subject to be overrun by enemy troops and gunboats. Those who did not wish to live under Federal rule or with the constant fear of enemy raiders were left with only the forlorn option of refugeeing to Texas, a location thought to be "the end of the earth" by most displaced Louisianians. "They believed," says Mary Elizabeth Massey, "that Texas had nothing to offer but heat, dust, wind, reptiles, insects, and uneducated boorish neighbors—nothing else, that is, but safety from the enemy." Most Louisiana and Arkansas refugees settled in the relatively more civilized eastern third of Texas, along the Brazos, the Sabine or the Trinity rivers or along the coast. The towns of Tyler, Rusk, Waco, Marshall and Corsicana were considerably swelled by the influx of refugees. An October 1863 issue of the Marshall newspaper, for example, reported that refugees from Arkansas and Louisiana were "pouring in,"

the roads into town being "lined with them, and the houses filled to their capacities." Mary Elizabeth Massey, *Refugee Life in the Confederacy* (Baton Rouge: Louisiana State University Press, 1964), pp. 90–93.

[60] George G. Rucker was second lieutenant of Company C, Seventeenth Texas Infantry.

[61] James Priest was second lieutenant of the Bastrop Volunteers Infantry, commanded by Captain George Washington Jones. He enlisted in the Confederate army on March 22, 1862, in Bastrop County and was mustered in on March 30, 1862, at Camp Terry. His age was given as 45. Confederate Index, Texas State Archives, Austin, Texas.

[62] Samuel Flemming was mustered in at Camp Terry on March 30, 1862, as a private in Petty's company. Confederate Index, Texas State Archives, Austin, Texas.

[63] During this period McCulloch's Division was reviewed on November 27 by General Holmes. Blessington described the "grand review": "Shortly after our arrival on the parade-ground, General Holmes, accompanied by his respective staff-officers, arrived on the ground from Little Rock. Several carriages, with citizens, accompanied him to witness the review. As he rode rapidly along the line to examine the condition of the troops, the bands struck up the tune of 'Hail to the Chief.' After taking his position, the column passed in review. At the head of the column was General McCulloch and staff, followed by Young's Brigade, then Randall's [Randal's], next Flournoy's, and their respective batteries. This review—the first real review of the Division—presented a dazzling sight. There they are, before you—the columns extending for about two miles marching along with their guns and bayonets glittering in the morning sun, and the gay flags and banners flaunting in the breeze—there they are, infantry and artillery, brigade and regimental commanders, dressed in gorgeous uniforms, and riding prancing steeds richly caparisoned; staff officers gay and sparkling, full of ambition and the hope of winning an honored name." Blessington, *Walker's Texas Division*, p. 62.

[64] On November 25 Holmes reported to Richmond: "At Helena the enemy has a force of 15,000. Last week they made a strong demonstration on my unfinished fortifications at the Post of Arkansas, but on trial their transports drew too much water, and the column they sent by land retired after reaching the White River, opposite. To defend the fortifications I have between 4,000 and 5,000 men, under General Churchill, and to cover Little Rock, I have three brigades at Brownsville, under General McCulloch, and a brigade of cavalry, under General Hawes, on White River, with heavy pickets always near Helena to watch the enemy's movements. The distance to the Post from Brownsville is about 80 miles and my hope is by keeping a close watch near Helena that I will be able to concentrate the two commands to resist an advance. If I leave here there is little doubt the valley of Arkansas will be taken possession of, and with it goes Arkansas and Louisiana, for there is nothing to subsist an army on between Arkansas and Red Rivers, the intermediate region having been depleted by the drought of last year." Theophilus H. Holmes to Samuel Cooper, November 25, 1862, *Official Records Armies*, series I, XIII, pp. 927–28.

[65] Colonel James Deshler's Second Brigade consisted of the Tenth Texas Infantry, Colonel Roger Q. Mills; Fifteenth Texas Cavalry (dismounted), Major Valerius P. Sanders; Seventeenth Texas Cavalry (dismounted), Colonel James R. Taylor; Eighteenth Texas Cavalry (dismounted), "Darnell's," Lieutenant Colonel John T. Coit; and Haldeman's Texas Battery. *Official Records Armies*, series I, XXII, p. 904.

[66] The site of the earliest French settlement in the lower Mississippi Valley, Arkansas Post was founded in 1686 by Henri de Tonti. Ceded to the United States by the Louisiana Purchase of 1803, it became the first capital (1819–1820) of the Arkansas Territory. Fort Hindman was built near the small village and was named for Major General Thomas C. Hindman, an Arkansas resident.

[67] Francis Richard Lubbock, a Houston businessman who had served as lieutenant governor during H. R. Runnels's administration, was a delegate to the Democratic National Convention at Charleston in 1860 and later favored secession. In August 1861 he was elected governor on a platform declaring for unstinting support of the Confederacy in the prosecution of the war. Lubbock defeated Edward Clark, the incumbent, by only 124 votes, 21,854 to 21,730. T. J. Chambers was in third place with 13,759. Before his inauguration Lubbock went to Richmond to confer with President Davis as to how Texas could best serve the Southern cause. As governor he did all in his power to place the whole state's strength behind the Confederacy. He succeeded in this effort to such an extent that within 15 months 68,500 Texans were under arms. Seth Shepard McKay, "Francis Richard Lubbock," in Webb, Carroll and Branda, eds., *Handbook of Texas*, II, p. 89; Ernest Wallace, *Texas in Turmoil, 1849–1875* (Austin: Steck-Vaughn Company, 1965), pp. 116–17; Herbert P. Gambrell and Lewis W. Newton, *A Social and Political History of Texas*, rev. ed. (Dallas: Turner Company, 1935), p. 292; Lubbock, *Six Decades in Texas*, pp. 326–27, 471.

[68] Van Dorn and Price's disastrous defeat at Corinth in October 1862 opened the way to Grant to move overland against Vicksburg, the Confederate bastion on the Mississippi. Leaving Grand Junction on November 4, Grant advanced toward Holly Springs, Van Dorn falling back before him. At the same time General John McClernand was concentrating a large Federal force at Memphis to move on Vicksburg by the river. Alarmed by these movements, the Confederate government instructed Holmes on November 11 to send 10,000 men to Vicksburg if possible. Holmes, on receiving this order, directed Thomas Hindman to abandon his projected invasion of Missouri from northwest Arkansas and return to Little Rock without delay. Instead, Hindman made up his mind to attack General James Blunt

in the vicinity of Fayetteville before obeying Holmes's order. He had already sent John S. Marmaduke toward Cane Hill with a division of cavalry. On November 28 Blunt attacked Marmaduke at Cane Hill and drove him back to the vicinity of Van Buren with considerable loss, giving the Federals a momentary edge. Blunt then took position at Cane Hill. Hindman resolved to attack him there with his whole available force. Snead, "Conquest of Arkansas," pp. 448–49.

[69] This news was a little premature. It was not until December 21, 1862, that three companies of the Forty-second Massachusetts Volunteer Regiment, 260 men under the command of Colonel I. S. Burrell, left New Orleans for Galveston; the remainder of the regiment, totaling approximately 1,000 men, were to follow within a few days. This first contingent arrived on December 25 and was immediately put ashore, taking up positions and quarters on one of the wharfs at Renshaw's recommendation. Cumberland, "Confederate Loss and Recapture of Galveston," p. 118.

[70] Holmes ordered McCulloch to hold his division in readiness to move to Vicksburg. Blessington, *Walker's Texas Division*, p. 63.

[71] John C. Pemberton, a native of Pennsylvania and a West Point graduate (class of 1837), who had been in command of the Department of South Carolina, Georgia and Florida, was promoted to lieutenant general ranking from October 10, 1862, and assigned to the command of the Department of Mississippi and Eastern Louisiana, an area which included Vicksburg. Warner, *Generals in Gray*, pp. 232–33.

[72] In a confusing battle at Prairie Grove (December 7), about 12 miles southwest of Fayetteville, Arkansas, on Illinois Creek, Confederates under Thomas C. Hindman attacked Federal forces under James Blunt and Francis J. Herron. Herron had been ordered to Blunt's support with two divisions of the Army of the Frontier. Hindman, advancing from Van Buren on December 3, attempted to defeat the two Federal units separately, but they managed to join after Herron's men made a hard march from Wilson's Creek, Missouri. The Confederates held their position, but bitter winter weather forced them to withdraw during the night. Blunt did not pursue. The Federals maintained control of northwest Arkansas. Federal casualties were reported as 1,251 out of an estimated 10,000 troops; Confederate losses were put at 1,317, also out of about 10,000 men. Long, *Civil War Day by Day*, p. 293.

Hindman sheltered his demoralized army behind the Arkansas River, opposite Van Buren, and tried to reorganize it. On December 28 Blunt dashed into Van Buren at the head of a small cavalry force and hastened the long-projected Confederate retreat to Little Rock, which was reached about the middle of January 1863. "During the long and dreary march thither the troops, who were not clad to withstand the snows and rains of winter, suffered severely," wrote Colonel Thomas L. Snead. "Sickness increased alarmingly; the men straggled at will; hundreds deserted; and Hindman's army faded away." "Several of Hindman's men froze to death and hundreds of mules," a Texas cavalryman wrote his wife. "Hindman's men is deserting every day they are here at Little Rock. They say twenty or thirty hundred has deserted since they left Fort Smith in coming down here." Snead, "Conquest of Arkansas," pp. 449–50; Ray, ed., "Civil War Letters from Parsons' Texas Cavalry Brigade," p. 219.

[73] On the morning of December 13 McCulloch's Division took up the line of march to Vicksburg, going 18 miles. After the arrival in camp a courier came in with dispatches from Holmes, countermanding the Vicksburg march and ordering the division to march to Van Buren. "Marched eight miles, through mud and water," J. P. Blessington grumbled in his diary on December 14. "The 'iron horse' on

the Memphis and Little Rock Railroad blew his whistle, as much to say: if we came to Arkansas with the expectation of riding on railroads we would find ourselves mistaken." Blessington, *Walker's Texas Division*, p. 63.

[74] One of the ways declining morale manifested itself was the evading of duty by feigning sickness. This subterfuge, referred to as "playing old soldier" by Rebs, made its appearance early in the war, as Surgeon Edward Cade discovered: "Great many are making efforts to get out of the service. Tomorrow I have [been] appointed to examine cases for furloughs and discharges and I suppose there are no less than a hundred who wish to go. There will not be more than ten though that I will recommend. Numbers are feigning to be exceedingly bad for that purpose. I have Surgeon calls at 6 o'clock every morning at which time the orderly sergeants of companies bring up their sick to me and every morning I order at last 20 on duty who are pretending to be sick." Anderson, *A Texas Surgeon*, p. 37.

[75] McCulloch's Division marched 19 miles on December 15. After getting about four miles above Little Rock the route of march was again countermanded. The division was ordered to camp nearly opposite Little Rock. On the evening of the 16th Speight's Regiment was ordered to the Indian Nation. Blessington, *Walker's Texas Division*, p. 64.

[76] John Bankhead Magruder, "Prince John" to all his acquaintances, was born at Port Royal, Virginia, May 1, 1807, and graduated from West Point in 1830. He was three times brevetted for gallant and meritorious conduct in the Mexican War as an artillerist. Appointed brigadier general in the Confederate army on June 17, 1861, and major general on October 7, Magruder distinguished himself in the early stages of the Peninsular Campaign, deceiving McClellan as to the true size of his small force at Yorktown. "He is handsome, perfectly uniformed, insistent, impatient and theatrical, and he always appears at a gallop," Douglas Southall Freeman wrote of Magruder. "Despite a slight lisp, he loves to talk and he writes ceaselessly to his superiors. A certain aptitude for independent command he possesses, and with it ability to bluff an adversary." On October 10 he was assigned to the District of Texas, New Mexico and Arizona, and took command on November 29. Warner, *Generals in Gray*, pp. 207–8; Douglas Southall Freeman, *Lee's Lieutenants: A Study in Command*, 3 vols. (New York: Charles Scribner's Sons, 1942), I, p. xxxiv.

[77] See note 72.

[78] "We remained encamped opposite Little Rock long enough to spend Christmas, and anything but a merry Christmas," Blessington remembered. "Many of us had intended to keep Christmas somewhat after the manner of our home style, but we could purchase neither eggs nor whiskey in Little Rock, to make an egg-nog. We were, therefore, compelled to make our Christmas dinner of a piece of corn bread and some blue beef. On Christmas night the citizens of Little Rock could witness fully 15,000 camp-fires, that glowed and sparkled like the gaslights of a city." Blessington, *Walker's Texas Division*, p. 64.

[79] On December 26 the division left camp at sunrise, recrossed the Arkansas River at Little Rock and encamped three miles from town on the Pine Bluff Road. In the evening an order from Holmes, dated December 23, was read on "dress-parade" to each regiment assigning Major General John G. Walker to command the Texas Division and McCulloch to command Flournoy's Brigade. The division was to move "without delay, and take post at Pine Bluff." Blessington, *Walker's Texas Division*, pp. 64–65. The original of Holmes's "Special Orders No. 121" is in the John G. Walker Papers, Southern Historical Collection, University of North Carolina at Chapel Hill (hereafter cited as Walker Papers).

[80] John G. Walker was born in Cole County, Missouri, July 22, 1822, and received his early education at the Jesuit College in St. Louis. Commissioned directly into the army in 1846, he served in the Mexican War and achieved the rank of captain by the time he resigned on July 31, 1861, to join the Confederacy. He was commissioned a major of cavalry and, after being appointed lieutenant colonel of the Eighth Texas Cavalry, was made brigadier general on January 9, 1862. His service in the Army of Northern Virginia, including participation in the capture of Harpers Ferry and the battle of Sharpsburg, won him promotion to major general on November 8, 1862. On November 11 he was ordered to proceed to Little Rock and report for duty to Holmes. Warner, *Generals in Gray*, pp. 319–20; John Withers to John G. Walker, November 11, 1862, Walker Papers.

[81] "Rearing Tearing Pitching Allen" was a nickname given the colonel by the cadets at the Bastrop Military Institute.

[82] Theodore A. Supple, first or orderly sergeant in Captain H. M. Bouldin's company, was from Bell County. He enlisted on March 24, 1862, at Belton and was mustered in at Camp Terry on April 11, 1862. He was 35. Confederate Index, Texas State Archives, Austin, Texas.

[83] Petty is referring to the battle of Fredericksburg, Virginia, December 13, 1862. General Ambrose E. Burnside, commanding the Army of the Potomac, threw away his troops in a series of futile, piecemeal frontal attacks against Lee's strong natural position on Marye's Heights. The Federals lost 12,700 killed or wounded. Confederate losses were only 5,300. Burnside wanted to renew the attack the next morning, but his commanders talked him out of it, and after remaining in position astride the Rappahannock River, December 14–15, the army was withdrawn on the night of the 15th. Long, *Civil War Day by Day*, pp. 295–97.

[84] "It was generally believed amongst the troops that General Holmes was advised by the Medical Board to give Walker's Division enough of exercise," wrote J. P. Blessington. "This may be the object of our marching and countermarching between Little Rock and Pine Bluff." Blessington, *Walker's Texas Division*, pp. 67–68.

[85] The Confederate Index in the Texas State Archives lists three men named Gorman in Petty's company: J. H., J. P. and T. W.

[86] Grant's first plan for the capture of Vicksburg envisioned an advance of 40,000 men due south along the Mississippi Central Railroad, combined with a movement by water of 32,000 troops under William Tecumseh Sherman against Chickasaw Bluffs, just a few miles north of Vicksburg. The overland advance was stopped by Van Dorn, who slipped behind Grant with 3,500 cavalrymen and captured his advance supply base at Holly Springs on December 20, 1862. Sherman attempted to storm the Confederate defenses on the bluffs on December 29 but was bloodily repulsed. On January 2, 1863, he dropped down to the mouth of the Yazoo River, where John McClernand, a former Illinois congressman, arrived and assumed command.

In the meantime William S. Rosecrans, who had succeeded Don Carlos Buell after the battle of Perryville, moved out of Nashville to attack Braxton Bragg's Army of Tennessee. At the desperate and bloody battle of Murfreesboro or Stones River, fought on the last day of 1862 and the first two days of 1863, the Confederates successfully halted the Federal advance. It was a tactical victory for the South, but Bragg lacked the strength to destroy Rosecrans's army or drive it from the field. On the night of January 3–4 Bragg withdrew toward Shelbyville. Rosecrans did not pursue. It was not until June 1863 that the Federals renewed operations in this area.

[87] McClernand arrived at Milliken's Bend on January 3, 1863, and the next day assumed command of Sherman's troops. He determined to capture Arkansas Post, which threatened Federal supply lines on the Mississippi River. On January 4 he embarked 32,000 men on transports and steamed for the Arkansas River, accompanied by Acting Rear Admiral David Dixon Porter's fleet of three ironclads and six gunboats. Reaching the vicinity of the Post on the 9th, he disembarked his men the next day. The garrison consisted of about 5,000 men under the command of Brigadier General Thomas J. Churchill. The fleet attacked Fort Hindman on the evening of January 10. The attack was renewed the next day by both army and navy; after a terrific bombardment the fort's guns were silenced, and shortly thereafter the white flag was raised. McClernand reported his casualties as 134 killed, 898 wounded and 29 missing — a total of 1,061. Churchill's incomplete return listed the dead as not exceeding 60, with 75 or 80 wounded. Confederate prisoners numbered 4,791. *Official Records Armies*, series I, XVII, pt. 1, pp. 708, 716–19, 782. One historian called the Federal losses "a striking illustration of the difficulty of storming fortifications even under the most favorable circumstances." John Fiske, *The Mississippi Valley in the Civil War* (Boston: Houghton Mifflin and Company, 1900), p. 206.

[88] Captain X. B. Saunders, Company A, Sixteenth Texas Infantry Regiment.

[89] Blessington reported the episode as follows: "At this camp [five miles west of Pine Bluff] the division was formed in line of battle to witness three soldiers belonging to McCulloch's Brigade, drummed out of camp for 'hog-stealing.' The band played 'The Rogue's March' along the line. The three soldiers marched along the entire line, followed by a file of soldiers, with fixed bayonets. This kind of punishment, inaugurated by General McCulloch, seemed to be a novelty to the Texas boys, and it created roars of laughter amongst the troops." Blessington continued with a question to his readers: "Boys, ask yourselves if you were ever guilty of 'hog-stealing' during the late unpleasantness?" Blessington, *Walker's Texas Division*, p. 68.

[90] Churchill gave the following account of the surrender in his official report: "The fort had now been silenced about an hour, most of the field pieces had been disabled, still the fire raged furiously along the entire line, and that gallant band of Texans and Arkansians having nothing to rely upon now save their muskets and bayonets, still disclaimed to yield to the overpowering foe of 50,000 men, who were pressing upon them from almost every direction. Just at this moment, to my great surprise, several white flags were displayed in the Twenty-fourth Regiment Texas Dismounted Cavalry, First Brigade, and before they could be suppressed the enemy took advantage of them, crowded upon my lines, and not being prevented by the brigade commander [Robert Garland] from crossing, as was his duty, I was forced to the humiliating necessity of surrendering the balance of the command. My great hope was to keep them in check until night, and then, if re-enforcements did not reach me, cut my way out." Thomas J. Churchill to Theophilus H. Holmes, May 6, 1863, *Official Records Armies*, series I, XVII, pt. 1, p. 781.

[91] On the morning of January 11 Walker's Division took up the line of march to reinforce Arkansas Post, about 55 miles distant. Passing through Pine Bluff, it marched down the riverbank for 25 miles before encamping for the night. During the march couriers continually passed back and forth between Walker and Churchill. At daylight on the morning of the 12th the march was continued for about five miles when news was received that Churchill had surrendered, and the troops encamped on the riverbank. Recalled Blessington: "From stragglers who made their escape from the Post, it was learned that, after a few hours' fighting, a white flag was displayed from a prominent point, unexpected to General Churchill and many of the troops of his command, as they were confident of holding the place until Walker's Division arrived." Blessington, *Walker's Texas Division*, pp. 69–70.

[92] The yellow flag means "quarantine" and hence indicates a hospital. Violation of such a symbol would be equivalent to a modern army firing on the flag of the Red Cross.

[93] Walker's Division remained encamped on the riverbank until the morning of the 19th, awaiting the enemy's advance. Holmes arrived from Little Rock to assume command. The camp was generally known as "Camp Freeze Out" because of the rain, snow and freezing temperatures. "We expected every moment to meet the enemy's fleet and forces," Blessington stated, "for the river, swollen by the rain, hurried its dark flood along with drift and foam, sweeping masses of snow from the banks, and seemed conspiring with the elements to hasten his advance. But the dark flood knew better the secrets of fate." On the morning of the 15th Holmes, anticipating the Federal gunboats coming up the river, backed by their army, began fortifying some two miles from the river. During the night of the 17th it was learned that the Federal fleet had left Arkansas Post and was on its way downstream. (McClernand had wanted to keep on to Little Rock, but Grant, aghast at having 30,000 men diverted from Vicksburg, ordered him back to the Mississippi.) The Confederates left "Camp Freeze Out" on the morning of the 19th and began their march back to Pine Bluff. Blessington, *Walker's Texas Division*, pp. 70–71, 75.

[94] Charles Leroy Morgan enlisted in September 1861 in Bastrop County and was first lieutenant in Captain C. Ferrell's Company D, Eighth Texas Cavalry (Terry's Texas Rangers). He later resigned and was given a cavalry command in the Trans-Mississippi Department. Blessington mentions "Major C. F. [L.] Morgan's Squadron of Cavalry." Confederate Index, Texas State Archives, Austin, Texas; Blessington, *Walker's Texas Division*, p. 64.

[95] Captain L. M. Nutt commanded an unattached cavalry company of about 90 men from Shreveport, Louisiana. Governor Thomas O. Moore of that state had authorized individuals to raise companies of Partisan Rangers. Nutt's command was also known as the Red River Rangers. *Official Records Armies*, series I, XIII, p. 881; Thomas O. Moore to George W. Randolph, July 8, 1862, *ibid.*, series I, XV, p. 773; Andrew B. Booth, comp., *Records of Louisiana Confederate Soldiers and Louisiana Commands*, 4 vols. (New Orleans, 1920), III, p. 1309.

[96] During the Civil War, Texas, which had printed its own money during the Republic period, began printing notes in denominations of $1 to $100. Since hard money had all but disappeared there was still a need for money of smaller denominations. At least 90 Texas counties attempted to solve the problem by issuing their own bank notes in denominations of 25 cents, 50 cents, $1, $2, $3 and $5. A few printed $10 notes. The notes were guaranteed by the county treasury, could be used only within the county and could be exchanged for Confederate money. The "county money" was printed mostly in 1862–1863. The notes are rare today because most were destroyed as soon as they were redeemed. Those that still exist

have a value to collectors many times greater than the amount shown on their face. Jack Maguire, "Confederate 'county money' filled gap after state seceded," "Talk of Texas" column in Austin *American-Statesman*, October 12, 1980.

[97] Camp Mills was located northwest of Pine Bluff. It was named for Colonel Roger Q. Mills of the Tenth Texas Infantry who was captured at Arkansas Post. Walker's Division remained at this camp until February 9, drilling and cleaning the campground. Walker issued orders that two men from each company in the division should be granted furloughs for a reasonable period of time which "gave general satisfaction throughout the division." Also, the weather changed to bright, clear and pleasant days; and tents and blankets to make the men comfortable soon arrived. Blessington, *Walker's Texas Division*, pp. 75–76.

[98] When appointed as Postmaster General of the Confederate States of America, John H. Regan of Texas was faced with the problem of creating a postal system in a land whose already overloaded transportation system daily deteriorated and lacked even the facilities for manufacturing postage stamps. He also was charged with the nearly impossible task of making this system self-supporting. Regan was, after March 1, 1863, able to do this largely because mail contractors were willing to accept "ridiculously low compensation" in order to escape the draft. Despite immense difficulties the Southern postal system was able to handle the mail, at least in the states of the Confederate heartland.

Mail day, to the armies in camp or field, was a greater event than pay day. Each brigade had its own mounted courier whose duty it was to deliver soldiers' letters to the nearest post office and to return with the mail for his unit. As letters to soldiers were generally addressed to no special post office but only to the soldier in care of his unit, the arrival of such mail was an uncertain affair at best, often following the ebb and flow of the war for as much as six months and more before being delivered. As armies in Tennessee and Georgia ranged over a much larger theater of war and marched over more wretched roads, the mails reaching them were much later than those addressed to their comrades in Virginia, and delivery in the Trans-Mississippi Confederacy was correspondingly slower still.

A great part of Confederate correspondence, "perhaps most of it," Bell Wiley speculated, was delivered without benefit of the postal service at all. Soldiers going home on furlough or sick leave, visiting relatives, politicians, clergymen and servants were entrusted with letters home, and soldiers returning to service at the end of furlough or leave often published the fact in local papers, offering to return laden with letters for the men of their units. This informal system of mail delivery took up much of the slack created by the steadily deteriorating Confederate postal service as the war progressed. Wiley, *Life of Johnny Reb*, pp. 200–1; Robert Selph Henry, *The Story of the Confederacy* (New York: Grosset and Dunlap, 1931), p. 93; Clement Eaton, *A History of the Southern Confederacy* (New York: The Macmillian Co., 1954), p. 59.

[99] Colonel George Washington Carter, Twenty-first Texas Cavalry, Parsons's Brigade.

[100] One of Walker's men wrote his mother at this time: "Our pickets captured several prisoners whill [while] we were down there and since we got back they have been coming in daily more or less about 125 have been paroled at the Bluff. Col. Carter who is below here with some cavalry has paroled about 300. They desert and come over and allow themselves to be taken in order to be paroled. They represent that Lincoln's Emancipation proclamation is having a very demoralizing effect on the Federal army, that numbers of them are going home swearing they will fight no longer for Abraham." David M. Ray to "Dear Mother," January 28, 1863, David M.

Ray Papers, The University of Texas Archives, Austin, Texas (hereafter cited as Ray Papers).

[101] Lincoln's final Emancipation Proclamation of January 1, 1863, putting into effect his preliminary proclamation of September 22, 1862, read in part: "I do order and declare that all persons held as slaves within said designated States, and parts of States, are, and henceforth shall be free." No slaves were freed specifically at that moment, for the Proclamation pertained only to areas "the people whereof shall then be in rebellion against the United States." These areas were indicated. However, as Federal troops advanced into those areas, the slaves were to be freed. The Proclamation further provided that former slaves would be officially received into the nation's armed services. Long, *Civil War Day by Day*, p. 306.

[102] "Morale seems to have been considerably better among the upper and middle classes than it was among less privileged groups," noted Bell Wiley. "This better spirit can be attributed not so much to the greater material stake involved as to intangible factors of education, travel, experience and self-confidence. A broad background led to a more wholesome point of view and to greater adaptability." Wiley, *Life of Johnny Reb*, p. 145.

Private William Elisha Stoker, a conscript from Upshur County, Texas, in Company H, Eighteenth Texas Infantry, wrote his wife from Camp Mills: "Betty, I dont write [of] the hardships & the ruff way we hav to liv to distrss you. I just want to let you know how soldiers had to liv. I hav heard lots of tails told about the hardships of soldiers life but the story hasent yet ben told. But, I would trye to grin & endure them all if they would let me come to see you occasionley, but they aint going to let knowboddy off unless they desert & they are doing that pretty fast. There has 19 left this companey & there has lots left other companes & other regiments. They are going to try to cut us out of our 60 dayes furlow that was promissed us in each & every year, but (since) it was in the contract & if they dont giv it to us, we will take it when the time rolls round, if they will ever pay us any money to bear our expences home. If I dont get the chance to come home before long, I am afrade Ile forget how you & priscilla looked. I would giv a $1000. this morning to see you, if I had it. There is no more pros spect of peace now than there was 12 months ago. Nothing more. Ile close by saying I remain your effectionate husband until death." Robert W. Glover, ed., "The War Letters of a Texas Conscript In Arkansas," *Arkansas Historical Quarterly*, XX (Winter 1961), p. 379.

Stoker was wounded at the battle of Jenkins' Ferry, Arkansas, April 30, 1864. A relative described to his wife how "Brother Elisha was shot just above the right nipple, the bullet coming out under his right shoulder." "He was in the hospital at the time but it is quite probable that he never recovered," wrote Robert Glover. "A close check of the Upshur County records and the Coffeeville cemeteries, plus the fact that there were no more letters written by him all tend to indicate that he never returned from Arkansas." *Ibid.*, p. 387.

[103] Confederate forces had evacuated Galveston in October 1862, and it was briefly occupied without resistance by a naval force under Commander William B. Renshaw and on December 25, 1862, was garrisoned by 260 men under Colonel I. S. Burrell, Forty-second Massachusetts. The Federals occupied Kuhn's Wharf and barricaded themselves against attack. The new commander of the Department of Texas, General John B. Magruder, determined to retake the city. Two small channel steamers, *Neptune* and *Bayou City*, armored with cotton bales, with 300 veterans of Sibley's New Mexico campaign under Tom Green serving as "Horse Marines," moved against it by sea. A land force was concentrated at Virginia Point opposite Galveston. The attack began at dawn on January 1, 1863. Renshaw was killed when

his grounded ship, *Westfield*, blew up prematurely after he had ordered it set afire to avoid capture. *Harriet Lane*, her top officers killed, was captured along with another ship filled with supplies. The other Federal ships quickly sailed away, and the Federal land forces surrendered. Galveston was once again in Confederate hands, and the blockade was temporarily disrupted. Joseph W. Young, "Battle of Galveston," in Webb, Carroll and Branda, eds., *Handbook of Texas*, I, pp. 662–63; Robert M. Franklin, *Battle of Galveston, January 1st, 1863* (Galveston: Galveston *News*, 1911); Cumberland, "Confederate Loss and Recapture of Galveston," pp. 109–30.

Rear Admiral David Glasgow Farragut, commanding the West Gulf Squadron, felt the loss of Galveston very deeply. He was anxious to go down to Texas in *Hartford*, but the state of the bar at Southwest Pass prevented him, and he returned to New Orleans. "Our disaster at Galveston has thrown us back and done more injury to the Navy than all the events of the war," he wrote despairingly. Loyall Farragut, *The Life of David Glasgow Farragut, First Admiral of the United States Navy, Embodying His Journal and Letters* (New York: D. Appleton and Company, 1879), pp. 305–6, 309.

[104] Edmund Kirby Smith was born at St. Augustine, Florida, May 16, 1824. He graduated from West Point in 1845. After serving with distinction in the Mexican War he was assistant professor of mathematics at West Point from 1849 to 1852. Later he served against the Indians on the Texas frontier. As major of the Second Cavalry in 1861 Smith refused to surrender Fort Colorado to the Texas militia under Ben McCulloch and expressed a willingness to fight to hold it. Nevertheless, he resigned his commission on April 6. He was made a lieutenant colonel in the Confederate army and served in the Shenandoah Valley under Joseph E. Johnston. On June 17, 1861, he was promoted to brigadier general and was severely wounded at First Manassas the following month. Promoted to major general on October 11, 1861, in 1862 he was in command of the District of East Tennessee, participated in Bragg's invasion of Kentucky and won a victory at Richmond (August 30). He was promoted to lieutenant general to rank from October 9, 1862. Warner, *Generals in Gray*, pp. 279–80.

Early in January 1863 Kirby Smith was suddenly called to Richmond, and on January 14 he was officially appointed to command of the Southwestern Army, "embracing the Department of West Louisiana and Texas." That same day Adjutant and Inspector General Samuel Cooper informed Holmes of Smith's appointment and that a "draft" would be made upon Holmes's troops for his army. "At least four brigades of Texas troops will be required for the Southwestern Army, and, looking at the composition of your forces, . . . it is thought that the division of General McCulloch, comprising the brigades under Colonels Young, Randal, and Flournoy, all Texas infantry, with a brigade of Texas cavalry, under Brigadier-General Hawes, would, by their withdrawal from your command, least derange your organization. . . ." However, Smith's appointment was shortly rescinded, and he was assigned to command in North Carolina. But not wishing to replace his friend Gustavus W. Smith, Kirby Smith insisted on a return to his first order and left for Louisiana. Before reaching his destination he received still another order, dated February 9, 1863: "The command of Lieut. Gen. E. Kirby Smith is extended so as to embrace the Trans-Mississippi Department." He thus replaced Holmes in that position. Samuel Cooper to Theophilus H. Holmes, January 14, 1863, *Official Records Armies*, series I, XXII, pt. 2, pp. 771–72; Joseph Howard Parks, *General Edmund Kirby Smith, C.S.A.* (Baton Rouge: Louisiana State University Press, 1954), p. 251 (hereafter cited as Parks, *Edmund Kirby Smith*).

[105] "Probably no body of troops has suffered so much from sickness during the present war as this Division," wrote a member of Colonel Overton Young's First

Brigade on February 5. "We have left upwards of 2,800 Texan graves at Camp Nelson alone. They mark the marches of our regiment all the way from Western Texas to Des Arc and Helena. Besides, we leave about one half of those alive at the Hospitals of Little Rock and Camp Nelson. A large number even of those in camps and determined to keep up with the army at all risks, are suffering from jaundice, mumps, and diarrhea, and should instead be under constant medical attendance and careful nursing." Bellville *Countryman*, February 21, 1863.

[106] E. P. Petty was not the only Rebel soldier sick of cornbread. As cornbread was the most constant item on the Southern soldier's menu, it was natural that he should soon grow weary of it. In 1863 a Mississippi private wrote to his sister, "I want Pa to be certain and buy wheat enough to do us plentifully — for if the war closes and I get home I never intend to chew any more cornbread." A Louisiana soldier was yet more pointed: "If any person offers me cornbread after the war," he threatened, "I shall <u>probably</u> tell him to — go to hell!" Wiley, *Life of Johnny Reb*, pp. 97–98.

[107] Colonel Xavier Blanchard Debray's Twenty-sixth Texas Cavalry.

[108] At the beginning of the Civil War the Confederate States Army based its court-martial proceedings upon those of the United States Army and instituted two types of military tribunal, the special court-martial and the general court-martial. Special courts-martial consisted of three officers and were limited in their jurisdiction to crimes of noncapital nature committed by enlisted men and junior officers. Appointable by regimental commanders and commanders of military installations, the power of the special court-martial was limited to fines not to exceed one month's pay or imprisonment at hard labor for no more than 31 days.

The general court-martial was comprised of from five to 13 officers and judged cases involving all ranks of the army and all civilians on military payroll. These courts were authorized to pass sentences up to and including death by firing squad. The findings of both types of court-martial were subject to review by the officer who had ordered the tribunal to meet, and it was his prerogative to concur with or to modify the findings of the court.

In October 1862 a third type of military court, composed of three judges of the rank of colonel and one judge advocate with the rank of captain, was instituted. One each of these special military courts was assigned to each corps of the army and vested with powers above those of the general court-martial. This new system began to take over the duties of the older types of court-martial, lessening the jurisdiction of both general and special courts-martial and tending to occupy the full time of the officers assigned to special court-martial duty.

Capital sentences in the Confederate army were rare, but frequent punishments assigned by court-martial included time in the guardhouse, wearing of a ball and chain or a barrel shirt, time at hard labor, public reprimand, bread-and-water diet, the stoppage of pay or, in extreme cases, branding. The courts were sometimes more imaginative, however, as in the case in which they sentenced a Texas cavalryman to walk from San Antonio to Austin in three days, a distance of some 80 miles. Wiley, *Life of Johnny Reb*, pp. 219–20; 231.

[109] Frank R. Tannehill of the Sixteenth Texas Infantry wrote his wife on March 11: "A sort of drouth prevails at this time in the way of news. We have got nothing certain from the other side of the river for a long time. . . . General Walker received a telegraphic dispatch from the Arkansas Post that the N. Y. Herald had been received there which states that there had been another engagement at Vixburg in which the Federals had suffered such disasters that it would not do to publish them. There was a rumor in camp several days ago that there had been another

battle there in which the Federals had lost eighteen thousand in killed and prisoners, but no one paid any attention to it. But since northern papers have made such admissions as the one above, it is regarded as an exception to reports that get into circulation without anyone knowing how they come." Anne Thiele Holder, *Tennessee to Texas: Francis Richardson Tannehill, 1825–1864* (Austin: Pemberton Press, 1966), pp. 117–18 (hereafter cited as Holder, *Tennessee to Texas*).

In fact, the rumor of a Federal attack on Vicksburg was false. On March 11, however, Confederate Fort Pemberton on the Yalobusha River near Greenwood, Mississippi, 90 miles north of Vicksburg, successfully repelled the first of several attacks by enemy gunboats seeking passage. By March 16 the Federals were forced to withdraw. Another of Grant's probes against Vicksburg — the so-called Yazoo Pass Expedition — had been foiled. Long, *Civil War Day by Day*, p. 328.

[110] As the war dragged on many Confederate soldiers found reason enough to leave the ranks, and desertion began to be the principal offense tried by court-martial. Although the courts were most often quite lenient in meting out their punishments for this crime — too lenient, many critics would claim — in the final years of the war the death penalty became increasingly common. When this sentence was executed commanding officers generally saw to it that the effect of the object lesson was not lost on the other members of their commands. In most cases the entire brigade or even division of the condemned soldier was drawn up in a hollow square, and the prisoner was hauled into its center in a wagon with his coffin as a seat. Removed from the wagon, he was compelled to stand or to kneel beside his freshly dug grave as a detail of 24 men, only half of whom had loaded rifles, was drawn up into a firing squad. A brief prayer was read, and the detail fired.

Bell Wiley observed that from the evidence of many letters home, the point was well taken by those who were compelled to watch, but it is questionable whether morale was improved or actually harmed by compulsory attendance. One Alabama soldier wrote to his wife: "I saw a site today that made me feel mity Bad. I saw a man shot for deserting. there was twenty fore Guns shot at him. they shot him all to pease . . . he went home and they Brote him Back and then he went home again and so they shot him for that. Martha it was one site that I did hate to see it But I could not help my self. I had to do Jest as the sed for me to doo."

Frank Tannehill, another witness to the execution reported by Captain Petty, was equally sympathetic to the plight of the condemned and at least as resentful of the authority which ordered the executions and forced him to watch them. "Six

deserters have been condemned by a court martial to be shot," he wrote to his wife. "The time was fixed for last Saturday the 7th, but at the request of a Catholic priest their time was extended three days to give time to prepare for death. The whole division was ordered to turn out to witness the shooting, but it rained very hard all day yesterday and night before last so that it would have been very bad walking, and the execution was put off again, this time to the 13th (day after tomorrow) when every man who is able is ordered to turn out. There will be a grand review on the same day. I have no taste for that kind of thing, even when the condemned deserve death, which, in the case of two of these I do not believe. True they deserted, but the officer who commanded them is a perfect tyrant and treated them very badly, and it is pretty certain that they deserted to escape the abuses to which he subjected them, and not from a desire to get out of the service. Their commander is . . . . . and has command of an artillery Co." Wiley, *Life of Johnny Reb*, p. 228; Holder, *Tennessee to Texas*, pp. 118–19.

[111] "General Walker, after taking command of the Texas troops, soon became very popular with them," J. P. Blessington stated. "His presence was always hailed with the wildest enthusiasm by both officers and soldiers." Blessington, *Walker's Texas Division*, pp. 72–73.

[112] Colonel Thomas L. Snead quoted the following about Hindman: "Hindman 'was a man of genius and could have commanded a department, or have been a minister of war; but he could not command an army in the field, or plan and execute a battle.'" Snead, "Conquest of Arkansas," p. 450.

General Sterling Price reached Little Rock on March 25, 1863, and was assigned to the command of Hindman's division. The state of affairs in Arkansas as seen from Richmond is depicted in a letter from Secretary of War James Seddon to Kirby Smith on March 18: "From a variety of sources, many of which I cannot doubt, the most deplorable accounts reach this department of the disorder, confusion, and demoralization everywhere prevalent both with the armies and people of that State. The commanding general [Holmes] seems, while esteemed for his virtues, to have lost the confidence and attachment of all; and the next in command, General Hindman, who is admitted to have shown energy and ability, has rendered himself by alleged acts of violence and tyranny perfectly odious. The consequences as depicted are fearful. The army is stated to have dwindled by desertion, sickness, and death from 40,000 to 50,000 men to some 15,000 or 18,000 who are disaffected and helpless, and are threatened with positive starvation from deficiency of mere neces-

saries. The people are represented as in a state of consternation, multitudes suffering for means of subsistence, and yet exposed from gangs of lawless marauders and deserters to being plundered of the little they have." Snead, "Conquest of Arkansas," pp. 454–55.

Unhappy with Holmes and distressed at the pending collapse of his work, Hindman applied for a transfer. In February 1863 he left Arkansas to serve on the Court of Inquiry investigating the loss of New Orleans. He subsequently commanded a division at Chickamauga, Chattanooga and in the Atlanta campaign, in which he received an incapacitating wound. After the war he moved to Mexico but returned to Arkansas in 1868 and resumed his law practice. On September 28, 1868, he was assassinated in his home at Helena by an unknown assailant, an act probably inspired by his determined opposition to Radical Reconstruction. Warner, *Generals in Gray*, p. 138; Michael B. Dougan, "Thomas C. Hindman: Arkansas Politician and General," in *Rank and File: Civil War Essays in Honor of Bell Irvin Wiley*, ed. James I. Robertson Jr. and Richard M. McMurry (San Rafael: Presidio Press, 1976), pp. 21–38.

[113] According to the return of the District of Arkansas for March 1863, Walker's Division had 484 officers and 6,202 men "present for duty"; 8,444 "aggregate present"; 12,577 "aggregate present and absent." *Official Records Armies*, series I, XXII, pt. 2, p. 810.

[114] Smith assumed command of his department at Alexandria, Louisiana, March 7, 1863. Richard Taylor was left in command of Louisiana, and Magruder in Texas. Holmes was made commander of the District of Arkansas, including Missouri, and the Indian Territory. In fact, this was the only position he had previously filled, for as Kirby Smith reported to President Davis, Holmes had remained at Little Rock and given his entire attention to the defense of Arkansas and a possible invasion of Missouri. "There was no general system, no common head; each district was acting independently." Holmes expressed pleasure at being relieved of his "elephant." On July 4, 1863, he ordered an attack on Helena, which was strongly fortified and garrisoned by 5,000 men, in a vain and much-too-late effort to aid Vicksburg. The assault failed from want of numbers and mismanagement. Holmes withdrew his army to the White River, and, being ill, turned over command of the District of Arkansas to Price on July 23. Bishop Henry C. Lay characterized Holmes, his parishioner, as "an easy old soul" who "appreciated soul questions," who cried during religious services, and who at 47 was "a very old man" with "memory, will, judgment all debilitated to a degree which incapacitates him for any efficient administration." Holmes later organized the reserves of his native state, North Carolina. Parks, *Edmund Kirby Smith*, pp. 257–58; Snead, "Conquest of Arkansas," p. 456; Warner, *Generals in Gray*, p. 141. Lay is quoted in Dougan, *Confederate Arkansas*, p. 93.

[115] "Col. Randal still commands our brigade," Surgeon Edward Cade told his wife. "Genl Hebert was sent here to take command of our brigade but Genl Smith & Walker have sent him back to Texas. Col R [Randal] is very popular with both men & his superior officers." Anderson, *A Texas Surgeon*, p. 44.

[116] Major General Sterling Price, called "Old Pap" by his men, was born in Prince Edward County, Virginia, on September 20, 1809. About 1831 he moved to Missouri where he served as legislator and congressman. During the Mexican War he was a colonel of the Second Missouri Infantry and brigadier general of volunteers and was appointed military governor of New Mexico by General Stephen W. Kearny. He was governor of Missouri from 1853 to 1857. In March 1861 he was president of the state convention that opposed secession, but he himself later

joined the Confederacy. Up to this time he had taken part in the battles of Wilson's Creek, Lexington, Elkhorn Tavern (Pea Ridge), Iuka and Corinth. Warner, *Generals in Gray*, p. 247.

[117] The Nineteenth Texas Cavalry Regiment was organized in 1862 and was commanded by Nathaniel Macon Burford of Dallas. Wright, comp., *Texas in the War*, pp. 26, 118n.

[118] Morgan's Texas Cavalry Battalion, commanded by Major Charles L. Morgan, was organized in early 1863 and was originally composed of the cavalry companies of Captains B. D. McKie, Milton M. Boggess and Alf Johnson. Johnson's company was known as a "spy company." Wright, comp., *Texas in the War*, pp. 33, 127n.

[119] "Pratt's Texas Battery" was commanded by J. H. Pratt, who was appointed captain, March 1, 1861, and major, February 19, 1864. The battery's second commander was Captain H. C. Hynson. During the war the battery served in the Indian Territory, Arkansas and Missouri. In 1864 it was assigned to the Second Artillery Battalion, Trans-Mississippi Department. Wright, comp., *Texas in the War*, pp. 43, 134n.

[120] General John Sappington Marmaduke, a native of Missouri and West Point graduate, commanded a division of Confederate cavalry. In mid-March 1863 he traveled to Little Rock to confer with Holmes. His division was to sweep through the Iron Mountains, destroying telegraphs, bridges and forts as it went, and then swing across to the eastern side of Missouri to demolish the Federal supply base at Cape Girardeau. It was also hoped that a large number of recruits would be picked up. Marmaduke returned to Batesville, Arkansas, early in April and began to concentrate his forces at Eleven Points River. On April 19 the division rode for Rolla, Missouri, on what is known as "Marmaduke's Cape Girardeau Raid." Trains slowed his march and, by bogging down in the Mingo swamps, prevented the Confederates from capturing Cape Girardeau. On May 31 the troops dismounted at Jacksonport, Arkansas. The raid had cost 30 killed, 60 wounded and 120 missing. One hundred

fifty new recruits accompanied the division. "In terms of strategic objectives, Marmaduke's second Missouri raid was a complete failure," wrote Stephen B. Oates. "The Federal supply depot at Cape Girardeau had not been damaged, and the Army of the Frontier was moving once again into northern Arkansas." Stephen B. Oates, *Confederate Cavalry West of the River* (Austin: University of Texas Press, 1961), pp. 121–31.

[121] "Soldiers life is notoriously conducive to degeneration of some standards of morality," wrote Bell Wiley. "Granting an impressive susceptibility to religious impulse, as witness periodic outbreaks of great revivals among the fighting men, objective study of soldiers' letters and diaries makes inescapable the conclusion that all the evils usually associated with barrack and camp life flourished in the Confederate Army." Wiley, *Life of Johnny Reb*, p. 36.

[122] Camp Wright was named for the owner of the land where it was located. Blessington gave the following description: "Our situation here was a good one, and, for the first time in the State, the troops were comfortably situated. And they appreciated it very much; for, if ever there was an army that had been harassed and 'used up' to accomplish nothing so far, it was this army. At this camp it was an imposing sight to see a long stretch of country, rich and beautiful as the sun ever shone upon; the deep pine forests; belts of wood, whose dark green foliage contrasted strongly with the white tents. Fields lately luscious with vines are drooping with amber-colored corn, all of them covered over with white tents, arranged with street-like precision, with regiments or battalions on parade or review, with martial music echoing along the river-bank, from splendid bands. Add to this the Arkansas River, flowing on in majestic grandeur, on its bosom numerous transports steaming up and down. Such was our encampment at Camp Wright." Blessington, *Walker's Texas Division*, p. 76.

[123] Constant K. Hall was a Bastrop business man who operated stage lines with the firm of Sawyer, Risher and Hall. It is unclear how Petty's coat pertains to him.

[124] John Bigland, *A Geographical and Historical View of the World, Exhibiting a Complete Delineation of the Natural & Artificial Features of Each Country* (Boston, 1811).

[125] Alexander Pope, *An Essay on Man* (1733), epistle I, line 284:

"All nature is but art unknown to thee,
All chance, direction which thou canst not see;
All discord, harmony not understood;
All partial evil, universal good;
And spite of pride, in erring reason's spite,
One truth is clear, Whatever is, is right."

[126] The Arkansas Post prisoners, instead of being exchanged at Vicksburg as the Dix-Hill cartel required, were sent up the Mississippi River to St. Louis. The officers were then sent to Camp Chase, Ohio, and the men to Camp Douglas at Chicago, Illinois, and Camp Butler at Springfield. While the officers fared well, there were many deaths from sickness among the men at Butler and Douglas. Exchanged at City Point, Virginia, in April-May 1863, the Arkansas Post prisoners were sent west to Bragg's Army of Tennessee and assigned to what later became known as Granbury's Texas Brigade in Pat Cleburne's division.

[127] Horace Haldeman was born in Pennsylvania in 1820 and was commissioned a second lieutenant in the United States Army on February 16, 1847. He served with the Eleventh United States Infantry Regiment during the Mexican War and was

promoted to first lieutenant. In the 1850's he was stationed on the Texas frontier, serving as commander of Fort Gates (Coryell County) from January 1852 to March 1853, and surveyed the road from Austin to that post. He also gained fame as an entomologist. In 1858 Haldeman resigned his commission and settled at Troy in Bell County, where he raised horses. During the Civil War he commanded a battery of light artillery in Walker's Division. After the war, as the battery was returning to Texas from Louisiana, the men buried their guns in the Red River. Haldeman settled at Belton and later moved to Calvert, where he died on September 10, 1883. Wright, comp., *Texas in the War*, p. 134n.

[128] This is the first stanza of one of Thomas Moore's "Irish Melodies" (London, 1839).

[129] Macbeth's challenge to Macduff in Shakespeare's *The Tragedy of Macbeth* (Act V, Scene VIII): "lay on, Macduff; and damn'd be him that first cries 'Hold, enough!'"

[130] An old hymn, popular at camp meetings and revivals:

"Jerusalem, my happy home
When shall I come to thee?
My sorrows when shall they have an end
Thy joys when shall I see?"

[131] The two lines quote William Cowper, describing the solitude of Alexander Selkirk, a sailor shipwrecked on the island of Juan Fernandez in the South Pacific:

"I am monarch of all I survey,
My right there is none to dispute:
I am centre all round to the sea,
I am lord of the fowl and the brute."

[132] This was a reference to the Arkansas Post prisoners.

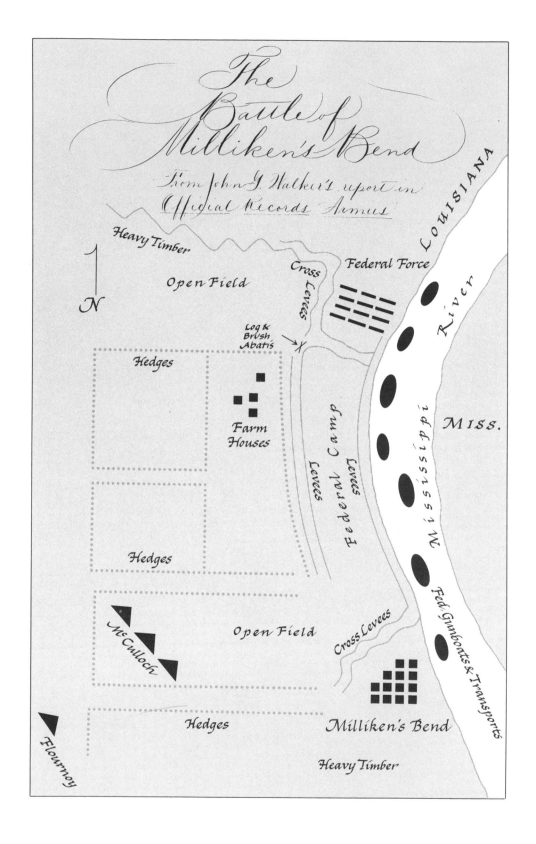

The Battle of
Milliken's Bend

From John G. Walker's report in
Official Records Armies

Heavy Timber

Open Field

Cross Levees

Federal Force

LOUISIANA

River

Log & Brush Abatis

Hedges

Farm Houses

Levees

Federal Camp

Levees

MISS.

Mississippi

Hedges

McCulloch

Open Field

Cross Levees

Fed. Gunboats & Transports

Hedges

Milliken's Bend

Flournoy

Heavy Timber

N

Walker's Greyhounds

ON APRIL 14, 1863, General Kirby Smith advised Theophilus Holmes that Federal General Nathaniel Banks had evacuated Baton Rouge, Louisiana, and was shifting his troops west of the Mississippi to Berwick Bay. He had already concentrated 15,000 men there, and everything indicated an intention to occupy western Louisiana. Another force of equal strength, commanded by General John McClernand, was reported at Richmond, Louisiana, ready to operate along Bayou Maçon. "Order General Walker without delay with his division to Camden, with instructions to move to Monroe should the movements of McClernand render it necessary," Kirby Smith instructed, adding: "I will delay to Little Rock until the plans of Banks and McClernand are further developed." A day later Holmes was ordered to send Walker's Division on to Monroe so that it would be in position to move to General Richard Taylor's assistance, should the latter be compelled to fall back to Alexandria. On April 19 Kirby Smith told Holmes that five gunboats had passed Vicksburg going down the Mississippi, and the enemy had one division on Bayou Vidal and one on Bayou Roundaway. "Please hasten Walker's movements," he urged. "When Walker starts, telegraph to Monroe and Camden for all the boats in the river to be at Camden to transport him. If the enemy advance toward Monroe, send a portion of your force to occupy Camden, to prevent the destruction of that depot."[1]

At Camp Wright, four miles north of Pine Bluff, Walker's Texans held their weekly dress parade on the evening of April 23. An order from Holmes to Walker to proceed with his division "without delay" to Monroe was read to each regiment. "In taking leave of Walker's Division, the commanding general of the district expresses his sincere regret," Holmes said. "It was instructed and disciplined under his supervision; and, having the fullest confidence in its strength, patriotism and valor, he hoped it would be his proud privilege to participate in the honor in store for it when it meets the enemy. Better officers and men no division can boast of. The Confederacy may well be satisfied with the security of its interests entrusted to them."[2]

The next morning the troops marched out of Camp Wright and took the road which led southward through Pine Bluff. Because recent heavy rains had flooded the Saline River and Moro Creek, the division moved directly toward Monroe instead of going first to Camden. The route of march was through Monticello and the villages of Lacy and Fountain Hill to Hamburg, Arkansas.[3]

Fountain Hill Ark Apl 29th 1863

My Dear Wife

We are now in Ashley County Arkansas 10 miles North of the town of Hamburg and 23 miles South of Monticello. We have just received orders to remain at this place until further orders. These orders may come at any moment and hence we hold ourselves ready to move at an instant warning. We received similar orders last night and on this morning started at 8 O'clock a m and came here making a march of 12 miles. This has been an average march since we left Pine Bluff. Through Drew County had an ovation nearly the whole way. The ladies in perfect swarms were on the road side at every house. At points the whole neighborhood would assemble and such waving of hankerchiefs and throwing boquets I havent seen hardly in my life. At

Monticello there were more ladies and prettier ones than I ever saw in
my life. Every house and every corner and every yard swarmed. At the
Court house there was a perfect crowd of them. Such a fluttering of
handkerchiefs, such a showering of flowers and boquets, such a rushing
of negroes and little boys bearing flowers and boquets to the ranks as
then and there took place did the hearts of the weary soldier good
and in return hats waved and cheer after cheer went up such as
Monticello and this portion of the Confederacy ever witnessed before.
The soldiers were hoarse with cheering when we got through.
Monticello has the right name. Its meaning is the "Heavenly City"
and from the number of angels I saw in it I believe that it is truly
named. If I could get to see such beautiful visions as I then saw every
day I would'nt care if I never saw a Yankee in my life.[4] Arkansas beats
the world (at least all that I have ever seen) for the number and beauty
of the women. I dont particularly know the reason of stopping here. I
have my opinion which however is not worth much. We are in about
40 miles of Gain's Landing on the Mississippi river where I learn there
is a large force of Yankees. The main road from that point west leads
to Monticello which is now in our rear. It may be and is quite probable
that the Yankees will attempt to move a force to our rear and cut us off
from the ballance of the Arkansas army leaving us in small bodies with
forces between us so as to prevent our reinforcing each other and then
attempt to capture or whip us by piece meal or in detachments. If we
stop here we can anticipate such movements and checkmate them. I
am inclined to think that we will wait here a few days to look into
these matters. At all events one thing I know that army movements
are uncertain and the soldier never knows his fate. I have no particular
news of federal movements. I hear that there has been fighting at St
Martinsville Louisiana between Banks army and our Genl Taylor[5]
in which Taylor was worsted.[6] If Taylor gets whipped the best part
of Louisiana goes into the hands of the feds. It is the principal sugar
region and has immense wealth in it. It is one of the richest and most
beautiful portions of the Confederacy. I hope the news is false. There
seems to be a lull in the storm which I interpret to be for the gathering
of the mighty forces for the impending struggle which I think will
be the hardest that we have yet witnessed. I think that there is to
be much blood shed this campaign. I hope not. The feds along the
Mississippi now having failed to take Vicksburg and Port Hudson[7] have
become mad and are now going out into the country bordering that
stream and are destroying everything particularly crops, provisions and
farming utensils; burning residences, gins etc; stealing negroes and
every thing that they can lay their infernal hands upon. They are in

fact carrying on a predatory war in its broadest and most barbarous sense. This they are not only doing there but every where else in the Confederacy and yet I see no signs or prospects of our Commanders ordering the <u>Black</u> Flag to be raised. I hope it will be raised & that I will get to fight under it. Whether it is raised or not I expect to make it by principal and act accordingly unless the booming of the cannon and the whistling of the minie balls shall sober and molify me verry much. I am told that it has a terribly softening influence upon a person. I expect before long to test it experimentally. Col Allen and Genl McCulloch have not rejoined us yet and I expect that they have gone on to Texas. I sent you by Col A $200 in two dollar Confederate bills — I can send you some more and if the prospect for a fight waxes good I will dispatch it by mail to you. I might accidentally be killed or taken prisoner then the money would go up and you would be the looser thereby. I am in fine health and am standing the march admirably. I improve every day. To day in addition to my own load I carried the knap sack and gun of a sick man. I came into camps in fine condition and verry little tired. How are all my little brats. God bless them. How I want to see them. Not an hour passes over me but what I think of them and you. I hope the time will speedily come when I can realize my bright visions of happiness when I shall rejoin my family and wander from them no more forever. Take care of them and of your money and property. A thousand kisses to you all. Flemming & Lum Owens and all the rest are with us and are well. John Wilson (Wash Jones Brother in law) was taken sick & left near Monticello. He is better to day. Respects to all.

Truly yours
E. P. Petty

Camp near Hamburg May 1st 1863

My Dear Wife

I wrote you a letter two days ago from Fontain Hill 11 miles above Hamburg and now I have concluded to send you a few lines from this camp which is 3 miles nearly west from Hamburg on the road leading to a little place called Mary Saline. I dont know when and while I will mail it but will send it from the first accessible post office. Since I wrote our direction has been changed and as I now understand it we are ordered to Shreveport La. to reinforce Genl Taylor who has been for several days fighting Genl Banks army and retreating before it not having sufficient force to make an effective stand. I am in hopes that in this adventure we will be more successful than in our attempt to reinforce the Arkansas Post and that we will be in time to help our friends and save our country. The feds have failed signally, failed at both Vickburg and Port Hudson and hence have concluded to move out upon some weak point and gobble it up as they did at the Post but in this I think that they will now be mistaken as we seem to be on the alert and are generally ready for them. I am disposed to think from what I can gather from the movements of the enemy that they intend to make a heavy campaign in the Trans Miss Dept and I now look forward to long weary marches, sleepless nights, hunger and hard fighting for our armies over here. If we do I hope to be in my proper place at all times and to fully discharge my duty with honor to myself and benefit to the country and if I should fail to do so by showing the white feather I hope that some friend will immediately shoot me so that the disgrace shall not attach either to my wife and children. We are having a lively time in our march so far. Wherever we go the ladies throng the road and literally strew our way with flowers. We camped 1 mile beyond Hamburg last night. The Lone Star Minstrels gave a consert which I attended for the purpose of seeing the beauties of the place.[8] They were out in crowds and after the consert they opened a ball which lasted until about 2 Oclock and strange to say — although I stayed and witnessed the dancing for some time I did not participate in it and for this reason. I was too modest. I saw it was a grab game. Men pitched in without ceremony or introduction and actually pulled the women out on the floor to all of which they did not object and Cheerfully submitted and so out of self respect and respect for my wife and children who were vividly present in my mind I stood aloof. I could not and did not go in but when I got tired witnessing the frolic I retired to my honest and virtuous couch for repose. On this morning we marched in good order through the town. The ladies and roses were there and the hankerchiefs and noise were there and it all went off well. Our march to day was just four miles. We came through a prarie that made me think of Texas. The boys when they saw it raised a shout. We have rested to day and have generally cleaned up. I have had all my clothes washed and am ready for a long march on to morrow. _____ does my washing and never will have a cent for it. He says that I have done him so many favours that he has long since been paid. He does any work of any sort that I want without charge. I am afraid Jo aint good grit for every time we start towards where there is a prospect of seeing the feds he gets sick. On this trip he has been complaining the whole time nearly. I believe that I will send you a one hundred dollar bill in this letter. I dont want to keep any money on

hand. I am afraid that I may loose it. I rather you would have it than the feds.

Love & kisses to my chaps and compliments to friends.

Yours truly
E. P. Petty

Near Hamburg May 1st 1863

My Dear Daughter

I have nothing particular to write more than I have written to your Ma but to show you that I have'nt forgotten you and that I fully appreciate you I have concluded to write you a few lines. I am in splendid health and am standing the March admirably. I dont much like the idea of having to march so much, to toil so much, to suffer so much etc. without ever getting so much as a sight of a Yankee but now as we are going full bent towards where we know that they are and are fighting I go in with more alacrity. I am now getting so I had rather fight a little than to march so much. On our march so far we have had a fine time. The ladies have thronged our road and strewed it with flowers and have encouraged and cheered us with smiles and words. We can fight better now than we could have done a week ago. On this trip we have passed through two towns Monticello and Hamburg. Monticello has a population (or has had before the War) of about 1600 & is a beautiful place — Larger than Bastrop and I never at any place saw more ladies and prettier ladies (except at Pine Bluff) than I did here. I gave Ma a description of our March through the place. Hamburg is a smaller town having only about 500 inhabitants but by the way quite a pretty little place. There were lots of ladies here also to see, see description in Ma's letter. How do you & Frank get on with your studies. I hope well. I want you to beat any other children and take the prize. I know you can if you will and I believe you will. God bless you all. How I wish I could embrace and kiss you all. And then stay with you for ever more but I must submit — I helped to make this war and I must fight it and so I will. Kiss Ma & the children for me. Write often. Dont wait for me. I have my hands full.

Yours truly
E. P. Petty

My Dear Wife

I wrote you and Ella both a letter about 5 days ago from near Hamburg Ark but having no good oppertunity to mail them put them in my trunk where they now are. I could not get at it as it was in the bottom of my wagon so I have concluded to drop you a line anew to let you know my whereabouts, my destination as far as I can learn it and how I am progressing generaly. We took boats at Washita (Ouachita) City about 50 miles by water above this place this morning and in 3 hours we debarked at Trenton a little place about 2 miles above here on the opposite side of the river. To morrow perhaps our waggons will start over land for Alexandr[i]a on Red River and we will start by water for same place. Our destination is therefore so far as we now know Alexandra where we expect to have to fight gunboats and all that sort of thing. In 3 or 4 days may be less we will be there.[9] I am in fine health and spirits. Hav'nt fagged in the least since the first day under the march though for several days we made about 20 miles per day which is considered a forced march. The Command is fine and eager for the fray. In my other letter I enclosed you a $100.00 bill. I now also enclose you one here. I dont want the money here. Use it to the best advantage. Address me now at "Shreveport Louisiana 17th Tex Regt Infty McCullochs Brigade Walkers Division" and it will reach me wherever I go. I will write more at more leisure if I have any. Kisses & compliments to Children etc.

Yours truly
E. P. Petty

Camp near Trenton La.
May 7th 1863

My dear Son Frank —

I was down at Monroe yesterday and wrote Ma a short letter from there — If I remember I dated it 5th when it should have been 6th May.

We will not move today. We are waiting for Genl Hawe's Brigade[10] which will be down to day I suppose and if so I expect we will start on boats tomorrow. We will go down the Ouachita and up Little river to within 16 or 20 miles of Alexandra and go over land to that place, where I expect in a very short time we will have a chance at the Yankees.

Night before last I went to a dancing party on Bayou Bartholomew and danced until 2 O'clock. I had on thin clothing and during the time it turned cold — I then rode about 3 miles to camp in the thin clothes and caught about as bad a cold as I have had for years. I have to whisper now not being able to talk louder but not withstanding the cold I consider that I got value received for it. I had a nice time and enjoyed my self finely.

This place of Trenton which is in about ½ mile of this camp is a small shipping port on the Ouachita. The rail road to Monroe which is two miles below has taken the wind out of this place and the war has just about finished [it].

Monroe is quite a pretty place — It is near the size of Bastrop (Texas) and quite handsomely built with the prettiest gardens and pastures you ever saw or that I ever saw. Flowers bloom on every hand and shade in great abundance prevails. It is a nice place in a very rich country on a beautiful stream where lots of steam boats come. I thought this morning I would send Ma the letter which I have had written for several days — also one for Ella at the same time write you a line — I sent in Ma's letter yesterday one hundred dollars — and now I send here in one hundred dollars for her.

Be a good boy Frank. Learn your books. Some of these days I will come home and see you all.

We are now comeing much nearer home every day and if the feds dont press too hard I can come home after awhile.

We are now beyond the confines of Arkansas. I must confess that I left the state with some feelings of regret. I had formed some attachments there. I had met some of my old Tennessee friends and renewed old acquaintance and hence I felt that I had to stay away from home that I had rather stay with my friends than strangers.

I dont like Louisiana as well as I did Arkansas. It is low, flat and sickly though it is rich, fertile and filled with wealth.

I have no news. I sent Ma yesterday the Monroe Register that contains all the news —

Write to me. Kisses and love for all.

Yours truly
E. P. Petty Capt. Co. F
Allen's Regiment

[Camp near Trenton La. May —? 1863]

[My Dear Wife]
This camp is 2 miles West of Trenton on the Shreveport road and four

miles West of Monroe. The Washita Valley is a magnificent farming section. There is immense wealth in it but the people are alarmed & this road is lined with negroes, wagons & families en route to Texas. They came from the Mississippi river and all the Bayous bordering on it. I never saw such an exodus before. Texas will be over run I fear with negroes. It immense capacities will be taxed too heavily and her own citizens will have to suffer for food. All the Sugar growing portion of Louisiana is now in the hands of the feds. Texas now has the only sugar region in Confederate Lands. We are nearly ruined on the Sugar question and if you hav'nt laid in enough you had better hast[e] on that subject. Sugar will be out of reach soon unless the war ends for if we even now drive the Yanks out no sugar can be made this year as they have devastated the Country & either stolen or run off all the negroes. So buy if you have to pay a big price for it. Also buy some molasses a barrell at least. Dont stand on any price for you cant do without these things & some coffee you had better buy and all other things that you prospectively will need for sometime. Things look equally in the Trans Miss Dept and will be worse unless we set on foot something that shall turn the tide and that soon. Vicksburg though it can never be taken is comparatively played out for with the Canal and gun boats they have passed all they need by it and now have control of the river below and between there and Port Hudson. Their troops have been marched round by land. So the effective power of Vicksburg has been shorn from it. It will stand to prevent the navigation of the river & tramels their Commerce but for war purposes they have eroded its force[11] — Our communication with the east is almost entirely cut off. What is done is by chance. So you see that by Yankee persistency and ingenuity that although checked yet they continue to encroach upon our borders and contract our limits. I therefore think that as we cannot possibly prevent all their raids that we ought to concentrate our troops at one point, give up all others temporarily and move upon them in one grand army and cut & thrash and lay wast as we go until we bring them to their senses or wipe them out from the face of the earth. If we concentrate so will the enemy and hence the country will be relieved from them except where the main armies are. If we would get all our army together it would be an irresistable force that could not be checked and would overrun the North. This is what ought to be done so that they could feel the stings of the war. If I could have my way now I would gather into one mass our whole army, hoist at its head the black flag and move via Washington City, Philadelphia, New York to Boston & elsewhere and cut & carve until not a Yankee soldier was left to tell the tale and not a seed of Abolitionism was left upon this continent. Even all this would'nt satisfy me for the wrongs

and injuries inflicted upon my own loved sunny South. Take good care
of my loved children — Spare no pains or money in their education.
Let them see and learn every thing that is worthy to be seen and
learned. Dont calculate the expenses when it comes to the matter of
the education and accomplishment of them. This is about all I ever
expect to be able to give them and if I were worth millions I would
expend it freely that way. I feel the want of it myself and as long as I
am able to move a hand or wag my tongue it shall be done for them in
that line. I will write to each of them letters as time & oppertunity
offers and give them such encouragement as they may need. A
thousand kisses for you & them. Write as often as possible.

Your's truly
E. P. Petty

Trenton La. Sunday May 10th 1863

My Dear Daughter
  I have no idea when I shall hear from you all again. We are now a
long way from Little Rock Ark. and intend to still go further but thank

goodness that as I lengthen my distance from Little Rock I shorten it
between me and the home of my loved ones and if I cannot go to see
them I can at least hear from them more frequently. Our Division left
this place on yesterday morning on Steam Boats to proceed by the
Washita river, Little river and Chatahoula [Catahoula] Lake to within
20 miles of Alexandra and then by land to that place to reinforce our
Army there and repel the invasion of Red River Vally. We filled 14
Steam Boats and it presented a grand scene to see us steaming one
after another down this beautiful river with banners fluttering, bands
playing, men huzzaing and cheering, with the bank lined with ladies
with palpitating hearts and fluttering handkerchiefs.[12] We proceeded
down the river about 70 miles when by a signal given from the pioneer
boat (which was about 3 miles ahead and on which was G^{enl} Walker
& staff) the boats turned and commenced steaming back up the river
each one trying to get ahead of the others and all running seemingly
for life. No one knew the cause of our retrograde movement. All
supposed that the gun boats were after us. Men were excited to a high
pitch — some got their guns, some loaded pistol and some did one
foolish thing and some another. This state of affairs continued pretty
much until the Signal Boat (B.L. Hodge) came up when the signal to
halt was given. Genl Walker then stated that the fleet would return to
this place in order & that there was no necessity for any excitement
etc. We then returned here where we arrived about 2 O'clock AM this
morning. We will leave here in the morning over land for Nachitoches
on Red River if our wagons get back. They had been sent on by land
and we have sent after them. I found out the cause of our return this
morning. A courier overtook our Genl. with the news of the fall of
Alexandra. This of course put the feds above us, and they could easily
have bagged us if we had proceeded by water.[13] We will now go by land
and get in above them. They are crowding us again. They seem to
be able to go wherever they please. I do hope that we can meet and
check them some where and that we may be enabled to <u>Massacre</u> the
last one of them that ever has or may hereafter place his unhallowed
feet upon the soil of our sunny South. This is the most beautiful
country on this river that I ever saw. Men wallow in wealth and
magnificence — There is also the finest prospect I ever saw for crops.
Every thing is Corn. If nothing happens enough corn will be raised in
this vally to support the Trans Miss Army but the river is high & deep
and there is nothing to keep the gun boats out and hence I expect to
hear of its entire destruction by Vandal hords. It is strange to me that a
Just God will suffer such a people and such a country as we have to be
Murdered and destroyed and wasted by such a Carping race of

Scoundrels as compose the Yankee army — I sent Ma a letter from Monroe La. with $100 in it. I also sent Ma, you & Frank one from this place with $100. Tell her to acknowledge the receipt of both if she got them. I perhaps will not write again until I get on Red River. Write to me at Shreveport La. I have no special news. A thousand kisses and manifold love for you all. I hope some time to see and embrace you all. Until then believe me

Truly yours
E. P. Petty

Camp Near Trenton La. May 15th 1863

My Dear Wife

I have been in this vicinity a little over one week and this is the 5th letter I have written home. In 3 preceeding I enclosed one hundred dollars cash making total sent you from this vicinity three hundred dollars. I hope that you will receive it all safe though it was rather hazardous to send so much money by mail. The owner however agreed to take the risk. Our train got back to us last Tuesday evening — about the time the train reached here we got orders to remain here three days longer. To day is the last of the 3 days & I await with impatience further orders. We have burned here about 10 days of most precious time which perhaps can never be recovered again. It looks like the same kind of Vacillation that lost us North West Arkansas and the Ark Post. One day Genl Holmes thought he would reinforce Genl Hindman and therefore send us east of the Ark river, the next he would believe that he would send us back to the Post and thus we would recross the river & so we crossed & recrossed until Hindman was whipped & compelled to evacuate North West Ark and the Post was captured. Well now here we are hesitating whether to remain here and defend the Ouachita river, go to Delhi near Vicksburg or go on & reinforce Genl Taylor on Red River and so I am afraid we will halt & hesitate until it will be too late to do any good in any quarter. If we would act the true policy we would concentrate our forces on Red River, whip & drive back Banks' Army and compel him to evacuate all Louisiana or at least a great portion of it. But we have hired our Generals to do our thinking and we must submit to them. They are behind the screen and are or ought to be posted and hence know perhaps more and better than we do. If they dont it is verry little advantage in being a General. I dont like this country here. It is going to be terrible on our boys again. A great many are already getting sick with a fair promise of a continuation of the same thing. The water is not healthy. The diarrhea prevails now extensively produced no doubt by the water. I have had it for two days and am somewhat weak & emaciated from it. I only weighed yesterday 132½ pounds which is considerable falling off in a few days. I have a most insatiable thirst for water which it does not gratify & yet it using me up to drink it. I am abstaining from food pretty well which will be of advantage to me and I am abstaining entirely from medicine. This you know I will do. I am just a little weak. Dont think I could march over 20 miles per day in my present condition. I hope we will get orders to day to go on to Red River. I believe that on a strain I could march in that direction 25 miles per day. There is no news here except as to the fight in Virginia on the Rhapahanock in which we are gloriously Victorious again.[14] What we gain in Va we loose in the Trans Miss Dept it seems. We had to give up nearly all our baggage on this trip. I left nearly all my blankets in Pine Bluff. We left several tents there. Then on the road near Hamburg we had to leave more and now at this camp we did a general business cleaning up. I sent back my trunk with nearly all my clothes in it together with some for L^ts Cunningham & Bearns. I ordered it to be sent by stage to Bastrop. It went from here to Camden Ark. where the man in charge said he would place it upon the stage for Bastrop. I advanced him 10 dollars to pay on freight. If this is'nt enough you must foot the bill at home. I hope it will get there safe. I am now nearly on the soldiers platform <u>naked</u>. See Judge Denny and get him to keep a look out for the trunk for you. I will send you the key by letter after awhile.

P.S.

I understand that Mrs James (Mary) Nolen has a guitar which is a verry fine one and that perhaps she has no use for it and it can be bought. Please see her and if it can be bought buy it for Ella. I want her to have one. It is fine music and the best accompaniment of the female voice. A fine guitar ought to cost in good times about $25 or $30. Get it as cheap as possible and then let Ella learn to play on it. I have sent you by mail $200. I enclose you here in $100 more.

Here are a thousand kisses for you.

Truly yours
E. P. Petty

Camp near Trenton La.
May 15th 1863

My Dear Son Frank,

I received your letter of the 15 inst. and you have scarcely an idea how much good it did me to get a letter from my good little son. Although you did not write it your self you I know you dictated it and endorsed the sentiment and hence it was almost as much satisfaction to me as if your own fingers had traced the letters. How proud I shall be, my son, when I get one in your own handwriting and I hope it will be so before long —

I know you could learn and would do it if you could just think about it right, but I was a little afraid that you thought more of play than learning, but since Ma & Ella & you have all written to me I am satisfied that you are doing your best to learn and learning fast. I am glad of it — I am proud of it and now I know that when I come home I will find a neat, gentlemanly educated boy instead of a street wandering, loafing, idle one.

Oh how proud I will be of you then Frank. So push on my son in the good way — learn all you can — help Ma and mind her — love your brothers & sister — be kind to every body & every thing and you will not only have the approbation of your parents who love you, and of man, woman & child but that of your own conscience and of God who rules every thing and who loves every good boy.

Much love & many kisses to you all.

Yours truly
E.P. Petty
Capt. Co. F Allen's Regiment

Camp 4 Miles NE. of Sparta Bienville
parish La May 19th 1863

My Dear Daughter

Yours of April 23rd and Ma's of the 28th April last have just now come to hand. We had our mail ordered to Shreveport La and sent a courier to that place after it and he met us to day with our mail. You can scarcely appreciate my feelings on the receipt of your letters. Imagine yourself far away from home & its sweets toiling in dust & sunshine, fatigued & footsore amidst rough & uncouth soldiers with oaths & obscenity on every hand and then in this moral desert to receive a sweet & endearing token from home from wife and daughter perfumed with love, purity & fidelity and then you will have but a faint idea of what were my feelings.

I have heard all the news etc of the Louisiana fighting and quite sad it was to me and detrimental to our struggling country and we are now on our way to reinforce Genl Taylor at Nachitoches on Red River so as to assist in driving these Vandals out of the country or dying in the attempt. We are now about 60 miles from Nachitoches and are making forced marches to get there.[15]

I have been a little unwell for about 6 or 7 days but have without much trouble or pain made out to travel at the head of my company and could now march 25 miles per day. We have some that are a little sick who could not do so and hence we have only made to day about 17 miles. Every body & every thing is now up at camp and preparing for our supper. The sun is about an hour high. The men have been in camp for about 3 hours & the wagons are now all in. The reason I write so bad is that I am sitting in a wagon writing on my lap. The mules are pulling at the tongue and the men are sifting meal in the hind part of the wagon and so with all things I have a shaky time of it.

I am sorry that you have an enemy at school and hope that it will be honorably adjusted between you but I am proud that you are so independent as not to bend or cringe to any body. When I do a person any rong and am satisfied that I am in the rong I will apologize for it. If that it satisfies the injured party all right and we will still be friends but if after I apologize they are still dissatisfied they can go and I will never put myself in their way again or have any thing to do with them. It then becomes theirs to approach me and make the necessary apologies or advances. If I have done them no rong I made no apologies. In your case if you were rong you did enough by offering to make friends and now if she wants to be friendly let her make the advances. Dont be stubborn but be independent. Let her come to you now. Never succumb to any person. Be always sure you are right and then die by the right. I am sorry that your preacher _____ got into a muss. He is too old a man and ought by this time to be so tempered by experience and age as not to let his hot blood get the better of his judgement and lead him in a harrang of abuse against other churches or denominations. He ought to be charitable enough to accredit as much honesty to others as he claims for himself and ought to know that every person cannot see or think exactly alike. This you (a child) have sense enough to know much more so a man of extensive learning & great experience. But Mr. _____ conduct I consider in the highest degree reprehensible. It showed a want of sense, taste, judgment & every thing else that characterizes a sensible man or even a half witted man. If he did not approve the discourse or the sentiment he could quietly get up and leave the house. This would have been the course of a gentleman. The most gentlemanly course he could have pursued would have been to remain in the church and listened as long as it was bearable and then if it became intolerable get up quietly and leave. To get up in a crowd of ladies, gentlemen & children and call an old man & a preacher in the midst of his sermon a liar was indication of low breeding and bullyism.

As great a traitor as [Andrew Jackson] Hamilton ought to meet the traitors doom death by hanging and a woman so base and hostile to our Cause as his wife ought to be escorted beyond our lines and sent to the federals. You have such a nice joke on me do you? No doubt Pass Turner told it all finely and in a laughable style but let me tell you my dear little daughter I never passed myself off to the girls as a single man. Whenever I was asked by any body whether I was married or single I always told them I was married. For my own sake, for your Ma's, for your's, for the children, for virtue and chastity & purity's sake and for the sake of humanity I would not do such a thing. I have frequently enjoyed myself with the young ladies without refering to the subject at all but when ever asked I always told the truth. The case you refer to occurred with Miss Mat Lytle a Cousin of Lum Owen and it was the first night I ever saw her. We went down to see Lum & the girls of course and during the conversation we spoke of the Texas ladies when Miss Mat said that Cousin Lum told her that you had a daughter. Lum had been staying there several days & had told her of me & my family. I am much pleased with your progress in music. Think you have done finely but dont let this take up too much of your time — you have more important studies to pursue. So give to music only the time that ought to be devoted to music. I exceedingly regret to hear of the death of Lieut Litle. A mighty good & honest man has been lost to the community in his death.

I am glad that John Person got home with my cloth. I have sent my trunk home with nearly all my clothing in it & hope it will get home in due time. Tell Ma it is all right on the Allen money question. I only wanted to know how she made her calculation that was all. I got a letter the other day from Pa written before yours. Tell Ma that as long as matters stand as they now do she need not look for me home. I will not desert my Country and under any pretext in her hour of need. Puryear said he intended to tell my wife how I was running after the women in Ark. He has'nt told her half what I have written her. I wrote to Ma to buy you Mrs Irvin (Mary) Nolen's guitar. She has a fine one and I understand that perhaps it can be bought — I will give you some songs I want you to learn to sing & play either on piano or guitar or both & the accordian "The Lone starry hours," "Bonny Eloise," "Bonny Jean," "Anna Laurie," "Do they Miss me at home," "The Wild Chamoise," "The Wild Ash Deer," "The Ingle Side," besides many others of the same sort. Off all these I like Bonny Jean, Anna Laura & The Lone Starry hours the best in the order mentioned. Get the songs & the music & learn them to play for me when I come home.[16]

I sent Ma $300 by mail in three different letters from Monroe & Trenton. I hope she got them. I now herein enclose fifty dollars more, $5 for Ella, $5 for Frank, $5 for Don, $5 for Van & $30 for Ma. You can spend it as you please only I want you to write how you all invest it so that I can see which has done the best with their money. Write to me at Shreveport La. I believe that I write pretty often and although as Puryear says the Ark galls are about to steal me yet I dont forget home and would not give my little home, loving wife & sweet children for all Ark & La & all the women in them both. Dont you & Ma be alarmed about me. I will come up all right. Love & kisses in abundance. Tom Bearns wishes to be remembered & wants his folks to know that he is all right. So of Lt. Flemming & Lum Owens.

Yours truly
E. P. Petty

Camp Near Black Lake Natchitoches
Parish La May 20th 1863

My Dear Wife
We have travelled to day some 19 or 20 miles and are now encamped on Bayou near Black Lake and about 25 miles from Campte [Campti] on Red River at which point I suppose we will cross that river and then move down by Grand E'Core to Natchitoches & form a junction with Genl Taylor. After which I expect that we will have some fighting to do. We have heard some cannons down the river to day & yesterday but dont know where nor the cause. I think that we will have warm times down here this summer. The fact is we dont care much. We have tramped so much until we prefer fighting to marching. Our boys (the most) are eager for a fight. I reckon one fight will sober them. I was for the first time in my life put under arrest yesterday but released in the evening. The evening before Lt Cunningham & myself after getting to camp concluded to go to a house about a mile off and get our supper (so as to get some milk & butter) leaving Lts McLester

& Beavers with the Company. After we left Col Jones wanted the Captains of Co.'s so as to communicate some orders. Lt McL. reported & Jones wanted to know where I was & where Lt. C. was.

He was told where we were. Next morning without comeing to our camp or making any enquiry about it he reported to Genl McCulloch that we had staid all night away from our Company without leave from him and Genl McC. ordered him to arrest us. Which he did just after we started on the morning march. Col Jones ordered us to report to Genl McC which we did upon reaching camp in the evening. When Genl McC. learned the facts and that we did not stay out at night but returned at an early hour he released us and said that he only ordered us to be arrested for staying all night. I asked Col Jones who reported the fact that we staid out all night to Genl McC. & he said that he did that he supposed it was so. I told him he ought not to act upon supposition and that he must report himself to Genl McC. for reprimand (this last was in a Joke) and so the matter ended. The fact are that we were inside of the picket line at the picket camp, took supper with Capt Miller who commanded the pickets that night, also with Col Gregg[17] Brigade Field officer of the day who had the authority to & did give us leave to stay & get our supper so that we were right & the ballance were rong. If the matter had been pressed I believe it would have resulted in getting Col Jones reprimanded but I did not wish that. I am thus particular in giving you the facts as no doubt the statement of my arrest will go back home and will be exagerated & magnified as is the case always and so that you may know for a certainty that I am all right as I ever have been & ever hope to be. I have no news to write. I am sorry that Lt Litle is dead. I loved him as well as I could well love a man. His trunk was carried to Belton Texas by Mr. George B. White. You had better write a letter to Mr W and find out all about it with charges etc. & have it sent to you at Bastrop. You can then see Mrs Litle & she will take the trunk & settle matters with you. I am well to day & feel fine and am able to eat as much & travel as far as any body and am as ready & willing as any body to meet & fight the Yankees.

Yours truly
E. P. Petty

Camp Near Campte Louisiana
May 22nd 1863

My Dear Wife
We are now in about 1 mile of Red River and the town of Campte

encamped in a beautiful grove on a considerable Lake the water of
which is not verry good however and is filled with alligators. We will
not travel tomorrow but will spend the day in cleaning our clothing
and arms, inspecting our arms & amunition etc. Day after tomorrow
we will go down Red River on steam boats to a point as I now learn
about 50 miles below Alexandra. The federals have evacuated
Alexandra and that vicinity after devastating the country, laying waste
farms, breaking sugar kettles, destroying farming utensils, household
furniture, beds, clothing, etc, stealing all the negroes & other
transportable property and carrying it away with them. We have a
cavalry force attempting to cut off their trains and try to get back some
of the plunder. Genl Moutons commands our Cavalry and I am
informed has near 8000 men.[18] I do hope he will be successful and that
a just retribution will soon overtake the plundering devils. I have long
prayed and petitioned as you know for the black flag. The authorities
and the masses were against me but such raids as this are fast bringing
them to their senses and I sincerely hope ere long to see its glorious
(though unchristian) folds floating at the head of our oppressed and
struggling nation. For myself it is my banner and to it I bend my knee
in adoration and if any luckless Yank should unfortunately come in my
way he need not petition for mercy. If he does I'le give him lead if he
ask for bread or water. I'le send his infamous soul to the regions below
where he will get melted lava for his parched lips. I am becomeing a
monomaniac on the subject of the black flag. I have seen my Country
& her sons & daughters suffer enough by vandal foes. You must excuse
the blots on the reverse hereof as I had an old & a miserably bad pen
which gave down too much ink besides it I have a miserable light to
write by. I have a better pen now and will do better on this side. I can
form no correct idea of the number of our forces here and in this
valley. It must however amount to some 12 or 15 000 men. Genl
Taylor has already left Natchitoches for Alexandra. Others have also
gone down. We will follow and I think we will have forces enough to
follow Banks up perhaps to New Orleans or at least to confine him to

the Mississippi River. We have had a hard time of it and a long one on this march. We left Pine Bluff 24th Apl but we lost about 6 or 7 days at Monroe. Take your map and follow us in the march — Beginning at Pine Bluff Ark — to Monticello — to Hamburg Ark down Bayou Bartholomew to its mouth at Washita City — down the Washita River to Trenton just above Monroe La — down the Washita to near Columbia — back up the Washita to Trenton — To Vernon, to Sparta and then to Campte or this camp — a part of the time we made forced marches. Is'nt this a tortuous & zigzag march. It is over 300 miles. Dont we infantry soldiers have a hard time. Dont you feel for us. Now we have got to steamboat it awhile and then perhaps march again and then perhaps fight and maybe skedaddle or pursue the enemy double quick etc. I think that I can fully appreciate the ease and comforts of home when I get there again at least I am more than willing to try it but as this is my war & one that I took some little part in making I must bear it all unmurmuringly & stand to my post though the fires do envellop me and though myself, my wife, children, friends, property and Country all all be swept away leaving not a wreck behind. Col Allen rejoined us to day for the first time since he started home about the 20th April. He met with rather a cool reception as they boys did'nt care much whether he came back or not. He informed me that he sent my letter to you with the two hundred dollars forward by Lt Coleman of Colorado County with instructions that if he could not see you to leave it with Mrs Allen — I suppose by this time you have got it all. I have also sent you by mail in four different letters $350 which I hope you may safely get. I wrote you to buy sugar, molasses, salt etc. You had better at once lay you in a full supply of these necessary articles as all the sugar regions nearly have fallen into federal hands and the crops destroyed so that there is no hope of sugar & molasses being any cheaper soon and as for salt, coffee etc that prospect is also unpromising. Invest your money in something, milk, cows & horses and land and buy corn & fodder etc to keep them up — They will all pay perhaps better than Confederate money as every body have set their heads to depreciate the money. You requested me to send you blank deed for Snellings interest in the Piney Land. Here in you will find it. Do the best you can with him. You had better now write to me at Alexandra Louisiana. I expect that will be our nearest post office. I have no special news to write. Send me a Texas news paper occasionly. I hardly ever see one. Much love & many kisses to the children & compliments to friends.

Yours truly
E. P. Petty

My Dear Wife

We reached Alexandra yesterday at about 2 oclock PM by steam Boat. From what we could learn on the way down we were highly elated with the idea that we would be landed in a day or so in the presence of the enemy and would have some active & exciting to do to compensate for our long and wearisome march but to our chagrin & mortification and surprise we received orders to debark on the north side of the river opposite to A. and go into camps as I learn to await the arrival of the ballance of our Brigade when we will proceed immediately to La Croix landing on Catahoula Lake, take steam Boats and return immediately to Monroe via Little River & Washita river the same route which we undertook to come to this place. Why all this boxing the compass this marching and countermarching I can hardly form a conjecture. The Feds have nearly all left this part of Louisiana and are drawing in from every where towards Vicksburg. So our forces seem to be gathering that way and ere long one of the hardest and most bloody battles of the world will be fought in that vicinity.[19] It may be that we are to go to Monroe then by Railway to a point as near Vicksburg as possible so as to be if possible in at the fight or near enough to assist in winding up the great ball. Vicksburg is in a critical condition but I have every confidence in the skill of our generals and in the heorism and bravery of our men and about the time the Yankees are certain of their gain something will turn up as it did it Richmond and we will knock their base from under them. Vicksburg will not fall. Vicksburg will come out all right or I will give up my judgement about such matters. Our recent & present movements convince me of the uncertainty of all military calculations & movements. To day we are ordered to one point and on tomorrow some movement of the enemy calls us to another. This would not be so hard if we had steam boats & Rail Road transportation over here but when we have to make long forced & weary land marches it wears the soldiers down. I only saw Alexandra from the River. It is a beautiful and quite a large place. The feds did verry little damage to the town. They destroyed the foundry and some shops, burned up some cotton houses & fencing. But in the Parish they destroyed all the crops, stole all the negroes, horses, mules, cotton, sugar, molasses etc. They did immense damage to the Parish. I am still bad off with diarrhea, dont get any better, quite weak though I stand square to my post. Dont take any medicine. Dont intend to if I can help it. This disease is quite prevalent. It is attributable to the water we have been

using. This is the first camp in La. where we have had good water. The water is cool & well tasted. We are in a high piney woods the long leaf pine. Write to me at Shreveport La. If we go to Monroe that is on the route. Give my love to my dear children & respects to friends.

Yours truly
E. P. Petty

P.S I saw John Hereford yesterday. He is the same old John & looks as natural as life.

On Steamer Doctor Batey
Tensas Bayou La May 30 1863

My Dear Daughter

I wrote Ma a letter from Alexandra dated 27th inst. The date was a mistake and should have been 28th. In a verry short time (say 2 hours) after I had written and dispatched that letter we received orders to cook 3 days rations and start at 5 o'clock PM same day.[20] We did so — travelled about 15 miles that night taking up at near 11 oclock. Next morning (yesterday) we travelled 10 miles (starting at day light) to Little River when we embarked at La Croix's Landing. Went down Little River to Catahoula Lake, through that Lake into Little River again (the river running through the lake) into Black river at Trinity, where the Washita, Tensas & Little rivers unite forming the Black — up Tensas river and are now on it steaming like life in the direction of Vicksburg. You will see by the map that Tensas (Tensaw) rises in lake Providence which lake is in about ½ mile of the Mississippi river and the falls have cut a canal out of that river into the lake. We are now in the region commanded by the feds and would not be surprised at an attack at any moment. We have been putting some artilery in position on our bow to reply to any thing of the kind and our men & guns are now in order. I dont know how far up this river we are going nor what our destination or the object of it but I do know that we are moving with great secresy and dispatch in the direction of the enemy. We left all our baggage nearly behind. I have a change of underclothing & my oil cloth to sleep on. I have no blanket. McLester & myself have one blanket between us. Many of the men have no change of clothing. I have one fry pan, one bread pan and one water bucket to the mess. So you see that we are now on the proper basis for fighting — I expect that before tomorrow night we will hear the enemy's guns. I am

writing this letter with very little prospect of sending it off but it will
be ready and if the chance offers I will send it. All is hurry, confusion
& bustle. We are beyond the line of Post offices. I dont know when
you will hear from me again. I am told by those who know that in
battle life is uncertain and that bullets and balls are wreckless & blind.
One by chance might hit me and stop my writing & thinking process.
I have no fears or misgivings however on this point for I believe that
until a man's time to die comes he is safe and that when it does come
he cannot resist it and so I go forward confidently trusting to my fate.
Dont be alarmed or uneasy on my account. I am all right or hope I
am. You shall hear from me just so soon as possible and as often as
possible. My present parting advice to you is to be the same good
sweet girl that you have ever been. To be kind & affectionate to your
Mother & your brothers. To be respectful to age, dignified & courteous
to your equals and kind & accomodating to the young & polite to
every body. To be studious — qualify yourself to take a high position in
society. Keep a loof from the vicious & low bred. Associate with those
of the first class in society & as much as possible with the educated.
Never do any thing that is mean & little & that would show a little &
low order of mind. Dont do any thing without asking your Ma's advice
and particularly dont correspond with any body unless it is agreeable to
her & let her see the letters. Dont write to any gentlemen or boy at all
until you finish your education and then only by consent of your
parents. On this last point be extremely careful. Take a high &
dignified stand in society & sink or swim by it. "There is plenty of
room above but it is crowded mightily below." Dont take deck passage.
The Cabin is commodious, airy, accommodating & pleasant and ladies
and gentlemen do travel therein. The Cream rises to the top while the
blue John remains below. In the selection then of associates and
companions choose such as will not drag you down but rather elevate
you in the scale of gentility & respectability. You cant be too cautious
on these important points. Let them occupy your mind sufficiently to
impress their importance upon you. Your family and your stock are as
good and fine as any body's. Then dont for God's sake and your own &
mine and your Ma's & all our family do any thing that will deteriorate
or degenerate it. Improve it if possible. You are not wealthy in one
sense of the word but you have a mine of wealth in brain & heart &
honor & virtue & character & quality that will outshine all the wealth
of this world that consists in glittering heaps of gold if you will but
keep it all pure and unalloyed and bright. Will you not do it? I will
answer for you Yes. I know you will for my sake. This may be my final
parting advice to you. If so cherish it as a memento of me. It comes

gushing from a heart that beats every stroke warm & true for the "loved ones at home" — which though wild & cheerful is as "true to you all as the needle to the pole." Port Hudson is completely surrounded & Vicksburg is in a precarious condition. I hope we will be able to relieve the one or the other. A man of Capt Edgars Battery on this boat fell overboard and was drowned in Little River. We could not save the poor fellow —

    I have two sick men this morning. Sam Wilson & Tom Gorman both have fever and I am afraid will have to be left. I left one sick near Alexandra. Sam Flemming is quite unwell to day. I am nearly well now. The orders to come on this trip acted better on me than medicine. I could hardly walk when it came & that evening & next morning I marched 25 miles by land & then boated it to this place & now feel pretty well. Give my very best love spiced with a thousand kisses to wife & children and write me.

Truly yours
E. P. Petty

I have no pen or ink & have to write with pencil. Mighty bad but best I can do.

E.P.P.

My Dear Daughter

I now finish another chapter in my letter — On the 30 ult (the date of my letter) we debarked from the Steam boats at a point about 9 or 10 miles from the Mississippi River and about 20 miles below Vicksburg. We spent the principal part of the night preparing rations for an early march next day. At about 2 clock AM next morning we were stirring & in a few moments were on the march for the Miss River.[21] I forgot to tell you that as soon as we landed on the evening of the 30th we sent out a scouting party who captured one federal soldier and several negroes with a cart & some tricks & provisions — another scouting party were fired into by federal pickets about 2 miles from our camp — This last thing gave the feds notice that we were at hand and they went to work for our reception. This prevented us from surprising them & capturing them with baggage etc. Well as I said we started at about 2 oclock and about 8 oclock we were halted & ordered to load — pickets and skirmishers were thrown forward some on horseback & some on foot. About 3 miles from the fed camp our skirmishers had some fun with their pickets etc who retreated as ours advanced. We captured some 2 more negroes about 2 miles from the fed camp. We were ordered to cap our guns. Our flags were thrown to the breeze and we marched boldly forward — They had been camped at Judge Perkins plantation about 1 mile or a little over from the Miss River. We came to Judge P.'s place and found that they had skeddaddled leaving some provisions & clothing etc. We took possession of these or a[t] least the men were generally did so each one appropriating such as he wanted. The ballance we left — a half mile further on & we discovered some boats raising steam. We could see that there were both gun & transport boats — We could see the men on board. They were about ½ mile from us — A long levee led from where we were down to & beyond the feds. Running nearly directly towards them a little bayou ran along in the same direction the mouth of which formed an inlet of the Miss in which were the boats. McCulloch's Brigade alone was on the ground — Randall's [Randal's] was about 6 miles off & Hawes on the Tensas about 10 miles. Flournoy's, Allen's & Fitzhugh's Regts formed close under the outside of the levee. Edgar with his battery supported by Waterhouses Regt went over to the left about 100 yards to feel of the enemy. Before Edgar got into position the gun boat opened upon us with shell. Edgar replied. This artilery duel was kept up about an hour the enemy beginning & ending it. They threw their shells high & wide. They did'nt know where to find us & hence sent them out generally some exploding high in the air, some as they struck & some not all. Their transport after being struck (as we suppose) several times ran the gun boat, withdrew to a more respectable distance. We dont know what damage we did them. They killed one man with shell & wounded one in the skirmish. After the shelling ceased we thought we saw them planting a land battery behind a levee to rake us with — Some determined to offer them battle charged their battery in the face of the gunboat & take [?] or drive them on to their boats. We threw forward a line of skirmishers, formed our line of battle & moved up in the open field to about 400 yards of where their boats were & then waited in line of battle for the word. Our skirmishers were called in, reported that they had all gone on the boats. We then marched back to this place on same reaching here before dark making over 20 miles march, an hour fight & about 3 hours exposure in the hot sun. This ends this expedition which was no doubt intended to cut off Genl Grants (Fed) supplies but which failed as he had none there. Well I have been in one battle at last. I stood it finely not a nerve twiched or muscle trembled — not a palpitation of the heart, not a misgiving. I was as cool, quiet & self possessed as you ever saw me. I thought no more of it than going to a frolic. Co F was all right so was the regiment — every body cool. Jokes & cute remarks about the shooting etc passed freely. If this is all the fear I dont mind a battle. We start again tomorrow. Where I cant say but hope we will do better. A big fight is going on at Vicksburg. I can distinctly hear the guns. They make the ground shake. Wash Jones wants you to tell his wife that he is well, that he left his paper in his trunk & hence cant write.

Yours truly
E. P. Petty
May 30th 1863

Bayou Mason below Delhi
[Bayou Maçon, Madison Parish, La.]
Thursday June 4th 1863

Dear Ella

I write a continuation of my letter having had no chance to mail it yet. We now have 3 days rations cooked in our haversacks and are on route for some point as I suppose to attack the enemy. There are lots of them in our vicinity now and we anticipate stirring times. We will perhaps get pay for our long season of inactivity. In our fight of <u>Sunday</u> 31st May our damage was one killed, one missing & one wounded. The federal loss we cannot positively ascertain. An old negro woman that was with them reports that we killed eleven. I dont fully credit this report however though no doubt but we killed some.

We got 2 wagons, 6 mules, a lot of clothing, blankets etc and about 100 beeves with one fed prisoner & 5 negroes. I will enclose you a minature diagram of the battle field which is however verry imperfect. When we formed our line of battle facing the enemy we were in about 800 yards of them and why they did'nt fire on us from their gun boats is more than I can imagine. I expected it every moment. We were in the open field with no obstructions in the way. It was the most dare devil banter that I ever saw. They had 3 gun boats and I dont know what else. I was highly amused at some of my boys when we were forming that line of battle. We had to pass through a verry fine dew berry patch and not withstanding we were expecting the fire of the enemy every moment some of my boys began to gather dewberries. I told them that it was no time to gather dew berries now, that we would get blue berries (bullets) as much as we wanted in a few moments. If you could have heard the jests sent around at the explosion of every shell and every thing else you would have thought that we were going to a frolic instead of a battle. Some few men in our regiment were frightened but very few. None of my men or of our regiment were hurt. I have several sick men along now. The hard marches, hot weather and bad water is the cause of the sickness. Another fight was going on at Vicksburg last night. We could plainly hear the guns.

We left Tensas Bayou yesterday morning and have been deep in the Mississippi swamps where snakes in abundance [*illegible phrase*].[22] We are now marching up Bayou Mason in the direction of Delhi and are about 18 miles of that place. I hope that I can get to mail my letter at that place. We are now in about 10 miles of Delhi & 20 of Richmond. At Richmond the feds have a force where I expect we will hear the music again. I have been sick with diarrhea for over 3 weeks. I am better now and am packing all my luggage and marching pretty hard. Write to Monroe La. Love etc to all.

Truly yours
E. P. Petty

Early in June 1863 the Confederates decided to attack Milliken's Bend on the Mississippi River, an assault destined to be their most serious threat from the west during the siege of Vicksburg. With Milliken's Bend taken, Young's Point, eleven miles below, would certainly fall, and thus Pemberton's army in Vicksburg would be covered if he chose to abandon the city and cross the river. In the meantime Kirby Smith instructed Taylor to keep Pemberton informed of his movements whenever practicable and "to spare no exertions in his efforts to throw supplies into Vicksburg from the west bank of the river."[23]

Lying immediately above the town of that name, Milliken's Bend was a Federal camp 15 feet above the right bank of the Mississippi. The camp, 150 yards wide, was sheltered by two levees, one on the riverbank and the other on its land side. In front of the forward levee the camp was protected by a thick hedge averaging 15 feet in height. To the right and left were open fields, trailing off in each direction into densely wooded areas. Supporting gunboats could protect the camp's rear. The garrison, commanded by Colonel Hermann Lieb, consisted of the Twenty-third Iowa Volunteer Infantry and the African Brigade (Ninth Louisiana, Eleventh Louisiana, Thirteenth Louisiana and First Mississippi), numbering in all 1,061 men. The ex-slaves had been mustered in at Milliken's Bend on May 22.[24]

By a roundabout route Walker's Division on June 6 moved to the vicinity of Richmond, Louisiana. Five miles above this place, J. M. Hawes's brigade took the road leading to Young's Point to destroy the Federal camp there while McCulloch's Brigade, numbering about 1,500 men, moved against Milliken's Bend. Horace Randal's brigade remained in reserve at the intersection of the roads. Between 2:30 and 3:00 on the morning of June 7, Colonel Isaac F. Harrison's Louisiana cavalry, serving as McCulloch's scouts, having approached within about a mile and a half of Milliken's Bend, were suddenly fired upon by the Federal pickets from behind a dense hedge. Many of the scouts broke and fled to the rear, throwing away their guns and losing their hats and coats. Mistaking Harrison's men for enemy cavalry, the Confederate skirmishers fired at them; fortunately, no one was killed or wounded. Now without the benefit of the cavalry, McCulloch immediately pressed his skirmishers forward and drove back the enemy pickets.

Upon encountering enemy skirmishers in considerable force under cover of a thick hedge, McCulloch ordered forward a portion of his command in line. The Confederates drove forward from hedge to hedge and ditch to ditch, through small running briars and vines that made a regular military advance almost impossible. Twenty-five paces from the first levee, on the Federal left flank, three regiments formed in line under a heavy fire. Allen's Regiment was on Waterhouse's left and Fitzhugh's, under the command of Lieutenant Colonel E. P. Gregg, was on Allen's left. Flournoy's Regiment was behind and to the right. The three regiments charged the enemy posted behind the levee with cries of "no quarter!" Many of the Negro troops were inexperienced in the use of a gun, some had had only a few days of drill, and, according to Federal Brigadier General Elias S. Dennis, their guns were "very inferior." As the Confederates charged up the first levee (which was ten feet high and crowned with cotton bales), most of the white troops and some of the Negroes in this line after one or two volleys fled back to the second line of defense, leaving the remaining Negro troops to defend the position. Hand-to-hand fighting with bayonets and clubbed muskets broke out. "This charge was resisted by the negro portion of the enemy's force with considerable obstinacy, while the white or true Yankee portion ran like whipped curs almost as soon as the charge was ordered," McCulloch reported. "There were several instances in this charge where the enemy crossed bayonets with us or were shot down at the muzzle of the musket." E. P. Becton, a surgeon in Waterhouse's Nineteenth Texas Infantry, wrote his wife that "the Yankee force at the Milliken Bend fight consisted principally of negroes & the boys say they fought bravely for a little while but when the charge was ordered they fled in confusion."[25]

Some of the Negro troops cowered below their works and were shot in the head. That afternoon Admiral David Porter arrived at Milliken's Bend in his flagship *Black Hawk*. What he saw he described in a letter to Grant: "The dead negroes lined the ditch inside of the parapet, or levee, and were mostly shot on the top of the head. In front of them, close to the levee, lay an equal number of rebels stinking in the sun. Their knapsacks contained four days provisions. They were miserable looking wretches."[26]

The Confederates drove the Federals into the open space between the two levees and through their camp to the riverbank, using their bayonets freely. "When we got to the top of the levee they bolted and ran to their gunboats," J. H. Pillow of Allen's regiment recalled many years later. "Then we put in our work. How many we killed I do not know, but there were dead ones all along to the river. I do not remember the number of men we lost. My only brother was killed." At the second levee nearest to the river the resistance stiffened. The gunboat *Choctaw* opened fire with a giant 100-pounder Parrott rifle and a 9-inch Dahlgren. "It was impossible for me to see the enemy on account of the high banks, and I could learn their position only by hailing our troops," reported Lieutenant Commander Frank M. Ramsay. McCulloch fell back to the first levee and took up position there. The wounded were removed to the rear. An attempt against the extreme Federal right was checked by two companies of the Eleventh Louisiana posted behind cotton bales and part of the old levee. In his official report Taylor criticized the Texans for retreating. "On mounting the second levee in pursuit, our men came in sight of the gunboat and transports (mistaken by them for gunboats), and at once fell back, and could not be induced to cross the levee. Confusion ensued, and the gunboat, which at the beginning had no steam up, brought her one gun to bear in the direction of our troops."[27]

McCulloch sent back some six miles to ask for reinforcements. At 9 o'clock the gunboat *Lexington* came up and threw a few shells into the woods. Walker hastened forward just after noon with Randal's Brigade but found that McCulloch had already withdrawn his troops out of range of the shells. His men were exhausted by the day's excessive heat and want of water. In the evening Walker withdrew the two brigades back toward Richmond instead of moving down to Young's Point to aid Hawes as Taylor had instructed — an action which the commanding general censured in his official report: "It is true the heat was intense, the thermometer marking 95 degrees in the shade; but, had common vigor and judgment been displayed, the work would all have been completed by 8 a.m."[28]

The Confederates captured 50 Negro soldiers and 2 of their white officers ("unfortunately," according to Taylor)[29] and brought back a number of horses and mules, commissary stores and some few small arms. McCulloch's losses were significant: 44 killed, 130 (or 131) wounded and 10 missing — 12.2 percent. The Seventeenth Texas had the highest losses in the brigade — 1 officer (Lieutenant Thomas Beaver) and 20 men killed, 4 officers (including Petty) and 64 men wounded and 3 men missing — a total of 92, half the casualties in the brigade. Colonel Allen was slightly wounded but remained at his post. Federal losses were reported to total 652. Of this number, 101 were killed, 285 wounded, and 266 captured or missing. Some of the missing straggled back into camp later.[30]

In the meantime General Hawes, who was to make a simultaneous predawn attack upon Young's Point while McCulloch assaulted Milliken's Bend, set out at 7:00 in the evening to cover the necessary 20 miles. He had with him 1,403 Texans, plus a small detachment of Harrison's cavalry to serve as scouts. His troop movement delayed by a destroyed bridge over Walnut Bayou, it was not until 10:30 on the morning of June 7 that Hawes came upon a small picket of Negro troops, peacefully fishing about two miles from their main camp. He captured several of them and drove the rest back. After a reconnaissance

reported three gunboats in the river at Young's Point (one of the vessels was actually a hospital boat), Hawes withdrew to the woods to his left and rear without making an attack or firing a shot. About 500 of his men were rendered unfit for duty from heat exhaustion. A short time later the gunboats *Petrel* and *Romeo* began shelling the area with shrapnel, and Hawes ordered a general retreat, leaving over 200 stragglers behind. Harrison's cavalry was sent to bring in these men. Taylor's orders to seize the camp and send the captured property to the rear were forgotten. "It is useless to state that the Brigade suffered no loss as a portion of my skirmishers only were engaged with a small detachment & picket of the enemy," Hawes reported.[31]

Taylor was quite severe on Walker's Division in his official report, writing:

General Walker's division was suddenly and secretly thrown within 6 or 8 miles of the enemy's line of camps on the Mississippi River, information of the most reliable character furnished to it of the enemy's strength and position, which in every instance was fully verified. Nothing was wanted but vigrous action in the execution of the plans which had been carefully laid out for it to insure such successes as the conditions of affairs would admit; besides, the division commander had weeks before expressed to the lieutenant general commanding his ardent desire to undertake this or a similar expedition. Unfortunately, I discovered too late that the officers and men of this division were possessed of a dread of gunboats such as pervaded our people at the commencement of the war. To this circumstance and to want of mobility in these troops are to be attributed the meager results of the expedition.

Of McCulloch's performance, Taylor remarked: "In this affair General McCulloch appears to have shown great personal bravery, but no capacity for handling masses." As for Hawes, "Should there be a court of inquiry or a court-martial, or would it be better simply to relieve Brigadier-General Hawes?" Secretary of War James A. Seddon asked after reading Taylor's report.[32]

Walker later learned from one of his staff who returned from Richmond that Taylor's report had reflected upon him. On October 15 Taylor asked Kirby Smith to convey to the War Department "the statement that nothing in the report was intended to reflect, directly or indirectly, on General Walker. The plan was mine, and the position held by General Walker was strictly in accordance with my orders. The misconception existing at Richmond is calculated to injure unjustly a meritorious officer, and I ask that this communication be forwarded." Walker had earlier written Kirby Smith that through General Thomas Waul he had learned that President Davis attributed the failure to relieve Vicksburg from the Trans-Mississippi to his (Walker's) advice. "It is but justice to a gallant and efficient officer that this impression should be removed," Kirby Smith admonished Davis. "The blame, if it rests anywhere, is with myself and General Taylor, the department and district commanders. General Walker, when on the march from Arkansas to Alexandria, asked permission to act with his division against Grant's communications opposite Vicksburg. Banks in force was at that time pressing General Taylor, and, the country east of the Bayou Mason Hills was too much under water to admit of operations."[33]

Disgusted with apparent failure and eager to get back to lower Louisiana, Taylor prepared to abandon the campaign for the relief of Vicksburg and to transfer Walker's Division south of the Red River. Kirby Smith's headquarters was notified to this effect on June 8, but three days later Taylor reported that for the present he had decided not to withdraw Walker "until the enemy's movements and the condition of affairs around Vicksburg are more fully developed. As there are troops enough in the lower portion of the State for the expedition against the enemy, who is opposite Port Hudson, it is not necessary at this moment to withdraw General Walker's division, as I contemplated at the time of my report from Richmond." On June 16 Kirby Smith wrote President Davis from Shreveport:

> General Taylor is commanding the troops within his own district, and is in person with the force operating for the relief of Port Hudson. General Walker was left in command of the force in Northern Louisiana, and operating opposite Vicksburg. They both have instructions to spare no efforts in throwing supplies into those places. All the disposable force of the department has been thrown to the relief of Port Hudson and Vicksburg, and is operating on the Mississippi to that end.[34]

Many of the sick and wounded of Walker's Division were moved west to Delhi, to which the railroad was still operating. Here Randal's troops boarded a train for the trip to Monroe. At Monroe they embarked on transports and had reached Columbus on the Ouachita River, when Randal was informed that the movement to Alexandria had been suspended and that he should rejoin Walker at Richmond.[35]

Meanwhile, on June 8 Grant ordered Brigadier General Joseph A. Mower to move his Eagle Brigade from Haynes Bluff across the Mississippi to Young's Point to reinforce Dennis. He was instructed to drive the Confederates from Richmond and to push on to Monroe. On the morning of June 15 Mower's 1,200 men were joined at the junction of the Duckport and Milliken's Bend roads by Brigadier General Alfred W. Ellet, with the Marine Brigade. The Federal force numbered about 2,500 men and two batteries. McCulloch's and Hawes's brigades, reduced by sickness to about 1,500 effectives, according to Walker, waited for the attack within about two miles of Richmond behind a wide ditch and a hedge of willows. The Fifth Minnesota was deployed as skirmishers while the other Federal regiments formed the line of battle, with the artillery placed in intervals in the lines and a section on the left flank. Advancing across an open field, the Federal skirmishers had approached within 30 yards of cover when Walker's men opened up a heavy fire. The Minnesotans at once fell flat upon the ground, seeking partial protection in the weeds and tall grass. For the next 20 minutes a sharp skirmish fight ensued. The Eighteenth Texas then fell back, pursued by the Fifth Minnesota and a portion of Ellet's command. The Confederates began to rake the open area with grape and canister. Mower sent two batteries forward, and a sharp artillery duel followed that lasted more than an hour. During this time Walker slipped his men across Roundaway Bayou, burned the bridge, obstructed the road and retreated towards Delhi. At the Tensas River Brigadier General James C. Tappan with his Arkansas Brigade, 1,300 strong, joined Walker.

"They informed us that they heard a great many of 'Walker's Grey-hounds' had been captured by the enemy," Blessington recalled. "After assuring them that the greyhounds were too quick for the enemy, they became reconciled."

The Federal cavalry forded the bayou and pursued the Confederate rear guard for six miles on the road to Delhi, capturing 25 stragglers. Mower rebuilt the bridge and burned Richmond to the ground, but instead of following the retreating Confederates, he returned to Young's Point, and Ellet's brigade returned to their boats. In this engagement the Federals lost 1 killed and 11 wounded. "We found 3 of the enemy dead upon the field, 2 mortally wounded and captured 11 prisoners and about 60 stand of small arms," Ellet reported to Admiral Porter. "The enemy was commanded by Major-General Walker, was a part of Kirby Smith's command and consisted of two brigades, containing seven regiments, 4,000 strong, with 6 pieces of artillery. They retreated toward Delhi, where General McCulloch is said to be posted with a command about equal in strength to the one we encountered."

"My division looked like a vast moving hospital," Walker said of his retreat. "We had sick men in wagons and carts, wounded men on litters, borne by soldiers, and a crowd of enfeebled and emaciated men for whom no transportation could be had, who were straggling along in front of the marching column, which accommodated its movements to their feebleness." He gave his losses in the morning's engagement as about 15 killed, wounded and missing.[36]

Walker remained encamped with his division near a spring of fine water northeast of Delhi until June 22. In the meantime Randal's Brigade rejoined. The Confederates presented a ragged and unkempt appearance. Wrote Blessington:

While we remained encamped in the Mississippi bottoms, Falstaff's ragged regiment was well uniformed in comparison with our troops. No two were costumed with any attempt at uniformity, and each individual stood forth a decided character. But few of the troops had shaved for weeks, and, as a consequence, there was a large and general assortment of unbrushed black, gray, red, and sandy beards, as well as ferocious mustaches and whiskers — enough to rig out an army of West India buccaneers. A more brigandish set of Anglo-Saxon forces has never been collected. Then as to costume, it is utterly impossible to paint the variety our division presented. Here would be a fellow dressed in homespun pants, with the knees out of them; on his head might be stuck the remnant of a straw hat, while a faded Texas penitentiary cloth jacket would perhaps complete his outfit. His neighbor, very likely, was arrayed in breeches made out of some cast-off blanket, with a dyed shirt as black as the ace of spades, and no hat at all. Then would come a man with a woolen hat made like a pyramid, sitting jauntily upon his head, while, to introduce his style of hat, he had it covered over with assorted buttons; and, to top the climax, had a red tassel sewed on top. Notwithstanding his gaudy hat, a part of a shirt, and occasional fragments only of what had once been a pair of military pantaloons, made up the rest of his attire.[37]

On June 22 Walker started on an expedition against Goodrich's Landing on the Mississippi between Milliken's Bend and Lake Providence. Traveling through the region east of Bayou Maçon, he broke up the plantations that were engaged in raising cotton under Federal leases, capturing some 2,000 Negroes, who were restored to their masters "with the exception of those captured in arms, and a few the property of disloyal citizens of Louisiana." The cotton they had picked was burned. On June 29 at Mounds Plantation, about ten miles south of Lake Providence, Colonel William H. Parsons's two cavalry regiments, joined by Randal's Brigade, surrounded a fort built on a high, ancient Indian mound, garrisoned by Negro troops. The three white officers agreed to surrender if they would be treated as prisoners of war and to surrender the armed Negroes unconditionally! The terms were accepted; and the officers, plus two companies of the First Arkansas Volunteers (African descent) numbering 113 men, were captured. "I consider it an unfortunate circumstance that any armed negroes were captured," Walker stated bluntly. Walker moved to the vicinity of Goodrich's Landing, continuing to burn plantations. Admiral Porter sent Ellet's marines to reinforce the Federals at Goodrich's Landing. Arriving at 2:00 in the

morning on June 30, Ellet found the countryside lighted by burning mansions, slave quarters and cotton gins set afire by Walker's men. He discovered the Confederates resting on the opposite side of Tensas Bayou, some 12 miles inland. Walker made a half-hearted attempt to cross the bayou and turn Ellet's right flank, but the Federal skirmishers and artillery thwarted this plan, and Walker slowly retreated back to Delhi.[38]

Taylor sent General C. LeDoux Elgee, a voluntary aide, to see Joseph E. Johnston at Jackson and on his return west of the Mississippi he wrote Walker from Delhi on June 24:

> Genl. Johnston considers it impossible to do more than extricate Genl. Pemberton & the garrison of Vicksburg. He desires all the aid that can possibly be given him by the troops on this side the river in cutting off supplies or reinforcements to the enemy by way of the river. If by any possible means a man may get into Vicksburg from above, he desires percussion caps may be sent Genl. Pemberton. It is of the greatest importance to get information to Vicksburg. Genl. Johnston hears from there by men floating on logs down the river at night — The same means might be adopted from above to get a man into Vicksburg. Should there be a probability of success attending such a plan, Genl. Johnston is extremely desirous of knowing it & requests you will communicate it to him as speedily as possible. He is also desirous that any information you may receive which would be valuable to him or any disposition or operations of your own forces which it would benefit him to know may be communicated.

Elgee suggested that a courier be sent at once to Natchez, Mississippi, from which point there was telegraphic communication. "It would therefore be necessary to use the cypher," he advised. "Genl. Johnston will communicate with us to Natchez by telegraph, care of A. Ferguson, who is our news agent & will forward dispatches by courier at once to Delhi."[39]

Meanwhile, Kirby Smith had received another urgent message from Johnston: "Our only hope of saving Vicksburg now depends on the operations of your troops on the other side of the river. General Pemberton says he has provisions for a fortnight; perhaps he has them for a longer time. Now, if you contrive either to plant artillery on the Mississippi banks, drive beef into Vicksburg, or join the garrison, should it be practicable or expedient, we may be able to save the city. Your troops up to this time have done nothing." An intelligence officer, who had brought dispatches from Pemberton, was quoted as saying that Vicksburg would be saved if Kirby Smith could send in an "abundance of cattle" and 8,000 men.[40]

On June 29 Kirby Smith left Shreveport for Monroe, sending in advance 300,000 percussion caps which he hoped could be transported to Pemberton. He inquired of Walker what could be done about throwing reinforcements and provisions into Vicksburg. Walker replied "I am reluctantly compelled to state that, with the force at my disposal, or within my reach, I consider it utterly impracticable." At no time since he had arrived in the region had he had more than 4,700 effective men, and at present, "such has been the deleterious effect of the climate and bad weather," that even with Tappan's Arkansas Brigade, he had not more than 4,200 "fit for duty." To get to Vicksburg would require 20 or 30 miles of marching down a narrow peninsula with overwhelming enemy forces ready to move into his rear and render his capture or destruction inevitable. And as for the proposed batteries on the banks of the Mississippi, Walker declared that there was not a single point from Young's to Lake Providence that could be held by his small force for more than a few hours. He concluded:

> If there was the slightest hope that my small command could relieve Vicksburg, the mere probability of its capture or destruction ought not, and should not, as far as I am concerned, weigh a feather against making the attempt, but I consider it absolutely certain, unless the enemy are blind and stupid, that no part of my command would escape capture or destruction if such an attempt should be made.[41]

Taylor, feeling a great need for Walker's assistance in lower Louisiana and despairing of any results from the campaign opposite Vicksburg, ordered him to proceed immediately to Berwick Bay, from which place Taylor intended to send him into the Lafourche country. Kirby Smith, now on his way toward Walker's headquarters at Delhi, countermanded the order. But, after talking with Walker, the departmental commander gave up all hope of relieving Vicksburg other than sending in the percussion caps. He notified Johnston to that effect on July 4.[42]

Walker's Division waited at Delhi to learn Vicksburg's fate. Against the enemy's reports that the city would surrender on the "Fourth of July," the soldiers took bets and on the night of the third almost the entire division, for curiosity's sake, stayed awake all night, listening to the cannonading. As the hours passed the sentries would cry out, "11 o'clock, and Vicksburg all right!" and so on. At seven the next morning, when they heard about a dozen shots in rapid succession, "a gloom of sadness appeared to have come over the troops." They feared the worst for

Vicksburg. The uncertainty was not relieved until the morning of July 7, when a Confederate officer arrived in Delhi with the awful news that Pemberton had indeed surrendered on July 4. Even then Walker did not credit it, and he had the officer arrested and put under guard until he was recognized by some of Delhi's leading citizens and released from custody. "As soon as it became known for certain, in camp, that Vicksburg had surrendered, a perfect storm of indignation burst forth among the troops," Blessington stated. "What! surrender, and that too on the 4th of July, above all other days? Impossible. The men broke forth in bitter denunciation of Lieutenant-General Pemberton, boldly proclaiming that he had sold it to the enemy. Surrender on the 4th of July! Why should that day, of all others, be chosen for our humiliation?"[43]

But even more bad news was to come. On July 9 Port Hudson, the last Confederate bastion on the Mississippi, surrendered to Banks after a six-weeks' siege. Federal gunboats could now range up and down the entire length of the "Father of Waters." The Trans-Mississippi states were isolated — for all practical purposes lost to the Confederacy.

On July 9 Surgeon Edward Cade wrote his wife a long letter, describing the fall of Vicksburg and the reaction to the news among the men of Walker's Division. "The army in consequence of the sad news is despondent and gloomy. There are however no feelings on the part of any one to abandon the struggle, but they had looked forward with so much hope to the time when Johnston should rout Grant and the attempt upon Vicksburg failing they confidently expected the day of peace to dawn. . . ." "Since the fall of Vicksburgh, the men are very low spirited," Sam Farrow of the Nineteenth Texas admitted to his wife. "It is the opinion of a great many that the war will soon close." Farrow was afraid that since the Confederates could hold no position the country would soon be overrun by the enemy and "that we had as well give up all for lost." He explained: "They have got full control of the Mississippi river from its fountain head to where it empties into the Gulf and the North Western states now will pour down their forces upon us in such number that we will be compelled to retreat before them as far as they choose to follow. And all we can do will be to Bush wack and cut off foraging parties a while longer."[44]

On July 7 Walker's Division marched 11 miles up Bayou Maçon to Monticello, returning on the 8th to Delhi. On July 11 the men boarded a train and rode the 40 miles to Monroe, where they remained until July 19, when they were ordered to Alexandria via Campti on the Red River. Part of the trip was made by water. En route General McCulloch was relieved from command of the Third Brigade and ordered to report to Magruder in Texas. He was assigned to the northeastern portion of the state, with headquarters at Bonham in Fannin County. Colonel George Flournoy took command of the Third Brigade.

Walker's Division remained encamped near Alexandria until August 10, when it moved to Camp Green in the piney woods about 20 miles southwest of Alexandria. "Released at length from the swamps of the Tensas, where it had suffered from sickness, Walker's division of Texas infantry joined me in the early autumn, and was posted to the north of Opelousas," Taylor wrote in his memoirs. "Seconded by good brigade and regimental officers, he [Walker] had thoroughly disciplined his men, and made them in every sense soldiers; and their efficiency in action was soon established."[45]

After recuperating at home from the shoulder wound received at Milliken's Bend, Petty left Bastrop on August 11, 1863, to return to his regiment. His first letter home while en route to Louisiana was written from Huntsville, Texas.

Camp Near Huntsville
Monday 17th 1863 Aug

My Dear Wife

I thought a line this morning would not be amiss. I am now in about 2 miles of Huntsville & will pass there this morning. We are generally having an agreeable trip. I have got a sty on my left eye and with this & for want of coffee I have had head ach nearly every day.[46] Two days I had the diarrhea from excessive use of peaches & watermelons. One night & part of a day I had fever and part of one day a pain in my right side this all besides what ails me so I am passing it all off agreeably. Except Sty I am all right this morning. I met Capt Mabry yesterday. He looks well. I find a general spirit of despondency prevailing all over the Country. People seem to be ready to give it up. I would'nt give a shuck for millions of such Scoundrels. Confederate

Money is fast declining in consequence there of. Invest your money in something as quick as possible. Old Father Armstrong's land & hogs. May be so you can buy Mrs Nicholson's stock of cattle entire. Try & do something and put yourself in a state of readiness to leave the accursed Country if it submits or is subjugated. Kisses for all.

Yours truly
E. P. Petty

Bluff Town Aug 22nd 1863

Dear Wife

The city of Bluff Town is situated on the Neches river in Tyler County Texas 14 miles from Woodville and 16 miles from Jasper. We will pass through Jasper today where I will mail this letter. I meet every day furloughed Soldiers from our Command on their way home. They are doing an extensive furloughing business[47] now. I met Adjutant Hunt[48] yesterday & he informed me that Col Jones had been furloughed and that we would perhaps meet him.[49] I am now quite well sty on my eye & all and am enjoying myself well. I dont eat at the wagon more than I can help. They boys are so dirty in their cooking. At a great many places they charge nothing. My face & brass passes me through. Then as a matter of course I know every body in the army and nearly every body along the road has relations in the army and hence I make it a rule to know every body's relation and to carry a letter all of which gets my breakfast and supper etc for me. Who would'nt know how to travel. One old lady sent money by me to her son and another sent a negro man by me to her son and gave me 3 days rations of corn etc. So you see that my face carries me through with the ladies. Who would'nt have a good honest face such an one as I have got. "Quin Sabe." It is about 120 miles from here to our Camp so we will be 6 or 7 days more on the road. Fom the Sabine River to camp about 75 miles the Country is full of Jay Hawkers[50] and the Citizens generally are hostile to our Cause and it becomes dangerous to travel through there. We will have to be on the alert. Watch as well as pray. I keep my pistol in good order and always at hand and the Jay Hawkers that gets this lay out will get six Shots first. Mine is the only shooting arms along. Lt McLester has got well & is in Camp. Lt Cunningham has gone home on sick furlough. I dont know who else from my company has gone home as they all went the upper route & I did not meet them. I can find out when I meet Col Jones. The people I mean the stay at homes & speculators are generally whipped. They seem ready to give it up. Our army is not in the best condition. Dissatisfaction and mutinous feelings exist to a considerable extent mostly however on account of rations etc and not against the Cause. Still you know it has a demoralizing effect and makes the army uncontrollable & inefficient. All this is ruining our money. It is depreciating every day. Invest your money or the most of it by all means. Dont stand long upon prices. Did Andy Highsmith let you have his poney etc. I will write again from Camp. Kisses & love to all.

Yours truly
E. P. Petty

Camp Texas Louisiana
Aug 28th 1863

My Dear Wife

I arrived at this camp safe & sound on yesterday evening (27). I came right through the Jay Hawkers' settlement. Saw lots of sign and at one place in a thick swampy ground saw one man who run like fury into the bushes and cleared himself before I could get a showing at him. I was the only man in the party armed and I had to do all the responsible picketing, scouting etc of the party which I did carefully, scientifically & boldly believing that a bold bluff game oftener wins than looses. I find some of my men sick viz Ras Barrett is bad off — I am afraid will die. Bunt Dabney is quite sick though not dangerous. Frank Meeks is sick. McLester is still sick having chills etc. Nearly every body have gone home on furlough.[51] There are but two field officers to our Brigade present. I am now in Command of the Regiment being promoted the verry first day here. I am cutting a high swell acting Colonel. Capt Miller has gone before the board to be examined for promotion to Major and this has left me in command of the Regiment. I found some half dozen or more letters here from you & Ella which I will read at my liesure and answer if it suits me or if I find any thing that needs attention in them. In Louisiana I find not only a despondent but a disloyal sentiment which is open and brawling and particularly so in the Jay Hawker neighborhood. There is a good deal of Mutinous elements in the army and some are deserting though I find as I always contended the army in good & cheerful spirits not despondent and not by any means in the least whipped but e contrarie [au contraire] sanguine of ultimate success etc. I find all the clothing which I left at Alexandra safe here except one shirt which Lt McLester gave to one of my men. We have a pretty camp here in the pine woods. Fine water and looks like it ought to be healthy. When I get more time and look about me a little more I will perhaps write more. Kisses etc to all.

Yours truly
E. P. Petty

Camp Texas La Aug 29th 1863

My Dear Wife

I am in fine health and splendid morale. The army here is improving tone. I find Company F in fine condition better than most other Companies. The boys are not whipped and verry little despondency prevails. I shall contribute largely to improve this sentiment and elevate the tone & feelings of the boys. The health of Co F is better generally than any other Company so far as I can learn as we report a greater number of men for duty according to the number present than any other Company. I sent you by Col Jones a lot of peach seeds. They are from the finest peaches I have ever seen in Texas and as fine I believe as I have ever seen any where. The peaches were as large as my fist and perfectly luscious — please plant them with care and away from other seed. Keep the seeds of the free stone seperated from the others. The reason is the seeds in part belongs to another man who will want some of the young trees and will want some of each kind. I also here in send you some tame indigo seed. It grows finely here and will do so I suppose with you — try it any how. It makes good indigo so the women tell me. Capt Pitts[52] starts to Texas in the morning and I will send this letter by him. In it you will find four hundred dollars Confederate money which you will do a fine business to invest as soon as the Lord is willing and you have the chance. C.S. money here rates at 15 to 1 gold & is growing worse daily. Buy some thing with it. There is nothing here to buy with it. I studied my "Medical Students Vade Mecum" [a book for ready reference] pretty well on my trip. Think I will make a splendid Doctor at least can kill greasers very fast etc. We have sent to Ark for our clothing etc. I got here to late to put in my claim to go so I wont get to see my Ark gals. I got a letter however from Matt Lytle since I got here which satisfies me on the Ark question verry much. She says that she is as pretty & interesting as ever "in a horn." I shall answer it some of these days if I get leisure. We had a good rain yesterday, heavy thunder & heap of lightning. I was paid up to 1st Sept 4 months making $520⁰⁰. You see I keep some on hand for emergencies. Start all the children to school. Let Don go but make a bargain with Orgain to pay for the times he goes. Write to Alexandra. Kisses & love to all.

Yours truly
E. P. Petty

Alexandra La Aug 31 1863

Dear Daughter

I started a letter yesterday by Capt Pitts to your Ma and in it enclosed four hundred dollars which I hope she will get in a few days. When that letter was written the prospect of a long continued stay at Camp Texas were flattering but in a verry short time I received orders to hold the regiment in readiness to march at a moments notice and yesterday at 12 o'clock we struck camps and came to this place arriving here at 10 o'clock PM last night marching from 12 PM to 10 PM 20 miles or more. To day we will not move. I am inclined to think at least that seems to be the case now as we are preparing for inspection of arms, amunition, muster etc but a soldiers fate is quite uncertain and if the emergency that brought us here continues to threaten we are liable to march at any moment. The causes of our sudden moves are that the federals are threatening both Little Rock Ark and Monroe La.[53] This is my best information. When we will move from here, what direction we will take and what our destination — are things sealed to me at present. I am still in command of the Regiment (Capt Miller and Gutlin[54] both being sick). It is in good condition and ready to meet the enemy again. If we are to have a fight soon I wish it would come off whilst I am in command as I wish to see how I could perform and try my hand at a brush with them. I believe that I could do as well as some others have done before me. The old regiment is ready to make its mark again and to be marked. I dont know what is in store for us in the next month but I am ready for any and every emergency.

> "Here's a smile for those who love me
> A curse for those who hate
> What ever sky's above me
> Here's a heart for every fate"[55]

Dont be alarmed for me. "Whatever is to be will be and whatever is is right." When you hear from us you will hear that I am at my post if that post be in the blazes of a thousand Yankee hells. I hav'nt been down in the city yet and cant tell you much about it. We are about a mile above it on the river and near the falls of the Red River. This is a

magnificent country here. A great deal of sugar cane is growing &
considerable preparation for making sugar.

I send herein some Muscadine [grape] seed taken from select fruit. I
want Ma to plant them with care and nurture the plants well. I want
to see if I cant raise Muscadines in Bastrop. I have no news of interest.
I am in fine health & spirits.

Yours truly
E. P. Petty

P.S. I send here in Robert B Wall's letter just received by me.

E. P. Petty

Camp La Sept 3rd 1863

My Dear Wife

I sent you a letter to day by mail but as I have a chance of sending
one by Lieut McLester who goes home after clothing and as the mail
has been uncertain I have concluded to write a few lines this way and
trust to Lt McL to give you all the minutiae and particulars. I hav'nt
had a line from either Bastrop or Seguin since I left those places. I am
quite uneasy as to Pa and his fate and would be glad for you to inform
me as soon as you can how his sickness terminated if terminated at all.
I am awfully afraid I shall never see my poor old father again — We
are now in a healthy and eligible camp 21 miles west of Alexandra on
the Texas Beef road on the waters of Bayou Rapides. The health of the
Command is only tolerable ie there is some sickness more or less. Ras
Barrett died on the 1st inst after a long & protracted illness. I am sorry
— He was a good boy and a true & faithful Soldier — It will be a
sore trial to his parents as they have lost a son in law in battle and a
grandchild by death and now a son. This war is a severe trial to the
Country. But it is said the Lord chasteneth whom he loveth and hence
I conclude he loves the Confederacy with a strong love. We are getting
along verry well. There is much murmuring now in camps. Men are
dissatisfied, want to go home. I dont believe that I have a man who is
mean enough to go home unless he can go right but there are men
here who will do so I am awfully afraid. I am in fine health about as
well as you ever saw me. I have sometimes since I have been in camp
the heart burn which is caused by the food I have to eat. I have had it
only slightly however. I have no news. Press the children at school.
God Bless them. I wish I could see them now. I want to see you all

worse now than ever but I will get weaned after awhile again. Love & Kisses to all.

Ever Truly Yours
E. P. Petty

Camp La Sept 3rd 1863

My Dear Wife
On the 31st I wrote Ella a letter from Alexandra. I then thought we were after Yankees and that before I could get another chance to write I would pass through scenes of carnage, bloodshed etc but alas for human calculations. We pulled up stakes at Camp Texas and marched over 20 miles in one evening and then struck camp and remained immoveable 1½ days and then moved back into the pine hills behind Alexandra 20 miles again and have gone into seemingly a fixed camp. We are like the King of France who with 20000 men marched up the hill & then marched down again. We are now 20 miles from A. on the Texas beef road in the pine hills. Have a pretty camp and splendid water. Ras Barret of my Company died yesterday of chronic diarrhea poor fellow. He was a good fellow and a fine soldier. Tom McDonald has been quite sick. Looks mighty bad but seems better now. There is some sickness in the command but not as much as could be expected. There is great dissatisfaction in the army here. Men are insubordinate

and between us I would not be surprised if this army was comparatively broken up. Men say that they will go home and let the Confederacy & war go to hell etc. Every effort will be make to prevent it and I hope with complete success but I deplore this state of feelings.[56] I hate to hear men speak of selling their honor & Country for selfishness in other words for a mess of potage.[57] I have no news. The cause of our movement was a raid by the Yankees on Monroe. They captured Monroe and carried away about 5000 negroes and all the mules & horses etc. When they left we returned.

I am quite well and doing well. I am still in command of the Regiment but expect to turn it over to Capt Miller in the morning. I hav'nt heard a word from home since I left nor from Seguin since I left there. Kisses & love to all.

Yours Truly
E. P. Petty

Bayou Rapides La
September 5 1863

My Dear Son

I have written two letters home in the last few days in which I gave all the news that I knew or could gather. I have just heard the news and I am afraid it is true that the federals have knocked Fort Sumpter [Sumter] all to pieces and now have their gun boats in shelling distance of the City.[58] Of course it too will go up. I believe that the Charlestonians will not be like the Citizens of New Orleans, give their City up so easily but will defend it to the last and then before leaving the city burn it to the ground.

We moved our camps from the pine hills yesterday on to the east side of Bayou Rapides so that we can hold ourselves in readiness either to go to Alexandra or up the river as the necessity may be. The feds are advancing on Alexandra from Trinity on the Washita river by the way of Little river and are now said to be in about 25 or 30 miles of A.[59]— Col Randalls with his Brigade is over confronting them. Genl Hawes Brigade has gone to reinforce them. We are held here with Polignac's Brigade[60] to reinforce those forces etc. Our batteries have been planted at A. The Commissaries & Ordnance stores etc have been removed from A and the people I understand are leaving. So you see that we have pulled off our coats and rolled up our sleeves for a fight. I hope no more running or falling back will be allowed but that we will now make the fight and if compelled to fall back will do so contesting every inch of ground.

I am afraid an invasion of our section is intended. If so I dread the consequences for my family. You must all take care of yourselves. Be prudent & discreet. There is no telling what the devils may do. But my son before they get to you all they will leave many a bloody track behind them. After they get into Texas their steps will all be bloody for we must & will contest every inch of ground, if we are true to ourselves, to our country and to our families. I want you and Ella & Don to go to school all the time possible. Learn all you can for before we know it you will perhaps have no chance to go to school.

So learn my boy all you can. The chances of education are growing more precarious every day.

Be a good boy. You may not have a father to advise you and support and protect you long and you may have to rely upon yourself. Resolve to be a man, a good man, a true man and let the calamities of war come and all that sort of thing. You will be able to pass along and be respected & honored by every body. The Yankees may rob or you may loose everything. You have some others but if you have a good & pure heart, a clear head and a good education you will rise and make your mark. So hurry up my boy. Dont let the precious moments waste.

Remember me kindly to all & give kisses & love to family.

Yours truly
E.P. Petty

Camp Shepherd La
September 11th 1863

My Dear Wife

I have no special interesting news to write but to pass my time pleasantly aye the most pleasantly that it is possible for me to do so I have concluded to write some any how. I have received but one letter and one paper from home since I left. It has just been one month today since I bid you all farewell and endured with patience and soldier like fortitude the pang of parting from the dearest objects of my life with which I am happy and without which — I came verry near saying miserable but you know that I have much philosophy about me and dont suffer myself to become miserable — It seems to me six months since I saw you. You have no idea how the time drags wearily and slowly along to me now. The brief time I spent at home rushes vividly upon me at all times and I feel the aching void which your abscense and their's make. However I try to keep as busy as possible always looking upon the bright side of the picture, frequently at your

ambrotype and when I have liesure time from my official duties I am
engaged in the hard study of anatomy, physiology and hygiene — I am
making some progress in my studies though I have not much time
to devote to them. What I contemplated before I left home I am
endeavoring to carry out. If our beloved Confederacy should be
unfortunate which I do not and will not believe I intend to expatriate
myself with my loved ones beyond its borders and then I will either
have to work or change professions and of course I do not want to
work — I am physically unable to do so successfully. I believe that it
will be advantageous to emigrate, let the war terminate favourably as
their will succeed a verry bad state of society for a long time. Affairs
will be desperate and to be out of it and to keep my sweet ones out of
it I believe I shall hunt some strange land and carve out a new fortune
with a new people. Take your map and hunt you a new home where
you think you would be willing to cast your lot. The Sandwich Islands
[former name of the Hawaiian Islands] are verry desirable — The
inhabitants are considerably civilized & christianized (not enough yet
for such wars as we have) and the soil is rich & climate salubrious.
The Americans have considerable influence amongst the nations etc.
Rio Janerio [Rio de Janeiro] in Brazil meets my highest admiration —
It is a large city — with fine society — great commerce and the
Brazilian Government (though a monarchy) is limited, mild and
liberal. It is a slave country and would suit my ideas of class etc. The
Argentine Confederation or Republic holds out great inducements to
emigrants yet its government is unstable. Study the question and post
yourself as I believe it will be better for us. I had rather go to Oregon
than any place but I am determined not to live in the United States
government.[61] What say you on these important suggestions.
I am going to press my medical studies all I can. It will be no
disadvantage to me let the matter go as it will. We seem to be in a
stationary camp again 21 miles from Alexandra in the piney woods.
We have fine water and the general health of the army is improving. I
have one verry sick man. Dave Morris with flux. Tom McDonald is
sick with Chills & fever. Eats so much that it keeps him sick all the
time. John W. Wilson is sick with an attack of billious fever. John
Perkins has been sick with flux but is nearly well now. There has been
some other sickness but of no consequence recently. McLester has gone
home on furlough. I hope he will carry my trunk which is now at
Shreveport. All our things that were at Monticello & Camden Ark
have been sent to Shreveport. I think that our tricks at Pine Bluff will
be sent for soon — I hope so as bedding is an object or will be this

winter. The feds who were threatening Alexandra have all retired and "all is quiet along Red River to night."[62] I hope that they will either allow us to rest awhile or that our officers will allow us to fight awhile and it does'nt make much difference to me which happens. I am ready for any & all emergencies. I am in fine health and in as good & hopeful spirits as ever you saw any one. Things looks black & gloomy now I confess but in nature the darkest hour is just before the dawn and why may it not be so in the Confederacy. I look forward with hope to the full establishment of the Confederate States amongst the first class powers of the earth. _____ has obtained a sick furlough to go home. If able he will assist you in any thing you may want. Jo does'nt make a good soldier. He is inherently a coward and he cant help it. He gets sick whenever there is a prospect or promise of a fight — He will prevaricate here and it is the only mean thing I know of him. With this exception he is a good, faithful and true man. At home he is a good trusty fellow. Dont say any thing about him or this to any body. It is <u>inter nos</u> (between us). I expect I will send this letter by him. He can give you all the particulars & minutia. I tried to get John Perkins a sick furlough but he did not get the recomendation of the medical board & hence failed to get one. Discontent & desertion is still the order of the day though the public post has been suppressed.[63] A few scoundrels are still going off and will constitute themselves I expect a set of Jay hawkers & thieves in Texas. None from our Regiment have left. We have the only regiment from which none have gone. Hurrah for the immortal and bloody Seventeenth. Old Co F is all right. My boys are tried, true & trusty. I can count on them day & night against federals or runaway Confederates.[64] They are nearly up to my standard. I intend to bring them up to it if possible. Do the best you can at home. Take awful good care of my little ones God bless them. Remember me kindly to friends and lovingly to the children. Kisses and all that for them.

Yours truly
E. P. Petty

Sept 13th — 1863

I am good well to day and all goes on well with us here. No more letters from you. I send my summer coat by Jo.

E. P. P.

Camp Shepard La
Sept 18th 1863

My Dear Daughter

I awaited the arrival of the mail to day with a great deal of anxiety hoping to receive a kind memento from the loved ones at home but lo the mail came, the letters were distributed and there was none for me. My greatest desire and chief pleasure is to receive, read and reread letters from home. A few days ago I received Uncle Charley's and Ma's bearing the melancholly tidings of the death of Pa. A sad tale it was to me. I can hardly realize the fact that he is dead and that I never shall see him any more. It requires all my philosophy and fortitude to reconcile me to his loss. I have written to Ma trying to console her as much as possible. I want your Ma and you to write to her also and cheer her up. If she needs any money etc I want your Ma to let her have it. We are still at Camp Shepard with a present prospect so far as I can see of remaining here some time. We have gone to drilling again for health & improvement. I am again in command of the Regiment Capt Miller having gone to the country on sick leave of abscense. There is some considerable amount of small sickness but none now fatal. All my boys are fast improving in health. The desertion furor has about ceased the prospect of getting shot having detered some and the bad material having most been expended. They have dubbed my Company as the fighting Company because we fell in with so much promptness and alacrity armed and equipped when we were called upon to quell the mutiny. Things look much better here now. We had a considerable rain yesterday and last night and to day a considerable

Norther which so chilled the air as demand of me to put on my overcoat. This is what I call decidely cool. I am studying Cutter's Anatomy, Physiology & Hygiene[65] and when I come home again I will be competent to converse with you about the Os frontalis, Os Occipitalis, Os hyoides, humeris, ulna raidias, carpus, metacarpus, phalanges etc etc etc. You must hurry up or I will leave you behind and you know that you began this study before I did and that you have more time than I have for study. I can even now begin and name nearly if not quite all the bones, muscles, arteries, veins, organs etc etc so you must take care. I will turn you down when I get in a class with you. My trunk is at Shreveport and my book is in it but I borrowed one here in the Regiment which I am now studying as closely as I have time.

There are some nice young ladies near here with whom I spend a pleasant evening occasional or semi occasionally. I have a nice social time playing cards & drinking wine with them. I have no news to write. Wish I had if it were good news. The army is a dull monotonous place. There is a continued sameness about every thing. Morning, noon & night it is roll call & drill etc etc each & every day. Write to me as often as you can and give me all the news. If Frank cant write do so for him. Remember me kindly & lovingly to Ma & the children & respectfully to friends etc.

Yours truly
E. P. Petty

Camp Shepard Louisiana
September 24th 1863

My Dear Wife
Your's of the 7th inst have just been received. I hear a great deal of complaints about mail irregularities etc. It is the reason why you dont get letters for I write regularly to you & Ella always once a week and frequently twice. I am sure that I dont get as many from you as are written though I hope they will come after awhile. Since I wrote last I have spent a few days in Alexandra attending on a Court Martial. I was defending a poor fellow who was charged with Mutiny etc in getting up this general desertion etc. I am sure that my services will save the fellow from being shot and perhaps may acquit him though I think from his indiscretions he ought to be punished some. Our army here needs the example of some more men being shot though just now they are doing better. Three men at last from Capt Mabry's Company

had to disgrace the old 17th by deserting. They are frontier men. I had quite a pleasant time in Alexandra. I found a nice boarding house with a nice young lady who sang sweetly and who took pains to entertain me most elegantly. I think that I shall go down there again if we stay here long. Though in less than ¼ of a mile from camp is a most estimable lady's house who generally has three or four young ladies (gay & lively) at her house and having a sick man staying there I visit there almost nightly and have a super-abundance of fun, frolic, wine & cake with any amount of card playing. I am having as gay a time nearly as I had at Pine Bluff. The ladies here although genteel & nice are freeer & easier than in Texas and make a man feel at home. They seem to appreciate the fact that a soldiers fate is a hard one at best and do all they can to relieve it of its roughness & tedium. I have no special news. We had a grand Review yesterday. It was magnificent and everything went off satisfactorily. Genl Walker seemed & talked proudly of his Command. He is a glorious General. I reckon you know that Genl McCulloch has left us. He has been taken away and placed in command of Northern Texas with his head quarters I suppose at

"Walker's
Greyhounds"

Bonham. I dont know who will be our Brigadier but suppose it will be Genl Scurry of Texas.[66] I hope it will though he is another head strong fighter but we want and need fighting men and Generals. I learn that the federals are massing a force at Brashear & Berwick City perhaps for a forward movement. They have also taken Little Rock and extend their scouts considerably this side. I look from all these facts an advance move in three columns, on Shreveport & Texas, one by Nibletts Bluff, one from Little Rock or Monroe & one by the Indian Territory.[67] If so we are destined to see hot times over in this army for I will look for a season of continued fighting in which many a poor fellow will bite the dust. I hope for better times though I bargain for worse. I am ready and willing to meet the shock if it has to come. About financial & home matters all I can say is do the best you can. Use your money to the best advantage and your pistol scientifically if necessary. Always be on the alert and shoot quick and to the mark. Look out for your horse or it will be stolen. Buy whatever you think you need — Keep the children at school — pay all your debts — dont let any body pay you any old debts — At the verry earliest

convenience lay in a full supply of provisions and even press a convenience to do so. Wilkinss negroes will be a good place to get corn I expect. You had better see them quickly. Keep in your bosom a strong heart & a determined will — a clear head and a firm & steady nerve. Watch as well as pray etc. Remember me kindly to Mrs Graves & my friends generally. Hug & Kiss the children for me and say that it comes warmly & truly from pa's heart that he would like to do so himself rather than by proxy — I am in charming health. Good God protect my wife & children and save my Country.

Yours etc E. P. Petty

In camp 20 miles below Chen[e]yville La
September 28 1863

My Dear Ella

Walkers grey hounds as the feds call us are again on the track. We left Camp Shepard 4 days ago and have been on forced marches ever since. What our destination is and what we are after is more than I can say. I suppose after feds as a matter of course.[68] We are now encamped for the night on Bayou Boeuf about 20 miles below Chenyville on the road leading to Washington and on down in the direction Brashear City & Berwicks Bay. Genl Green[69] is on the Atchafalaya Bayou near Morganza and was fighting or skirmishing a few days ago. We may be going to reinforce him. We are now on the road that the feds came up from Berwicks Bay to Alexandra. From Alexandra here is the finest & richest country I have ever seen. It looks like the garden spot of the world. I see in the neglected fields & deserted houses & burned bridges the effects of war and federal invasion. The sugar crops though extensive have been neglected and are not so abundant as they would have been. If the feds are kept back now a good deal of sugar will made. It would do you good to travel through this section to see the extensive farms, beautiful residences, fine shrubery, immense wealth etc. How much more so would it be in times of peace and quiet. I am trying to write on my roll of bedding. It is raining & everybody is comeing in my tent bringing in their tricks to keep them dry as we have but two or three tents for the Co. Besides Henry Perkins has just arrived, is in my tent & it a perfect babel of sounds every body talking at once. Perkins is sick with Chills & fever. Looks quite bad and is on his way to Chenyville to see his sister I believe. I have no news to write as I can learn nothing. When I get through with this expedition I will give you a history of it with its results. Dont be uneasy about us. I will be in to whatever turns up and dont be afraid that I will not be at my post let that post be where it may whether in the Cannons Mouth, at the point of the bayonett or in some place of safety. Wherever they tell me to go or whatever they tell me to do I am going to that place and to do that thing. You must do the best you can. Get as good an education as you can. It will be important & useful to you as you pass through this troublesome world. Cultivate your moral as well as your mental character and principles. Be pure in thought and action. Be chaste in thought & word. Remember all the advice I have given you heretofore. Remember me lovingly to Ma & the children and kindly to my friends. I will write again when I get time & chance.

Yours truly
E. P. Petty

Camp Saw Dust St Landry Parish
La October 3rd 1863

My Dear Wife

I am writing more from the same Camp that I addressed Ella from 4 days ago. We went one days march below here. Stayed 2 or 3 days in the swamp and have just returned here on our way up the Country. Maybe to Alexandra. Maybe to Simsport [Simmesport] on Red River — We came down here to back Genl Green in a fight which he had on the 29th Sept beyond the Atchafalaya and within 7 or 8 miles of the Mississippi river.[70] He crossed in two flat boats and attacked a party of about 7 or 800 feds who were behind a levee & in a sugar house. About 100 men killed and wounded on both sides when near 500 of the feds surrendered with two small cannon, some mules and their small arms etc. Our forces fell back on this side the Bayou leaving pickets over there who I learn went in to a mile of Morganza on the Miss river and reported no advance of the feds in that direction. We did not get nearer than 20 miles of the fight. The fed prisoners were marched through our camp yesterday on their way to Alexandra. They are Indianians & other Western men. Fought like devils and seem to think that the rebellion is nearly crushed out. They are in fine spirit or seem so.[71] It rained incessantly for two days & nights on us down here and oh the mud & slosh. No one can form an idea of it unless he has once been in the swamps of Louisiana. I have seen the most of Frank Hogan's Company and such another haggard and sickly looking set I hav'nt seen. They dont look like we do. When they were ordered down to reinforce Green there were but 3 that could or would go & they were privates. Not an officer went. They were able however to run about over the country and much more able than we were when we went to Milliken Bend. Josy Wilkins is no longer a captain. He has been dismissed from the service & from office for long continued abscense. A secret I have to tell you but it is no secret in the army here. After the capture of Brashear City and all the negroes etc that were there & thereabouts the officers generally began to steal & run off negroes & mules to Texas. One Colonel ran off as high as 25 negroes with mules & wagons etc. _____ ran off 2 negroes and about 20 mules and sold them for $8000 in Confederate money near Nibletts Bluff in Texas and I learn invested his money in cattle. These things has caused his long abscense and he was stricken from the roll for it. I do not want his family for whom I have the greatest respect to know or suspect that I know or have said any thing about it. But such rascality deserves exposure and the severest condemnation of all honest men. How can our cause prosper when those in high places have turned out to down right & open stealing. When this war ends no one can say of me in truth that I have either stolen or extortioned one Cent upon my fellow man or soldier. I have no news of interest to write. I think that we will figure around in here some where until we get to smell gun powder again. I met down in the swamp Sam Thompson the blacksmith who lived at Bastrop 4 or 5 years ago and who run off for shooting at Bob White. We camped two or 3 days at his house. His daughter is now grown, still walks with a crutch and looks tolerable well. They were very glad to see their old Bastrop acquaintances. I did'nt hear Ellen curse like she did at school nor see her use her crutch on any of the boys but she said God dem it several times and threatened Steve Snelling & the boys with her crutch etc whilst they were devilling her. They are about as no count as they were at Bastrop. Our mail courier will be in this evening and I hope I will get some letters from home. Oh how I would like to hear from you and see you. You can hardly imagine my pleasure at getting a letter from home and my dejection at not getting one. God bless the Young ones. Kiss them for me & consider yourself kissed a thousand times.

Yours truly
E. P. Petty

Bayou Rouge Oct 4 1863

Dear Wife
    We travelled about 10 miles to day on the road to Simsport and are

encamped about 6 miles on Bayou Rouge from Evergreen a little insignificant town. We are no doubt en route for Simsport to try and surprise another Yankee force. The boys have just found & cut a bee tree and I stopped to eat some honey. It was a tremendous sycamore and there was a good deal of honey. Oh we soldiers have a fine time. We have as much sugar cane as we can eat and find that it is quite healthy as well as palateable. We are living finely now potatoes in great abundance. I have eaten bread but a few times in the last ten days and if I can get potatoes I dont want corn bread. We have beef, some times mutton, corn Bread, sometimes flour, sugar, molasses, sugar cane, Sweet potatoes etc. That etc does not cover much this time as I about enumerated all we have. The boys are sick some. I sent back 2 sick to day. Tom Irvine is behind sick at Sam Thompsons. The 2 sent back are Alfred Moore & John Miller. Tom McDonald still has chills & some others also. I am in blessed health as fine as you ever saw me and can out travel a horse and stand as much as a mule. I hope we may soon meet and wipe out the feds. No Charly Nichols (our courier) yet and hence no good news for me. God bless & protect you all.

E. P. Petty

Bayou De Gla[i]ze La
October 5th 1863

Dear Wife

No mail yet. We are now in 4 miles of Simsport Avoyles [Avoyelles] Parish La Camped on Bayou De Glaze. We travelled 16 miles to day.[72] 3 regiments of our Brigade and 2 Cannons are here. Where we are going and what we hope to accomplish is more than I know. I expect that we are going on a raid of some sort to the Mississippi river. If we do I expect this time to take a drink of water out of the "father of waters." I am in enviable health & spirits. Will write you more when I know more. God save & protect my wife & children.

E. P. Petty

Bayou Rouge Oct 6th 1863

Dear Wife

Charly Nichols has just arrived and has brought me yours & Ella's of the 15th Sept. So you see that I am nearly a month behind in mail. We left this camp yesterday morning & marched 16 miles to within 4 miles of Simsport. Last night we got orders to return back to Bayou Boeuf to reinforce Col Lane[73] who was retreating before the feds and to day we are encamped again on the same ground. I expect we will get orders to go somewhere else before to morrow morning. Such is a Soldiers fate not to know where or when he is going or how nor when he dies. I cant advise you more than I have about financial matters — do the best you can. If you can send Don to school it will give him a start & enlarge his ideas generally. I left sick at Camp Shepard Dave Morris, Bunt Dabney, Ben French and John Perkins. They were not much sick but not able to travel. I sent 2nd day to Alexandra sick Henry Biggs. Tom Irvine is at Sam Thompsons quite sick as I learn. John Miller and Alfred Moore are at Evergreen sick. Tom McDonald, John W Wilson & John I Chilwick are present sick have to go on the wagon. The ballance are navigable. I have only about 30 men along for duty. Wont I make a big fight — as large as ever that number made before.

Give my love to all my friends & a thousand embraces & kisses to my darling little ones. God & Liberty.

E. P. Petty

Bonny Eloize

1 Oh Sweet is the vale where the Mohawk
gently glides
On its clear winding way to the sea
And dearer than all the storied
Streams on earth besides
Is this bright rolling river to me.
Chorus — But sweeter dearer yes
dearer far than these
Who charms when all others fail
Is blue eyed bonny bonny Eloize
The belle of the Mohawk vale.
2 Oh sweet are the scenes of my boyhoods
sunny years
That bespangle this gay valley o'er
And dearer are the friends seen
through memories fond tears
That have lived in the blest day of
yore.
Chorus — etc

3 Oh Sweet are the moments when dreaming
I roam
Through my loved haunts now
mossy and gray
And dearer than all is my child-
hoods hallowed home
That is crumbling now slowly
away.

Camp Palmetto Oct 7th 1863

Dear Wife

We are again down on Bayou Rouge just above the Town of Big
Cane and near Thompson's on our way down the country toward
Washington and the Teche Country. The feds are advancing from
Berwick Bay and our forces are falling back.[74] I see that they are now
organizing a large expedition in New Orleans for Texas and I tremble
for the consequences. Look out for breakers ahead and do the best you
can. I will do my best to send them to hell as they come. I wrote a
long letter to your mother last night and gave it to a citizen here who
says he will carry it or send it in the federal lines and mail it for me —
I enclosed also yours & Ella's of the 15th ult in mine. I hope she will
get it and write to me in return. No special news — Bully for Bragg.[75]
Kisses & all that.

Yours truly
E. P. Petty

Big Cane Louisiana
October 8th 1863

Dear Wife

We are now encamped on Bayou Rouge ½ mile from the Town of
Big Cane an insignificant little place. I went down to Sam Thompsons
this evening and brought Tom Irvine to camp. He looks verry peaked
but seems to be much better. If we have to go out of here I dont want
to leave any of my men for the federals to catch. We only marched
about 6 miles to day and will remain here for further orders. The feds
are falling back on the Teche I learn. I hope that the whipping Braggs
has given Rosencrans [Rosecrans] is so complete that it will prevent an
invasion of Texas and cause a general falling back of our enemies.

Charly Nichols starts for Alexandra in the morning so I will have to conclude my series of letters in one and send it forward. This is the first & only chance I have had to send it. My boys are all improving & in fine health. I am <u>bully</u> excuse the army expression for <u>fine</u>. I have no special news. I go out serenading every favourable chance and make it pay in the way of fine suppers etc.

God bless & preserve my wife & my children.

E. P. Petty

P.S. 1 hour later — Orders have just been published to the command to move at 6 O'clock AM tomorrow. Oh the Certainties of a Soldiers life. I am in <u>Splendid health tomorrow</u>.

E. P. Petty

Bayou Huff Power Louisiana
October 11th 1863

My Dear Daughter

Yours by Capt Mabry of the 26 ultimo has just been received. Ah! ha! My sweet little daughter is getting jealous of me because she thinks I have written to Ma and Frank and not to her. Well in the first place I have written to you more than one letter and that you hav'nt received them is no fault of mine and in the second place when I write a letter home (it matters not to whom it is addressed) it is intended for you all and I want you all to read it and consider it your letter so far as it pertains to you. Hence dont you see you little duck your Pa hasnt slighted or neglected or overlooked or forgotten you nor would he do so for the world for he thinks too much of you. If any man loves his family I believe I do for I believe I have a family that is in every sense worthy of the most exalted love and that loves me fully in return. I have not neglected and will not neglect you, my little sweety, so dont fret & chide me any more about it. I am better pleased with this last letter of yours than any you have written to me. You seem have taken more pains with it. Your hand writing is good, spelling good, composition fine and your grammar nearly perfect. There are two or three sentences that could have been improved in grammar which I cannot now point out to you. One thing you entirely overlook and that is punctuation and you are somewhat defective in the use of capital letters. I am not attentive myself to punctuation as you will see but this [is] nothing [to] you — it was neglect in my early education and as you are now receiving yours I want you to attend to this part of it. It is necessary in reading and writing and nothing so helps a person as being a good reader and writer. I am afraid that you have more studies on hand than you can do justice by. It would seem to me that a fewer studies well and diligently pursued would accomplish a person quicker and more perfectly than to have such a mixture on hand at once. Of this however I do not profess to be a judge as I never taught school. My Cutters Anatomy is in my trunk which when I last heard of it was at Shreveport and hence I could not send it by Mr Weber. I have one borrowed which I am now studying and if you dont mind I will be the better anatomist & phisiologist when I see you again. I was in hopes that Lt McLester would carry my trunk home with him as he knew it was at Shreveport and knew that I wanted it at home. I am sorry that you have so bad an opinion of your neighbor Mrs. Ploeger as to think that she would poison your pig and I would be much more sorry to know that you had so bad a neighbor as one that would be guilty of so mean and low an act as the poisoning of a neighbor's hog. Good neighbors are great blessings but bad neighbors are annoyances and curses.

I never have thought that the Confederacy would be whipped. I am sure it never will be subjugated as long as her sons and daughters are true to her but any person who will travel over it as I have and see and hear as much defection and treason as I have seen and heard can but once in a while feel a little despondent and feel that extortioners and traitors are trying to sell out this government and if it was not for the Army I mean the Volunteer Army not conscripts & drafted men and feather bed soldiers but the Army I would loose all hope of the Confederacy. In view of all these facts and in anticipation of the status of society after the close of the war whether we were successful or not I thought it would be better for us all to hunt a new home amongst a new people and try and carve out a new fortune in a new way and I am not so sure but what it would be the best thing now and that I will try and do so. Hence I wrote to Ma to be looking out a place that she would like and not because I thought that the Confederacy would be whipped.

We are encamped on Bayou Huff Power 10 miles below Cheneyville and 1 mile above Evergreen on the road leading from Alexandra to Morganza on the Mississippi river. We are awaiting the movements of the enemy who have been advancing up the Teche as far as Vermilionville where I learn that Genl Green has checked this advance for the present. We are at a point when we can meet them if they advance either up the Teche by Morganza or by Simmesport. We are ready, eager and anxious for a fight and aint at all particular when or how it comes. Our army is in good health, fine spirits and good moral, better than it has been in three months and if the fight does come off the federal fur will most certainly fly.

I wrote Ma a long letter this week in which I sent you a song "Bonny Eloize." It is pretty and I want you to learn to sing and play it.

I have no special news. Remember me kindly to Mrs Graves & family, Mrs Dewy & family & in fact to all my friends. A thousand howdies & kisses to wife and children.

Yours truly
E. P. Petty

Bayou Huff Power Louisiana
October 13th 1863

My Dear Wife

Just a few lines is all you must expect now. We (Walkers gray hounds) are again on the trail. I headed this letter as above but we are now encamped on Bayou Rouge near Big Cane on our way to meet the federals who to night as I learn will reach Washington. Genl Green is fighting and falling back. The forces of the enemy are variously estimated at from 15 to 50000. I expect that they number about 30000. If so it will be as much as we can conveniently handle with our gloves on. For my part I am going to pull my gloves off. I think I can do better. I am now bargaining for some weeks of hard active Service mixed up with considerable fighting. I dont know when I can write again as I dont expect to have much if any oppertunity. When I get a chance or get through with this lay out I will write long & minute. If I get killed or taken prisoner be of good cheer. The fates have so decreed it and it is all right. Take care of yourself & my children and raise them as they should be and as I know you are capable. Do the best you can under all the surrounding circumstances. I hope that we will make a triumphant raid upon them down here. Our trains & sick have been sent back. We are now prepared for any emergency. Some of my boys who were detained at Shreveport have come in and I now have 40 enlisted men & 2 commissioned officers present and all for duty. I have the largest & most efficient Company present and every man is ready, willing and anxious to make the wool fly. I wish I had all my men present. Tom Irvine is sick again & has been sent to the rear. This is according to his Mothers wish which was that he should get sick before every fight. Tom however is really sick now. I can only refer you to what I have always said about yourself, family & property. I will do the best I can for myself & my Country over here. I would be thrice happy to be at home with my loved ones but my country is bleeding at every pore. The valdals [vandals'] feet are on her soil, his torch is on her temple door. She pleads, she implores me.[76] I must go to her relief. With Curses & Maledictions upon the vandal wretches and love aye much love & kisses for you & yours.

I am truly yours
E. P. Petty

Bayou Boeuf St Landry Parish Louisiana
October 19th 1863

My Dear Wife

Yours of the 23rd ult has just been received. I have a boil on my lower lip which is intensely painful. I slept but little last night with it and am now almost in an agony of pain. It seems that every nerve in my face & head are more or less effected by it. In this condition I cannot write much of a letter. Neither have I much to write if I were in a proper fix to do so. We are now on Bayou Boeuf 5 miles above Washington.[77] Our command is in fine health and fine spirits. The federals in heavy force are 16 miles below on Car[r]ion Crow [Carencro] Bayou. They have neither advanced or retired for several days. Genl Green is confronting them with his Cavalry whilst we rest here on our arms ready to support him in case he can draw them into an engagement. Although he has daily skirmishing with them he has so far failed to draw them out in a general engagement. How long we will lay in this fix is more than I can say. Both parties seem to be maneuvering for advantages. If we do fight we must whip it. It would'nt do to have our army here defeated. It would demoralize them so our Genls seem to feel and realize and hence I think that no unnecessary fight will be made. If we do get hitched in there will be an awful battle for this side of the river. I have the largest Company in the Regiment and they are ready and eager for the fight. Except my boil I am quite well and this will only tend to make me the more mad and furious. I hope that I may be all in perfect trim as I desire to do more execution than I can hope I did at Milliken Bend. I had no idea that there was such a Country under the sun as this. I have never seen such. It is the garden spot of the Confederacy a real garden of Eden. But war has touched it with its blighting influence and it wasting away. I would like to have seen it before the war. It would have done the

heart good. I wish you could have seen it or even see it now. It would be worth a years experience to you. Oh such pain in my lip! Whew! We have been here four days and hold ourselves ready for orders day & night. I would like to hear from Mrs Graves. Remember me kindly to her & to Mrs Denny & family and my friends generally. Flemming got here two days ago. He was well except a boil on his leg which was quite painful. Tell Jo Weber that he must return here promptly at the expiration of his furlough as I wish to furlough others and will have to wait until they return. Kisses and all that for my you & my children. Do the best you can with the money you have. I dont know when I will get any more. There is no money to pay with now.

Yours truly
E. P. Petty

Bayou Boeuf La Oct 26th 1863

My Dear Wife
I received yours of the 1st inst yesterday. Since yesterday at 12 O'clock we have marched 40 miles from about 8 miles above Washington to this place which is about 6 miles below Cheneyville.[78]

The enemy is at Washington and his pickets extend to Moundville 3 miles above. This was the condition yesterday. Day before yesterday their Cavalry advanced 3 or 4 miles above Moundville and had a heavy skirmish with ours. Ours fell back & they advanced. Two of our Brigades (McCulloch's & Hawes's) went down, formed line of battle, planted cannon etc in about 1½ miles of the enemy and waited for his advance until near Sundown when the whole of the troops except Allen's Regt., 2 pieces of artilery (Parrott Rifle guns) and some sharp shooters were withdrawn and sent away to Camps some 4 or 5 miles. We were in the edge of an old sugar farm full of ditches & cross ditches all of which we cleared out so that we could pass from the one to the other without being too much exposed. Our sharp shooters & skirmishers were in advance in the sugar houses, Negro houses and skirts of timber. Our cannon were posted behind in the edge of some timber. Here we remained all night & until 12 Oclock yesterday when we got orders and fell back here. I think the cause of the sudden fall back is that the feds are attempting to flank us by comeing up Bayou Rouge which lies to the east of this. Here the roads by both Bayous meet and here Bayou Boeuf is bridged which will give us considerable advantage and here I expect and hope that our Generals will find it advisable & advantageous to fight them. The Yankees are to strong for us in a fair fight. They have not less than 25000. Nearly all Western men and good fighters. Genl Scurry has been assigned to our command in place of Genl McCulloch — He has reached here and assumed command.[79] I am well pleased with him. I knew him well in Texas. He is a fighter and those who follow him will go to the Cannon's Mouth. Since I wrote to you I have suffered a half dozen deaths with a rising on my lower lip. I had no good sound sleep in 7 days & nights though I took opium once. It is now much better — getting well fast though my lip is yet as thick as a Negroes. I did duty & marched all the time. The health of the boys is generally good. We have got rid of nearly all the drags and have a pretty good set of fellows who will do duty and fight. Jim Rowlett has just reached here. Ole Carlson got sick & returned home. The weather has been quite cold for a few days past. I got Mrs Sewells letter was verry glad to hear from her — Will answer it just as soon as I can. Tell her to wait patiently and the answer will come. Tell her that I will answer it if you have no objection to my corresponding with young widows. Love & kisses & all that to the Children and respects etc to friends.

Yours truly
E. P. Petty

Bayou Boeuf La Oct 28th 1863

My Dear Daughter

Cousin William King has promised to come by and see you all and bear my letter to you. Genl Scurry brought his staff with him from Texas and Genl McCulloch's old staff are relieved here and will report to him in Texas for duty.[80] Cousin William intends to avail himself of this change to visit his home and family. I am glad he gets to go home but I regret exceedingly his leaving here. He is a fine Quarter Master, an honest, conscientious, upright, agreeable gentleman such a man as we need in that office and to me he has been clever and kind and I hate to part with him. He is the only relative I have in the service here and to loose him goes hard with me now. Cousin William can give you all the items of interest which would be too tedious to write in a letter. I have no news of special interest to write to you. The Yankees are still at Washington and are not now advancing that I know of. Occasionally we take some of them in out of the wet and cold. Yesterday 33 prisoners were taken below here, who were captured by our Cavalry. Our boys dressed in Yankee uniforms and went in behind the Yankee pickets then turned and came back to them. The Yankees thought it was their own Cavalry coming to relieve them and did not fire or attempt to escape. In fact they did not know that it was the Confederates until our boys were upon them and ordered them to surrender which they did without firing a gun. This is out Yankeeing the Yankees themselves. If they head our boys in tricks of that kind they will have to begin quite soon.

We are now resting for a day or two. Washing and cleaning up clothes etc and waiting for the enemy to move either to advance or retreat. I expect that we have retreated as far as we will without a fight. I had rather fight than run any farther now. At least I am in favour of feeling of them and seeing how strong they are. When any thing happens I will write to you all about it unless that same thing happens to me and in such a manner as to disqualify me from writing in which event some kind friend will think enough of me to write for me.

I have written Mrs Sewell a letter which I enclose with this. I wrote it in pencil before I got my trunk in which I had pen and ink. It is too much to write it over besides paper is scarce and hence she must now excuse the pencil writing. It can be easily read and it is the original manuscript is about as funny as I could make it by writing it over and I know she likes some thing funny. In fact I think it would spoil it to copy. The originality (on which I pride myself) of the writing would be destroyed. In letter writing it is like most other things with me. I must feel in the humor and then if I can hit upon a humorous vein I can write as amusing a letter as any body but if I am in the dumps or hav'nt much time and chance to write or if I am bothered whilst writing, my writing becomes confused and uninteresting even to myself. There is much in practise in letter writing. About the time I quit school and began to study law I had a large circle of correspondents and from my frequent practice I could write a much more grammatical and a better letter than I can now. I took more pains to have every word spelled right, every sentence of the right measure and grammatically arranged etc but after I got to practicing law although my correspondence was much more extensive it became hurried & hasty and my pains were lost in brevity and haste. I like brevity when it doesnt spoil composition. An idea expressed in short sententious words or language goes home with me but it may be entirely destroyed or its beauty impaired by not using language to develop its full meaning & beauty. The Diamond is more sparkling and brilliant when polished but it too may be worn away by to much cutting. A blaze is much brighter, warmer & more cheerful than a smothered, smouldering, smoky fire. So ideas expressed in brief but ample language is much more impressive than when mistified with far fetched & high sounding phrases or words. Remember this in your composition and endeavour to develop the one style and avoid the other. I am in fine health. My lip has nearly recovered. It is getting down now to a kissing thickness. I am glad that there was no one here to kiss while my lip was so large and sore for I should have been compelled to forego the pleasure but if they come along now I am ready and you know I am always willing so look out pretty girls and nice widows or some body will be kissed. But Oh sha what is the use of being foolish. I have a nice wife and a sweet little daughter at home to kiss and must I waste my "perfume upon the desert air"[81] by expending my kisses on these way off Louisiana women.

My Confederate gray pants are completely worn out. The cloth was rotten and scarcely worth any thing. Col Jones got his fine gray Confederate coat burned nearly up a night or two ago. His bed caught on fire & burned his bedding & coat & shoes pretty badly. It will take more than Irvins liniment to heal the wounds.

I have just learned by report from the front that the enemy has fallen back from Washington and are now 14 miles below that place. This puts a distance of about 60 miles between us now so that the prospect of an immediate fight is greatly lessened.

Lieut Cunningham reached Camp yesterday. He is in fine health & looks quite well.

Oct 29 1863

It rains to day & promises bad weather. We are in a bad place for wood but water is abundant. No news from the feds to day. Love & kisses to family & respects to friends.

Yours truly
E. P. Petty

Bayou Boeuf La. Nov. 2 1863

My dear son [Frank], —————————

I thought I would drop you a line. I am a little tired having just got in from the show of shooting a deserter. He belonged to Col. Randle's Brigade — attempted to get to the Feds — was arrested today — at 11 o'clock payed the penalty by being shot in the presence of the army. Such is the deserved fate of the man who attempts to desert and betray his country.

We are lying still here 7 miles below Cheneyville. I dont know what the Federals are doing, but I do know we are catching prisoners every day and whilst I am writing I saw some on the opposite side of the Bayou just being brought in by our boys.

Black Don's father left here today to cross the Mississippi river and I wrote another letter to your grandmother Pinner and sent by him hoping that it may possibly reach her. I hope too that she will write to me or your mother as I want to hear from her very much.

I have the largest and best company in Allen's Regiment. The boys are generally well and in fine spirits. It does seem that this thing here is going to blow over an we get no fight out of it. It is truly shocking, my boy, just to think of it. We are here to fight — it is our trade and yet lay in the immediate presence of the enemy 5 or 6 weeks and get no chance — is truly shocking, but whatever is is right and we must submit, my boy.

I wish you were here awhile, my boy, to see the soldiers and eat sugar cane. It would be a good to you, but your Ma needs your services at home and you must also go to another sort of school and you may yet have time and opportunity to witness all these scenes.

This war looks like it is getting hitched in good. There is no opening yet for its settlement and I am afraid wont be soon. I mean one honorable to the South, and I never could consent to a settlement that would tarnish our honor.

How do you get on at school? I hope you are using your time to the best advantage.

I want my boy Frank to be a good boy, an honest boy, a noble boy
— one that will scorn a mean act and have a contempt for everybody
and everything mean — a dutiful boy who will honor, love, protect
and cherish his sisters and brothers — and have respect for older
persons.

Multiplied kisses and love to you and the balance of the family —
Respects to all friends.

Yours truly
E.P. Petty
Capt. Co. F. Allen's Regiment

[*Fragment, no date.*]

I waited two days last week to be put under arrest by Genl Scurry aye I
courted it and bartered for it but without success. They have been
in the habit of detailing my men whenever they wanted without
consulting me on the subject. They have now at Division & Brigade
Head Quarters 9 of my men including Lt Cunningham. One morning
last week they detailed John Perkins to drive an ambulance and cook
for some of them around Hd Qrs without letting me know any thing
about it. I was blazing mad and wrote a verry tart note to the Adjutant
Genl in which I not only remonstrated but even menaced [?] them. It
was returned endorsed that it was "disrespectful both in substance and
form" and I was warned that such offensive language would not be
over looked again by the Genl. I immediately replied, disavowed
disrespect — but insisted upon an answer to my question and closed by
asking "if that Courtesy that should characterize officials in their
intercourse with each other did not require that the Captain should be
consulted before detailing his men." This was a little tighter than any
thing contained in my first communication and I did it with the
purpose of vindicating myself or being put under arrest and I didnt care
which. I hunted up my old rusty sword that was full of grease and mud,
the belt all chewed up by the mules and all in a most deplorable fix to
have it ready to send up to the Genl but instead of an order of arrest I
received a reply to my note not however in verry Courteous terms but
yet a full answer to my question. He claims the right to detail my men
without my knowledge and consent. I was almost mad enough to send
up my resignation. But I hardly think I will now upon reflection. You
ask me what I mean by the ladies being <u>free and easy</u>. I mean that they
are easy to get acquainted with and free and agreeable in conversation.
They are not shy but trusting and confiding and much more fun for the
same length of acquaintance can be had with them than with Texan

girls. I did not use it in an improper sense. All the ladies that I
associate with are so far as I have been able to learn or know of the
right stripe. On the substitute question I acknowledge that I was once
verry bitterly opposed to substitutes but as our Government has
established the law and as I am opposed to too much change in laws as
it leaves every thing in uncertainty I have concluded to conform
myself to it and abide by its provisions. Therefore the first pretty
woman I can find with clean nice Children I will (if they are willing)
receive your kisses. On the Meat & bread question you must do the
best you can. I have sent you the money. You must use it. I cannot
verry well direct you in the premises except that if you have specie
hold on to every cent of it. Dont let a dime go for any thing. I have
no news nor can I get any here. I am in the most excellent health. I
send love and kisses to you & the children and respects to friends.

Yours truly
E. P. Petty

Bayou Boeuf Louisiana
November 5th 1863

My Dear Wife
I understand that the Yankees are falling back towards the Bay. So
you see that our prospect of a fight at present is growing beautifully less
every day. I was so sure that we would have a fight for a few days. In
fact it was so imminent that I double shotted my six shooter and
otherwise made the necessary dispositions for the fight one of which
was throwing my sword away or sending it to the rear with the wagon
which is equivalent. We were formed in line of battle once the ditches
were cleaned out. The advance of the enemy was with in 3 miles of us.
Citizens were flying by us to the rear. Our Cavalry were driving back
all the cattle and other stock left by the Citizens in their flight to keep
the feds from getting it. The sick, the halt, the maimed, the blind
with the wagons were sent to the rear. The horns (brass band) were
sent away and the musicians transposed into an infirmary corps to pack
off the wounded. The guns were furnished, amunition inspected,
cannons planted, sharp-shooters and skirmishers thrown forward, every
officer and man at his post and on the lookout. All that we liked
[lacked] of a battle was the advance of the enemy which he prudently
failed to do thereby spoiling a great battle in the Trans Miss Dept —
much anticipated fun on our part and escaping a good sound thrashing
upon his part. "There's many a slip betwixt the Cup and the lip." The

enemy retired back and we retired back mutually saying no fight my boys this time "patience and shuffle the Cards,"[82] the time may come yet when your desires may be more than gratified. If we do fight dear wife woe be unto the luckless federal army that comes in contact with Genl Walkers Division. We are still camped on Bayou Boeuf (beef) 7 miles below Cheneyville between a large canefield & the Bayou in a narrow compass. The cane in the field was sugar and we have consumed it by turning in our horses & feeding it away. The fence we burned for cooking & other purposes so the field is now like a prarie. On the opposite side of the Bayou is an extensive sugar cane plantation — a great place of resort for the boys. They cut down trees and made a bridge. It is destroyed by orders from the Head Quarters. The destroying party hardly gets away before it is rebuilt. It is again and again destroyed & rebuilt in rapid succession. A guard is then placed at it with orders to let no one pass without orders from Brigade Hd Qrs. Two men from each company are only allowed passes per day. They get them in the morning and go over to the sugar cane and bring over large loads. Their passes are handed to two men who do likewise and so it goes on through the day. The Camp is full of sugar cane and the orders are laughed at so you see the daily routine of camp life on Bayou Boeuf. We are all in fine health & spirits, have plenty to eat & drink (Boeuf water) and plenty of amusements to while away the hours. Who would not be a Confederate Soldier in Louisiana? Echo answers who?! It is now raining again. The ground of course is muddy for whenever it thunders here the ground gets muddy. My company is pretty well fixed up for winter and rain so far as tents are concerned. Mine is the only company in the regiment that has any thing like tents enough to keep the men dry. I have five good tents and that will shelter all my men in the day and nearly all sleeping. It is due to my own industry and energy that we have them. The other Brigades after we returned from Milliken Bend grabbed all our tents. I got an order from Hd Qrs, made a [illegible] and got the most of mine and several for our regiment. The other Captains seem indisposed to do the same and I shall do no more for them. I wrote to your mother again and sent the letter by Mr Davis (Black's father) who left here last Monday for Genl Bragg's army. Black went with him to the Mississippi river and saw every necessary preparation for his father's crossing before he left. There are scarcely any federals now on the river except gun boats. Our pickets going to it on both sides so I think that in all probability your mother will get the letter. The gentleman with whom I entrusted the other letter to her sent me word by Black that he had gone in the federal lines and had mailed my letter. I hope she may get them both and I hope I may hear from her soon. I send this letter to you by Mr. Carter (Black Carter) who is here on a visit to his son and who will start back in the morning. I shall request him to call and see you and answer such other questions as you may see fit to propound. I learn by Carter that Confederate money has gone up considerably. I hope that you have been lucky enough to proffit by this advance and have disposed of some of your surplus money to advantage either by investment in property or gold. I wish I had a chance to send you some sugar and syrup home. Good sugar can be bought here at from 10 to 15 cents per pound and the best kind of Sugar house molasses from 75 cents to one dollar per gallon. I will watch and if I can possibly get a chance will send you some. I weighed 136 pounds yesterday in my shirt sleeves. I cant yet get up to my Arkansas weight but hope I will soon. I know that I am in good health as I am up there. Multiplied love & kisses to you & all & regards to friends.

Yours truly
E. P. Petty

Novr 6th 1863

Dear Wife

We had a fight with the feds a day or so ago below Opelousas in which we had 3 regiments of our infantry engaged and our Cavalry I suppose. Our loss as reported is 140 killed, wounded and missing. The enemy's loss is about 1000 being 600 prisoners. We took 2 parrot Cannons. I cant give any more particulars now as I dont know any.[83] No other news. Health of myself fine.

Your's truly
E. P. Petty

Bayou De Glaze La
Near Moroville [Moreauville]
Novr 9th 1863

Dear Wife

Your's of the 26th ult with Ella's of the 24th ult has been received this evening. It finds me again on the road to Simmesport and within 15 miles of that place. We broke up Camps on Bayou Boeuf yesterday 11 O'clock AM.[84] Our whole army here is moving. There is something on hand. If I am allowed to conjecture (and who says I shant) I believe that we will cross the Atchafalaya at Simmesport and sweep down the Mississippi river through the Fordoche, the Plaquemine and Lafourche Country breaking up the Government plantations and recovering as much stolen property as we can and destroying the ballance. Nearly all the federal troops on the river have been carried to Tennessee to reinforce Genl Rosencrantz leaving it verry near Clear of troops.[85] Now is the time for us to make a ten strike. The army that was down on Bayou Boeuf have nearly all retreated to the Bay and Genl Green is following them up capturing, whipping and scattering them generally. I dont think that they will be able to interfere with us much. I wrote to you by Mr Carter that there had been a battle below Opelousas. The substantial fruits of that victory is over 600 prisoners, near 300 killed & wounded, 300 mules captured, 1 parrot cannon, several hundred small arms and the destruction of their Camp with a large number of tents & other property. I hear another report to day that Green had captured 500 more of them. Our loss in the fight was about 20 killed, 80 wounded & a few missing. If we can sweep down between them and New Orleans we can perhaps capture them and take the city. Would'nt that be glorious but I dont hope for any such. We will damage them some however. This I expect will be the last oppertunity that I may have for writing to you until we return from this expedition. There are no mails through here now and our courier will perhaps have no chance to follow us up in our rapid marches. Of this however I cant say positively. You know that I will do the verry best I can and write every chance. I take broad grounds here and enjoy myself to the full limit with the women but I am ever mindful and never neglectful of the loved ones at home who are more dear to me than all on earth besides. I am sorry to hear of the troubles that Ma is seeming to have. I dont believe that either Cochran or Howerton would advise to her to or do themselves any thing that they did not think was for her good but if she objects then I think they ought and certainly will have nothing further to do with her affairs. The property is hers during her life and under her control alone. Cochran is to assist and advise her in carrying out the will such as the payment of debts etc. I think it will all be right with them after awhile. Ma must learn not to be too sensitive and they must not to be too officious. I am in the verry finest of health never better in my life. The boys are generally well. Tom McDonald still has chills but stays with the command and does duty when I will let him. I can write you no other news now. Remember me kindly to friends and lovingly and affectionately to the children.

Your's truly
E. P. Petty

Novr 10 1863 Simmesport

Dear Wife

We are now on the Atchafalaya river at Simmesport. Our troops are now crossing. We will cross in the morning. The feds left one house standing here and many chimneys. They burned the town. I am in fine health today. All gay & lively.

Yours etc
E. P. Petty

Bayou Letsworth or Lake De Passo
La Novr 16 1863

Dear Ella

When we crossed the Atchafalaya I did not think I would have another chance to write until we came out of this place but our courier goes back to Alexandra on tomorrow and I have concluded to send you a few lines. We crossed the A last Wednesday. We came on to this Bayou or Lake on Friday and will remain here for several days I expect.[86] We are now in 3 miles of the Miss river. Have been busy day & night in planting our batteries on the river. They are now ready 12 guns planted and I am now anxiously listing [listening] for the opening of the ball. 5 transports passed yesterday but we were not ready but woe to the unlucky one that attempts to pass to day. There are two gun boats in about ¾ mile of one of our batteries anchored near the opposite shore. They look grizly & dismal & when the fight opens will make I presume merry music. They dont have any idea that we are here notwithstanding we have been at work night & day in their vicinity. The levy is so high they cant see us. I hope they wont until we open the ball which will be as soon now as we get a chance. The infantry will remain here in supporting distance of the batteries a few perhaps going in as a guard etc. Oh how anxious we all are to hear the music. We are like gallants at a ball waiting for the fiddler who is seemingly late in comeing. This is a magnificent country over here. I like it better than Bayou Boeuf. The people are more liberal and patriotic than any we have found any where. Every thing is in abundance. Corn & potatoes are rotting in the fields. We are living finely. I eat out of the Camp with the citizens half my time and live like a Lord. They have suffered awfully here and hate the Yanks with a vengeance. If any thing turns up to day I will postscript it in this letter. I am in fine health. The boys are generally well. Tom McDonald was left at the A river he being still sick with chills. Dr Gorman was also left sick. I have about 42 men now with me. Jim Cunningham has been promoted to asst Commissary of Subsistence for the Brigade with the rank of Captain. So I have lost my Lieut.

We can get no news in here. I cant write much now. Remember your poor old daddy and be a good, cheerful, nice girl. Kiss Ma and the children for me and recolect me to friends. Write oftener than you do.

Yours truly
E. P. Petty

Sun Set Nov 16 1863

P.S. I went out to the river this evening and have just returned. I visited our Bateries. I saw the gunboats. They looked fearful. A transport came down the river & stopped at the gun boats. After staying 3 hours she went back up stream — Our cannon were loaded ready to send her under but she did not come. Oh how much I was disappointed. I itched for the ball to open.

E. P. Petty

Point Coupee La
Novr 23rd 1863

My Dear Wife

Your's of the 5th inst has just been received. Since I last wrote we have been on the tramp for four or five days threatning and daring the enemy — Our batteries near Red River Landing (Mouth of RR) have been firing upon transports and fighting gun boats for several days. One transport laden with Commissaries I learn has been burned & sunk, another injured. The gun boats shelled some of our batteries out. About 5 days ago the 17th Regt (Allens) with a battery of artilery and some Cavalry in all about 500 strong were ordered to take position near Morganza on the Miss River and fire upon transports etc. It seems that the orders were not properly understood and so we did not stop near Morganza but turned it and went way down some 10 or 15 miles below (the battery & Cavalry going some 25 miles) W on the Fordouche on the road leading to Plaquemine putting ourselves in a complete trap but as it happened the enemy did not have forces enough and we held the triggers of the trap and were not caught. The enemy will never have another such a chance at the 17 as they then had. Genl Walker recalled us and we are now stationed with batteries planted 4 miles above Morganza and about 25 miles above Port Hudson. The gun boat of the enemy came up today & anchored right opposite to our batteries but did not see us as we were well hid under the levy. After staying an hour she went back. We are waiting for a transport who we will open the ball. We are rather in an exposed place and I dont feel quite easy but I have long since made up my mind to go & do without question or hesitation whatever & whenever I may be ordered — Oh what a Country this is. It is the garden spot of the world. Egypt in its palmyest days was nothing to Louisiana. But the rude hand of war has been lain heavily upon it. We planted our battery in front of a fine house. The owners and the neighbors all skeddaddled quick. The place will be torn to pieces when the shelling commences and I look for that all the time. They had to abandon much and so it is over the whole Country. You cant imagine how it is injured & such will be the fate of Texas if it is invaded. I am in fine health and good cheerful spirits so are all my boys & the company. Love to all & respects to friends.

Yours truly
E. P. Petty
Nov 23 1863

Bayou Letsworth La
Nov 27 1863

Dear Ella

I will write only a few lines now. Last Wednesday (the 25) the enemy shelled us out from the river above Morganza and on the next day returned to our Command here. We did not get any body hurt. The only damage done was a shell tore the coat sleeve off of a negro without hurting him much. Our sharp shooters are now along the river annoying them very much and occasionly we send in a battery to fire at them. They are excessively annoyed and shell the woods hunting for us every day. We had quite a pleasant though risky trip of 8 days down the Country and I was sorry when we got the orders to rejoin our Brigade. One Dutchman deserted & went to the feds. We suppose with this exception we lost not a man. I am in fine health & weighed to day 140 pounds. The boys are quite well generally. Good spirits & humor prevails in our entire command. There seems to be no feds on this side of the river. I am afraid that you will see some trouble in Texas — Col. Allen has petitioned Genl Smith to have our Regt sent

to Tyler to guard fed prisoners. I have no idea that will be done & I dont care much to go there.[87]

Kisses & love to all.

Yours truly
E. P. Petty

Bayou Letsworth Louisiana
November 30th 1863

My Dear Wife

I hav'nt any thing of much importance to write to you. I sent you a letter a few days ago and a day or two ago one to Ella since which no change has taken place in the position of things here of any moment. We are still in the Trans Atchafalaya District — Still annoying the enemy on the Miss River by firing into their gunboats and transports with sharpshooters etc. We give them great trouble. Have killed several men, wounded many others, partly burned one steamboat. Somewhat injured a gunboat. Caused several desertions from the boats and otherwise injured and knocked them about. We intend to hold this Department until the waters run us out. This is the finest Country in the world and I am willing to help hold it at all hazards. We are now moving one of our Pontoon Bridges from Simmsport to Morgan's Ferry.

It is designed no doubt for us to make a raid down towards Plaquemine and on the La Fourche Bayou and will have a crossing nearer to us so that in case of haste we can cross more conveniently. I saw another new sight to day. Some men were caught stealing a hog. Genl Scurry had a hog skinned and fitted upon them so that the skin of the head made a cap, the snout making the vizor or brim, the ears sticking up naturally, the forelegs clasping across the breast and the ballance forming a cloak and thus dressed they were marched back and forth before the entire Brigade to the amus[m]ent of all and the mortification of themselves — While passing some called hogs, some squealed and grunted like hogs whilst all crowded to the roadside and induleged in remarks, laughs etc. I think that it was enough to cure all hog stealing propensity. I am in fine health. Weighed a day or so ago 140 pounds. Am getting along finely. Am making some good and substantial friends amongst the citizens here and particularly amongst the ladies. I will write as often as I can. I have some money to send you and only wait for a chance to do so. I am afraid to risk it by mail as it is so irregular now. Our mail will be in this evening and I hope to get a letter from you. Write as often as you can. Love & kisses to children & respects to friends.

Yours truly
E. P. Petty

Bayou Fordouche Louisiana
Sunday December 6th 1863

My Dear Wife

On the 1st inst our whole command left Bayou Letsworth and after 3 days marching we arrived at a point about 12 or 15 miles below this on Bayou Grosse Tete and on the road leading direct to Plaquemine. We all thought that Plaquemine was certainly our destination and we had bright visions of Yankee goods, clothing, Boots etc but on the 4th we were halted for further orders and on the 5th marched back to this place where we now await further orders.[88] This place is on the road from Morgans ferry on the Atchafalaya to Morganza on the Miss river & is about 2 miles below the Fordouche battle ground and is one of the prettiest sections of this beautiful & magnificent Country. I understand that the Feds got notice of us and rendered Plaquemine impregnable to our forces by reinforcements, gun boats etc so that our visions of goods etc have proven like all other visions a baseless fabric. We will stay here perhaps a few days when I think we will fall back to

Morgans ferry and recross the Atchafalaya. The feds are too busy in Tennessee to notice us much. We were in hopes of making a diversion here and calling some troops away from [George H.] Thomas thereby weakening him so that Bragg could use him up but I am afraid that we shall fail as we did on our attempted diversion on Vicksburg.[89] We can only get the gun boats to notice us and we keep them pretty busy shelling the woods etc. It is amusing to see them expending their amunition. They shell every day every point where we have ever been. I am not so fond of the music as I am that of our band or of a piano. I believe it was the poet Ossian[90] who said the "music of the shells resounded through the halls of our fathers." Mr Davis has returned from beyond the Miss river and says that he had my letter to your invention and also of Modern Civilization but be it what it may our children can exclaim in the same language "the music of the shells resounded through the halls of our fathers." Mr Davis has returned from beyond the Miss river and says that he had my letter to your Mother mailed in the federal lines and I have no doubt but that she will get so that at least she can hear from us if we do not from her. I have just heard that Corpus Christi Texas has been taken by the feds. I am fearful that Don went up with it and his family also. Please let me know if it is so. Send me your paper every mail so that I can keep posted on Texas matters. I get no news here from there that I can tell much about. I want to hear more & oftener. I am fearful that Texas is now to be overrun unless her citizens who are at home will show that heroism that is characteristic of her name. You had better buy you such articles now as you need. The trade with Brownsville is gone. The salt works are gone I fear. The sugar crop is light — I cant send you any from here because I cant get any transportation for it. Every thing will now be higher & scarcer. Money will be more depreciated so that you had better without delay lay in salt, sugar, molasses, clothing etc while you can if you can and while you have money. For fear your money may run short I have concluded to stint myself again and send you all I can. I dont need it much here and can get along any way. I can rough it. I am in splendid health & cheerful spirits, get plenty to eat & have plenty to wear. Dont need much of any thing and can get money if I need it here. So I send you all I can herein. Use it to the best advantage. If you have any gold or silver cling to it. Dont let your right hand know that your left hand has it. Be careful with your property & effects. Keep the children at school under any & all circumstances. Feed & cloth them well and teach them to know & appreciate their position and relations in life. I wish I were in Texas if it should be invaded so that I might be enabled to give you personal

assistance but I fear that I am wedded to the soil of Louisiana during the ballance of the war but while I fight & struggle in Louisiana I know that it is for Texas and I am reconciled. I understand that my trunk has been sent from Shreveport to me and is now at Morgans ferry. I wish it were at home but must try and take care of it. I will write as often as I can to you. I want you all to write. I hav'nt had a letter in two weeks or longer. Love & kisses to children & respects to friends.

Yours truly
E. P. Petty

P.S. I send by Mʳ· Geo W Davis (Black's father) this letter with Three hundred ($300) dollars in it. I have just weighed and my weight is 141 pounds.

E. P. Petty

My Dear Wife

I started you a letter day before yesterday by Geo W Davis of Travis County (Black's father) with three hundred ($300) dollars in Confederate money but I expect that Mr Chambliss who is the bearer of this will reach home before Mr Davis does and if I had been certain when Mr C would start would have sent the letter and money by him. In due time however you will get the letter & money. By yesterdays mail I received your letter of the 15th October last. Now isnt that late news from home. I got however some time ago a letter from you of the 6th Novr and through a letter from Cousin Wm G King I heard from you on the 10th Novr & from Seguin on the 16th Novr. It seems that I can now get nothing from home in regular time. I hear that McLester reached Morgan's ferry on the Atchafalaya on yesterday and will be here to day so I hope that I will again hear directly from home. I know that it is not your fault and if you dont get letters it is'nt my fault as I write often at least once a week and every other private chance. I sent by Davis and now by Chambliss so you see I loose no available oppertunity. Well I write I say it will either be repetition or foolishness and as you are fond of foolishness may be so some will be palateable to you. We are here and eating up our rations and in good health is about the whole that would be necessary to be written as that Comprehends every thing but I will add that our object in being here is two fold. One is to forage this section which is the best foraging country we have found and will soon have to be abandoned to the feds whenever the waters arise and another is to annoy the commerce of the Miss river etc all of which we are doing daily. I learn that the Atchafalaya is rising. If so perhaps we will have to go out of here for if it gets high enough to let a gun boat in our pontoon bridges will be destroyed and we may be cut off. We keep our eyes open to all these things. I heard a cannonading going on at the river yesterday evening. I suppose our river batteries are at work. We are making the river rather warm for comfort. I hope that we may succeed in setting the river on fire. It has been so low this summer that I learn the feds refused to allow the Citizens of Memphis to use water out of it for fear that it would be exhausted. Low as it is it is terribly in our way and while it is in our way we will make them uneasy about it some. Love & kisses etc.

E. P. Petty

Dec 9th 1863

Dear Ella

I send also by Mr Chambliss some New Orleans papers of a tolerable late date. There are later ones in camp but I cant get hold of them. I also send a map of Louisiana which will give you some idea of our whereabouts. Our range has been from Camp Shepard on Bayou Rapides above Alexandra down Bayou Boeuf to where near Opelousas over to the mouth of Red River and down the Miss River to near Baton Rouge on Bayou Grosse Tete to where Bayou Marengoen [Maringouin] and G.T. [meet]. I also send you the flags of all the principal powers & nations. I wish I could get some thing worth sending. I wish I could have sent you a birthday present but I could not get any thing to send in time.

I am in splendid health. I have just heard that the firing at the river yesterday was at a large transport which was greatly damaged seriously.[91]

Yours truly
E. P. Petty

PS In ½ hour or so we leave here for Morgan's ferry.

EPP

Simmesport Louisiana
Sunday Dec 13th 1863

My Dear Daughter

You will see by the heading that I am at another place and so we go hither and thither and back again verrifying the name that the feds gave us "Walkers grey hounds." I do reckon that Walkers Division has travelled more and fought less than any troops in the Confederacy. We made a campaign of one month in the Trans (beyond) Atchafalaya Department. We did a good deal of damage and an immense amount of annoyance to the feds. I cant of course accurately estimate their damage but as far as I know we shut the ports of one gunboat by shooting into them with sharp shooters, damaged her some with our cannons and ran her off. We destroyed or rendered valueless 3 steam boats, fired into others with our sharp shooters. We know of several men killed and wounded and 30 deserted off of one boat and joined the Confederates. We made quite uncertain the navigation of the old father of waters. In fact a steamboat dared not pass unless under convoy of a gun boat. It reminded me of a young gallant taking a young lady on his arm and escorting her through the streets crowded with men she poor thing knowing that all eyes were upon her and trembling with fear lest some rudeness should be offered.

The feds have also wasted amunition etc enough shelling the banks to knock down Vicksburg nearly. Our damage is 2 men killed and 2 wounded by the feds, the bursting of one cannon and slightly wounding 3 men thereby. As an offset to this we subsisted one month in a section where the feds would have got the subsistence if we had not and we lived better than we have any where else. The rivers began to rise a few days ago and have now risen near 5 feet. This rendered the shores of the Cis-Atchafalaya (this side) more attracting and its atmosphere more salubrious as it was well known that gun boats could very soon enter the A and by destroying one pontoon perhaps capture us. So we crossed over and have to night just reached our camp one mile back of Simmesport where I expect we will remain a few days. If the waters go down we will perhaps go back on the Miss river. If they continue to rise the Campaign of the Trans Atchafalaya has ended for the season. I am sorry of it. I had become attached to that Country and its people for it is the prettiest & finest country and most hospitable people that I have been with or seen in La or elsewhere so I leave it with many regrets. We have considerable rains now and the roads are getting quite bad — to day it rained some but this evening cleared up with a brisk norther and the prospect is promising for some open and pleasant weather. God speed it.

I have no particular news to write. The news of Genl Bragg's great victory over Grant you will see published before you get this letter. If it is as good as we have heard and hope it will end the Campaign on this side of the river and may be so the war for they will be compelled to draw their troops from here to make an army in front of Bragg. If they do not Tennessee, Kentucky & Cincinatti is exposed and open to an invasion. These little places here are of minor importance to them and will be overlooked for the present. This is the foundation of my hopes that Texas will escape for the present. Our army here is in fine health and spirits. I never saw men looking better and more cheerful. We are in better condition and humor for fighting than we ever have been — some of my boys have a chill occasionly but it does'nt unfit them for duty. Jim Wilson, Tom Irvine & Jim Loftin & John Smith are the only ones so effected. Tom McDonald has got well & is fat again. I am in superfine health. McLester has arrived but is not well yet. He left my letter in his Carpet sack at Alexandra and I dont know when I will get it. It will be old when I do, I am afraid.

Write me a long letter giving me all the items & incidents of
Bastrop, your school, Grand Ma's visit etc etc etc. Remembrances,
Loves, Kisses etc to each & all of the family and respects to friends.

Yours truly
E. P. Petty

Camp Near Simmesport Louisiana
Tuesday December 15th 1863

My Dear Son Don

Pa has verry little news to write to his little boy. I have written so
many letters home in the last week and nothing having transpired
worthy of notice since that I am as the saying goes about "out of soap"
but I could'nt help writing a few lines by way of being remembered and
to show you that I hav'nt forgotten you and I hope yes I know that you
hav'nt forgotten me. You hav'nt forgotten what I have written and
told you I know. Uncle Charley says that you are a good match for
_____ . I hope that you are equal to him in sense, good
breeding, good manners and all those qualities that make a good boy
but I do hope that in mischief and badness and cruelty that you are
not equal to him. Dont be a bad boy — Be a good boy. Learn your
book. Obey your mother. Love your brothers & sister. Respect older
folks than yourself — When I come home I want to see my smart,
good little boy Don and then any and every thing I can do for you that
is right to be done I will do it. You know I furnish you with plenty to
eat, plenty to wear, a good home and I want you to have a good
education. So that when you grow up to be a man you will make a
good, intelligent, smart, useful citizen and be a pride to your parents, a
blessing to your country and an ornament to society. Now wont you do
all this. Yes I believe you will. Now try and do so. If you will try it will
be easy for you to do so. Try and learn to write so you can answer my
letter without getting any body else to do it for you. In the meantime
get Ella or Ma to write to me for you. Tell them what to write and
make them write it in your own language just as you say it for I dont
want any of their polish to it. I want just from Don so that I can see,
feel and hear my boy. I am mighty well now. Getting along finely.
There is a heap of rain and mud here. I have to go out in the rain and
wade in the mud. We dont stop for the weather. Whether the sun
shines or the rain pours, whether it be warm or cold it is all the same
to us. Orders and marches are like time and tide. They wait for no
man and for no weather. I expect we will remain near this place some

time as we have commenced fortifying at Yellow Bayou about one or two miles further up Bayou De Glaze than our present Camp.[92] I was in hopes that we would go back to the pine hills as this country will be awful muddy this winter but I expect we will have to stay here. There is more honey in this Country than I ever dreamed of. Our boys cut down 10 or 15 every day and sometimes get as much as 160 pounds of honey out of one tree. It readily sells at 50 cents per pound so you see money is made at [it.] Persimmons are plenty and I have enclosed here in some of the seed. Tell ma to plant them in the garden and take care of the trees if they come up. I dont know any more now to write. Love & kisses to all.

Yours truly
E. P. Petty

Camp on Bayou De Glaze La
Tuesday Decr 22nd 1863

My Dear Wife

The letters you sent by Lieut McLester have just been received. Lt M^cL came in over a week ago but left his Carpet Bag with the letters at Alexandra. Our clothing has not reached us yet. M^cL has gone with a wagon after it and will be down within a few days. I have been (as

also the entire regiment & others besides) to day at work on our fortifications about 1½ miles from here in the junction of Yellow Bayou with Bayou De Glaze. The works are about 3 miles from Atchafalaya (at Simmesport). We have an eligible position and are putting up strong works. We have again made another pontoon bridge over the Atchafalaya and have orders to cross tomorrow at 9 O'clock. The A. & Miss river have fallen and we are going back to pitch into transports & gunboats.[93] The furloughing system has been again started and Lt. Charles Keton leaves for home in the morning & will carry you this letter together with a birthday present for Ella which is a small but beautiful volume of Baxters Poems.[94] Also a work on Anatomy, Phisiology & Hygene by Cutter which is for Ella. It is the book I promised to send her long since but have had no good chance before. I also send you herein one hundred dollar Confederate bill. I sent you by George W. Davis of Travis County some two or three weeks ago three hundred dollars which I hope you will receive soon or have received. I thought that I had sent you all the money that I would be able to soon but when I learned how near you were out of money and how much you seemed to think of me I relented and have concluded to strip myself again and send you all I can spare. My wife and my children must have money and live whether I do or not. I wish I had more to send but you must try and get along with what you now have until I can make & collect more. The notes executed by Ma & Pa are all right. If I had written them I would have written them a little different but I am satisfied —— If I get over on Bayou Letsworth in time I expect to have a Christmas dinner and an egg nog. I have some warm, substantial friends over there male & female. I get word every day or so from them. I think that I shall have a good time over there. I am in the enjoyment of splendid health. I weigh now 143 pounds — more than I weighed at Pine Bluff by 2 pounds. I think that I will go up higher unless some accident happens to me. The boys are generally well. Tom McDonald & Jim Wilson still have the chills. I tried to get them a furlough the other day but failed. They have both been sent to the hospital at Evergreen. There are some others chilling occasionaly. Col Jones is quite well.[95] So Bob Wilkins. I expect it will be difficult to get William Wilkins transfered to my Company. It rains here every week. It now rains & we will have mud tomorrow. Walt Farmer & Dave Morris will leave in a few days on furlough. I will send the ballance of Tom Bearns clothing by them. Mrs B. & Mrs Erhard can then converse with Dave Morris (who staid with Tom til he died) and learn the true facts of the case. I hope that they will satisfy themselves

with him. Dave & Walt will call to see you and give you all the items.
I have no news to write. Flemming is quite well. I will write again by
Dave & Walt. Love, kisses and all that to my little ones & respects to
friends.

Yours truly
E. P. Petty

Bastrop Dec 24th 1863

Captain Petty!
Dear friend!
    If you please will let Mr. Hoffman have $10.⁰⁰/₁₀₀ Teen Dollars paper
money to Buy him some Tobacco, I will pay it To your Lady here in
Bastrop. I oblige, your friend.

[*Signature illegible.*]

Bayou De Glaze La
Saturday Decr 26 1863

My Dear Daughter
    Christmas Gift[96] to you all and a Merry Christmas besides. I
expected on Christmas eve to spend mine in a fight as 1200 negroes &
federals had landed on the Mississippi river & were comeing out as we
supposed in an advance movement: Genl Scurry rallied his brigade and
started us over to attack them. We marched about 10 miles after night
to a point on Bayou Letsworth in about 6 miles of this landing place
intending to open Christmas morning with a fight but lo, the
scoundrels embarked at about 8 o clock at night and left for points
unknown. Instead then of fighting all day I called on some Lady
friends on Letsworth, got an egg nog, a fine breakfast & had a gay
time. We thus returned to the Atchafalaya. Spent the ballance of the
day until 12 o clock at night at a nice place, had a magnificent dinner,
fine music, pretty & charming ladies, intelligent gentlemen, songs,
cards etc. So you see my Dear Daughter that I have had a gay time and
that I have not forgotten the loved ones at home. The young ladies
have promised to give me a dance etc on my birthday. I am afraid the
river will be up so that I cant attend as it is rising now pretty fast so
much so that we thought it prudent to come back over here.
    I am in fine health never better in my life. The boys are generally

well and keen for a fight. Rheum Castleman is here & will carry this
letter to you & will give you the news. Love, kisses etc to all.

Yours truly
E. P. Petty

Bayou De Glaze La
December 27 1863

My Dear Wife
   I wrote to Ella yesterday (26) by Rheum Castleman. I loaned
Castleman one hundred dollars to be paid to you when he gets home.
Receive the money and enter it to my credit on my bill of expenses
with you. I also sent you one hundred dollars by Lt Charles H. Keton
some two or three days before and about a week before that I sent you
three hundred dollars by George W Davis of Austin making total 500
dollars which I have sent you in about 2 weeks. The government has
paid me up to the 1st of this month and I have sent all to you retaining
verry little if any for myself. Thirty dollars per month will pay my
expenses and there is nothing here to waste money in buying besides I
dont want to waste it whilst I have so much use for it at home. I am
not living for myself alone. I have dedicated myself to my Country and
my means to my family. I hope the time may speedily come when my
Country will no longer need my services and when I can devote and
dedicate both person and property to my family. I gave Ella the
particulars of my Christmas day engagements. I spent the day gaily,
drinking Egg nog, Wine and eating fine viands. I flitted & flirted in
gay society of men, women & children and enjoyed myself hugely but
amidst all this hilarity I thought of home & family.

> "Well I can prize this happy scene
> "And feel its sweet control
> "And every word & smile can find
> "A place within my soul
> "I love them all but there is <u>one</u>
> "Is dearer still to me
> "Without whose presence this fair earth
> "A dreary waste would be
>
> "She spreads a charm through every scene
> "That mocks the cares of life
> "She leans her trusting heart on mine
> "My own <u>endearing wife</u>

"For her I'd leave friends, kin & place
"All I have known before
"Not that I love them ought the less
"But that I love her more.

These lines breath my true sentiment and although I dive deep in pleasure as it passes and make the most of everything as it comes yet of thee I am ever thinking, and of those who call me by the endearing name of <u>father</u>. I have the promise from some young ladies (voluntarily given) to give me a birthday party. The Atchafalaya is rising some now and last night it rained hard which I fear will increase the rise. If it gets a little higher the gunboats can enter it and then my birthday party will dissolve like a vision as the ladies reside in the Trans At. Dept. I shall live in hope if it ends in fruition. I am better pleased with the Trans At Dist than any place I have found. Its people are kind & hospitable. Its ladies pretty & intelligent. Its soil rich & fertile and every thing suits me. I wish I could stay over there whilst I had to stay in the army. There by way of variety we can every day get a shot at the enemy and can hear the sweet music of whistling & bursting shells. They sound sweet when you are safely ensconsed under a ten foot levy & the shells are high up in mid air. Variety is the spice of life and there is such a variety to be found in the Trans At. Dist as to render life quite spicy and some times a little uncertain. I wish I had you & Ella with me here in the Trans At Dist a little while. I know you would fully appreciate it and enjoy it as I have done and hope to do again.

December 28th 1863

This has been a clear, cold day. The ground has dried off wonderfully. The At River has risen considerably. It is four feet higher than it has been. It is sufficiently high for gun boats but none have come in yet. We loosed our Pontoon Bridge to day as the river was getting to high for its use. My birthday party has gone up. How I hate it. I had anticipated great pleasure.
"Pleasures are like poppies spread,
"They bloom a moment, their flowers are fled."[97]
Some more of my bad luck you see. I have no news from across the Miss. Our Brigade now occupies the advance post all the ballance having been removed back to Marksville some 20 miles from us. I had rather be in the advance than rear. There is some novelty in being in front. We see and hear and <u>risk</u> more but it all pays. Give me the front always. Cicero Nash has just arrived. He looks badly though he says that he is much better than when he left home.

December 29 1863

Walt Farmer & Dave Morris have their furlough's this morning &
will start some time during the day so I will have to close up my
journal as they are the bearers hereof.

This is a cold, frosty though a brilliant clear morning. The air is pure
and healthy and it seems strange and rong that man should be warring
upon his fellow man and desolating all that is fair and lovely on earth.
The poet[98] has truly said "That man clothed in a little brief authority
cuts such fantastic tricks before high Heaven as make the angels
weep." Man alone of all created nature seems to be in incessant
destructive war. "Oh God I blush for my own species." I am in
excelsior health and spirits. The boys are generally well. Genl Rum has
had a merry time with our Command this Christmas. No news from
any where that I know. The Miss & At Rivers are rising rapidly. Our
Trans At Campaign is truly at an end & I am sorry. Love, kisses & all
that to Children.

Yours truly
E. P. Petty

My Dear Son Don

I have received your letter. Ma said you cried because you could'nt think of any thing to write. I wanted your own sweet little prattle is the reason why I made this exaction. Why couldn't you tell me something. How mischevious you have been. How you pulled the cats tail, throwed rocks at the chickens, roped the calves, rode the pigs and bit the dogs ears. How you romped and played. How you followed after Frank whenever he went and all that sort of thing. This would all interest me. I wanted to see if you could think. I know that you could have told me all these things if I had been there. Then why could'nt you tell Ella and let her write them but it is all right. Try it again. Next time you will do better and next time better and next time still better. As it was I was glad to get it and hope you will send me another. I dont want Ella to fret my boy and make him cry again. She must write without that. I did'nt mean for her to be so hard with my boy. Try and learn to read and write and you wont have to depend on her. Here is a kiss for you and Van and all the rest.

Yours truly
E. P. Petty

Bayou De Glaze La
Jany 4th 1864

Dear Sister Sally[99]

In two months I have sent addressed to you & your Mother two letter which I hope you have received. I hav'nt heard a word by letter or otherwise (except an indistinct & unintelligible message from John Claiborne) from any of you or my relations in Tenn or Ky since the war commenced or even since secession and you can well imagine my anxiety on the subject. I would give almost any thing to have a letter from you. I want to hear all the news from you all. How has the war used you? Have you yet married? Are you still living at the old place? Where is Mat Northington & Mary? Where is William, Elbert, Joseph and Thomas? How fares the old lady our Mother? Did the Yankee's according to their inherent desires and rascally proclivities steal any of your negroes and other property! What has become of our other relatives and friends? If you have received my other letters you know how and when I stand and if you did not receive them I will state that I was a Secessionest per se. Spoke, electioneered and voted for it. Helped to carry Texas triumphantly out of the accursed old Union.

Have been in the army over two years. Have fought and bled in our glorious Cause and am now ready to fight and bleed again. Am a soldier for this war determined to be a free man or a dead man. Never expect to sheath my sword or cease fighting until our independence is acknowledged and our glorious Chivalrous Confederacy takes her stand as proud nation among the nations of the earth. I am Captain in the 17 Tex Reg Infty now stationed on Bayou De Glaze in Louisiana. Have a fine company in good health and exuberant spirits determined to die or be free. My family at home are doing quite well, have plenty of money, provisions, property, friends etc. I send you a letter herein from my wife, the latest I have from home. It will give you the particulars of family matters.

Ella is learning finely. She has progressed considerably in various studies and plays well on the piano. She is as large nearly as her mother. Frank is a good, fine boy learning finely. Don Green is one of the smallest & most mischievious boys in the Confederacy. Van Alvin is a perfect Petty for mischief etc. I have a great wife and the finest of children so I think & do you blame me. I wish you could see them. I have no news of interest. Address me as follows, Capt E P Petty, Co F, 17 Tex Infty, Scurry's Brigade, Walkers Division, Alexandra Louisiana and envellop it and address the envellop to "Mr James DeValle, Williamsport Point Coupee Parish La" who will get it & send it to me. Love & respects to relations and friends.

Yours truly
E. P. Petty

I have just written a letter to your Aunt Sally Pinner at Dover.

Bayou De Glaze La
Jany 4th 1864

My Dear Daughter

I sent a long letter to your Ma yesterday with a letter from Miss Mollie E Moore the poetess of Tyler Texas. She is a nice and most estimable young lady and writes a splendid letter. I send it that you may read and pattern after her style. It is a poetic style, fine in imagination and clothed in beautiful drapery of fancy and poesy. I shall continue to correspond with her and send you the letters. When I say I want you to pattern after her I dont mean that I want you to ape the peculiar phraseology or style of any body but that it is a good pattern for you to improve upon or adapt to your own original ideas.

All we know we learn from others and she seems to be capable of setting a good copy for young ladies. Her style is elegant, her ideas pure and dignified, her language chaste & beautiful. I imagined that she could write a beautiful letter and having a slight acquaintance with her for the benefit of myself and Lts. Cunningham and Miller to address her she replied and I feel that I am amply repaid for my trouble and any thing that is so good & elegant I dont feel like withholding from you and Ma. As our tastes are of similar mould (having been adapted to each other) I feel and know that you can and will appreciate it.

I have had a terrible day to day. We have been to the fortifications to work to day and it has been raining on us nearly the whole time. It was mud and slosh all the time which made it hard & disagreeable work. I could have remained at Camp being officer of the day but chose to do other wise and took my chances with the boys. I understand that the Yankees are landing Negro troops again on Racarce [Raccourci] Island over on the Miss River but the At. river is so very high that it would be unsafe for us to go over after them again. I suppose we will not do so. I have no news to write, only do so because I have a chance to send it to Texas. Tell Ma to make use of that Confederate gray cloth I left to clothe the boys. I have got a fair piece and shall not need it. Prosecute your studies. Love & kisses to all the family & compliments to my friends. Write every chance you have & oftener too.

Yours truly
E. P. Petty

PS Tom McDonald is nearly well again.

Petty

Bayou De Glaze La Jany 7 1864

My Dear Wife

We are still near our fortifications on this Bayou. One Brigade of four regiments are doing all the work here. Our regiment working every fourth day. Day after tomorrow will be our day. We start at 6 O'clock, march 3 miles and work until 4 O'clock and return to camp. We work by reliefs. Work one hour and rest one hour. We have a verry cold spell upon us now. It has been quite cold and wet for over a week. Some little snow fell the other night. It rains at least once a week and frequently two a week. It is a miserably wet time and mud mud mud is

all the go. We are having a rough time for soldering. My Company is the largest present in the Command. I have 50 men present and nearly all for duty. Tom McDonald had returned from the hospital. He still has chills occasionly. John Wilson (not Wash Jones' Brother in law) is sick a little. These are about all that are sick and they only slightly. We are living tolerable well. Have plenty of Corn bread & poor beef all the time with occasionly pork and potatoes. Have plenty of sugar and molasses with occasionly some flour. We have to send along ways for forage & provisions. From 15 to 30 miles our waggons go. The roads are getting so bad that the mules are worked nearly down. If we had to run out from here now nearly all of our baggage would be lost. I expect however that we are destined to see the trees bud and the grass grow in this section unless the Yanks will make haste and run us out. It will take a pretty considerable force to make us skedaddle from here now. I weighed to day 146 pounds none of your swashy dropsical but genuine substantive flesh.

Bayou DeGlaze La Jany 9 1864

My Dear Wife

I am still in Superfine health. Have been to the fortifications hard at work to day. Shovelled up a heap of dirt to day. We would'nt work at Galveston but now we link in to it as though our lives depended upon it. I have no news to day. Hav'nt seen either Presidents Davis or Lincoln's messages or the proclamation of Abe which I learn is a ponderous document.[100] Wipes our state governments, frees the negroes and offers amnesty to all below the rank of Colonel who will lay down their arms and take the oath of allegiance to the U.S. I am below the rank of Col & of course am included in his amnesty. But I would see the sun fall from its socket, the Moon refuse to shine, the stars go out, the Heaven fall, Hell burst up from the depths of earth, God almighty turn his back upon the world and many other Calamitous things happen before I will take the oath of allegiance which he requires. There is great deal of despondency in the army and amongst the people. If the question of war or peace on any terms was submitted to this army the side of peace would get a heavy vote. I hate to believe this but am pretty sure it would be the case although the army is in fine spirits and would fight an awful fight now. Yet they sigh for peace, peace, peace, home and family etc etc. This is between us & I would'nt have it circulated for any thing so be mum upon this subject. I sometime when I hear the soldiers talk feel blue and despondent. I feel that there is very little reliance upon any body or set of men however patriotic they may pretend to be. It is enough to discourage the most sanguine patriot in the land. I know a man's family is dear to him but it makes me blush to see how men will prostitute honor and the honor of their family's to the little gratification of being with them without country or honor. I love my family but not with such an intensity.

Jany 11th 1864

Last night it rained and we have slosh and mud to day. It is a safe rule to say that it will rain at least once a week here. I received yesterday Ella's of Nov 10 and Yours of the 17th & Ella's of the 16 Decr last. It seems that the County fund is to be grabbed by the rich and although it is exceedingly humiliating and mortifying to me for you to get any thing in that way yet I must say <u>do as you please</u>. You have as much and more right to get it than Mrs Oliver. I leave you entirely free to do as you please.

Bayou De Glaze La
Jan 14 1864

My Dear Wife

And still I am in superb health weighing 147 pounds. I am getting so fat that I am almost an incumbrance to myself. I had no idea that I should ever be so fat in my life and yet I am on the improve and there is no telling what I will yet weigh if I dont get sick. I have taken your advice in taking good care of myself though you can scarcely form an idea of the amount of mud and slop that we are now living in. It rains every few days and we are in a flat sticky mud. It is producing more or less sickness amongst the men and I am afraid that if we have to stay here long that a great deal of sickness will be the consequence. The roads are so heavy, the water so high etc that the mails are getting quite uncertain and I am afraid that you and I both will not get letters as often as is desirable though I shall continue to start one or two every week and then at every favour chance by hand. They will come to hand some time. Even now occasionly I get a letter over two months old from you and yet I devour it with as much delight as if it had the fresh perfume of your sacred heart just breathed into it. Ben Decherd reached here the 12 inst after being a month on the road. I suppose he was doing his best to keep away from the service. I had received several later letters from you and yet I was just as anxious to get the one he had as if I had not heard from home in more than a year. The mail day here is an era in our lives and we watch the comeing of Charley Nichols with as much anxiety as the Christian's watching the comeing of the Savior. We are still at work on our fortifications. Next Sunday will be our day again. Dont be surprised at our working on Sunday for it is the busiest day in military circles. We know no Sabbaths. We rest when we can and work when we are compelled to. To give you an idea of our whereabouts etc. take the map of Louisiana and find the town of Marksville in Avoylles Parish. Fort De Russy is on Red River in three miles of that place. There is where we have two Brigades stationed viz Genl Hawes' and Col Randle's. They have a large negro force at work there. You will then discover a little serpentine Bayou running (south of Marksville) east towards & entering into the Atchafalaya at Simmesport which is not far from the mouth of Red River. This is Bayou De Glaze on which we are now encamped. Another Bayou runs in to De Glaze about 3 miles from Simmesport from the South. This is Yellow Bayou. On the west bank of this Bayou and on both banks of De Glaze we are fortifying. Genl Scurry's Brigade is doing the work here. Our Camp is still 3 miles higher up De G than the works. We have laid off extensive works extending for near two miles in length. Such as forts, glacis, rifle pits etc etc. This is one of the routes by which Ft De Russy can be flanked. But there are 3 other routes by which it can be flanked either of which is as good or better than this and why this alone is defended is more than I can tell. The other routes that I refer to are 1st By the way of Berwicks Bay, New Iberia etc the way that Genl Banks approached Alexandra last spring, 2nd By the way of Morgan's ferry up Bayou Rouge by Cheneyville etc, and 3rd and best route is up Red River, up Black river, up Little River through Cataloula lake and by water to within 18 miles of Alexandra. If we had a force and works to guard all these routes I could see some practicability in the work that we are doing here. Otherwise it appears nonsensical. But we have no right to think. Others have been appointed to think for us and we like the automation must kick (or work) when the wire is pulled. This is Genl Taylor's Country. He has set his heart to defend it and none could do so as well as Texans. We will therefore have to stay here and defend La whilst Texas is overrun and in agony. This however is all right. Many a true son of Louisiana had to remain in Virginia & Tennessee when his own home & fireside was invaded and desecrated. With me I want to be where I can do the Confederacy the most good and the Yankees the most harm. If you should all be overrun which I pray God may not be the case although I shall grieve in spirit and agonize beyond conception yet I will remain at my post and with renewed oaths, energy etc endeavour to strike the accursed invader the harder licks possible.

Sunday Jany 17 1864

We are just from the fortifications to night. We have spent our devotions to day in working. The boys dont work well on Sunday. They dont have the vim that they would on another day. Yours & Ella's of the 26th ult came to hand this evening. We are not quite so green as you supposed for as soon as the river rose we recrossed the Atchafalaya & broke down our pontoon brid[g]e. The river is now falling and I expect that we will recross the Atchafalaya again. Your opinion of our position here and of the war is pretty good & correct so far as your information goes, but being so far removed from us and not being posted as to the minutia of course it cant be expected that you should be altogether correct. As to fortifying the City of Austin I believe that the only good to be accomplished in doing so will be to keep in subjection its own tory population. I dont believe that it will ever be of much benefit against the Yankees. The place to defend Austin and Texas is on the Coast never to let them penetrate to the interior. Just about as much as I expected of Charley. He is not as patriotic as I could wish for a kinsman of mine. I am afraid that you will have some trouble about your meat. Do the best you can and dont depend on such fellows as Kige. He never thinks or cares about such small matters as meat & bread if he can get a frolic. I am truly glad that you have enjoyed Christmas as well as you have. I know that the dancing part suited Ella and I am proud that she was gratified in this to her hearts content [*next page lost*].

Bayou De Glaze La Jany 18 1864

My Dear Daughter

Yours of the 26 ult came to hand yesterday. It affords me exquisite pleasure to learn that you have had so good a Christmas and enjoyed yourself so well. May your enjoyments never be less and may your next Christmas be enjoyed in company with your father whilst peace reigns over our land. But my Dear Daughter you must not let the glitter & bauble of the ball room, the dance and the party seduce your mind from your studies. You are now learning fast. You are the right age to learn with facility and nothing must now divert your attention from your books or divide your time with them. The boys must have no

place there for the present. If you dance & enjoy yourself with them
it must be [that] a ball room scene must vanish before the light of
books & science. It must be only a ball room acquaintance & nothing
more. Thats no place to form attachments. You can tell nothing about
them there. It is all glitter and glare fixed to order, made to sparkle and
dazzle for the moment. No girl of sense will be caught with such if she
reflects. Tis the moths and silly flies that dazzled by the light of the
Candle plunge into it and are burned to death. Dont play the moth
now. Dont be taken in by the glitter and glow of what you call beauty
unless it has something substantial to back it up. What is beauty unless
it have worth and purity and character to sustain it but an idle show of
doubtful meaning. The Poet Shakespear[e] says of it

> "Beauty is but a vain and doubtful good
> "A shining gloss that fadeth suddenly
> "A flower that dies when first it 'gins to bud
> "A brittle glass that's broken presently
> "A doubtful good, a gloss, a glass, a flower faded
> "Lost, broken, dead within an hour.[101]

When you form attachments and associations with men or women
let worth, honor, purity of character, goodness of name and heart,
character of family etc be your guide. Dont fix your affections and
heart on unworthy creatures. Never look down hill always aloft. "It is
crowded mightily below their is plenty of room above." You can breath
freer above. The air is close, hot & sultry below. Look aloft. Look
aloft. You are a nice, good, sweet girl, a blooming pretty rose. "Dont
waste your perfume on the desert air." Dont be dazzled by a little
beauty if it does deck the outward form of a _____ . You dont know
him or his people. Appearances are deceitful. He is no doubt a nice
man, pretty enough for any of his class, but our sort dont herd with his
sort. The horse cant wallow in the mud with the hog. His qualities are
too noble, his blood to high, his spirit too exalted, his career too
grand. Neither can my stock herd with the _____ stock. There is too
much high blood and mettle for that. Look aloft. Study your books,
endow your mind with wisdom, qualify your self for society. Learn
human nature to do which you must study yourself thoroughly, dive
into the labaryinths of the human heart, its secret recesses. It is
deceitful and full of guile. All these things you must learn to know the
good from the bad, the pure from the impure, the true from the false
before you think of the boys, before you think of falling in love with
any body. When you can do all these things then it will be time think
of love & love affairs. I say all these things to you in fatherly kindness.

I love you beyond compare. I'd do any thing (you know) in the world for you to make you honored & happy. You are the apple of my heart my sweet my loving daughter, my hope, my happiness and hence I write to you in all earnestness not chidingly but lovingly, hopefully, confidingly. I know that you would not do any thing intentionally to hurt me but you are young and perhaps unthoughted. You havn't as much experience as I or your Mother and you must advise with & trust to us. This as a good & dutiful daughter I know you will do. I know every body in the County and you or your mother can always find them out by writing to me. Dr. _____ is a tolerable clever old fellow of not much character, gets drunk frequently, is common stock and just such folks as I dont want any alliance offensive or defensive with. I have said enough lest I weary you.

I have written ma a long letter. You can read it. It is for both of you, but I thought I would write this also. I gave her all the news if there is any except that I learn that Genl Bragg is comeing West of the river to take command of the Trans Miss Dept. I dont believe that it will be a good change. He is too tyranical, too strict to suit our wild western men. Then he has lost his caste and would come without prestige. I hope it may prove untrue and that he will not come.[102] I send you another nice letter elegantly written in fine diction, beautiful periods, chaste language, pure sentiments. Try and take pains and come up to these letters by the time you get as old. I know that you have the capacity and trust that you will do so. With such ladies I am proud to be acquainted and reckoned as a friend. With such correspondence my feelings will be exalted, my thoughts enobled, my character purified. I send them to you & ma that you too may enjoy them as I have enjoyed them. I will try and do nothing that will make my cheek tingle with shame and that I would be unwilling for my wife & children to know. I haven't anything more worth writing. Health fine, spirits good, body fat, face round, whiskers long, provisions abundant & good and all that. Love, kisses etc to ma & the children and my sweet, good, nice daughter.

"May a thousand liveried angels lackey her"
"Driving afar each thing of sin or guilt."[103]

Yours truly
E. P. Petty

Bayou De Glaze La Jany 21 1864

My Dear Daughter

I sent a tremenduous long letter home a few days ago written to both your Ma and you. Since then nothing has happened here or elsewhere to my knowledge of much interest. I find out that the rumored statement that Genl Bragg was comeing west of the river is not true. It was Col [John L.] Logan of Louisiana Cavalry whose crossing gave rise to the report. I am glad that it is so. For a few days we have had clear and pretty weather. To day is spring like and if we had our Texas runner lizzards here I should look for them to be out. I am afraid it is only a weather breeder. The regiment are at work on the fortifications today. I remained at camp not choosing to go. Whilst I had nothing better to do to day (and how could I have anything better to do than to think and write about my sweet little daughter) I penned the following <u>acrostic</u> on your name and for you. It is not very good but is the best my muse could furnish on this occasion.

> Ella my own, my sweet little daughter
> Lovingly now in my vision I see thee
> Like a "thing of life" on times bubbling water
> All graceful and buoyant thou seemest to me.
>
> Pene my charming, my darling, my sweet one
> Even now in exstatic delight I embrace thee
> Nor will I e'er number this moment a fleet one
> E'n tho in a wink from my mind it difuse thee.
>
> Petty be the ills of life that beset thee
> Evanishing like meteors leaving no traces behind
> Tripping thro life may the good Lord e'er let thee
> Turning each evil which perchance you may find
> Your sours to sweets, Your storms to sunshine.

When I get to be a poet like Burns or Byron I will improve on the above and give you something better but altho it is mere dogeral verse and not perfect in feet & measure it has one merit. It is from the heart warm and fresh and I hope you will appreciate it for that if not for its beauty. I wish you could see me now. I am getting so fat. I weighed to day 148 pounds. I hardly know myself when I wash my face. It feels like I am washing somebody else's. My ribs are covered with a roll of fat so that you can hardly feel them and my back bone is completely hid and still I seem to be improving, fattening every day. I am afraid that I shall become an incumbrance to myself. I dont feel near as active as I did before. I am in superb health. The boys of my company are generally well. Occasionally some of them have chills. Col Jones is in fine health and fat. We have a game of cards occasionally. This must needs to be a short letter. My Love & kisses to Ma & the Children. Respects to friends.

Yours truly
E. P. Petty

P.S. I sentenced Ben Decherd to 30 days roots & forfeiture of 2 months pay for his absence without leave.

Bayou De Glaze La Jany 24 1864

My Dear Daughter

I received your's of the 27 ult and 1st inst also Ma's of the 26 ult and 1st inst with[in] a few days. Those received previously I have answered. I also received your composition and although you seemed to regard it as perfect yet you will observe by my pencilling upon it (for I herein return it) that I have dissected and torn it considerably to pieces. I will say that for a girl of your age it is a fine composition and with fewer mistakes and better sentiment than is usual. Yet there were several mistakes some in grammar, some in Orthography, and some in elegance & choice of expression. I have not attempted to touch or correct the sentiment. All my corrections are made with pencil. The 1st line was grammatical but I changed to make it more elegant. So you will see in some other places. There is nothing so beautiful as a smooth flowing, well rounded sentence. It is like putting the sugar, the spices, the tinctures, the eggs etc in the cake. Flour and water & sugar will make cake but it will be tough and unpalateable but add the other ingredients & you have light, spongy, nice, well seasoned cake so in writing a sentence may be grammatical and the words all well spelled but the language may not be choice and elegant. The same sentiment expressed in good, well selected phrases & choice words elegantly arranged pleases the fancy, charms the eye or ear and shows taste & style in the writer. You write very well and with a little more practice and careful attention to a few simple rules will write elegantly a thing much to be desired. Keep your dictionary by you and learn to spell every word correctly and give to it its proper meaning in the sentence. Attend to your capital letters beginning each sentence after a period and all proper names with capitals. Punctuate your letters. In this I am deficient. And attend well to the grammatical construction and arrangement of each sentence. Have plural verbs to plural nouns &

vice versa. Use a free, easy, liquid, flowing, elegant, tasty style. Don't cramp up and smother and destroy your sentiments in uncouth, inelegant language. Observe these rules carefully and you will soon make a fine writer. Take a little more pains in the formation of your letters. Improve your hand write. I have sent you two letters which I received from young ladies Miss Moore* & Miss Fitch. They will do for models. They are fine in sentiment, chaste & select in language and elegant in style. The rules of Orthography, Syntax and prosody are carefully observed. You can with a little patience and pains equal if not excell either of these. Study hard and read everything that is useful and ornamental and store your mind well with facts as well as language and fancy and you will have no trouble to excel in writing. I have thus criticised your composition and called your attention to certain rules for your improvement. If you have any more good compositions send them to me for like purpose. Dont be afraid. It will be for your good for it is the constant rubbing of the diamond that brings forth its brilliancy. Your mind is a rich and rare diamond and I wish by polishing it to devellop its beauties. I am glad to hear that you have had so pleasant a time during Christmas & New Year hollidays but you musn't let parties and boys take your attention from your studies.

You quoted a verse in your last letter something about whistle daughter whistle etc etc. I do not see the point or object of its quotation. A quotation when it is appropos or illustrates any thing or when it gives strenght and beauty to your sentiments is to be much admired but in this case I cannot see that anything of the sort was accomplished. You seemed to have thrust it in with[out] any particular object in view except just to have the verse in. This is not in good taste. This I say to call your attention to style of writing. I should think that if Oly Coulsber was able to dance and frolic that he could return to his command. I am afraid that he is throwing off some. He is a first rate young man and made a splendid soldier and I would be sorry for him to throw off. When you talk about nice young men he will do for he is a number one boy himself and has worthy, high toned, respectable parents & family etc. If you got to dance so much with him I dont think that you ought to envy Puss Wallace the Turner boy. Let her rejoice in it without envy my dear daughter and for John Perry you know that he nor his connections are worth noticing in elegant & high toned society. It was well enough to give them the benefit of a party and to treat them courteously but let the acquaintance <u>end</u> with the <u>ballroom</u>.

*Mollie E. Moore's letter follows this one.

Rheum Castleman is now a member of my company I having swapped Henry Fontaine for him. Henry is a fine soldier and a splendid young man and I hated to part with him but he wanted to get with his father. I have no news to write. We are still fortifying here without any present prospect of a fight. If there was a prospect of a fight I would'nt mind staying and working here but to expend labor for nothing is trying on my patience. It looks like "loves labor lost." There is very little preparations in this part of the country for farming. Everything is now scarce and I fear that necessity if not the Yankees will run us out. We are expecting and hoping to cross the Atchafalaya soon as it is falling. Give many Kisses & much love to Ma & the Children and many kind regards to friends.

Yours truly
E. P. Petty

Sylvan Dell
Jan 15th [1864]

[To E. P. Petty]

Christmas has come and gone and old Winter has wept his snows upon the grave of the departed year — a "merrie Christmas" would sound somewhat misty and ghostlike in the midst of January but it is not too late for a "happy New Year" — let mine descend like a blessing upon you. May the "happiness" which I wish you linger with you all through the shadow and sheen of the twelvemonth — through Life's long and weary pilgrimage! Happy New Year! Shall I recount to you the pleasures of the past holidays? How the days were one glow of sunshine (save that Shadow cast from the gloomy wings of War) and the long winter evenings too short to careless hearts? How musics

"Voluptuous swell charmed the senses into forgetfulness of care and taught the glowing feet to chase the flying hours"! It is surely useless to describe it all for it would be but a counterpart of yours — no scarcity of gentlemen nor any lack of glittering uniforms, lighted halls and warm hearts keeping time to the quick sound of elastic feet! You have seen — felt the picture! The climax of my enjoyments however was a musical soiree which I attended last Monday evening and which was presided over by Professor Sigmosky who is not only a fine musician but a composer of marked ability — We had some elegant music from amateur performers and some sweet wild "fantasias" improvised by the Professor — I love music — so constituted that my whole being sways before the least excitement. It could hardly be supposed that I could remain passive before the magic power of the "poetry of sound"! There are some strains that seem to bear my very soul aloft and scarcely pause before the gates of Heaven itself with their wild triumphant harmony — Others with their

"dying fall ————— like the sweet South

Breathing over a bank of violets —" lull my whole spirit to repose or send it wandering into the past with a feeling

"like the songs of Carryl pleasant though mournful to the soul"! We had a songstress with us too, from the orange groves of Louisiana whose voice had surely caught something of heaven amid those placid lakes and sunny skies for it had a melody about it such as we imagine the angels possess when they sweep the golden lutes in paradise! She sang the "Marseillaise" and the most stolid among us would, in the inspiration of the moment, have gladly died beneath the banner of his country. She sang "Lorena" and "La Deux Anges" and we felt it no shame to weep such is the power of "music, and her sister Song!" A few evenings ago, however I attended a regular country party which at least wore the charm of novelty for ere — I would like to conduct you there and carry you thro the enjoyments of the evening — but I fear it is out of my power — beggars description. Suffice it to say that it lasted from "dewy eve to easy morn" — the country belles and rustic beaux tripped the "light fantastic toe" after the scraping of a miserable "fiddle" with as much zest as they took forfeits in honest round kisses when they indulged in the classic game of "Old sister Phebe"! A country party did you ever attend one! If not I envy you the enjoyment in store for you. There is a dearth of war news in this vicinity now — I fear it is but that calm that precedes the storm and that ominous stillness fortelling the coming thunderbolt — nor can we tell where or how it will strike. Heaven send that our own lovely State may not feel the blow! Charleston, our sea goddess, yet braves the fire

of the foe and looks upon them with a stern passionless gaze which though not possessing the power of Medusa to turn them into stone possesses that equally as appalling — of laying them mangled and bloody at her feet! Glorious Charleston! The sacred hand of Liberty has surely been laid upon her! And will protect her to the end of her fiery trial! From our coast we hear but little — we only know that Tom Green and his gallant command are there and <u>we are content</u>! Late at night —

I have been sitting before my fire for some time with an <u>omnium gatherum </u>in the heart

"While pleasant things the wind did whisper As I sat dreaming in my chair" but my day-dreams have ended as they usually do with the downfall of my fiery castles and having laid aside with a sigh of relief Bulwer's [Edward Bulwer-Lytton] "Last Days of Pompeii" which I have just finished I summon you up from the "vasty deep" of memory — Unlike Glendower's spirits mine always come to my bidding and hold converse with me and angels and ministers of grace! What a cloud of "bright eyes, music, song, toasts, pretty faces, cakes, goodies & egg-nog" you bring with you! But stay — Like Prometheus indeed your "godlike crime" consists in "being kind" and since you scatter sunshine so profusely I forgive your malicious attempt to make me envy you your joyous Christmas! Have you ever read the "Last Days of Pompeii." I do not like it so much as I expected having heard it very highly commended — Its descriptions are good, sometimes rising to the sublime but I do not admire it — Of Bulwers novels "Rienzi" and the "Pilgrims of the Rhine" are my favorites though they differ widely as to style — But [Charles] Dickens is my favorite novelist — it has been complained that there is no <u>point</u> to his stories — I confess that I do not read them for the plot at all but for the humor and pathos — the knowledge of human heart which is discoverable in every line he writes. Bleak House, Dombey & Sons, David Copperfield and Nickolas Nickleby — I think are incomparable — do you like him! If not remember in saying so that I am prepared to shiver a lance in his defence!

I am of the opinion that whatever you may do with the fire as it falls, you understand the art of flying kites to catch it! Are you a Chinaman!

Having displayed the light of my countenance to him who styles himself mine humble servant I hereby command him to lay by his sword and do battle with his pen "for the space of an hour"!

Very truly yours
Mollie E. Moore

Jany 24th 1864

My Dear Wife

I have received two or three letters from you this (one by Bunton) thereby heaping up my sweets of pleasure mountain high. I sent you and Ella some this week that will offsett all you can write and that is'nt all. I keep a stream going homeward all the time by mail and private hand. If it does you as much good to receive a letter as it does me (and I believe that it does you more) I dont regret a single line that I write. I have to give from 5 to 10 dollars per quire for paper but what care I for expenses when the pleasure is so great and what care I for the time and trouble. The happiness of my own "gude wife" pays me all. I am glad to hear that you are in such good health and cheerful spirits. You have much cause for rejoicing I think. You have suffered comparatively little. Good health, plenty money, plenty victuals, plenty clothes etc and have lost no near relatives that I know — This war has fattened me. I weighed yesterday 149 pounds. Dont I thrive — You know how loose my jeans coat was for me. It was nearly large enough for an overcoat. Now I can hardly button it on me without a vest. My shirt sleeves & collar are painfully tight for me. You can hardly realize my condition. I wish you could see me now.

You spoke of getting some meat from Levi Moore. I am glad you have the meat as you needed it very much but I think he ought not to charge more than the market price as the debt which he owed is a gold and silver debt. I expect that he owes Jones & myself over one hundred dollars as Executor of Aldridges Estate so that you will have to pay him nothing. I will settle with him when I come home. Be sure to secure provisions enough for your family by some sort of hook or crook. Dont spare your confederate money but hold with a deathly gripe to any gold or silver which you may have. We work on fortifications tomorrow. No news. Love & kisses

Yours truly
E. P. Petty

Jany 26 — 1864

Quite well today. The smallpox is in our vicinity having been brought over the river. We have quarantined the house to keep it from spreading. No news. Henry Fontaine left me yesterday for Braggs Army.

Yours truly
E. P. Petty

My Dear Wife

   Your's of the 8th inst came to hand on the 27th inst. You have no
conception how much good it does me to learn therefrom that "you
are all well and doing well." I am always well satisfied when I see such
statements — I am quite well and doing quite well. Now aint you
satisfied too. If I write an incoherent letter dont be astonished. I have
been out dissipating again — hav'nt slept any in 24 hours. Danced all
night last night — Was at the finest party (on a small scale) that I ever
attended. The young ladies who promised to give me a birthday party
owing to high water & cold, rainy weather did not do so until last
night. They told me that it was for my birthday. We had about a dozen
of each sex, the elite & flower of the Trans At. Dept and you may
depend they were nice, pretty, sensible and superb. The finest supper I
have sit down to in a long time it looked like a wedding supper. We
danced until after three oclock and it was day light before I reached
Camp then I had to work all day on the fortificatons and now after
night I write this letter. Amongst the ladies was Mrs. Judge Merrick
wife of Chief Justice Merrick of this state and her two daughters — I
hav'nt see such ladies for brains or as the fatalists call it sublimate
animal matter.[104] As I was a lawyer I was soon on the most favourable
terms with them and afterwards enjoyed myself to the highest pitch.
Before breaking up Mrs M. and daughters said "that when I wrote
home that I must give my wife their love that they knew I had a good
wife for I most certainly deserved one etc." I replied that I had and
that I would write a letter full of love to her and would tell her that
Mrs M & daughters shared it with me etc. So you have the letter as
promised in the language as it occured. Was'nt I flattered and did'nt I
enjoy it. I have found out one thing that women love flattery and
another that men dont hate it. This is a green spot in my memory and
I shall the more love the Trans At. Dept and shall seek every effort to
visit it and as often as I can. The party was given at the house of Mr
Tessier 2 miles above Simmesport in the Atchafalaya Bayou. I wish
that you & Ella could have been with me. I know that you would have
enjoyed it. The boys are generally well. Some two or three having
chills whose names I have already given you. There is no news that I
can learn. All quiet on the other side of the river and on this also. I
have a chance of sending this letter by hand to Brenham. Will have to
be short as I am orfully sleepy about this time. Will write again in a
day or two. Keep a perfect stream of letters going to you — Hope that
you will be satisfied with the lenght of some of them. Love & kisses to

the children, for me exclusive of M^rs M's to you etc. Keep writing all
the time.

Yours truly
E. P. Petty

Bayou De Glaze La
Febry 3rd 1864

My Dear Wife

    Owing to an abscense of four days in attendance upon a court of
inquiry at Marksville I have not written any in that lenght of time.
Marksville is about 20 miles from this Camp. In going there I passed
thru the towns of Moroville, Mansura and Cocoville all little places
but verry pretty. Mansura, Cocoville and Marksville are near each
other and are in a beautiful prarie. The prarie is about 10 or 12 miles
long and some mile or so wide and from beginning to end is nearly like
a continued village on both sides of the road nearly all French and
Catholic. At Cocoville there is a Convent for the education of
females.[105] It is a verry fine school, thorough in education and perfect
in discipline. Of all places for the education of young ladies a Convent
is the best. Male society are excluded except on proper occasions. No
chances for mischief are allowed. Whilst a young lady is acquiring her
education [she] does not need the society of young men to detract and
distract her attention. After she has acquired her education & is ready
for society she can then be placed in the parlor a complete & perfect
lady. In a convent all those influences calculated to excite and
influence the passions are withdrawn and the mind and virtues of the
heart are developed and nurtured. It is no objection that they are
Catholic institutions and under the influence of the Nuns and Sisters
of Charity as no influence of a religious kind are exercised over the
pupils. They are perfectly free in this respect. I wish it were so that I
could send Ella a year or two to a convent to finish her educations. It
would be the best thing in the world for her. I was acquainted with
one young lady a teacher in the Convent. I had seen her once and
spent an evening in her company at her father's. I sent her my card
stating that I would call upon her at 6 Oclock in the evening. The
rules of the Convent prevent the reception of Company after 6. This I
did not know and the young lady knew that I did not. So she went to
the Mother Superior, informed her that an old friend would call upon
her at 6 oclock and that she must waive the rule and allow her to
receive him. The M. S. kindly did so and I was received and

entertained in style. I was then informed by the young lady how near I
had come of being repulsed, how she had interceded for me and
obtained a special dispensation. She then told me when to visit and
how I could find her. So you see that in my raid on the Convent I
came off first. With a scholar I could not have received this privilege
only with the teacher. I visited also Fort De Russy and the water
battery near it.[106] The fort is 3 miles above Marksville, is situated on a
high plateau which is a continuation of the same as the prarie only it is
covered with timber. It controls the river for about 1½ miles. It is a
strong work and there are some fine guns there but it is incomplete.
The water battery is immediately on the river bank some 600 yards
from the Fort incasemated. Will be verry strong when finished. There
will be some fine guns here. It will take a month to complete the Fort
and Battery. When completed no gun boat will be able to pass and
they can only be taken by a land attack. Two of our Brigades are there
to defend them. Lt Col Byrd is in Command of the Fort & Batery with
13 companies. Capt Mabry's company being one having been detailed
for that purpose. If we get ready before the waters get up the enemy
will find a snag in these parts if they attempt to go to Alexandra or
Shreveport. Our work goes slowly on. We hope to have it done some
of these days. For 15 or 20 days we have the most delightful weather
with very little rain. Spring is beginning to show itself and farmers are
making some little preparations for crops etc. I am in fine health. I
weighed the other day 151 pounds but now I dont weigh as much by
several pounds. I have had no cause to loose flesh that I know of tho I
must have done so. I was in hopes that I would continue to fatten
until I weighed 160 pounds then I would have been fully satisfied. The
boys are nearly all well. Col Jones is in fine health. So is Flemming

and Lum Owens. Nash has been promoted to Captain. His health is mighty bad. Capt Gutlin has sent up his resignation. So they go one by one. Only two of the original Captains here now, Capt Mabry & myself. Capt Miller is here but promoted as Major so I dont count him. Seth & myself are rivals to see who is the hardiest and can stand this service the best. He is Senior Captain and there is no chance for my promotion unless I can kill him off. God grant that he may live a thousand years, that his shadow may never grow less nor his face less brilliant. Oh he is a jolly good soul. God bless him and Major Miller is one of the best little big souled men you ever saw. I love him & Mabry next to Wash Jones. I could praise others but will not do so now.

Bayou DeGlaze Feby 7 1864

I have been expecting to send this letter by Charley Purcell who will I suppose get a furlough in the course of a day or so.

Since I wrote the foregoing part of it I made a raid in to the Trans At. Dept. and spent almost 6 hours wandering to and fro in labarynthine pleasures and mazes. I hav'nt enjoyed myself better on any trip or on any occasion than on this. I charged the Commissary Department verry heavily and laid in a good supply. I am still in the enjoyment of the finest health and am getting back to my best weight having weighed today nearly 149 pounds. I send a song for Ella which is exquisite. The words are fine and the air delightful. I want her to get the music and learn it. My friends Mrs Ferguson & M^{rs} De Valle of Bayou Letsworth sing & play it to perfection. They have made it one of my favorites.

3 Oclock PM Sunday 7 Feb

Yours & Ella's of the 17 & 18 & of the 22nd ultimo have just come to hand. I was more than glad to receive these as I hav'nt had a letter from you in over a week. I expect that I receive all the letters that you write but some times I forget to mention them in mine [illegible]. Now I know you was'nt mad and you certainly did not have your feelings even a little hurt any did you. I never thought of firing back as you call it. I only committed what we call repartee. I thought I had a right to perpetrate a joke and did so. Never was in a better humor in my life than when I wrote nor further from wanting ever to hurt or abraid [abrade] your feelings. I was in an excellent humor and was humorous in my letter and wanted you so to consider it.

Molly Bawn

1. Oh Molly Bawn why leave me pining
   All lonely waiting here for you
   While the stars above are brightly shining
   Because they've nothing else to do.
   The flowers late were open keeping
   To try a rival blush with you
   But their mother nature set them sleeping
   With their rosy faces washed with dew.
   Oh Molly Bawn why leave me pining
   All lonely waiting here for you
   While the stars above are brightly shining
   Because they've nothing else to do.
   Molly Bawn Molly Bawn

2. Now the pretty flowers were made to bloom dear
   And the pretty stars were made to shine
   And the pretty girls were made for the boys dear
   And may be you were made for mine.
   The wicked watch dog here is snarling
   He takes me for a thief you see
   For he knows I'd steal you Molly darling
   And then transported I should be.
   Oh Molly Bawn why leave me pining
   All lonely waiting dear for you
   While the stars above are brightly shining
   Because they've nothing else to do.
   Molly Bawn Molly Bawn

Bayou De Glaze La
Febry 8 1864

My Dear Daughter

Yours of the 18 & 22 ultimo have been received. I was glad to hear that you enjoyed your Christmas hollidays so well but sorry to hear that it had made you sick. Was glad to hear that you had again resumed your studies with some prospect of success but sorry to hear that you had let your festivities come between you and your studies. Hope that now nothing will interfere to mar or molest them again but that you will go on steadily step by step until you reach the achme of fame and science. I am glad that those gentlemen whom you mention

have been enabled to get home on furlough. I am not envious of the pleasure of others but am all ways pleased to hear of their success & luck. Envy and jealousy are bad passions and I am proud to say have no resting place in my heart.

You say that you think Ma & myself are getting quite loveing etc. Well now aint that all right. I think I ought to love her. She is my own true wife: she is the mother of my children, my sweet little children and she is doing all she can to take care of, raise and educate them. Who could help loving her. I cant and I do not want. It does me good to express it to her and I have no doubt does her good to have it expressed. That is what we live for to love and cherish each other. I wish I could have a chance to kiss her instead of her Ambrotype. I must beg leave to differ with my daughter about Miss Mollie E. Moore. While I do not think her hand writing the best I have seen I think her composition is inimitable. Her grammar is good and her sentiment is fine. I never studied Quakenboss [Quakenbos][107] but I know something of grammar and diction. I am glad however to see you have an independent notion of your own with a spirit of criticism. It will do you good if you properly exercise it.

I am mighty sorry that you will be compelled to quit music or at least quit taking lessons. If Mr Yates thinks fit to depreciate the currency I have the right to refuse to send to him. You must not however give it up. Get permission to practice on somebody's piano occasionly thereby keeping up your music. You can do this by sometimes visiting where there is a piano.

I have no idea that I shall see Mr McNeil and if I did would have no chance to send any sugar and molasses as I expect he will have his own load. Sugar and molasses have now considerably advanced in price though it is cheap here to what it is at Bastrop. We are having fine weather here now — are making active preparations for the opening of the Spring Campaign. We expect fighting here and will try and be ready for it. You need not expect us in Texas at all unless they invade it with a large force. I sent a long letter to Ma this morning by Lt Denson[108] who will mail it at Belton. Charly Purcell will carry this and will perhaps call at your house is so he can answer all your questions about me satisfactorily. I have posted him fully and given him power and authority to answer.

I am in fine health as the boys say "as fine as a woman." Lt Cunningham is still my 1st Lieut but is now detached at Brigade Head quarters as assistant Commissary of Subsistence that is he feeds the officers while the Chief Commissary feeds the men. I have no war news. Love & kisses to all and particularly to Ma and dont you be jealous my little minx. I love you too dearly.

Yours truly
E. P. Petty

Bayou De Glaze La Febry 15 1864

My Dear Wife
The mail has come and with it no letter for me from my wife or children but with one from C.C Howerton from Seguin dated 28 Jany 1864. I also the night before got a letter from Wm. G. King at Bonham Tex. dated Febry 7 1864. So I have some letters to read but they do not suffice. If I dont get one from home each week I feel like I have lost something. I will now have to wait a week unless some lucky chance by hand or by Brigade Courier brings me in one. Yesterday (being Sunday) we worked on the fortifications and I did the hardest days work that I have done in 12 months. I feel the effects of it in my

right shoulder. I fear that it is weaker by reason of my wound though I
have never felt it until I set to work to spading. It would seem to be
perfectly sound & well and yet it hurt me to spade hard. I am a first
rate irish man. I can throw dirt 10 feet high with my spade. I am as
sound as a dollar weighed yesterday 148 pounds in my shirt sleeves. I
am like the ballance of you at home however. I've got that infamous
itch. McLester brought it from Bastrop & gave it to me. I have done
nothing for it yet but scratch. I have verry little news to write. The
Atchafalaya and Mississippi rivers are getting up quite high. No gun
boats have yet entered the A. though there is plenty of water for them
to do so. Beyond the A. they have landed and caught some of our
pickets and one of our Captains (Capt Allen of Waterhouse's Regt)[109]
and several officers & others crossing from beyond the Miss. riv. I
learned yesterday that the waters were nearly on a stand — if so the g.
boats will not visit us here this time and soon we will be able to go
back beyond the A. and annoy them again. They also captured some
cotton (30 bales) for us on Old river beyond the A. The government
is winking at a considerable cotton trade here.[110] A lot of Jews are
running the blockade and bringing out goods and some medicines for
the army. I look upon it as an infamous trade contrary to law and
demoralizing in its consequences and if I were in command a little
while I'd rid the country of both the trade and the Jews that carry it
on. They take the oath of allegiance (I suppose) to both governments
so that they can pass in & out and smuggle and steal. They care
nothing for obligations or any thing else but the almighty dollar. They
have neither country, character or honor. These are the fellows that
get all the contracts and feather their nests with the proffits. I fear that
there is something rotten in Denmark and that government & other
officials are quite deeply interested (privately) in the trade. I am glad
the Yanks steal it from them when they can and often it is delivered to
them. I am glad that we burn it sometimes. Last week we burned 200
bales above Morganza on the other side of the Miss river. Genl Scurry
sent a party across to burn it. So you see we trade and steal and burn
all in good harmony. Fine times these. If the country is'nt cursed it will
not be for the want of rascals to bring down the ire of God almighty
upon it. The health of the boys is about as last reported by me.

Febry 16th 1864

We had quite a row in Camp last night. Some of the men thought
to have some fun burying some beef that was too poor to eat and so set
out with the beef with horns, bells, pans and etc all beating & ringing

& created quite a general excitement. Col Jones got mad and ordered all under arrest. Some 50 were arrested when nearly every body got mad and something serious was apprehended. When Col Jones found out that it was no disrespect intended for him but was only for a little fun he had the men released but there is much murmuring & discontent in the camp. I am quite well. No news.

Yours truly
E. P. Petty

P.S. Please send Sally or your Ma this letter with hers.

E.P.P.

Bayou De Glaize La
Febry 16 1864

Dear Brother Thomas[111]

I had not heard a word from you (until I saw Mr Shemwell this evening) since secession. I have been more than anxious to hear from you and have started two letters inside of the federal lines to your Mother and Sister Sally. The third one to Sally I prepared and was disappointed in getting it off so I now conclude to trust it to Mr. Shemwell to be handed to you or to be sent by some other hand to her. I hope that they will get some of them and that I will be enabled to get a letter from some of you. I hardly know how to write you a letter. The part that I have taken in the present struggle in brief may no[t] be uninteresting to you — Well then I was a Breckenridge & Lane Sub Elector for the 2nd Judicial District of Texas. Then upon the election of Lincoln I took the stump for Secession — spoke, electioneered, legged wire, worked and voted for Secession. Attended the Texas Convention and lobbied for it and when Texas over the opposition of Gov Houston and his satelites went out of the Union on the 2 March 1861 (just 2 days before Lincoln was inaugurated) I rejoiced and shouted. I was sworn into the Confederate Service 1st Novr 1861 and have been in ever since except 13 days. Have tramped all over Texas, Arkansas & Louisiana, Have been in several battles, shellings, bombardments etc. Was severely wounded in the Battle of Milliken Bend in the Shoulder. I am a soldier for the war. Never expect to cease hostilities until our country is free and if I outlive the Confederacy will not remain in the Union. Will beg my bread and drag my family out of the country in poverty and rags. Have Hamilcar-like sworn my children to eternal hostility to the Yankee race etc

etc.[112] I am in the finest health. Weigh about 150 pounds which is 25 pounds more than my usual weight. My face is not near so angular as when you knew me. I have fattened up so that Mr Shemwell hardly knew me. We have been here on the Mississippi river for about 3 months annoying its free navigation by firing into transports, gun boats etc and have done them some considerable damage and a deal of trouble. The waters having got up we had to fall back for the present but will as soon as we can give it to them again. We have a fine army here in good health, good discipline, well fed, well clad, well armed, well munitioned and confident and woe to the unlucky feds who provoke us to strike them. I am Captain of Co F, 17 Tex. Vol Infty, Scurry's Brigade, Walker's Division, Trans Miss Dept. So you may know how to address me. I enclose you the letter to Sally. Do not address me as I have ordered her to do as that plan will now fail me but as I have shown you above. I also send a letter from home. I have had later dates but have burned them up. My family were well and doing well. My children were learning quite fast. Luckily I had plenty to live on when the war opened and thank God and my own carefulness I have plenty yet. My father is dead. Died 23 August 1863 just 12 days after I left home for my command after being on furlough. Dewit and my two brothers in law are in the service in Texas. One brother in law is not in the service is hiding behind a little office. I want you to write to me specifically about all your family and our relations and my relations as far as you know — Send my letters to Sally and let them write to me through you. You can have a chance to send it to & from me. My love to all.

Yours truly
E. P. Petty

My Dear Wife

Your's of the 31 ult & 1ˢᵗ inst came to hand on yesterday. I have a
chance in the morning of sending you a letter by hand. I started you a
letter two or three days ago by mail. You speak of a Mr Allen who is at
Bastrop pressing horses etc and state what he said about my fattening
up etc. I cant conceive who he is from your description. If I ever knew
him I cant now fix him up. One thing however is sure that is he over
did the truth considerably. I have fattened up considerably but hav'nt
grown any taller that I know of and my feet hav'nt grown any as I still
wear with ease no 7. My shirt collars and sleeves however have
become tight and my pants & drawers had to be loosened. I weigh
now about 150 pounds which you know is about 25 pounds more than
my ordinary home weight. My face is some less angular than formerly
and I can shave on my cheeks without so much danger of cutting my
face. When I hear small men spoken of I never think that I am at all
included. Sure enough according to your prediction I wrote home for
some shirts not thinking of the amount of trouble and expense it
would be for you to get and send them. As it is you [need] not send me
any. I will try and get some here as we have a trade going on with the
federals. So I countermand the order. I have plenty of money on hand.
Have drawn two months more wages to include December and
January. I would send you some more money home but wish to keep
enough on hand to meet expenses and to try and come home during
the ensueing summer. Although it is exceedingly humilating to my
pride for you to have to call on the County for any thing yet I must say
that I am not sorry that you did so. I will have my part of the taxes to
pay and I learn that others not near so necessitous as you have drawn
on the County for articles and there can be no good sense in not doing
so. If the money was disbursed as it was intended to those alone who
were necessitous then I should have regretted very much your having
done so. As it is I am content. It stands you in hand to save all the
money you can for there is no telling the moment when your supply
from this direction may be cut off — The waters are already in motion.
The thundering of artilery and the clash of arms are resounding.
Terrible fighting is in store for the Confederacy. Figuratively speaking
blood enough will be shed the ensueing Campaign to make an
impassable river between both sections about whose free navigation no
questions will arise — In these pastimes somebody will get hurt and

may be that somebody may be me. My opinion is that there will be awful fighting east of the Miss river and but a small amount on this side. I hope that I may not be wrong. I am sorry that Orgain and Yates have adopted the course they have. It is an imposition and a trick to keep from taking our currency. I reckon that Ella knows enough of music to quit taking lessons but she must practice every oppertunity she can get. The other education of the children must not be neglected under any circumstances so they must be sent whether ever paid for or not — Therefore stop Ella's music lessons and send to Orgain is my advice. Of this however you must to some extent judge and I leave it to you. My daughter if possible must be educated and accomplished. At the same time poverty is a hard task master. As to sending Don to school be the judge but if he does'nt go have him learned some at home. Encourage him to learn by some device, some hope of reward. Jo Webber has deceived me I must confess. Although I knew him to be an arrant coward yet I thought he had some honor. I will put him through when I get him here. I have been to the breast works to day and done a verry hard day's work. I am a used up man to night tired to nervousness. Cant hardly write. Cant hardly think but cant forego the pleasure of sending you a letter by the chance offered however desultory it may be. To know that I am well and doing well will be some pleasure to you I know and if I could only say that much every week it should be said amidst all my toils, labors, pains and turmoils, frolics, gaieties, fetes, feasts etc my wife and my children are not forgotten and are never out of my mind. Nothing but sleep removes them and that not always. I look around me and grasp at every thing for pleasure and when in its full enjoyment I think of you all and wish that you could enjoy it with me. The boys are generally well. My love and kisses to the home circle and respects to outside friends.

Yours truly
E. P. Petty

P.S. Here's a letter from a Louisiana Lady friend who is a teacher at the Convent at Cocoville near Marksville. What do you think of that as a specimen. She is a magnificently nice & sensible young lady.

E.P.P.

Convent of the Presentation Feb 15th 1864

Captain E. P. Petty
    I certainly could not reject friendship offered in so sincere a manner

as you have done, and I shall consider myself happy if I succeed in relieving in a measure the tedium of your camp life. You say you hope I will not consider it improper to correspond with a male friend! No, I do not, though it is true that the rules of etiquette might condemn the promptness with which our acquaintance has ripened into friendship; yet I am not a slave to etiquette and set her laws at defiance when reason and good sense tell me there is no impropriety in doing so.

You wrote during the calm and quiet of night: tis the time I love best — when sleep has fallen over earth, and the stars watch with ever wakeful eyes upon the universe. What scenes do they witness? Is it always the serene repose of innocence and peace? Alas! no — I used formerly to think so, but I have been disabused of my sweet Dream — Oh! if we only knew the sufferings endured during the silent hours of night! Now, above all, I picture to myself our poor soldiers, the wounded — the sick — pining, dying, far from home and loved ones. The noble youth, who with bouyant step, and high wrought purpose, girt himself with steel, for the defense of his country — Behold him! The light fading from his once flashing eye, his majestic form, wasted with fell disease, stretched on that couch of pain! Mothers! Sisters! see the darling of your hearts, the pride of your life! These are woman's thoughts, woman's sufferings . . . aye! and bear them she will, with unflinching courage! Yes, brave defenders, of our once happy land, and wherever you go, you are followed by her ardent prayers, and every one would be willing to sacrifice her heart's best blood for the triumph of our cause.

Ah, my friend, it seems that I have forgotten myself a little, I should remember that I am writing to a soldier, who perhaps does not know how to sympathize with me; therefore excuse me, and let us to another subject.

I am very willing to receive such incense, as you offer, though remember, if I must be a deity, I am one who likes neither flattery nor insincerity.

You spoke of our difference in religion. It is to be regretted — yet I am glad you are not prejudiced, for that, I consider the mark of a narrow mind — of a mind misinformed! The Catholic religion has been very much misrepresented by Protestant writers. I have read some myself, which, were I not perfectly convinced, and firmly confident, that my religion was the true one, might have shaken my faith. It is true, unfortunately, that some abuses do exist in the Catholic Church but that does not make her doctrine false nor prove that she inculcates wrong principles. As to the mummeries of which you speak, there is not a single one of them without its meaning. Every ceremony is connected with some event of our Savior's Passion, which render it a religion of heart felt Devotion to those who understand it. I could tell you many things, but I do not like to speak on a subject which I fear may be displeasing to you.

You complement too highly on my qualities as a teacher. Three years ago when I left school I little thought, I would ever have the charge of directing young minds in the paths of knowledge. I feel much more like a child, than like a person having the care of children, and though all my pupils seem very much attached to me, I am tired of teaching; but I am not on this account less exact in the fulfilment of my duties, than I was when all was novelty. So you see I have no merit for what I do.

I am much obliged to you for delivering the letters. I send others to you, which if you can send or take to their destination, will be rendering me another favor. You had better be careful, you have got a troublesome little friend in me. I am delighted to know that you had a pleasant time on the Atchafalaya. I think every one should strive to make the position of our soldiers as agreeable as possible, remembering the great debt of gratitude toward them. I must now bid you good night as my paper is finished & I have no envelopes. When you write again tell me if there is any news with regard to the movements of the enemy.

Your friend
Amelia Tessier

Bayou De Glaize La
Febry 22 1864

My Dear Daughter

I have concluded to send you a line by the mail in the morning — I wrote to Ma a day or so ago by hand which I hope she will have no trouble in getting. I am in finer health and condition than you ever saw me. I wish you could see your poor old dad now. You would think that he was not so poor as he had been but I have spoken enough about my self.

I have no news of interest neither local or general.[113] The feds I hear are bombarding Mobile.[114] I expect that the next grand move will be on Mobile. Genl Sherman seems now to be moving in that direction from Vicksburg via Jackson Miss. to act in concert with Farragut's fleet which is now before it.[115] I dont think that we will have much fighting in the Trans Miss Dept this campaign but on the other side the welkin will ring and the earth tremble beneath the mighty tread of armies and roaring of contesting cannons. I apprehend very little danger from the Yankees in Texas. The failure of crops and consequent starvation of its inhabitants is my greatest dread — I will have to leave you all in the hands of the good Lord for protection and safety giving to him such help as I can in a feeble way hoping and trusting that by our joint efforts we may all survive the war and be again happily united in a proud glorious Confederacy. I am again at my old business — I am defending Lt. Col Redwood Tex Infty[116] before a Court of Inquiry. Capt Marshall[117] preferred a series of charges against him for things which occured while Col R was Commander of our advanced post at Simmesport on the Atchafalaya. He called upon me to conduct his defense which I consented to do. I expect that I will be engaged in the case about a week. This looks like my old business only I dont intend to charge any fee.

I haven't been to any frolics or amongst the women for two or three weeks now. I am spending my time in reading poetry & novels. I am devouring with rapacity any amount of light literature. I sent you my anatomy etc and have nothing of that sort now to read. Did you receive it and Did you receive my birthday present for you a nice little volume of poems by Baxter. I sent it by Charly H Keton. I am sorry that difficulties are environing your course of studies and music — I wish you to be educated and accomplished. You are my only daughter and I wish you to be accomplished in learning and manners.

> "What the stars are to the night my love"
> "What its pearls are to the sea"
> "What the dew is to the day my love"
> "Thy beauty is to me."

But beauty unaccompanied with sense and culture is worse than nothing. I would willingly therefore make any & every sacrifice for you were it not for the equal claims of others upon me. Your little brothers are just as near and dear to me and they have yet received none or scarcely any education and so I will have to look after them also. In this you can aid me materially. You can assist in teaching them at home and while you press forward in your own studies you can teach their young ideas how to shoot. We are having splendid weather now. The waters are again receeding and no gun boats yet in the Atchafalaya. I hope they will not rise again this year and that no invasion may occur here. I am not so bad off for a fight as I was though I am ready and willing to do so if nothing else will do the Yankees. Love, kisses, good wishes & hopes for the family circle and for you my sweet loving daughter.

"Ah! Never may a heavier shadow rest —"
"Than thine own ringletts on that brow so Fair"

is the sincere prayer of

Yours truly
E. P. Petty

Bayou De Glaize La
Febry 29th 1864

My Dear Wife

Your's of the 6th & of the 9th & 10th & Ella of the 6th & 13th inst have all been received. Of course you thanked Mrs Duvall for the shirts. Now for me tell her that I will with pleasure receive them and consider my self under many obligations to her. My old shirts which are wearing out here I will send home if I can. They will do finely to make others for the children. You say that you will send me two shirts to work in on the fortifications and one to visit the ladies in. Why did'nt you not the reverse the number and send me one for fortifications and two for ladies as I had rather visit the ladies twice than to work on the fortifications once. I am sorry that Ella showed Miss Fitch's letter. I dont want to give any publicity to our correspondence. She might hear of it and be offended. She lives at Chappell Hill. Carmer lives there. The Allens are intimate with Carmer and by that sort of means it might reach her and what would she think of me. The same of Miss Moore's letters. She is a connection of the Blacks and a knowledge that I was making her letters public might reach her. I sent them to you and Ella that you might enjoy them as I have and that Ella might improve thereby. Dont even let Mrs Jones know any thing about them. Upon reflection you will see that I am right. By the way that was a magnificent letter of Miss Fitch. Its style was elegant, its composition fine and chaste and its grammar and orthography are perfect. I like Miss Moore style and composition verry much and I have sent you another from Miss Amelia Tessier which is inimetable. She is in the Convent at Cocoville and is a splendid young lady. Now you seem to be dispairing about the war and the Seasons. Christians ought not to repine at the providences of God. He will do all things in his own right time and his own peculiar way. Dont be alarmed but cheer up. All things will work for the best in the end. Be more hopeful and dont yield to despondency. He who feeds the ravens and sees even the fall of the little sparrows will protect the

children of his own Creation. If I could go the Christian figure to the full lenght that you do I would be the most hopeful and cheerful creature alive. The Angels in heaven would envy me. I am sorry to hear that the small pox is so near you. It is in about 1½ mile of this Brigade. There are now two cases and one died yesterday and one has recovered making four cases in total that has been here. It is not amongst the soldiers and we have it quarantined and hope to prevent its spreading. If all is quiet in these quarters I intend to try and come home. Dont cook for me however as it is all uncertainty with a soldier. I made another raid into the Trans Atchafalaya Department yesterday (Sunday) and like the honey bee returned laden with pleasure. It is a glorious Country over there and gloriously did I enjoy it. The river is now falling fast and is getting quite low. I made also a raid on Saturday on to Choupique Bayou into the French Settlement over there. It is a fine place and finely did I enjoy it. The French ladies are so charming and pretty and play Cards well. I am in fine health. To day is our review and muster and inspection and I am quite busy. No news of moment. The boys are all well. Kiss and love to the children.

Yours truly
E. P. Petty

Night Febry 29 1864

My Dear Son Don
    How is my little son to night. I know he must be well. He has'nt forgotten his Pa has he? Oh no I know he has'nt. He is a good boy yet aint he! Yes I know he is. I am told that you did'nt want to go to

school. Why did'nt you! You aint too lazy I know but you think you are too young. Well you could learn some any how. Make Ella and Frank learn you at home and Ma will also learn you. You must make a smart boy of yourself and then a smart man. Dont be too mischevous. Dont rock the chickens nor pull the old cats ears too much. Now wont you write to me again. I will see. My best love to you.

Yours etc
E. P. Petty

Febry 29 1864

My Dear Son Van

Dont you know that your pa loves you and will write you a little letter. Here it is you must take care of it and learn to read it and learn to write and write me one. Tell ma to kiss you for me and hug you and all that. Tell her to give you a pretty and some Cake and Candy for your pa. Oh how I love you.

Yours truly
E. P. Petty

Bayou De Glaize La Febry 29 1864

My Dear Daughter

Your's of the 13th inst has been received. I am right glad to know that you are studying so hard but I hope that you will not be so completely absorbed as to cease writing to me. You must write to me if you have to burn the midnight lamp to do so. You asked me to find out who was writing to Miss Laura Hardeman. Well I knew without having to find out. I showed the young gentleman your letter and asked him if I should tell you and he begged me not to do. I will tell you and Ma and I would not have you to hint that you know to any body and for nothing would I have you hint it to Laura for then she would know that it came from me. Then inter nos (between us). Sub rosa (under the rose) it is William H. Black. Now as you love and respect me dont hint this to any body. I am willing to trust you with any & every thing I know. Ma says that you showed Miss Fitch's letter to Mrs. Orgain. I am sorry that you did so. I did not want it known out of the family. It is betraying confidence to get a letter from a lady and then expose it. Dont never do so again. What if she should find it out? What would she think of me? That I was an unprincipalled scamp. The ladies had confidence enough in me to write to me and I wouldn't for the world expose them to public censure.

We have just been stirred up for the first time in a long while. Whilst I was writing I was ordered to hold my Co in readiness to move at a moments notice — all is agog again. Wherefore and for what I have just learned that five gun boats have passed up Red River in the direction of Ft. De Russy and it may be that we will be called to defend that point. I will find out after awhile I suppose. When I do I will write to you all about it and will as I have ever done keep you posted. You must put up with a small letter now for to day we have marched 8 miles, had a Brigade review and inspection and marched and I am quite tired to night.

Kisses & love to all.

Yours truly
E. P. Petty

March 1st — 1864

There is a cold norther and rain this morning. We did not have to move last night. Maybe will to day — hope not.

EPP

CHAPTER THREE

Notes

[1] E. Kirby Smith to Theophilus H. Holmes, April 14, 1863, *Official Records Armies*, series I, XV, p. 1041; Smith to Holmes, April 15, 1863, *ibid.*, pp. 1042–43; Smith to Holmes, April 19, 1863, *ibid.*, XXII, pt. 1, p. 828.

[2] Blessington, *Walker's Texas Division*, p. 78.

[3] *Ibid.*, p. 79.

[4] "In this county [Ashley] and the one above the people have showed a great deal of sympathy and interest for us, the only place in Arkansas they have," Frank Tannehill wrote his wife from the camp near Hamburg. "Crowds of women (and there are more women in this part of the state than any place I ever saw) collect on the sides of the streets and roads and wave their handkerchiefs and throw bouquets of flowers into the ranks. Some old ladies prayed aloud for us as we passed through Monticello, while some middle-aged ones wept as if some near and dear relative had died; I suppose they were women who had lost their all in the army. The men are all gone to the army from this part of the country nearby; it is a very rare thing to see a man down here able and of an age to be in the army." Holder, *Tennessee to Texas*, p. 123. Blessington also noted that "As we passed through Monticello, the ladies were on the sidewalk, waving their handkerchiefs as a token of admiration for the Texas boys." Blessington, *Walker's Texas Division*, p. 79.

[5] Richard ("Dick") Taylor, the son of President Zachary Taylor and brother of Jefferson Davis's first wife, was born on the family estate near Louisville, Kentucky, January 27, 1826. Much of his early life was spent in frontier posts where his father was stationed. He studied in Europe and at Harvard and graduated from Yale in 1845. He established himself as a sugar planter in Louisiana in 1850 and served from 1856 to 1861 in the state senate. At first a Whig, he joined the Democratic Party and voted for secession at the Louisiana convention. Appointed colonel of the Ninth Louisiana Infantry at the beginning of the war, he arrived too late for First Manassas. He was promoted to brigadier general on October 21, 1861, and major general on July 28, 1862. He served with distinction under Stonewall Jackson in the Valley Campaign of 1862 and in the Seven Days Battle, and was assigned that summer to command the District of West Louisiana. Warner, *Generals in Gray*, pp. 299–300. See also, Jackson Beauregard Davis, "The Life of Richard Taylor," *Louisiana Historical Quarterly*, 24 (January 1941), pp. 49–126.

[6] Taylor had about 4,000 troops between the Teche and the Atchafalaya, his flanks protected right and left by two captured Federal vessels, the gunboat *Diane* and the armed ram *Queen of the West*. Banks had four Gulf Squadron gunboats with which he planned to neutralize these two ships, and he intended to capture Taylor's army by sending one division from his 15,000-man command across Grand Lake to Irish Bend, an eastward loop of the Teche near Franklin, to attack the Confederate

rear while he engaged them in front at Bisland, below Franklin, with his other two divisions. On April 11 Banks moved William H. Emory's and Godfrey Weitzel's men from Brashear City across the Atchafalaya to Berwick, and while they were advancing up the left bank of the Teche the next day, skirmishing as they went, Cuvier C. Grover put his 5,000 troops aboard transports, escorted by the four gunboats, and crossed the lake. Landing at Hutchin's, he advanced to the Teche, pushing the Confederates back and through Franklin. Taylor, who was fighting Emory and Weitzel at Bisland, got wind of what was up and reacted quickly. Leaving a handful of mounted men under Colonel Thomas Green of Texas to hinder pursuit, he moved back with the rest to cut his way through Grover's force and to move to safety at New Iberia. In a heavy fight on April 14 the battle of Irish Bend or Nerson's Woods, Grover was held in check while Taylor slowly slipped away up the Teche, foiling the carefully laid plan for his destruction. But as Taylor retreated his army grew smaller and smaller from straggling and desertions. Continuing with his three divisions up the Teche, Banks marched into Opelousas on April 20 and Alexandria on May 6. Admiral Porter's fleet had preceded him into Alexandria by a few hours. Taylor kept up his retreat toward Natchitoches. His exhausted, dispirited men continued to desert until he had hardly a thousand infantry. Richard Taylor, *Destruction and Reconstruction: Personal Experiences of the Late War* (New York: Appleton and Company, 1879), pp. 127–37 (hereafter cited as Taylor, *Destruction and Reconstruction*); John D. Winters, *The Civil War in Louisiana* (Baton Rouge: Louisiana State University Press, 1963), pp. 221–35 (hereafter cited as Winters, *Civil War in Louisiana*); Morris Raphael, *The Battle in the Bayou Country* (Detroit: Harlo Press, 1975), pp. 86–157.

[7] Port Hudson, Louisiana, was a Confederate strong point guarding the Mississippi approximately 25 miles north of Baton Rouge. The first action here took place on March 14, 1863, when Admiral David G. Farragut bombarded the place during his passage up the river to Vicksburg. The U.S.S. *Mississippi* was lost in this action. Boatner, *Civil War Dictionary*, p. 663.

[8] "Theatricals not only afforded great amusement in the preparation and showing, but also provided topics of conversation and subject matter of letters for days to come. After attending 'a kind of Negro Show called the Lone Star Minstrels' in the Pine Bluff Court house by Flournoy's Texans, a member of that regiment wrote to his sister: 'Bully for Flournoy's Regiment we are some punkins, Youll Bet.'" Wiley, *Life of Johnny Reb*, p. 166.

[9] After crossing into Louisiana the division marched in a southwesterly direction, arriving at the mouth of Bayou Bartholomew, where it emptied into the Ouachita River, on May 5. Opposite the mouth of the bayou was Ouachita (or Washita) City, consisting of a store and warehouse on a high bluff. Here about a dozen transports stood ready to carry the men 36 miles downriver to Trenton, nearly opposite Monroe. After disembarking at Trenton the division marched two miles and encamped in the rear of the town. Here it remained until the morning of May 9. Blessington, *Walker's Texas Division*, pp. 79–80.

[10] At Pine Bluff Brigadier General James M. Hawes had succeeded Colonel Overton Young as commander of the First Brigade. Hawes had formerly commanded a brigade of cavalry under Hindman and had taken part in many cavalry raids throughout Arkansas. Young resumed command of his regiment, the Eighth Texas Infantry. Warner, *Generals in Gray*, pp. 128–29; Blessington, *Walker's Texas Division*, pp. 77–78.

[11] Vicksburg sat on a high bluff overlooking a sharp bend in the Mississippi. It

proved unapproachable from either west or north. On March 29 Grant ordered Mc-Clernand to march south from Milliken's Bend on the west side of the Mississippi to New Carthage, below Vicksburg. On April 16 Acting Rear Admiral David Dixon Porter's fleet of 12 vessels ran downriver past the Vicksburg batteries to aid Grant's crossing. All but one of the warships got through safely and concentrated near Hard Times on the west side of the Mississippi. On April 25 skirmishing occurred near Hard Times as Grant's forces continued to push south. The fleet followed the army down. By noon on April 30 Grant's first forces were across the Mississippi at Bruinsburg south of Vicksburg and were preparing to move inland.

[12] Kate Stone, whose family had abandoned its large cotton plantation, Brokenburn, in what is now Madison Parish, to seek refuge from the Federals at Monroe, recorded in her journal: "Several thousand of our soldiers are now at Monroe under Maj. Gen. Walker. Two of the officers spent yesterday evening here and told us the whole command would get off this morning and that there were some splendid bands with the regiments. So this morning we rode out to the river opposite Monroe to see them off, starting before sunrise. We saw crowds of soldiers, talked to a number of them, and heard inspiring music. . . . The troops after embarking received counter orders and are again in Monroe, expecting to march at any minute. There is another panic in Monroe. The Yankees are looked for at any time. They could not make anything out of this poor family. We have been too thoroughly plucked by the river Feds." John Q. Anderson, ed., *Brokenburn: The Journal of Kate Stone, 1861–1868* (Baton Rouge: Louisiana State University Press, 1955), pp. 207–8 (hereafter cited as Anderson, ed., *Brokenburn*).

[13] Wrote J. P. Blessington: "Nothing worthy of notice transpired on our trip down the river, until we were near the town of Harrisonburg, when a courier, from General Dick Taylor's head-quarters, hailed General Walker, and handed him a dispatch informing him that the enemy had crossed Red River at Alexandria, and were likely to attack Fort Beauregard at Harrisonburg in the rear; and that four gunboats had left Alexandria for the purpose of making an attack by water. He sent a dispatch to Colonel Logan, commanding the fort, to burn his last cartridge in its defence. Colonel Logan replied that he had as much force as he wanted, and that he would hold the fort with 'God's blessing.' General Walker at once ordered his boats to 'about ship' on hearing the news from Colonel Logan. So we took the back track once more for Trenton, where we arrived about 3 o'clock the next morning, after an excursion of one hundred and twenty-five miles." At daybreak the troops again disembarked. In accordance with instructions from General Taylor, Hawes's and Randal's brigades immediately took up the march for Natchitoches. Walker with McCulloch's Brigade stayed at Trenton for a few days in order to support General Paul O. Hébert's state troops in the event that Federal gunboats en route up the Black River forced their way past Fort Beauregard. Blessington, *Walker's Texas Division*, p. 81.

"On approaching Monroe, we passed through the camp of Walker's division (8000 strong)," Lieutenant Colonel Fremantle noted in his journal on May 10. "It was on the march from Arkansas to meet Banks. The division had embarked in steamers, and had already started down the Ouachita towards the Red River, when the news arrived of the fall of Alexandria, and of the presence of Federal gunboats in or near the Ouachita itself. This caused the precipitate return and disembarkation of Walker's division. The men were well armed with rifles and bayonets, but they were dressed in ragged civilian clothes. The old Matagorda man recognized his son in one of these regiments — a perfect boy." Lord, ed., *Fremantle Diary*, p. 69.

[14] Following his victory at Fredericksburg, Lee held strong positions below the

Rappahannock. General Joseph Hooker, who succeeded Burnside as commander of the Army of the Potomac, began crossing the river on April 28 with 70,000 men and prepared to turn Lee's left flank. Lee boldly split his forces, sending Jackson through the Wilderness with 26,000 men to hit the Federal right, while he confronted the enemy's left and center with 17,000. Jubal Early remained in Fredericksburg with 10,000 men to oppose John Sedgwick's 40,000. Jackson struck on May 2, completely surprising the Federal troops under O. O. Howard and sending them reeling back in confusion. On May 5 Hooker pulled his battered army back across the Rappahannock. Chancellorsville was a costly victory for the South. Among the casualties was Stonewall Jackson, mistakenly shot by his own men during the night of May 2. He died eight days later of pneumonia, which developed after his left arm was amputated.

[15] Walker with McCulloch's Brigade remained in camp four miles west of Trenton until the morning of May 16, waiting to hear further news of the enemy. If they succeeded in capturing Fort Beauregard, it was expected they would advance on Monroe or Trenton. Walker kept his communications open with Logan. During the bombardment of the fort word was received from Delhi that about 1,000 Federals had crossed Bayou Maçon and were advancing on Monroe. When Logan succeeded in forcing four Federal gunboats to withdraw, and news was received that the enemy had recrossed Bayou Maçon, abandoning their raid on Monroe, Walker was at last free to join Taylor on the Red River. On May 16 McCulloch's men started for the town of Campti on the river. Hawes's and Randal's troops were bivouacked at nearby Black Lake. The 120-mile march was through Vernon, Woodville and Sparta. This distance was covered in seven days, at an average of 17.1 miles per day. On arrival near Campti word was received that the Federal army under Banks had evacuated Alexandria and was falling back to the Mississippi. Banks had left Alexandria for operations against Port Hudson in cooperation with Grant's final push against Vicksburg, which was then underway from south of the city and was achieving a striking success. Walker's Division proceeded by boat to Alexandria, arriving on May 27. Blessington, *Walker's Texas Division*, pp. 82–83.

Before hearing of Banks's withdrawal Kirby Smith had complained to Holmes of Walker's slowness in reaching the Red River. "General Banks' advance has as yet only reached Monette's Ferry, 40 miles below Natchitoches. Walker delayed most unjustifiably at Monroe, and has probably defeated the possibility of a junction with Taylor at Natchitoches. He has been ordered to move directly to this point [Shreveport], on which Taylor retreats in the event of being forced to evacuate Natchitoches. The length of the march, and the danger to his communication, may check the enemy's farther advance, and give us time to prepare for him. Should we be compelled to evacuate this place, it will be with an immense loss of material, and with no base to fall back on."

Holmes's response to Kirby Smith's complaint was to request that Walker be sent at once back to Arkansas to command the cavalry division now under Marmaduke, "who is not equal to it." McCulloch could command Walker's troops well. Smith directed Taylor to consult with Walker "as to his wishes, and, if he desires it, order him at once to General Holmes." Walker evidently did not desire it, for he remained in command of his division. E. Kirby Smith to Theophilus H. Holmes, May 16, 1863, *Official Records Armies*, series I, XXII, pt. 2, pp. 839–40; William R. Boggs to Richard Taylor, May 22, 1863, Boggs to Theophilus H. Holmes, May 23, 1863, *ibid.*, pp. 846–47.

[16] The outbreak of the Civil War made martial and patriotic music and sentimental war songs the order of the day, and sheet music from presses in New Orleans,

Richmond and Augusta found their way into the Trans-Mississippi Department. A. E. Blackmar & Bro. of New Orleans and Augusta printed such pieces as the love song "Bonny Eloise, the belle of the Mohawk vale," with words by George W. Elliott and music by J. R. Thomas; old Scottish songs like "Annie Laurie" by Brinkerhoff, and "Bonny Jean" written by George Linley and composed by Charles Osborne; and the lush, sentimental period piece, "Do They Miss Me at Home?," "as sung by the Amphions, at their principal concerts throughout the country." The original lyric of "Do They Miss Me at Home?" was written by Caroline Atherton Mason, a minor mid-century poet in the genteel tradition. The music was composed by S. M. Grannis, whose other works included such typical period titles as "Sparking Sunday Night" and "Your Mission," the latter reputedly one of Lincoln's favorite hymns. Marjorie Lyle Crandall, *Confederate Imprints: A Check List Based Principally on the Collection of the Boston Athenaeum*, 2 vols. (Boston: Boston Athenaeum, 1955), II, pp. 562, 569–70, 582; Irwin Silber, comp. & ed., *Songs of the Civil War* (New York: Columbia University Press, 1960), p. 119; Lota M. Spell, "Music in Texas," *Civil War History*, 4 (September 1958), pp. 301–6.

[17] Edward (or Edwin) Pearsall Gregg, lieutenant colonel, colonel, Sixteenth Texas Cavalry Regiment (dismounted). Wright, comp., *Texas in the War*, p. 26.

[18] Jean Jacques Alfred Alexander Mouton was born at Opelousas, Louisiana, February 18, 1829, the son of ex-governor and United States senator Alexander Mouton. He received his early education in the schools of Vermillionville (now Lafayette) and graduated from West Point in 1850. He resigned almost immediately to become a railroad construction engineer and brigadier general of Louisiana militia. He was elected colonel of the Eighteenth Louisiana Infantry in October 1861 and rendered outstanding service at Shiloh, where he received a nearly fatal wound. He was promoted to brigadier general to rank from April 16, 1862. After his recovery he was given a brigade of Louisiana cavalry regiments in Richard Taylor's department and was frequently commended by that officer for his ability and skill. Mouton was killed at the battle of Mansfield or Sabine Cross Roads, April 8, 1864. Warner, *Generals in Gray*, pp. 222–23.

[19] After crossing the Mississippi Grant abandoned his communications and supply lines and pushed inland. First he struck at Jackson, the capital of Mississippi, driving back the small Confederate force General Joseph E. Johnston had collected there, and then he turned on General John Pemberton's army, defeated it in two battles, Champion Hill (May 16) and Big Black River Bridge (May 17), and forced it into Vicksburg. After two ill-advised assaults the Federal army settled down to besiege the city, while gunboats kept up a bombardment from the river.

In the meantime Pemberton frantically called upon Kirby Smith for cooperation with the Confederates east of the Mississippi. "My force is insufficient for offensive operations," he explained on May 9. "I must stand on the defensive, at all events until re-enforcements reach me. You can contribute materially to the defense of Vicksburg and the navigation of the Mississippi River by a movement upon the line of communications of the enemy on the western side of the river. He derives his supplies and re-enforcements for the most part by a route which leads from Milliken's Bend to New Carthage, La., a distance of some 35 or 40 miles. To break this would render a most important service."

Since Banks had now crossed the Mississippi to besiege Port Hudson, Kirby Smith felt compelled to do what he could for Pemberton. If Taylor, reinforced by Walker's troops, could move up the Tensas and destroy Grant's line of communications between Young's Point and New Carthage on the west side of the Mississippi, he might be effectively checked, "if not frustrated," Smith suggested on May 20. He was conscious of Taylor's desire to recover lower Louisiana and threaten New Orleans, Kirby Smith said, "but the stake contended for near Vicksburg is the Valley of the Mississippi and the Trans-Mississippi Department; the defeat of General Grant is the <u>terminus ad quem</u> of all operations in the west this summer; to its attainment all minor advantages should be sacrificed." If Bayou Vidal could be seized and held for a ten-day period, Grant's whole army would be endangered. Should Grant have already been defeated before Vicksburg, it "insures his destruction." Had Grant's supply line been where the Confederate high command expected it to be, Smith's hopes might have been realized. But Grant had now abandoned his base at Milliken's Bend and was opening a new supply line on the Yazoo, far beyond the reach of any Trans-Mississippi force.

Taylor later stated that he remonstrated against being sent on such a campaign, pointing out the impossibility of approaching Vicksburg from the west. The way to relieve the Confederate forces east of the Mississippi, he insisted, was with Walker's force to capture Berwick Bay, overrun the Lafourche, interrupt Banks's communications with New Orleans and threaten the city itself. Banks would be compelled to rush from Port Hudson to the defense of New Orleans. Port Hudson's garrison could then unite with Joseph Johnston behind Grant. But Kirby Smith, Taylor explained, was under too much pressure to give this plan serious consideration. To Taylor he remarked that "Confederate authorities in the east were urgent for some effort on our part in behalf of Vicksburg, and that public opinion would condemn us if we did not <u>try to do something</u>. To go two hundred miles and more away from the proper theatre of action in search of any indefinite <u>something</u> was hard; but orders are orders." "Taylor's account was no doubt colored by subsequent events," wrote Kirby Smith's biographer, "but Kirby Smith was definitely under pressure. His duty with regard to the lower Mississippi had been stressed upon him from the time he was appointed to his new post." John C. Pemberton to E. Kirby Smith, May 9, 1863, *Official Records Armies*, series I, XXIV, pt. 3, p. 846; Smith to Richard Taylor, May 20, 21, 1863, *ibid.*, XXVI, pt. 2, pp. 12–13, 15; Taylor, *Destruction and Reconstruction*, pp. 137–38; Parks, *Edmund Kirby Smith*, p. 270. For a detailed study of the attempt to relieve Vicksburg from west of the Mississippi, see Edwin C. Bearss, "The Trans-Mississippi Confederates Attempt to Relieve Vicksburg," *McNeese Review*, 15 (1964), pp. 46–70; 16 (1965), pp. 46–67.

[20] Time was so important that Taylor determined to run the risk of moving Walker's Division by water, although the enemy could bring gunboats into the lower Red and Ouachita as well as into the Tensas, and had some troops in the region between the latter and the Mississippi. On the evening of May 28 the division left camp near Alexandria for Little River, about 20 miles distant. Here transports were waiting to carry the men up the Tensas. The boat that had Taylor, Walker and their staffs aboard led off, followed by the rest of the transports. After crossing Catahoula Lake the transports arrived at the mouth of Black River during the night of May 29 and ascended it to the mouth of the Tensas. "To prevent a surprise from the enemy, sentinels were placed upon the hurricane deck of all the transports to keep watch, lest the enemy should be lurking about," wrote Blessington. "We were only twenty-five miles from the Mississippi River. The country between the two rivers was invested with the enemy's pickets." The transports carrying McCulloch's and Randal's brigades arrived at Buck's plantation, the head of navigation on the Tensas, on the evening of May 30. The distance from Little River was about 250 miles. The men went ashore on the right bank of the river and made camp. Here Major Isaac F. Harrison's 15th Louisiana Cavalry Battalion met them. For safety the transports were sent down the Tensas to its junction with the Ouachita and up the latter above Fort Beauregard; bridges were thrown over the

Tensas and Bayou Maçon to give communication with the terminus of the Monroe railroad. After supper the men received orders to be ready to march at a moment's notice. Blessington, *Walker's Texas Division*, pp. 85–86; Taylor, *Destruction and Reconstruction*, pp. 138–39.

[21] Arriving on the evening of May 30 at Buck's plantation, the Confederates marched at a little past midnight for Perkins' Landing on the Mississippi, near the town of New Carthage and about 15 miles from Vicksburg. Expecting to surprise the Federals at daybreak, the Texans executed a terrifying night march through enemy-held territory. "After leaving the river," Blessington wrote, "the route of the troops was through a cane-brake, dark and dismal, and as desolate and dreary as the imagination could picture, and highly musical with croaking of frogs; to these add reptiles of every hue and species, and you have some idea of the ground. . . . That was a night that tried men's souls. Although moving slowly forward, in momentary expectation of being attacked, nothing special occurred."

On the morning of the 31st McCulloch's Brigade, which had the advance, formed a battle line in a skirt of timber adjoining Perkins's plantation and advanced on the enemy's camp, only to find that the Federals had fled, leaving their provisions and cooking utensils. "Our troops helped themselves to the enemy's 'hardtack' and coffee," Blessington stated. "The coffee they found very palatable, and more nourishing than corn-meal coffee." The Federals formed in line of battle behind the levee of the Mississippi under the protection of the ironclad *Carondelet*, and an artillery duel took place between the gunboat and Edgar's Battery. "The intervening valley was one dense cloud of smoke, which rose in floating canopies over it," Blessington remembered. "We could behold the sheets of flame, followed by volumes of smoke, jump out from the mouths of the brazen monsters, while the loud reverberating sounds echoed through the river valley." At 11 a.m. Taylor and Walker arrived with Randal's Brigade. When the gunboat dropped down the river and the Federal troops scrambled aboard the transport *Forest Queen*, the Confederates marched back to the Tensas. Before dark the steamboats with Hawes's troops aboard arrived, and the division was reunited. McCulloch's Brigade lost one killed, two wounded and two missing, and McCulloch reported unofficial sources as saying that "the enemy had eleven killed and several wounded on the land, besides those which must have suffered similarly on the transports." Blessington, *Walker's Texas Division*, pp. 86–92. Blessington reprints McCulloch's report.

[22] "On our march through the swamps we beheld several large rattlesnakes, that had been killed by our advance guards," Blessington noted. "Very frequently, in the swamps of Louisiana, a soldier wakes up in the morning and finds that he has a rattlesnake for a sleeping partner; but there is one excellent trait in the character of these reptiles: they never bite unless disturbed, and will get out of the way as soon as possible, except in the month of August, when they are said to be blind, and will snap at anything they may hear about them." *Ibid.*, p. 93.

[23] E. Kirby Smith to John C. Pemberton, May 30, 1863, *Official Records Armies*, series I, XXIV, pt. 3, pp. 935–36. See also, Smith to Joseph E. Johnston, June 4, 1863, *ibid.*, p. 948.

[24] Benjamin Quarles, *The Negro in the Civil War* (Boston: Little, Brown and Company, 1953), pp. 220–21 (hereafter cited as Quarles, *Negro in the Civil War*); *Official Records Armies*, series I, XXIV, pt. 2, p. 447.

[25] *Official Records Armies*, series I, XXIV, pt. 2, pp. 447, 467; E. P. Becton to Mary Becton, July 1, 1863, E. P. Becton Papers, The University of Texas Archives, Austin, Texas (hereafter cited as Becton Papers). "The news of today is that our

men were repulsed at Milliken's Bend and are falling back to Delhi," Kate Stone recorded in her journal on June 10. "A very different account from the first. It is hard to believe that Southern soldiers—and Texans at that—have been whipped by a mongrel crew of white and black Yankees. There must be some mistake." Kate joined the other women in making mattresses for the wounded soldiers expected at Monroe. "It is said the Negro regiments fought there like mad demons, but we cannot believe that. We know from long experience they are cowards." Anderson, ed., *Brokenburn*, pp. 218–19.

Charles A. Dana, the managing editor of the New York *Tribune* who resigned in 1862 and joined the staff of the War Department, was for a time special commissioner at Grant's headquarters in the West. In his memoirs he stated: "The bravery of the blacks in the battle at Milliken's Bend completely revolutionized the sentiment of the army with regard to the employment of negro troops. I heard prominent officers who formerly in private had sneered at the idea of the negroes fighting express themselves after that as heartily in favor of it. Among the Confederates, however, the feeling was very different. All the reports which came to us showed that both citizens and soldiers on the Confederate side manifested great dismay at the idea of our arming negroes. They said that such a policy was certain to be followed by insurrection with all its horrors." Charles A. Dana, *Recollections of the Civil War: With the Leaders at Washington and in the Field in the Sixties* (New York: D. Appleton and Company, 1913), pp. 86–87.

[26] David D. Porter to Ulysses S. Grant, *Official Records Armies*, series I, XXIV, pt. 2, pp. 453–54.

[27] Yeary, comp., *Reminiscences of the Boys in Gray*, pp. 609–10; *Official Records Navies*, series I, XXV, p. 163; *Official Records Armies*, series I, XXIV, pt. 2, p. 459.

[28] *Official Records Navies*, series I, XXV, p. 163; *Official Records Armies*, series I, XXIV, pt. 2, pp. 459, 464. On the battle of Milliken's Bend, see Winters, *Civil War in Louisiana*, pp. 199–201; Quarles, *Negro in the Civil War*, pp. 221–24; Dudley Taylor Cornish, *The Sable Army: Negro Troops in the Union Army, 1861–1865* (New York: Longmans, Green and Co.), pp. 144–45.

[29] "Antipathy toward ordinary Yankees was deep and pervasive, but it was mild in comparison with the hatred which most Rebs felt for Negroes who wore the blue," wrote Bell Wiley. "The mere thought of a Negro in uniform was enough to arouse the ire of the average Reb; he was wont to see in the arming of the blacks the fruition of oft-repeated Yankee efforts to incite slave insurrections and to establish racial equality. Anticipation of conflict with former slaves brought savage delight to his soul. And when white and black met on field of battle the results were terrible. Negroes were taken prisoners in several engagements, but if the wishes of the private soldiers who fought them had prevailed, no quarter would have been granted. Most of the Rebs felt as the Mississippian who wrote his mother: 'I hope I may never see a Negro soldier,' he said, 'or I cannot be . . . a Christian Soldier.'" Wiley, *Life of Johnny Reb*, p. 314.

[30] *Official Records Armies*, series I, XXIV, pt. 2, pp. 448, 470.

[31] J. M. Hawes to R. P. Maclay, June 8, 1863, Walker Papers; *Official Records Armies*, series I, XXIV, pt. 2, pp. 471–72.

[32] *Official Records Armies*, series I, XXIV, pt. 2, pp. 459–60, 465.

[33] Richard Taylor to William R. Boggs, October 15, 1863, *Official Records Armies*, series I, XXIV, pt. 2, p. 462; E. Kirby Smith to Jefferson Davis, June 5, 1864, *ibid.*, pt. 3, p. 1070. "Taylor attempted to place the blame for the failure of

the mission upon his timid commanders, but it was Taylor himself who was largely at fault," wrote John D. Winters. "By consolidating his forces he could have pushed over five thousand men against Milliken's Bend and Young's Point. As he did not trust his subordinate officers, he should have led his men into the field instead of remaining in the rear at Richmond." Winters, *Civil War in Louisiana*, p. 202.

[34] Richard Taylor to William R. Boggs, June 8, 1863, *Official Records Armies*, series I, XXIV, pt. 2, pp. 457–62; H. P. Pratt to Taylor, June 15, 1863, *ibid.*, XXII, pt. 2, p. 868; E. Kirby Smith to Jefferson Davis, June 16, 1863, *ibid.*, XXII, pt. 2, pp. 871–73; Taylor, *Destruction and Reconstruction*, p. 138.

[35] Blessington, *Walker's Texas Division*, p. 123. "Take a map and see our travels since April 26," Surgeon Edward Cade wrote his wife on June 14. "Commence at Pine Bluff and go to Monroe, 180 miles. Go down Ouachita river 80 miles [and] back, making 160; thence to Alexandria, 210 miles; thence to the Mississippi in 15 miles of Vicksburg, 220 miles; thence to Milliken's Bend, 50 miles; thence to Monroe, 100 miles; then down the Ouachita river 120 miles & back, 240 miles — in all, 1170 miles in 49 days." Anderson, *A Texas Surgeon*, p. 59.

[36] *Official Records Armies*, series I, XXIV, pt. 2, pp. 451–53; *Official Records Navies*, series I, XXV, pp. 175–76; Blessington, *Walker's Texas Division*, pp. 110–12, 123–25; Winters, *Civil War in Louisiana*, pp. 202–3.

[37] Blessington, *Walker's Texas Division*, p. 115.

[38] *Official Records Armies*, series I, XXIV, pt. 2, pp. 450, 466; Blessington, *Walker's Texas Division*, pp. 113–15; Winters, *Civil War in Louisiana*, pp. 202–4. "Three men have come in from the command, one of which is slightly wounded,"

Henry Orr of the Twelfth Texas Cavalry wrote his sister from Bayou Maçon on July 2. "The news they bring in as follows: That the command stormed a Negro fort on last Monday, and after a short fight they surrendered their fort [which] was an Indian mound fifty or sixty feet high with steps or pegs on one side to descend. In it were 150 commanded by four Federal officers. The others, some 800 in number — big, little, old, and young — were around the quarters; all that tried to escape were killed. They were sent to Monroe. I think those with uniforms and arms should share the fate ordered by Col. Parsons when he told the boys to charge them, which was to kill them [illegible] take none with uniforms on. Only four of [our] command were killed, eighteen wounded at this place. Some of my acquaintance got a good many mules, and I am told the boys [illegible] valuable articles and burnt everything they had. Gen. Walker with his command came up just about the time the fun was over." Anderson, ed., *Campaigning with Parsons' Texas Cavalry Brigade, CSA*, pp. 111–12. See also George W. Ingram to Martha F. Ingram, July 18, 1863, Ingram, comp., *Civil War Letters*, pp. 55–56.

"There are quite a number of Yankee prisoners at Tyler [Texas], captured while in command of black troops," an indignant Kate Stone noted in her journal on September 1, 1863. "It does seem like they ought to be hanged, and they are so impudent too. The detestable creatures!" Anderson, ed., *Brokenburn*, p. 239.

[39] C. LeDoux Elgee to John G. Walker, June 24, 1863, Walker Papers. See also, Elgee to Richard Taylor, June 22, 1863, *Official Records Armies*, series I, XXII, pt. 2, p. 914; Elgee to Walker, June 22, 1863, Walker Papers.

[40] Joseph E. Johnston to E. Kirby Smith, June 26, 1863, *Official Records Armies*, series I, XXIV, pt. 3, p. 979.

[41] John G. Walker to E. Kirby Smith, July 3, 1863, *ibid.*, XXII, pt. 2, pp. 915–16.

[42] Richard Taylor to William R. Boggs, June 27, 1863, *ibid.*, XXVI, pt. 1, pp. 211–12; Guy M. Bryan to Paul O. Hébert, June 30, 1863, *ibid.*, pt. 2, p. 97; E. Kirby Smith to Joseph E. Johnston, July 4, 1863, *ibid.*, XXII, pt. 2, p. 904; Smith to Samuel Cooper, July 10, 1863, *ibid.*, p. 913; Parks, *Edmund Kirby Smith*, p. 276. In his memoirs Taylor wrote that "General Kirby Smith reached Monroe direct from Shreveport, countermanded my orders, and turned Walker back into the region east of the Tensas, where this good soldier and his fine division were kept idle for some weeks, until the fall of Vicksburg. The time wasted on these absurd movements cost us the garrison of Port Hudson, nearly eight thousand men; but the pressure on General Kirby Smith to do something for Vicksburg was too strong to be resisted." Taylor, *Destruction and Reconstruction*, p. 139. In fairness to Smith it should be noted that Taylor first ordered Walker's Division south of the Red River in early June but withdrew his order on June 11; that Randal's Brigade actually started south but turned back at Columbus on the Ouachita River; and that Taylor did not again order Walker's Division to lower Louisiana until June 27 (the order Smith countermanded), just eight days before Vicksburg surrendered and much too late to save Port Hudson. However, it was Taylor's contention that Walker should never have been ordered to operate opposite Vicksburg in the first place.

[43] Blessington, *Walker's Texas Division*, pp. 116–17.

[44] Anderson, *A Texas Surgeon*, pp. 67–68; S. W. Farrow to Josephine Farrow, July 11, 1863, S. W. Farrow Papers, The University of Texas Archives, Austin, Texas (hereafter cited as Farrow Papers).

[45] Blessington, *Walker's Texas Division*, pp. 127–31; Taylor, *Destruction and Reconstruction*, p. 179. McCulloch took leave of his brigade at Vernon, Louisiana, July 22, 1863.

[46] Captain Petty was not the only Southern soldier to suffer "coffee hunger headaches." In July 1862 another Texas Confederate suffering from chronic headache lamented: "How much I miss the good coffee I use to get at home. I would cheerfully pay one dollar for as much like it as I could drink. . . . We got some ground coffee from the Yanks in the Seven Days fight," he said, but since then he and his comrades had "to pay two dollars and a half a pound." Steep as this price seemed to the coffee-starved Rebel, worse was yet to come with Fremantle reporting the cost of coffee at $7.00 a pound in San Antonio in April 1863.

Around army campfires, on hard-scrabble farms and on the great plantations, blockaded Rebels were experimenting with varieties of ersatz coffee. An amber liquid, somewhat euphemistically called coffee, was brewed from parched corn, peanuts, rye or peas and even dried apples. A beverage which many Southerners were pleased to call "tea" was made of corn bran, ginger and herbs of various sorts, with sassafras especially reaching such heights of popularity that it is still drunk today by many rural Southerners. Wiley, *Life of Johnny Reb*, p. 103; Lord, ed., *Fremantle Diary*, p. 41.

[47] The sixty-day furlough was by long odds the most desirable benison which any soldier might hope to receive and was consequently a tremendous source of discontent to those who failed to receive one. The application process was toilsome, and the waiting period while those in authority decided on the petition's merits seemed interminable. Adding injury to insult, the request for leave was most often refused, leaving the disheartened soldier with the feeling that his superiors were "heartless and unreasonable."

So unpopular were the Army's policies concerning furloughs that, when Thomas Jefferson Chambers ran for governor of Texas in 1863, one plank in his platform called for their revision. "I am of the opinion that married soldiers should be given the opportunity of embracing their families at least once a year, their places in the ranks being taken by unmarried men," he proposed. "The population must not be allowed to suffer."

Although the promise of a two-month leave was the immediate impetus which caused many Confederate volunteers to sign on for a second tour of duty, often for the war's duration, many Southern patriots, most of whom were safely behind the lines, decried this expedient as actually a weakening factor in the Confederate armies. "This extraordinary measure was inspired by the military genius of President Davis," snarled Richmond *Examiner* editor Edward A. Pollard, "and was directly recommended by him. It depleted our armies in the face of the enemy; it filled our military commanders with consternation; it carried alarm, confusion, and demoralization everywhere." This argument and others like it caused a number of commanders in the field to disregard the government's policy and to deny furlough to newly reenlisted veterans. These provocations, coupled with more-than-occasional evidence of favoritism in dispensing furloughs, caused more than one Rebel soldier to take leave whether those in authority approved or not. Wiley, *Life of Johnny Reb*, pp. 133–39; Pollard, *The Lost Cause*, p. 220; Lord, ed., *Fremantle Diary*, p. 50.

[48] T. M. Hunt, Adjutant, Seventeenth Texas Infantry.

[49] George Washington Jones went home on sick leave on August 19. Compiled Service Record of George Washington Jones, National Archives, Washington, D. C.

[50] Leo E. Huff stated: "The term 'Jayhawker' seems to have originated back in about 1849 in Illinois when members of a wagon train starting for the California gold fields remarked that they would just jayhawk their way across the plains. This train became somewhat famous and its members became known as jayhawkers. The

expressions 'to jayhawk' and 'jayhawkers' spread and were applied to the roving bands of Kansans in the bloody pre-Civil War days. Early in the war the term was revived and was used to designate the meanest and lowest specimens of mankind. A jayhawker was a robber, a thief, a rogue and an assassin. The term seems to have been applied initially to General James Lane and the men of his Kansas brigade, who achieved notoriety for their indiscriminate plundering and burning in Missouri. The Confederates later applied the term to Union guerrillas, to outlaws, to Federal soldiers who engaged in looting, and even to some of the Union generals themselves, Samuel R. Curtis and John McNeil, for example. The Federals occasionally used the term 'jayhawkers' when referring to Confederate guerrillas or outlaws. But in general, the expression was used principally by the Confederates, while the Federals more often used the term 'bushwacker.'" Leo E. Huff, "Guerrillas, Jayhawkers and Bushwackers in Northern Arkansas During the Civil War," *Arkansas Historical Quarterly*, XXIV (Summer 1965), p. 129.

[51] The Bellville *Countryman* of July 4, 1863, noted Colonel Allen's arrival at Hempstead, "direct from the Mississippi nearly opposite Vicksburg."

[52] Captain William A. Pitts was from San Saba City, Texas.

[53] On August 20 Brigadier General John D. Stevenson, with the Third Division of the Seventeenth Corps and three batteries of artillery plus a battalion of cavalry, set out from Vicksburg on an expedition to Monroe. The purpose of the expedition was to clear out partisans and to break up a reported troop encampment at Monroe. Debarking at Goodrich's Landing, Stevenson crossed Bayou Maçon on August 24 and arrived at Monroe four days later. General Hébert had withdrawn his small command from the town and was on his way to Shreveport. As he withdrew Hébert burned 5,000 bales of cotton. Stevenson left Monroe on August 28 and returned to the Mississippi, arriving back in Vicksburg on September 2. On August 31 Walker's men heard that the Federals had occupied Monroe and that 7,000 more had crossed Bayou Maçon from the direction of Lake Providence and were advancing towards Bayou Bartholomew, while another force of Federals was within a few miles of Little Rock, Arkansas. Winters, *Civil War in Arkansas*, pp. 301–2; Blessington, *Walker's Texas Division*, p. 131.

[54] Captain Thomas H. Gutlin, Company C, Seventeenth Texas Infantry Regiment.

[55] Petty changed the words of these lines from Lord Byron's *To Thomas Moore*, St. 2:

Here's a sigh to those who love me,
    And a smile to those who hate;
And whatever sky's above me,
    Here's a heart for every fate.

[56] "I really do not know what to say to you about the continuance of the war," Surgeon Edward Cade confessed to his wife. "There is a great deal of bad feeling being exhibited in our division. I think I may safely say there has been 300 desertions in the last month and they still continue to go. I am happy to say however that not more than 7 or 8 has deserted from our brigade. One from Martin's company. Nothing but quick, stern and unrelenting punishment will stop it. I am sorry that in this dark hour of our country when the services of every man are so much required that men can desert her cause." Anderson, *A Texas Surgeon*, p. 73.

[57] On this same day (September 3) Kirby Smith lamented to Taylor: "The diffi-

culties of my position are well known to you — a vast extent of country to defend; a force utterly inadequate for the purpose; a lukewarm people, the touchstone to whose patriotism seems beyond my grasp, and who appear more intent upon the means of evading the enemy and saving their property than of defending their firesides. The policy which must influence me in ordering the movement of troops or in adopting any general plan of operations adds in a tenfold degree to these difficulties; it is not only as a military man, but as a statesman that they have to be considered. The President impresses it upon me, the representative and the leading men of the States urge it upon me, that the States must be defended; that, once in the hands of the enemy, they will be irretrievably lost to the Confederacy. But for these considerations, I would long since have followed the military principle of abandoning a part to save the whole, and, concentrating in advance, been ready to strike decisively and boldly when the campaign would have been materially influenced." He was convinced, from his own observation, "that the withdrawal of the troops and the abandonment of the Arkansas Valley would be followed by the defection of the Arkansas regiments. The Missourians might be relied upon, but the Indian allies are in the same category." E. Kirby Smith to Richard Taylor, September 3, 1863, *Official Records Armies*, series I, XXII, pt. 2, pp. 988–90.

[58] On August 17, 1863, 11 guns of the Federal batteries on Morris Island, South Carolina, aided by naval armament, fired a total of 938 shots in the first major bombardment of Confederate-occupied Fort Sumter in Charleston Harbor. Sumter's brick walls crumbled under the heavy blows, but the rubble and sand formed an even more impregnable bulwark against Federal fire. The first bombardment of Sumter ended on August 23, after 5009 rounds had been fired. Only one gun was left in good condition in the fort, by then a mass of rubble and wreckage. Long, *Civil War Day by Day*, pp. 398–400.

[59] The next Federal raid into north Louisiana got under way from Natchez, Mississippi, on September 1. The expedition, under the command of Brigadier General Marcellus M. Crocker, consisted of the Second and Third Brigades, Fourth Division, Seventeenth Army Corps; Company F, Second Illinois Artillery; the Fifteenth Ohio Battery; and the Seventeenth Wisconsin Infantry (mounted). The troops moved inland in the direction of Trinity on the Black River. A small steamer, the *Rinaldo*, was captured and burned. On the morning of the 4th the command moved to Harrisonburg. When Lieutenant Colonel George W. Logan, Chalmette (Louisiana) Regiment, commanding Fort Beauregard at Harrisonburg,

learned that the Federals numbered between 10,000 and 15,000 men, he decided to evacuate the post, although he knew that Randal's Brigade of 1,100 men was approaching Harrisonburg from the direction of Alexandria. At 3 a.m. on September 4 Logan evacuated the fort after destroying the works and started toward Alexandria on the Centreville and Natchitoches road. "Having only 40 effective men in garrison, I have only been able to save all our wagons, horses, and mules, and four of my best pieces of artillery," he reported. Randal skirmished with the Federals east of the Brushy Bridge, 12 miles west of Harrisonburg, and then he too slowly retired by the Alexandria road. He reported: "The object of the expedition having failed, the superior strength of the enemy and the remoteness of any assistance, and the facility with which the enemy could gain my rear, induced me to retire to the line of Little River where I am now encamped." Taylor ordered Hawes's Brigade with a battery to reinforce Randal.

The Federals arrived at Harrisonburg between 10 and 11 a.m. on September 4. They found that Logan had burned his commissary stores, ammunition, a large quantity of small arms, and had left eight guns in the burning casements. Crocker removed two of the guns and further demolished the remaining six that could not be moved. Leaving Harrisonburg that afternoon, the Federals recrossed the Black River at Trinity on the 5th and on the 7th recrossed the Mississippi at Natchez, "without anything of interest occurring on the march." *Official Records Armies*, series I, XXVI, pt. 1, pp. 273–83.

[60] Camille Armand Jules Marie, Prince de Polignac, was known as the "Lafayette of the Confederacy." A native of France and veteran of the Crimean War, he joined the Confederate army in July 1861 as a lieutenant colonel and served on the staffs of Beauregard and Bragg in 1862. Transferred to the Trans-Mississippi Department early in 1863 after being promoted to brigadier general, he was given command of a brigade of Texas troops.

Because of the difficulty in pronouncing his name, the irreverent Texans soon dubbed him Prince "Polecat." Richard Taylor wrote in his memoirs: "In the winter there joined me from Arkansas a brigade of Texas infantry, numbering seven hundred muskets. The men had been recently dismounted, and were much discontented thereat. Prince Charles Polignac, a French gentleman of ancient lineage, and a brigadier in the Confederate army, reported for duty about the same time, and was assigned to command this brigade. The Texans swore that a Frenchman, whose very name they could not pronounce, should never command them, and mutiny was threatened. I went to their camp, assembled the officers, and pointed out the consequences of disobedience, for which I should hold them accountable; but promised that if they remained dissatisfied with their new commander after an action, I would then remove him. Order was restored, but it was up-hill work for General Polignac for some time notwithstanding his patience and good temper. The incongruity of the relation struck me, and I thought of sending my monte-dealing Texas colonel to Paris, to command a brigade of the Imperial Guard." Taylor, *Destruction and Reconstruction*, pp. 183–84. On Polignac, see Warner, *Generals in Gray*, p. 241–42; Roy O. Hatton, "Prince Camille De Polignac and the American Civil War, 1863–1865," *Louisiana Studies*, III (Summer 1964), pp. 163–95 (hereafter cited as Hatton, "Polignac and the American Civil War"); "Polignac's Diary," *Civil War Times Illustrated*, XIX (August 1980), pp. 14–18; (October 1980) pp. 34–41.

[61] Petty had considered moving to Oregon before the war. In reply to his letter of December 1859 Senator Joseph Lane of that state, writing from Washington, D.C., had lauded the new state's natural beauty, crops and stock raising, and moderate climate. He was confident that Petty could succeed well in his profession in many

localities. "Portland is the principal town, has thriving commerce and an enterprising population," Lane stated. "It is on the Willamette river. On the same river are Oregon City in Clackamas County, Eugene City in Lane County. In other counties are Albany, Salem and Corvallis. In the Southern portion of the State are Roseburg, Jacksonville and Kerbyville. In all these towns much business is done, and consequently there is litigation, the attractive feature for gentlemen of your profession is good." Petty had evidently made some reference to a Republican paper in Oregon, for Lane confirmed: "You have judged the 'Oregon Argus' correctly. It is black as the ace of spades, and as little reliable as a paper can be." Joseph Lane to E. P. Petty, January 4, 1860, in possession of O. Scott Petty, San Antonio, Texas.

[62] Petty is referring to the popular poem "All Quiet Along the Potomac," the authorship of which was disputed throughout the war between Ethel Lynn Beers of New York and Lamar Fontaine of Texas:

> "'All quiet along the Potomac tonight!'
> Except here and there a stray picket
> Is shot, as he walks on his beat, to and fro,
> By a rifleman hid in the thicket."
> etc.

[63] Blessington noted: "While encamped here, application was made by company commanders to division headquarters to grant them the privilege of furloughing two men from a company. Their application was referred to district headquarters, and refused. There was much excitement and dissatisfaction in camp. After long months of severe service, enduring untold hardships and trials, fighting several battles with a courage and bravery which had made their name distinguished everywhere, the only boon asked, the only favor which could have been conferred on them as a recompense for their deeds, was refused. Now they could look forward only to a life in the army until the termination of the struggle. The disappointment was most bitterly felt, and it is not surprising that it found expression in still more bitter words." Blessington, *Walker's Texas Division*, p. 132.

[64] Efforts were made at this time to check the number of desertions. In accordance with instructions from President Davis, Kirby Smith offered pardons to those who would return to their commands by September 30. Preparations were made to send cavalry to arrest those who failed to return. There had been an "unparalleled number" of desertions among Texas troops serving under Taylor. The only way to stop such "disgraceful abandonment of colors," Kirby Smith advised Taylor, was to use "the most summary punishment." General Orders No. 38, August 26, 1863, *Official Records Armies*, series I, XXII, pt. 2, p. 980; E. Cunningham to Sterling Price, September 7, 1863, *ibid.*, p. 997; S. S. Anderson to Richard Taylor, September 19, 1863, *ibid.*, XXVI, pt. 2, p. 241; Parks, *Edmund Kirby Smith*, p. 319.

[65] Calvin Cutter, *First Book on Anatomy, Physiology, and Hygiene for Grammar Schools and Families*, rev. stereotyped ed. (New York: Clark, Austin, and Smith, 1860).

[66] William R. Scurry was appointed to command the Third Brigade. Born in Gallatin, Tennessee, February 10, 1821, he moved to Texas in the late 1830's and settled in San Augustine. He studied law and was licensed to practice before he was 21. Enlisting as a private in the Second Texas Mounted Volunteers during the Mexican War, he was mustered out with the rank of major in Colonel George T. Wood's regiment. For a time after the war Scurry practiced law at Clinton in DeWitt County. About 1850 he moved to Austin and bought the *State Gazette*, which he

owned until 1854. In 1859 he was appointed commissioner from Texas to fix the Texas-New Mexico boundary and was a member of the Texas secession convention, representing DeWitt County. He entered the Confederate army as lieutenant colonel of the Fourth Texas Cavalry and took part in Sibley's New Mexico campaign, seeing action at Valverde and commanding the Texas troops at Glorieta Pass. "Scurry's conduct was most gallant," the Houston *Telegraph* said of his performance at Glorieta. "He never flagged, and was always the same Bill Scurry, full of humor, we all knew so well. He always carries the same laugh on the battle field he does everywhere. He was wounded in both cheeks by minnie balls." Scurry was promoted to brigadier general to rank from September 12, 1862. He commanded the land forces in the recapture of Galveston on January 1, 1863.

Scurry commanded a brigade in Walker's Division in the battles of Mansfield and Pleasant Hill, Louisiana. He was mortally wounded in the battle of Jenkins' Ferry, Arkansas, April 30, 1864. According to L. W. Kemp, "He refused to be removed from the field, directed the soldiers who were bearing him off to return to their places, and ordered the officers to advance the brigade. Overwhelming numbers forced General Scurry's command back about fifty yards. This ground was not regained until two hours later, when the enemy was repulsed and the Confederate forces were victorious. During all this time, General Scurry lay between the combatants. His first question was, 'Have we whipped them?' Upon being answered in the affirmative, he said, 'Now take me to a house where I can be made comfortable and die easy.'" Warner, *Generals in Gray*, pp. 270–71; Wright, comp., *Texas in the War*, pp. 92n–93n; Houston *Telegraph*, n. d., quoted in Bellville *Countryman*, May 10, 1862; L. W. Kemp, "William Redi Scurry," in Webb, Carroll and Branda, eds., *Handbook of Texas*, II, p. 584.

[67] General Nathaniel Banks planned to occupy Texas by invading the state at the mouth of the Sabine River on the Louisiana border, but a Federal expedition of four gunboats and 22 transport ships carrying 5,000 troops was turned back by only 47 Confederates led by Lieutenant Dick Dowling on September 8, 1863. Firing their six small cannons from a dirt fort, Dowling's men destroyed two gunboats, disabled another, drove the remaining vessels away and captured 350 sailors. But this stunning defeat did not cause Banks to abandon the idea of gaining a foothold in Texas. He decided to move up the Teche to Lafayette or Vermillionville, over the grass plains to Niblett's Bluff and into Texas. William H. Emory's and Godfrey Weitzel's divisions of the Nineteenth Army Corps, under the command of William Franklin, supported by Cadwallader Washburn's and George McGinnis's divisions of the Thirteenth Corps, under Edward O. C. Ord, were concentrated at Bisland on the lower Teche in preparation for the new move into Texas. Albert L. Lee's cavalry division guarded the front at New Iberia. Francis Herron's division, 2,500 strong, sent down by Grant, was stationed at Morganza to prevent the Confederates from operating in the Upper Atchafalaya. An advanced detachment under Colonel J. B. Leake held a position at Sterling's plantation, seven miles from Morganza on the road to the Atchafalaya. Leake's orders were to reconnoiter the area constantly and keep back the Confederate forces. Richard Lowe, "Battle of Sabine Pass," in Roller and Twyman, eds., *Encyclopedia of Southern History*, p. 1071; Winters, *Civil War in Louisiana*, pp. 296–97.

General Frederick Steele's Federal expedition from Helena, Arkansas, occupied Little Rock on September 10, 1863. Sterling Price's Confederates withdrew to Rockport and Arkadelphia. Two brigades of Steele's cavalry under Colonel Lewis Merrill started in pursuit but, after following Marmaduke's cavalry for a day, returned to Little Rock. Snead, "Conquest of Arkansas," pp. 456–57.

[68] On the morning of September 26 Walker's Division received orders to proceed

to Washington, St. Landry Parish. The troops marched via Cheneyville, Evergreen and Big-Cane, and on the 29th encamped within four miles of Washington. It rained incessantly during the march, making the roads impassable to travel. Blessington, *Walker's Texas Division*, pp. 132–33.

[69] Born July 8, 1814, in Buckingham County, Virginia, Thomas Green moved with his parents to Tennessee in 1817 and was graduated from the University of Nashville. In the fall of 1835 he came to Texas and fought at San Jacinto. He was a member of the House of Representatives in the Fourth Texas Congress and secretary of the Senate in the Sixth and Eighth Congresses. In 1841 he became clerk of the Texas Supreme Court, a post he held until the outbreak of the Civil War. In addition to his other activities Green found time to participate in nine Indian and Mexican campaigns during the period of the Texas republic. During the Mexican War he served as a captain of Texas Rangers under John C. Hays, distinguishing himself for bravery at the battle of Monterrey. Green entered the Confederate army as colonel of the Fifth Texas Cavalry in the Sibley Brigade and commanded the brigade at the battle of Valverde when Sibley became ill. He subsequently commanded the Confederate fleet at the battle of Galveston. After Colonel James Reily was killed in the battle of Bisland, Louisiana, Green as senior colonel assumed command of the "Old Sibley Brigade." He was promoted to brigadier general from May 20, 1863. Green's exploits soon made his name a household word throughout the Trans-Mississippi Department. He participated in the battles of Mansfield and Pleasant Hill and was killed in action at Blair's Landing, April 12, 1864, when a shell from a Federal gunboat tore away a portion of his skull above the right eye. Odie B. Faulk, *General Tom Green, Fightin' Texan* (Waco: Texian Press, 1963); *idem*, "Confederate Hero at Val Verde," *New Mexico Historical Review*, XXXVIII (October 1963), pp. 300–11; Captain E. B. Millett, "When General Green Was Killed," *Confederate Veteran*, XXIV (September 1916), pp. 408–9; Alwyn Barr, "The Battle of Blair's Landing," *Louisiana Studies*, II (Winter 1963), pp. 204–12.

[70] Green crossed the Atchafalaya during the night of September 28–29 and moved upon Leake's position at Sterling's plantation in three columns. Mouton's and Speight's infantry brigades, 1,400 strong, moved on a muddy trail through the swamps and took position behind the Federals on the Morganza road. Green's own brigade, consisting of the Fourth, Fifth and Seventh Texas Cavalry (dismounted in this operation), with Edwin Waller's and Leonidas Rountree's Texas cavalry battalions, and Semmes's Battery, moved over the main road to Fordouche bridge in front of Leake's position. One of James P. Major's cavalry regiments, Phillips's, was sent against the Federal left flank to cut off any retreat to Baton Rouge, crossing the Atchafalaya at Lyon's Ferry 20 miles below Green's position.

The Confederate cavalry reached the bridge by 11 a.m. and began skirmishing with the Federal pickets. Half an hour later a brisk fire was heard in the rear of Sterling's plantation. Green pushed forward through the muddy fields, driving the enemy's advance cavalry back. One mile from the bridge at Norwood's house, Rountree charged the Federal cavalry drawn up in line of battle; the blue coats scattered and disappeared through the turnrows and a secret lane leading around the Confederate trap back to Morganza. Major Hannibal H. Boone took two cavalry battalions to Sterling's and rode down the enemy artillery. The engagement was over, and the Federal infantry were rounded up as they fled in the rain over the muddy fields and through the wet bushes.

Federal losses in the battle of Bayou Fordouche amounted to more than 500, with 16 killed, 45 wounded and 462 captured. Green claimed he lost only 121 men — 26 killed, 85 wounded and 10 missing. "We have again given the enemy a wholesome lesson, and I have so far been exceedingly fortunate as commander, beginning with

Val Verde," Green proudly wrote his wife. "The last <u>four</u> battles fought in Louisiana have been under my command, three of which are splendid victories, and the other one of the most desperate fights on record, for the numbers engaged, and one where there was more <u>fruitless</u> courage displayed than any other, perhaps, during the war." Winters, *Civil War in Louisiana*, p. 297; "Battle of Atchafalaya River — Letter from General Thomas Green," *Southern Historical Society Papers*, III (February 1877), pp. 62–63. See also, Cooper K. Regan, ed., "The Diary of Captain George W. O'Brien, 1863," *Southwestern Historical Quarterly*, LXVII (October 1963), pp. 235–42. Confederate and Federal reports are in *Official Records Armies*, series I, XXVI, pt. 1, pp. 320–32.

[71] "The day after our arrival in camp, about 500 Yankee prisoners passed through our camp, escorted by some of Green's Cavalry, en route for Alexandria. They were captured at the battle of the Fordoche." Blessington, *Walker's Texas Division*, p. 133.

[72] "Marched eighteen miles; passed through the village of Moreauville," Blessington noted on October 5. "At this place we met Mouton's Division of Louisiana troops, who were nearly all dressed in Federal uniforms that they had captured at Brashear City. They were a fine body of troops, and did good service in the Attakapas country. We arrived at camp, without four miles of Simmsport." *Ibid.*, p. 133.

[73] Colonel Walter P. Lane's Third Texas Cavalry Regiment (South Kansas-Texas Regiment). Wright, comp., *Texas in the War*, pp. 23–24.

[74] Early in October General William Franklin began a slow movement westward from Bisland toward Opelousas and Washington in what was known as the Bayou Teche Campaign. At the same time General Edward O. C. Ord, reinforced by General S. G. Burbridge's division, left Berwick Bay and on October 14 joined Franklin at Carencro Bayou. Franklin now had 19,500 men for the overland move against Texas. Taylor, with about half the Federal strength, fell back slowly to Opelousas, fighting several minor skirmishes with Franklin's men. The Federals pushed into Opelousas and took possession of the surrounding territory, which they continued to occupy until the end of the month, but they failed to reach the Sabine River. Winters, *Civil War in Louisiana*, pp. 297–98.

Back in New Orleans, after a brief visit to Franklin on the Teche, Banks began organizing a second Texas expedition to go by water. Under the command of General Napoleon J. T. Dana, the Second Division of the Thirteenth Army Corps, the Thirteenth and Fifteenth Maine, and the First Engineers and Sixteenth Infantry Regiment of Negro troops left New Orleans on October 26 for Texas. Early in November this expedition landed on the island of Brazos Santiago off the mouth of the Río Grande and proceeded to occupy Brownsville and Point Isabel. Several other points in the interior and Corpus Christi, Aransas Pass, Indianola and other points along the coast of Texas were occupied in the next month. Forts Quintana and Velasco (at the mouth of the Brazos), Galveston and Sabine Pass were the only important Texas coastal positions left to the Confederates. At last Banks had a weak foothold in Texas. *Official Records Armies*, series I, XXVI, pt. 1, pp. 395–447.

[75] In the so-called Tullahoma Campaign William S. Rosecrans's Army of the Cumberland maneuvered the unresourceful Braxton Bragg out of middle Tennessee and Chattanooga without a battle. Alarmed at the loss of this key point, the Richmond government rushed a portion of General James B. Longstreet's corps from the Army of Northern Virginia to reinforce Bragg. The armies clashed at Chickamauga (September 19–20), where the Federal line broke and fled in considerable disorder. General George H. Thomas earned for himself the sobriquet, "Rock of Chick-

amauga," by fighting the great defensive battle of Snodgrass Hill, repelling assault after assault until nightfall. The Federals retired into Chattanooga, and Bragg invested the city.

[76] Compare James Ryder Randall's poem, "Maryland, My Maryland," written at Pointe Coupee, Louisiana, April 26, 1861:

> "The despot's heel is on thy shore,
>   Maryland!
> His torch is at thy temple door,
>   Maryland!
> Avenge the patriotic gore
> That flecked the streets of Baltimore
> And be the battle-queen of yore,
>   Maryland, my Maryland!"
>   etc.

[77] Blessington gives the following account: "Oct. 17th. Marched three miles, and encamped along-side Mouton's Division, and a portion of Green's Cavalry near a little village named Moundville. Shortly after our arrival in camp, the 13th Dismounted Cavalry, commanded by Colonel Burnett, was ordered on picket, below the town of Opelousas. While encamped near Moundville, we learned that the enemy, numbering about 27,000, under command of General Franklin, was encamped within seven miles of Opelousas. General Tom Green's Cavalry were daily skirmishing with them. On the evening of the 18th, General Dick Taylor and staff arrived in camp from Alexandria, to take command in person of the entire army that was concentrated at this place. . . . Owing to his arrival in camp, the troops

anticipated being brought into action every day. Preparations were made by him to give the enemy a warm reception if they should advance. Many were the rumors afloat in camp about the advance of the enemy; occasionally we would hear that they were within a few miles of our camp; then, again, we would hear of their retreat." Blessington, *Walker's Texas Division*, pp. 134–35.

[78] On the morning of October 21 the Sixteenth Texas Infantry, commanded by Colonel Flournoy, was sent to Green's assistance and also to relieve the Thirteenth Texas Infantry, which was on picket below Opelousas. Early the next morning the Federals advanced on Opelousas, driving the Sixteenth Texas and Green's cavalry before them. The Sixteenth Texas arrived in camp in the evening. They reported that the enemy had taken possession of Opelousas at about 10 a.m. and was advancing on Washington. On October 23 the Federals took possession of Washington; Green's cavalry fell back towards Moundville. The Eleventh Texas Infantry, commanded by Colonel O. M. Roberts, and the Eighteenth Texas Infantry, commanded by Colonel Wilburn H. King, were ordered to reinforce Green at Moundville. Taylor formed his line of battle in a position to sweep the road that the advancing Federals would be most likely to use; parks of artillery were planted; the infantry was sheltered by a ditch in their front. "Every minute seemed like an hour to us, till the ball should be opened," Blessington remembered. The Federals advanced to Moundville but, seeing the Confederate pickets, fell back to Washington, followed by the Eleventh and Eighteenth Texas regiments, who were continually skirmishing with them. They were assisted by all of Green's cavalry, except his Old Sibley Brigade, which was left in position on the infantry's right flank. There were several batteries of light artillery present, including the Valverde, Semmes's, Edgar's, Daniels's, Mesh's and Haldeman's. The Confederates numbered in all about 11,000 men.

The Eleventh and Eighteenth Texas regiments, reinforced by Colonel James E. Harrison's (formerly Speight's) regiment, the Fifteenth Texas Infantry belonging to Mouton's Division, formed themselves into a brigade commanded by Colonel Roberts and advanced on Washington, accompanied by Green's cavalry. On their arrival the enemy was observed rapidly retiring across the prairie to Opelousas. In the meantime Taylor established his headquarters at Moundville. Hearing of the retreat, the balance of Walker's Division fell back about two miles to a better campground. On October 26 the troops fell back some 12 miles and camped near the village of Holmesville where they remained until November 8. Blessington, *Walker's Texas Division*, pp. 135–37.

[79] "Through respect towards him, the bands of the brigade serenaded him," Blessington said of Scurry's arrival in camp. "After the music had ceased playing, several of the officers, and the majority of the men, called upon him to make a speech. He informed them that he despised speech-making nowadays, but in a few days expected to meet the enemy, and then he would address a few remarks to them, and he expected the troops of the 3rd Brigade to respond to them as brave soldiers should do." *Ibid.*, pp. 136–37.

[80] Scurry's staff consisted of the following officers: Major T. J. Scurry, Quartermaster; Major H. H. Haynie, Commissary; Captain S. F. A. Bryan, Ordnance Officer; Captain J. F. Wooford, Commissary of Subsistence; Captain James Clarke. Aide-de-Camp; Captain A. N. Mills, Assistant Adjutant-General. *Ibid.*, p. 137

[81] Thomas Gray, *Elegy in a Country Churchyard* (175), St. 14:

"Full many a gem of purest ray serene
The dark unfathomed caves of ocean bear:
Full many a flower is born to blush unseen,
And waste its sweetness on the desert air."

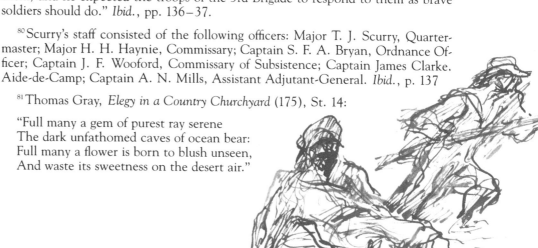

[82] This is a Spanish proverb, "*digo, paciencia y barajar*," originating in Cervantes's *Don Quixote*, II. 23. The meaning is, "if you don't like the situation, wait for the next round."

[83] When the Federals retired from Opelousas Taylor ordered Green to pursue and harass them, and to strengthen his command also ordered forward on November 2 the Eleventh, Fifteenth and Eighteenth Texas Infantry regiments, led by the senior colonel, O. M. Roberts. At noon on November 3 the Confederates caught an infantry brigade and some cavalry detachments commanded by Stephen G. Burbridge napping in their camp near Grand Coteau on Bayou Bourbeau. Green immediately formed his troops for an attack with the infantry regiments on the left between the bayou and the road; the Old Sibley Brigade, now commanded by Colonel Arthur P. Bagby, partially dismounted, in the center west of the road; and James P. Major's cavalry brigade, mounted, on the right. Green's artillery was a rifle section of Daniels's Battery and a section of the Valverde Battery. Green's men swooped down upon Burbridge from all directions before he could form his troops. "The firing of the enemy extended along our whole line and therefore seeing no part of it from which any reinforcement could be drawn I ordered a charge," Roberts reported. "Our whole line responded at once and rushed towards the enemy, and continued it through the enemy's camp, they having fled before us." The Confederate cavalry then swept down on the enemy's flanks and completed the defeat. After a near rout a short and bloody contest was fought in the woods, and a portion of the Federal troops succeeded in escaping to two other brigades of infantry three miles in the rear. Reinforcements were rushed forward to Burbridge, but after a hot skirmish Green retired with his prisoners and booty to Opelousas. The next day, November 4, Franklin resumed his retreat, fighting minor skirmishes every day or two until he arrived back at New Iberia on November 17 and went into camp. Federal losses in the battle of Bayou Bourbeau were 716 — 25 killed, 129 wounded and 562 captured or missing out of 1,625 men in action. Green's totals — 22 killed and 103 wounded — were slightly lower, and only 55 of his men were missing. Winters, *Civil War in Louisiana*, pp. 298–99; Alwyn Barr, "The Battle of Bayou Bourbeau, November 3, 1863: Colonel Oran M. Roberts' Report," *Louisiana History*, VI (Winter 1965), pp. 83–91; Blessington, *Walker's Texas Division*, pp. 138–49. Federal and Confederate reports on the operations in the Teche country are in *Official Records Armies*, series I, XXVI, pt. 1, pp. 332–95.

[84] On November 8 Walker's Division took up the line of march for Simmesport, passing through Evergreen and by Moreauville and continuing beyond Simmesport to the banks of the Atchafalaya. On the morning of the 12th the troops crossed the bayou on flatboats, a bridge not having been finished. The crossing was completed by sunset, and camp was made for the night near Colonel Simmes's residence opposite Simmesport. Blessington, *Walker's Texas Division*, p. 150.

[85] On September 22, 1863, 37,000 men, three divisions of the Fifteenth Corps of Grant's army, left Vicksburg for Chattanooga. Long, *Civil War Day by Day*, p. 413.

[86] On November 13 the march was continued in the direction of the Mississippi River, and the troops camped on Bayou Letsworth within four miles of the river. Cannon were installed along the bank to harass enemy ships. Several transports were fired upon, but the only vessel to suffer severe damage was *Black Hawk*, which floated down the river and burned to the waterline. Gunboats shelled the troops, but only one man was killed. Blessington, *Walker's Texas Division*, pp. 150–52.

[87] Colonel Robert T. P. Allen commanded Camp Ford, the Confederate military prison near Tyler, Texas, from November 1863 to May 15, 1864. A New York colonel regarded Allen as "conscientious" and "an educated gentleman," and most of the prisoners seem to have felt that he was strict but fair. One prisoner noted with

some sarcasm Allen's first orders to the newly arrived captives. Each regiment, he said, would be allowed the length of ground it occupied, plus 15 or 20 feet. After informing them of other camp rules he then invited them to feel perfectly at home and to make themselves as comfortable as possible.

One of the guards, Sergeant W. W. Heartsill of the W. P. Lane Rangers, who had spent some miserable months in a Federal prison, witnessed Allen carrying dried peaches, eggs, butter and other delicacies to the Yankee officers in the stockade. He remarked that "this is quite different from the treatment that our officers received at Camp Chase [Ohio]; I think it would do Col Allen good to stay a few months in [Federal] Fort Delaware."

Mrs. Allen's kindheartedness towards the prisoners earned for her their highest regard and the simple sobriquet "Mother Allen." "We all respected her; a plain, good matron — really 'a mother in Israel' to the sick or sorrowful prisoner, whoever he might be," wrote one. One of the three issues of the prisoner newspaper, *The Old Flag*, contained a flowery poetic tribute to Mrs. Allen written by a Federal officer. Augustine Joseph Hickey Duganne, *Camps and Prisons: Twenty Months in the Department of the Gulf*, 3rd ed. (New York: J. P. Robens, Publisher, 1865), pp. 408–10; W. W. Heartsill, *Fourteen Hundred and 91 Days in the Confederate Army*, ed. Bell Irvin Wiley (Jackson: McCowat-Mercer Press, 1954), p. 198; Leon Mitchell Jr., "Camp Ford: Confederate Military Prison," *Southwestern Historical Quarterly*, LXVI (July 1962), pp. 13–14; F. Lee Lawrence and Robert W. Glover, *Camp Ford C.S.A.: The Story of Union Prisoners in Texas* (Austin: Texas Civil War Centennial Advisory Committee, 1964), pp. 42–44.

After the war Colonel Allen returned to Kentucky, where he resumed his position as superintendent of the Kentucky Military Institute, 1866–1874. He drowned while swimming in the Kissimmee River, Florida, on July 9, 1888. He was 75. Wright, comp., *Texas in the War*, p. 101n; Cullum, *Biographical Register of the Officers and Graduates of the U. S. Military Academy*, I, p. 569.

[88] Walker hoped by rapid movements to carry Plaquemine by a coup de main with his own and Mouton's divisions before the enemy learned of his plan or received reinforcements, but at Lavina he received "the most exact and entirely reliable information in regard to the strength of the garrison, and the nature of the defenses." In addition an enemy spy had reported his advance to the garrison, which left no hope of a surprise. "We are still forty miles from the point to be attacked," he noted. "There is an absolute certainty that we will meet such resistance as will render the capture of Placquemine, if not impracticable, only possible at an expense of life that we cannot afford. I am fortified in this opinion by the unanimous concurrence of Brigadier General Mouton, commanding division, and his brigade commanders, and the brigade commanders of my own division." Walker's report appears in Blessington, *Walker's Texas Division*, pp. 155–56.

[89] Following the battle of Chickamauga, September 29–30, 1863, William S. Rosecrans's routed Army of the Cumberland streamed back into Chattanooga where they were invested by the victorious Confederate army. General Braxton Bragg, however, failed to exploit his enemies' demoralized condition, and by the end of the month the 35,000 Federals besieged in Chattanooga determined to "fight it out here at all hazards."

Within days the War Department pulled 20,000 men from the Army of the Potomac and 17,000 more from Sherman's army in Mississippi and sped them to the aid of their beleaguered comrades in Tennessee. Rosecrans, having been thoroughly demoralized by his severe thrashing at Chickamauga, was yet in no condition to lead his army, however reinforced, from under the Confederate guns glowering down from Lookout Mountain and Missionary Ridge, so, in mid-October, he was removed from command and replaced by General Ulysses S. Grant. By the end of October Grant had opened a supply line into the city and gained the initiative over the lethargic and outnumbered Bragg.

For most of the month of November Grant's new army gathered strength, while Bragg wasted his in fruitless operations far from the focus of the theater at Chattanooga. Then on November 24 the Federals struck out at the Southern lines, held now by a force one-half as great as their own. General "Fighting Joe" Hooker led two corps of the Army of the Potomac against the Confederate left on Lookout Mountain, while William T. Sherman threw his veterans of Vicksburg against Bragg's right on Tunnel Hill. The Union center, under George H. Thomas, was to keep a steady pressure on Missionary Ridge, the line which connected the two Confederate wings. Hooker found the going easy against lightly held Lookout, but Sherman was severely checked and bloodily repulsed at Tunnel Hill. To take pressure off of his favorite lieutenant, Grant ordered Thomas forward against the Rebel center on the morning of November 25. Hoping merely to draw Confederate strength away from Sherman, Thomas's troops not only took the row of Rebel rifle pits at the foot of Missionary Ridge as ordered, but continued up the ridge and over Bragg's artillery. The Confederate line was broken cleanly in two, its grip on Chattanooga irretrievably lost, and Braxton Bragg's military career irreparably damaged.

A gallant rearguard action by General Patrick Cleburne's division held the North at bay while the remainder of the Army of Tennessee slipped back into Georgia, but with the gateway to the Southern heartland firmly in Union hands the stage was set for the drive on Atlanta.

Ironically, all of these events had already taken place as Captain Petty, on far-off Bayou Fordouche, dreamed of aiding Bragg in bringing his siege to a successful close. So poor was the mail service between the states of the Deep South and those of the Trans-Mississippi Department that it was not until December 13 that Petty mentioned the fighting around Chattanooga to his wife, and in that instance he erroneously referred to the Confederate disaster as "Genl Bragg's great victory over Grant." Fairfax Downey, *Storming of the Gateway: Chattanooga, 1863* (New York: David McKay, Inc., 1960).

[90] Ossian was a legendary Irish hero, subject and putative author of a number of "ancient Gaelic poems" which were actually produced by Scotsman James MacPherson in the 1700's. This was one of history's most celebrated literary hoaxes. The minstrel Carryl is Ossian's brother in the cycle. "The music of the shells" in the Ossianic poems refers (as Petty surmises) not to artillery, but rather to revelry and celebration. MacPherson imagined that the ancient Celts used shell drinking vessels in their victory feasts.

[91] This was the steamer *Van Pool.* While opposite Daniels's Battery and the Sixteenth Texas Infantry, she was summoned to surrender. When her captain did not comply with the request the Confederates opened fire, killing the pilot and wounding the captain and several others. She finally made her escape, in Blessington's words, "considerably the 'worse for wear.'" The Confederates then withdrew and rejoined the command. Soon after they left three gunboats came down the river and shelled "where they supposed the rebels were." Blessington, *Walker's Texas Division,* pp. 153–54.

[92] On December 29 Surgeon Edward Cade, writing from "Camp on Bayou Des Glaise," commented unfavorably on the fortifications and on Confederate strategy in general: "Our command is engaged in throwing up quite an extensive line of earth works, though I think it labor thrown away as they are perfectly useless. In fact I have always thought it an error to keep the best portion of the army in the

Department in southern Louisiana, as the country is deserted by the inhabitants and there is nothing in it to defend while the enemy are so seriously threatening Texas from the coast and driving Price out of Arkansas. There is a council of war now being held at Alexandria composed of Generals Smith, Taylor, Price, and Walker. Some change of policy I think will be adopted. Greens Brigade of cavalry I understand is now on its way to Texas." Anderson, *A Texas Surgeon*, p. 85.

[93] On December 15 Hawes's and Randal's brigades were ordered to Marksville, there to go into winter quarters. Scurry's Brigade remained behind to protect the Atchafalaya country. They moved the following day from their camp on Bayou De Glaize, where "they took possession of some negro cabins (then vacated), making themselves perfectly at home." A company from each regiment in the brigade was sent on picket to Simmesport to protect the pontoon bridge over the Atchafalaya and to be on the lookout for the enemy. On the morning of the 23rd Scurry's men crossed the Atchafalaya and proceeded in the direction of the Mississippi, in order to capture an enemy foraging party that was playing "general havoc" along the riverbank. The Sixteenth Texas was sent in advance to ascertain their strength. On the morning of the 24th the Confederate pickets reported that the enemy had gone on board their transports during the night. The brigade soon returned to its old campground. Blessington, *Walker's Texas Division*, pp. 158–59.

[94] Most likely Petty means Richard Baxter (1615–1691), English nonconformist (Presbyterian) divine and religious writer.

[95] George Washington Jones took command of the Seventeenth Texas when Allen was assigned to Camp Ford. Major General John Forney, commanding Walker's Division, promoted Jones to colonel in Special Order No. 78, issued at Monticello, Arkansas, September 27, 1864. Major J. B. Miller was promoted to lieutenant colonel. Compiled Service Record of George Washington Jones, National Archives, Washington, D. C.

The men of the Seventeenth Texas wanted a commander easygoing enough to understand that they chafed under excessive discipline but qualified to be a capable combat leader. Certainly Jones had the physical presence for command. "Wash Jones was one of the most impressive looking men I ever saw," wrote Dr. J. B. Cranfill, who as a young man heard him give a Fourth of July address at Cistern, Texas, in 1875. "Jones was tall and angular and stately. His hair and beard were jet black and up to that time were not even sprinkled with gray. Nothing escaped his piercing black eyes." Jones, with a tin cup filled with whiskey on one side of the stand and a drinking glass of water on the other, spoke for three hours. "During that time not a man left the audience," Cranfill recalled, "and, notwithstanding the fact that many of his hearers on the outskirts were standing in the blazing sun of a hot July day, they lingered there intrigued by the spell of his matchless oratory and as many as could, when he had finished his address, rushed forward to grasp his big, strong hand." J. B. Cranfill, "Col. Wash Jones in His Palmiest Days + + + + Independence Day Oration in 1875 + + + + Dr. Cranfill Recalls Great Speaker," Houston *Chronicle*, August 7, 1927.

Frank G. Carpenter, a Washington correspondent, described Jones's arrival in the capital to take a seat in the House of Representatives as a member of the Greenback Party. "When Mr. Jones, of Texas, came to Washington he was about as raw a specimen as ever struck the town. He was the typical Westerner of the stage. He wore a woollen shirt and rawhide boots, and he showed not a sign of a collar or cuff. His red cotton handkerchief was often in evidence, as it still is today." Jones lived in a second-class boardinghouse, and these surroundings, together with his long silence at the first of the session, created the impression that he was a nonentity.

However, according to Carpenter, "one day an exciting political discussion arose in the House and to the surprise of everyone, Mr. Jones took the floor. He made a most eloquent speech, commanding the applause and attention of both Republicans and Democrats. It was full of good sense and possessed a certain quaint, old-fashioned humor that took the House by storm. Since that occasion, Mr. Jones has had a different status. His Washington experience has improved him. He now dresses like a civilized citizen and has lost much of his Western roughness. It is not every man who is improved by his experience in Congress." Frank G. Carpenter, *Carp's Washington*, arr. and ed. Frances Carpenter, intro. Cleveland Amory (New York: McGraw-Hill Book Company, Inc., 1960), pp. 23–24.

[96] The shouting of "Christmas Gift!" to friends and family (and especially by Negroes to their masters) is an old plantation custom. The first to shout this greeting to another on Christmas morning is thereby entitled to some trifling present. The custom is still often observed in the rural South, although the giving of the gift is now more honored in the breach than in the observance. Calvin S. Brown, *A Glossary of Faulkner's South* (New Haven: The Yale University Press, 1976), p. 52.

[97] Compare Robert Burns, *Tam O'Shanter*:

"Pleasure are like poppies spread,
You seize the flow'r, its bloom is shed."

[98] William Shakespeare, in *Measure for Measure*, II:2.

[99] Sarah Olivia Pinner, Margaret Pinner Petty's youngest sister.

[100] On December 8, 1863, Lincoln issued his Proclamation of Amnesty and Reconstruction, pardoning those who "directly or by implication, participated in the existing rebellion" if they took an oath to the Union. Exceptions included high-ranking military officers, members of the Confederate government, all who resigned commissions in the United States Army and Navy to join the Confederacy, and those who treated Negroes or whites "otherwise than lawfully as prisoners of war." If at least one-tenth of the citizens who voted in the election of 1860 so wished, a state government would be recognized in any seceded state, provided those citizens took an oath to support the United States and barred slavery. Long, *Civil War Day by Day*, p. 444.

[101] William Shakespeare (?), "The Passionate Pilgrim," canto xiii.

[102] A Louisiana Confederate, Felix Pierre Poché, in camp near Monroe, Louisiana, also recorded in his diary on January 23, 1864, the rumor that Bragg was coming to take command from Kirby Smith and was expected shortly. "The lax discipline of this department will be improved by Genl Bragg's presence and authority," Poché commented approvingly. Edwin C. Bearss, ed., *A Louisiana Confederate: Diary of Felix Pierre Poché*, trans. from the French by Eugenie Watson Somdal (Natchitoches: Louisiana Studies Institute, Northwestern State University, 1972), p. 76 (hereafter cited as Bearss, ed., *A Louisiana Confederate*).

There was no truth to this rumor, however. Bragg had stepped down as commander of the Army of Tennessee on December 1, 1863, but was reassigned to duty in Richmond as military advisor to President Davis.

[103] These lines are from John Milton, *Comus*, 1. 453:

So dear to heav'n is saintly chastity,
That when a soul is found sincerely so,
A thousand liveried angels lackey her,

Driving far off each thing of sin and guilt,
And in clear dream and solemn vision,
Tell her of things that no gross ear can hear,
Till oft converse with heav'nly habitants
Begin to cast a beam on th' outward shape.

[104] A native of Massachusetts, Edwin T. Merrick practiced law in Ohio and Iowa before settling in New Orleans. He was admitted to the Louisiana bar in 1839 and rapidly acquired a large practice and recognition throughout the state. In 1840 he married Caroline E. Thomas, the daughter of Captain David Thomas of Jackson, Louisiana, and they had four children — two daughters and two sons. In 1845 Merrick was elected judge of the Seventh District, and in 1846 the Whigs nominated him for justice of the state supreme court, to which position he was elected by a large majority. Though opposed to secession, Merrick believed that the people had a right to secede and stood with them when Louisiana left the Union. During the war he lived with his family on his plantation at Pointe Coupee, occupied with his duties as chief justice. In 1863 he was reelected and in 1865 returned to New Orleans to live. His property had been seized by the Federal authorities, but he succeeded in recovering it. In 1871 he published a brilliant treatise on the "Laws of Louisiana and their Sources." He died at his home in New Orleans, January 2, 1897. Alcée Fortier, ed., *Louisiana: Comprising Sketches of Parishes, Towns, Events, Institutions, and Persons, Arranged in Cyclopedic Form*, 3 vols. ([Madison:] Century Historical Association, 1914), II, pp. 145–46.

[105] When Bishop August Martin of Natchitoches went to France in 1854 to get missionaries for his diocese, he also made arrangements for a few nuns of the Order of Daughters of the Cross to come later. In a letter to them before their coming he said: "Your mission here will be such as becomes the holy state of the Daughters of the Cross. Grand and beautiful indeed is the task which falls to your lot — to be the first Religious Community to offer the blessings of Christian education to young girls living in ignorance as their mothers have been for 150 years, since the first Europeans came to settle among the Indian tribes of Avoyelles. The field of your labors is as large as the largest diocese in France. It is encircled by the Mississippi, the Red, and the Atchafalaya Rivers."

Ten Sisters were sent from Treguier, France, to form the American Foundation of the Daughters of the Cross. Mother Mary Hyacinthe Le Conniat was elected first Superior. They left France on October 24, 1855, and after a rough sea voyage arrived in New York City on November 6. From New York they traveled by train to St. Louis and there took a boat to New Orleans. After a day or so in the city they took a boat up the Mississippi and Red Rivers, landing five miles from their destination. Father Hyacinth Tumoine, rector of the Hydropolis church, met them with four carriages. Since both Marksville and Mansura had wanted the convent, it was decided to put it between the two towns, a mile from Marksville, in the village of Hydropolis (now Cocoville). On November 28 the contract was completed, and Bishop Martin confirmed the selection. Thus the Convent of the Presentation was founded. The buildings consisted of a dilapidated one-story house, a small brick building and a few Negro cabins.

In the early days of the convent the following notice appeared in the local paper, the *Avoyelles News*: "Convent of the Presentation — A Young Ladies' Academy Conducted by the Daughters of the Cross. This newly established institution is situated on a healthy, elevated prairie at Hydropolis, in the parish of Avoyelles, near the state road from the Mississippi River to Alexandria and Texas, five miles from Gorton's Landing on Red River.

"The plan for the Institution is that it combines with valuable benefits of a

Catholic Christian education every advantage that can be derived from a punctual and conscientious care bestowed on the pupils in every brand of science suitable to the sex. The most painstaking attention is given to the pupils in the pursuit of their studies. The health of the pupils is an object of the most anxious solicitude.

"The general course of instruction embraces the English, and the French languages, Orthography, Reading, Writing, Grammar, Rhetoric, Arithmetic, the elements of Geometry, Bookkeeping, Sacred and Profane, Ancient and Modern History, Geography, the elements of Astronomy, Natural Philosophy, as well as Music, Drawing, Painting, Embroidery, Sewing, Tapestry, Lace Work, and Artificial Flower Work.

"Young ladies who are not Catholic are admitted on condition they conform exteriorly to the religious exercises prescribed for the pupils.

"The classes begin every year on the first Monday in November, and finish on the fifteenth day of September. (Custom in France.)

"Terms:

Board and Tuition per year	$140.00
Bed and Bedding per year	24.00
Music Lesson with use of instruments	60.00
Vocal Music per year	20.00
Laundry	12.00
Half-Boarders who study and dine at Convent	60.00
Day pupils per year	40.00"

There were not many pupils the first year, but gradually people learned of the school and sent their daughters. The attendance at the end of the second year was 45 boarders, besides the day students. The school was flourishing when the Civil War began. Mrs. Henry Gaines described the Convent as follows: "There were two buildings several hundred yards from each other connected by an elevated walk. Halfway between the two was the chapel, where they heard mass each morning. The rear entrance to the chapel was on the platform, or walk, so that the girls always entered from the rear to keep from getting their feet wet. The front entrance of the chapel was used by the town people, or anyone else who wished to attend services." Corinne L. Saucier, *History of Avoyelles Parish, Louisiana* (New Orleans:

Pelican Publishing Company, 1943), pp. 64–67. See also, Sister Dorothea Olga McCants, Daughter of the Cross, ed., *They Came to Louisiana: Letters of a Catholic Mission, 1854–1882* (Baton Rouge: Louisiana State University Press, 1970).

[106] Fort De Russy was situated three miles from Marksville, on the Red River. The garrison was composed of detached companies, one from each regiment in Walker's Division, numbering about 400 men, and was under the command of Lieutenant Colonel William Byrd. Blessington, *Walker's Texas Division*, p. 174.

[107] George Payn Quackenbos, *Advanced Course of Composition and Rhetoric; a Series of Practical Lessons on the Origin, History, and Peculiarities of the English Language . . . Adopted to Self-Instruction, and the Use of Schools and Colleges* (New York: D. Appleton and Company, 1855).

[108] First Lieutenant M. M. Denson of Captain C. L. Marshall's Company D, Nineteenth Texas Infantry (Waterhouse's Regiment). He enlisted in Davis [Cass] County on March 30, 1862, for three years of the war. Confederate Index, Texas State Archives, Austin, Texas.

[109] Captain A. C. Allen, Company C, Nineteenth Texas Infantry. Blessington, *Walker's Texas Division*, p. 58.

[110] Trade with the enemy was frowned upon from time to time and was forbidden by both sides. When the Confederates were hard pressed for supplies trade regulations were often relaxed. "I am glad you are increasing the amount of supplies introduced into your district in exchange for cotton," Kirby Smith wrote Taylor on January 15, 1864. "It should be extended so as to meet the wants not only of your district, but, if practicable, the other portions of the department. The interruption of the Rio Grande trades makes the introduction of supplies through the enemy's lines the <u>sine qua non</u>." The United States Treasury Department strongly endorsed trade in occupied areas, especially in cotton. In September 1863 the Mississippi River was completely open to trade "subject only to such limitations as may be necessary to prevent the supply of provisions and munitions of war to the enemies of the Country." Cotton or other products could be brought to military posts along the Mississippi "without restraint." "Poorly paid treasury agents could be bribed to issue trade permits for

almost any item anywhere in Louisiana, and they sometimes accompanied speculators outside the lines to lend an air of validity to the illicit trade," wrote John Winters. "Even the military winked at certain violations. Cotton poured into New Orleans from all parts of the state. From March to the first of November 30,500 bales were shipped north from New Orleans, and some 8,000 bales awaited shipment." E. Kirby Smith to Richard Taylor, January 15, 1864, *Official Records Armies*, series I, XXXIV, pt. 2, p. 871; Winters, *Civil War in Louisiana*, pp. 308–9.

J. P. Blessington wrote that while Walker's Division was camped on the Atchafalaya during December 1863, orders were read to the troops at dress parade forbidding anyone to cross the river without permission from district headquarters. "If this caution had prevailed from the commencement," he explained, "it would have kept out the Yankee spies, who were acting in the garb of cotton buyers, and at the same time gathering all the information necessary for the enemy to profit by." Meetings were held among the men protesting the cotton-buying scheme as an act of treason to the honest and patriotic people of the South. "Many of our men that were taken prisoners at Pleasant Hill, afterwards recognized some of the said cotton-buyers acting in the capacity of staff officers to General Banks, the Federal commander." The troops were assured that no more cotton would be sold to the enemy. Yet the following February, when Felix Pierre Poché visited General Scurry and his staff in Eugene Oubre's house (the brigade was camped on the Norwood plantation), he noted disapprovingly: "The General and his staff are well provided, not only with the necessities, but with all the delicacies of the New Orleans market. They even have coal oil lamps, which are one of the principal profits of the speculators in the large trade in cotton with the enemy, and our Brigade [Gray's] composed of natives of the soil and in part the true producers of this cotton who are at this moment almost naked, gains nothing from that tremendous commerce." Blessington, *Walker's Texas Division*, p. 162; Bearss, ed., *A Louisiana Confederate*, p. 89.

[111] Thos. Jefferson Pinner, M.D., Margaret's brother.

[112] Hamilcar Barca was a Carthaginian officer who in 247 B.C. was given the chief command in Sicily during the First Punic War between Carthage and Rome. He seized in succession two natural strongholds, Mt. Hercte near Panormus, and Mt. Eryz by Drepana, from which he conducted a successful guerrilla war against the Romans. At the conclusion of the war in 241 he brought his mercenaries back to Africa to be paid off, only to have them break into open mutiny in a quarrel over their wages. In 238 he was given the chief command and completely restored Carthaginian sovereignty in Africa. He then obtained a commission to extend the Punic dominions to Spain, by way of compensation for the territory lost to the Romans. In the remaining nine years of his life he laid the foundations of a Punic empire, which his son-in-law Hasrubal and his son Hannibal extended to the Ebro and the Sierra de Toledo. After Carthage was defeated by Rome in the Second Punic War, Hannibal left his native land and went to the court of Antiochus. According to the historian Polybius, in order to prove that there was nothing he would not do against the Romans, Hannibal told the king the following story: "He said that at the time when his father was about to start with his army on his expedition to Spain, he himself, then nine years of age, was standing by the altar, while Hamilcar was sacrificing to Zeus. When, on the omens being favourable, Hamilcar had poured a libation to the gods and performed all the customary rites, he ordered the others who were attending the sacrifice to withdraw to a slight distance and calling Hannibal to him asked him kindly if he wished to accompany him on the expedition. On his accepting with delight, and, like a boy, even begging to do it besides, his father took him by the hand, led him up to the altar, and bade him lay

his hand on the victim and swear never to be the friend of the Romans." Polybius, *The Histories*, Book III. 11.3.

[113] On February 11, 1864, Brigadier General James Hawes was relieved from command of the First Brigade at his request and ordered to report to Magruder in Texas for assignment to duty. On February 16 Taylor asked Kirby Smith to retain Hawes in command of the First Brigade. "I have just made a minute inspection of Hawes' and Randal's brigades of this division, and have never seen any troops in finer condition," he stated. "No troops ever exhibited greater improvement in all the qualities of soldiers, and their present condition reflects great credit on the division and brigade commanders. . . . General Hawes' brigade is in splendid order. A change would be very unfortunate." However, the order was not rescinded, and Hawes, after reporting to Magruder, was placed in charge of the troops and fortifications on Galveston Island, Texas. Thomas N. Waul (late of Waul's Texas Legion) was relieved from duty in Texas and given command of the First Brigade. He had surrendered with his Legion at Vicksburg and was promoted after his exchange to brigadier general to rank from September 18, 1863. Special Orders No. 34, February 11, 1864, *Official Records Armies*, series I, XXXIV, pt. 2, p. 961; Richard Taylor to William R. Boggs, February 16, 1864, *ibid.*, p.971; Blessington, *Walker's Texas Division*, pp. 164–65; Warner, *Generals in Gray*, pp. 328–29; "General Thomas N. Waul," *Confederate Veteran*, III (December 1895), p. 380.

[114] On January 9, 1864, President Davis warned his commanders in Alabama, Georgia and Mississippi of reports that Admiral David Farragut was preparing to pass the forts at Mobile as he had at New Orleans in April 1862. On January 20 Federal vessels made a reconnaissance of Forts Morgan and Gaines at the mouth of Mobile Bay. Some minor Federal probings and ship-and-shore operations, including bombardment of Fort Powell, took place until late March around Mobile, aggravating the Confederate fear of an attack. Long, *Civil War Day by Day*, pp. 454, 456, 464–65.

[115] Meridian, Mississippi, represented the seat of Confederate military power in the state. Lieutenant General Leonidas Polk had his headquarters there, and the city served as the hub of Confederate efforts to supply their forces in western Mississippi. William T. Sherman decided to strike eastward through Jackson to Meridian. He sought to isolate Mississippi, prevent supply efforts westward and break the only railroad connection between the state and the East. General William Sooy Smith was to strike south from Memphis with 7,000 cavalry along the Mobile & Ohio Railroad and link up with Sherman at Meridian. After some skirmishing en route Sherman's 25,000 men entered Meridian on February 14–15, 1864. For five days they destroyed roads, bridges and railroad tracks in the area. Not hearing from Smith, Sherman withdrew his force on February 20 to Canton, Mississippi, and thence to Vicksburg. Smith was late starting south and was routed by General Nathan Bedford Forrest at West Point, Mississippi, on February 21, 1864. John G. Fowler Jr., "Meridian Campaign," in Roller and Twyman, eds., *Encyclopedia of Southern History*, p. 813.

Taylor had informed Walker on February 8 that Sherman had reached Vicksburg with some 12,000 men. "My opinion is that Sherman will move east from Vicksburg and attempt to reach the Mobile and Ohio Railroad and the Tombigbee River," he stated. "This would have an important influence on the Georgia campaign. Connected with this movement Banks may threaten Mobile, but I do not believe he will subordinate his plans to Grant's if he can avoid it." On March 1 Scurry, at Norwood's plantation, sent Walker a pencilled note concerning the various rumors coming from New Orleans and Mississippi relating to Sherman's movements:

> From Confederates I learn that [Leonidas] Polk was crossing the Tombigbee and moving in the direction of Selma, at which point he would be strongly re-enforced by [Joseph E.] Johnston; that a column had moved out of Mobile and was at State Line. . . . If Sherman advances upon Mobile, Polk moves upon his rear while the Mobile troops engage him in front. If he follows Polk to Selma the thing will be done in the same way . . . by inversion. . . . It is well known that the Federal officers regard him as being in a perilous position, in which he must either capture Mobile immediately or lose his army.

Of course, none of this came to pass. Richard Taylor to John G. Walker, February 8, 1864, *Official Records Armies*, series I, XXXIV, pt. 2, pp. 950–51; William R. Scurry to Walker, March 1, 1864, *ibid.*, pp. 1016–17.

[116] Lieutenant Colonel William H. Redwood, Sixteenth Texas Infantry Regiment. Wright, comp., *Texas in the War*, p. 21.

[117] Captain C. L. Marshall commanded Company D, Nineteenth Texas Infantry Regiment. Confederate Index, Texas State Archives, Austin, Texas.

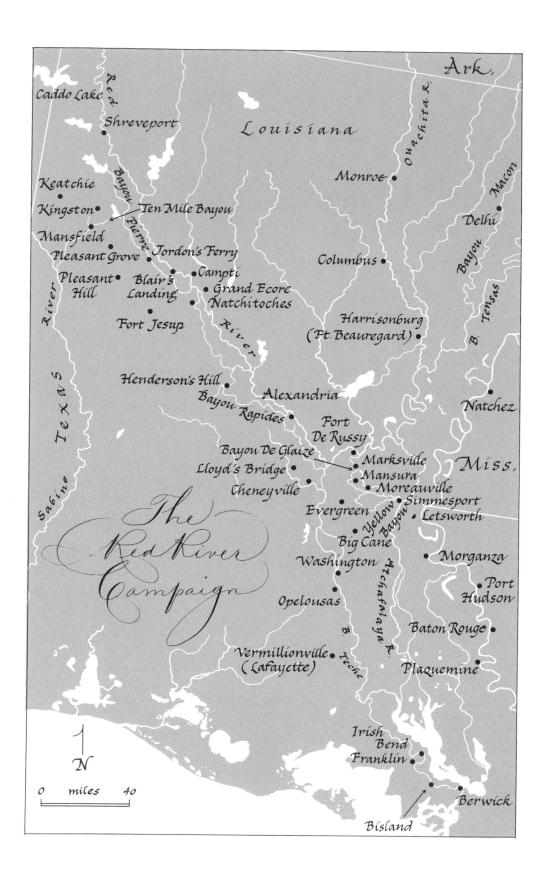

CHAPTER FOUR

The Red River Campaign

THE RED RIVER CAMPAIGN of 1864 represented Federal efforts to acquire cotton, to stimulate Texas Unionism, to disrupt the Confederate trade with Mexico and to protect against French activities in that country. On January 4 General Henry Halleck, Lincoln's military advisor and General-in-Chief, wrote Nathaniel Banks: "Generals Sherman and Steele agreed with me in opinion that the Red River is the shortest and best line of defense for Louisiana and Arkansas and as a base of operations against Texas." Halleck ordered Banks to "operate in that direction" as soon as there was "sufficient water in the Atchafalaya and Red Rivers." Steele's army at Little Rock, some of Sherman's men in Mississippi and Porter's gunboats would join Banks in the enterprise. Banks had strongly objected to using this route, but the General-in-Chief reassured him on January 11: "The best military opinions of the generals in the West seem to favor operations on Red River, provided the stage of water will enable the gun-boats to co-operate."

Although Banks wished to join Sherman and Farragut in a move against Mobile, he bowed to Halleck's decision. The desire for cotton played no small part in Banks's decision as did his ambition to be the Republican nominee for president in 1864. On March 1 Sherman traveled down from Vicksburg to confer with Banks in New Orleans and promised to send 10,000 of his best men along with Porter's fleet to him at Alexandria on March 17. He stipulated, however, that these troops must be taken no farther than Shreveport and must be returned to him by about April 15. It was understood that Steele would move from Little Rock to join Banks near Shreveport.[1]

   In addition to being Kirby Smith's military headquarters, Shreveport was the heart of a military-industrial complex that extended west to Marshall, Texas, and northwest to Jefferson, Texas, 50 miles from Shreveport to which it was linked by steamer through Cypress Bayou and Caddo Lake. There were large stores of arms, ammunition and other war materials at both Shreveport and Jefferson, and several arsenals also existed at both places. The steam ram *Missouri*, the only ironclad warship which the Confederates west of the Mississippi ever attempted to construct, was perched on the ways in a Shreveport shipyard, still awaiting her armor. Slightly more than 100 miles west of Shreveport was Tyler, Texas, site of an ordnance plant and of Camp Ford, a Federal prisoner-of-war camp. East Texas was a vital granary, and an estimated 150,000 cotton bales were scattered along or near the Red River's banks. In sum, Shreveport with its surrounding region was an important prize for the Federals.[2]

Bayou De Glaize La
March 3. 1864

My Dear Frank

I have concluded to write you a few lines to night although I have nothing of any interest to communicate. I started by the last mail letters to Ma, Ella, Van & Don and reserved this for you. I stated to them that we had received marching orders. The reason of the orders was that some five or more gun boats had gone up Red River in the direction of Fort DeRussy and it was thought that an attack was intended. The boats however proceeded up Black River and on the evening of the 1st inst and morning of the 2d inst verry heavy cannonading was heard in that direction which was supposed to be at Fort Beauregard which is at Harrisonburg on Washita River. We can tell nothing about it.[3] I learn that two transports proceeded up RR to day without troops however. I expect it is a thieving expedition and that the Transports have gone up after cotton which they will steal.

Before I send this away I may find out — The gun boats are still figuring in Red River. I can hear occasional firing in that direction but what at and what for I cannot yet learn. The gun boats are also in Rackasel Bend of the Miss river and occasionly fire on our pickets over [there]. We sent a raid over there two days ago to prevent them stealing some government sugar & molasses. We had to knock the heads out of 150 barrels of splendid molasses to keep them from getting it. They occasionally land and steal cotton, molasses, sugar and burn houses & sugar mills. You can form no idea of the state of the country on the border where both parties have access to it — both destroy and steal and the citizens are between the frying pan & the fire as the saying is.

I understand that the feds are sending a large force up the Teche from Berwick's Bay. If so we will have to skedaddle from here or they will be in our rear. Then our works here will be of no service. We are still under marching orders — i e we are ordered to hold ourselves ready to move at a moments notice — and our work on the fortifications have been suspended. I am afraid that all our work here will come to naught and I am now rather of an opinion that we may have some work to do on this side of the river. I see that Genl Sherman's expedition through Miss towards Mobile has returned and it may be that they will give us a visit. I cant tell much about things yet as all is rumor in these Camps. I will keep you posted as well as I can. There is no other news of interest. I am in fine health and we are all living tolerable well. Rations of good meat is short — We are living on pickled beef mostly which is shipped to us from Jefferson Texas and have to subsist on ¾ lb per day — Our fresh beef is too poor to eat. ¾ lb with bone & salt is rather short rations for laboring men — Well my boy how do you get on at school. Are you learning fast? Are you availing yourself of the oppertunity now given to get an education? I hope so as the time may come when you will no longer have such a chance. I want you too to try and learn Don and Van to spell and read. Dont keep all you know to yourself. Learning does no good unless a person shows it to others and uses it to advantage. What good would your learning do you if you did not use it to advantage and if you locked it up in your own mind? None. Thus learn all you can yourself and learn your little brothers all you [know.] Be kind and good and patient with them — If they cant understand a thing at once remember that their minds are young & feeble — that yours was once that way and that you had to learn slowly. Give my love and respects to all.

Yours truly
E. P. Petty

P.S.
Cant you write yet?

March 5 1864

My Dear Wife

Yours per Walt Farmer with shirts was received. Thank you. Thank you again. The domestic shirts are coarse but I am glad to get them and will wear them with pleasure. The Nankeen shirt is fine. Thank you. Thank you again. You told me to wear it to see the ladies. That very day I concluded that I would do so and christened it accordingly by wearing it to a [storm?] or surprise party and dance in Bayou De Glaize Bend. I danced all night and had what I call a good time but amidst all my pleasure and gaiety my thoughts are ever running back to home and to thee.

> "My thoughts are happier oft than I"
> "For they are ever love with thee"
> "And thine I know as frequent fly"
> "O're all that severs us to me"
> "Like rays of stars that meet in space"
> "And mingle in a bright embrace"

At your earnest request I have stopped fattening — I cant get over 150 lbs. and am now under it. I fluctuate according as the beer barrell now holds out from 145 to 150 lbs. Walt Farmer told me how hard you were to find at home but he could'nt give me the cause of your absence — I suppose it's all right and I wont question you on the point. Farmer & Morris were over their time 8 days. They were Court martialed and Farmer sentenced to 6 days extra fatigue and Morris to 15 days extra fatigue. We are putting them through now when they are over their time as they keep others from home. I send you by John Wilson some old shirts and some old socks. The shirts will do for the children, the socks some of them will do to heel and toe for me and the other you can dispose of as you like. I showed Jones your letter with reference to his wife and negros trouble. I know that you must get more letters than any body for none write so much or so often as I do. My chiefest pleasure is in writing to you. All are well. Love, kisses and respects to all. News in Frank's letter.

Yours truly
E. P. Petty

March 7th 1864

Dear Wife

I have just learned that the federal expedition against Fort Beauregard proved a failure. That Genl Polignac held the places and repelled 3 efforts to land by them, that his loss was 3 killed & 11 wounded — The federal loss and damage not known. I regard this as reliable. Hurrah for Texas again. I have no other news. The amount of molasses destroyed by our party on Old river was about 300 barrels which belonged to the federals as I now learn instead of to our people — The beer barrell is full to day and my clothes fit me rather tightly now. We brew beer for use instead of water as our water is getting rather bad. Charming health today. My paper & envellops are exhausted. I wish you would send me a good supply from your old blank books. Paper is 12 dollars per quire and envellops 5 dollars per pack here now and scarce at that. We will start a lot of fellows home on furlough in a day or two.

E. P. Petty

Bayou De Glaize La
March 10 1864

My Dear Wife

I have no news to write of interest. The feds have gone back out of Red River after having been repulsed at Fort Beauregard. The last news from them there were 12 gun boats at the Mouth of Red River. The river is now getting low and I hardly think they will try it again until the waters rise. The waters are still receding. We have stopped work on our fortifications here and the spades etc have all been sent to Fort De Russy so as to complete the works there.[4] It has been raining all day and it is quite muddy. We have had a beautiful spring up to this time and it is not cold now but wet and muddy. We are drilling nearly every day. We want to drill for a new flag as ours is worn out. There is some considerable planting on this Bayou but not enough I am afraid to subsist an army. We are now living on corn bread and pickled beef.

The beef comes from Jefferson Texas and is good. We get also sugar and molasses. These are becomeing scarce and high. We use the most of our sugar and molasses in making beer. It is fine and I hardly ever drink any water now. I weighed to day 151½ pounds. This is the effects of the beer. I hav'nt been out to see the girls this week. As we are under marching orders I do not think it prudent to leave Camp although it is a sore tribulation to me for there are so many nice ladies here who look as though they "had been fed on roses sopped in silver dew" that I can hardly content myself away from them. The boys are generally well. Nobody in the Regt much sick. We have no deaths now hav'nt had over 3 in over 4 months. We are Veteran Soldiers now. Col Jones is in fine health and loves to play cards as much as ever. Tell those who may enquire that we are all well. There is a great deal of dissatisfaction in the army here growing out of the cotton trade. I am afraid it will ruin our army and demoralize the citizens. I am seriously alarmed about it. This is inter nos (between us). Love, kisses etc to the children.

Yours truly
E. P. Petty

La Near Carroll Jones
Mar 17 1864

My Dear Wife

I wrote you a hasty note a few days ago but could not send it. I have therefore concluded now to write more at lenght and not send the other. On last Saturday the 12th inst 54 gun boats and transports entered Red River with felonious intent up[on] us Confeds. 28 of the number entered the Atchafalaya and about 1 Oclock landed at Simmesport. The ballance went up R R to Ft De Russy. On that night I was at Ft D R and stayed with Capt Mabry. Sometime in the night a courier bearing the news reached there and at day light on Sunday the 13 Capt M was sent into the rifle pits 2 miles below the fort — I started immediately & without breakfast to my command. I met our Brigade on the retreat before a verry large and superior force.[5] I met them 12 miles above our old Camp on Bayou De Glaize. I learned from them that about 2 Oclock Saturday they were ordered down towards the Atchafalaya, that they moved down immediately and below our fortifications when they met our Battalion of pickets retreating from Simmesport. They all fell back to our works where they remained until near dark when they retreated to the place where I had met them getting there about 2 oclock at night making about 18 miles which they had travelled that evening. All our tents were abandoned, all the cooking utensils of Co's B (Capt Nash), Co D (Capt [A.J.] Ridge) and Co H (Capt McDowell) with the books & papers of some other Companies besides a good deal of loose stuff generally. After getting to Camp that night several wagons were sent back after the articles left as above stated. The feds having reached our Brigade Hd Quarters before the wagons etc gave chase to Capt [Allen F.] Flowers, Lt Cunningham & others who were then on the look out, ran them pretty clean for 6 miles. They escaped into the swamp & got off clean. The wagons & wagoners were not so fortunate. They got 2 wagons from our Regt, 1 from Fitzhugh's and 1 from Flournoy's. They captured also Ben A Brundige who used to live in the River Bend above Bastrop, Jim Harris wagoner of our Regt with Walt Jones & Wash Fellows of Capt Nash's Company and Perry of Co D with some others from the other Regts. The command from where I met it on Sunday morning then fell back across Bayou De Glaize and took position about 12 Oclock on the Magnolia Hills burning 2 bridges behind us. We remained there in line of battle or ready to be formed so until Monday morning about 9 Oclock. We heard the feds beat reveille and heard them beating their drums of the march — about 8 oclock we heard picket firing in front and the Shout of battle. We fired 3 cannons and then fell back about a mile in the prarie at Mansura and formed line of battle.⁶ Genls Hawes & Randle's commands having joined us here we remained about an hour. It was a grand and magnificent sight to see our troops filing into line of battle on an open prarie. It was cool, the sun shone brightly and guns & bayonets glistened. Men were cheerful and merry. We then heard big guns & the direction of Ft DeR — Saw the smoke of several boats in that direction. We fell back towards Cheneyville leaving the fort to our right about 8 miles. At about 12 miles crossed the Bayou De [Du] Lac at its junction with Pearl Lake. However as we were about leaving the prarie about 5 mile from Bayou DeL. the fed cavalry came up with our rear and we had some little skirmishing. The only damage on our side being 1 horse wounded slightly. About 3 oclock the thunder commenced in earnest at Ft De Russy and continued until about 5 oclock without much intermission. The fort was surrounded by land and an attack from both sides went on and at 5 oclock the garrison surrendered Capt Mabry & Company I suppose included — Lt Col Bird [Byrd] commanding at the fort was killed as well as I can learn. There were besides Col Bird a Lt and 6 privates killed. What damage was done to the feds I have not been able to learn. About 60 men who were in the water batteries escaped. About 300 I suppose were captured. Thus fort De Russy at its garrison went up on Monday Mar 14th 1864 at 5 oclock P.M. — at AM o'clock [midnight?] Monday night we began our grand skedaddle again and by 2 oclock Tuesday evening were about 5 miles above Cheneyville on Bayou Boeuf.[7] Here we stopped for dinner and rest. At sun down we started again and went about 8 miles where we rested until 3 oclock that night when we started and by Wednesday 4 oclock had travelled about 30 miles to a point above Hinestone on the Colcassiu [Calcasieu] in the Piney Woods. Here we rested all night and to day we have marched to this place (20 miles) which is near Carroll Jones on the Alexandra & Burr's ferry road about 35 miles above Alexandra and about 7 or 8 miles from Bayou Rapides and about 40 or 50 from Natchitoches where we will remain as I learn 2 or 3 days. We have as you will see travelled day and night for 5 days & nights and we have had an average of about 1 good meal per day. The men are weary and foot sore, broke down and jaded. Even the horses have fagged under it. After the feds took the fort they rushed their boats etc to Alexandra and took possession of the place. This threw them above us and hence we had to march so hard and take to the piney woods. They were also sending a large force up Bayou Teche from Berwicks Bay to cut us off so you see that if we had'nt been Walkers gray hounds we would have been now federal prison[er]s perhaps. The following is the best estimate that I can get at their numbers — Genl Sherman's Core [Corps] on Red River 25000 and Genl Franklin on the Teche 12000[8] — To meet these forces we had about 7000 all told if we could have got them united. We will now I suppose as we have got above them and out of danger of being captured contest the country falling back towards Natchitoches & Shreveport — Genl Green is coming to us from Texas.[9] Genls Fagan and Tappan I learn from Arkansas[10] so that we will have some 15000 or more men. With these we must fight — We can't run always & give up all the Country. I am quite well except my feet — they bruised and sore & road foundered. I think that the fatigue etc of the trip has made me fall off and that I am not so fat as I was. I think that you will hear stirring news from these parts soon. Dont be uneasy about me. It will do no good to be so. If I am to die for my Country I hope it will be in a blaze of glory that will shine upon my wife & children. I will try and take care of myself. I have no news further than I have [written]. All my nice associations etc on the Atchafalaya & Bayou De Glaize have been broken up. This hurts me worse than the march and the sore feet. It is getting so dark I cant see how to write. We go on picket soon in the morning. Our Brigade is in front & our Regt will be in front of that. "The post of danger is the post on [of] honor" & we Court it. Give much love and many kisses to my darling little ones. I will write again when I can. The muss has broken into our mail arrangements. God bless you all.

Yours truly
E. P. Petty

Piney Woods La March 19 1864

My Dear Wife

On the 17th inst I started you a letter of 8 pages by mail giving you a full and correct narration of the federal advance upon us at Yellow Bayou and at Ft De Russy and on our grand skedaddle to this place. That letter I hope you will get in due time. Now I will continue the tale to this evening with such items as I may have enabled to gather. Since the 17th inst we have been stationary here — Our troops are getting over their heavy march — My feet are getting over their soreness and I am not quite as stiff with a bad shoulder as I was. I am about ready to fight or run as the occasion may require and so I believe is the whole command. I believe all are cheerful and willing to fight if they can get a half a chance. All our troops are now in a few miles of each other so as to reinforce if attacked at any time. Scurry's Brigade as usual occupy the extreme front of the infantry. We have some Cavalry in front of us who now picket to within about 5 miles of Alexandra — We are about 2 miles in front of the nearest infantry camped in order of battle with all our baggage, wagons, sick etc sent 18 miles to the rear. We send out 1 regiment every day to picket for us 1 or 2 miles to the front. They in turn send out a company or more to from ¼ to ½ mile in their front and they in turn send out videtts to their front so you see that we picket and guard pretty well. Our Regt was out yesterday & last night and returned to camp this morning. Our future movements I presume will depend on those of the enemy. They are in heavy force at Alexandra. Supposed to be over 20000 strong. They have there 6 gun boats and 37 transports — Besides this force Genl Franklin has in the neighborhood of Opelousas an estimated force of 6000 men. If they advance with these forces we of necessity must retire until reinforced. If they retreat we will perhaps dog after them and try and bite their heels. From what I can learn they are ravaging Alexandra with an unsparing hand. Considerable farming was going on here in La by now. This will be broken up. The people have fled with every thing possible. The ballance they will steal. They have considerable negro force with them. Some 60 or more escaped from Ft De Russy. Capt Mabry no doubt was captured and now is a prisoner with the most of his Company. We are living pretty hard right now on poor beef and corn bread not being able for the present to do any better. I hope a better day will come soon. Our Regt has 15000 lbs of bacon above Natchitoches if we can get to it or it to us. I cant for the present form an opinion as to whether the feds intend to advance or not. I will have to wait events with patience. We have foraging and meal grinding parties 15 miles to our front under heavy guard to protect them. They are bringing out considerable corn etc. They boys are generally well. Some 5 or 6 of my company went to the rear with the wagons viz Tom Adkins, Bunt Dabney, Sid Person, Cox. I believe these are all. I can give you no other news now — Oh Tom McDonald also went to the rear. Still has the chills & fever — I cant get him off home yet. Rest easy about me. The Lords will not thine nor mine be done. I am in fine health though having fallen off a few pounds on this trip. I only weigh to day 146 pounds. I am in splendid trim for any thing fighting or running. Kiss my children for me God bless them. Tell them to always think of their poor ol daddy in his trials & tribulations for his country. That he is ever thinking of you & them. I wear your ambrotype next my heart. May it shield & protect it against the machinations and evils of my enemies as it has ever from the evils of passion etc. Write often. God bless you.

Yours truly
E. P. Petty

Camp 22 Miles from Natchitoches
La March 24 1864

My Dear Daughter

We have had another grand run since I wrote to your Ma on the 19th inst. The 21st inst being equinoxical day it was as it generally stormy and rainy and quite cold. We were without tents in the piney woods about 35 miles above Alexandra. The boys stretched blankets etc. and made out the best way possible though I dont think that we have ever spent as uncomfortable a time in the service. We had to build pine knot fires and such another smoked set of creatures you have never seen. I know that the Yanks would have thought that we were fighting negroes against them if a battle had come off. About 3 oclock on that evening we heard a heavy cannonade about 10 miles in our front which continued until about 4 or 4½ o clock pretty rapid and regular. This proved to be a fight between Edgar's Battery (Confed) and a force of Yankee Cavalry making a reconnaisance. Some of our Louisiana Cavalry was also engaged in it. I dont know the casualities of the skirmish.[11] Two of the Yankees rode up to one of our men and endeavoured to capture him. He knocked one off his horse with his gun and shot the other, put spurs to his horse and ran off. While running off he was shot two or three times (by the man whom he had knocked off his horse) with a six shooter but succeeded in getting away and I suppose is not dangerously wounded. The night of the 21 was particularly boisterous and rainey. About 10 o'clock at night the Yankee Cavalry (being piloted by somebody perhaps a negro) passed round our pickets and went into our Cavalry Camp on foot (having hitched their horses out), waked up our boys and took about 150 prisoners. The others escaped by running off in the dark. They also

went into the camp of Edgar's Battery and took the whole Company with one or two exceptions and captured all the guns being four brass guns 2. 6 & 2. 12 pounders.[12] We got the news about 3 oclock and were ordered into line of battle immediately. It was quite cold and dark and the ground was covered with water. We stood in line of battle expecting an attack about an hour when we took up again the line of retreat and such another march as we had till day light you have perhaps read of in history of our revolutionary war. We marched without much stoppage until about an hour or two after dark on the night of the 22 making near 30 miles that day. A great many of the men did'nt have a mouthful to eat the whole day and with no prospect of any thing when they reached camps but cornbread and beef so poor that it had to be held up to be knocked in the head. I need not tell you that there was much murmuring for there was a great deal. There was much discontent many men's patriotism rising no higher than their stomach's and their love of country and honor being measured and ballanced with a good dinner or a full belly. I wouldn't give a snap of my finger for such patriotism and for such men yet we have many of that sort here with. I can now understand the trouble Moses had with the children of Israel in his travels of forty years through the wilderness as I presume that human nature in that day was the same that it is now. I know too what is meant by "sighing for the flesh pots of Egypt."

Wed the 23 —

We marched to this camp being about 3 miles march. Here we got some flour and bacon and I dont hear so much murmuring in camp today. The men are full and I believe would now fight. To tell you the truth Ella since we started on our grand skedaddle from Bayou De Glaze on the 11th inst till last night we have fared horribly having nothing but coarse cornbread and the very poorest quality of beef. If we could have got sugar and molasses we could have done well. We have marched about 200 miles on bad fare and it takes a good patriot not to murmur under such circumstances. I have no news for two days from the Yankees. At the last accounts they had not left Alexandra with their gun boats. The river is now rising and I expect that they will attempt to ascend the river. We are now in 22 miles of Natchitoches still in the piney woods. We are laying up to day but expect at any moment to receive orders to march. Our next destination will be Natchitoches or Grand E'Core on Red River I dont know whether we will make a stand then or not. I think that we ought to make a fight soon. It looks like giving up the entire Country without a struggle to run so far before them. At the same time we ought to be in a good condition and as near on equal terms as possible with them before risking too much for a defeat of this army i.e. a bad defeat would ruin the Trans Miss Department. The enemy's forces are too heavy for us now numbering from 15 to 20 thousand or more. Our time will come after awhile and when we do strike I want to make it count. I am tired as the boys say of issuing men to the federals as we did at Fort De Russy and near Alexandra on the 21 inst.

The clouds seem to be lowering over the Trans Miss Dept Louisiana. Sur[e]ly Louisiana is gone up and the foot of the despoiler is hung upon her neck now. For us it looks gloomy but I console myself singing my favorite air "Maggie by my side."

> "Storms can appal me never when her brow is clear
> "Fair weather lingers ever when her smiles appear
> "An when sorrows breaking around my heart shall bide
> "Still may I find her sitting by my side etc."[13]

You know the song. I want you to learn it and sing it for me when I come home. I will try and come this summer unless the federals are crowding us too closely. Then I must be at my post. You can say that your poor ol daddy was in the grand skedaddle from Bayou De Glaize in March 1864 and that for 5 days and nights he never pulled off his over coat or shoes, but slept with all on and that he marched day & night and lived on coarse cornbread & poor beef etc., was weary and foot sore etc etc and all that sort of thing and whether we have our historian or not our deeds etc will be remembered for years. I havn't had a letter from home in over two weeks. The mails & offices were broken up at Alexandra & Natchitoches. On tomorrow our course [couriers?] will start to Shreveport after our mail.

My chances for writing are not so good as I could wish but I will do the best I can. I want you all to write as often as usual. I will get them some time.

My love, kisses etc to ma & your brothers. Respects to friends.

Yours truly
E. P. Petty

Kisatchie Creek
Natchitoches Pa La
Mar 28th 1864

My Dear Wife
Our Regt is now on picket 10 or 11 miles in advance of our

Command and my company is on picket in advance of the Regt at a bridge over the Kisatchie a large creek which runs into Red River. We are in a pretty place to be captured as we are beyond supporting distance from our Command. I understand that we will move up the Country on tomorrow. I am sorry. I had rather go down if we could. Some of Genl Greens men reached our Camp last night.[14] I wish they were all here. We would make the feds draw in their pickets and be particular how they foraged. There is no news from the front that I know of. We are living hard now but will be in the better humor to fight. It is awful dark times in Camp.[15] I have been out to day solitary & alone nearly a mile in advance of our videtts prospecting. Some lucky fed or Jay hawker might have grabbed me up if he had known it but I watched as well as prayed. I must see ahead if I can. I want to know what is in front. Some of the boys are now having a chill occasionally viz Tiffany, Billy Craft, Frank Meeks, Polk Condry & Lt McLester. I am in fine health though I believe that with hard living & hard service I am falling off in flesh a little. I dont weigh over 145 now I suppose. Love & kisses & etc to children. Respects to friends. Hastily

Yours truly
E. P. Petty

Bellwood Natchitoches Pa
La March 30 1864

My Dear Wife

We are again on the move up the Country towards Shreveport. Our Regt was on picket 8 or 10 miles from the Brigade and is consequently some 15 or more miles behind. The Brigade moved yesterday and we started this morning. We are entirely in the rear of every thing except a little squad of Cavalry. I have just learned that Green & Majors Commands camped near Fort Jessup on last night which is about 20 miles from here. Our Brig will camp at Ft Jessup to night. We will get there some time tomorrow. The federals are now advancing on Natchitoches. They have crossed at Monets [Monett's] ferry which is on Cane river 40 miles above Alexandra & 40 miles below Natchitoches. I expect that there will be a concentration of our army at Shreveport when the big fight of the Trans Miss Dept will come off and that before a great while. I look for a hard struggle here now — I once thought that they did not intend advancing farther up the country than Alexandra but it seems now that relying on their numbers and gun boats they will still press up the country. We must unite and fight them at or before they reach Shreveport. We have already run away & given up nearly all and quite the best part of Louisiana and Arkansas. We must fight them and whip them. This we are certain to do I think.[16] I have no news other than above written. I am in fine health. We are hard up just now for rations but will have plenty soon. Dont be uneasy about me. I will keep you posted all the time if I can. Love etc to the children.

Yours truly
E. P. Petty

My Dear Wife

Desha Bunton reached our camp yesterday and brought me letters from the whole family. I cant express my feelings at receiving letters from all the loved ones at once. God bless them I wish I could embrace them all at this moment. But I cant tell now when that happy event is likely to occur as the Yanks have been pressing us verry heavy for several weeks and even now as I write I hear the booming of the Cannon in the direction of Fort Jesup. We sent Genl Mouton's Division down in that direction yesterday to stop the advance of their Cavalry and this is no doubt a fight between them. I believe that I wrote to you from Belwood by Lieut Stallings. After leaving B. we march 20 miles to Fort Jesup and 20 miles to Pleasant Hill in the direction of Shreveport. We are now in 60 miles of Shreveport and about 5 miles from P. H. rather in the direction of Natchitoches. The enemy have taken Natchitoches & Grand E'Core[17] — Two of Genl Greens Regts had a fight at or near Natchitoches two days ago and had 3 men killed & several horses killed & wounded — a pretty rough reception to Louisiana as they had only been in a day or so.[18] Their gun boats are above the falls but the river is falling rapidly I hear. They seem to be determined to try and go to Shreveport if possible. Our reinforcements are just beginning to arrive — 2 of Greens Regts are here. Genl Price with about 5 or 6 000 men were at Shreveport two or 3 days ago. Other Regts from Texas are in hearing distance. We are now in the high piney and oak hills of La where in all probability we will attempt to make a stand. I think the earth will shake and the wool fly in these parts in a few days if not sooner. I am sanguine of success whenever our Genls think that the time has come to put us into it. Although I dread the amount of suffering and anguish of woe that will result from such a collission yet I fear not and am keen for the issue to be made and met. We have run already unconscionably and the Country has been devasted thereby. I have had to stop writing to load up everything and get ready to march in a moment.[19] I dont know what the news from the firing is but our mules have turned to the rear and perhaps another skedaddle as on hand for to night. It is nearly 4 oclock now. I had rather advance than retreat if we are ready for the fight and so I believe is feelings of the most of us. We have run until our patience has oozed out. A fight I think will help us now. We shall see soon. I am in fine health and so are the most of the boys and eager for a fight. No other news.

Love etc.
E. P. Petty
April 2 1864

On April 3 Walker's Division marched ten miles in the direction of Mansfield. Camp was made near a sawmill, about halfway between that point and Pleasant Hill. The next day the troops marched 12 miles, leaving the Mansfield road to the left and taking the Kingston road. On the way they passed 20 wagons loaded with flour for Green's cavalry. They encamped in a swampy bottom four miles north of Mansfield about 37 miles from Shreveport. Here they remained until April 7.[20]

Meanwhile, on the Arkansas line Steele was becoming a serious threat. Kirby Smith was busy calculating. On arriving at Washington Steele could advance by two directions — move directly down the east bank of the Red River, or cross the river near Fulton and join Banks either at Shreveport or Marshall, Texas. At present the two Federal generals were too far apart to make any calculations for concentration. In the meantime Taylor must fall back since he was not strong enough to fight a battle on which the fate of the department depended. Price had 7,000 cavalry and 1,500 infantry and would be instructed to hold his command ready for rapid marching as circumstances required. "A decision must now soon be taken upon which the fate of the department must rest." The commanding general would like to have Taylor's "views and opinions before taking a step which is alike pregnant with weal or woe for us individually as well as for the country."

Taylor, not being familiar with the country beyond Shreveport, was not in a position to designate the place to meet Steele, and he was more afraid of him than of Banks. The latter he considered "cold, timid, easily foiled." And since Banks depended heavily upon the river for transportation, low water and the sinking of the Confederate steamer *Falls City* as low down as possible would delay him. Steele was "bold, ardent, vigorous" and, being independent of river transportation, would probably "sweep Price from his path." As the more dangerous of the two, he "should be met and overthrown at once." In either case prompt and vigorous action was required. "While we are deliberating the enemy is marching. King James lost three battles for a mass. We may lose three States without a battle." Taylor would hold himself ready to move in such direction as Kirby Smith might order. Looking to the possibility of being ordered to Shreveport, he began repairs to the road via Kingston. On the evening of April 4 Churchill's and Parsons's divisions of Arkansas and Missouri troops, 4,400 effectives, were ordered to march from Shreveport to Keatchie, report to Taylor and await his orders at that point.[21]

The fact that Steele had crossed the Little Missouri was not yet known to Kirby Smith, and on April 5 he advised Taylor that the distance between the two Federal columns was over 200 miles — "far too great for us to concentrate on either column." Moreover, Steele had not yet committed himself to a line of march. Since the fate of the department was at stake the battle must be decisive, whether with Steele or Banks. By holding the interior line the smaller Confederate army had the advantage, and as long as "we retain our little army undefeated we have hopes." The advantage of position must not be given up by any ill-advised movement. "When we fight, it must be for victory."[22]

On April 5 Brigadier General James P. Major, with Lane's Cavalry Brigade, Hardeman's and Waller's regiments of Arthur Bagby's brigade, along with Brigadier General Hamilton P. Bee with two regiments of his cavalry division, Buchel's and Terrell's, reached Mansfield. On April 7 Major, with Lane's Brigade and three regiments of Bagby's, engaged a numerically superior Federal cavalry force under General Albert L. Lee in a "severe skirmish" at Wilson's Farm three miles north of Pleasant Hill and then withdrew to Ten Mile Bayou, leaving a small force to impede the progress of the Federals. Each side lost about 75 in killed and wounded. Suspecting that this enemy advance might be the forerunner of general movement, Taylor wired Kirby Smith for instructions. Should he "hazard a general engagement at this point?" An immediate answer was requested, "that I may receive it before daylight to-morrow morning." Taylor later stated that he notified Kirby Smith he would "fight a general engagement the next day if the enemy advanced in force, unless ordered positively not to do so." As Kirby Smith's biographer noted, "his telegram does not reveal such a positive intention."[23]

It is not known when Kirby Smith received this telegram. He replied on April 8, too late to restrain Taylor. "A general engagement now could not be given with our full force," he advised. "Re-enforcements are moving up — not very large, it is true. If we fall back without a battle you will be thrown out of the best country for supplies. I would compel the enemy to develop his intentions, selecting a position in rear where we can give him battle before he can march on and occupy Shreveport." He promised to order down all the armed cavalry from near Marshall, Texas, and forward Pratt's Battery from Shreveport with every available man before a battle was fought. "Let me know as soon as you are convinced that a general advance is being made and I will come to the front," he urged. Taylor could not have received this message before the fighting began.[24]

On the night of April 7 Walker's Division received orders to cook one day's rations and to be ready to leave at four o'clock the next morning. William P. Head, the chief surgeon of the Sixteenth Texas Cavalry (dismounted), informed his wife:

I have just received orders to be ready to march at daylight in the morning, & do not know which direction but from the character of the orders I think we will go in the direction of Natchitoches, the federals are within twelve miles of Mansfield on the Natchitoches road. In what force I am unable to tell, though it is presumed to be very large, & suppose thirty thousand. We now have twenty thousand men, thirteen thousand Infantry and seven thousand cavalry

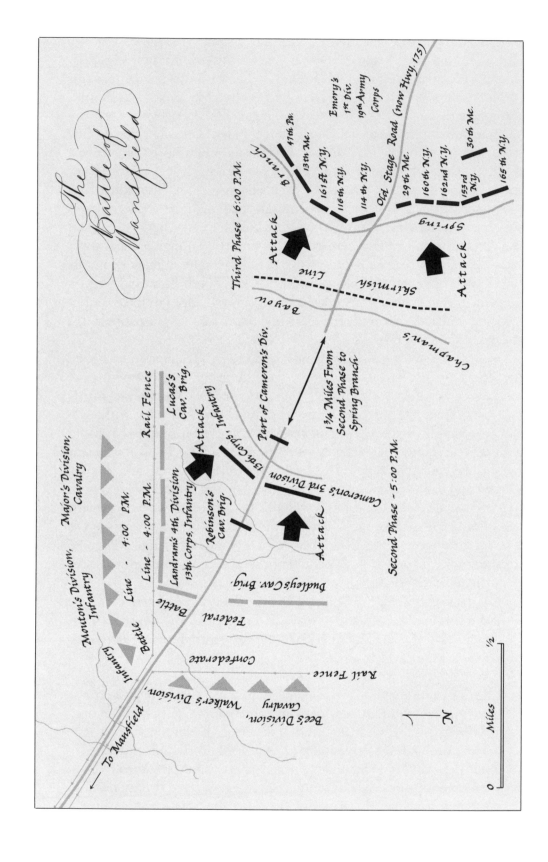

The Battle of Mansfield

we have enough; at least, all of the men think so and you know that will be [a] great help to us. I think they will fight like veteran soldiers.[25]

The Federals did not fall back during the night, and Green reported them advancing the next morning (April 8). Hours passed as Lee's cavalry and Colonel Frank Emerson's First Brigade of Colonel William J. Landram's Fourth Division, Thirteenth Army Corps, pressed ahead against a skillfully conducted withdrawal. In answer to a plea from Lee, the division's Second Brigade, commanded by Colonel Joseph W. Vance, was ordered forward to reinforce the weary van; but it was considerably delayed by Lee's wagon train which practically blocked the road for miles. Taylor, meanwhile, ordered Mouton's Division to the front and prepared to bring Walker's and Churchill's forward from Keatchie to Mansfield. "I am not sure whether the enemy's whole force is in my front; if so, and he means to move on Shreveport, I consider this as favorable a point to engage him as any other," he wired departmental headquarters at 9:40 a.m.[26]

Arriving near Mansfield, Walker formed his division in line of battle. The road from the camp to Mansfield was over a high ridge, flanked by ravines, which were covered with a dense, almost impenetrable growth of blackjack oaks and hazel bushes. Many of the men went to work with their knives, lopping off the branches of the trees and bushes which obstructed a good view of the road, in order to make their aim and fire more effective. The division remained in this position until 11 a.m., when Taylor ordered Walker to move forward through Mansfield to meet the enemy, who were reported about halfway between that point and Pleasant Hill. The head of the column moved off, the bands playing Dixie. The inhabitants of Mansfield appeared to be astonished when they saw Walker's men marching proudly back to meet the enemy before whom they had so long retreated. Colonel T. R. Bonner of the Eighteenth Texas Infantry described the scene:

> As we passed through the streets of the beautiful town, they were thronged with fair ladies — misses and matrons — who threw their bright garlands at our feet, and bade us, in God's name, to drive back the Yankees and save their cherished homes. As their cheerful songs of the sunny south fell in accents of sweetest melody upon our ears, we felt that we were indeed "thrice armed," and though greatly outnumbered, would drive back the foe.[27]

"General Walker's men are in fine condition for fighting, and will no doubt have a showing on this very day," a courier on General Major's staff noted approvingly as they passed him on the road.[28] The troops saw Taylor, Walker, Mouton and Green on the right of the road, apparently in deep consultation about the forthcoming battle. After marching some three miles below Mansfield to Sabine Cross Roads (or Crossroads) on the Pleasant Hill road, Walker's Division filed off to the right of the road through a skirt of timber, Waul's Brigade in front. Next came Randal's Brigade, with Scurry's bringing up the rear. "The men in this brigade appeared to be in splendid condition," Blessington remembered. "They were full of fun, led by their gallant chief, who looked every inch a soldier." One of Scurry's regiments was ordered forward to a ravine, some 600 yards in advance of the main line, in order to ambush the enemy, should they advance before the main line of battle was formed. The balance of Walker's Division, after marching and countermarching and maneuvering, was formed in line about 12 p.m. at the edge of a large field behind a rail fence which enclosed the Moss Plantation; the left of the division rested on the Pleasant Hill road — Scurry's Brigade on the right, Waul's in the center and Randal's on the left. After the line was formed the command was given to "stack arms." The troops remained inactive for about three hours, awaiting the enemy's approach. The Federals were reported to be in line of battle about one mile to the front. Each minute the firing of the cavalry skirmishers became more and more distinct. Presently, the regiment of Scurry's in the ravine double-quicked across the field to join the rest of the brigade.[29]

On Walker's right were two cavalry regiments, August Buchel's and Alexander W. Terrell's, commanded by Hamilton P. Bee. Alfred Mouton's division, consisting of a brigade of Louisianians commanded by Colonel Henry Gray and Polignac's Texas Brigade, occupied the left side of the road with a division of dismounted cavalry, under James P. Major, made up of Major's own brigade (Lane's) and Arthur Bagby's brigade. Xavier Debray's Twenty-sixth Texas Cavalry was held on the road a little to the rear. Two batteries, Horace Haldeman's and James M. Daniels's, were posted on the right with Walker, and Florian Cornay's and Nettles's batteries were with Mouton on the left. In front with the cavalry skirmishers was McMahon's Battery, which soon was to be withdrawn to the rear to act as a reserve. The entire Confederate force at Sabine Cross Roads, according to Taylor, totaled 8,800 men — 5,300 infantry, 3,000 cavalry and 500 artillerymen. Taylor waited for Banks to advance. As he rode along his line he called out to Polignac, "Little Frenchman, I am going to fight Banks here, if he has a million of men!"[30]

Brigadier General Thomas E. G. Ransom, the 29-year-old commander of the Thirteenth Army Corps, placed the mass of the Federal infantry under Colonel Landram on the right of the Pleasant Hill road. The troops occupied a narrow belt of timber dividing two large plantations, with open though broken ground in front and in the rear cultivated fields which descended to a small creek, then rose to the edge of the timber one-half mile to the rear of the line. Ormand F. Nims's Second Massachusetts Battery was posted on Honeycutt Hill on the left or south side of the road, about 200 yards to the left of the belt of timber, and was supported by the Twenty-third Wisconsin Infantry, also on the left of the road and behind the crest of the hill with open fields in front. The Sixty-seventh Indiana supported the battery on the north side of the road, joined by the Seventy-seventh Illinois, both regiments facing in a westerly direction, and, facing north behind a split rail fence, the One Hundred and Thirtieth Illinois, Forty-eighth Ohio, Nineteenth Kentucky, Ninety-sixth Ohio, a section of mounted artillery and the Eighty-third Ohio, totaling 2,413 infantry. The cavalry and mounted artillery under Lee were posted on the flanks and rear, with Colonel Nathan A. M. "Gold Lace" Dudley's brigade on the left and Colonel Thomas J. Lucas's on the right, and with skirmishers deployed in front of the infantry. There were about 4,800 Federals of all arms on the field. About 3 p.m. Banks himself arrived in company with Major General Franklin. Despite Ransom's conviction that an advance would "finish him," the army commander overruled him and Lee. The cavalry leader predicted an assault could only result in the Federal forces being "gloriously flogged," but Banks was adamant that pressure be put upon the Rebels.[31]

Shortly after 4 p.m., having completed his deployment, Taylor stated that he became "impatient at the delay of the enemy in developing his attack, and suspecting his arrangements were not complete, I ordered Mouton to open the attack from the left." Mouton said to Polignac, previous to the attack, "Let us charge them right in the face, and throw them into the valley." The Louisianians and Texans swarmed to the attack against rifle fire and guns that belched grape and canister. Felix Pierre Poché described the beginning of Mouton's assault:

At 2½ Genl Mouton ordered Col Grey to increase his sharpshooters and to follow the enemy. Immediately after that we were ordered to leap over the fence, and with resounding yells we began running and stormed the enemy. At a distance of one hundred fifty feet the enemy opened fire and a really terrific cannonade. The balls and grape shot crashing about us whistled terribly and plowed into the ground and beat our soldiers down even as a storm tears down the trees of a forest.[32]

Ransom saw the lead Confederate attackers fall back in "confusion" only to recover their courage and run forward again. This time they "halted about 200 yards from our front, where many . . . laid down and returned our fire." Rebel losses were severe. The gallant Mouton was killed, but Polignac rode forward, took over the command and pressed the shattered division steadily forward. "With tears of grief and rage in their eyes, the yelling men followed Polignac," wrote John Winters. "They ran on through the deadly hail, determined to avenge the death of their leader." Landram's men held firm and took a terrible toll. Colonel Leopold Armant of the Eighteenth Louisiana, Colonel James Beard of the Crescent Regiment, Lieutenant Colonel William Walker commanding the Twenty-eighth Louisiana, Lieutenant Colonel Sebron Noble of the Seventeenth Texas Consolidated Regiment, and Major Canfield of the Crescent Regiment were killed, and Lieutenant Colonel F. H. Clack of the Crescent was mortally wounded. Seven standard bearers fell one after another with the flag of the Crescent, which sustained 200 casualties. Over one third of the division was lost. Meanwhile, Major's dismounted men moved forward on Mouton's left. Impeded by dense woods, much to Green's impatience, they gradually turned the enemy's right flank. Randal's Brigade, now on the left of the Pleasant Hill road, supported Mouton's right by advancing in echelon from the left. As soon as the left attack was well developed, Taylor ordered Walker to send Waul's and Scurry's brigades forward on the right of the road. Bee, on Walker's right, was to push forward with Debray's and Buchel's cavalry and gain Banks's rear. Scurry was ordered to drive in, turn the en-

emy's left and take up position on the high road beyond the main Federal line of battle. "The dense wood through which Bee advanced prevented him from gaining much ground, but the gallantry and vigor with which that accomplished soldier (Walker) led his fine brigade into action and pressed the foe had never been surpassed," Taylor reported.[33]

Walker gave the command: "By the right of companies to the front, forward march!" The line of march was through a large field in front, then through a skirt of timber and into another field. Resting a few minutes in the timber, the command was given: "By companies, into line!" After the line was formed orders were given to fix bayonets. The men passed Walker and marched steadily forward. Soon the command was given to double-quick. The enemy was found strongly posted behind a rail fence, and, in Colonel Bonner's words, "greeted our coming with a perfect shower of leaden hail, from both artillery and small arms, but we dislodged them without firing a gun." Blessington described the advance:

> When our army had arrived within about fifty paces, and before we had fired a shot, a general flash was seen along the enemy's line, and a storm of bullets went flying over our heads. They had aimed too high. Onward our troops advanced, pale with excitement, compressed lips and blazing eyes betokening the spirit of their determination. Casting your eyes along the column, you behold the flags of the various regiments floating on the breeze, and each regiment trying to be the first to scale the fence. Nearer our troops advance; the color-sergeants flaunt their flags at the enemy, and fall; others grasp them and fall, and they are then borne by the corporals. In this fearful charge, there was no flinching nor murmuring — nothing but the subdued talk of soldiers, the gritting of teeth for revenge, as they saw their comrades falling around them. At last the fence is gained; over it our troops go, like an avalanche of fire! A loud and prolonged Texas yell deafens the ear; their cheers rise in one great range of sound over the noise of battle, and are heard far down the lines to the left, where the Louisiana boys are at it.[34]

General Albert L. Lee described the Rebel assault from the Federal side in testimony before the Joint Committee on the Conduct of the War:

> There was very brisk picket firing, and the whole line of the enemy advanced on our flanks and on our front and marched straight up to our line. We opened upon them with artillery, with canister, and with musketry, and fought in line perhaps twenty minutes,

when they charged right straight up to our line. They were repulsed two or three times, but the end of the thing was that in twenty minutes our line was just crumbling everywhere and falling back. I ordered my batteries off when the infantry support gave way; but three guns of one of my batteries had to be left on the crest of the hill, as every horse and almost every man had been killed.[35]

The Texans, "yelling like infuriated demons," brushed aside the Third Massachusetts Cavalry and swept up Honeycutt Hill, flanking and driving back the Sixty-seventh Indiana and Twenty-third Wisconsin. Nims's Battery lost over half its horses and had to abandon three guns. Walker's men turned them on the fleeing Yankees. Captain Nims reported the action:

Upon the approach of the enemy, who came out of the woods and on the right flank, the battery opened fire, using shell and canister with good effect, repulsing three successive charges of the enemy. Within twenty minutes from the time when the action commenced, the battery was ordered to retire from the hill, the infantry support having previously retired in disorder. Three pieces were taken to the rear in good order. Three pieces were left on the field, being unable to remove them on account of the horses being disabled.

Lieutenant Pinckney Cone's Chicago Mercantile and Captain Martin Klauss' First Indiana batteries had arrived on the field and were now under such heavy fire from Walker's infantry that they were withdrawn from an advantageous position on a ridge near the center, where they could fire to the left and to the right. Ransom, while trying to organize a rally around the Mercantile Battery, was struck in the left knee by a ball. He fell from his horse but still shouted out orders until two sturdy infantrymen carried him to the rear on their shoulders. Ransom later described how the Confederates "came at him like the wings of a V, the open part covering his front and flanks, and that every time he attempted to form a line of battle the wings of the V enveloped his flanks and closed down on them like a nut-cracker."[36]

The rout of the Federal left exposed the rear of the center behind the rail fence, and disorderly flight followed. Landram summed up the situation in this way:

Seeing that the capture of the entire force was inevitable unless I withdrew, I ordered the remainder of the shattered regiments to fall back, which they attempted, but were unable to accomplish with entire success. The list of the killed and wounded of my command cannot be ascertained, inasmuch as the enemy retained possession of the field, but that we suffered severely there can be no doubt.

Meanwhile, Brigadier General Robert A. Cameron, commanding the Third Division, Thirteenth Army Corps, about 1,300 officers and men, had formed the second Federal line about one-half mile from the first near Sabine Cross Roads, a short distance west of the Antioch Church at about 5 p.m. He deployed his troops on either side of the Pleasant Hill road and advanced them through the woods to the edge of the Birdwell Field, where they were able to fire on the Confederates from the woods behind a rail fence as the Rebels advanced across open ground. But Lucas's cavalry on the right was overwhelmed by Major's cavalry; Dudley suffered the same fate on the left at the hands of Scurry's and Waul's brigades, and the Federal infantry in the center of the line was pushed back by Mouton's Division and Randal's Brigade. The second Federal line was soon crumbling along the entire front; the infantry, throwing down their arms and all other equipment that would slow them down, fled in panic. All semblance of order disappeared as the sole line of retreat — the Pleasant Hill road — was blocked by an abandoned wagon train hopelessly mired in a small creek. Seventeen more guns had to be abandoned, making a total of 20. General Lee reported the loss of 156 wagons and about 800 mules. "We have driven the enemy at this hour 3 miles, with a loss to him of six guns, and, as far as ascertained, many hundred prisoners," Taylor informed departmental headquarters at 6 p.m. "We are still driving him. . . . Churchill's troops were not up in time to take part in the action, and will be fresh in the morning. I shall push the enemy to the utmost."[37]

The Federals were driven back two miles to Chatman's (Chapman's) Bayou where the First Division, Nineteenth Army Corps, commanded by Brigadier General William H. Emory, met the fugitives. "Still thicker and denser came the frightened crowd, rushing past in every possible manner," wrote the historian of the One Hundred and Fourteenth New York Regiment. "Men without hats or coats, men without guns or accoutrements, cavalrymen without horses, and artillery men without cannon, wounded men bleeding and crying at every step, men begrimed with smoke and powder — all in a state of fear and frenzy, while they shouted to our boys not to go forward any farther, for they would all be slaughtered." Emory's division made a successful stand at Pleasant Grove on a ridge overlooking the stream, checking the victorious Confederates in an action that lasted only 20 minutes before darkness fell. Many Rebels called it the Peach Orchard Fight. "Fatigued and disordered by their long advance through dense wood, my men made no im-

pression for a long time on this fresh body of troops," Taylor wrote in his memoirs, "but possession of the water was all-important, for there was none other between this and Mansfield. Walker, Green, and Polignac led on their weary men, and I rode down to the stream. There was some sharp work, but we persisted, the enemy fell back, and the stream was held, just as twilight faded into darkness."[38]

Colonel Bonner described the "terrible shock" of the sudden encounter at Pleasant Grove with Emory's men:

> Volley after volley resounded from the hill, and shower after shower of bullets came whizzing down upon us. It was utterly impossible to advance, and to retreat beneath the range of their long guns seemed equally desperate. Never shall I forget that moment, and what soldier that was there can ever cease to remember the "Plum [sic] Orchard" fight. We lay down, arose again, and then involuntarily sought such shelter and protection as the ground afforded. Encouraged by their leaders, our brave men attempted again and again to charge, but human fortitude and human bravery were unequal to the task. Even Napoleon's "Old Guard" itself must have quailed before that terrible fire. The very air seemed dark and hot with balls, and on every side was heard their dull, crushing sound, as they struck the swaying mass, tearing through flesh, and bone, and sinew. The position of our line could have been traced by our fallen dead — Within a few short moments, many a gallant spirit went to its long home.

> We were compelled to retire. As soon, however, as we reached the timber, the men were rallied, and though the sun had gone down behind the hills, and night was fast closing upon that bloody scene, still it was resolved to make another effort to take the hill. Again the line was formed and the order given to charge. Right gallantly did we commence the task, but the enemy was fully prepared for our reception and reserved their fire until we had advanced to within 100 yards of their position. Then their rifles belched forth a bright red sheet of flame along their whole line, lighting up the expiring day with an unearthly glare, while the thunders of 10,000 guns resounded through the heavens, and seemed to shake the earth to its very center. For our wearied and almost exhausted troops to oppose such fearful odds with success, was utterly impossible, and the attempt to dislodge the enemy from his stronghold, proved as unfortunate as it was ill-advised. Many a brave man, for there were no craven hearts in this last charge, whose life might have been saved to his country and his family, was slain in this vain

attempt to drive the enemy. Had the battle closed when we first received our check in the orchard, no page in the history of the war would have recorded a more brilliant Southern victory than that of the battle of Mansfield. As it was, much of the prestige of success gained in the day, was lost in the blood of the fearless, undistinguished heroes, who fell in this deadly night charge.[39]

The historian of the One Hundred and Fourteenth New York Regiment gave a northern view of the engagement:

> Presently, a long line of rebel infantry came out in full view, directly in front. The over-confident and undaunted enemy, flushed with the excitement of victory, advanced exultingly forward, not knowing that concealed behind that fence steady arms and cool eyes aimed many a muzzle at their breasts. Every minute seemed an age. Nearer and nearer they came, when the order was given, and one terrific, blinding, stunning crash of fire sent many a man to the dust.
>
> The rebels were appalled. They reeled and staggered, their lines quivered for a moment, and then they fled in discomfiture to the woods. Again the maddened and desperate foe came up in line after line, to be cut down like grass before the mower's scythe. For every one killed, two stepped forward to take his place. Our men loaded and fired with such rapidity, that it seemed not like the usual tremulous rattling of musketry, but like one continuous explosion. Such discharges from such rifles would check a stronger rebel force than this. The musketry of Champion Hill and Shiloh did not exceed that of Sabine Cross Roads.[40]

Banks held a hasty council of war where it was decided — supplies, food and water all being in short supply — to fall back to Pleasant Hill, where A. J. Smith and his fresh troops could reinforce the army. All night long the retreat continued. Taylor granted his exhausted troops a well-deserved rest by the stream. Waul's Brigade, placed in line of battle across the road, occupied the front of the army during the night, only 300 yards from the enemy's line. "The remainder of our infantry forces, 'watch-worn and weary,' truly slept upon their arms," wrote Bonner, "and silence — save the moans of the wounded and the groans of the dying — soon fell upon that field where late was heard the din and crash of battle."[41]

Leaving instructions for Green to pursue at dawn with the cavalry, Taylor rode to Mansfield to look after the wounded and meet General Churchill, who, having been put in command of Parsons's Missouri Division as well as his own, put Brigadier General James C. Tappan in command of the Arkansas Division. Churchill came and reported his two divisions in camp four miles from Mansfield on the Keatchie road; he was told to prepare two days' rations and march toward Pleasant Hill at 3 a.m. At 1:30 a.m. Taylor sent Walker the following letter from Mansfield:

General

Churchill and Parsons are starting. Churchill has been warned to take position on the right of the road, Parsons will march by his left, and take position on the left of the road. They will lead the attack at early dawn. Time is every thing to us. Dispatches just received from the river show that the enemy has troops on the east side, and is again trying to get transports covered with troops up the river. This shows the enemy has divided his forces. We must take advantage of this error. Your men and Polignac's will have some relief as Arkansas and Missouri have the fight in the morning. They must do what Texas and Louisiana did today. Show this to Genl. Green, and tell him we must push our left vigorously to occupy the road from Pleasant Hill to Blair's landing as this road is the shortest for the enemy to reinforce upon, and it is important to push him behind Pleasant Hill, which forces him to return to Natchitoches to unite with his column on the river. Gl. Major should push some cavalry on the Blair's landing road as soon as possible — even a squadron, as it would materially delay the enemy should he attempt to cross Bayou Pierre at Jordons Ferry. From the nature of the position any resistance at Jordons would be fatal to an attempt to cross. The enemy cannot receive any thing from the river before late in the day tomorrow, so it is all important to push him vigorously. He has nothing in our front but the troops we beat today, and the 19th Corps — all Yankees, whom we have always whipped. This corps is about seven thousand strong — many recruits who will make no fight. Should the enemy have disappeared in the morning, which is probable, the cavalry must make an active pursuit, at least to Dupont's bridge, and further if possible. One or two Regts of cavalry will be in from Logansport early in the day. I will be in the field at early dawn, but if detained a little later, the attack must be pressed at early light. The safety of our whole country depends upon it. Marmaduke has badly damaged the enemy on the Little Missouri, taking many waggons in his rear.

Yo. Obt. Servt.
R. Taylor
Major Genl[42]

Taylor then returned to the front. The cavalry, with a battery, moved early to Pleasant Hill, 14 miles distant, leaving Walker and Polignac to follow Churchill's command as soon as it had passed. At 7:30 a.m. Taylor notified Kirby Smith that he was pursuing the enemy with cavalry, followed up by infantry. "If the wind holds and circumstances will admit, will follow the enemy to Natchitoches." Taylor rode with Green and found many stragglers, scattered arms and burning wagons, showing the haste of the enemy's retreat. The vicinity of Pleasant Hill was reached before a shot was fired. The enemy was found a mile in front of the town, and as the cavalry's rapid advance had left the infantry far to the rear, feints were made to the right and left to develop his position and strength.[43]

En route to Pleasant Hill Walker's Division met a squad of Green's cavalry escorting to the rear some 300 or 400 Zouaves who had been captured. Some of the soldiers, noting their exotic, bloomer-like uniforms, speculated that the war must soon be over, as the Rebels had whipped all the men in the Northern states, and Lincoln was filling up his ranks with women. On their arrival in Mansfield the "Joabs," as the Zouaves were called, were informed that they would all be paroled, the Confederacy having scarcely enough provisions to feed their own troops without providing for women prisoners.[44]

From two miles above the village, at 10:40 a.m., Taylor reported to departmental headquarters that the enemy's burning wagons, abandoned arms, knapsacks and other property along the road furnished "ample evidence of the haste with which he is endeavoring to get away. He is now making something of a stand here for the purpose of gaining time and possibly to cover the Blair's Ferry road." Taylor would do his best to force the enemy to retreat by the Natchitoches road around the head of Spanish Lake, "which road is a desert for many miles."[45]

Pleasant Hill was a small village of about 200 inhabitants occupying part of a plateau, a mile wide from east to west, along the Mansfield and Fort Jesup road. It boasted a Methodist Church, post office, hotel, three storehouses, a school building for girls and Pearce Payne Methodist College for boys. The highest ground, called College Hill, was on the west, and here entered a road from the Sabine River, which struck the Red River at Blair's Landing 16 miles to the east, while, from the necessity of going around Spanish Lake, the distance to Natchitoches and Grand Ecore was 36 miles. The Confederate reconnaissance showed that the Federal lines extended across the open plateau, from College Hill on their left to a wooded height on the right of the road to Mansfield. In front of this position was a ditch cut by winter rains but now dry, bordered by a thick growth of young pines with fallen timber interspersed. This was held by the enemy's advanced infantry, with his main line and guns on the plateau. Separating the ditch and thicket from the forest toward Mansfield was an open field, several hundred yards wide near the road but diminishing in width toward the west. Banks had about 11,000 effective infantry and artillery plus 1,000 cavalry.[46]

Shortly after noon the Confederate infantry began to appear, Churchill in advance, but Taylor saw at a glance that his men, having marched 45 miles in two days, were too exhausted to attack immediately. Walker's and Polignac's divisions had been heavily engaged at Mansfield and Pleasant Grove, and all the troops were suffering from heat and thirst. Accordingly, they were given two hours to lie down and rest. Taylor had just above 12,000 men.[47]

General Hamilton P. Bee stated in 1880 that "General Taylor himself told me at three o'clock of the day of the battle of Pleasant Hill, that the superb line of battle which I had watched all day, with his serried lines compact and entrenched, and which he had not seen, 'was a mere feint to cover the retreat of their wagon trains.' On this hypothesis, he formed his plan of attack. . . ." Taylor completed his dispositions around 4 p.m. On the east side of the Mansfield road were Debray's and Buchel's cavalry brigades, under Bee, supported by Polignac's small, battered division in reserve. Walker's Division was west of the road. On Walker's right were Tappan's Arkansas and Parsons's Missouri divisions, under Churchill, with Hardeman's, McNeill's and Terrell's regiments of cavalry and Etter's and Daniels's batteries. Major, with Lane's Brigade and most of Bagby's, was to dismount and move forward on the left to outflank the enemy's right, and gain and hold the Blair's Landing road, thus keeping Banks from escaping in that direction.[48]

At 3 p.m. Churchill was directed to move his troops to the right and turn the enemy's left. His route was through the forest for two miles to the Fort Jesup road coming from the Sabine. The enemy's left outflanked, he was to attack in a northeasterly direction, keeping his cavalry regiments well to his right, and Walker would attack on his left. At 4:30 he was reported nearing the position from which he would attack; and to mask his movement, Major Brent advanced his 12 guns into the field within 200 yards of the enemy's lines and opened fire. Soon the sounds of Churchill's attack were heard, and the cheers of his men indicated success. Walker at once led his division by echelons of brigades from his right, Brent advanced his guns, and Major gained possession of the road to Blair's. Green ordered Bee to charge with Debray's and Buchel's regiments across the fields and up the opposite slope, but he was repulsed by close and deadly musket fire from the dense woods on either side of the Mansfield road. Buchel was mortally wounded. In a letter to his parents a Federal soldier described the charge:

> About 300 rebel cavalry came dashing along at full speed with their sabers drawn & yelling at the top of their voices. Capt. Jones who was then in command of our regt. (our Lieut. Col. being killed) ordered us to lay still untill he gave us orders to fire. When they got within about 100 yards from us Jones hollows "To your feet & boys let them have it." He had hardly got the words out of his mouth when every man was on his feet & such a roll of musketry I never wish to hear again. Out of that 300 cavalry I will guarante not 50 got back to their friends alive. I could see the poor fellows fall from their horses at ever shot we fired at them. They were truly brave fellows or they never would have ventured up so close. But they were engaged on the wrong side & met their just punishment.

Upon returning to the Confederate lines Debray's regiment was ordered to dismount and support Walker's Division, which was hotly engaged in the woods on Debray's left front.[49]

Forming his line of battle with the Missouri Division on the right and the Arkansas Division on the left, Churchill moved forward, only to discover after advancing three-quarters of a mile that he was not far enough to the right. He ordered his command to move by the right

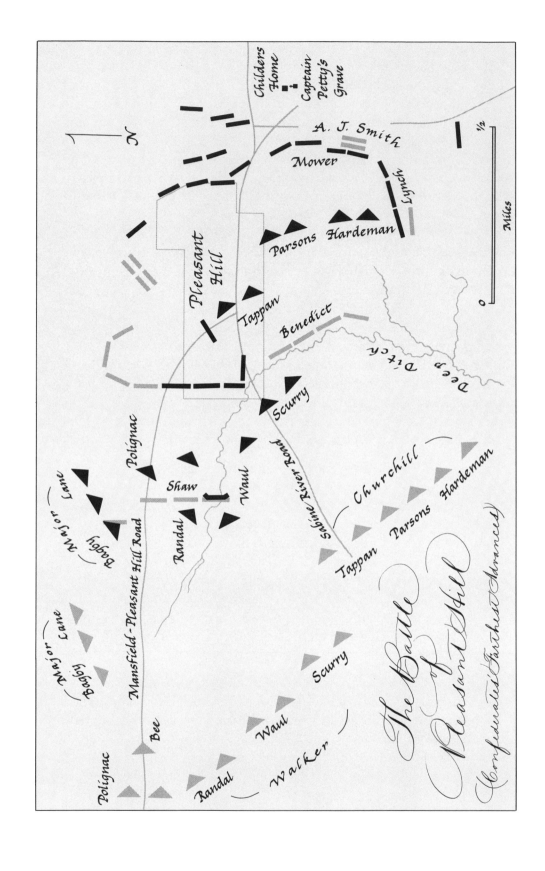

The Battle of Pleasant Hill

(Confederates Farthest Advanced)

flank, but again, because of the undergrowth and his unfamiliarity with the country, not far enough for a flanking movement. He made his turn to the left by the Sabine River road instead of the Fort Jesup road as planned. Shortly before 5 p.m. Churchill drove in the Federal skirmishers and hit Colonel Lewis Benedict's Third Brigade, First Division, Nineteenth Army Corps, which was posted behind the deep ditch, on the left flank and diagonally across the front; it broke and fled to the rear. During the Rebel assault Colonel Benedict, while occupying a conspicuous position on top of the slope in the rear of his brigade, had his horse shot from under him. He dispatched his aides to various portions of the brigade and during their absence was shot dead, a minié ball passing through his head. In all, five balls pierced his body. Colonel Francis Fessenden, commanding the Thirtieth Maine, which was on the left of Benedict's line of battle, described Churchill's attack in a letter to his wife:

> About 5 P. M. the company of colored skirmishers attached to the 16th Corps. were observed coming across the open ground to the left of the 3rd Brigade, passing the interval between the Brigade and the woods and disappeared. They were soon followed by the skirmishers of the 3rd Brigade who came in from the woods in front. The officer in command of the left company of skirmishers reported a Rebel Column in the woods, advancing without skirmishers and that he heard the command of their officers to halt, dress, and load at will. Col. Benedict commanding the 3rd Brigade, ordered some companys of skirmishers into the ditch in front of the line of battle and the company of skirmishers from the woods had <u>hardly</u> had time to form when the sharp zip zip of the minnie balls foretold the approaching assault. In a moment a heavy column emerged from the woods and dashed down the slope. The instant the firing commenced, the skirmishers in the ditch opened their fire and as the head of the column appeared, the skirmishers fell back and the line opened its fire along the front of the Brigade. With great impetuosity the rebel column surged down the slope, crossed the ditch, and driving the 3rd Brigade before it advanced almost in rear of the centre of the Army and gained short possession of a battery. The 165th, 173rd and 162nd fell back towards the centre of the position while the 30th Maine retreated to the cover of the woods upon its rear and left and was reformed upon the right of Mowers Brigade.

The Confederates captured 300 prisoners, got possession of a battery whose horses had been killed and reached Pleasant Hill, failing in their moment of triumph to see the dark blue masses of A. J. Smith's troops poised dangerously on their right flank. Parsons's Missourians were taken in flank and rolled up by the First Brigade, Third Division, Sixteenth Army Corps, under the command of Colonel William F. Lynch. Seizing the opportunity, Smith ordered his whole line forward. As Parsons's Division was driven back the right of Tappan's was exposed, and it too was forced to retire. The Federal advance now became a grand right wheel, pivoting on Pleasant Hill.[50]

Seeing Churchill's two divisions falling back in disorder, Walker ordered Scurry's Brigade to reinforce them. Wrote J. P. Blessington:

> The brigade stripped themselves of their blankets and knapsacks, in order that nothing might impede their work, and then swept down the hill, across the field, and on towards the enemy, delivering fire after fire on the enemy's forces. Batteries opened on them right and left, hailing grape and canister into their very faces, while from the woods, a stream of lead was poured before them. As their line swept along, the heroic General Scurry galloped towards the head of his column, halloing, "Come on, boys, you have got your chance at last." The order was quickly responded to, and with a desperate onset the whole line rushed forward upon the enemy. It was a fine sight, that charge of Scurry's Brigade to the death struggle.[51]

Scurry drove back the Fifty-eighth Illinois of Lynch's brigade for a quarter of a mile until they struck the full force of Smith's advancing line. The retreat of Tappan's left brigade (Gause's) threw Scurry's lines into disorder and hindered his advance. To relieve Scurry, Walker ordered Waul and Randal to charge across the field in two lines against the Federals fronting them. Robert S. Gould of Gould's Battalion in Randal's Brigade later described the advance:

> We moved on in beautiful order across the field. Our front as we moved was changing obliquing to the left. By degrees as we advanced a fire of small arms was opened on us from the woods on the opposite side of the field. As we came nearer the fire became hotter, and men began to fall. The noise of the firing and cries of the wounded filled the air. I remember noticing about this time Capt. Tullos of Co. S. crying out as he fell. No regular fire was returned on our side as yet, though some, I think, fired of their own accord. Gaining the shelter of a slight hollow or depression, the men pressed forward to a fence in front and from this point returned the fire briskly.[52]

Awaiting Waul's and Randal's men was Colonel William T. Shaw's brigade from Mower's Third Division, Sixteenth Army Corps, consisting of the Fourteenth Iowa, Twenty-seventh Iowa, Thirty-second Iowa and the Twenty-fourth Missouri. "Then came on the infantry, in solid column, with reckless daring, marching with their guns at right shoulder shift, until they arrived at the crest of a hill about twenty rods in front of our line," recalled H. N. Brockway, a sergeant in the Thirty-second Iowa. "At the command to fire they melted away. Again and again they rallied, aided by fresh troops, and came on with fierce yells to the charge, but each time were driven back from our front." Heedless of its losses, Walker's second line advanced over its dead and wounded comrades in the first line and began bending Shaw's left flank, passing around to the left of the Thirty-second Iowa into its rear and relieving Scurry. Smith, seeing Shaw's plight, ordered him to fall back. The three right regiments retreated in confusion, but the Thirty-second Iowa was cut off by Walker's troops pouring through on all sides. "My lines now faced in three directions," its commander, Colonel John Scott, reported. "I was completely enveloped, without orders, and virtually in the hands of the enemy had he dared to close in and overwhelm us with his masses now around us."[53]

In the meantime Scurry was urging his men forward, exclaiming aloud in his stentorian voice (according to Blessington), "Scurry's brigade may be annihilated, but must never retreat." A rifle ball glanced his cheek, slightly wounding him, but, hat in hand, he cheered on his men. "Brigadier-General Scurry . . . behaved most nobly," Taylor said in his official report, "and speaks highly of Colonel Waterhouse, commanding one of his regiments."[54] But A. J. Smith's advance was irresistible. Polignac was ordered forward to reinforce Walker. Standing in his saddle, the Frenchman shouted: "My boys, follow your Polignac." His men made several charges, but the Federals repulsed them, at times "as if by a resistless and superhuman power." Walker's troops fell back to the low ground and the ditch, where they put up a brave but useless resistance. Walker was shot in the groin, and Taylor ordered him to leave the field. Scurry's Brigade, while crossing the ditch, was attacked, and 247 men were captured. "The enemy made a stand at a ditch, which was about three-fourths of the width of the field from my original position," reported General Mower. "They lost largely in killed and prisoners here, and were, after a desperate resistance, dislodged and driven back into the woods." Noted Francis Fessenden: "The Rebel column in some confusion from its rapid advance was thrown back greatly shattered beyond the ditch, where a fresh Brigade coming to their support, they made a temporary stand. With the whole line advancing the enemy fled and disappeared in the woods. The line advanced nearly a mile but found no enemy." After nightfall the Confederate units separated in the dense woods and began firing at each other. Taylor, to prevent more confusion, withdrew his troops and fell back six miles to a water supply. Most of his cavalry continued on to Mansfield for water and forage. As the last Southerner disappeared into the woods Banks rode up to A. J. Smith and took his hand. "God bless you, general," he said. "You have saved the army." [55]

Taylor, with some cavalry, remained near the battlefield, where he was joined a few hours before midnight by Kirby Smith, who had ridden down from Shreveport. "Our repulse at Pleasant Hill was so complete and our command was so disorganized that had Banks followed up his success vigorously he would have met but feeble opposition to his advance on Shreveport," the department commander later claimed. However, after holding a council of war Banks retreated to Grand Ecore, where he could reunite his army with Porter's fleet, thus converting a tactical victory into a strategic defeat that sealed the fate of the Red River Campaign. "For what reason Banks retreated I don't know unless it be through mear cowardise," an Iowa soldier wrote from Grand Ecore:

> Nearly every officer & man condemn him for the act for the rebels retreated the same night. Had we followed up the next day I believe we could have got the whole lot of them. Just before night the tide of battle turned in our favor & we captured one Brigade of them [Scurry's] which still discouraged them more. So far this Red River expedition has been an entire failure. We have accomplished simply nothing & have lost a great number of men, besides teams & stores out of number. If what our officers say in regard to General Banks & his Red River Expedition be true, then there will be a heap of disgrace fall upon his head for every officer & man condemn him for retreating, as they consider it a burning shame & disgrace & numbers of them say they will never fight under him again. [56]

Ludwell Johnson wrote that Taylor's plan failed "because Churchill did not form his line of battle far enough to the South, with the result that instead of rolling up the Union flank, he crossed his right in front of the enemy's left and was himself rolled up." Churchill realized the chance that he had missed, and he said in his report that "Could our lines have been extended a half mile farther to the right it would have been a most brilliant success; but they were then stretched to their utmost tension." In his memoirs Taylor shouldered the blame for the failure of Churchill's attack. "Instead of intrusting the important attack by my right to a subordinate, I should have conducted it myself and taken Polignac's division to sustain it. . . . All this flashed upon me the instant I learned of the disorder of my right. Herein lies the vast difference between genius and commonplace; one anticipates errors, the other discovers them too late." However, the immediate responsibility was Churchill's. "A worthy gallant gentleman, General Churchill," said Taylor, "but not fortunate in war."[57]

Banks's total losses in the battle of Mansfield or Sabine Cross Roads were 115 killed, 648 wounded and 1,423 captured — a total of 2,186. Taylor reported that he had captured 2,500 prisoners, 20 guns, several stands of colors, many thousands of small arms and 250 wagons. He gave his own loss as around 1,000 men. At Pleasant Hill Banks suffered 1,506 casualties — 152 killed, 859 wounded and 495 captured. Taylor's killed and wounded came to 1,200 and prisoners to 426 — a total of 1,626. Walker's Division casualty returns for the two battles, although incomplete, showed 69 killed, 404 wounded and 141 missing, for a total of 614. Scurry's Brigade had 22 killed, 104 wounded and 124 missing. In his memoirs Taylor placed the missing from the brigade at 247 "at the time it was so nearly overwhelmed." Petty's regiment, the Seventeenth Texas, reportedly lost 16 dead, 35 wounded and 60 missing, and the number of missing was probably higher. George Washington Jones was taken prisoner. "I tell you it was a terrible time and the old soldiers say it was a harder fought battle than the battle of Shiloah [Shiloh]," an Iowa soldier in Shaw's Brigade said of Pleasant Hill. "But my prayer is that I may never witness another such a sight. Dead men & horses literally covered the ground for rod after rod, while the grones and cries of the wounded were too awful to listen to. We could hear them all night begging & praying for water."[58]

Two young boys, Richard Joshua Wilson and his brother Bob, were thinning corn in new ground near Pleasant Hill when the battle opened. Richard told his grandson, Waylon Maroney, that "It sounded like fire coming through a canebreak; cannons roared like thunder. We heard mama call us on the horn for dinner, but we had to find out what was going on." When they reached the battlefield men were lying everywhere, and smoke and dust were hanging over the area. Confederates and Federals were mixed up "like salt and pepper, horses were spinning like windmills, some without eyes, some looking like shells had gone clear through them. Men were crying for water." The two boys carried water in a five-gallon demijohn from a spring three-quarters of a mile down the hill to give drinks to the wounded and the dying. An unidentified doctor working on the wounded cautioned the boys to give only a little swallow to each man. They carried water all day, until the wounded were placed under roofs in the area.

The next day they watched as the ground was opened up with turning plows, and the dead of both armies were laid head to foot all the way around the south side of the Wilson place, and the whole hillside was "wrapped up with soldiers and the unburied dead." When the earth began to warm later in the season, huge cracks appeared in the ground. It swelled up in ridges, like a big mole run, and the entire hillside turned green with flies, according to Richard Wilson, who told his grandsons he never forgot that time.[59]

Among the dead at Pleasant Hill was Captain Elijah P. Petty. In 1913 T. F. Mays of Waco, who had been a sergeant in Petty's Company F, described in a letter to Don G. Petty how his father had been mortally wounded:

> . . . now this was the 9th day April 1864 and after the Battle was almost won your dear Father Capt. E. P. Petty was killed. He was in the front of the battle with only a few of his men as we were badly scattered. He was shot through the breast with a grape shot about 3:30 in the evening and one of our men by the name of L. P. Barrett was by his side and he gave him a drink of water out of his

cantina. He fell on his pistol. He asked Mr. Barrett to turn him over and take his pistol off as he was laying on it and it was hurting but he was suffering so much that he couldnt bear to be moved and the Yanks came and captured Mr Barrett although Barrett could have made his escape and your father urged him to do so but he would not for he loved him so that [he] stood by him to the last, and he was carried to a home a short distance off and I think placed on a cot in a Widow Ladies yard and he died there sometime that night and was buried close to that house. . . .[60]

Two years later Mays, now living in Deansville, Texas, wrote a letter to the editor of the Bastrop *Advertiser* on the 51st anniversary of the battles of Mansfield and Pleasant Hill. "Those two days, fifty-two [sic] years ago, were bloody days for some of the dear old Bastrop boys," he recalled. In giving his recollections of the fighting Mays again recounted the circumstances of Petty's death and paid him the following tribute: "A braver man or a purer soul was never sacrificed on a battle field than Captain E. P. Petty. Wash Jones was our Colonel and I have heard him say that Petty was the coolest and bravest man in battle that he ever saw."[61]

The home that Petty was carried to was the Childers House in Pleasant Hill, Banks's headquarters during the battle and a temporary hospital afterwards for the wounded of both armies. It was two-storied, with eight large rooms; there was a spacious hall in front and a very large dining room and kitchen in the back. A balcony graced the front of the frame house, with a wide gallery, supported by four round pillars with fluted ornamental work at the top and bottom. Mrs. Maria Childers, a widow, owned the home, which had been built in 1859 by her husband, John S. Childers, at a cost of $10,000, not including the labor which was done by slaves. During the battle the family members took refuge in the cellar in the rear of the house. Several minié balls passed through the walls of the house, and one 10-pound round bomb lodged between the ceiling boards but did not cause much damage. Soon after the battle wounded began to fill the house, using every hall and room except the dining room, kitchen and two bedrooms. After three or four days' delay the two brick wings of the unfinished college were utilized as a hospital for the Federal wounded, except those in a camp near a house two miles east of town; and at Mrs. Childers's request, her home was then given up to the Confederate wounded.[62]

On June 2, 1864, Major Charles Morgan of Morgan's Texas Cavalry Battalion in Parsons's Brigade wrote Margaret Petty the following letter concerning her husband's burial:

Mrs Petty

I would have written to you long before this time, but have been so busily Engaged following & fighting the hated Enemy that we had no time or opportunity of writing & I thought that you Whould have heard long since from the numerous friends of your lost Husband the full particulars of his death. What a loss not only to his bereaved & loving Family but also to his Country, which needs the brave & gallant such as he was to defend her rights & avenge her wrongs. But he has gone & it should be a consolation to his bereaved Family & friends that he died so bravely, gallantly charging & driving the hated Vandals that would over run our Country & avenge themselves on Children & Women. God Grant that they may soon meet with their just reward such as a just God will deal to such Savages. None but those who have witnessed their cruel deeds can imagine the extent or cruelty of them.

Truly do I sympathis with you in this your greatest Tryal the loss of a devoted & loving Husband but it was the will of God & we should all try and bear with patience his decrees. I with my command came to the Battlefield about dark & learning of his death I left the command & went to look for his body which I found in a yard near Pleasant Hill. He had been dead 24 hours. Not having any men with me to dig his grave my command having gone on in pursuit of the Enemy I waited until morning & got a detail from Capt Highsmiths Co & he was buried near the House in a corner of the yard selected by us & that Grave received one of the nobles & braves men that ever went from our State. I got his Sash, Handkerchief, knife, Comb & have them in my wagon & will send them to you as soon as possible. I would send them by some of Highsmiths furloughed men but my wagon is still up in Pleasant Hill. The things will be taken care of and sent to you. He was shot with a Grape Shot in the center of the Breast 3 inchs below the neck the ball Passing through his body. He was buried as well as we could have him in his cloths that he wore when he was shot. He had on the Gray [*word illegible*] Coat he wore from home. You have many friends who mourn with you in this great loss. [*Word illegible*] that you may meet him in a better world. I am, Mrs Petty

Your friend & fellow mourner
Charles L. Morgan

My love to my Mother, Relatives & friends. I am doing well.
Charles[63]

Thus, Petty's wife and children knew how, when and where he was killed, but for 25 years not the exact place of his burial, only that it was in the yard of a house near Pleasant Hill. In 1889 Don G. Petty, in conversation with a Mr. Ruffin of the firm of Curtis & Co. in St. Louis, Missouri, learned that his father was buried in the yard of W. D. Gooch's home in Pleasant Hill and that Ruffin had had the grave shown to him. Petty made arrangements to visit the site with his wife and mother. Gooch, who had married one of the Childers girls and now owned the Childers House (Maria Childers had died in 1886) was then living at New Pleasant Hill, or Sodus, two miles from the old town. He took the Pettys out to the house, showed them the battlefield and pointed out Captain Petty's grave, saying: "That is undoubtedly the grave of Captain Petty." "My father was buried in the south east corner of Mr. Gooch's yard, and for over twenty years the family had kept up the grave, and pointed it out to visitors as that of 'Capt. Petty from Texas,'" Don Petty wrote the editor of the Bastrop *Advertiser*. "They were very kind to all the Confederate soldiers, but particularly to my father." "It seemed," Petty quoted Gooch as saying, "that Capt. Petty had somehow gained the confidence and love of the family in the short time that he was there, and that they could not forget him; that as he lay on his bed of suffering and requested that he be buried in that beautiful spot that he could see from the window, that they resolved to carry out his every wish, and they did it."

As Don Petty stood on the porch of the Childers House the battlefield stretched before him, and he imagined he could see the "raging battle":

Immediately in front facing from the house was Gen. Banks army, and advancing upon it the "One hundred thousand mad Texans" as General Banks afterwards expressed it. To the right, facing the Federals, was the Texas cavalry, and to the left my father's company, while immediately in front was the brave Texas and Louisiana infantry. There was the ruins of the old church, and to the far left the brick college, afterwards used as a Federal hospital. Above my head could be seen the hole in the wall made by a shell thrown by the Confederates which cut the pillow on which the head of Gen. Banks had lain the night before. To my side could be seen the holes made by the minnie balls. Walking over the field I could see the incline where my father fell. To the extreme left is still to be seen the old Natchitoches road along which the Federals retreated after their ignominius defeat. In my imagination I could see the great battle, and how I wished I had been there and fought, and shared in that great victory. After quite a while looking over the battle field, we returned to Sodus, a sad party; there the mother who, after twenty five years of waiting had come to a strange land to claim her dead and the one who had been deprived of a fond father's love and protection.

It was the family's intention to remove Petty's remains to Bastrop; and in his letter to the *Advertiser*, Don Petty stated that "it would afford us great pleasure to have his old comrades and friends accompany his remains to Fair-View Cemetery." However, the body was too badly decomposed to move.[64]

In its May 25, 1889, issue the *Advertiser* had carried a story about the Petty family's trip to Pleasant Hill to visit Captain Petty's grave, which it copied from the Orange (Texas) *Tribune*.[65] This prompted a Hutto man, H. A. Highsmith, a member of M. D. Highsmith's Company D, Twelfth Texas Cavalry, Parsons's Brigade, to write the paper an account of Petty's death and burial. The brigade had remained in the Shreveport area until April 4 when it was ordered to join Taylor; it was held in reserve at Keatchie, missing the battles of Mansfield and Pleasant Hill. Taylor ordered it to the front on the night of April 8. Wrote Highsmith:

> Capt. E. P. Petty was fatally wounded in the battle of Pleasant Hill, La., and after the close of the battle he was carried to the Federal hospital, where he died. The hospital was established in a two-story residence, about one-fourth of a mile south of the village, and Capt. Petty was found there among the dead, by Major C. L. Morgan. My regiment reached the battleground about dark and some of Highsmith's company meeting Major Morgan, learned Capt. Petty's whereabouts. Being Sergeant-Major of the 12th Texas cavalry I had [a] detail made from Highsmith's company, under Sergeant Freeman Faust; the detail as follows: M. S. Hughes, Frank H. Perkins, Wm. Faulkner, and others whose names I do not remember. The remains were wrapped in M. S. Hughes' blanket and the burial took place at night, by torch light. He was buried in the southwest corner of the inclosure in which we found him, and was placed there all alone. For further reference will refer you to the above named parties, some of whom are living in your county.[66]

After reading Highsmith's letter in the *Advertiser*, Frank Petty, who was living in Orange, Texas, wrote him, seeking additional information on Captain Petty's burial and the present whereabouts of the burial party. On June 6, 1889, Highsmith replied:

> Yours 3d inst to hand and duly noted and in reply will answer as near my memory serves me Mr M S Hughes resides at Elgin Bastrop Co Texas Frank H Perkins is a brother to Mrs J H Goodman of

Bastrop and the outher parties I am unable to give you any information of them. Your Father was buried the next night after the Battle of Pleasant Hill [w]raped in his own coat and M S Hughes Blanket and unless things have been changed I think I can find the spot allthough he was buried at night. I cut his name in a board an[d] placed it at his head but I still think it must have been in the S W corner of the yard although it was at night. The bu[i]lding at which we found his corps[e] was a frame building and fronted the vilage of Pleasant Hill which was north of it and he was laid in the yard with 25 or 30 dead Yanks with his over coat over his face and if the lady [Maria Childers] mentioned had him buried according to his request it appears he would have had better attention than we found him in. He had the appeerence of having been dead several hours as the flies had blown his face and ther[e] had been no blood washed from him. In regard to his being conscious when he was brought off the field I can only give you the statement of wounded C S Soldier that was in the Hospitle that we saw stated that your Father was brought in the evening before and died the morning of the night we buried him and that he never spok[e]. The over coat we found with his remains was one that I had seen him wear manny times before the war. It was in Color either a brown or Snuff Col and in pattern a talma. I am a brother of M B Highsmith and was born and raised in the town of Bastrop and known then as Albert Highsmith and knew your father from the time I was a small boy until I went in the army. Mr Hughes & Perkins knew him well. Perkins was raised in Piney Creek about 1½ miles from the town of Bastrop. My communication to Capt Cain [editor of the *Advertiser*] was not to raise any controversy but to give correct information to the children of one I considered a good friend of mine during his life and it has allways greaved me that I was unable to even procure a roughf box if no better for him — the Regiment to which I belonged was not in the Battle but marched there the next evening to my recolection about one hour by sun and the next morning was ordered forward to follow up the retreat of the enamey and I have never seen the vilage of Pleasant Hill since. If there was any Ladies or men eather there that were Citizens I never saw them and as to cimpathy for the wounded or dead Soldiers there was non[e] give it only comrad[e]s even at the late hour that I reach there — there was a wounded C S Soldier shot through the temples with his brains running out at the bullet holes and still living and no one to look after him—Your father was Shot in the breast about 2 or 3 inches below the sink in neck where the breast bone joins the neck and the wound had the apearence of being made with a grape shot as it was very large and the men with me expressed a surprise that he lived any length of time after being wounded. My reason for neaver saying any thing in regard to this matter was that the first time it was mentioned that members of Highsmith Company buried your father it was contradicted & what little part I took in his burial was not for honor or a big name but for the regard I had for your father and the duty we owe to each outher and not wishing to se[e] your boys remove the remains of some one of no relation to you. I would be glad for you to Communicate with Mr Hughes and se[e] how his memory serves him in regard to this matter. Likely he will be able to refer you to outhers. Any outher information you think I can give to you it will give me pleasure if in power.[67]

Highsmith thus called into question Gooch's story that the dying Petty had requested that he be buried in the yard of the Childers House and that the family had carried out his wish. His account of the burial tallied with Charles Morgan's description in his June 2, 1864, letter to Margaret Petty. However, in an October 1906 article in the *Annals of Iowa*, "Reminiscences of the Battle of Pleasant Hill," Henry H. Childers, Mrs. Childers's grandson who was living in the house with her at the time of the battle, confirmed and embellished Gooch's story:

One Confederate soldier who was brought to our house for treatment was Captain Petty of Bastrop, Texas. His case was hopeless and just before his death, upon being told that he could not live, he was raised in his bed and allowed to look out the window for the last time. His eyes fell upon a piece of green sward in the corner of the small yard around the house, near by which stood a large oak. He asked to be buried in that little corner, stating that he did not care to be buried with the other soldiers, as his identity might be lost in the confusion of indiscriminate burial. His request was granted, and to this day the dust of his bones is in that same spot, returned to its native element and now mingled with the soil that made the grass green for his fading vision. The last time I saw this grave, it was unmarked by stone or board, but the neighborhood knew that it was the last resting place of Captain Petty, the bravest of his regiment.[68]

It is clear from the Morgan and Highsmith letters that Petty was not buried by the Childers family, contrary to Gooch's statement that "they resolved to carry out his every wish, and they did it," and Henry Childers's that "his request was granted." Moreover, the burial party selected the grave site without consulting with Mrs. Childers, whose whereabouts at the time are unknown (she may have been asleep in the house). However, these facts in themselves do not necessarily invalidate the Gooch-Childers account of Petty's request. Highsmith's description of the condition of Petty's body ("no blood washed from him") and his statement that in regard to Petty being conscious when he was brought off the field, "a wounded C S Soldier" in the house "stated that your Father was brought in the evening before and died the morning of the night we buried him and that he never spoke," while casting further doubt on the story, are also not conclusive against its validity. Perhaps it was not Petty, but another soldier that the wounded Johnny Reb saw. Highsmith's charge that only their comrades showed any sympathy for the wounded or dead soldiers is contradicted by Captain Solon F. Benson of the Thirty-second Iowa, who lost an arm in the battle. Benson, one of the 400 severely wounded Federal soldiers left behind when Banks retreated, later paid tribute to "the kind-hearted southern ladies" who "were frequent visitors at the hospitals and generously supplemented the bill of fare with such delicacies as their slender larders afforded, for they, too, had been plundered by both armies, and were almost constrained to part with the widow's last mite." Among these "noble ladies," he identified "a very chief among them all, Mrs. Maria Childers, mistress of the Childers estate."[69]

Although the possibility certainly exists that the story was fabricated by the Childers family to explain the presence of a solitary grave in their yard (which, it should be noted, they kept up and pointed out to visitors

as Captain Petty's), there is no conclusive evidence to contradict it; and it has an established and honored place in local tradition. Mrs. R. A. Rembert, born Sallie Chapman, daughter of Postmaster Stephen Chapman, was living in the middle of Pleasant Hill at the time of the battle. Interviewed at age 89 by Mrs. L. C. Bridges, Mrs. Rembert, who was thought to be the only living eyewitness of the battle, recalled, in Mrs. Bridges's words, that "Captain Petty was buried near the Childers home where he was shot down. He lived only a short time and asked to be buried near where he was wounded."[70]

Some time before the Petty family visited the Childers House, the village of Pleasant Hill was moved to the nearest railroad station two miles southwest, called Sodus by the New Orleans and Pacific branch of the Texas & Pacific Railroad, though retaining its old post office name of Pleasant Hill. W. D. Gooch had the Childers House torn down and used some of the materials in the construction of a new home at Sodus. After an absence of many years Henry Childers, now a New York lawyer, returned to the battlefield in May 1895, just in time to see the dismantled remains of the old mansion. Cast down with sadness at the fate of this historic relic, he asked Gooch why he had not asked the United States government to buy the house and the adjoining battlefield as a government reservation. Gooch replied that he had contemplated that very thing, but the government had moved slowly; he had become impatient and decided to put the building to a practical use, only to learn after the demolition had begun that if he had waited a little longer, the government would have taken action. "Nothing remains of the old Pleasant Hill," Childers stated in 1906, "and I am informed that the main street now forms part of a field cultivated in cotton or corn. The buildings were torn down and moved to Sodus station."[71] By that date the Petty family had bought the land on which the Childers House had stood and marked Petty's grave with a gray granite monument (the only one on all the battlefield) surrounded by a black wrought-iron fence. Inscribed on the tombstone are the words:

E. P. Petty
of
Bastrop, Texas
Captain of
Co. F 17th Vol. Inf.
Scurrys Brigade
Killed at the Battle of Pleasant Hill Louisiana
April 9, 1864
Erected by his sons[72]

[1] Henry W. Halleck to Nathaniel Banks, January 4 and 11, 1864, *Official Records Armies*, series I, XXXIV, pt. 2, pp. 15–16, 55–56, 481, 494, 496–97; Johnson, *Red River Campaign*, pp. 325–26. On the origins of the Red River Campaign, see Johnson, *Red River Campaign*, pp. 3–86.

[2] Kerby, *Kirby Smith's Confederacy*, pp. 71, 284; Waldo W. Moore, "The Defense of Shreveport — The Confederacy's Last Redoubt," in *Military Analysis of the Civil War: An Anthology*, Editors of *Military Affairs* (Millwood: Kto Press, 1977), p. 396; William A. Albaugh, *Tyler, Texas, C.S.A.* (Harrisburg: Stackpole Co. 1958).

[3] On March 2 two Federal gunboats shelled Fort Beauregard at Harrisonburg, but Polignac's Texas Brigade and a field battery hugged the riverbank and held the town while damaging *Fort Hindman*. After the warships passed upriver Polignac withdrew his men to their camps a mile from town. However, the gunboats returned an hour later, and Federal sailors set fire to some buildings in Harrisonburg before being driven out by the Thirty-first Texas. The fires were extinguished under a steady bombardment from the warships, and all but three houses were saved. The next day the Federal gunboats dropped down to Trinity, where they destroyed the pontoon bridge across Little River and captured three hidden 32-pounder cannon before steaming for the Red River. The Confederates lost six killed and ten wounded, as compared to two killed and twelve wounded aboard the Federal gunboats. "Loss of the big guns made the expedition a Confederate defeat of sorts," wrote Alwyn Barr. "But rain had made the roads nearly impassable for infantry; removal of the heavy guns had been virtually impossible under the prevailing conditions. Again the Texas brigade had proved it could operate effectively under its new commander and had also cleared away most lingering doubts about the fighting qualities of the retrained dismounted cavalry regiments." Alwyn Barr, *Polignac's Texas Brigade*, Texas Gulf Coast Historical Association Publication Series, VIII (November 1964), pp. 37–38.

[4] On the evening of March 4 the gunboats that had been bombarding Fort Beauregard appeared off the Atchafalaya Bayou. Captain Haldeman's battery was placed in position at Simmesport, supported by Scurry's Brigade, to await the enemy's approach. Late in the evening a courier informed Scurry that the gunboats had left. On the morning of the 5th the brigade quit work on the fortifications on Yellow Bayou. According to Blessington, they were known as Fort Humbug, "which proved afterwards a very appropriate name." On March 6 all the division's sick were ordered to Alexandria, there to be transported on boats to Shreveport. On the evening of the 7th Scurry's Brigade was notified to hold itself in readiness to march at a moment's notice; news was received that Banks's army, numbering some 30,000, was at Brashear City and that its destination appeared to be the Red River country. On the 11th it was learned that the Federals were near the town of Franklin, on Bayou Teche. Blessington, *Walker's Texas Division*, p. 166.

Banks concentrated his troops on the Teche under Franklin. On the evening of March 13 the cavalry advance moved out on the road to Alexandria. Two days later the First Division of the Nineteenth Army Corps under William Emory and Thomas Ransom's division of the Thirteenth Army Corps began their march up the Teche. Grover took the Second Division of the Nineteenth to Alexandria by steamer. On March 10 General A. J. Smith, with 15 infantry regiments and two batteries of light artillery from the Sixteenth Army Corps, and six infantry regiments and one battery of artillery from the Seventeenth Army Corps, sailed from Vicksburg for the Red River, accompanied by Ellet's Marine Brigade. After arriving at the mouth of the river about midnight, March 11, Smith received a dispatch from Banks advising him that heavy rains had so delayed his troops that he would not be able to reach Alexandria before March 21.

On conferring with Admiral Porter, who had assembled a fleet of 19 gunboats at the mouth of the Red River, Smith learned that Fort De Russy would have to be taken before they could proceed to Alexandria. It was decided to attack the fort in conjunction, the army in the rear by land and the navy by river. Leaving the mouth of the Red River about midnight, March 12, Smith proceeded up the river to the mouth of the Atchafalaya and then down that river to Simmesport, which was reached about 5 p.m. the same day. The troops were preceded by nine gunboats; the other warships went on up the Red River to clear away the heavy obstructions the Confederates had placed in the river and to "amuse" Fort De Russy until the army could land at Simmesport and reach its rear. Winters, *Civil War in Louisiana*, pp. 326–27; A. J. Smith to William T. Sherman, September 26, 1865, *Official Records Armies*, series I, XXXIV, pt. 1, p. 304; David D. Porter to Gideon Welles, March 15, 1864, *Official Records Navies*, series I, XXVI, pp. 24–26.

[5] On the evening of March 12 Scurry's Brigade, numbering about 1,400 men with Haldeman's Battery, took position at "Fort Humbug." It was learned that four of the enemy's gunboats and transports loaded with troops had arrived at Simmesport, before the infantry pickets were informed by the cavalry of their approach. The pickets were taken completely by surprise and narrowly escaped being captured. Pickets above Simmesport reported that the entire enemy fleet of gunboats and a large number of transports were coming down the Atchafalaya. Scurry immediately informed Walker of the enemy's landing by courier. "4 gunboats landing troops in Simsport," his scrawled note stated. "I have advanced to the works & will try to check their advance. Troops in fine spirits & moving down handsomely." Walker, at his headquarters in Marksville, informed Taylor that he would move at daylight with Randal's and Hawes's brigades to support Scurry on Yellow Bayou, but he admitted the position was untenable because it could be turned at the present low stage of water. "I am embarassed to know how to cover Fort De Russy," he admitted, "as against such a force as the enemy evidently has. It would be extremely hazardous to risk an engagement on this island around Marksville, out of which there is no egress except by the bridge over Bayou Du Lac."

Meanwhile, Scurry arranged his line of battle to inflict heavy casualties on an attack across Yellow Bayou in front of his fortifications. The bridge across the bayou was destroyed by the pioneer corps after the infantry pickets had crossed. "General Scurry and staff appeared to be in the height of their glory, as they rode along the lines," Blessington remembered. "General Scurry made a brief remark to his troops, informing them that, although he did not make a speech to them when he took command of the brigade, when called upon to do so, he would now address them a few words, and the sum and substance of his remarks were, 'that he expected every officer and soldier of his brigade to do his duty.'" The men gave three hearty cheers for Scurry, three for Walker and three for "Fort Humbug." After the cheering stopped the troops waited anxiously behind their breastworks for the first sight of the enemy. William R. Scurry to John G. Walker, March 12, 1864, Walker Papers; Walker to Richard Taylor, March 12, 1864, *Official Records Armies*, series I, XXXIV, pt. 1, p. 597; Blessington, *Walker's Texas Division*, pp. 166–77.

But Scurry decided that the fortifications could not be held. As he reported: "These works were rendered almost useless for purposes of defense; the swamps, which, from being usually impassable at this season of the year, had been relied on to protect their flanks — otherwise without protection — having dried up, and being perfectly practicable for troops." The brigade left their camp about 10 p.m. that night and fell back slowly. After marching 12 miles they made camp near Moreauville. The following morning (March 13), after burning the bridge over the Bayou De Glaize, they marched five miles and joined the rest of the division at the Long Bridge near Moreauville. On the morning of March 13 A. J. Smith sent the two divisions of the Sixteenth Army Corps, under command of Brigadier General Joseph A. Mower, forward with directions to move out about five miles on the Fort De Russy road, capture or disperse any parties of the enemy in the vicinity, and gain all the information possible of the state of the roads and position of the enemy. The division of the Seventeenth Army Corps was ordered under arms in readiness to support Mower if necessary. During the day the Federals advanced about five miles, capturing some wagons and about 20 men belonging to Scurry's Brigade, who had been sent back to their old camp after baggage. Smith then ordered Mower to return to Simmesport. "I shall endeavor to hold the enemy in check here [Long Bridge]," Walker informed Taylor at 12:30 p.m. on March 13, "but it will be unsafe to linger here should Fort De Russy be reduced, which would enable the enemy to throw his whole force up Red River as high as Alexandria, and in that case we would be thrown back upon the desert toward the Sabine. I should be glad to have your views upon the situation." A. J. Smith to William T. Sherman, September 26, 1865, *Official Records Armies*, series I, XXXIV, pt. 1, pp. 304–5; John G. Walker to Richard Taylor, March 13, 1864, *ibid.*, p. 492.

Earlier in the day Taylor advised Walker that if he could attack the enemy at Simmesport "with the least hope of success, the sooner you attack him the better. He should be attacked, if possible, before his landing is completed." However, if the enemy was in such "largely superior force" as to compel a retreat, Walker should retire by the De Glaize road in the direction of Evergreen. Mouton's Louisiana Brigade, commanded by Colonel Henry Gray, was at Lecompte and would be ordered to form a junction with Walker by way of Bayou Huffpower. Polignac's Brigade would probably arrive in Alexandria that day and would be ordered to his support as soon as possible. If compelled to fall back by the De Glaize road, Walker would be covering Fort De Russy to some extent, as "it is not likely the enemy would march immediately in toward the fort, leaving you on his flank. Every hour that the enemy is held in check by your presence in his front or on his flank must be improved to get everything in complete readiness at Fort De Russy." A. H. May to John G. Walker, March 13, 1864, *ibid.*, pp. 492–93. Walker's report of his operations, March 12–19, 1864, is in *ibid.*, pp. 597–601.

⁶On the morning of March 14 Walker's Division, numbering about 6,000 men, marched to a point about five miles west of the village of Mansura, built in the middle of a prairie, and about two miles from the Long Bridge, which was burned. Walker selected level ground for his infantry to maneuver on, while the site was solid enough for the artillery. "This morning I arrived at Mansura in time to see General Walker's preparations for a fight with the Yankees," Felix Pierre Poché noted in his diary. "The latter were advancing on his position this morning and show signs of engaging in combat. Walker formed his line of battle on the Mansura

prairie with his left wing placed on Mansura and his right in the woods at Grand Pont. Being anxious to see the fight, I offered my services as aide-de-camp to General Scurry who accepted immediately, and I fell in line with his general staff, helping to transmit his orders. The army was making preparations to fight, the regiments lined up one behind the other, the commands were given and promptly obeyed by the various commanders, the Batteries came at a gallop dispersing here and there among the regiments, the aides-de-camp of the various generals on their beautiful horses, galloped between the lines, and transmitted the orders of their superiors, the male nurses of the hospitals with their identification marks consisting of a white cloth attached to their arms, carrying their boyards, formed a spectacle at the same time interesting, sublime and sad to observe by those who know that soon the cannon will begin to rumble and belch forth their deadly missiles on that band of men and in a few minutes the ground will be covered with bloody corpses." Bearss, ed., *A Louisiana Confederate*, p. 94.

A. J. Smith left Simmesport with his whole command at about 9 p.m. March 13, bivouacking for the night after going four miles. The next morning at 3 o'clock he moved toward Fort De Russy. Instead of attacking Walker, Smith tore down an old cotton gin and used the timber to bridge Bayou De Glaize at Mansura. Using the bridge and a ferryboat, he crossed the bayou and moved north and west, going around Walker and leaving him on his left. Smith directed General Thomas Kilby Smith, who was at the rear of his column, "to keep well closed up and watch carefully the left flank and rear." Walker fell back to Bayou Du Lac, marching 28 miles closely followed by the Federal cavalry. The bridge across Bayou Du Lac was burned after all the troops had crossed. In the meantime Smith invested Fort De Russy. The Confederate artillery opened fire with five guns. Just before sunset a Federal charge carried the fort, and the garrison surrendered. The Federals lost only 3 killed and 35 wounded; they captured 10 guns and 319 prisoners, killed 5 and wounded 4. Nothing was saved from the fort but two large 32-pounder Parrott guns, which were removed before the Federal troops arrived and accompanied Walker's Division on its retreat. "These huge guns, transformed into field pieces, and each drawn by a

dozen oxen, presented such a novel appearance that, when first seen by our troops, they created no little merriment," Blessington commented. "They were christened by the name of the 'Bull Battery,' by some of the troops and were afterwards thus known during the entire campaign." *Official Records Armies*, series I, XXXIV, pt. 1, pp. 598–99; Blessington, *Walker's Texas Division*, pp. 172–74; Winters, *Civil War in Louisiana*, p. 328; Wm. Byrd, "The Capture of Fort De Russy, La.," *Land We Love*, III (January 1869), pp. 185–87. In his memoirs Taylor remarked sarcastically of the capture of Fort De Russy: "Thus much for our Red River Gibraltar." Taylor, *Destruction and Reconstruction*, p. 155. General A. J. Smith's account of the capture of Fort De Russy is in *Official Records Armies*, series I, XXXIV, pt. 1, pp. 305–6. General Joseph A. Mower's report is in *ibid.*, pp. 316–17. He gives the number of Confederates captured as 260.

⁷Taylor's entire force on the south side of the Red River consisted of 5,300 infantry, 500 cavalry and 300 artillerymen, and General St. John R. Liddel, on the north side, had about the same number of cavalry and a four-gun battery. "From Texas, if at all, the delayed reinforcements must come, and it was vital to cover the roads from the Sabine," Taylor noted in his memoirs. Walker's Division remained at Bayou Du Lac until the evening of the 14th when, without waiting for instructions from Taylor, it made a march of 20 miles to Lloyd's Bridge on Bayou Boeuf, some 25 miles south of Alexandria. Accompanying the division was Mouton's Louisiana Brigade, which Walker found camped on the Huffpower, 19 miles south of Fort De Russy, under orders to reinforce his division. Taylor assumed command on the Boeuf. On the 18th he marched from Bayou Boeuf on the Burr's Ferry road to the plantation of Carroll Jones, a wealthy free Negro, which was reached on the evening of the 17th. Here, where the Burr's Ferry and Natchitoches roads separated, was a depot of forage, and he encamped. Taylor determined to remain at Carroll Jones's plantation until the last moment, "hoping to hear of re-enforcements which . . . I had reason to expect." On March 15 Polignac's Brigade left Alexandria to join Walker. His brigade and the Louisiana Brigade were united in a division for General Mouton. Colonel W. G. Vincent's Second Louisiana Cavalry, from Opelousas, joined on the 19th. In the meantime the advance of Porter's fleet arrived off Alexandria on the 15th, and the town was occupied the next day. Thus Porter and Smith were at Alexandria ahead of time. Banks's cavalry arrived on the 19th, followed by the infantry and artillery on the 25th and 26th. *Official Records Armies*, series I, XXXIV, pt. 1, pp. 561, 600; A. H. May to John G. Walker, March 15, 1864, Walker Papers; Taylor, *Destruction and Reconstruction*, p. 156; Richard B. Irwin, "The Red River Campaign," *Battles and Leaders*, IV, ed. Johnson and Buel, pp. 349–50 (hereafter cited as Irwin, "Red River Campaign").

⁸A. J. Smith's command on loan from Sherman consisted of two divisions of the Sixteenth Army Corps under Joseph A. Mower and Thomas Kilby Smith's division of the Seventeenth Army Corps, numbering about 10,000 men. There were 3,000 troops in Alfred W. Ellet's Marine Brigade which accompanied Smith. Banks's forces on the Teche under William B. Franklin consisted of William H. Emory's and Cuvier C. Grover's divisions of the Nineteenth Army Corps, about 10,500 strong; Robert A. Cameron's and Thomas E. G. Ransom's divisions of the Thirteenth Army Corps, about 4,800; and a division of cavalry and mounted infantry under Albert L. Lee, numbering 4,600, for a total of 19,900. The grand total was 32,900. Petty's estimate of 37,000 was thus only 4,100 high. Irwin, "Red River Campaign," pp. 349–50.

⁹The cavalry coming from Texas under the command of General Thomas Green was organized into two divisions, commanded by Hamilton P. Bee and James P. Major. Bee had the brigades of Xavier B. Debray and August C. Buchel, and Major

those of Walter P. Lane and Arthur P. Bagby. Lester N. Fitzhugh, "Texas Forces in the Red River Campaign, March-May, 1864," *Texas Military History*, 3 (Spring 1963), p. 20 (hereafter cited as Fitzhugh, "Texas Forces in the Red River Campaign").

[10] Sterling Price's infantry from Arkansas, 4,000 to 5,000 strong, arrived at Shreveport on March 24. Parks, *Edmund Kirby Smith*, p. 380.

[11] On March 20 Taylor sent the Second Louisiana Cavalry, led by Vincent, into the Bayou Rapides valley to scout towards Alexandria. Federal cavalry sent out by A. J. Smith skirmished briskly with Vincent's troops on the 20th and the next morning. Taylor sent Edgar's Battery of light artillery, which was attached to Scurry's Brigade, to assist the Louisianians. Vincent encamped on Henderson's Hill, some 23 miles above Alexandria; the hill commanded the junction of Bayou Rapides and Bayou Cotile. Winters, *Civil War in Louisiana*, p. 330; *Official Records Armies*, series I, XXXIV, pt. 1, p. 561.

[12] On the rainy night of March 21–22 General Joseph Mower, guided by some Jayhawkers, attacked Vincent's camp from the rear of the hill, taking the Confederates without firing a shot. Vincent and a few of his men succeeded in escaping, but Mower took over 200 prisoners and Edgar's Battery. "This sad news fell like a thunderbolt on our division, as each brigade exhibited considerable jealousy towards the others concerning the Nonpareil Battery," wrote Blessington; "all three of the brigades claiming it as their battery." Walker's and Mouton's divisions formed in line of battle near Carroll Jones's for about an hour, but hearing no news from the enemy (Mower marched back to Alexandria), marched towards Pleasant Hill by way of Fort Jesup and on the morning of April 1 encamped near the town. Taylor arrived there the same day. That evening Thomas Green arrived from Texas and joined Taylor; he informed him that Debray's Twenty-sixth Cavalry Regiment, and Moseley's and McMahan's batteries, were moving up from Many to Pleasant Hill. *Official Records Armies*, series I, XXXIV, pt. 1, p. 562; Blessington, *Walker's Texas Division*, pp. 177–79; Winters, *Civil War in Louisiana*, p. 336.

[13] A song, words and music by Stephen Collins Foster.

[14] Colonel Henry C. McNeill's Fifth Texas Cavalry, numbering 250 men of whom 50 were unarmed, and Colonel Philemon T. Hebert's Seventh Texas Cavalry, numbering 350 men of whom 125 were unarmed, were the first reinforcements to reach Taylor since the opening of the campaign. *Official Records Armies*, series I, XXXIV, pt. 1, p. 562.

[15] "We are getting along badly here," S. W. Farrow of the Nineteenth Texas Infantry complained to his wife. "We are getting nothing to eat except bread. I have not had enough to eat for more than one meal a day for seventeen days, except two days. There is a great deal of dissatisfaction in camp. The men are literally starving here. A great many are talking of leaving the field and they will do it if they are not better fed very seasonable. Sensible men can see that we had better quit before times get any worse. The existing laws in our State is one great cause of discontent. When times get so that your women and children are to be put on half rations, and to take away a great portion of the cloth they make it will be time for us to wind it up." S. W. Farrow to Josephine Farrow, March 29, 1864, Farrow Papers.

[16] Because their ammunition was defective, Kirby Smith decided not to send Price's infantry to Taylor until it had been replaced. Meanwhile, Price's men were reorganized into two small divisions under Thomas J. Churchill and Mosby M. Parsons. Taylor was spoiling for a fight, but Kirby Smith wanted to delay as long as possible and not risk a general engagement "without hopes of success." Steele had

left Little Rock on March 23 and was marching toward Washington, Arkansas, with around 8,000 men and 16 guns. If he continued his swift advance, Kirby Smith thought it would be better to take Price's men to rejoin the remainder of Price's infantry and cavalry and fight Steele. If victorious, Taylor could then receive around 13,000 instead of 5,000 men. When Taylor read this dispatch he was furious with Kirby Smith, writing him on March 30: "I respectfully suggest that the only possible way to defeat Steele's movement is to whip the enemy now in the heart of the Red River Valley. . . . To decline concentration when we have the means, and when the enemy is already in the vitals of the department, is a policy I am too obtuse to understand." Taylor was also upset because the reinforcements from Texas had not arrived. "Had I conceived for an instant that such astonishing delay would ensue before re-enforcements reached me I would have fought a battle even against the heavy odds," he admonished. "It would have been better to lose the State after a defeat than surrender it without a fight. The fairest and richest portion of the Confederacy is now a waste. Louisiana may well know her destiny. Her children are exiles; her labor system is destroyed. Expecting every hour to receive the promised re-enforcements, I did not feel justified in hazarding a general engagement with my little army. I shall never cease to regret the error." Richard Taylor to William R. Boggs, March 30 and 31, 1864, *Official Records Armies*, series I, XXXIV, pt. 1, pp. 514–15; E. Kirby Smith to Taylor, March 31, 1864, *ibid.*, pp. 516–17; Winters, *Civil War in Louisiana*, p. 336.

[17] Banks's cavalry entered Natchitoches on March 31, and his infantry arrived on April 2, Franklin moving by land and A. J. Smith on 26 transports by the river to Grand Ecore, four miles distant. "Our troops now occupy Natchitoches," Banks proudly informed Washington, "and we hope to be in Shreveport by the 10th of April. I do not fear concentration of the enemy at that point. My fear is that they may not be willing to meet me there." Should the Rebels refuse to fight he would pursue them "into the interior of Texas." "I am sorry to see this tone of confidence," Lincoln said when he read Banks's boastful dispatch. "The next news we shall hear from there will be of a defeat." Nathaniel P. Banks to Henry W. Halleck, April 2, 1864, *Official Records Armies*, series I, XXXIV, pt. 1, pp. 179–80; Shelby Foote, *The Civil War, A Narrative*, 3 vols. (New York: Random House, 1974), III, p. 34 (hereafter cited as Foote, *The Civil War*); Irwin, "Red River Campaign," p. 351.

[18] The Twenty-sixth Texas Cavalry unexpectedly encountered the Federals before reaching Pleasant Hill and had "a brisk skirmish" with them, which resulted in a loss of five men and several horses wounded. "Such was Debray's regiment's baptism of fire," Debray wrote later. At the same time Arthur Bagby's cavalry brigade was skirmishing with the Federals who were advancing on the Natchitoches road. *Official Records Armies*, series I, XXXIV, pt. 1, p. 563; X. B. Debray, "A Sketch of Debray's Twenty-Sixth Regiment of Texas Cavalry," II, *Southern Historical Society Papers*, XIII (January-December 1885), pp. 155–56 (hereafter cited as Debray, "Sketch of Debray's Twenty-Sixth Regiment"). See also, Thos. H. Edgar, *History of De Bray's (26) Regiment of Texas Cavalry, 1861–1898. Embracing Roster and Casualties* (Galveston: Press of A. A. Finck & Co., 1898), pp. 10–11.

[19] On the morning of April 2 Walker's Division marched five miles in the direction of Bayou Pierre, southeast of Pleasant Hill. Heavy cannonading was heard in the direction of Natchitoches. As the men were preparing to cook supper an officer from Walker's staff arrived in camp to notify brigade commanders that the enemy was rapidly advancing, and it now became a race between their men and the Federals to get to Pleasant Hill first. Recalled Blessington: "The division was formed in line rapidly; regimental commanders received orders to double-quick their regiments to Pleasant Hill, distant about five miles. On we sped, like lightning —

every man for himself, and the 'devil take the hindmost.' To add to the excitement of the moment, courier after courier came galloping on their fast steeds, informing us that the enemy had surrounded our wagon-train, and that there was a possibility of our losing it, unless we hurried up. On we sped. Night overtook us in the race. We fell pell-mell over stumps and roots of trees, arriving at Pleasant Hill at 7 o'clock, making the distance of five miles in one hour, carrying our knapsacks and accouterments." The troops formed in line of battle under the crest of the hill and remained there all night, expecting every minute to be attacked, but when morning dawned, "bright and glorious," no enemy was in sight. "They seemed to be perfectly worn out with the marching and countermarching," Blessington said of the disappointed Confederates. "They preferred meeting the enemy in a fair field, small as their number was, rather than to be harassed and annoyed by them." Blessington, *Walker's Texas Division*, pp. 179–80.

[20] *Ibid.*, pp. 180–81. Felix Pierre Poché noted in his diary on April 5: "Today the army remained stationary and the troops were given a much needed rest, after such a long march of two hundred miles, overwhelmed with great fatigue and by privations without parallel in history. And especially humiliated by having to flee before an implacable enemy and leaving homes and lands to be pillaged and their women and children to their insulting violence." Bearss, ed., *A Louisiana Confederate*, pp. 100–1.

[21] E. Kirby Smith to Richard Taylor, April 3, 1864, *Official Records Armies*, series I, XXXIV, pt. 1, pp. 521–22; Taylor to William R. Boggs, April 4 and 5, 1864, *ibid.*, pp. 522–23; *ibid.*, p. 563.

[22] E. Kirby Smith to Richard Taylor, April 5, 1864, *ibid.*, pp. 525–26.

[23] Richard Taylor to William R. Boggs, April 5 and 7, 1864, *ibid.*, pp. 524, 526; *ibid.*, p. 563; Parks, *Edmund Kirby Smith*, p. 386.

[24] E. Kirby Smith to Richard Taylor, April 8, 1864, *Official Records Armies*, series I, XXXIV, pt. 1, p. 528; Parks, *Edmund Kirby Smith*, p. 389. According to Sarah A. Dorsey, Kirby Smith's dispatch came to Taylor in the midst of Mouton's charge at the battle of Mansfield or Sabine Cross Roads. "' Too late, sir,' said Taylor, to the courier who brought it; 'the battle is won. It is not the first I have fought with a halter around my neck.'" Sarah A. Dorsey, *Recollections of Henry Watkins Allen, Brigadier General Confederate States Army, Ex-Governor of Louisiana* (New Orleans, 1866), p. 263 (hereafter cited as Dorsey, *Recollections of Henry Watkins Allen*).

[25] William P. Head to Nancy C. Head, April 7, 1864, William P. Head Papers, The University of Texas Archives, Austin, Texas.

[26] Richard Taylor to William R. Boggs, April 8, 1864, *Official Records Armies*, series I, XXXIV, pt. 1, p. 526.

[27] Blessington, *Walker's Texas Division*, pp. 182–83; T. R. Bonner, "Sketches of the Campaign of 1864, I," *Land We Love*, VI (October 1868), p. 462.

[28] Rebecca W. Smith and Marion Mullins, eds., "The Diary of H. C. Medford, Confederate Soldier, 1864, I," *Southwestern Historical Quarterly*, XXXIV (October 1930), p. 216.

[29] Blessington, *Walker's Texas Division*, pp. 183, 185–86.

[30] Winters, *Civil War in Louisiana*, p. 340; Taylor, *Destruction and Reconstruction*, p. 162; Dorsey, *Recollections of Henry Watkins Allen*, p. 261.

[31] *Official Records Armies*, series I, XXXIV, pt. 1, p. 266; James T. Huffstodt,

"Ransom at the Crossroads: One Man's Ruin on the Red River," *Civil War Times Illustrated*, XIX (December 1980), p. 13 (hereafter cited as Huffstodt, "Ransom at the Crossroads").

[32] *Official Records Armies*, series I, XXXIV, pt. 1, p. 564; Dorsey, *Recollections of Henry Watkins Allen*, p. 263; Bearss, ed., *A Louisiana Confederate*, pp. 106–7.

[33] *Official Records Armies*, series I, XXXIV, pt. 1, pp. 266, 564–65; Winters, *Civil War in Louisiana*, pp. 342–43. "Minnie balls like hail," Lieutenant Colonel A. W. Hyatt of the Crescent Regiment noted in his journal. "The fire of the enemy was so terrible that almost every man in the direct attack of Mouton's Brigade was struck with a bullet. All of the troops in front would have been shot down but for the timely turning of the enemy's flank by the troops sent by Taylor to get round them. Mouton was killed at the head of his brigade. Armand at the head of his Creoles received three wounds, the last one killing him dead while waving his sword. The men of Mouton's Brigade charged at a double quick for twenty-five minutes. Out of 2,200 men it lost 762, principally in a ravine where the Federals had been driven and where the Brigade was torn to pieces by grape and cannister at close range." Napier Bartlett, *Military Record of Louisiana Including Biographical and Historical Papers Relating to the Military Organization of the State* (New Orleans: L. Graham and Company, 1875; Baton Rouge: Louisiana State University Press, 1964), III, "The Trans-Mississippi," p. 13.

[34] Bonner, "Sketches of the Campaign of 1864, I," p. 464; Blessington, *Walker's Texas Division*, pp. 187–89.

[35] Testimony of Brigadier General A. L. Lee, January 11, 1865, *Red River Expedition* (Millwood: Kraus Reprint Co., 1977), p. 37.

[36] Winters, *Civil War in Louisiana*, p. 343; *Official Records Armies*, series I, XXXIV, pt. 1, pp. 266–67, 462–63; Huffstodt, "Ransom at the Crossroads," p. 15; William H. Heath, "Battle of Pleasant Hill, Louisiana," *Annals of Iowa*, VII, Third Series (October 1906), p. 518; Reuben B. Scott, *The History of the 67th Infantry Volunteers, War of the Rebellion* (Bedford: Herald Book & Job Print., 1892), pp. 71–72.

[37] Winters, *Civil War in Louisiana*, p. 344; *Official Records Armies*, series I, XXXIV, pt. 1, pp. 292, 458; Richard Taylor to William R. Boggs, April 8, 1864, *ibid.*, p. 527; Alonzo H. Plummer, *Confederate Victory at Mansfield*. Published by Kate Beard Chapter No. 397 United Daughters of the Confederacy (Mansfield: Ideal Printing Company, 1969), pp. 24–26. According to Plummer, who was Superintendent of the Mansfield Battle Park, "The battle was called the Battle of Mansfield by the Confederates. The Federals called it the Battle of Sabine Cross Roads. There is some confusion as to the location of the crossroads from which the name of this battle was derived. There were two roads that intersected the main road which were over a mile apart, one was about three miles out of Mansfield, a short distance west of the Mansfield Battle Park, and the other a short distance east of this park near the intersection of Highways 522 and 175. Both General Taylor and General Banks wrote of the former as a Sabine Cross Road. The latter was known as Sabine Cross Road locally. Both had some significance in the battle. The former was used by General Taylor to deploy his troops for the first phase of the battle, and General Cameron used the latter for the same purpose in the second phase" (p. 27).

[38] Dr. Harris H. Beecher, *Record of the 114th Regiment, N.Y.S.V. Where It Went, What It Saw, And What It Did* (Norwich: Published by J.F. Hubbard Jr., 1866), p. 311 (hereafter cited as Beecher, *Record of the 114th Regiment, N.Y.S.V.*); Taylor, *De-*

struction and Reconstruction, p. 164. An artilleryman in Daniels's Battery reported that he "went over the battle ground and traveled the road next day on which the Yankees were slaughtered; for ten miles the dead Yankees were lying on the side of the road; a great many of them were stripped of their coats, pants and boots, while others had their pockets turned wrong. I don't blame our men who were needing clothing for so doing." J. J. Wilson to Mag Wilson, April 12, 1864, "Lamar County Artilleryman Recounts Battle of Mansfield in Letter," Mansfield *Enterprise*, April 2, 1964.

According to Plummer, both names of the battle "probably had to do with parts of the Chatman (Chapman) farm. A bloody part of the fighting took place in the Peach Orchard. A grove of stately oaks that adorned the home site probably accounted for the name Pleasant Grove." Plummer, *Confederate Victory at Mansfield*, pp. 26–27.

[39] Bonner, "Sketches of the Campaign of 1864, I," p. 465.

[40] Beecher, *Record of the 114th Regiment, N.Y.S.V.*, p. 313. See also, John M. Gould, *History of the First-Tenth-Twenty-ninth Maine Regiment* (Portland: Stephen Berry, 1871), pp. 412–19.

[41] Winters, *Civil War in Louisiana*, p. 347; Bonner, "Sketches of the Campaign of 1864, I," pp. 465–66.

[42] Taylor, *Destruction and Reconstruction*, p. 164; Richard Taylor to John G. Walker, April 9, 1864, Walker Papers.

[43] Taylor, *Destruction and Reconstruction*, p. 165; Richard Taylor to William R. Boggs, April 9, 1864, *Official Records Armies*, series I, XXXIV, pt. 1, p. 528.

[44] Blessington, *Walker's Texas Division*, pp. 193–94.

[45] Richard Taylor to William R. Boggs [April 9, 1864], *Official Records Armies*, series I, XXXIV, pt. 1, pp. 528–29.

[46] "Battle of Pleasant Hill, Recollection of Mrs. R. A. Rembert, interview by Mrs. L. C. Bridges," p. 1, enclosed in Mrs. L. C. Bridges to Mrs. N. W. Jenkins, May 14, 1938, copy in editor's possession (hereafter cited as Rembert, "Battle of Pleasant Hill"); Taylor, *Destruction and Reconstruction*, pp. 165–66; Johnson, *Red River Campaign*, p. 168, gives the Federal numbers.

[47] Taylor, *Destruction and Reconstruction*, p. 166.

[48] H. P. Bee, "Battle of Pleasant Hill — An Error Corrected," *Southern Historical Society Papers*, VIII (April 1880), pp. 184–85; Taylor, *Destruction and Reconstruction*, pp. 166–67; Winters, *Civil War in Louisiana*, p. 349. According to Winters, "because of the great distance from the main supply base at Alexandria and the serious lack of sufficient drinking water for an entire army, Banks could not hold his position for any length of time. . . . Without making a final decision concerning the future of his campaign, Banks sent his wagon trains, convoyed by most of Lee's cavalry and Dickey's brigade of the Corps d'Afrique, on the way toward Grand Ecore. At the same time messengers were sent to Porter and Kilby Smith to tell them of the battle and to instruct them to fall back to Grand Ecore" (p. 348).

[49] *Official Records Armies*, series I, XXXIV, pt. 1, pp. 566–67; Debray, "Sketch of Debray's Twenty-Sixth Regiment of Texas Cavalry," p. 159; W. C. Littlefield to Albert and M. J. Codwell and Emeline Littlefield, April 15, 1864, W. C. Littlefield Papers, Illinois State Historical Library, Springfield, Illinois (hereafter cited as Littlefield Papers).

[50] Winters, *Civil War in Louisiana*, pp. 351–52; *Official Records Armies*, series I, XXXIV, pt. 1, pp. 308–9, 350; Francis Fessenden to Nelly Fessenden, April 12, 1864, Francis Fessenden Papers, Bowdoin College Library, Brunswick, Maine (hereafter cited as Fessenden Papers). Fessenden's official report, dated April 13, 1864, is in *Official Records Armies*, series I, XXXIV, pt. 1, pp. 429–32.

[51] Blessington, *Walker's Texas Division*, pp. 195–96.

[52] Winters, *Civil War in Louisiana*, p. 352; Blessington, *Walker's Texas Division*, p. 196; "Biography and Diaries of Robert Simonton Gould," p. 67, typescript in Robert Simonton Gould Papers, The University of Texas Archives, Austin, Texas (hereafter cited as "Biography and Diaries of Robert Simonton Gould"). See also, T. R. Bonner, "Sketches of the Campaign of 1864, II," *Land We Love*, VI (November 1868), pp. 7–12. "At the battle of Pleasant Hill my Captain, [Joe] Tullos, was shot down by my side," recalled Preston B. Maxey, a private in Company A, Gould's Battalion. "I asked him if I could do anything for him and he said, 'No, they have killed me. Go on and do all the good you can.'" Yeary, comp., *Reminiscences of the Boys in Gray*, p. 475.

[53] John Scott, comp., *Story of the Thirty-Second Iowa Infantry Volunteers* (Nevada: John Scott, 1896), p. 154; *Official Records Armies*, series I, XXXIV, pt. 1, pp. 355–56, 366. See also, A. J. Barkley, "The Battle of Pleasant Hill, Louisiana. Recollections of a Private Soldier," *Annals of Iowa*, III, Third Series (April 1897), pp. 24–28 (hereafter cited as Barkley, "Battle of Pleasant Hill"); William T. Shaw, "The Battle of Pleasant Hill," *Annals of Iowa*, III, Third Series (April-July 1898), pp. 401–16; "Judge Charles T. Granger's Statement," *Annals of Iowa*, III, Third Series (April-July 1898), pp. 416–19; "An Army Letter by Quartermaster T. C. McCall," *Annals of Iowa*, III, Third Series (April-July 1898), pp. 419–23; S. F. Benson, "The Battle of Pleasant Hill, Louisiana," *Annals of Iowa*, VII (October 1906), pp. 490–99 (hereafter cited as Benson, "Battle of Pleasant Hill").

[54] Blessington, *Walker's Texas Division*, p. 196; *Official Records Armies*, series I, XXXIV, pt. 1, p. 568.

[55] Winters, *Civil War in Louisiana*, pp. 354–55; Hatton, "Polignac and the Civil War," pp. 175–76; Taylor, *Destruction and Reconstruction*, pp. 168–71; *Official Records Armies*, series I, XXXIV, pt. 1, pp. 309, 317; Francis Fessenden to Nelly Fessenden, April 12, 1864, Fessenden Papers.

[56] *Official Records Armies*, series I, XXXIV, pt. 1, p. 568; E. Kirby Smith, "The Defense of Red River," *Battles and Leaders*, IV, ed. Johnson and Buel, p. 372; W. C. Littlefield to Albert and M. J. Codwell and Emeline Littlefield, April 15, 1864, Littlefield Papers. "The safety of the army, as well as the success of the expedition, seemed to justify this movement," Banks explained to Grant. "Leaving Pleasant Hill, it was 15 miles before any water was found. It would have been impossible for the army, without supplies of water and rations, to have sustained another battle, in the condition in which it was then placed." Nathaniel P. Banks to Ulysses S. Grant, April 13, 1864, *Official Records Armies*, series I, XXXIV, pt. 1, p. 185.

[57] Johnson, *Red River Campaign*, pp. 167–68; *Official Records Armies*, series I, LIII, p. 478; Taylor, *Destruction and Reconstruction*, pp. 167, 170–71.

[58] Winters, *Civil War in Louisiana*, pp. 347, 355; Taylor, *Destruction and Reconstruction*, p. 171; Alwyn Barr, "Texas Losses in the Red River Campaign, 1864," *Texas Military History*, 3 (Summer 1963), pp. 104–5; Compiled Service Record of George Washington Jones, National Archives, Washington, D.C.; W. C. Lit-

tlefield to Albert and M. J. Codwell and Emeline Littlefield, April 15, 1864, Littlefield Papers.

[59] Liz Chrysler, "The Battle of Pleasant Hill — From a Boy's Viewpoint," Mansfield *Enterprise*, May 17, 1977. "Green flies swarmed everywhere," recalled Alonzo J. Barkley, who had been left behind with the other Federal wounded. "Buzzards blackened the sky after feasting on the miserable remains of hundreds of dead horses lying on the field. The stench was most intolerable." Barkley, "Battle of Pleasant Hill," p. 30.

[60] T. F. Mays to Don G. Petty, February 19, 1913, in possession of O. Scott Petty, San Antonio, Texas.

[61] Bastrop *Advertiser*, April 23, 1915.

[62] Liz Chrysler, "Marie Childers: 'Kind Hearted Southern Lady,'" Mansfield *Enterprise*, May 24, 1977; Mrs. J. H. Davis to David Blackshear, n. d., copy enclosed in O. Scott Petty to Mrs. Mary Estelle Tucker and others. June 13, 1972, copy in editor's possession; Henry H. Childers, "Reminiscences of the Battle of Pleasant Hill," *Annals of Iowa*, VII, Third Series (October 1906), pp. 507, 515 (hereafter cited as Childers, "Reminiscences of the Battle of Pleasant Hill"); Benson, "Battle of Pleasant Hill," p. 500.

[63] Charles L. Morgan to Margaret Petty, June 2, 1864, Captain Elijah P. Petty Papers, Mansfield Battle Park Museum, Mansfield, Louisiana (hereafter cited as Petty Papers).

[64] Don G. Petty to Editor, May 6, 1889, Bastrop *Advertiser*, June 8, 1889. This issue also carried the following notice: "Don G. Petty, of Orange, Texas, wishes the address of Doctors Christian and Herndon, confederate Surgeons, at the battle of Pleasant Hill, Louisiana."

[65] Bastrop *Advertiser*, May 25, 1889.

[66] H. A. Highsmith to Editor, May 26, 1889, *ibid.*, June 1, 1889. M. S. Hughes, F. H. Perkins, W. M. Faulkner and F. S. Faust are listed as members of M. B. Highsmith's Company D, in the muster and pay rolls for the Twelfth Texas Cavalry Regiment, for the months of September, October, November and December 1863. Parsons' Texas Cavalry Brigade Association, *A Brief and Condensed History of Parsons' Texas Cavalry Brigade Composed of Twelfth, Nineteenth, Twenty-First, Morgan's Battalion, and Pratt's Battery of Artillery of the Confederate States. . . .* (Waxahachie: J. M. Flemister, Printer, 1892; Waco: W. M. Morrison, 1962), pp. 55–56.

[67] H. A. Highsmith to C. F. Petty, June 6, 1889, Petty Papers.

[68] Childers, "Reminiscences of the Battle of Pleasant Hill," p. 514.

[69] Benson, "Battle of Pleasant Hill," pp. 501–2.

[70] Rembert, "Battle of Pleasant Hill," p. 2.

[71] Childers, "Reminiscences of the Battle of Pleasant Hill," pp. 505, 516. Solon F. Benson of the Thirty-second Iowa, who spent some time in the Pleasant Hill area interviewing people who were there during the battle, noted that "the forest has claimed much of the old abandoned battle-field, and rail fences traverse the old streets, while cotton and corn celebrate the 'blood stained' fields. The old Camp Meeting Ground, one and a quarter miles east of old Pleasant Hill, where the 16th Corps bivouacked the night before the battle, is now cultivated to corn and cotton to the very margin of the graves in the cemetery, while brambles, brush and tall trees dispute with marble shaft and slab the dwelling of the dead." Benson, "Battle of Pleasant Hill," p. 504.

[72] Don G. Petty to Mrs. B. D. Orgain, January 10, 1908, Bastrop *Advertiser*, February 15, 1908. In this letter to Mrs. Orgain, the president of the T. C. Cain chapter of the United Daughters of the Confederacy in Bastrop, Petty contributed $100 toward the erection of a memorial to the Confederate soldiers who enlisted in Bastrop County. "I wish there could be erected there a small monument in memory of the Bastrop soldiers, and by the Bastrop people," he said, speaking of Pleasant Hill. He asked her to have her chapter get "EACH living Bastrop soldier, who was in the battle of Pleasant Hill, to write a paper . . . and have it read before your Chapter, and preserved. After being read, I would like to get a copy of each. Be sure to get one from Major [Joseph B.] Sayers. If any of the Veterans can not write it up, get some good writer to do it for them, letting them sign it and I will pay the expenses. It makes no difference what they write, so it is their own experience and remembrance of that battle." Mrs. Orgain promised to "try to get all the information possible in regard to battle at Pleasant Hill. My brother John O. Johnson of Austin was wounded at Mansfield and I may be able to get something about it from him." She added a postscript: "I would like to have your letter to me published in 'Advertiser' if you will allow me that publicity may be given to your desire to have papers written in regard to Pleasant Hill battle. Old soldiers who might not be reached otherwise might see the letter and respond to your request." Mrs. B. D. Orgain to Don G. Petty, January 31, 1908, letter in possession of O. Scott Petty, San Antonio, Texas.

Vandals toppled Captain Petty's monument from its position over his grave about July 28 or 29, 1973. It was believed that the stone was defaced at the same time the Mansfield Battle Park was damaged. The vandalism was discovered by Otis Lee and his grandsons of Pleasant Hill and reported to the *Sabine Index*. *Sabine Index*, August 16, 1973. The monument was set back over the grave.

In front of the Mansfield Battle Park Museum are three flagpoles, one given by the Children of the Confederacy, one by the Daughters of the Confederacy and one by the Petty family in memory of Captain Petty. Inside the museum is a wall display case with Captain Petty's sash and other personal articles and letters.

Walker's Texas Division
The Last Year

AFTER PLEASANT HILL Walker's Division was ordered back to Mansfield. The Third Texas Infantry was attached to Scurry's Brigade to rebuild its strength. On April 15 the division crossed the Red River at Shreveport on a pontoon bridge and marched via Minden against Frederick Steele's Federal force at Camden, Arkansas. The Texans arrived near Camden on April 26 and found that Steele had started back for Little Rock. About noon on April 30 the Federals were overtaken while crossing the Sabine River at Jenkins' Ferry. It was here, in a sea of mud, that pursued and pursuers fought a battle novelist-historian Shelby Foote called "a miry nightmare of confusion and fatigue."[1] Kirby Smith, in command of the Confederate army, committed his troops as fast as they arrived, first Churchill's Arkansas and then Parsons's Missourians. They made little headway, for the Federals had stout log breastworks in a position whose access was restricted on the left by Toxie Creek and on the right by an impenetrable swamp. Walker's Division came up about 9 a.m. and was ordered to turn the enemy's left flank. Committed piecemeal, just after Churchill and Parsons were thrown back for the second time, the Texans attacked furiously but did no better in the end than the Arkansans and Missourians before them. Randal and Scurry were both mortally wounded; Waul was also injured. The Federals crossed the Sabine and returned to Little Rock unmolested. "Kirby Smith commanded in person & the general impression is that he didn't do any big things," Surgeon E. P. Becton wrote his wife. "The Feds continued their flight to Little Rock and suppose we might claim it as a victory." "It was a bloody little fight for us and nothing accomplished," an elderly veteran of Walker's Division wrote in 1910, "and I never could figure out why our commander ran up against such a hard proposition."[2] The losses in Walker's Division, again incomplete, were 74 killed, 266 wounded and 1 missing, for a total of 341. Losses among the Missouri and Arkansas troops were reported as 542 killed, wounded and missing, bringing the total known Confederate casualties to 883.[3]

On May 3 the Confederate army was ordered back to Camden, which was reached on the 5th. On May 9 Walker's Division started for Alexandria to rejoin Taylor, who was trying (unsuccessfully as it turned out) to trap Banks's army and Porter's fleet before they could reach the Mississippi River. The march was continued over muddy roads until May 22, when the Texans arrived at Pineville, opposite Alexandria. The division, from the opening of the campaign at Simmesport to the time of its arrival at Alexandria, a period of about ten weeks, had marched 700 miles and fought three pitched battles. While the division was encamped there Taylor informed Walker that the prisoners taken at Pleasant Hill had been exchanged and were doing guard duty at Natchitoches. On June 17 the troops learned, much to their surprise and dismay, that Walker had been assigned to the command of the Department of West Louisiana, in place of the short-tempered Taylor who had been relieved from duty at his own request by Kirby Smith. Brigadier General Wilburn H. King took temporary command of the division.[4]

On July 9, 1864, General Stephen D. Lee informed Kirby Smith (erroneously) that Banks's successor, General E. R. S. Canby, was moving on Mobile with 20,000 troops and that it was "of vital importance that a part of your troops are crossed over the Mississippi, or you co-operate in such a manner as to divert their troops. General Bragg directed me to confer with you as to crossing troops."[5] In the latter part of July it was decided to send Walker's and Polignac's divisions to the east side of the Mississippi River where they would form part of Taylor's new command, the Department of Mississippi and East Louisiana. Walker's men were moved near Harrisonburg on the Black River where they remained encamped for nearly a month. The order to cross created much dissatisfaction among the home-sick Texans. "As for my part I take crossing in mine although it is a bitter pill," one said. "I cant believe the present Suffering of the Soldiers will last long. This Hell roaring war cant exist long . . . it is rather cool for a man to leave his home exposed to the enemy an[d] go to protect one that is all reddy over run though I cant tell what is best neither do I give a darn blew button." As a consequence, there were hundreds of desertions.[6] "We learn today that because of our contemplated move, the infamous Texans have deserted in great numbers yesterday and last night," Felix Pierre Poché fumed in his diary on August 19. "Two hundred out of Walker's Division returned of the four hundred that had deserted and one hundred thirty-five deserters of the Texas Brigade in our [Polignac's] Division."[7] J. E. Harrison, the commander of the Texas Brigade in Polignac's Division, admitted that "there has been a greadeal of excitement in my Brigade. I have lost 123 deserted, [who] wont cross the River. There are many others who dislike it extremely. . . ."[8]

Taylor blamed the Texans' discontent on several factors: the "non-payment of the troops for a period of twelve months," the absence of a "very large proportion of the field officers," recent changes which had taken place in the commanders on the division and brigade levels, and the inactivity of the command for the last two months. In addition, the crossing of the Mississippi would be fraught with difficulties, and once across the river soldiers would find it hard to return for the defense of their homes if needed. These problems satisfied Taylor that if he marched the two divisions any nearer the Mississippi, he would lose by desertion "at least one-half the entire command." To intercept the deserters, at least 200 of whom were armed, checkpoints manned by cavalry were established at various Red River ferries from Cotile to Grand Ecore.[9]

On August 1 Kirby Smith wrote Walker: "Your influence with your old command is deservedly great, and can be made a powerful auxiliary in securing its cheerful acquiescence in the movement. I believe that even though you finally remain in the district you should at least temporarily resume command of your old division and assist in putting it across the Mississippi." But just two days later Walker was ordered to assume command of the District of Texas, New Mexico and Arizona. Major General John Forney, who had commanded a division under Pemberton at Vicksburg, left Shreveport on August 12 to assume command of Walker's Division. Learning that many of the Texans were opposed to Forney, Kirby Smith ordered that as soon as the troops crossed the Mississippi, Taylor was to relieve him and order him to Richmond. Forney's arrival served to inflame the Texans, who regarded him as too strict a disciplinarian. In view of their feelings he did not formally assume command of the division until September 4.[10]

On August 18 Taylor issued orders temporarily cancelling the attempt to cross the Mississippi. He had received information from his scouts that the Federals had learned of the undertaking. Gunboats had taken position between Vicksburg and Red River at intervals of about 12 miles, while other gunboats constantly patrolled between those points. A crossing under such circumstances would, in his opinion, be "impracticable" and would result "only in injury to the whole command. . . ." Kirby Smith concurred, sending Taylor word on August 22 "to immediately suspend the movement of the troops across the Mississippi River." Taylor was to send the two divisions to Monroe "without delay." He was "relieved from the command" and was to cross the river alone. A few days later Taylor with his Negro servant and a guide crossed the Mississippi in a light canoe. "A gunboat was lying in the river a short distance below," Taylor stated in his memoirs, "and even the horses seemed to understand the importance of silence, swimming quietly alongside of our frail craft."[11]

Following Taylor's decision to postpone the crossing of the Mississippi, David M. Ray of the Sixteenth Texas Cavalry (dismounted) wrote his mother from the camp near Harrisonburg:

> I have little news to write except there is a probability of this division and Polignac's crossing the Miss river and we had expected to go before now but the move is postponed for the present. There has been a good many desertions on the strength of it about 50 from this Brigade, 200 from Wauls and about the same from Mc-Clays. We only lost one from this regt, another started but was caught, but there are several in the guardhouse for talking about it from our Regt: they have a great many in the guardhouse, some with irons, they have handcuffs on some and what they call stiff knees on others, which is done by putting a ring around the ankle and another around the thigh with a bar of iron extending from one ring to the other. I do not know whether there has many deserted from Polignac or not as they are on the other side of the Wachita.[12]

On the morning of August 30 Forney's (formerly Walker's) and Polignac's divisions took up the line of march for Monticello, Arkansas, in anticipation of a Federal raid from Pine Bluff which did not materialize. Forney was disturbed by the amount of straggling prevailing in the division. To correct the situation, he ordered that each company's roll be called at every rest halt. The men didn't like this at all as the roll call consumed all the time of the halt. On September 20 the troops reached Monticello. "The command is in fine spirits — Genl. Walker has gone to Texas & Major Genl. John H. Forney is in command of the Division," Surgeon E. P. Becton wrote his wife. "Of course we can know but little about him but so far he has not made the most favorable impression — he however may be an excellent officer. I will not pass upon him yet awhile —"[13]

The troops were reviewed on the 26th by John B. Magruder, who was commanding the District of Arkansas. Churchill's and Parsons's divisions were also present. On October 2 the Confederate army was ordered west to Camden, where they were put to work building fortifications to repel any Federal advance south from Little Rock. On the evening of the 16th the troops witnessed the shooting of Captain John Guynes, Company F, Twenty-second Texas Infantry, who was convicted by a general court martial of encouraging his men to desert when they were ordered to cross the Mississippi. After completing the fortifications around Camden Forney's Division marched to Camp Sumter (named by the Missouri troops) on the Red River north of Shreveport. With supplies so scarce in the Red River area, Kirby Smith ordered Forney's and Polignac's divisions to take up winter quarters at Camp Magruder near Minden, Louisiana.[14]

On the evening of November 12 the troops received two months' wages, the first money they had received in two years. On January 8, 1865, they participated in a "sham battle." "Everything passed off pleasantly, and to the entire satisfaction of the ladies, who assembled in large numbers to witness the scene," wrote Blessington. "We returned to camp late in the evening, strongly convinced that it was easier to participate in a hundred 'sham battles' than one sure-enough battle." On January 17 Kirby Smith arrived in camp to review the troops. He was accompanied by General Simon Buckner, then commanding the District of Louisiana. After passing in review and taking their former position in line, Buckner put the troops through Hardee's tactics[15] for about two hours, "which proved highly gratifying to the ladies who had come from all parts of the country to witness the grand review."[16]

Forney's men remained at Camp Magruder until January 26, when they departed for Shreveport, arriving two days later and encamping about a mile east of the city. About 4 p.m. a terrific storm of wind, rain and hail from the northeast struck the camp. The next morning, according to Blessington, it presented "a most lamentable spectacle":

Only two tents were standing, out of all the officers' tents in the division. The men were huddled together in groups, endeavoring to keep warm. The fires, having been extinguished, could add nothing to their comfort; and the poor fellows, wet, supperless, and without the fragment of a chance for breakfast, presented a most wretched appearance indeed.

The storm continued to rage until the evening of the 29th when the wind changed, and it cleared off piercingly cold. The next day, "apparently to warm the troops up," Forney held a grand review. "The parade-ground was about five miles from our camp," wrote Blessington. "On our march to the parade-ground, many of the soldiers, worn out by exhaustion, and unable to march with their companies, were picked up and placed under guard by General Forney's body-guard (consisting of a company of cavalry). On their arrival on the parade-ground they were compelled to march a ring until the review was over. This treatment of the sick was loudly denounced by both officers and men." On the morning of February 7 camp was again moved, convenient to a drill ground, and drills were performed every day.[17]

A move of Forney's Division to Texas was contemplated at this time because of a rumored Federal expedition fitting out at New Orleans for the Texas coast, Galveston or Sabine Pass. Departmental headquarters advised John G. Walker, who was commanding in Texas: "The greatest energy should be employed in strengthening the position at Houston, where in the event of an invasion from the coast you will receive the support of Wharton's and Forney's divisions." However, a movement of the Federals in the direction of Monroe, Louisiana, prompted Kirby Smith to retain Forney's Division in the vicinity of Shreveport, awaiting further developments.[18]

While encamped near Shreveport the division was visited daily by ladies from the city and vicinity "who always had pleasant smiles and cheerful words for the soldiers." On February 18 thousands of spectators thronged to the parade ground to witness a review followed by a mock battle. Kirby Smith and Magruder were present. The troops advanced in columns of attack, and, after deploying, broke to the rear, forming two lines of battle. After changing front to rear on the first line, they advanced to the attack. First was heard the skirmisher's scattering fire, then volleys of musketry mingled with the roar of artillery. "The maneuvering was well executed, and, but for the gala appearance of the scene, a spectator would have imagined that one of those bloody dramas so frequent in those war-like days was being enacted," recalled a participant. "As it was, some fair ladies screamed, and down the cheeks of others coursed tear-drops, either of sympathy for a soldier's dangers, or from some memory brought up by this warlike scene." After the sham battle arms were stacked, and, following "short and stirring addresses" by Colonel L. Bush of Louisiana and Colonels George Flournoy and Richard Hubbard of Texas, the soldiers were treated to a jigger of whiskey each and a barbecue.[19]

On February 21 Forney's Division marched toward Natchitoches, covering ten miles and making camp near the old Mansfield road. It remained there until March 6. At this time the Second Partisan Rangers, Thirty-fourth Texas Cavalry, "Well's Regiment" (no number) and the Twenty-ninth Texas Cavalry, all from Tom Green's old cavalry division, were dismounted and assigned to the division. A fourth brigade was organized, and Wilburn H. King, who had been reassigned to the division, was placed in command. Americus Leonidas "Lee" Nelms of the Thirty-fourth Texas wrote his wife Minerva Jane on March 1:

> We dident start today. I went to town this mornin. I heard there that the fedrel piquets were in the neigborhood of Alexandria and that they had had several skirmishes with them. We had orders to day from Genl Forney to send off all our bagage to Shreveport except what we could carry on our backs and if any private baggage was found in the wagons they would be thrown out by the road side and burnt; this is pretty tight but if its for the good of our country I shant grumble. I recen we will start in the morning. I shall try to carry all my things with me and if they have to be burnt I will have the pleasure of burning them my self. It is the opinion of a good many that we will go across the Miss River and I dont care much if we do. I am going to try not to care for any thing that happens these times. . . .

Nelms also informed his wife that "they are dismounting a goodeal of the cavalry down here" and that it was being done by force. "It took 3 regments to dismount one and 15 companies to dismount an other. They pressed their horses for artillery horses. There was 60 of them run off the night after they were dismounted from one regiment." The soldiers were getting "tolerable plenty to eat of meat and bread and some sugar and peas, and we can buy potatotes once in a while and get turnip greens."[20]

In early March Walker wired Kirby Smith from Houston that a secret service agent had just arrived from New Orleans, bringing important information from Catholic Bishop John Marie Odin and others — a Federal force of 40,000, commanded by Canby, would sail for the coast of Texas within three days! Actually Canby's expedition was to move against Mobile, Alabama, but Walker and Kirby Smith did not know this. The departmental commander relayed the message to Buckner and President Davis and began preparations to meet the invasion. Forney's infantry was ordered to Huntsville, Texas, to await further developments. Churchill's Arkansas Division was sent to Marshall, Texas; Parsons's Missouri infantry and Jo Shelby's cavalry were ordered to move closer to Shreveport from which point they could be rushed to Texas if needed. Since Forney was Walker's senior in the rank of major general and would expect to assume command of the District of Texas, Kirby Smith, having little confidence in Forney's ability and conscious of his unpopularity with the troops, transferred Magruder back to Texas. Walker was given his choice of either taking command of an infantry division or the District of Arkansas.[21]

On March 6 Forney's Division started for Huntsville. It passed through Mansfield, crossed the Texas state line on March 15, the Sabine River at Grand Bluff on the 17th, and passed through Rusk and Crockett. On entering Texas the men found game plentiful and enjoyed themselves hunting. The Trinity River was crossed on April 3, and the division reached Camp Groce near Hempstead on April 15. "We have been at this camp 4 days and every thing leads to the conclusion that we will stay here sometime," Americus Nelms wrote his wife.

We have cleaned off our camp ground and are drilling. We have orders to drill 3½ hours a day. The regiment is out drilling now. We are camped on a high sandy post oak ridge with a nice clear running branch close by and a small Prairie on the south of us. We have a pleasant breeze nearly all the time and a shower of rain nearly every night, we can hear the cars [of the Houston and Texas Central Railroad] whistle every day. I hear nothing more of an invasion. I am in hopes that there will be no fighting on this side of the river this Spring.[22]

Six days before Forney's Division arrived at Camp Groce Robert E. Lee had surrendered the Army of Northern Virginia to Ulysses S. Grant at Appomattox Court House, Virginia. Although stirring addresses to stand by their colors to the last moment were made by Kirby Smith, Magruder and Forney, the men could no longer be relied upon to resist. "The most of the men in this part of the army are whiped," Nelms admitted.

They say there is [no] use in holding out any longer, and that it would be folly in us to fight on this side of the river now. There is a good many that thinks the war is about over and that we will all be home in a few months. Confederate money is not worth anything here now. It was going at 3 cts on the dollar till the news of Lee's surrender reached here and then it went right down to nothing. I dont believe that a man could get 50 cts for a hundred dollars of it; one man in our company offered all his wages for ½ cent on the dollar and couldent get it.[23]

On May 12 Walker, displaced from his district command by Magruder, was ordered to relieve Forney in command of the Texas Division. Forney was posted to Shreveport pending further assignment. Douglas French Forrest, the Assistant Paymaster on the commerce raider C.S.S. *Rappahannock*, had slipped into Galveston on May 2 from Havana, Cuba, on board the blockade-runner *Wren*. One of his fellow passengers was Mrs. John G. Walker, who was traveling with a child and nurse. She interceded with her husband and secured Forrest an appointment to his staff. "I like him exceedingly & am delighted at the prospect opening up before me," Forrest recorded in his diary on May 15 after conversing for the first time with Walker.

The Genl. is the most popular General in the Trans Mississippi & has acquired his popularity by gallant service in the field & an equal & regular, but very rigid discipline. Genl. Forney's Divisions have clamored so loudly for their old General that Forney has been relieved from the command & it has been tendered to Walker to whom they are warmly attached. He is a small spare man, very quiet, courteous in his deportment to all, of great force of character & great capacity.[24]

But not even Walker could hold the soldiers to their duty. "I have seen letters from intelligent officers in Walker's infantry division who state that those troops will fight no longer," Magruder wired Kirby Smith from Houston on May 16. "I have sent for General Walker and he will be here to day; will add what he may say after I see him." Walker added this postscript:

P.S. — I entirely concur in the foregoing. I will say in addition that my observation convinces me that the troops of this district cannot be relied upon. They consider the contest a hopeless one, and will lay down their arms at the first appearance of the enemy. This is the unanimous opinion of the brigade and regimental commanders of Forney's division whom I have this day consulted. The cavalry are still firm and quiet, but only waiting for what they consider the inevitable result, viz, surrender.[25]

The soldiers now took matters into their own hands, and this period in Texas was long known as "the breakup." Military units disbanded with incredible rapidity. In some commands there was not a man left on the scene of a former encampment in an hour's time, the soldiers seizing wagons, mules and other government property and scattering in squads, couples and singly, to their homes. In some cases the troops defied officers who pleaded with them to remain; some left without consulting with their officers. Lieutenant Colonel Fontaine, in charge of three batteries of artillery, awoke one morning to find the men in only one remaining; the members of the others had departed with the horses, wagons and camp equipage, leaving the guns and caissons. In some commands, notably in Hardeman's and Debray's, the soldiers stood by their colors until their officers agreed that it was useless to remain longer and went through the form of giving them honorable discharges from the service. The different units of the army had been scattered during the winter for subsistence, and there was no concert of action; but as the tidings of the "breakup" elsewhere reached a command, it followed the general movement either at once or after a short delay.[26]

By May 19 a majority of the soldiers in Walker's Division had either left for their homes or were preparing to do so; and the following day the remaining men at Camp Groce were furloughed, which was the equivalent of a discharge. "The parting among the troops was most affecting," wrote J. P. Blessington. "Many put their arms around each other's necks,

and sobbed like children; others gave the strong grasp of the hand, and
silently went away with hearts too full for utterance; while still others
would mutter a huskily-voiced 'Good-bye' or deep oath." But Douglas
French Forrest's diary told a grimmer story. "This has been a most event-
ful day & one most disgraceful to us, the darkest chapter in the gloomy
history of this War," he noted on May 20.

> The Army dispersed to-day contrary to orders and in a manner
> most lawless & unsoldierly. By evening the <u>whole</u> country for miles
> around was filled with predatory bands, utterly irresponsible, recog-
> nizing no rights of property, utterly demoralized. They stood about
> in squads, breaking into every depot of Q[uarter] M[aster], commiss-
> ary & ordnance stores, robbing them of everything they c[ould]
> possibly use & destroying what they could not use. Wagons &
> teams were stolen in every quarter & the little town of Hempstead
> was utterly sacked, not only public stores carried away but shops &
> private houses entered & robbed. . . . About eleven o'clock news
> came to us of the scenes that had been enacted at other camps like
> ours. Everything at Genl. Waterhouses Hdqrs had been stolen &
> the like fate had befallen Genl. Forney's.

Walker sent orders about midday to move his camp to the headquarters
of the II Corps about a quarter of a mile distant. But before the headquarters party could leave, a band of "desperados" appeared and quietly
drove off a team. "It seems that we formed no exception to the rule that
obtained to-day," Forrest lamented. "There was no instance of opposition to their <u>reasonable</u> (?) demands. 'They only wanted transportation
home & why sh[oul]d Genl. Walker who was now no better than any
other man have four wagons & an ambulance & they return afoot.' We
soon after started for our new quarters & reached there in safety."[27]

"In the adjacent village of Hempstead men assembled, seized trains loaded with clothing and stores and distributed them among themselves," Major Robert S. Gould, the commander of Gould's Battalion, wrote in his memoirs. "Wild stories were told of other commands having no transportation, who were marching with arms to claim a share of ours. It was feared that terrible outrages would be perpetrated over the country by desperate and reckless men." Gould's men determined to act otherwise.

Finally, by consent of the commanding officers, a time was set when it might be considered right for us to dissolve and go home. The ordnance stores, guns and ammunition, were divided. Every man of my command was furnished with arms and ammunition.

For the last time they were drawn up in line. I spoke to them briefly. Company A, to reach their homes, would take from the outset a different route from the others. I bade them good bye. To the others I stated that I no longer claimed any authority over them, but if they wished it I would assume control and we would march as if there had been no change, so long as our routes lay together.

It was the unanimous request that I should retain command, and I was promised obedience to my orders.

We marched as usual, camped and placed guards for the protection of our mules and transportation, with even more than usual strictness. Through the town of Anderson we marched in order; I was told, the only command that did so. Here the men obtained large supplies of powder (public) and lead. As we entered Madison county, men of Company B. and E., having reached the vicinity of their homes, left us. In the vicinity of Madisonville we camped for the last time. Here, most of Company B, and E had gone and here Company C, from Houston County took their departure. With my old original company from Leon County we reached Centerville that day, and separated.

I kept nothing save my tent, the equipment of a soldier and a spade. Wagons and mules were divided by others. Lieut. Goodwyn took the ambulance.[28]

H. D. Pearce, Company D, Sixteenth Texas Cavalry (dismounted), got a four days' pass on May 19 to go to Houston and went down on the train. On the evening of May 21 a number of his comrades came in on the train with the news that their regiment had dissolved. The next morning Pearce went to Magruder's office and found a very depressed "Prince John" and his Adjutant General sitting at a table talking. Pearce presented his pass to Magruder, remarking that his regiment had broken up and gone home and that he had come to report for duty. Magruder said to his Adjutant: "Fill out the soldier a complimentary discharge." When it was completed the General signed it.[29]

On May 21 at Crockett, Texas, Kirby Smith received a wire from Magruder, stating that Walker's Division had disbanded. Four days later he arrived at Hempstead, "having been compelled to remain 36 hours in Huntsville to escape the mob of disorderly soldiers thronging the roads." At Hempstead he found another telegram from Magruder; the cavalry had disbanded, and all control over the troops had been lost. Still grimmer news came from Walker. His infantry had mutinied on May 19, seized all transportation and supplies, and carried off to their homes everything they could get their hands on. "In a word," he announced, "there is not an animal, or wagon, or public stores of any description left in their track." By the time Kirby Smith arrived at his new headquarters in Houston on May 27, he was a general without an army. On May 30 he issued his last message to the soldiers of the Trans-Mississippi Department. It said in part:

> Soldiers! I am left a commander without an army — a General without troops. You have made your choice. It was unwise and un-patriotic, but it is final. I pray you may not live to regret it. The enemy will now possess your country, and dictate his own laws. You have volunteerly destroyed your organizations, and thrown away all means of resistance.

> Your present duty is plain. Return to your families. Resume the occupations of peace. Yield obedience to the laws. Labor to restore order. Strive both by counsel and example to give security to life and property. And may God, in his mercy, direct you aright, and heal the wounds of our distracted country.

On May 25 Simon B. Buckner, chief-of-staff to Kirby Smith, Sterling Price and J. L. Brent conferred with General Canby in New Orleans and agreed to surrender the Confederate forces in the Trans-Mississippi, subject to Kirby Smith's approval. The following morning a military convention was signed which stipulated essentially the same terms as those given to Lee. On June 2 Kirby Smith, accompanied by Magruder, went on board the Federal steamer *Fort Jackson* off Galveston harbor and signed his name to the agreement, endorsing thereon that he understood that "officers observing their parole are permitted to make their homes either in or out of the United States."[30]

General Walker had tried to persuade the officers and men of his division to go to Mexico with him but was unsuccessful. "The Genl. & Mrs. Walker rode the cars up this evening," Douglas French Forrest noted in his diary on May 21. "Poor Mrs. Walker seems to be laboring under great anxiety superinduced by the defection of men who had volunteered undying devotion to the General & had enrolled in his Mexican band. It seems as if no confidence can be placed in anyone at this time." General King and Colonel Flournoy had gone without giving notice of their intention or informing Walker of the fact. "Others have left him & our scheme languishes." On June 1 Mrs. Walker, who had been "quite unwell," left for Houston to go by flag of truce to New Orleans and then to Mexico via Havana. On June 6 Walker, Forrest and four other men left Colonel Kirby's residence near Hempstead for San Antonio. From there Walker continued his journey with a party of 40 men which included Generals William Preston and Hamilton P. Bee and Colonel P. N. Luckett. Forrest, who was ill with a "raging fever," had to remain behind. "I bade him 'goodbye' with regret," he said of his parting from Walker, "for I greatly admire this quiet little man." After his unsuccessful attempt to escape to Mexico, Forrest returned to Virginia. Walker returned to Winchester, Virginia, in the late 1860's, where he was in the mining and railroad business before serving as United States consul-general at Bogotá, Colombia, and as special commissioner to the South American republics on behalf of the Pan-American Convention. He died in Washington on July 20, 1893.[31]

At one point when Walker had seemed "very undecided as to his future moves," Forrest, who never lost faith in "the Mexican scheme," had vowed in his diary that "I am determined whatever move he has decided on, to leave the country without ever being a prisoner paroled or otherwise of our detested foes."[32] Captain Elijah P. Petty had expressed similar sentiments before his death; he had talked in letters home of going to Brazil if the Confederacy was defeated. Had Petty been present when Walker's Division disbanded, his feelings in all probability would have been akin to those of Major Robert S. Gould, who wrote, more than six years after the war:

> I reached my home a down-spirited man. I had felt that it was ignoble in us to lay down our arms with no foe near us. I thought we owed it to the cause we had embraced to fight to the bitter end. I thought and said that history would brand our "break-up," our yielding up the cause as disgraceful. I felt as if I wished to show, by contending to the last, that I was not unworthy of liberty.[33]

Whether Petty would have carried out his wartime decision to leave the South rather than live under a hated flag can never be known. More than likely, he would have returned to Bastrop and resumed his law practice, struggling, like hundreds of thousands of his comrades, to eke out a meager livelihood for his family in the post-war South.[34]

Petty left to posterity some official documents; his wallet, sash and other personal effects; a lonely grave in the woods at the end of a dirt track off a secondary road; and a collection of letters which testify that in his service to the Confederacy, he was, in the words of the motto inscribed on his company's flag, "Fearless and Faithful."

Notes

[1] Blessington, *Walker's Texas Division*, pp. 241–58; Foote, *The Civil War*, pp. 74–75. On the battle of Jenkins' Ferry, see Edwin C. Bearss, *Steele's Retreat From Camden and the Battle of Jenkins' Ferry* (Little Rock: Civil War Centennial Commission, 196-?), pp. 114–62; Ira Don Richards, "The Battle of Jenkins' Ferry," *Arkansas Historical Quarterly*, XX (Spring 1961), pp. 3–16.

[2] E. P. Becton to Mary Becton, May 7, 1864, Becton Papers; R. S. Wilson, "The Battle of Jenkins' Ferry," *Confederate Veteran*, XVIII (October 1910), p. 468. One of Walker's men described the battle in a letter to his mother: "The morning of the fight we started from Camp at 2 o'clock and marched 15 miles through one of the hardest rains that I ever saw fall and a great many of the men were exhausted and unable to get up to the fight and the last 3 miles was through the worst sort of a swamp and the battle was fought on the same sort of ground the enemy had thrown a bridge across the river and had posted his troops in such a position that we could not effect much our men shot a way about all their ammunition which was 40 round. the enemy then decamped across the river leaving his dead and wounded in our possession. Genl Price's army first engaged the enemy, before we got there. our brigade fought something over 2 hours the firing was very heavy and almost uninterrupted the whole time. our regt. had 2 men killed and 10 or 12 wounded." David M. Ray to "Dear Mother," May 7, 1864, Ray Papers.

[3] Barr, "Texas Losses in the Red River Campaign," pp. 106–7. In a letter to his mother, dated May 8, 1864, Lieutenant Colonel Henry Gerard Hall of the Twenty-eighth Texas Cavalry Regiment (dismounted), Randal's Brigade, reported that "out of 84 killed in Walker's Division our Brigade lost nearly half, 39; and of these our Regt. lost nearly half, 16. Four of our wounded have since died making our dead 20 and leaving our wounded 40. In Walker's Division it was 84 killed, 360 wounded, and 3 missing. (One of these 3 was John Arnason wounded and taken off by the enemy.) The loss in our division is about ⅓ of all for there were 2 other divisions. I know not the enemy's loss. Some were buried on the field next day. 210 have since been fished out of the creek from whose banks they fought. 310 wounded were carried into our hospitals and left under the treatment of our and their surgeons and nurses. About 800 wounded Federals have been found in houses beyond the Saline River. Having a pontoon over the river in their rear they could readily remove their slightly wounded and the dead who were of importance." Dotson, comp., *Who's Who of the Confederacy*, p. 86.

All three brigades in Walker's Division were left without commanders. Colonel Wilburn Hill King of the Eighteenth Texas Infantry was promoted to brigadier general by Kirby Smith and assigned to the command of the First Brigade (Waul's). Major Robert P. Maclay (McClay), Walker's chief-of-staff, was promoted to brigadier general and assigned to the command of the Second Brigade (Randal's). Colonel Richard Waterhouse of the Nineteenth Texas Infantry was promoted to brigadier general and assigned to the command of the Third Brigade (Scurry's). Maclay's and King's promotions were never approved by President Davis. Waterhouse's commission was approved by Davis to rank from March 17, 1865, and was confirmed by the Confederate Senate on the last day that it was in session. Wright, comp., *Texas in the War*, pp. 85n, 94n; Warner, *Generals in Gray*, pp. 326–27, 351.

[4] Blessington, *Walker's Texas Division*, pp. 259–71; S. A. Smith to Jefferson Davis, August 28, 1864, *Official Records Armies*, series I, XXXIV, pt. 1, p. 486.

[5] Stephen D. Lee to E. Kirby Smith, July 9, 1864, *Official Records Armies*, series I, XLI, pt. 1, p. 89.

[6] Winters, *Civil War in Louisiana*, p. 381; Wiley, *Life of Johnny Reb*, pp. 137–38. "The transfer of men to places far from their homes was a common cause of desertion," noted Bell Wiley. "This was not true early in the war, because it was generally thought that the struggle would be short, and a trip to Virginia or Kentucky was regarded by Louisianians, Texans and others as a sort of holiday excursion. Nor were single men as much affected as those who were married. But after it became apparent that the war was to be long, and that various portions of the South were to be invaded, the thought of being far away from families who were helpless and in danger caused many a Reb to cast longing and uneasy glances toward home."

[7] Bearss, ed., *A Louisiana Confederate*, pp. 155–56. On August 21 Felix Poché noted in his diary: "Crossing the ferry at Harrisonburg I had a very animated discussion with a Lieut. Rister of Walker's Division, who spoke in very rebellious language regarding our movement to the other side. In view of the fact that the division is in a state of mutiny I considered his remarks very dangerous and very helpful to the enemy. I went to Genl Polignac's headquarters and denounced the Lieutenant in question. Genl Polignac told me that he would immediately arrest him and have him court martialled." *Ibid.*, p. 157.

According to Edwin Bearss' notes, Samuel T. Rister had entered Confederate service as a private in Company C, Seventeenth Texas Infantry. He had been promoted to second lieutenant of his company on February 25, 1863. "Rister's service record contains no information concerning his arrest," wrote Bearss. "This leads to the conclusion that if he were placed under arrest, he was released without having to stand a court martial." *Ibid.*, p. 305n.

[8] Barr, *Polignac's Texas Brigade*, p. 48.

[9] Richard Taylor to E. Kirby Smith, August 19, 1864, *Official Records Armies*, series I, XLI, pt. 1, pp. 111–12; Simon B. Buckner to William R. Boggs, August 20, 1864, *ibid.*, p. 113.

[10] E. Kirby Smith to John G. Walker, August 1, 1864, *ibid.*, pp. 94–95; John G. Meem Jr. to Richard Taylor, August 12, 1864, *ibid.*, p. 105; Will M. Levy to Judah P. Benjamin, September 15, 1864, *ibid.*, pp. 120–21; Blessington, *Walker's Texas Division*, p. 276.

[11] Richard Taylor to E. Kirby Smith, August 19, 1864, *Official Records Armies*, series I, XLI, pt. 1, pp. 111–12; William R. Boggs to Taylor, August 22, 1864, *ibid.*, p. 117; Bearss, ed., *A Louisiana Confederate*, p. 159; Taylor, *Destruction and Reconstruction*, p. 197.

[12] David M. Ray to "Dear Mother," August 24, 1864, Ray Papers.

[13] Blessington, *Walker's Texas Division*, pp. 275–77; E. P. Becton to Mary Becton, September 20, 1864, Becton Papers.

[14] Blessington, *Walker's Texas Division*, pp. 277–81.

[15] The years between the war with Mexico and the Crimean War saw the advent of the rifled cannon, the delayed-action fuse, the Borman fuse, shrapnel, the revolver, the percussion cap and the minié bullet which extended the accurate range of a rifleman to 300 yards while enabling him to reload and fire much faster than with a conventional rifle ball. Secretary of War Jefferson Davis felt an urgent need to reshape United States Army tactics to fit this revolution in military technology. In 1853 Davis hand-picked and began working very closely with Brevet Lieutenant Colonel William J. Hardee of Georgia on a new manual of drill and tactics designed to provide speed and flexibility for infantry units in battle where, within range of so many new weapons systems, time had literally become life. Hardee's *Rifle and Light Infantry Tactics*, completed in 1854 and adopted by the United States Military Academy when its author was appointed as Commandant, was especially innovative in its emphasis on the use of a fluid line of self-reliant skirmishers advancing in open-order formation as opposed to the more rigid, lock-step formations favored in the age of Napoleon.

A simple, practical guide for company and regimental infantry commanders in the regular army of the 1850's, "Hardee's Tactics" became the bible for both Northern and Southern volunteer officers during the Civil War. As one Union volunteer officer recalled in 1900, Hardee was "the authoritative guide of our army drill, and by that means his name was familiar to every officer and man among us." Hardee's lessons in how to mass firepower and increase accuracy, together with the rifle's replacement of the smoothbore musket as the standard infantry weapon revolutionized American tactics during the Civil War, changing them from a contest of assault and counter-assault, relying upon the bayonet to shatter the enemy line, to a contest of maneuvering for position. During the last years of the Civil War, however, technology once again surged ahead of tactical doctrine, and the breech-loading and repeating rifle drove armies into a phase of trench warfare wherein the spade was rated as the equal of the gun. This ascendency of firepower over maneuver and shock in military doctrine remained in effect for 75 years until the development of the tank and the airplane rendered warfare mobile once again. William J. Hardee, *Rifle and Light Infantry Tactics* (Philadelphia: Lippincott, Bramb, and Co., 1854); Nathaniel C. Hughes Jr., *General William J. Hardee: Old Reliable* (Baton Rouge: Louisiana State University Press, 1965), pp. 41–50.

[16] Blessington, *Walker's Texas Division*, pp. 281–85.

[17] *Ibid.*, pp. 286–87. "Our Division Genl [Forney] is ahead of any yet in this Department," Bruno Durst, a lieutenant in the Thirteenth Texas Cavalry (dismounted), wrote his friend Captain Jet Black on February 25, 1865. "He is what the boys call a Dead'ner on the field. Brigade and Division drill is all the go with sham battles, in which we fire one round then change [charge?]; reviews, etc. Has a Squadron Cavalry to follow the Division during drill, whose duty it is to pick up the drags and those who step momentarily aside to attend the calls of nature. These are collected and made to walk a ring while the drill goes on. But the boys take it all in fun." Leon Durst, "A Confederate Texas Letter: Bruno Durst to Jet Black," *Southwestern Historical Quarterly*, LVII (July 1953), p. 96 (hereafter cited as Durst, "Confederate Texas Letter").

[18] J. F. Belton to John G. Walker, January 22, February 2, 1865, *Official Records Armies*, series I, XLVIII, pt. 1, pp. 1339, 1363; Parks, *Edmund Kirby Smith*, p. 453.

[19] Blessington, *Walker's Texas Division*, pp. 288–90. Bruno Durst described the review and barbecue as follows: "There was a grand festival and barbecue given to this Division on the 18th inst., by citizens of Caddo and Bassier, and also Harrison County, Texas. We had a sham battle. Was reviewed by General E. Kirby Smith,

and after speeches by several distinguished gentlemen. Then they issued a jigger of whiskey to each of us. Then came the barbecue. Imagine 16 tables 70 yards long filled with all the substantials, necessary to make us relish our grub for instance. 140 hogs, light bread and potatoes to match, mutton, turkeys, chickens, cake, pie, etc. and etc. There were near 4000 of us present and almost as many visitors. There were preparations made also for a grand dance, but it proved a failure as the thing was too big." Durst, "Confederate Texas Letter," pp. 95–96.

[20] Blessington, *Walker's Texas Division*, pp. 291–92; Robert S. Weddle, *Plow-Horse Cavalry: The Caney Creek Boys of the Thirty-fourth Texas* (Austin: Madrona Press, Inc., 1974), p. 153 (hereafter cited as Weddle, *Plow-Horse Cavalry*). Forney's Division was to be constituted as follows:

First Texas Infantry Brigade — Brigadier-General Waul commanding: Eighth Texas Infantry, Twenty-second Texas Infantry, Thirteenth Texas Dismounted Cavalry, Twenty-ninth Texas Dismounted Cavalry.

Second Texas Infantry Brigade — Acting Brigadier-General Waterhouse commanding: Third Texas Infantry, Seventeenth Texas Infantry, Nineteenth Texas Infantry, Sixteenth Texas Dismounted Cavalry, Chisum's regiment dismounted cavalry.

Third Texas Infantry Brigade — Eleventh Texas Infantry, Fourteenth Texas Infantry, Gould's battalion Texas dismounted cavalry, Martin's regiment Texas dismounted cavalry.

Fourth Texas Infantry Brigade — Acting Brigadier-General King commanding: Sixteenth Texas Infantry, Eighteenth Texas Infantry, Twenty-eighth Texas Dismounted Cavalry, Thirty-fourth Texas Dismounted Cavalry, Wells's regiment dismounted cavalry. William R. Boggs to Simon B. Buckner, February 27, 1865, *Official Records Armies*, series I, XLVIII, pt. 1, pp. 1405–6.

[21] E. Kirby Smith to Jefferson Davis, March 7, 1865, *Official Records Armies*, series I, XLVIII, pt. 1, pp. 1411–12; John G. Walker to Smith, same date, *ibid.*, p. 1412; William R. Boggs to John G. Magruder, March 8, 1865, *ibid.*, p. 1416; J. F. Belton to Simon B. Buckner, March 9, 1865, *ibid.*, p. 1417; Smith to Walker, March 11, 22, 1865, *ibid.*, pp. 1419, 1442; Parks, *Edmund Kirby Smith*, pp. 454–55.

[22] Blessington, *Walker's Texas Division*, pp. 275–301; Weddle, *Plow-Horse Cavalry*, pp. 156–57.

[23] Blessington, *Walker's Texas Division*, pp. 303–6; *Official Records Armies*, series I, XLVIII, pt. 2, pp. 1284–85, 1294; "Gen. Forney's Address To His Men," *Confederate Veteran*, XII (November 1963) p. 533; Parks, *Edmund Kirby Smith*, pp. 456–57; Weddle, *Plow-Horse Cavalry*, p. 158.

[24] *Official Records Armies*, series I, XLVIII, pt. 2, p. 1300; Douglas French Forrest, *Odyssey in Gray: A Diary of Confederate Service, 1863–1865*, ed. William N. Still Jr. (Richmond: Virginia State Library, 1979), p. 306 (hereafter cited as Forrest, *Odyssey in Gray*).

[25] John G. Magruder and John G. Walker to E. Kirby Smith, May 16, 1865, *Official Records Armies*, series I, XLVIII, pt. 2, pp. 1308–9.

[26] John C. Walker, "Reconstruction in Texas," *Southern Historical Society Papers*, XXIV (1896), p. 48.

[27] Blessington, *Walker's Texas Division*, p. 307; Forrest, *Odyssey in Gray*, p. 309.

[28] "Biography and Diaries of Robert Simonton Gould," pp. 81–82.

[29] Yeary, *Reminiscences of the Boys in Gray*, p. 595.

[30] Parks, *Edmund Kirby Smith*, pp. 473–78.

[31] Forrest, *Odyssey in Gray*, pp. 310–21; Warner, *Generals in Gray*, p. 320; Jon L. Wakelyn, *Biographical Dictionary of the Confederacy* (Westport: Greenwood Press, 1977), p. 424.

[32] Forrest, *Odyssey in Gray*, pp. 316–17.

[33] "Biography and Diaries of Robert Simonton Gould," p. 82.

[34] Margaret Petty survived her husband by 47 years, dying at the home of her son Van in San Antonio on August 15, 1911. She was buried in Bastrop. Petty, "Memo of the family of Elijah P. and Margaret E. Petty." In the mid-1870's Margaret took the two young daughters, Gertrude and Grace, of her brother Joseph Pinner to raise, when he married his second wife. Gertrude was born on April 24, 1871, and Grace on February 18, 1873. Joseph enclosed sums of money ranging from $5 to $50 in most of his letters to Margaret. It is not known how long the children remained with her. Both girls married and were living in Baton Rouge, Louisiana, in 1927. Joseph C. Pinner to Margaret E. Petty, June 28, August 7, 14, 20, September 17, October 26, 1875; January 11, April 17, December 16, 1876; March 18, May 1, 30, June 13, December 15, 1877, copies enclosed in Wilfred Richardson to O. Scott Petty, May 23, 1981; Van Alvin Petty to Kitty Ford, July 8, 1927, in possession of O. Scott Petty. Margaret's brother Tom wrote her in August 1879: "When I came home from Hot Springs I went by to see Joe at Dyersburg. I stayed with him four days in all. He seemed to be getting along very well. His wife was not in good health. She seemed to be delicate." Thomas Jefferson Pinner to Margaret E. Petty, August 9, 1879, enclosed in Wilfred Richardson to O. Scott Petty, May 23, 1981.

Ella Pene Petty married John T. (Tom) McDonald, a member of Captain Petty's Company F, on December 3, 1868. The couple had eight children: E. Petty, W. T., Idel, Mary E., Hugh A., Frank G., James E. and one dead in infancy. After returning home from the war McDonald helped his father run a ferry and sawmill at Bastrop, later farmed, and in 1870 opened a store at Hill's Prairie, which he operated for 15 years. In 1887 the McDonalds moved to a 215-acre farm in Bastrop County. Two years later McDonald was elected County Commissioner of Precinct No. 2, Bastrop, and was reelected in 1892. Ella died at her country home on March 13, 1890.

Cyr Frank Petty married Hattie P. Reynolds in Bastrop on August 4, 1880. They had a daughter Maggie. Frank engaged in the manufacture of staves in Gibbsland, Louisiana. He died there on June 19, 1923.

Don Green Petty married Mary Sherman Reynolds on October 4, 1880. There were seven children: Kitty, Don Green Jr., Ella, Sherman, Frank, Lenna and Daisy. Don was a successful lumber manufacturer in Orange, Texas. He later moved to Mansfield, Louisiana, where he died on May 13, 1913.

The youngest son, Van Alvin, married Mary Cordelia Dabney of La Grange on November 10, 1887. The couple had three children: Van Alvin Jr., Dabney E. and O. Scott. Van went to work in 1882 for Olive, Sternenberg & Company, a lumber firm in Beaumont, Texas. By 1890 he had acquired a financial interest in the company, which was reorganized as the Olive-Sternenberg Lumber Company in 1905. In 1901 Van moved to San Antonio. It was largely through his efforts that the Gunter Hotel was built, and he served as a director of the hotel company. President of the Mission Wood and Coal Company of San Antonio and vice president of the Campbell-Petty Lumber Company, he was connected with a number of other business enterprises in Texas and Louisiana. One of the largest real estate holders in San Antonio, Van also owned two large ranches, one of 15,000 acres in Webb County and one in Zavala County. He died in May 1929.

Biographical information on the Petty children came from the following sources: Frank W. Johnson, *A History of Texas and Texans*, ed. and up-dated by Eugene C. Barker with the assistance of Ernest William Winkler, 5 vols. (Chicago and New York: American Historical Society, 1914), V, pp. 766–67, 2256–57; San Antonio *Express*, May 20, 1915; L. E. Daniell, *Texas, the Country, and Its Men: Historical, Biographical, Descriptive* [Austin?, 1924?], pp. 682–86; Wilfred Richardson to O. Scott Petty, May 23, 1981.

APPENDIX A

A Soldier's Last Letter

On April 7, the eve of the battle of Mansfield, Sergeant John Samuel Bryan, Company B, Sixteenth Texas Dismounted Cavalry, Walker's Texas Division, wrote his wife Nancy, who lived at McKinney, Texas, from Walker's campsite a few miles north of Mansfield.

Camps in the field
April the 7th 1864

Dear Nancy

Again I am permited to drop you a few lines to let you know that I am yet on the land of the living well and hearty cincearly hopeing this may reach and find you all enjoying the same good blessing. The helth of the boys hear is tolerbly good at present. Nancy we have had some pretty heavy marching to do lately. We have retreated some two hundred and fifty miles that is what I call giving back considerable. We are now within thirty miles of Shreveport. We have had no fight with them yet and I think it unsertin wheather we do have any unless they try to take Shreveport. Nancy I have had the bad luck to loose all my blankets that was any account. I sent them back with the rest of our baggage and thay eather lost off the wagon or was stolen or missplased someway but I will have to buy some more. We lost one man from Co B on the retreat I do not know weather he was stolen or not. He went off in the night. His name was R. H. Brown. He lived near clear lake. I said we have had no fight with the feds. I mean no general engagement. Our cavalry have had some skirmishes with them. We have considerble cavalry hear now though it has lately come in that is it is not write hear but within strikeing distance. Bill Smithey came into camps yesterday. Some of the boys claim a furlough on him as a recruit. Smithey ses the goverment officers in collin are taking all the wheat, corn and meat except six months provisions for the sitisins. That is pretty heavy. Perhaps we will all starve together at the end of six months. Nany I have nothing that will interest you to write.

Neather have I any news but lies or thay says whitch is all the same thairfore as it is a bad rainey day I will write but little. Nany I have not received any letters from you yet. Tell Mr Ballou to write to me and give me all the news. Give all my best wishes to all enquiring friends. Nany write soon and often for it is but little plesure that we see and thair is nothing more pleasant out hear than to get a friendly letter so no more at presant but remain as every yours truly untill death.

J S Bryan
to N B Bryan

My love to Willey and Mary

This letter, in the archives of the Indiana Historical Society, was the last written by Sergeant Bryan to his wife. Bryan was wounded in the fighting on April 8–9 and died on April 16, 1864. His wife never knew where he was buried but assumed it was around Mansfield. After Bryan's death Nancy's brother came to Texas and brought her and her children back to Shelby County, Indiana. She later remarried and died at the age of 89 on November 11, 1931. Terry G. Waxham, "A soldier's last letter," Mansfield *Journal*, March 28, 1977.

John Samuel Bryan letter courtesy Indiana Historical Society Library, Indianapolis, Indiana.

A Chief Has Fallen

Head Quarters Dist. Western La.,
Mansfield, La., April 13th, 1864

General Orders,)
    No 58   )

Soldiers! A Chief has fallen. A Warrior of Warriors has gone to his home. On the 12th inst. fell Thomas Green. After braving death a thousand times, the destroyer found him, where he was ever wont to be, in the front line of battle. His spirit has flown to the happy home of heroes, where the kindred spirit of Alfred Mouton awaited it. Throughout broad Texas, throughout desolated Louisiana, mourning will sadden every hearth. Great is the loss to family and friends; much greater is the loss to this army and me. For many weary months these two have served with me. Amidst the storm of battle; by the lonely camp-fire; at the solitary outpost, my heart has learned to love them. Their families shall be as mine; their friends, my friends. To have been their beloved friend and trusted commander is the highest earthly honor I can ever attain. Soldiers! the fall of these heroes shall not be in vain. Inspired by such examples, this army will achieve great things. Moistened by the blood of Mansfield, Pleasant Hill and Blair's Landing, the tree of national independence will grow apace and soon overshadow the land, so that all may repose in peace under its grateful shade. The memory of our glorious dead is a rich legacy to future generations, and their names will be remembered as the chosen heroes and martyrs of the chivalric Southern race. The Colors of the Cavalry corps of this army will be draped for thirty days, in memory of the late heroic commander.

R. Taylor,
Major-Gen'l Com'd'g.

Original printed order in Mansfield Battle Park Museum

INDEX

Bayou De Glaize La
March 10. 1864

My Dear wife

I have no news to write
of interest   The feds have gone
back out of Red River after having
been repulsed at Fort Beauregard
The last news from them there were 12
gun boats at the Mouth of Red River
The river is now getting low and I
hardly think they will try it again
until the waters rise.   The waters
are still receding   We have
stopped work on our fortifications
here and the Spades &c have all been
sent to Fort DeRussy so as to Complete
the works there,   It has been raining all day. and it is quite muddy
We have had a beautiful Spring up
to this time: and it is not Cold now
but wet and muddy.   We are drilling nearly every day - we want to drill
for a new flag as ours is worn out